The Opera House

PETER FITZSIMONS

The Opera House

The extraordinary story of the building that symbolises Australia
— the people, the secrets, the scandals and the sheer genius

hachette
AUSTRALIA

Published in Australia and New Zealand in 2022
by Hachette Australia
(an imprint of Hachette Australia Pty Limited)
Gadigal Country, Level 17, 207 Kent Street, Sydney, NSW 2000
www.hachette.com.au

Hachette Australia acknowledges and pays our respects to the past, present and future Traditional Owners and Custodians of Country throughout Australia and recognises the continuation of cultural, spiritual and educational practices of Aboriginal and Torres Strait Islander peoples. Our head office is located on the lands of the Gadigal people of the Eora Nation.

10 9 8 7 6 5 4 3 2 1

A catalogue record for this book is available from the National Library of Australia

ISBN: 978 0 7336 4133 6 (paperback)

Cover design by Luke Causby/Blue Cork
Front cover images courtesy BG-Stock72/Adobe Stock and Architectural Prints
Front cover quote by Louis Kahn from *Sydney Opera House: Utzon Design Principles*, Sydney Opera House, 2002
Back cover images (top) Max Dupain Collection, courtesy Mitchell Library, State Library of New South Wales; author photo courtesy Peter Morris/Sydney Heads
Typeset in 11/14 pt Sabon LT Pro by Bookhouse, Sydney
Printed and bound in Australia by McPherson's Printing Group

Where noble headlands submerge under seas of red bungalows, it seems a bit odd that the people should perform a cultural act of faith and build an opera house, and they had nothing to put in it. How did it happen here?[1]

Bob Ellis, narrating *Autopsy on a Dream*

The sun did not know how beautiful its light was, until it was reflected off this building.[2]

Louis I. Kahn, architect

I think it looks like an untidily sliced apple, or perhaps a bunch of toenails clipped from some large albino dog.[3]

A *Daily Mirror* columnist, surveying the winning entry for the
Opera House

To the late, great, Jørn Utzon. Sir, thank you.

And to all the others whose skill, courage and resolve made it happen. I cite, particularly, Premier Joe Cahill and Peter Hall.

CONTENTS

INTRODUCTION AND ACKNOWLEDGEMENTS

I like to be on the edge of the possible.[1]

Jørn Utzon

In 2015 I read a story in the *Paris Review* about the American author David McCullough, who wrote an enormously successful book on the history of the Brooklyn Bridge: where it came from, how it was conceived and built, and incorporating all the personal stories that were the inevitable foundation stones for such an iconic structure.

The book had become an American classic and I was instantly entranced with the idea of doing the biography of a building. Which one, in my case? Well, that was easy. The Sydney Opera House, of course!

As much of a doe-eyed neophyte as I am in the world of architecture, the wonder of the masterpiece had never left me from the first moment I gazed upon it, and always with an attendant question. For originally – and *still*, seeing as you asked, but I uncustomarily lost the battle with the publisher – I wanted to call this book, *The Opera House: Where the Fuck Did That Thing Come From, Anyway?*

Despite a more genteel title, the above vulgar theme remains. And I mean it. Though raised at Peats Ridge an hour north of Sydney, I was educated down in the Big Smoke itself, starting high school in the year the Opera House was opened in 1973 and I remember well the first time I saw it on a school excursion. So fresh, so sparkling, so different, so . . . extraordinary!

About 10 years later, they opened the Regent Hotel at the bottom of George Street and I was also impressed. It was also so fresh, so modern, so much more sophisticated than the Hilton Hotel, just up the slope, which had previously been the last word in hotels. And the Regent had such interesting architecture!

But how are they viewed now, in the third decade of the twenty-first century? With the greatest respect . . . the Regent, now the Four Seasons, looks as tired and dull as a wet Wednesday afternoon in winter. But the Opera House? It *still* looks as sparkling, fresh and new as a shining Sunday morning in the year 2525.

The wonder lies not just in the glory of the architect's stunning design. It is that somehow, after the Dane had come up with the concept, 16 men of the NSW Cabinet – who were led by a Premier who liked nothing more than going to the Wentworth Park dogs on a Saturday night – who ate meat and three veg every day, went to church on Sundays, and lived behind white picket fences, could have a look at the plans and say, 'Yes, let's build the bastard!' Sorry, *what*? How did that happen?

To get started, I put one of my researchers, Noel Boreham – known to the rest of us as Noel the Diary Mole – on the hunt to spend some months trawling the archives, and over breakfast in August 2015 he gave his first report to my principal researcher, Dr Libby Effeney, and me. We sat entranced for a couple of hours as Noel took us through it all, and Libby got to work thereafter, digging ever deeper and wider.

The further we went, the more blessed I felt to have Libby's intellectual horsepower placed at the service of this book. The things she found! The complex concepts she helped make explicable! The esoterica she brought to the surface! We have worked together for nigh on ten years, and as a forensic force of nature, researcher and friend, she is as good as it gets. I also offer my deep gratitude to my other key researcher on this book, Barb Kelly, from Bunbury in WA. As always, Barb engaged in the subject with great passion and brought precious detail to the account. Trying to wrestle to the ground precisely what happened, and how it happened, would not have been remotely possible without Libby and Barb, and this book and author are forever in their debt. And as with all of my recent books it was great that Barb's son Lachlan was able to lend valuable assistance throughout this massive exercise. For it was six years after beginning – a record for me, from writing the first words, to getting a knock on the door from the courier – that this book took to complete. It has been difficult, particularly to get my head around complex architectural and engineering concepts, but in this venture I was at least helped by experts. First and foremost, and with my deepest thanks, was my eldest brother, David, a civil engineer of 50 years standing who explained some of the mysteries to me in language he knew even I could understand, and then vetted my entire book looking for errors in my own explanations.

Another enormous help was 77-year-old engineer Ron Bergin, who had worked on the Opera House for the entire time the roof was built and went on to work for the next three decades with many of the key figures I was writing about. He was happy to share with me his views, lend me books and documentation, and regularly meet with me to take me through it one more time – before hitting every sentence of this book with a hammer to see if it rang true to him. Through him, I was able to get input from other Opera House engineers like John Kuner and Ian Mackenzie – all of them members of 'The Originals', a group of senior engineers who took part in the Sydney Opera House construction, and now consult with Sydney Opera House management whenever advice is needed on the original method of construction, so it can be taken into account in heritage and conservation planning for the future.

I was equally blessed to be able to be draw on the work and research of previous authors. Beyond the bibliography where they are all listed, I particularly acknowledge and commend to you these works: *Opera House Act One* – David Messent; *The Saga of Sydney Opera House* – Peter Murray; *The Sydney Opera House Affair* – Michael Baume; *The Other Taj Mahal* – John Yeomans; *The Masterpiece* – Philip Drew; *Ove Arup* – Peter Jones; *Utzon's Sphere* – Yuzo Mikami; *An Engineer's Tale* – Jack Zunz; *Letters From Sydney* – Mogens Prip-Buus; *The Poisoned Chalice* – Anne Watson; *The House* – Helen Pitt; *Utzon and the Sydney Opera House* – Elias Duek-Cohen; *Building a Masterpiece* – Anne Watson; *Utzon and the Sydney Opera House* – Daryl Dellora.

On everything to do with the Thorne kidnapping, I was blessed to be helped by my friend the former NSW Crown Prosecutor Mark Tedeschi, who wrote the book *Kidnapped: The Crime that Shocked the Nation*; just as I was also blessed to have the famed ABC journalist David Salter help me on the story of Eugene Goossens and the 'witch of Kings Cross'. This included David handing me a precious folder of documentation that had, fabulously, been smuggled out of the Vice Squad office at Balmain Police Station secreted in the hubcap of an FJ Holden! I warmly thank them both.

Some of the people I cover in this book are still alive, and it was particularly wonderful to be able to talk with John Weiley. I also thank the progeny of Peter Hall – Willie, Rebecca, Antigone, Henry – as well as his second wife, Penelope; the son of David Littlemore, and the very man who used to strike terror in my heart, Stuart Littlemore of *Media Watch* fame; the son of Ted Farmer, Peter Farmer; the daughter of John Nutt, Cheryl; the daughter of Davis Hughes, Sue Burgoyne; and the brother of Ron Gilling, Doug. All were extremely helpful in giving me new perspectives and filling out what I most love: fine detail! My deep thanks also to the Opera House CEO, Louise Herron, who could not have been more encouraging and supportive. It was also a particular privilege to be shown all over the labyrinthian internal structure of the Opera House by engineer and Executive Director Ian Cashen. I also thank Opera House staff Claire Gammon, Laura Matarese, Valerie Ng, Julie Carrol, Al McCarty and Alex Zamorano, who were helpful across the board.

As with all my books, though this is a history, I want it to read like a novel so that you, the reader, will feel like you are *in* the story, not merely reading about it. To do it, I put the whole thing in the present tense, and use dialogue – but backed up by 1700 footnotes as the pinpoint pillars on which the story rests. For the sake of the storytelling, I have occasionally created a direct quote from reported speech in a journal, diary or letter, and changed pronouns and tenses to put that reported speech in the present tense. One more time for the road, I cite the late, great American novelist E. L. Doctorow, 'The historian will tell you what happened. The novelist will tell you what it felt like.'[2] It is for you to judge whether I have pulled it off, but I have tried to do both. As much as possible I have remained faithful to the language of the day, using contemporary spelling with only the odd exception where it would create too much confusion otherwise. To spare confusion, various spellings in various quotes have been converted to a single spelling, such as Jørn instead of Jorn and Joern, and Bennelong rather than Benelong.

I was blessed by the help of various experts. The architect and Opera House historian Eoghan Lewis gave me early valuable direction.

As ever, my long-time sub-editor Harriet Veitch took the fine-tooth comb to the whole thing, untangling hopelessly twisted sentences, eliminating many grammatical errors and giving my work a sheen which does not properly belong to it. In this book, she was as strong as ever, and I record my gratitude, just as I do to my eldest son, Jake, who gave valuable input.

My thanks also, as ever, to my highly skilled editor Deonie Fiford, who was as assiduous as ever in painstakingly polishing the whole thing from top to bottom, and my warmest thanks to Senior Editor Jacquie Brown for guiding the book through the editorial and publication process.

I am also grateful to my friend and publisher, Matthew Kelly of Hachette, with whom I have worked many times over the last three decades, covering a gamut of subjects.

Peter FitzSimons
Neutral Bay, Sydney
29 July 2021

DRAMATIS PERSONAE

Jørn Utzon, Danish architectural genius.

Ove Arup, British engineer of Danish heritage who founded Arup & Partners, now known as Arup Group. Considered to be among the leading structural engineers of his era, he joined Jørn Utzon in undertaking the mammoth task of bringing the architect's design sketches to reality.

Woollarawarre Bennelong, leading man of the Eora people of Port Jackson. Bennelong was abducted by Governor Philip and served as an interlocutor between the Eora and the British.

Eugene Goossens, English musician, conductor and composer. He spent nine years in Australia from 1947 until 1956. During that time, he conducted the Sydney Symphony Orchestra and was director of the New South Wales Conservatorium of Music. Goossens was first to champion and lobby for the idea of building a dedicated opera house in Sydney on the site of the old tram depot at Bennelong Point.

Charles Moses, General Manager of the ABC from 1935 to 1965. He was responsible for the establishment of Australia's first full symphony orchestras in all state capitals.

Joseph Cahill, long-serving New South Wales politician, railway worker and trade unionist. He was elected Premier of his state in 1952.

Norm Ryan, New South Wales Labor Party politician who served as Minister for Public Works from 1959 to 1965, and acted as Minister overseeing the Sydney Opera House project during Stages I and II.

Robin/Robert Askin, Premier of New South Wales from 1965 to 1975.

Davis Hughes, New South Wales politician representing the Country Party. In 1965, upon the election of the Askin Liberal government,

Hughes became Minister for Public Works, taking on responsibility for the management of the Sydney Opera House at Bennelong Point.

Mogens Prip-Buus, Danish architect and loyal colleague of Jørn Utzon, who began working with Utzon's team in Denmark in 1958. He subsequently accompanied Utzon to Australia in 1963 where they planned to work on Stage III of the Opera House project.

Jack Zunz, civil engineer from South Africa who was the principal design engineer of the shell structure for Stage II of the construction of the Sydney Opera House.

Michael Lewis, South African structural engineer, who, as lead site engineer, represented Arup & Partners in Australia from 1963 until the completion of the project.

Corbet Gore, the Director of Construction for MR Hornibrook Limited, the company charged with building the Sydney Opera House from the beginning of Stage II onwards.

Peter Hall, one of the top Australian architects of his generation, who trained and worked in the Government Architect's branch of the New South Wales Department of Public Works before taking on the job of head design architect for Stage III of the Sydney Opera House.

David Littlemore, Australian architect who partnered Peter Hall and Lionel Todd to complete Stage III of the Sydney Opera House. Littlemore took on the position of supervising architect for the remainder of the project.

Lionel Todd, Australian architect who partnered Peter Hall and David Littlemore to complete Stage III of the Sydney Opera House. Todd oversaw documents and contacts associated with construction during the final stage of the project.

PROLOGUE

Having passed between the capes which form its entrance, we found ourselves in a port superior, in extent and excellency, to all we had seen before.[1]

Captain Lieutenant Watkin Tench, Sydney Harbour, 26 January 1788

It must not ... be imagined that building, considered merely as heaping stone upon stone, can be of advantage, or reflect honour either on countries or particular persons. Materials in architecture are like words in phraseology, which singly have little or no power, and may be so arranged as to excite contempt; yet when combined with art, and expressed with energy, they actuate the mind with unbounded sway. A good poet can move, even with homely language; and the artful dispositions of an able architect will give lustre to the vilest materials, as the feeble efforts of an ignorant pretender must render the most costly enrichments despicable ...[2]

Sir William Chambers, Swedish-Scottish architect,
A Treatise on Civil Architecture, 1759

1770, Tubowgule, white shells on the point

Peer closely now. The banks of the great harbour burst with the bounties of nature, sustaining the many clans of the Eora Nation who have thrived here for millennia untold. Not far west of the harbour's lofty headlands is Gadigal territory. Look how the Gadigal women launch themselves from the banks of Warrane – a deep-water cove – gliding along the dark water in their *nawi*, canoes made of stringybark from nearby trees. See the Gadigal men stand poised and patient on the shore awaiting the perfect moment to strike, sharpened points cutting through the water, piercing the scales of fat and juicy fish that lurk in the shallows. At low tide, women with children amble out along the cove's eastern arm to a tidal island known as Tubowgule and – singing in rhythm all the while – pry delicious sea meat from jagged shells, which they add to the middens

XVII

of pearlescent white shells that abound all around this tongue of land; each pale pile telling a tale of the point's past. The Gadigal people are fond of Tubowgule, jutting out into the harbour, and often perform their ceremonial feasts and sacred rituals here.

To the west of Gadigal territory live the Wangal people, who roam along the south bank of *Burramatta*, meaning place of the eels. Peer closer still and you can see on that very bank a wiry fellow by the name of Woollarawarre Bennelong, named after a fish. He is a proud boy, six years old, recently free of his mother's *nawi*, he walks the shoreline himself, thinking himself a man.

Unbeknownst to the precocious boy, there are strange visitors to these lands who are watching the Eora people. They disappear almost as quickly as they appear, pallid people carried on the tides by great boats that make the *nawi* look like leaves in a creek. Bennelong is told of them some weeks later by his kin.

The Eora wonder what these white men mean, how their thread fits into the weave of the grand tapestry of the Dreamtime, but they are left wanting.

•

Those strange-looking interlopers are the officers, gentlemen and sailors of Captain James Cook's *Endeavour*, on the soon-to-be famous British mariner's first circumnavigation of the globe. And nearly two decades later, more of their kind are back in force, as a rough thousand souls – the bulk of whom are convicts – arrive on 11 ships under the overall command of Captain Arthur Phillip, who orders his men to sail through the lofty heads into what he describes as 'one of the finest harbours in the world, in which a thousand sail of the line might ride in perfect security'.[3]

For the actual place to plant the first seed of Britain's new penal colony, Governor Phillip picks out a cove boasting not only a tidal island brimming with oysters on the eastern side, to provide further shelter from the sea winds, but 'a spring of water, and in which ships can anchor so close to the shore, that at a very small expense quays may be constructed at which the largest vessels may unload. This cove is about half a mile in length, and a quarter of a mile across at the entrance. In honour of Lord Sydney, it [is named] Sydney Cove.'[4]

On 26 January 1788, the Union Jack is raised on the shore, as the Governor and his officers gather round and drink to the King's health.

Bennelong, now a strapping warrior in his mid-twenties, watches in horror with the rest of his people, as the trees of their ancestors are felled with great sharp axes, darker and bigger than any of the stone *mogo* that Bennelong is familiar with. With their transgressions, word of the white men – the *Berewalgal* – spreads like a bushfire with the great south wind behind it: the strange white beasts are back. The Eora have never seen anything like it. The trees continue to fall, the large huts to rise, and, among the many outrages, these interloping ghouls are soon herding four-legged fat clumsy animals out onto Tubowgule.

The beasts with the cloven hooves wandering on this sacred ground pay the middens of pearly white shells and the seagulls that perch on them no mind, occasionally knocking them down with their fidgeting tails, only to be startled by their own racket.

More than ever, the Eora realise they are dealing with reckless and dangerous savages, as foreign to these lands of the Dreaming as the foul-smelling beasts they herd, even taking milk from their breasts.

'Cattle,' the *Berewalgal* call them, and it isn't long before Tubowgule – the ceremonial grounds of the Gadigal – has been retitled in their discordant tongue: 'Cattle Point'.

And see now, the white women in dirty rags walking out to the point and collecting oysters They are slow to do it, not practised like the Eora – and they certainly don't sing – but they don't want the plump shellfish for eating, no, they want the shells, which they crush to a fine dust and burn to make lime for what they call 'cement mortar'. It isn't long before the tidal island is again renamed by the capricious whites, now going by 'Limeburners' Point'. The shells provide enough lime to construct Government House on the eastern edge of Sydney Cove.

Governor Phillip orders the waterway of the tidal island filled in with rocks and rubble so that it becomes a point proper where a very small fortification is built and two cannon from His Majesty's ships are mounted, should the French ever try to invade. The Union Jack is hauled up, above its ramparts, on New Year's Day, 1789.

25 November 1789, Sydney Town, the capture of Bennelong

Almost two years have passed since the *Berewalgal* arrived, and Bennelong's people are riddled with lesions and sores. 'Smallpox', the whites call it, a vicious virus running rampant through the Eora, killing them in droves and decimating the population. Bennelong is stout and healthy and survives the epidemic, but his beloved wife is not so fortunate.

On the other hand, it is because of his health that the strangest thing happens to him on this day . . .

He and his Gadigal friend Colebee had been offered some freshly caught fish by the white men, and had eagerly taken it, when the sailors fall upon them, bind them with rope and take them back to Government House. The officer in charge of the troop that had captured them records they 'were shaved, wash'd & cloathed; an Iron shackle was put on one leg with a rope made fast to it & a Convict charged with each of them, they were very sullen & sulky . . .'[5]

It is Bennelong who attracts most attention, 'judged to be about 26 years old, of good stature, and stoutly made, with a bold intrepid countenance, which bespoke defiance and revenge . . .'[6]

Both attitudes manifest themselves within a few months when Bennelong follows Colebee's lead and not only escapes, but is a part of the mob that manages to spear Captain Phillip in the shoulder. Yet the Governor has the self-restraint to insist that his men do not retaliate, and days later Bennelong returns to the Sydney settlement with Barangaroo, his reluctant second wife in tempestuous tow.

Bennelong becomes the Governor's intermediary with the Eora people, and soon adopts European dress and ways, and is trained in the English language. At Bennelong's request, some time in 1791, Governor Phillip builds him a brick hut 'on a point of land fixed upon by himself'.[7] He chooses Tubowgule. His hut is 12 feet square and covered with the colony's finest kind of sandstock clay tiles – made in wooden moulds in the colony's brickyards at Brickfield Hill, later to be part of Surry Hills – and from this time forth the eastern point at Sydney Cove is known as 'Bennelong's Point'.

When Barangaroo dies not long after giving birth to their child, Bennelong becomes more settled in his brick box on the point, and ever closer to Governor Phillip, who Bennelong seems to now trust – perhaps because the Governor has a tooth missing, rather like Bennelong's comrades who lose a front tooth as part of their initiation to manhood.

One night, Bennelong even invites the Governor and his senior officers down to his point to watch a sacred ceremony, a kind of singing and dancing performance called a *corroboree*. The whites have only seen this unusual performance art at a distance and refer to it among themselves as 'bush opera'[8], a kind of Indigenous version of the extravagant musical theatre – complete with singing, dancing, acting, costumes, scenery, an orchestra, the lot – that sprang up in Italy in the sixteenth century and is now all the rage across Europe, especially in London, where ladies in fine silks and gentlemen in powdered wigs have the pleasure of attending opera at a new opera house of their own – Theatre Royal, Covent Garden.

After the sun falls behind the blue-hued mountain range that lines the western horizon, and Sydney Town is blanketed with a thin, fading light that seems to amplify the shrieks of the sulphur-crested cockatoos feeding in nearby trees, an extraordinary thing happens. Governor Phillip and his men arrive from Government House to find a score of the Gadigal people happily scooping white clay from a hardwood *coolamon* and smearing it on their faces and naked bodies.

They are 'without even a fig leaf'[9] to protect their modesty. The painting ritual continues until nightfall, at which point the white men are ushered over to an open clearing by the side of Bennelong's hut. Several small fires burn in the darkness, each one tended to by the Gadigal adorned with the ethereal white body-paint. They glow in the gloom, spectres in the night. The Governor is thrilled, burning with curiosity, overjoyed he has finally been invited to something so private, but the dull ache that remains in his speared shoulder tempers his passion and urges caution. He motions to his officers to check the scrub nearby, 'to see that there are no armed lurkers'.[10]

Satiated with the sense of safety, the white men look to Bennelong and Colebee, who seat their guests in a semi-circle, facing a row of young boys standing, glowing, ready to begin. To one side sits an older man with two hardwood sticks, *bilmi*, one of which he has brought up to his breast before *clack . . . click . . . clack*. It is a rudimentary metronome and while he holds it 'in the manner of a violin' he also 'strikes it in a good and regular time'.[11]

As the old musician's *bilmi* beat rings out, the boys begin to bounce in time, their feet apart and their knees bent as they move with the music.

Another man standing near the musician – a 'performer, who was a stout strong voiced man'[12] – begins to sing, frequently applying, 'those graces in music, the piano and forte'.[13] He is soon 'assisted by several young boys and girls, who sit at his feet, and by their manner of crossing the thighs, made a hollow between them and their belly, upon which they beat time with the flat of their hand, so as to make a kind of sound which will be better understood from the manner of its being produced, than from any verbal description.'[14]

As the music rises and grows, so too does the ritual revelry. Before long there are some 26 men and a few women dancing with such prac-tised passion and fervour that the fires they have lit become hindrances to movement, so the feverish dancers simply 'dance through them'.[15]

The rhythm rolls on through the night, their songs sailing out to the sea beyond and the stars above as the white men sit silent, hypnotised.

At the end of each performance, the dancers crowd the white men, looking for feedback from the most transfixed audience the Eora people have ever had.

'*Boojery!*'[16] Governor Phillip and his officers cry, meaning, from the language they have learned from Bennelong, 'Good!' and '*Boojery cariberie!*'[17] meaning – the white men believe – 'Good bush opera!'

Or something like that ...

Captain Hunter records, 'These signs of pleasure in us seemed to give them great satisfaction, and generally produced more than ordinary exertions from the whole company of performers in the next dance.'[18]

(It is, in fact, a lot more than a mere dance to amuse them, and in actuality a ritual performance of stories and myths through fusion of song, story, music and dance that has evolved in a highly sophisticated manner since the dawn of the Dreamtime.)

After hours of song and cheer and carry-on, Governor Phillip is as impressed and enthralled as he is ... suddenly tired. He rises to his feet but is met by Bennelong, who tells him he must stay. Too weary to argue, the Governor agrees and the final song begins, more frantic and wilder than anything so far.

'Neath the ethereal light cast by the moon, the Governor squints slightly to see a faint glint by the water's edge. Dull and destitute in the gloaming, middens of pearly white shells, rebuilt by the Eora people, who continue to forage on the point, are now lightly gleaming in the night, expressive, as if they are alive ... There could be few more idyllic places in nature for such a performance. He sits back down.

•

Bennelong and Governor Phillip continue their close relationship. Bennelong calls the Governor '*Beanga*', meaning father, and Phillip in return calls him '*Durung*', meaning son.

The two become so close that, after more than four years in Sydney Town, when it is time for the Governor to head home in December 1792, back across the seas, he takes Bennelong with him, along with his friend, Yemmerawanne.

Six months later, they arrive in London. Oh, to see Bennelong's jaw drop and his eyes widen as they see such wonder. Such things as he has never seen in his life, like the ruffled shirts, breeches and spotted waistcoats he is made to wear – none of which fools *Lloyd's Evening Post*. For as that journal archly notes, 'they appear to be a race totally incapable of civilization, every attempt to that end having proved ineffectual ...

That instinct which teaches to propagate and preserve the species, they possess in common with the beasts of the field, and seem exactly on a par with them . . .'[19]

While there is much more in London that completely stuns Bennelong – the carriages pulled by horses; the long parade of white tribal elders to whom he is presented, with their extraordinary garb and hats, one of whom has a shiny crown; the Tower of London and St Paul's Cathedral, whose peaks and dome soar as high as the birds, in which giant bells – 'Big Ben' and 'Old Paul' – chime a clanging cacophony on the hour, causing Bennelong to jump in his breeches 24 times a day. But that's not the only thing not pleasing to his ears.

When his hosts take him to a 'Drawing Room concert', the pianist and singers have no sooner begun a piece by Handel – a famous opera composer – than the Eora Nation man grimaces wildly and brings his hands to his ears.[20] The sound is like that of a grand crackle of cockatoos and kookaburras, crying and screeching out into the dusk – but not half as pleasant!

He prefers the simplicity of two *bilmi* and the harmonious singing and humming of his own clan. As to who is killing who to make that dreadful noise, he knows not – only that he wants it stopped.

Oh, how he longs for his home, to return to Tubowgule, the point where his hut still stands.

Yemmerawanne clearly feels the same, not wanting to live in a world where such noises can be made, and after a prolonged illness, dies in May 1794. It is with great relief that Bennelong finally departs for home aboard the *Reliance* on the white man's calendar of 2 February 1795, arriving back in Sydney on 11 September 1795 . . . only a short time before his hut is demolished on the orders of the new Governor, John Hunter, while the towering white middens that once stood upon Bennelong Point are no more than a fading memory.

Returning to an approximation of his old life, Bennelong soon fades from the annals of the Sydney colony's history – though his death on 3 January 1813 at Kissing Point on the Parramatta River, and his burial in the orchard of the friendly ex-convict brewer James Squire, at least attracts notice. But his namesake point does not fade. In fact, its significance only increases.

1 January 1810, Sydney, a city for the settlers

As it happens, Governor Lachlan Macquarie, who takes up his duties at Sydney Cove on New Year's Day 1810 – a neatly symmetrical day for the beginning of a new era – is one who comes to sees the potential of 'Bennelong's Point', as he calls it.

Much of Macquarie's energy throughout his Governorship goes to laying the foundations, literally and metaphorically, for a free settler society. To that end, he establishes a government precinct on what will one day be called Macquarie Street, and the Bank of New South Wales, which stabilises the local currency even as the Governor forbids all further use of rum as tender – for it is simply too much trouble on too many fronts when a man's wages can be drunk as soon as spent. To tap into the skills of the colony, including those skills held by convicts, he encourages free colonists to make sure that emancipists – those convicts who have seen out the duration of their sentence – are treated no differently to anybody else. Macquarie thereby lays the path for the country's own self-styled egalitarian ethos, the idea that all men are equal beneath the Southern Cross. Or at least, all white men.

One such emancipist – who comes at the recommendation of the former Governor Phillip as an 'architect of eminence'[21] – is a convicted forger by the name of Francis Greenway, who Macquarie employs as the first 'Colonial Architect' and charges to design such important public buildings as a Town Hall and Court House, and a new Government House.

By the time the next decade is just starting to peek over the horizon it is time for Macquarie to turn his attention to the defence of Sydney against foreign powers who might invade. And where better to build a fortification than on that central tongue of land jutting out into the harbour, Bennelong's Point?

Part of Macquarie's inspiration may well have been what he had seen on a visit to Denmark just a couple of years before heading to Sydney. For it was on that trip he had visited the famous castle of Kronborg in the town of Helsingør. Established on a sandy finger of land jutting into the narrowest part of the Øresund, the key waterway between the Baltic Sea and the North Sea, the castle had inspired William Shakespeare's Elsinore, the setting of his masterpiece *Hamlet*. Macquarie had been entranced.

'We first went to have a good view of the old and gothic castle of Kronborg,' he had chronicled. 'From the tower there is a most delightful view of the Town of Elsinore and the Castle of Kronborg . . .'[22]

Why not something similar for Sydney Town?

Macquarie writes to Greenway on 4 July 1817, requesting him, 'to draw out a ground plan and elevation of a neat handsome fort – intended to be erected, as soon as possible, on the lower part of Bennelong's Point with ten embrazeurs . . . the fort is to be entirely built of the best stone that can be procured near the spot . . .'[23]

Greenway begins, as ever guided by his spirit of doing original, beautiful buildings, not mere copies of others that Mrs Macquarie finds in books.

(After all, as Greenway had written to the Governor back in 1814, when first asked to design Sydney's Town Hall and Court House based on a picture of the Temple of Theseus at Athens that Mrs Macquarie had found: 'I will immediately copy the drawing your excellency requested me to do, notwithstanding it is rather painful to my mind as a professional man to copy a building that has no claim to classical proportion or character . . . [yet] in any public work, I will exert myself in every way to do your excellency credit as a promoter and encourager of the most useful art to society.'[24])

Yes, there is some light grumbling around Sydney at the idea of a fortification on Bennelong's Point – it is unnecessary, an extravagance and, frankly, the whole thing is ill-conceived, more for display than defence – but Governor Macquarie proceeds regardless, filling out the site with more rubble then levelling the rocky promontory such that late on the morning of 17 December 1817, attended by his Lieutenant Governor, his entire staff and the leading officers and ladies, he lays the foundation stone of what will become known as Fort Macquarie.

The Union Jack is raised.

Cannon are fired in salute, with three volleys booming out in a Royal Salute.

To the King!

The King . . . The King . . . The King . . .

Alas, however good the architect Greenway's intent, not everyone is pleased with what is going on down on Bennelong's Point. There is bitter criticism of the unnecessary embellishments of the design, the amount of labour needed to construct it, the *time* it is taking and most particularly the *cost*.

'I should presume it to be,' one senior British official will complain, 'from the length of time it has been in progress and the very large number of hands it has almost incessantly employed, the most expensive of any of the public buildings. This building is contemptibly defective. It has already been the butt and jest of every foreigner who has visited this part of the world . . . (and) is so badly contrived that from four different directions it is of no defence to itself or the harbour . . .'[25]

Francis Greenway doesn't care and stands by his design. But while he has your attention, Governor, allow him to make the case to you one more time on the virtues of building a bridge across the harbour to join up the southern shore to its northern counterpoint. As ever, Governor Macquarie says . . . no, Mr Greenway. It is an interesting idea but beyond the resources of this colony.

When Fort Macquarie is finally complete in 1821, it is to yet more scathing reviews.

The report of John Thomas Bigge, the Commissioner of the Colonial Office – sent to Sydney Town by the powers in London as something of a spy, although ostensibly to review the affairs of the growing colony – is so scathing, he wonders whether Sydney Town needs an architect at all, insisting that 'an Officer of the Corps of engineers' could come up with plans just as good, and spare the cost. Upon that advice, Greenway the architect is indeed shown the door on 15 November 1822 – which still does not lessen the criticism.

'It is hardly necessary to remark,' the editor of the *Sydney Gazette* notes, 'that all military and scientific men have regarded Fort Macquarie as perfectly useless as a fortification . . .'[26]

Well, if the building out on Bennelong's Point is not performing its intended function, why not use it for something else? On 8 January 1830, a group of officers cum actors do just that, treating a raucous and riotous crowd of drunks to two lowbrow plays: *Raymond and Agnes; Or, the Bleeding Nun* and *The Miller and His Men*. Among some of the colony's first serious theatrical performances, these plays are as hideous to good taste as they are hilarious to the audience. (Another story claims the first performance had been held at Bennelong's hut many years before – a production of George Farquhar's *The Recruiting Officer*.[27])

For all the carping and criticism, still the fort stands, surveying with a weather eye all newly arrived ships until it can be established that they come in peace.

Come the dawn of the new century, it is finally decided to demolish Fort Macquarie, and another use is conceived for what is now called Bennelong Point – an overnight shelter for Sydney trams.

The interesting thing?

No sooner has Fort Macquarie been pulled down than Sydneysiders realise anew just what a spectacular site it is.

'Although it was a wrench to pull down old Fort Macquarie,' one paper notes, 'its demolition marks a decided improvement. Now that only a little of it remains, and that is fast disappearing, the advantages of a clear space at this particular spot are apparent, and the only thing to be apprehended is the erection of an unsightly building in its place.'[28]

After all, why build *anything* on such a glorious spot? Or if we must, a beautiful statue may be better suited?

'It is sincerely to be hoped that with such an improvement as the removal of the fort will make at this particular spot, [the Minister for Public Works] Mr O'Sullivan will rise in his artistic strength and claim a little park, with a loopline tram round it. To erect a shed would be a manifest insult after injury, though it may be remarked that nothing would be said against a statue, for which this particular point appears to be most suitable.'[29]

Such fears and frivolities are not remotely listened to, however, and the tram depot – a raised red-brick box building, 307 feet long by 131 feet wide that looks suspiciously like . . . Fort Macquarie's ugly cousin, complete with castellated ramparts in homage to the previous building – is duly built, its construction following a familiar pattern of public lament. 'While the work was in progress,' the *Sydney Morning Herald* notes on the day the building is handed over to the tram authority, 22 September 1902, 'the designs were altered and the nature of the structure elaborated until it ran into a cost of nearly double the original estimate. The whole work was designed and carried out by the Government departments . . .'[30]

Despite the controversy, at least it stands as a symbol of modernism thanks to the electric tramcars it houses and the intricate network of tracks that encircle it.

As it happens, while those railway and tram tracks are the arteries which pump the lifeblood of Australia's growing industrialisation in the first decades of the twentieth century, the men who work on them are in the cradle of a certain kind of politics and industrial action, which reasserts we white men are all equal under the Southern Cross and even the workers, *particularly* the workers, are not to be pushed around, do you hear?

In this white working man's paradise by the sea, the men have *rights* and they will not be given up easily, Great War or no Great War. Their grievances are many – a new 'card-based costing system intended to streamline production and measure the workers' performance'[31] at the onset of the war has led to strict oversight of each man's daily output, increasingly onerous work schedules, and widespread retrenchments. And the fact they have to request their tools from a central tool room is an insult to their dignity!

'Scientific management,' declares the railway union newspaper, *The Cooperator*, in 1916, 'seeks to make the task of the worker more monotonous than it ever was, to take from his work the last vestige of individuality, and to make him a mere cog in the machinery of production.'[32]

The brewing trouble comes to a climax on 2 August 1917, when workers in the Randwick Workshops and Eveleigh Carriage Workshops walk off the job – *we are out, comrades, so spread the word!* – quickly followed by tens of thousands of workers across the country. In short order, the largest industrial dispute the country has ever seen, known as 'the Great Strike', is underway as just under 100,000 workers – including waterside workers, coal miners and transport drivers – down tools and walk off the job. The trams grind to a halt, streetlights flicker and die as darkness descends, all while the shelves in shops start to empty of even the most basic supplies.

Undeterred by the Chief Railway Commissioner James Fraser calling them, 'pernicious mischief makers', whose unions are 'barbarous' and 'diseased',[33] the unionists march through the streets of Sydney, singing loudly.

> *Tramp, tramp, tramp, can't you hear the marching feet,*
> *As the sturdy sons of labour come swinging down the street?*
> *With manly step and bearing and faces shining bright,*
> *They have taken up the gauntlet in the battle for the right.*[34]

They number some 10,000, 'and in the vanguard there were close on 200 women, who laughed and cheered as they marched'.[35]

The Eveleigh rail-yards are silent. With tram workers on strike, Bennelong Point comes to a silent halt, too.

Such processions quickly become a daily event, always culminating in huge strike meetings at the Domain, where union leaders and Labor parliamentarians exhort the workers to never buckle, to stand up to the bosses. Sometimes the workers themselves speak, men who, though not occupying any elected position, are so passionate for the cause it encourages the other workers to become even more committed.

Like this young fellow. His name is Joe Cahill, he's the 26-year-old son of Irish Catholic parents and an apprentice fitter in the Eveleigh railway workshops, and on this occasion . . . rises to it. Standing in front of the unruly 10,000 on this winter's day, this proud young member of the Amalgamated Society of Engineers, who never finished high school so spends his evenings at Workers' Educational Association lectures and at debates, lets fly with passion, as the workers lean close.

There is no doubt about it. The young fellow speaks well – with eloquence, zeal and commitment, but in the common vernacular of the workers. He's got no tickets on himself, this bloke, and as he continues to speak in coming days, it looks like he might go a long way.

Well, in the view of his employers, the NSW Government, the key hope is that he will go a long way . . . away, and once the workers capitulate and this seminal strike is over on 8 September, after 82 long days, he is given a 'No. 2 notice', meaning he is 'never to be re-employed'.[36]

Against that, the fact that he had never wavered and stayed on strike to the end gives him a badge of honour among the workers. Men such as him, who stayed true to the cause, will ever after be known as 'Lily Whites' and given actual badges to commemorate their efforts – a silver horseshoe with a lily in the middle. Another to be given such a badge is a young engine driver from Bathurst by the name of Ben Chifley, who had also been given a No. 2.

Yes, ill will from the Great Strike in Sydney endures for decades after the war, but in the end the city decides to build a bridge and get over it . . .

19 March 1932, the Sydney Harbour Bridge, Sydney's red-letter day

In what has become a tradition attached to all ambitious public works in Sydney Town, there has been a good deal of controversy over predictions that it could never stand – Sydneysiders watching in horror and wonder at the great steel fingers of some deep-sea monster reaching out from both sides of the harbour towards each other – not to mention cost blow-outs. (The original estimate had been £4,217,721, 11 shillings and 10 pence, give or take, though £10 million if you count land resumptions and building the approaches – but look at them now!)

The metallic beast's fingers finally touch, forming a grand arch of cold grey metal bringing forth the memory of a long-gone polymath by the name of Leonardo da Vinci: 'An arch consists of two weaknesses which, leaning one against the other, make a strength.'[37]

On this, the day of opening of the mighty Sydney Harbour Bridge, 19 March 1932, there is barely a critic to be found as the crowds flock forward, 750,000 strong, on the bridge itself and within viewing distance from the shores, some humming the tune and mouthing the words of a newly popular song:

Behold the Arch of Wonder
With sunset all aglow
When sea and sky bring heaven nigh
And tides eternal flow;
O bridge of Light to greater height
Thy call shall ever be
Where beauty dwells and casts her spells
In Sydney by the sea.[38]

The noise! The buzz of excitement. The sheer *numbers*!

Still more people keep pushing in from either end as the big ships and small ferries go back and forth beneath, tooting till they can toot no more, even as trumpets blare, sirens sound, rockets fire and more songs are sung. But now to the big moment, as the dignitaries and public press ever closer to see the moment that Labor Premier Jack Lang cuts the ribbon, which will mark the official opening.

Wireless announcer Conrad Charlton is beside himself with excitement, describing the whole event live to the nation – as part of the new concept of 'actuality broadcasts' on the wireless, *live* from an actual event.

Up goes the shout. A horse dashes out. Out from the ranks so blue . . .

It is Captain Francis de Groot, a member of the shadow quasi-fascist group, the New Guard, and he is furious to have witnessed, as he will recount, 'several hundred of the occupants of the official "A" stand remaining sitting with their hats on, talking, laughing, and smoking'[39] as the band had played the National Anthem, 'God Save the King'. He is equally incensed that the Premier is cutting the ribbon, and not the representative of His Majesty King George V, the NSW Governor His Excellency Sir Philip Game. Traitors!

It is outrage he can no longer endure, and with his sword held high, de Groot forward dashes and downward slashes.

'On behalf of the decent and respectable citizens of New South Wales,' he roars, slicing the blue ribbon, 'I hereby declare this Bridge open.'[40]

Uproar!

'Stand back – I am a King's officer.'[41]

Which is true, but he is soon a King's officer under arrest for having, 'on March 19 behaved in an offensive manner in Bradfield Highway, a public place.'[42]

In sober-suited, buttoned-down, patrician Sydney, whose closest idea of rebellion is not to go to church every Sunday, it is the best approximation the town can come up with for a revolutionary act, and will be talked about for decades to come.

The whole thing is so dramatic in the midst of a huge event, perfect for an actuality broadcast over the wireless, so of course the newspapers are left behind, reporting it the next day. Still, however, the *Sydney Morning Herald* outdoes itself in terms of the wonder expressed by the glory of the whole thing.

A COLOSSUS OF THE SOUTHERN HEMISPHERE

WORLD'S GREATEST ARCH

Across Sydney Harbour has been thrown the greatest arch bridge of the age, a commanding structure with stately towers that stand like the Pillars of Hercules bestriding the tide. No matter by what standards of comparison we measure it, its place is assured as one of the greatest of its age throughout the world. It is an outstanding feat of engineering because, though since rivalled in length, it is the heaviest, the widest and the greatest single span arch yet constructed by man.[43]

At which point the paper is barely clearing its throat.

Its vast, sweeping curves, from wherever one may view it, give a sense of rhythm and harmony, of strength combined with lightness and grace.[44]

Beyond the sheer facility of the structure to increase traffic flow exponentially between the shores of the city, and lift the economy in the Depression years, it equally lifts Sydney's confidence and pride. If we can build something as beautiful and revolutionary as this – what *can't* we build?

It is enough to invoke the words of a poem written by Charles Darwin's grandfather, Erasmus Darwin, not long after he had heard of the establishment of Sydney Town, way back in 1788.

Where Sydney Cove her lucid bosom swells,
Courts her young navies, and the storm repels;
High on a rock amid the troubled air
Hope stood sublime, and wav'd her golden hair . . .

'Hear me,' she cried, 'ye rising Realms! record
Time's opening scenes, and Truth's unerring word. —

There shall broad streets their stately walls extend,
The circus widen, and the crescent bend;

There, ray'd from cities o'er the cultur'd land,
Shall bright canals, and solid roads expand. —
There the proud arch, Colossus-like, bestride
Yon glittering streams, and bound the chasing tide . . .'[45]

Oh, and what a proud arch she is!

So quickly does 'the Bridge' capture the public imagination that before many moons have passed the visiting American author James Michener will be emphatic in his advice to other visitors.

To get on in Australia, you must make two observations. Say, 'You have the most beautiful bridge in the world,' and 'They tell me you trounced England again in the cricket.' The first statement will be a lie. [The] Bridge is big, utilitarian and the symbol of Australia, like the Statue of Liberty or the Eiffel Tower.[46]

Just quietly though? Michener adds a rider. 'But it is very ugly. No Australian will admit this.'[47]

ONE

'THE MOST BEAUTIFUL SITE IN THE WORLD'[1]

My heart just loosens when I listen to Goossens.[2]

Noël Coward, English playwright and composer, of his great
friend, the world-famous conductor Eugene Goossens

*He did not look for ideas in architectural magazines which feature
the works of his contemporaries. Instead, he hunted for architectural stimuli all over the world, particularly among time-honoured
cultures. In this way, he was not just a lone wolf in the beech
forest in Denmark, but an excellent hunting wolf who trotted
around the globe on his own, eagerly looking for new stimuli to
enrich his imagination.*[3]

Yuzo Mikami, architect who worked with Jørn
Utzon on the Opera House project

*My mother meant everything to my father. I don't think he could
have had such a positive, creative life without her. People would
ask where he'd like to live. 'Where Lis is.'*[4]

Lin Utzon on her father Jørn's love for her mother, Lis Utzon

1 July 1932, Sydney's General Post Office, Martin Place, an Australian BBC

Ring, mighty bells; make up lost time;
Ring all the changes that you know.
We want more changes here, I trow.
That you can give: begin to chime.[5]

The sound of five tons of bronze being struck ripples out into the chilly
Sydney sky. A deep reverberating A note coming from the General
Post Office at Martin Place. 'Great Harry' they call it, an antipodean
echo of Big Ben and Old Paul – after the Father of Federation, Henry
Parkes, whose initials are cast on its inside – its dark metal shuddering
and shivering in the cold of the 240-foot Hawkesbury sandstone tower

1

it calls home. Each clang cascades down the stony corridors of the city, alive, echoing and changing as it boings and bounces from surface to surface before passing away in the silent night. It is a familiar sound to Sydneysiders. But on this teeth-chattering July eve, there is one key difference. For the first time, Great Harry's sonorous ring can be heard from as far south as Melbourne, as far north as Cairns and as far west as Perth. Hear it now, crackling and popping as its pealing notes ring out through the static on wireless sets far and wide.

Once. Twice. Eight times.

It is 8 pm, and in perfectly proper BBC English, Conrad Charlton announces into a boxy black microphone: 'This is the Australian Broadcasting Commission.'[6]

With which, the ABC is officially launched – simultaneously broadcast on eight 'A-Class' stations across Australia – with several goals, but one so important that ABC Chairman Lloyd Jones, grandson of iconic Sydney retailer David Jones *himself*, highlights it in this first broadcast.

'The establishment of an Australian National Orchestra is under consideration and this is a dream that the Commission hopes to accomplish.'[7]

And with that, a new era is ushered in.

Australian minds and hearts light up as they sit around the wireless this night – listening to concerts and plays, which are broadcast after the many speeches – wondering what on earth might sail over the horizons of possibility next.

By the end of the 1930s, the power and reach of the ABC has grown, with 26 stations across the country broadcasting 16 hours a day, every day, and putting out no less than 132,000 hours of content a year, making it the most reliable news and entertainment service for all Australians. Those stations are lauded as beacons of enlightenment, fonts for music and drama, debate and discussion, carriers of culture to the far corners of the country, a great unifying force for the people of Australia. From Darwin to Deniliquin and Perth to Proserpine, Australians could repeat the words of writer George Farwell as he looked back on the 1930s.

'But for the ABC,' he wrote, 'we would have inhabited a land of perpetual drought.'[8]

8 April 1940, Copenhagen, storm clouds approaching

As twenty-first birthday parties go, this one will be remembered ever after by nigh everyone there, and not just for the champagne and revelry but for what will follow directly afterwards.

For now, though, focus on the couple in the corner, who have just met.

She is the striking, smiling blonde, Lis Fenger, commercial arts student and the birthday girl of the moment. And doesn't she seem *very* content to be chatting playfully with that handsome, blue-eyed architecture student of the Royal Danish Academy of Fine Arts, the young yet towering Jørn Utzon?

As it happens, only a few days earlier, Jørn had been striding down the street with his elder brother, Leif, when he had spied this same sparkling lass with long limbs striding barefoot the other way – and had been so gauche as to offer a playful wolf-whistle. She had imperiously stuck her nose in the air at the likes of him, and that was the end for Jørn. He was once bitten, twice smitten.

Now, after sorting out an invite to her birthday party via a mutual friend, there seems some chance they are no longer moving in opposite directions.

They form an immediate bond over their shared feeling of being outsiders among the cosmopolitan Copenhageners. They both hail from northern Jutland – Lis an hour north of Aalborg, Jørn's hometown – and laugh about what it feels like to be the country bumpkins among the sophisticated urbanites. They are both artists, and they almost share a birthday, for had they met the day after, it would have been at Jørn's birthday party instead. But mostly, they share the night, the two of them laughing and flirting into the wee hours of the morning, playful and giddy as children, until they must bid farewell, promising each other they will meet again soon.

But as they walk home beneath the soft lamplights on the cobblestone streets of Copenhagen, there are boots marching through the darkness.

Over the border, across the way, and under the cover of night, thousands of German soldiers are preparing to launch *Operation Weserübung*. Before long, the Denmark Jørn and Lis know will be occupied by strange faces.

The Danish early birds are the first to learn of the German attack, thanks to the shrieking engines of the Luftwaffe circling over the royal Amalienborg palace, mechanical vultures searching for carrion.

By 6 am, Danish ports are *crawling* with German infantry. The Danes know resistance is futile, and the palace gates and the Royal Guard who protect them are quickly overwhelmed. King Christian X surrenders on the proviso that he may retain political independence in domestic matters.

The Germans are fine with it, for the Danes are proud Aryans after all, so why not let them govern themselves?

All up, the operation is a six-hour affair. It is a 'peaceful' invasion, at least that is how the Germans tell it. Their real strategic aim is to use Denmark as a springboard to Norway, which Hitler needs for access to the Atlantic.

The Germans lose just three men with 30 wounded, while the Danes lose 16 soldiers and 10 civilians, with 23 wounded overall.

Not surprisingly, Jørn Utzon's twenty-second birthday party that day is cancelled and a strange new reality takes hold of the young student's life. He continues his studies under relatively austere circumstances – food shortages, blackouts and curfews – but at least he and his friends soon find ways to express their resistance to the occupation by catching pigeons in Copenhagen's Kongens Nytorv Square and painting British roundels on their wings before setting them free. It is typical Utzon: imaginative, courageous and with a sense of fun, which comes complete with a certain irreverence that causes the bubbly Lis Fenger, now his girlfriend, to fall deeply in love with him.

And for those Danes under occupation, there is one point of inspiration – King Christian X. Cycling the streets each day, among his people, without any guard detail at all. He talks to all he meets, encourages endurance and lifts spirits. Though Danish Jews are not rounded up as they are in Germany, the King personally facilitates their transport to neutral Sweden.

(In fact, even in Britain some Jews are interned, though not *because* they are Jewish. An example is a teenaged Jewish boy by the name of Harry Seidler, who had fled Austria in 1938 to escape the Nazis, only to be interned in England in 1940 as an 'enemy alien'. It is only by agreeing to go to Canada that, after another period of internment, he will be released to begin to study architecture, just like Jørn.)

Come December 1942, Jørn and Lis are married, and their estimation of Britain is growing every time they hear the British Prime Minister Winston Churchill addressing Europe. Before long, they are imitating him, and begin to develop a rather jowly pronunciation of the English language. Jørn graduates from the Royal Danish Academy of Fine Arts after successfully completing a daunting task for all aspiring architects: designing his first building. The end result is a plain, pine weatherboard cottage along the seawall of his grandmother's house at Ålsgårde, a fishing village on the north-east coast of Zealand, a little way north-west of Helsingør where his beloved father, Aage Utzon, a naval engineer and shipbuilder, is in charge of a shipyard.

Despite the simplicity of his first building's design, Jørn's fellow graduates often whisper to each other about his remarkable eye and his unorthodox methods.

For Jørn Utzon does things differently.

'The start of all architecture,' he is to say, 'is an act of love.'[9] (For yes, Jørn is a romantic – he credits his sensitive side, his *emotional* side, to his affectionate half-Russian mother, Estrid.)

He begins every design with a sober sense of reverence for the space from which his building must spring. He sits alone, sifting through his rich visual memory to conjure up, with slight flicks of his wrist, freehand sketches as detailed as they are delicate; works of art in themselves. Satisfied with his ideas, Jørn develops and tests his designs further by building wooden models with his own hands.

Unheard of! Ingenious!

He tells his friends it's the best way to see his ideas and explain them to others – to show in three-dimensional space what he visualises, and to check his ideas are viable, buildable – just as it is for his father when designing boats and ships.

And therein lies one root of his unusual methods. For Jørn's father, Aage, designer of sleek and innovative sailboats using the latest advances in shipbuilding techniques, has always taught him to work just so. As wee boys, Jørn and Leif would spend countless hours in their father's workshop at home and in the shipyards, helping him to draw his ideas – *Neater, Jørn, we can't have sloppy curves for our boats!* – then turn them into hand-crafted wooden models. Aage Utzon is an idealist of sorts, his workshop walls plastered with sketches of curved hulls, magazine articles about his innovative '*spidsgatter*' racing class yacht and a poster that declares: 'Happiness is not owning but creating.'[10] It rubs off on young Jørn.

Aage repeats his central lesson to his boys over and over – the best idea may be just around the corner ahead. And he lets his designs evolve with the help of his handsome timber models – tweaking the hull's curvature here, refining the arc of the ribbed skeleton there. Jørn, looking on, is excited to take it out sailing when it finally comes into being – and if that means the final result must also evolve through undoing previous work, so be it. And woe betide yacht builders who don't keep to exactly what Aage has designed, down to the last plank. He doesn't just hand over the designs and move on to the next one. He personally works with craftsmen, working out the details, supervising the construction, perpetually hovering, tweaking, improving.

And so Jørn makes no apology for his own methods. As an architect, he is certain he can reckon a design better if he knows what it will look like off the page as well as on.

It's the Utzon way, and it works well for him – perhaps also powered in part by the fact that, as he is dyslexic, he is simply more comfortable in the visual, hands-on world than the world of the written form.

Another strong artistic influence since childhood is his uncle, Aksel Ejnar Utzon-Frank, who is no less than the Sculpture Professor at the Royal Danish Academy.

From Uncle Aksel, young Jørn obtains many things, not least of which is an appreciation of *global* art, most particularly from his uncle's collection of Chinese antiquities.

'Search for inspiration among the unknown Eastern cultures,' Uncle Aksel tells him. 'Instead of the West, with which we are already all familiar.'[11]

Young Jørn loves his uncle, and takes the advice to heart.

Apart from time spent helping his industrious father and visiting his sculptor uncle, Jørn's artistic abilities and eye for composition and materials have been further guided during summers spent as a child at his grandmother's house. There he befriended an elderly neighbour, Danish artist Poul Schrøder, who taught the curious child to draw, aided one particular summer by Schrøder's friend, the Swedish painter Carl Kylberg, who has himself been influenced by both the philosophy of Hinduism and the bright colours associated with those who embrace it. As Utzon would later recall, 'For me it was a great inspiration to speak to Carl Kylberg. He taught me about the introspection in nature that he knew so well. He constantly dealt with this theme in his work: longing and expectation. I repeat it again and again to myself, that Kylberg found a source of great wealth in his inner being, as can anyone who dares to open themselves up. There was a sense of timelessness in him, like that of water and life.'[12]

And yet, by its nature, time demands change. So the freshly graduated architect Jørn Utzon and his lovely Lis decide to leave the rapidly deteriorating conditions in Nazi-occupied Denmark and cross the narrow Øresund to live in still neutral Sweden. There Jørn gets a job in the Stockholm architectural practice of the notably innovative, though now deceased, Swedish architect Gunnar Asplund, who had been one of the chief architects of the famous 1930 Stockholm Exhibition – devoted to displaying the virtues of modern design and production, over solid, stolid, ancient craft. Asplund is one of Utzon's design heroes for his pivotal role in the Scandinavian movement from traditional to modernist architecture.

'[The Stockholm Exhibition] was the exhibition where Scandinavian functionalism had its breakthrough in the Victorianism of the time,' Utzon would later recall. 'Here they experienced the new simple white architecture that demanded light and space, that let the sun shine in and rejoiced in the functional, the unconcealed.'[13]

And it didn't just influence him.

'My parents returned home [from the Exhibition] completely carried away by the new ideas and thoughts. They soon commenced redoing our home. The concept was space and light. All of the heavy, unpractical furniture was moved out and simple things were brought in. We developed new eating habits: healthy, green and lean. We began to exercise, get fresh air, cultivate light and the direct, so-called natural way of doing things. We were made to sit upright on good, practical furniture. We children had a swimming pool we could visit each day and use our bodies like fish in water. We got bicycles so we could get out in the fresh air and see what nature had to offer. We learned to admire the working man. Decent, well-done work was emphasised. Conventions were dropped, it was a question of us as people. There were no longer rules and sets of manners. I believe at this time we learned to see, and this quite naturally was of great importance. The empty, dead museum-like feeling about architecture disappeared and it became a living reality.'[14]

It had even influenced Aage Utzon's work, as he began studying fish to improve his boat designs.

The way forward, both father and son come to understand, is to find the answers to design in nature, while using modern industrial methods to build them.

And if in doubt, go back to that first principle Aage taught his boys: innovate. Forget orthodoxy – what is the best, most modern way to do it? What might work? Give it a *go*. Oh, and son? Understand this: no matter if you think you have found a solution to a particular design problem, modify it, tweak it, look for improvements on the solution you've found, and maybe even try out an entirely different solution altogether. Trial and error . . . it works!

After all, look what that approach had done for the Swedish capital. Oh, how Stockholm has come on as the Mecca for innovative architecture in the decades since! No longer must they live in dull, dark brick boxes of buildings, catastrophic cubes of orthodoxy. They can loosen up a little, embrace creative structural expression – crisp lines, curves, well-chosen materials, natural light and forms. They can lift the human experience of architecture.

At Asplund's architectural practice, Jørn Utzon begins to learn the daily practice of architecture – the nuts and bolts of client briefs, consultants and working drawings – and to build on his more aspirational ideas about the need to contemplate nature and human sentiment when conceiving a design.

Young Utzon hears one story about the late Asplund that sticks fast in his mind, and which he goes on to repeat often in his life, concerning a beautiful building the great man had designed and begun building on the edge of Stockholm. The client had been insufficiently appreciative of the masterpiece now under construction and made constant complaint about the cost and delay, whereupon Asplund, like clockwork, would resign – which would in turn see the client give way, Asplund take up the job once more, and the result was the most beautiful building in Sweden!

Utzon's theories continue to take shape in precisely the manner of his proposed buildings, with each iteration becoming ever more emblematic of humanist ideals and 'organic theory' as it is known in architectural circles – the idea that structures should almost look as if they grew naturally in whichever landscape they are planted; the buildings adapted to the landscape rather than the landscape being ravaged to make way for the building.

The bible in the field is D'Arcy Wentworth Thompson's magnum opus *On Growth and Form* from three decades earlier, which holds that nature has already solved the key design problems of how to build the most beautiful forms with the most resilient structures, so by studying nature, you could, and should, improve design.

Jørn, acting on Uncle Ejnar's advice, becomes equally fascinated by architectural traditions around the world and studies them avidly. From the Chinese tradition he becomes captivated by the work *Yingzao Fashi (Chinese Building Standards)*, from early in the twelfth century, which notes the virtues of producing a simple form in bulk and then using it in different ways to make entirely different structures. Yes, the most obvious example is the simple house brick, but *Yingzao Fashi* demonstrated how that simple principle could be expanded exponentially to make wondrous forms. It is, perhaps, the key breakthrough in Utzon's understanding of the architecture that he wants to pursue: with the right repetitive materials, you can achieve the perfect harmony of style *and* production economy.

Another Chinese influence is Lin Yutang, whose 1935 book *My Country and My People* exposes Utzon to the essence of the wisdom of the ancients when it came to incorporating the glory and strength of nature into your work.

'The artist,' Yutang writes, 'must absorb impressions from the myriad forms of nature, its insects and trees and clouds and waterfalls. In order to paint them, he must love them, and his spirit must commune with them. He must know and be familiar with their ways, and he must know how the same tree changes its shade and colour between morning and night or between a clear day and a misty morning, and he must see with his own eyes how the mountain clouds "entwine the rocks and encircle the trees".'[15]

In the modern world of architecture, with his love of nature – an avid sailor, hunter and swimmer since he was a child – it's no surprise Jørn Utzon soon becomes a devotee of the great American architect Frank Lloyd Wright – the quintessential organic architect whose approach to housing design rubs off on the young Dane.

But Jørn's work in Stockholm is interrupted by the war, which looks certain to end in a decisive victory for the Allied powers. He and many of his Danish friends in Sweden join the 'Danish Brigade', or Danforce, a Swedish military unit made up of exiled and self-exiled Danes who wish to return to Denmark the moment they can.

Mercifully, Jørn is only separated from his Lis and their new baby boy, Jan, for a freezing fortnight north of Stockholm, his long feet poking out the bottom of his poky army green tent as he trains with the others, before, on the evening of 4 May 1945 they hear the wonderful news on the BBC: the commander of the German troops occupying Denmark and Holland has unconditionally surrendered to Field Marshal Montgomery.

The next evening, Jørn Utzon and the rest of Danforce are returning to liberate their homeland. In a memory that would never leave him, he is so petrified driving a truck loaded with dynamite, that he strains to sit as far forward on the seat as possible in the absurd belief that if it all exploded he might be spared. It really is something though, to drive into the Danish capital, to see their fellow Danes lined up both sides of the street, cheering and waving their flags.

1945 to 1946, Sydney, an orchestra of our own

World War II now over, it is an older and wearier Charles Moses – a tall Englishman who had risen like a bounced ball from being an ABC cricket commentator to become the ABC's General Manager back in 1935, before he'd gone off to fight the war – who has returned, a man whose grit now matches his wit. It is *Lieutenant Colonel* Charles Moses, if you please, who resumes control of the ABC. Having commanded Australian troops in everything from the Fall of Singapore to the routing of the Japanese at the conclusion of the Kokoda campaign, he had been summoned to resume his post while still in his hospital bed in Port Moresby, at the direct request of Australia's Labor Prime Minister John Curtin. Curtin needs a strong man of intellect and influence to head the Australian Broadcasting Commission, and he has no doubt that Moses – quickly dubbed 'The Colonel' upon his return – is that man.

Indeed, a man for his times, Moses judges the time is right to move on from wartime austerity and half-measures when it comes to lifting the mood of the people. He wants no more half-sized ABC studio orchestras. Let us move forward with full-time, full-sized ABC orchestras across Australia, in every state, for annual concert seasons.

But how to come up with the money?

Very simply. By 'hoodwinking'[16] – his word – the ABC's board of directors on just how much it will actually cost to run six ABC symphony orchestras, one for every state.

A bargain, I tell you!

What counts for now is that the commissioners agree to his plan.

By the end of 1945, Moses has successfully convinced both the NSW State Government and the Sydney City Council to pool their efforts and fund a 'Sydney Symphony Orchestra'.

The ABC proudly announces the news:

Sydney Sets Example
SYMPHONY ORCHESTRA IS LEAD FOR NATION

A watershed moment for music in the country, there is now a Symphony Orchestra that Australia can call their own. Or rather, New South Wales can call their own, and so they do. Moses would note of Sydneysiders' enthusiastic reactions: 'They didn't know much about classical music but they liked the idea of their children attending symphony concerts.'[17]

The NSW Premier of the day, Mr William McKell of the Australian Labor Party, gleefully tells reporters: 'The establishment of the Sydney Symphony Orchestra represents a further advance in a planned scheme for providing the people of New South Wales with every opportunity for the enjoyment and study of the fine arts . . . Appreciation of good music, as of literature and dramatic art, is an essential to the full enjoyment of leisure hours by a people who claim for themselves a high standard of living.'[18]

But what good is a fine orchestra without an equally fine place to perform? The Victorian-era Town Hall is fine for now, but surely Sydney could do better, like a grand concert hall or one of those extravagant, multipurpose 'opera houses' so fashionable in Europe and the New World, a home for all the performing arts.

But, an opera house in Sydney? It's actually an old idea. As far back as 1928, the English-born theatrical entrepreneur and influential broadcaster, Sir Benjamin Fuller, had proposed an opera house for Australia and suggested that the great opera singer Dame Nellie Melba herself – the first Australian to achieve international fame in the world of classical music – might make another comeback to get behind the project.

After all, he asks: 'What could be a better monument to her fame and name than a national grand opera house?'[19]

And now, Premier William McKell flags his commitment to the cause: 'My Government in its post-war reconstruction design envisages the building up of a National Opera House project, the expansion of the tutorial services of the Conservatorium, and the encouragement of a deep love of all that is worthwhile in music and the associated arts.'[20]

As to the head of the ABC, Charles Moses, he proudly tells reporters:

> We have already engaged the first guest conductor for 1946 – Karl Rankl, one of the leading conductors in Britain to-day; and negotiations are proceeding for the engagement of another famous overseas conductor. Sydney can now proudly take her place musically with the world's great centres.[21]

And so it begins, with 82 musicians rehearsing and practising, pouring blood, sweat and tears into their instruments in anticipation of the upcoming concert season in Sydney's Town Hall, the best venue Sydney currently has to offer.

26 May 1946, Sydney, a celebrity conductor in the Antipodes

On this glorious day of late autumn 1946, the conductor of the Cincinnati Symphony Orchestra touches down with a screech of tyres on the tarmac at Sydney's Kingsford Smith Airport. He comes by *aeroplane*, this Eugene Goossens III, a modern man with many commitments for whom maritime travel is far too cumbersome. He is here on the invitation of Charles Moses and the ABC to make a tour of the country as the second guest conductor for the brand-new Sydney Symphony Orchestra.

The press pack crowd the terminal windows, watching the conductor make his way down the swaying staircase and across the tarmac. He is large but lithe, imposing but elegant, with skin like porcelain and a strong straight nose set upon an otherwise delicate face that wears a deliberate gaze. Immaculately dressed in the finest fashion of the day, he is a sight to behold. His saunter, his insouciant swagger, his *presence* suggests a man of fine music and culture, a friend of Stravinsky, Toscanini and Beecham.

The truth is, in the world of music, Eugene Goossens is a native and to the musical manner born, emerging from his British opera-singer mother's womb with a violin under his chin and a bow in hand, just as his Belgian father, a famous conductor himself, had hoped. This legend in his early fifties, a third-generation conductor surpassing even the reputation of his father and grandfather, once went fishing with Picasso.

Indeed, Goossens is a renaissance man of many passions. Painting, photography, trains (model and otherwise), horticulture – the man is a jack-of-all-interests. The journalists stir as they watch him walk through the gates, fedora tilted to a precise angle and his beautiful third wife, Marjorie Goossens, on his arm, a New York socialite two decades the maestro's junior, every bit as elegant and alluring as her husband.

(Cue Raymond Chandler: 'She was a blonde – a blonde to make a bishop kick a hole in a stained glass window for.'[22])

Cameras click, each flash the promise of a photo in tomorrow's pictorial tabloids, which are the latest rage, growing more popular with every edition. The press call out questions and scribble in their notebooks, men in boxy suits and mismatching hats, looking like backcountry boofheads compared to these divine, floating foreign visitors.

'I am looking forward to coming to grips with your Australian orchestras,'[23] Eugene Goossens the Third booms out in a deep baritone, a human tuba expertly played. He speaks with those perfectly round British vowels, though there is a hint of something else, something further flung. French maybe? A German? A Yank? Perhaps all of the above – wherever his elsewhere is, it places him *above* the rest of us; it is a hybrid accent, an amalgamation of the pronunciations and cadences of a high-flying, high-society 1940s cosmopolitan man. A man of purpose and culture, a superior man we are so lucky to welcome to our far-flung shores.

'It is said that your Melbourne and Sydney symphony orchestras are now equal to those of America and England. I would be glad to find an original orchestral work by a young Australian composer.'[24]

A ripple of wonder rolls through the assembled press.

He wants . . . an Australian?

'I *also* want,' Mr Goossens follows up, 'to meet young Australian musicians who think and write music. I want to know their ideas, and their intentions. If I find a really original work, I will certainly play it in Australia, and will take it back to the States with me.'[25]

Mr Goossens, Mr Goossens!

'And what of your own compositions? Your operas?'[26]

Goossens smiles to know his work is recognised all the way down here. 'Yes, I composed two operas in collaboration with the late Arnold Bennett, the novelist and playwright. *Judith* and *Don Juan de Manara*,'[27] he graciously replies.

Eugene Goossens is hurried away to begin his tour of Australia, for all of Perth, Adelaide, Melbourne and Brisbane await with a return to Sydney – maestro, please – as the grand finale.

It is no exaggeration to say he takes the country by storm, with the review by Perth's *Sunday Times* music critic emblematic of the general reaction. He is so beside himself he could be twins.

> After years among venerable but hackneyed classics, Perth Symphony Orchestra last night dropped an atom bomb of modernity on Winthrop Hall musical conservatives . . . Many a reactionary whisker must have been singed, for Stravinsky's *Firebird* proved itself an incendiary fowl in more ways than one. Goossens fanned each spark to blazing point and the orchestra bombarded the audience with a fiery revelation of hitherto unsuspected powers.[28]

Encore! Encore!

Goossens arrives back in Sydney and conducts the Australian premiere of Stravinsky's *The Rite of Spring* at the Sydney Town Hall, which is a treat. But most exciting for the conductor is what he showcases next . . .

It is a beautiful, riveting, original 16-minute orchestral suite taken from a 45-minute ballet score titled *Corroboree*, written by the Australian composer John Antill. It is a tribute to the Indigenous culture of the Dharawal people he had seen at La Perouse, and from the moment Goossens lifts his baton with a flourish, the audience are enthralled.

One of ours wrote it?

But while Sydneysiders are heartily impressed, one who is much less so is . . . Eugene Goossens.

This is the best venue that Sydney has got for its Symphony Orchestra?

This draughty, cavernous Town Hall?

He finds it pitiful.

It had been built as an administrative base and assembly hall the better part of a century earlier, with no view – and more to the point, no *ear* – to the acoustics needed for the performance of a first-class orchestra. Alas, playing fine music in Sydney's old and echoing Town Hall is like drinking fine champagne from a pewter beer stein; it's fine, it still works, but there's something just *not quite right*.

What is the point of having a world-class conductor like (*sniff*) himself, if there is no place to play?

Delicately, Charles Moses reminds him that the orchestra is itself brand new.

But Eugene Goossens is not a man with time for excuses, he is a man of action and purpose, a man of momentum. There must be a proper concert hall in Sydney if the calibre of its culture is ever to improve and the heights of true aural ecstasy are ever to be reached.

And what of opera, Colonel Moses?

Well, I know there are a few small opera companies around Sydney who make do with whatever venue they can find, but . . .

Not good enough, the music man tells the ABC General Manager. The people deserve better. The musicians deserve better. The *music itself* deserves better!

Now this, this is a burning passion in a fiery man, if ever Colonel Moses has seen one . . . which gives him an idea.

Well then, Mr Goossens, given just how strongly you feel about our new orchestra here in Sydney, what if you were to become the resident conductor?

The master conductor counters, a warning to Moses that has since been forgotten – I am too expensive for you.

Something to think on, then . . .

And as for that unique Australian composition that Goossens had come looking for, that piece so singularly Australian in essence that it would be like taking a piece of the country home with him to show off, he has found it in John Antill's *Corroboree*.

(Cue a collective swoon from the press pack once more – that something written by an Australian could be so highly regarded by someone of Goossens' eminence that he promises to promote it in Europe.)

With Antill's score wrapped up safe and sound in his suitcase, Goossens is ready to fly back north with his cherished wife, back to London, back to Berlin, back to the grand symphony orchestras of Europe, then home to America. It will be the first Australian composition to be performed abroad; a lone, beautiful tendril of a quintessentially Australian sound reaching out from the Southern Hemisphere.

•

Charles Moses knows that securing public funds from the preening powers-that-be can feel like plucking feathers from a peacock. A certain amount of cunning and a little hoodwinking is always needed, lest there be a great deal of unpleasant screeching and no little scratching. And so, just as he has succeeded in pulling the state orchestras into existence, Moses now sets his mind to making a case for recruiting the great Goossens.

It isn't easy, but every rich and powerful room that Colonel Moses enters, he schmoozes. He works the room, gently prodding and probing and even proselytising, letting Sydney high society know that Goossens is the golden goose, the ticket to *really* putting Australia's cultural scene on the map.

Moses pulls off a miracle of biblical proportions and the sea of red tape opens up before him.

One night, Sydney time – early morning in Ohio – he has the man himself on the other end of a crackly line to Cincinnati.

Moses reveals all the perks he's scraped together and bundled into an enormous salary package for the maestro.

It is not that there is a sharp intake of breath on the other end of the line. But there is at least a pause.

And like that, an unheard-of public salary in Australian history is organised, and Eugene Goossens gives his notice to Cincinnati, where he has been for the last 16 years. From here on in, he will be the head of the Sydney Symphony Orchestra *and* the NSW Conservatorium of Music.

•

Back in Denmark, 28-year-old Jørn Utzon is now the proud father of three-year-old Jan and a new baby girl, Lin, named for the Chinese architectural seer Lin Yutang.

He has quickly picked up his career in architecture – mostly designing big factories as part of the post-war effort in Denmark, to pay the bills – and soon picks up a Minor Gold Medal from the Royal Academy of Fine Arts for his efforts in an annual competition for architects younger than 30, in recognition for his work designing a concert hall which, although never built, is innovative and beautiful.

It is the beginning of a lifelong passion for entering architectural competitions where one's imagination can flow freely without needing to fit in with dull parameters imposed by clients and budgetary constraints. And sometimes, should you win, great things can happen!

In a story that Utzon will delight in telling, back in 1907 the city of Stockholm had held an architectural competition to design the new City Hall right on the waterfront in central Stockholm, on the site of an old mill. The result had been an innovative wonder, halls and courtyards – inside and outside – towers and galleries, all of them a reflection of the city, its people and the landscape on which it was built. So beloved was this City Hall, designed by Ragnar Östberg, that it came to affect the face of the entire city. As public confidence grew, other architects began to understand the possibilities of design beyond the traditional, and the citizenry began to appreciate the sheer beauty of the waterfront as never before. Östberg had come up with a building that did, in and of itself, change the culture and lift the people.

Jørn aspires to do just the same with his own architecture, so keeps learning everything he can, wherever he can, and working his way up in his trade.

In early 1947, he works a while with Scandinavia's most acclaimed modernist architect, Alvar Aalto, in Finland – famous for combining Nordic Classicism with modern organic form, a forward-thinking proponent of the 'International Style'. Alvar Aalto, Utzon learns, is a man to be emulated.

2 July 1947, Sydney, Goossens rules the roost

There he is!

And there's his sophisticated wife, Marjorie, or, as they are soon to be known in Sydney: 'Eugene Goossens the Third and the third Mrs Eugene Goossens.'

Just behind them on the stairs coming down onto the tarmac are the two youngest of Goossens' five daughters, Sidonie and Renée – 'Donie' is 15 and Renée is seven – the progeny of his second marriage, and Sidonie already a wonderful harpist in her own right.

Mr Goossens wastes no time, setting out his latest grand plans for the crowding press.

'Visiting artists,' he says in that entrancing cosmopolitan lilt, *which just kinda oozes classiness, ya know?*, 'would speak about the great Sydney Orchestra, and it would spread Australia's fame overseas. It is my ambition not only to build a fine orchestra, but to have a fine home for it, with the right acoustic properties and seating accommodation for 3600 people. I want to see established in Sydney a musical centre housing a big hall for a symphony orchestra, a small hall for chamber music, and a fine home for an opera company. I want a home for opera where Australian composers will learn and will go on to write Australian operas.'[29]

Oh yes, nothing by halves for Mr Goossens.

But let us not tarry, Harry, and hurry instead, for Goossens is likely to worry if you don't scurry! Though not a sporty man, he certainly hits the ground running and is soon something close to the toast of the town, as the Sydney Symphony Orchestra rehearsals take on a refined quality – Goossens and his baton, driving them from splendid crescendo to splendid crescendo.

After being recalled four times at the end of his first performance with his new orchestra, Goossens does not hold back, saying, 'I look forward to making it one of the conspicuously great orchestras of the world. I feel that, with the material I have, I can do it.'[30]

Although his musicians find he has a certain 'Godalmightyness' about him, and he has a tendency to 'talk down to colonials', there is no doubt they flourish under his tutorship.[31]

Between times, that imperious figure sailing down the corridors of the Sydney Conservatorium, an enormous fur coat around his shoulders, surely more for the effect than the wintry chill? That, too, would be Eugene Goossens, newly installed as the director of 'the Con', the highest-ranking person there.

Watch now as his youngest daughter, Renée, runs towards his outstretched arms, as she comes on her first visit to the Conservatorium.

'Is this really your room, Daddy?'[32] she burbles, gazing around at the 'The Director's Studio', as it is called, an enormous space boasting a shining grand piano, a stylish leather sofa and French doors opening straight out to a tropical garden, beyond which both the Botanic Gardens and the sparkling waters of Sydney Harbour are apparent.

'Yes, my little one,' Goossens replies, holding her tightly. 'This is where I work. Piano students come here for auditions. I rehearse with the chamber music groups, rest before concerts, and talk to members of the staff and the orchestra. The sofa is comfy enough for an afternoon nap. It's a quiet place for composing, too. I rather like it . . .'[33]

Yes, Goossens' impact on the Conservatorium is immediate, as he sets standards that not all students or staff reach. In one burst of peak pique, the man they have come to call 'The Boss' – he even signs his professional letters as such – fails an entire class of senior students who did not get remotely close to his standards.

But if you happen to be a prodigious talent, well then, allow him to open the door to the world for you.

Speaking of which, it is while judging an eisteddfod at Sydney Town Hall not long after he arrives, that a young woman steps onto the stage to sing an aria.

Goossens is seen to stop still the moment she begins. He stares, he leans forward, he turns his ear towards her. In all his days, he has rarely if ever heard such control in one so young. Her voice stays perfect over an extraordinary range, going from a low G to hitting a high C, seemingly without effort. His jaw drops as she begins to 'spin lyrical phrases with elegant legato, subtle colourings and expressive nuances'[34].

He looks at his program notes.

What is the name of this virtuoso?

Joan Sutherland . . .

Amazing. In such a town as this, such a talent. And she is, he finds out, a *stenographer*. Well, not for much longer she won't be. Hers is far too precious a talent to waste tapping a typewriter, and he soon finds a place for her at the Conservatorium, where another talent, young Richard Bonynge, is emerging as a conductor. Goossens adds him to his coterie – and he is delighted when Sutherland and Bonynge start courting, as they can look after each other.

In response to the whole Goossens persona, Sydney reels. So brilliant! So sophisticated! Such a master of his craft!

And in fact, it is not just him; his glorious and always fashionably attired wife Marjorie causes her own sensation, becoming the last word – the *last word*, I tell you! – in *haute couture*.

No social pages are complete without photos of the two of them attending functions, inevitably surrounded by what must pass for high society in what they clearly regard as a backward provincial city, though they are quite gracious about it. No matter how close the crowd presses around them, still they take on all comers until it is time to go, at which point Mr Goossens – get this – loudly whistles the opening chords of Beethoven's Fifth Symphony, at which point Marjorie knows to extricate herself from the pressing flesh and make an exit with him every bit as grand as their entry had been.

The swish receptions at Government House are precisely the sort of events that Goossens has prepared for. He varies between whispering into influential ears and chewing some of them off in his eagerness to make those who count understand: Sydney *must* have an opera house to call its own. The grand capitals of Europe have them, why shouldn't Sydney, a city of – it's amazing but it's true – one and a half million people?

He tells one reporter: 'I'm starting an "opera house" and a "concert hall" movement . . . The spirit and enthusiasm behind this public is immense but it needs constant kindling.'[35]

Hearing of Goossens' interest, it is not long before Dr Karl Langer, an architect engaged by the Council of Sydney to prepare plans to remodel the Circular Quay area, contacts him to arrange a meeting and, in the company of Sidney Luker, the Chief County Planner for the Council, takes him for a small walk down the hill and over to Mrs Macquarie's Chair.

There it is, Mr Goossens.

There *what* is?

'How would you like to have an opera house there!'[36]

The conductor sees some rather dilapidated tram sheds on the point jutting out into the harbour at the east end of Circular Quay, the Harbour Bridge in the background, but Dr Langer and Mr Luker – trained for such things – see the *possibilities*!

Move the tram sheds somewhere – who cares? – and look at what you have! An open, flat spot, right next to the city, surrounded on three sides by the glorious harbour.

Before Eugene Goossens' very eyes, the tram sheds fall to dust, a grand opera house arises, and yes, just faintly, he can hear the music. The percussion and the strings and the brass and wind . . . all building to a superb climax.

As they walk back up the hill, the conductor is impassioned, proclaiming, 'It's incomparable!'[37]

Who can he talk to, to get this done?

He will start by whispering words of wisdom into the silky ears of those in the know and then to the press at every turn.

As it happens, the NSW Government already has a policy to build a 'National Theatre', which is a good start, and the Minister for Local Government, Joe Cahill – who had so overcome his 'No. 2 notice' from the Great Strike of 1917 that he has successfully entered politics and been prospering there for the last 22 years – is apparently on side to take it from being a policy to actually doing something, all of which is promising. But what is needed is for a critical mass of decision-makers to match Goossens' enthusiasm.

'I am confident of winning the interest and sympathetic co-operation of the Government in this regard,'[38] Goossens tells the *Herald*. 'Only the prize-winning architectural design of an international competition (which I hope an Australian wins) will be worthy of such a site. An opera house we can be proud of will focus the international spotlight of culture on Sydney. Without it we'll stagnate in outer darkness. But we must get started, or else it will be too late.'[39]

Joe Cahill is not sure, telling the *Herald* in response that the government's 'master plan for Sydney made no provision for an opera house on Bennelong Point but that it did provide for cultural centres to be built.'[40]

Which is about as far as it goes for the moment.

Not far enough, says Mr Goossens!

'We *must* have the Opera House within five years,' he says. 'Sydney Orchestra is taking its place among the world's major symphonic groups. A fine hall is essential if the public is to hear the orchestra at its best. If my plan succeeds Sydney will have, with the co-operation of those in authority, a great opera house. There is substantial support for the site and we intend to follow it up.'[41]

He does so by talking to such people as Professor George Molnar, from the Faculty of Architecture at the University of Sydney, who doubles as a cartoonist in the *Sydney Morning Herald*. Goossens convinces him to set his students the task of designing a theatre complex for Bennelong Point.

Goossens meanwhile commissions his artist friend, Bill Constable, to illustrate his personal vision, his dream, for the site – what he will come to call the 'Australian National Theatre'. It will be in an Art Deco style, with a grand Grecian amphitheatre, in the same vein as the Hollywood Bowl, famously situated in a concave canyon, providing a natural amphitheatre, and it will have modernist trimmings, like rounded P&O windows.

Next in his relentless campaign, he heads off to the Sydney City Rotary Club – base camp to the pinnacle of Australian cultural life – to set out the grand future that awaits, if the people get behind matters cultural.

'I want,' he says, 'Sydney people to look upon members of the Sydney Symphony Orchestra as they look upon members of cricket and football teams. As my flautist or trumpeter moves about the city, I visualise traffic being held up and people whispering, "There goes Mr White" or "There goes Mr Robinson" in the same way that they speak of Don Bradman. There is an amazing interest among ordinary folk in the Sydney Symphony Orchestra, and youth especially has succumbed to the spell of good music. I believe that eventually the youth of the city will take the matter in their own hands and give the same degree of recognition to musicians as is given today to cricketers and footballers.'[42]

And where else could they, should they, perform but in an opera house on Bennelong Point?

'I hope to see the opera house built in five years,' he repeats one more time for the road, before adding a little sniffily, 'I won't wait longer than that.'[43]

For a good chunk of the population the only thing that gets through is the conductor's idea that violinists could be as famous as the greatest man who ever lived, Don Bradman.

Yeah right, in this country you'd get more points for hitting a ball over a picket fence with a violin than coaxing fine music from it.

None of which dissuades the maestro.

1948 to 1949, North Africa to North America, stepping outside the box

In this rising summer of 1948, Jørn Utzon continues to move fast, pushing ahead in his on-the-road school of architecture, starting with the glories of Paris – the Eiffel Tower, the Arc de Triomphe, the Louvre, Napoleon's Tomb, the Avenue des Champs-Élysées! The Dane soaks it all up and, among others, is deeply honoured to meet the charming Swiss–French architect and artist, Le Corbusier, a leader in the modernist movement's International Style, who is currently designing the United Nations headquarters. Utzon would have loved to stay longer, but must now head to Morocco, where he is impressed by the way the Moroccans build manmade oases that blend in with the dry, hot, dusty landscape yet function to keep those harsh realities at bay with their beautiful shaded courtyards. Touring the cities of Marrakesh and Casablanca, he is enamoured of the colourful ceramic tiles that line the soaring domes of mosques, looking as brilliant as the day they were laid . . . hundreds of years ago. Incredible, and much the same as what he had seen on an inspiring trip to Persia earlier in the year – the Great Mosque at Esfahan, with its exquisitely tiled domes and inner vaults had left a strong impression.

Next stop for Jørn and Lis is America, courtesy of a grant Jørn wins from the Danish Government, and the best part is they manage to take their children, Jan and Lin, with them.

As Lin Utzon would later say of her parents: 'After the war, they hungered for life. And all that was forward-looking. They were eager to see the new society of America and its architecture.'[44]

Through his connections, Aage manages to secure them passage on a freighter bound for New York in return for Jørn working in the hold as a carpenter for the duration – allowing them to save the grant money for travel!

Better still, when they arrive in New York, it is to find a brand-new Studebaker waiting for them dockside, courtesy of the efforts of Lis's father, who had recently performed nasal surgery on the CEO of Studebaker and formed a friendship through it – giving the young family the perfect start to their months-long architectural odyssey.

They take in all the sights and sites, including the buildings of another architectural hero and proponent of modernist architecture, Mies van der Rohe, before travelling out to the Midwest to look at the buildings of the cutting-edge Finnish–American architect, Eero Saarinen – initially known as the son of the famed Finnish architect Eliel Saarinen who had emigrated to the US 24 years before, but now becoming famous himself.

The Utzons drive west to Taliesin East, the Wisconsin school of the most revered modern architect in the world, Frank Lloyd Wright, where the young Dane spends a few weeks with other up-and-coming architects studying at the great man's knee – nature is the key lesson of the revered Wright: a building should sit in unity with its natural surroundings.

At the end of their US tour, Jørn, Lis and the kids cross the southern border into Mexico, where they visit the buildings of Felix Candela, an innovative Spanish architect designing curved roofs from three-inch thin concrete shells. Utzon equally studies the architectural wonders wrought by the ancient Mayans, becoming fascinated by their temples in the Yucatan and Oaxaca, impressed by the notion of building sacred stone pyramids, with grand stairways, rising up and up on each side to a flat top poking out of the jungle canopy towards the skies.

'As an architectural element, the platform is fascinating. I lost my heart to it on a trip to Mexico . . .' Utzon will recount. 'By building up the platform on a level with the roof of the jungle, these people had suddenly conquered a new dimension that was a worthy place for the worship of their gods.'[45]

The Utzon family spends hours walking around these ancient sites, which demand reverence from even the most uninterested visitor, Jørn loping up and down the giant staircases like a giant kid, up and down, clicking away at his camera to get photos from every angle before calling out to Lis over and over just how magnificent these ancient edifices remain.

It's a trip Jørn will one day describe as, 'One of the greatest architectural experiences in my life.'[46]

Arriving home in Denmark, ready to settle, Jørn and Lis buy a wild plot of land tucked away in a beech forest on the outskirts of a tiny village called Hellebaek – meaning 'Holy Stream' – not far from where Aage Utzon works at Helsingør shipyard, some 40 kilometres north of Copenhagen and just a long stone's throw across the Øresund to Sweden.

In spare time from his paid work, Jørn puts enormous effort into designing the family home – a key milestone and oft foundation stone in any architect's career – trying to incorporate many of the wonderful architectural concepts he has learned from his studies and his travels. At work's end, in early 1952, the building of his vision completed, the young family move into Denmark's first 'open-plan' home. For all the seeming humility of this small, brick mid-century home hiding in the nook of an unknown forest, it causes a sensation among Scandinavian architects, who travel from afar to take a look at this entirely new concept, with the kitchen, lounge and living rooms all in one light-filled space!

'It's human nature to respond to nature,' Jørn is fond of saying. 'Up north, we want sunlight. In the Arab countries, they want shade. If you take basic things like that into consideration, you can create good environments for people.'[47]

To that end, Jørn had specially designed two huge 'skylights' for the flat roof – windows on the roof! – which are so admired that they are soon put into commercial production. If you can believe it, there's even heating built into the floor, a boon for fighting off the bitter cold of the northern winter.

The whole thing is just like the man himself: fresh, new, original, innovative and *exciting*!

Young Jan Utzon, nine years old at the time, will later recall of this period in their Hellebaek home: 'People said it was like living on Mars. It was the first of its kind in Denmark . . . Everybody wanted to see it. Busloads of architects came.'[48]

Jørn Utzon becomes the talk of the town.

No less than the great Arne Jacobsen – far and away the most famous architect in Denmark, thanks mostly to his iconic egg chair – comes for a visit. After just one look he remarks to Jørn's father, Aage, who happens to be there when he stops by: 'He sure is talented. More than me.'[49]

Aage's ear lobes turn pink with pleasure at his own thoughts being confirmed by the man himself, and humbly agrees.

And then there is the old man who lives on the other side of the woods who one day comes ambling, shambling up to their front yard and stares for a little while. The Utzon family, nothing if not hospitable, welcome him inside where he stops again and this time exclaims: 'Oh! People live like this, too?'[50]

Well, the Utzons do, and they are a weird mob; different from other families and everyone in the area knows it. Why, do you know their kids barely have toys – aside from a few Lego sets, another of Denmark's iconic exports – but they *are* given free rein to draw and paint on the walls of their home, and to play with sand on the floor . . . inside! Getting outside, though, is one of their greatest joys, as there's so much to explore – and their beloved father regularly takes them on trips through the forest, out hunting, down to the beach or out on his sailing boat, not to mention summers spent with Uncle Leif and the cousins, sailing mostly – everything in nature can be made into fun. As Lin will later recall: 'It was a creative home. Creativity ran through everything. [My parents] really did have a very different approach. Everything they did was different. I loved the unconditional approach that particularly Dad had. Mum had it, too, but Dad more so.'[51]

1951, Sydney, a star is born

That virtuoso moonlighting as a stenographer who Goossens had discovered at a Town Hall eisteddfod?

Look at her now!

Joan Sutherland in the starring role of Eugene Goossens' own opera, *Judith*, performing at the Con.

'Joan Sutherland is one of the most promising voices I have ever heard,' Goossens declares to all who care to listen. 'She will become famous, she deserves to.'[52]

Backstage, Joan blushes as the musicians and performers sing her praise. (Her life has been filled with sorrow of late, after her beloved sister Barbara jumped to her death at the Gap. Singing is Joan's only escape from the heavy loss – and her success some salve for the soul of her grieving mother.)

Young Renée Goossens, now 11 years old, runs up to congratulate her.

Joan thanks her dearly and asks, 'Are you proud of your father, for his opera?'

'Very proud of him,' the young girl replies. 'You were good, too.'[53]

Not everyone is convinced.

'Joan Sutherland sang the title role broadly and boldly,' *The Sun* reports, 'but was histrionically defeated by a part that would take the resources of a Sybil Thorndike to present plausibly.'[54]

Quite.

'It was a worthy debut by local standards,' it will later be noted, 'though not disposed to point the way to international status.'[55]

No matter. It is not the local critics who count. It is Eugene Goossens who continues to believe in Sutherland's extraordinary potential and, after more intense training with her, he is happy to send her to an audition at Covent Garden in London with a reference by him: 'The bearer of this letter has a magnificent dramatic operatic soprano voice, and has done excellent work here (Australia) in concert and operatic performances. Her voice is in the true Australian tradition, and she made quite a sensation here recently in her creation of Judith in my opera of that name. Her departure for Europe will be a great loss to Australia for such grand natural voices such as hers are all too rare nowadays.'[56]

She is accepted and soon launched, a bird flown the nest and out from under the wing of Goossens, the Sydney press be damned.

1952, Glebe Point Road, Sydney, he's so esoteric

Eugene Goossens' slender fingers fossick through the shelves of a dark Glebe bookstore – a touch bohemian, a little gloomy, a lingering whiff of old dusty volumes, and very anonymous, just the way he likes such stores. He has no specific title in mind, just a genre . . .

What is *that*?

Yes, he had been taught never to judge a book by its cover, but Goossens has never seen a cover quite like *this*.

A long-faced woman adorned with a starry pendant, anthropomorphised swine with all too human eyes, a man with the beak of an ibis and a coiling winged serpent bearing down on them all. Whatever this is, Eugene Goossens is transfixed.

It is called *The Art of Rosaleen Norton* and is filled with poetry and esoteric . . . in fact, erotic . . . artworks.

Time stops. Goossens' breath shortens. He glances nervously to the left and right. Has anyone recognised him? No, no-one even glances his way, and he is able to dig deeper into the book, turning the pages with rising excitement. Each image is more alluring than the last.

This artist, this poet, this Rosaleen, this woman who has cast a spell on him; what manner of Faustian bargain must she have made to bring forth such beauty and horror to the page?

Who knows the origins of a man's or a woman's sexual psyche, the things that stir from deep within, placed there by experiences of long ago? What is certain is that as a child, Goossens had, as his younger sister would later note, a 'sort of mania about gargoyles'[57], which would see him spending hours, days and *weeks* doing impressive drawings of the little devilish figures. So it's little wonder the conductor is transfixed by this devilish publication, devoted as it is to those very same gargoyles and other pagan and occult images, but in highly sexualised poses. All these naked hermaphroditic beings, these massive phalluses with serpent heads, searching for any crevice they can find . . . while pitch-black panthers prowl close. It is all part of a world he had first become absorbed in 50 years earlier when packed off to a Catholic boarding school in Belgium. There had been little outlet for it in his adult years but, here in Sydney . . . who knows?

A few furtive glances and a quick transaction later, the deed is done. The distinguished-looking gentleman with the great fur coat around his shoulders is walking out with a brown paper bag tucked guiltily under his arm.

•

In the realm of powerful gentlemen live many secrets.

The more powerful the man, the more secrets he knows. The more secrets he knows, the more dangerous they are.

As one positioned at the pinnacle of that very realm, Eugene Goossens may ask discreetly of his peers . . . who is this Rosaleen Norton?

Well, there is no other way of putting this, Gene.

She is a witch.

'The witch of Kings Cross,' they call her, the latter being that strip just east of the CBD where the desperate and the depraved, the dreamers and the drug addicts, the radicals, revellers, poets and politicians muster to mingle with American sailors, drunken yobbos, working girls and private school boys at the Hasty Tasty, the Roosevelt and other joints.

The witch is a fine example of the dangers of the place, Gene. And she's a witch all right, even if she hails from leafy Lindfield, up where you live, on Sydney's affluent North Shore. They say she spent a good part of her youth living in a tent in the backyard, when not in the principal's office at Chatswood Girls High, before being escorted firmly to the gates of expulsion.

But, no matter for Miss Norton that her God-fearing Protestant parents, and seemingly everyone else, resisted her embrace of an ancient calling. They will *never* understand that she did not choose to be a witch, she was *born* one – in a thunderstorm in 1917, seeing as you ask. And so she had maintained her childhood crush on Dracula with no more apology than she offered for keeping pet spiders – her favourite being a 'big furry night-spider . . . named "Horatius"'[58] skilled at weaving scary webs at the entrance to her tent – and had kept going until . . .

Until just after privately taking an Oath of Allegiance to the Horned God – Pan – by drinking wine mixed with her own blood and some green leaves, she left the family home and sustained herself by writing horror stories before studying art for two years under the noted sculptor Rayner Hoff, and modelling her naked form for Norman Lindsay, who called her . . . 'a grubby little girl with great skill'[59].

Quite.

Go careful into that dark night, Eugene's peers warn him, seeing the spark of arousal in his eye.

With a thrill of guilty pleasure, double-checking with the maid that Marjorie is out for the rest of the day, Eugene Goossens writes to Miss Rosaleen Norton, care of her publisher.

Scarcely believing that it could be coming from the famed Eugene Goossens who she has read about, whose daily rehearsals with the Sydney Symphony Orchestra are conducted in a Darlinghurst Road studio no more than 500 yards from her flat, she is quick to write back, inviting him for tea and . . . whatever.

•

The toast of Sydney, Eugene Goossens, arrives at Rosaleen Norton's door with his heart in his mouth, a lump in his stomach and an unmentionable stirring storm that comes from deep within. The conductor takes his first step into the witch's lair – which admittedly looks more like a poxy flat with flaky paint, holes in the roof, and wafting stalactites of cobwebs. Upon the dusty floor-boards stands a ritual altar covered in blue cloth and bearing the image of a toothy devil, painted by Miss Norton herself, while through the clouds of incense smoke he can just see that the walls are covered with more murals of Pan, 'the Horned God', together with an array of alluring rubber masks. A rather seductive-looking couch lies against one wall, while a bed in red is against another.

But forget all that.

For here is the witch herself, wearing the mask of a cat. And she is so exotic – so *erotic* – Goossens can see she is topless beneath her loosely slung black and red silk shawl. And though she wears a witch's black apron from the waist down, protecting what little is left of her modesty from front and back, it simply doesn't exist on the sides!

'Roie,' she says, offering a pale hand of introduction.

Goossens takes her hand and enters her shadowy world – a devilish covenant – ethereally lit by the brass lamp she holds and the red lamp in the corner, whose shade is decorated with demonic visages.

Goossens loosens, tightens, stiffens, and loosens some more, his breathing coming in short gasps.

Her form, her figure!

Her dark, wild, curly hair! Her ebony eyes so wonderfully set off by sharply triangular eyebrows!

And now, appearing as if from thin air, is Roie's sallow meets callow younger warlock lover, one Gavin Greenlees, a poet, who wears the mask of a toad but still manages to puff away with the same kind of long cigarette holder as Miss Norton.

And so it begins, Eugene's journey into Roie Norton's mystical world, helped along in the early months by the fact that his wife Marjorie has just left for one of her many extended trips to Europe.

Other Sydney gentlemen are part of the same secret coven, including a well-known radio announcer, and an extremely wealthy bookmaker. After several more visits to the coven, the covenant demands Eugene Goossens take his Oath of Allegiance to the Horned God. The special incense is lit and he kneels before his witch and warlock. Bowing his head and placing one hand on his crown and the other beneath the sole of his right foot in total submission, he swears to hereafter observe the four Elemental Powers of air, fire, water and earth.

Goossens is initiated with the occult name of 'Djinn' – a word hailing from pagan ancient Arabia, popularly translated as 'genie' in English, and a play on his familiar name, Gene. Roie hands him a small belt of green leather with silver buckles lined with blue silk, the Witch's Garter, which he must keep on him at all times.

He addresses the witch of Kings Cross by her own occult name of Thorn, and she is the all-conquering Queen of her domain. Arise, Warlock.

His secret double life takes on ever newer dimensions, filled with ever more rituals – all of them devoted to worshipping the Horned God, by engaging in the sins that please him most – while wearing everything from . . . nothing at all, to robes and hoods and masks.

Something else that binds the three, after the ribald rituals are realised, is a common love of classical music, with Thorn being particularly fond of Mozart and Beethoven. They plan to collaborate on a musical rendition of Edgar Allan Poe's famed short story, 'The Fall of the House of Usher'. Yes, Greenlees could write the words, Thorn could use her painting skills for the backdrops, while Djinn could compose the music. Who knows, one of these days it might even play at Bennelong Point!

TWO

'AN ACT OF RARE IMAGINATION'

The public buildings of Sydney are not very distinguished. Especially their settings are mean. (This does not apply to tram sheds) ... The site of an opera house should be generous, to give scope to imaginative design. It should be a commanding site. It should take advantage of the natural beauty of its surroundings.[1]

George Molnar, on the selection of a site for
Sydney's Opera House, October 1954

Manchester by the Sea.[2]

Neville Cardus, classical music broadcaster and famed
cricketing journalist, characterising Sydney in the 1940s

2 April 1952, Sydney, agitator to Premier

While NSW Premier James McGirr curses his illness and misfortune – something not quite right with his arteries it looks like – he watches, helpless, as Joe Cahill, the man from Marrickville, who had first made his name addressing his fellow workers in the Domain back in the Great Strike, becomes his successor. Joe is just starting out on his seventh decade, but still carries the energy of a man half his age, and at 34 votes to 14, he is the New South Wales Premier.

'I am here as one who has worked in industries right through early boyhood,' he said back in 1925, in his maiden speech to parliament, his laconic Australian accent as broad as the Nullarbor. 'As one who understands what the struggle for existence really means, as one who has not had the advantage of education of some men.'[3]

And though his life has changed in the 27 years he's spent in the NSW Parliament, 11 in the capacity of Minister, from Public Works to Local Government to the Deputy Premiership, he's still the same old Joe.

Yes, of course his hands have softened since his days on the tools, and his slicked-back silvering hair now lends him an ambassadorial air befitting a state Premier, but he has no airs or graces, not an ounce of swagger about him, and this genuine man of the people still goes to the department store barber every fortnight, where he waits his turn like everyone else. He still lives in the red-brick three-bedroom house in the Irish-Catholic stronghold of Marrickville where his parents had raised him. And he continues that tradition, raising five of his own in the same house with his dearly beloved wife of nearly 40 years – till death do them part – Esmey. One of their daughters has even become a nun in a convent, a proud manifestation of the deep religious roots the Cahill family have put down in Sydney.

For, just as he'd thundered back then in parliament, giving notice that he will be devoting himself henceforth to making sure that those, like him, born without easy advantages, can also rise and prosper in this world, so he fights on today. So let you rich folk be told.

'If you men who are so skilled in running your businesses, if you are able to reap such huge profits,' he'd said, 'why do you not take into consideration the most important part of production today – the people who produce the wealth and the luxuries in which you are indulging? . . . You regard those whom you employ in your workshops as mere pieces of machinery . . . your experience only reaches as far as your office, where you sit in the midst of luxury.'[4]

But his thinking is beyond mere populist attacks on the capitalist class.

'When we say we want an improvement in the industrial conditions of the workers today, we also mean we want to find out what change is going to be best for the people . . . we have to study and analyse the position to see if we cannot make the lot of the toiling masses easier than it is at the present time.'[5]

Yes, that is what Joe Cahill stands for, then and now, he echoes the call to the 'Light on the Hill' by the late great Labor Prime Minister, Ben Chifley, a man who cut his political teeth at the Great Strike of 1917, just like Joe. They want an end to the finer things in life being the bailiwick of the rich alone. Why can't everybody enjoy some of the finer things?

Things are going to have to change around here, and Premier Joe Cahill devotes himself to doing just that.

And he moves fast.

In the normal way of things, appointing judges to the Supreme Court takes many months. In Cahill's first three weeks in office, he appoints three. He has the backing of the parliament, and the impetus of being a new Premier, so why not get things done quickly that need to be done? (Joe Cahill is a can-do man. More than that, he's widely viewed as, 'an iron man who is impervious to the heaviest pressure of work'.[6])

One thing that Sydney most clearly needs, in his view, is modernisation, an influx of fresh blood, fresh ideas. In these post-war years, money has been a little hard to come by for many, and there is a certain battered, tattered feel about the place. The arrival of tens of thousands of European immigrants has helped bring a different sensibility about the possibility of the finer things of life being attainable, but so far, the state has not got to grips with providing them.

'Sydney in the fifties, despite its location, managed to look dowdy,' the great Australian writer Bob Ellis will one day utter. 'Cahill felt it needed a focal point for its increasing wealth and sophistication. Until then, it was a city without a centre. Some felt they could have built a sports stadium.'[7]

Others have other ideas, a little more imaginative, and Joe Cahill listens to them. Just three months into his Premiership, he approves a grant of £5000 to the NSW National Opera, which so gets the goat of the Country Party member from Armidale, one Davis Hughes – former teacher and RAAF squadron leader in World War II, a self-styled country man, originally from Tasmania, given to attack public spending in the city – that he goes on the attack in parliament, suggesting that expenditure earmarked for the city be spent to benefit country electorates.[8]

Come July, Davis Hughes is on the attack over government spending again. Addressing a meeting of the Country Party Executive, he says: 'Last year £123 million was spent in and around Sydney and about £20 million for the rest of the State. Can anyone suggest that this is fair treatment for country people?'[9]

Premier Cahill replies personally in the *National Advocate* newspaper: 'Mr Hughes, when he begins to talk in millions apparently becomes bewildered in some financial miasma. His statements are very, very, wide of the mark – completely divorced from fact.'[10]

Davis Hughes responds to Premier Cahill in his own electorate's main rag, *The Armidale Express*, charging the Premier with being, 'cheaply sarcastic, belittling the intelligence of country people and reducing the stature of the Premier of NSW',[11] before going on to quote old loan estimate figures and ministerial statements in parliament, rather than laying out real costs paid that support his attack.

Cahill wastes little energy in slapping the spotlight-seeking Hughes down, but at least dashes off a quick reply that is published in the *Express*:

> The second wild thrust by the Member for Armidale into political
> journalism should serve as a grave warning to his fellow party

unsophisticates. He and they would be better advised to leave all propaganda efforts to their party machine, even though it does miss on a couple of cylinders and its big-ends are worn out. The syndicated Country Party advertisements, which have been flooding the provincial press in recent months, inaccurate and misleading as they may be, are models of logical reasoning compared with the pathetic ramblings of Mr Davis Hughes.[12]

Davis Hughes will keep. Joe Cahill has him pegged.

March 1954, Sydney, conductor insists Minister is on the wrong tram

Yes, Eugene Goossens knows rare potential when he sees it – Joan Sutherland, for one, has become the toast of London's musical society – and, as ever, he goes after it like a hungry lion on the hunt – furtively, relentlessly. At every turn, he kindles the flames of his simmering 'opera house movement', describing his seven-year-old dream of a fine opera house on Bennelong Point as 'my dream child'[13].

And, yes, it's true, the Minister for Transport, Ernest Wetherell, continues to insist that Mr Goossens may dream and say what he likes, but the only building being raised on Bennelong Point is the newly planned modern bus depot to replace the old tram depot. It is to house *bus* conductors, Sir . . .

Goossens does not care. His opera house dream demands Bennelong Point or nothing. After all, as the conductor points out, just imagine visitors to Sydney in the future, arriving by ship.

'First you will see the Opera House, then you will see the bridge.'[14]

Can you imagine the glory of it all? Newcomers to old New York are greeted with Ellis Island and the Statue of Liberty, but here, in Sydney, they will see an opera house beyond compare!

The idea of it consumes him. So obsessed is he that often during the lunch-hour at the Conservatorium, he prevails upon his secretary, Phyllis Williams, to walk around the Botanic Gardens to the northern end of Bennelong Point where, again and again and again, he would gaze upon the tram depot – all hideous industrial, bricked-box ugliness – amid so much natural splendour.

'This is where it must be,'[15] he tells her. Every time.

Yes, Mr Goossens. Time to get back to the Conservatorium.

But first a quick stop at Rosaleen Norton's Brougham Street flat, where he can transform from Gene to Djinn and be oh so happily masked, naked, tied up, tongued and tantalised, surrounded by secretive hedonism rather than dull, official matters.

But still he harps on, even with her delectable witchy self, about his want, his *need*, for a world-class venue in Sydney.

As the months pass, however, with still no action, the conductor's frustration starts to fester, resulting in the odd acidic outburst in the press, where he openly attacks the government. What are these 'Philistines doing in government anyway?'[16]

Another focus for his angst, a man who could do something but does nothing – at least as far as he can see – is Charles Moses at the ABC.

Ah, Mr Moses?

It is Eugene Goossens again. On line one. He says it is an 'urgent matter'.

Yes, Gene?

'You should do something about getting a new opera house built.'[17]

Yes, Gene.

'He used to get quite heated,'[18] Moses will recall.

Which is one thing. But while taking heat himself is manageable, Goossens' continued comments attacking the NSW Government cannot be allowed to continue.

Yes, Miss Williams?

It is Mr Moses. He would like to see you right now at the ABC's head office at Pilgrim House on Pitt Street.

Though Moses is normally a genial man, the subsequent conversation is as short as it is terse.

'Gene, look, what you are doing is very embarrassing to the Government. They're employing you, really in a dual capacity, partly with the orchestra and as a Director of the Conservatorium. And even the City Council is partly your employer, they are on the Advisory Committee for the orchestra and it is certainly very embarrassing for us as partners of the Government and the council that you should be critical of our partners in this way. Frankly, I don't think you can continue making remarks like this.'[19]

What remarks?

Comments like, 'the people of Sydney [are being] fobbed off by specious promises and evasive talk',[20] remarks to the press that government officials have shown 'little or no reaction'[21] on the matter are *not* appreciated, Eugene.

Fair enough.

But that very subject reminds Mr Goossens of something.

'Something ought to be done [about building an opera house],' he says.

'Yes, well, something ought to be done,' snaps Moses. 'I don't think this is the proper way to do it, to do it publicly in the press. I think the best thing to do is for us to go and have a talk with the Premier.'

'I'd be delighted. Can you arrange it?'[22]

Well, he can at least try. Charles Moses can't recall ever having seen the staunch Labor man Joe Cahill 'at any concert or operatic performance'[23] in Sydney – so it will be no surprise if the reply comes back that the Premier has no interest in the matter, but . . .

But, to Moses's amazement, a quick phone call to the Premier's office sees him immediately put through to the man himself, and the answer crackles down the line.

'I would be delighted to see you,' says Premier Joe Cahill.[24]

In so many ways, it is an extraordinarily unlikely meeting. Certainly, everything in Eugene Goossens' background has steered him towards pre-eminence in his field. But the same cannot be said of Joe Cahill becoming the Premier of his state. And as to discussing something like an opera house? Well, what chance a man who has never been to an opera or ballet in his life; a man whose favourite song is 'The Donkey Serenade' from a once-popular 1937 musical film; a man whose experience with musical instruments goes no further than watching dust collect on his late mother's pianola in the corner of his living room; a man who relaxes at the races chewing on a sausage sandwich, while Sunday evening is spent listening to Lux Radio Theatre on the wireless . . . would seriously embrace the idea of his government building such a thing? This fellow is so much a man of the people he not only still has his home phone number listed in the people's phone book, under J. J. Cahill, he often answers the phone himself!

And yet, stranger still, the two get on well from the first, and Eugene Goossens is able to make his impassioned case with typical eloquence. Their conversation is gone with the wind, but given the conductor's penchant for loquacious lectures on the virtues of opera, there is no reason to think he didn't regale the Premier with at least a quick burst, focusing on how, since its birth in Renaissance Italy, it has seen a veritable reincarnation of community-forming Greek drama, while displaying the power and prestige of those states that sponsor its production. 'Opera', in fact, comes from the Latin word 'to labour'. Premier, it fits!

'Well, I tell you,' the Premier tells him at meeting's end, 'we've got to get on and do something. I'll call a public meeting . . .'[25]

Goossens comes away pleased that at long last – after nearly a decade of his distinctly agitated agitation – someone of real power is taking this seriously.

The reaction of Moses, who had accompanied the conductor to the meeting, has a different tone. 'I was amazed at [Cahill's] reaction,' Moses will later recount, 'you see, when all is said and done, one didn't expect a Labor Premier – and he came from a working background . . . I didn't expect his reaction to be what it was.'[26]

Moses is not a Labor man. His background and social circle is composed of the well-heeled, well-educated, cut-above, British-backgrounded, Prime-Minister-Robert-Menzies-loving middle-class folks, the 'Forgotten People' and the wealthy. Many of this ilk have an instinctive distrust of the ALP in general – organised labour, dangerous commie pinkos! – and a Labor Premier like Cahill in particular. And yet, here he is, not only agreeing to see Eugene Goossens, who had been attacking him, but seeming to enthusiastically embrace the whole idea of an opera house for Sydney!

As good as his word, by the end of the year – having researched the political possibilities of the idea by consulting widely, talking to people – Premier Cahill is confident enough in its worthiness to raise it in parliament.

'It is the policy of the Government to promote the cultural development of the State and we consider that an opera house is essential,' he says in his gnarled tones, as Australian as a kookaburra. 'It is generally considered that a city the size of Sydney should have an opera house and that the work should be put in hand despite the difficulty that we found in the completion of building projects . . . In the first place I should call together all those bodies that are interested in the development of the opera . . .'[27]

November 1954, Lecture Room, Mitchell Library, Sydney, an enterprise of great pith and moment

As promised, today is the day.

Milling about in a heady cloud of luxuriant pipe smoke, cologne and perfume are the good and the great of Sydney's arts, press, business, political and architectural worlds, including such luminaries as Eugene Goossens, Colonel Charles Moses, Frank Packer, Warwick Fairfax and NSW Government Architect Cobden Parkes, who happens to be the *seventeenth* and youngest child of Sir Henry Parkes.

'Ladies and gentlemen,' Premier Joe Cahill begins the meeting.

'The fact that so many of you have responded to the invitation to be present is a demonstration of your interest in the cultural development of our State. As you are aware, the Government has decided that an opera house shall be established in Sydney and that it will be worthy of this city. Approaching this building this morning one was conscious of the fact that the Mitchell Library is a credit to this, the mother city of the Commonwealth. A hall of culture such as an opera house should merit a similar type of building . . .'[28]

The way forward, he says, is to form an Opera House Committee chaired by Mr Stan Haviland, Under-Secretary, Department of Local Government – a bureaucrat of good character with whom Joe had worked closely as Minister of that department – and guided by Mr Goossens, who can advise on functional aspects of an opera house, along with Charles Moses, head of the ABC, and Harry Ashworth, Professor of Architecture at the University of Sydney.

There is a slightly restless stirring among those figures named, but Premier Cahill does not pause, moving straight on.

Make no mistake, he tells his esteemed audience, they will be embarking on a matter of great importance – coming up with a building that will change the whole city, if not the country!

'In Sydney a wonderful opportunity is offered to build a musical tradition which, in time, can equal anything the older countries can produce. The basis for that tradition is already firmly established by the Sydney Symphony Orchestra under the able direction of Mr Goossens . . .'[29]

As to how he plans to turn this castle in the air into a physical reality, Joe is more than aware that the agony brigade and the professional knockers will say the time is not right, and that funds are too scarce. But he's not fussed as he's heard it all before.

'I have been in public life for thirty years and there was never a time when a similar criticism would not have been offered against any great national venture of this nature. If such a criticism was valid one wonders how London ever got its Covent Garden; Paris, New York and Vienna their fine opera houses; Milan its La Scala. The State cannot go on without proper facilities for the expression of talent and the staging of the highest forms of artistic entertainment which add grace and charm to living and which help to develop and mould a better, more enlightened community.'[30]

Yes, there are those who will see the venture as highfalutin, high-brow, city-dwelling rubbish, but Joe wishes to be clear: 'The Opera House should not be regarded as the special preserve of Sydney people. It should be regarded as something which belongs to the people of New South Wales as a whole – or, for that matter to the people of Australia.'[31]

For is it not time we take this step, as a country?

'Australia has had experience as a young nation in two world wars and other theatres of conflict and has proved itself. Industrially Australia has shown the world that its skill and products equal those of any country. Surely it is proper in establishing an opera house that it not be a "shandy gaff" place but will be an edifice that will be a credit to the State not only today but for hundreds of years. If we in our lifetime did nothing more than express our love of the arts by providing a building worthy of them, even when names are forgotten, the building will always remain as a testimony to what was done in the year 1954 by a group of citizens for the encouragement of talent and culture.'[32]

For inspiration, it is a speech that is hard to follow, but Eugene Goossens is a performer at heart. He opens by thanking and congratulating the curtain-raiser act for today's affair, the Premier, on his 'splendid decision to build an opera house'[33].

Momentarily preening, as he is ever wont to do, he goes on in his posh English accent.

'When I came here in 1947 I was invited by the Australian Broadcasting Commission to speak as a guest of honour, and I submitted then that Sydney must have an all-purpose building to house its different cultural activities, similar to opera houses in Europe and in the United States of America.'[34]

As to its location, Goossens has no doubts, and lets out the bee that has taken up full-time residence in his bonnet: 'Bennelong Point,' he practically blurts out, 'the tram shed at Fort Macquarie.'

He goes on, fleshing out his own vision for the building to come.

At the end of his impassioned speech, Goossens admits, 'I speak only as a musician; my function in this city is not administrative. I do my best, and hope that it meets with approval, to contribute to the city's musical culture . . .'[35]

There's hearty applause as the charismatic Goossens resumes his seat. Various other speakers follow before Premier Cahill interjects, steering the meeting back to the more important matter at hand: 'I do not wish to curtail discussion,' he says, 'but we must be careful not to spend all our time discussing details before we have got a building . . . we must now make a decision on how to get the building of an opera house underway. Should we make an appeal to citizens to join in a combined effort? Should we now say, "The Opera House will cost £1,000,000 or £1,500,000. Who shall we interest in it?" If we merely leave these matters to the Government they do not always go as well as they should . . . We are all anxious to make a start. Can someone tell us how we can get going quickly in the matter?'[36]

A long discussion ensues, with several ideas put forward, including from Warwick Fairfax who says: 'We wish to pull together in the matter and do what we can to help building it as quickly as we can. You have mentioned the very ticklish question of finance and the fact that it might cost £1,000,000 or £1,500,000. I do not doubt that it will. You mentioned, also, the possibility of it gaining public support. While no doubt there will be great public support for it, you might have trouble getting that much money . . . I think that if you expect to get hundreds of thousands of pounds for it from the public, you will have an uphill fight. Of course, I might be wrong.'[37]

Premier Cahill, seasoned politician that he is, knows well that for this project to go ahead, it must be rushed through, not mulled over. It cannot be placed into the gaping maw of the political machine that is the State parliament to be chewed up and spat out – a real risk in that adversarial world so far removed from the creative aims of the arts.

And so, the meeting ends, as Premier Cahill takes his leave and Sydney's most notable music and arts enthusiasts stay on at the scene of triumph, scarcely believing that after so many years in the wilderness the promised land is right up ahead.

Of the shocked and surprised, none are so astounded as the members of the newly named 'Opera House Committee' that Premier Cahill has just named. They are three Englishmen and just one Australian – Stan Haviland – proof of journalist Charles Buttrose's observation about the 'well-observed Australian precept that when you have to fill an important cultural job, get an Englishman'[38]. After the announcement, they gravitate to one another to compare notes. *You didn't know either?* They quickly confirm that no, not one of them had been consulted!

'There we were,' Professor Harry Ashworth will recall years later, 'with no money allocated, no plans and nobody with any idea where the funds were to come from. All we had was just an instruction to build an opera house.'[39]

Ashworth at least looks the part as Sydney's doyen of dons architectural, his perky bow tie – the architect's sartorial tell – and black-rimmed 'milk-bottle glasses' bespeaking a rather superior-sounding Englishman of deep learning who has been around long enough to have served with distinction as a lieutenant colonel in India and Burma in World War II, before heading to Sydney in 1949 to take up the newly established position at the University of Sydney – the Chair of Architectural Design and History.

As for Stan Haviland, he is a public servant of the old school who has been scrupulously serving the public in various forms for the better part of *40 years* – risen in no small part due to his view that his own views count for little, and it is always better to defer, silently, to the views of his Minister. A little like P. G. Wodehouse's character who looks as if he had 'been poured into his pants and forgot to say when', this stocky fellow from down St George way seems rather out of place in his short sleeves and boxy brown trousers beside the well-dressed and elegant frames of Colonel Charles Moses and Sir Eugene Goossens towering over him, but so be it. A proud public servant, he is here to serve the public and cares little for appearances in the first place.

Stan Haviland gives his new colleagues a handshake and a close-lipped smile, nodding along as they talk easily with one another, saying nothing until they bid each other farewell, unsure how it is all to go ahead.

But Joe Cahill, of course, has a plan in mind.

•

The editor of the *Sydney Morning Herald* – the city's bible – the Scottish-born John Pringle, heaps praise upon Joe Cahill in his paper the next day.

'That Sydney requires an opera house is beyond dispute. That the State Government should take the lead in providing it and bear the major part of the cost would also be accepted without question, in any European country. Yet the British tradition is very different and today England is still contemplating building its first civic theatre at Coventry. For Sydney to go one better and build a splendid opera house would indeed be a feather in her cap.'[40]

Reading about it over toast and tea, Sydney loves the idea of having its own opera house. The times are changing. The war has been over for a decade. We are a modern people now, and we are connected to the *world*. And we want a modern opera house, that will be like us – global, fresh, arrrrrrrtistic!

2 December 1954, Department of Local Government, Sydney, starting somewhere

Two days after the public meeting, Stan Haviland receives a letter from the Premier's Department.

> The Premier is most anxious that the Committee should meet immediately and commence its functions at an early date, and I should be glad if you would kindly arrange accordingly.[41]

Although Stan knows not the first thing about creating a fine opera house from scratch, this meticulous member of the public service can certainly arrange a meeting, and that part at least is so quickly sorted it takes place just five days later, around the table in the Under-Secretary's

Ante Room at the Department of Local Government, a plate of Milk Arrowroot biscuits in the middle.

First order of business: selection of a site.

To get things underway, Goossens states what they already know.

'I think,' he says, 'the best site is Bennelong Point.'[42]

A chorus of nodding begins from one end of the table and ripples out to the rest. They all seem to be in agreement. Among them is Professor Harry Ashworth, who has brought along one of his senior lecturers in the architecture faculty at Sydney University, the beloved *Sydney Morning Herald* cartoonist, the Hungarian–Australian, George Molnar, who is here for this very question.

Molnar, thanks to Goossens, is a step ahead of the game, having already commissioned cliques of senior architecture students to design an opera house on a number of sites – with a personal preference for Bennelong Point.

As the chorus nods, it is clear there's one man at the table who's shaking his head. It's Stan Haviland, that man of order and process, especially in matters governmental.

'Well,' he starts regretfully, 'that's a bus depot. The Department of Transport, they've got that. And apart from that, the Harbour Board Trust have taken that side of the Quay for the overseas shipping terminal . . . I think they have already drawn up specifications for the terminal to be on that side.'[43]

Charles Moses sees his point. Bennelong Point is a nice idea, of course, but with the Department of Transport already in residence on the site – and the harbour's shipping authority having their own designs for the place – it seems like a stretch to try and wrangle it back from them, especially with so lofty an ambition as an opera house.

So, Bennelong Point is put down as the desired spot, albeit with not much hope that it can be accomplished.

End of 1954, Kings Cross, Sydney, sorcery, sex and epistolary

Djinn only wishes he could be there more often. And yet his workload and his life abroad as consummate cosmopolitan conductor are taking a toll on his free time.

In lieu of searing seances and fleshy ecstasy on Kings Cross, he makes do with wraiths and spirits, experiencing the magic of Thorn by proxy, exploring the eldritch tomes she has shown to him in his private abode in the gentleman's Upper North Shore suburb of Wahroonga, and writing letters. Lots of letters. Filled with vivid descriptions of magic-induced apparitions.

> A strange hoofed creature was in the room with us – upper and
> middle parts female, lower centaur and a pretty crustacean crea-
> ture with large milky breasts.[44]

He writes to her in tongues, their private language, known only to them:
unguents, materia magica and the osculum infame, and his need for
'S. M.,' as in 'Sex Magick', another way of saying, well . . . never mind.

He leaves most of these letters unsigned, or signed with his craft name,
Djinn, for safety's sake.

He exhorts Thorn to be careful with these letters, that his anonymity
is paramount.

Thorn understands, she knows the importance of running a clandestine
operation. But on the other hand, Rosaleen Norton is not a woman who
does what she's told just because she was told. Instead of destroying the
letters, she wraps them in a bundle and stuffs them down the back of
her lounge. Nice and safe.

February 1955, Sydney, site for sore eyes

It is the first of what will be many meetings between Premier Joe Cahill
and what has become known as the 'Sydney Opera House Committee'.

The Premier's furrowed brow of worry and his lack of pleasantries
at the beginning of the meeting have nothing to do with him being
anything less than a warm and caring man. It's just that he is anxious
to get a move on.

And anyway, as far as this wily veteran of the game is concerned,
a little feigned frustration and exaggerated urgency is a great way to
get what he wants. (As a Sydney judge would later recall of the Premier,
'Many times at the races or some other sporting function, such as cricket,
when the score is Australia three for 18, or when three favourites had
lost, I would say to him: "Don't look so worried." He would say: "I'm
not worried, I'm enjoying myself. If I don't look worried people will
come and worry me about political matters."'[45])

'Now look . . .' he begins on this occasion, brow furrowed. 'I want to
talk to you and see how you're getting on – you know, what's holding
you up – where are you [at]?'[46]

Well, Premier. We are going fine, thank you. We all agree that the
best site for an opera house is Bennelong Point, but Mr Haviland has
pointed out that the Department of Transport has got dibs on it and
they clearly don't want to move.

'Oh, I can't see any reason why they shouldn't – we can move them over the other side of Pyrmont where the railway goods yard is . . . they can move there. That's all right.'[47]

The Committee is stunned.

'No hesitation,' Charles Moses will recount. 'He was going to move them there!'[48]

But hang on. What about the Overseas Passenger Terminal, which the Sydney Harbour Trust is putting on the eastern side of Circular Quay, which would also interfere with plans for an opera house there?

'Oh well,' says Premier Cahill casually, 'they can go on the other side of the Quay.'

Without blinking, Joe Cahill makes the apparently impossible, possible.

Next time, can they give him a hard one?

Again, Moses is stunned.

'[It was] just like that,' the ABC impresario will recount. 'He was a man who, once he got his mind made up, right here was a site he could visualise. Here was some exciting place. We felt so keenly about it, but here were these impossible obstacles to be overcome, but to him they weren't obstacles, these are things – "right, we'll fix that," and he did . . . the Harbour Board Trust, they had to start planning for the shipping terminal to be on the other side of Circular Quay. So, he was very determined, very forceful. There was no arrogance about him – I've got to say this he was not – when I say he was forceful – but he was determined in his quiet way, and the things we saw as obstacles, he saw that those were something he could get rid of. And so, he went ahead, and with his help, we got the site we wanted. No-one else gave us any support at all – it was the Premier.[49]

It's not for nothing, Moses sees, that Joe Cahill has earned himself the nickname, 'Old Smoothie'.[50]

Will that be all?

No, Premier, just one more thing. We've settled the matter of where, but the matter of *how* is now the pressing issue. Premier Cahill's practised eyes quickly flick to the thrust of a report from the NSW Chapter of the Royal Australian Institute of Architects: '[We] recommend that this great architectural project should be the subject of an open competition (national or international) and that the Chairman of Assessors should be an architect of international repute, not resident in Australia and having special knowledge of similar projects.'[51]

And the Committee bolsters that choice in their own report.

Cahill knows just as much about international architecture as he does about opera and ballet; sweet motherless nuffin. That's why he set up the Committee, so the experts can advise the government what to do, not the other way around. In that spirit, he supports the idea to hold an international competition, so that this whole project may receive the most expert input on the planet.

After all, both the Sydney Harbour Bridge and the layout of Canberra had been the result of an international competition, and both had been great successes – even if the designer of Canberra, Walter Burley Griffin, who had beaten 136 competitors in the competition to plan the city of his dreams, had finally resigned with rancour. (It was a long story, but after vicious disputes over cost blow-outs and delays, Griffin had lost control to the bureaucrats and politicians placed in positions of authority over him, and he couldn't bear it.)

17 May 1955, Opera on Bennelong Point, smooth sailing

When Old Smoothie Joe Cahill says he's going to do something, he does it. And this move is particularly bold – every bit as politically risky as that long-ago decision to build Sydney's harbour bridge after World War I, which, despite endless political and public bellyaching, had worked out perfectly. Not only had it joined the harbour's southern and northern shores, it had transformed the image of the city and the self-image of Sydneysiders!

And, Joe insists, there's no reason this opera house on the harbour should be any different.

Come May 1955, Bennelong Point has gone through Cabinet, and the *Sydney Morning Herald* editor, John Pringle, takes up the first trowel in the service of the new building, and starts laying it on.

> By its choice of Bennelong Point as the site for Sydney's opera house, State Cabinet yesterday performed an act of rare imagination. No finer site for a great theatre exists in the world . . .
>
> Sydneysiders will remember [Mr Cahill] with gratitude if in a few years' time they can share with the citizens of Stockholm and Venice the civilised pleasure of hearing great music in a perfect setting beside the waters of their own matchless harbour.[52]

Early 1955, Sydney, knight of the night

Life just keeps getting better and better for esteemed conductor, renaissance man and obscene occultist Eugene Goossens. The maestro receives a prim and proper looking envelope in the mail. Inside is an invitation to be *knighted* at Buckingham Palace in early June for his longstanding services to music in the Commonwealth.

Oh, send him victorious, happy and glorious!

He can hardly wait.

'There can be no-one,' the *Sydney Morning Herald* enthuses in an editorial, 'who will not applaud the knighthood which had been awarded to Mr Eugene Goossens, the conductor of the Sydney Symphony Orchestra. Few services to the community are more fitted for such distinction than this. No man has done more to deserve it.'[53]

And the timing could not be better as he is actually in England at the time to receive his knighthood, while on one of his European summer conducting sojourns.

Of course, he still makes time to regularly write to Thorn, his fevered prose laying bare his obsession with this dangerous liaison.

> Contemplating your hermaphroditic organs in the picture nearly made me desert my evening's work and fly to you by first aerial coven. But, as promised, you came to me early this morning (about 1.45) and when a suddenly flapping window blind announced your arrival, I realised by a delicious orifical tingling that you were about to make your presence felt . . .
>
> I need your physical presence very much, for many reasons. We have many rituals and indulgences to undertake. And I want to take more photos.[54]

Goossens, as always, signs with his craft name, Djinn – he is newly knighted after all, the stakes are even higher.

And he constantly exhorts her to be careful with these letters.

> Anonymity is still best, without mentioning my name (which you will never do, in any connection).

And now . . . beneath a lewd sketch, he insists on the most important thing of all:

DESTROY ALL THIS.[55]

But this witch is not so disposed. Something within her refuses to destroy such precious documents and so, instead, she adds his latest letters to the growing bundle stuffed down the back of her lounge.

•

Rosaleen Norton's Kings Cross flat is a haven for heretics, a sanctuary for Satanists, and a roof over the head of all number of misfits and miscreants with nowhere else to go, including one particularly derelict chap by the name of Francis Honer, from over Glebe way. One night as he melts into the raggedy lounge in the middle of Roie's flat, listening to Beethoven's *Leonore* overtures, his wandering hands rest themselves on a small plastic canister. Ever curious – he has come to the devil's den because he'd heard of the strange goings-on – he pries open the cheap plastic lid and sees . . . photos. His eyes dart upward to see Roie and Gavin Greenlees distracted by the Devil knows what. Quiet as a rat about to dart, Francis Honer slips the canister into his pocket. Late that night, after he has returned to his dirty lodgings on Glebe Point Road, he pulls out a magnifying glass to have a closer look at just what he has stolen. He raises the film up to the light, leans into the glass and looks to see . . . *shocking* images.

Shocking is an understatement. These are stills from a flagellation, some sort of ritualistic sex in which Roie is strapped by her wrists and ankles to a pedestal in every photo. Mr Greenlees, masked, circles her, each photo in a different pose, performing everything from spankings to whippings to . . . an *awful lot more*.

Honer calls his friend Roy Ager to come and have a look himself, two peeping Toms, sticking their noses where they have no business being.

'They're dirty, aren't they?'[56] asks Ager, as aghast as he is excited. Honer nods; it goes without saying. But the real question is, *what* to do with them now that they've seen them?

26 July 1955, Sydney Opera House Committee, thinking outside the box

It is the seventh meeting of the Sydney Opera House Committee, and the Chairman, Stan Haviland, clears his throat before turning to Eugene Goossens. No, make that *Sir* Eugene Goossens. Ahem . . .

'On behalf of the Committee, congratulations upon the honour recently conferred upon you by Her Majesty the Queen.'[57]

Goossens gives a gracious and refined half bow as thanks.

And now back to the Opera House . . . This competition? What's it to be like?

George Molnar, writing for the *Herald*, has already answered that.

'A competition has three main elements: The program (that is, the requirements), the assessors, and the competitors. To get a good result all three have to be the best possible quality. It does not matter how good the competitors are if the program is too vague or too precise, or if the assessors lack courage and imagination . . .'[58]

Keeping that in mind, the Committee begins.

First things first – will it be a national or international competition?

The NSW Chapter of the Royal Australian Institute of Architects have already made their thoughts on that question known. It's going to be an Australian building, it needs an Australian architect.

But Molnar has his own counter to that, and repeats what he'd said in the *Herald*: 'If Australians think they're getting the best opera house in the world, because they're just as good as anybody else overseas, then what's wrong with asking [the overseas architects] to compete?'[59]

Touché.

'And how much greater the glory if an Australian architect wins. We have some definite advantages over our overseas colleagues. We know the site, our building conditions, our ways of living better than they do.'[60]

(Privately, Molnar knows it is one particularly vocal member of the Institute, Walter Bunning – a well-connected architect in his own right, with his own firm and a steady flow of projects – who has been agitating the loudest on the issue. 'It was Bunning,' Molnar would later say, 'miserable Bunning who was all for just to have an Australian competition. That was already a step down because he thought it should be given to Bunning, not to anybody else.'[61])

The Committee men agree with Molnar. An international competition, open to all architects.

But what of the guidelines?

Following the advice of Goossens, they more or less agree that the Opera House will need two halls – a big one for symphony concerts and grand operas and even choral festivals, and a smaller, more intimate stage for ballet, drama, and chamber music. Further decisions can be made once we seek advice from the Institute.

And the assessors? Well, Molnar notes that 'Every competition is as good as its jury.'[62]

But the problem for Australia is that there is no such opera house or even sufficient performance hall to look at as an example. This is virgin territory; there is no operatic playbook for the lucky country.

Professor Ashworth speaks up: 'There should not be more than five assessors, preferably three. The three assessors should be one from Australia and two from overseas. A majority of overseas assessors would inspire confidence in competitors from overseas.'[63]

Stan Haviland asks, 'Does anyone have any ideas respecting the proposed Australian assessor?'[64]

Well, he's sitting right here. The members put forward Professor Harry Ashworth himself, who responds, 'Yes, okay, I would be prepared to act in that capacity.'[65]

As to the other assessors, they refer the question to the Royal Australian Institute of Architects for discussion at the next meeting.

Before the meeting's end, Charles Moses says, 'I suggest the assessors co-opt Sir Eugene Goossens for advice respecting the functional aspects of the Opera House.'[66]

Indeed.

Come the next discussion, the Committee assesses the Institute's list of possible overseas assessors. They settle on Eero Saarinen from the USA – recently featured on the cover of *Time* magazine as one of the leaders in the interesting new field of using thin concrete shells to make free-form curved roofs – and the venerable Dr Leslie Martin from the UK, architect of London's Royal Festival Hall and a close friend of Professor Ashworth, the two having studied architecture together back in Manchester.

The Committee agrees to also invite Mr Cobden Parkes, NSW Government Architect, who is highly regarded not just for his lineage and his work but also because the missing two fingers of his right hand are a constant reminder that he had stormed the shores of Gallipoli at dawn on 25 April 1915!

Within days, all three men accept their phoned invitations to become assessors for the competition.

('The first thing that came to mind,' Saarinen will later recall, 'was that when my father was asked to be a juror in the Canberra City plan contest in 1911, he refused because he wanted to compete.'[67] Well, not this time. Saarinen is far too busy to draw plans for buildings that might not ever be built, but he can at least make time for a quick, glorious trip to Australia.)

This all bodes well for Joe Cahill, who is content to see things are progressing at his preferred speed – breakneck.

24 September 1955, *The Sun* office, lewd, crude and undesirable

We want to see the editor!

You two rough nuts, *what*?

We have something he's gonna wanna see.

With one grizzled eyebrow, the secretary sizes up the two knockabouts standing before her. They are – if nothing else – *The Sun*'s exact readership. Very well then, you can have a minute. The two are escorted upstairs to the editor's office, where one of the coves pulls the photo film from the canister and lays it on the editor's desk.

We want £200 for it, Sir. Fair price that is, this'll be story of the year, worth every penny.

And what, might I ask, is on the film? The editor asks with a raised eyebrow of his own.

Uhh . . . well. We can't say for sure actually, something rotten we think, we sto– . . . we FOUND it in a witch's house in the Cross. You heard of her? Old Roie Norton, that artist, up to no good she is.

Yes, he's heard of her, the world of tabloid reporting *thrives* on the salubrious, the scandalous, the salacious.

Very well, chaps, we'll take the film.

With the grins of boys who stole bickies from the bickie jar and got away with it, Honer and Ager practically skip out of *The Sun*. Two hundred pounds! They're going to be richer than Lord Muck!

•

Good God.

Having had the film developed upstairs in the photographic department, the editor of *The Sun* is both shocked and disappointed.

The shock comes from the sexual poses before him – the disappointment because he can't possibly run them in the paper.

What he can do, however, is send his senior crime roundsman, Joe Morris, over to Kings Cross to try to get access to the flat.

No breaking in, ya hear, Joe? Just find something we can use.

September 1955, Kings Cross, cracking the coven

No, Joe Morris doesn't *break* in. He has talked his way in, allowed through the door by Roie herself, once he professes to be a follower of the occult. And now he strains his eyes to get a feel of her place, the only illumination provided coming from a line of sputtering candles on top of a stone altar. Darting from fetish to curio to trinket to terrifying mural, Morris begins taking mental notes of everything before him; a skull, a piece of driftwood, bones, a tuft of hair, a small wooden box with intricate carvings and a burning stick perched atop it.

Morris feigns interest and acceptance. But truthfully, he is *mortified*. Taking a seat to better calm himself, he feels something sticking into his lower back. Terrified it is another esoteric bibelot, he slowly reaches behind the cushion with his eyes closed . . . only to feel . . . a bundle of envelopes? Well, that will do. Morris stuffs them under his shirt and apologises to Roie on account of a prior engagement that he has only just remembered, and would it be all right if he went on his way right this moment? He doesn't breathe properly again until he is out of the witch's lair. He races back to the editor with the envelopes and hands them over without a second thought.

Good *God*, that is the last time he'll ever go that far for a story.

•

If it sells papers, *The Sun* will print it.

But these letters, no different from the photos before them, are *really* pushing it. So racy that they are surely illegal. Just possessing them is a scandal.

Well . . . maybe *these* letters can't be printed, but who's to say this scandal won't provide something that *is* publishable?

The editor decides to hand everything he has on Rosaleen over to the Vice Squad at the Criminal Investigations Branch, in return for the promise that they will give the tabloid the inside running on whatever raids they might do. Would they be interested?

Are we what!

Vice Squad Detective Bert Trevenar takes one look at the photos and recognises the subjects instantly. It is, of course, those prime examples of the flotsam and jetsam that drift along the gutters of the Cross, Roie Norton and Gavin Greenlees, who have already come to the Squad's attention on various obscenity charges.

Clearly, they are still at it! (And in every position possible on God's green earth, as well as a few that can only have come from hell.)

Detective Trevenar now starts going through the letters Joe found.

Well, well, well.

What have we here?

There are 11 of them, written in a careful and clearly educated hand, and judging from the postal stamps, written in Sydney and London. They frequently refer to magic and, more intriguingly '*sex magick*'. Some are signed with the name 'Djinn', while others are left blank.

Shall we pay the witch a little visit, then?

•

As Sir Eugene heads to the Conservatorium this sunny spring morning, many of his fellow commuters are absorbed in their copy of *The Daily Telegraph* with its blaring headline, complete with photo and inside stories.

The Witch of Kings Cross

'I've served the Horned God since I was 13'
Together with sensational, revealing
Photographs: POST brings you this
Startling story as told by a disciple
of Lucifer[68]

Goossens blanches, as his whole world falls away.

In the city now, he buys a copy of the paper. Locking himself in his office, he devours the report: 'Vice Squad detectives have been investigating alleged sex orgies and witch cults for a week.'[69]

Could they know about *me*? Will she speak?

For now, he makes a vague excuse to his secretary and hurries home. Thankfully, Marjorie is overseas. Again.

He takes out his collection of pornography and black magic paraphernalia and burns it in the incinerator out the back.

November 1955, Criminal Investigation Branch, Sydney, a gander at the goose

I beg your pardon, ma'am?

Rosaleen Norton repeats herself.

Sir Eugene Goossens.

The detective pauses to collect himself.

Sir Eugene Goossens? *The* most celebrated visitor to this fair city in recent times?

Roie wonders if the detective will make her repeat herself again, but he settles for her silent nod.

Well. *Well*, that is something. Just quite what secrets the canary of Kings Cross sang that day are now lost to history, but we do know that Rosaleen held nothing of note back when it came to Goossens.

•

Sir Eugene Goossens sits lost in thought, staring morosely out the window of a taxi taking him to the airport as Sydney slips behind in the soggy morning. Has Roie said anything? Has she snitched? Squealed? Surrendered salacious secrets? Well . . . nothing has reached him yet. Perhaps his secrets will keep. For the moment, a flight to England and a five-month conducting tour of Europe will help take his mind off things.

•

Detective Trevenar thinks on this carefully. Were the author of these sordid letters any regular Joe, the law could come down on them with all guns blazing. But a highly respected conductor and a knight? He will have to approach this case with the utmost care.

The Vice Squad has more than enough evidence for Detective Trevenar to obtain a warrant for Sir Eugene's arrest on the grounds of 'scandalous conduct'. However, precious little good will a warrant do when the culprit is not in the city, much less the country or even hemisphere.

The detective picks up the phone and gets Joe Morris of *The Sun* on the line.

Joe, we need your help. Now.

Joe presses the phone closer to his ear, curious to know what this is about.

That conductor, the knight. Eugene Goossens, the Opera House fellow. Looks like he might be wrapped up in all that buggery and witchery over at Kings Cross. Get in contact with your pals at The Sun *in London, and have them follow the fellow around town. If they've got someone who can chase him through Europe, even better. We want to know where he goes, what he does, who he sees and what he buys. Whatever they can get their hands on.*

Joe Morris pauses on the other end.

And what's in it for us, what's in it for me?

An easy one for the detective.

Why, you'll get the exclusive story when he touches down in Australia. All right, Bert, you're on.

15 February 1956, Sydney, the conditions

On this bright summer's day, February 1956, Premier Cahill launches the 25-page 'Brown Book', its dull beige cover embossed in white with the New South Wales Coat of arms and its title:

An International Competition for a
NATIONAL OPERA HOUSE AT BENNELONG POINT
SYDNEY, NEW SOUTH WALES, AUSTRALIA[70]

Architects from around the globe can pay a £10 fee and they will receive a copy of the book in the post, detailing the guidelines of the competition, the site details and nine black-and-white photos of Bennelong Point and surrounds.

In terms of what the building requires, the Committee inform prospective competitors they want a scheme with two halls.

A large hall seating between 3000 and 3500 people, to be designed for 'symphony concerts, large-scale opera, ballet and dance, choral, as well as pageants and mass meetings'[71].

And a small hall seating approximately 1200 people, to be designed for 'dramatic presentations, intimate opera, chamber music, concerts and recitals and lectures'[72].

But the needs do not stop with the major halls. An opera house of this grandeur needs a tremendous cast of ancillary facilities: rehearsal rooms, amenities, a broadcast centre, offices, refreshment rooms, meeting rooms, bars and a restaurant.

As to the designs required, they are to be conceptual: 'The Assessors do not require elaborate drawings and would prefer them to be unrendered line drawings finished in black ink or pencil.'[73]

It is as open a brief as it is a demanding one. All submissions are to be postmarked by 3 December 1956.

Finalised, the notice for the Opera House competition is distributed wherever good architects are likely to be found reading international newspapers and architectural magazines.

•

In his small design studio, below his home in Point Piper, the fast-rising Austrian-born, Australian-dwelling architect of Australia's first modern Bauhaus residence, Mr Harry Seidler – one of the more dashing and best-dressed young men about town – immediately sets to work.

The Harvard-educated Harry is soon completely immersed, habitually working on his opera house design into the silent watch of the night, as both ends of his habitual bow tie usually sag before he does.

Each day and night his vision forms up beneath his hands, all of it in the Bauhaus tradition that had been so prospering in his native Austria when he fled from Nazi prosecution before the war.

And of course he is not the only Sydney architect excited by the prospect of becoming *the* architect of Sydney's Opera House, dozens are devoting themselves to creating the most magnificent building they can conceive. Among them, 'Miserable' Walter Bunning – a large, lumbering man with a shock of nearly grey hair and such a lugubrious air it would put a hound dog with a sore paw to shame – is bristling with confidence, quite sure that his feathered architectural cap and connections to Sydney's elite will count for something. He is certain that the competition is his for the taking.

George Molnar, who has a good head start on his competitors, having solved the problem of an opera house on Bennelong Point with his students at Sydney University, gets to work on his own design. (He had taken part in the preliminary meetings of the Committee, but has withdrawn as he wishes to compete, instead.) He is inspired by the 'lights of the Manly Ferry, scurrying across the water',[74] and works over several months with two other architects to transform his steamship-like concept into a detailed submission worthy of presentation.

In the rushed final few days before submission, Molnar is able to call upon some of his former students to help as draughtsmen, the most promising of the lot, one Peter Hall, now a resident at the university's prestigious Wesley College, who is for the first time exposed to the 'complex field of theatre design'.[75]

Late February 1956, Hellebaek, Denmark, 'the fault, dear Brutus, is not in our stars, but in ourselves'[76]

Jørn Utzon does not really have downtime. He is a man as passionate for his work as for his family, his sailing, his travel and leafing through architectural magazines. He is *not* looking for the work of his contemporaries, because for the most part their work doesn't interest him. Building houses and factories on traditional lines in modern times – who cares?

No, rather he is looking for two things.

Firstly – fresh ideas, architectural stimuli.

And secondly – architectural competitions from around the globe, giving him a forum to flesh out his more original architectural ideas and solve big design problems.

Sipping on his morning coffee, Utzon's blue eyes begin to widen. It's not the caffeine either, it's a . . . *competition*.

And not just any architectural competition. He has entered more than 21 such competitions – earning himself a reputation in Danish architectural circles as having, 'entered numerous competitions . . . not so much concerned about their terms and conditions; he was interested in the problems to be solved'[77] – and won seven of them with his innovative architecture. And yet – *dot three, carry one, subtract two* – none of his designs have actually been built.

But so it goes, that's just how these contests tend to operate, especially in the post-war 1950s, which has seen his profession elevated by a lofty, optimistic, creative spirit that is too often marred by broken economic realities. It is especially true of the public competitions with open-ended briefs. You can pour your blood, sweat and tears into a design, and win the competition hands-down, but there is never any guarantee that the project will ever advance beyond the drawing board. After all, politics often gets in the way of practicality, and there are few crueller mistresses than the public purse. But this competition is taking place in the newest of new worlds, Australia. Perhaps they are more open and understanding of a truly creative visionary down there?

It niggles at Jørn to know that, of his designs, apart from his own open-plan home, he has only fully executed and completed a house for his grandmother, and an estate of 60 townhouses on the outskirts of Helsingør, where Erik and Henry Andersson, two Swedish brothers and founding partners of Arton, the architectural firm where Utzon works, reside. Oh, and the 20 townhouses that he's currently designing and constructing don't fully scratch his creative itch, either. Sure, he has worked on countless other projects over the years – houses, factories, even a performing arts venue when he was at the Academy of Danish Fine Arts – but it is not enough. He'd never speak openly about his discontent – it isn't the Danish way to complain so brazenly – but he feels that the time has come to do *more*, to make something *unique*.

And look at the site proposed!

It is to be a building devoted to the arts, taking pride of place in the centre of Sydney on a flat piece of land jutting out into a beautiful harbour with no other buildings nearby.

All put together, it means that rarest of all things for an architect – nearly total artistic freedom. Whatever building he comes up with does not have to fit in with nearby structures, it could be a new start on urban land reflecting only the superb natural world surrounding it! In Europe, such land has been built out centuries ago.

Utzon regards it like an explorer who has just reached the top of a range to see a splendid vista of green pasture criss-crossed by bubbling brooks up ahead.

The possibilities are *endless*.

And he needs to do this.

'I felt I simply had to participate,' he would later reminisce. 'This programme had all an architect could wish for. It had a fantastic site, with a beautiful and demanding position on Bennelong Point. This caused me to start on the project immediately . . .'[78]

Coming home from the bank with 10 English pounds nestled safely in his pocket, Jørn walks through the door and begins to assemble the envelope. He marvels at the journey it is about to take, all the way from his cold village in far north Denmark to sunny Sydney, Australia, in the Southern Hemisphere.

THREE

EXIT THE MAESTRO

Who would have thought that the man who was standing up receiving all those ovations would be literally run from the country . . .[1]

Sir Charles Moses

There are more things in Heaven and Earth, Horatio, than are dreamt of in your philosophy.[2]

William Shakespeare, *Hamlet*, Act I, Scene 5

You employ stone, wood and concrete, and with these materials you build houses and palaces. That is construction. Ingenuity is at work. But suddenly you touch my heart, you do me good, I am happy and I say: This is beautiful. That is Architecture. Art enters in.[3]

Le Corbusier, pioneer of modernist architecture

One of his great genius traits is that he could take nature, take the lesson from nature, but not imitate it.[4]

Richard Leplastrier, Australian architect who worked with Utzon

7 March 1956, Sydney, the spider weaves the web

Give me the rundown, Joe?

Detective Trevenar, seems that your man Goossens has been hanging around 'grubby newsagencies and bookshops in Soho and around Leicester Square'.[5] *There's word that he 'probably has indecent photographs' – he'll have them in a briefcase when he returns.*[6]

After taking down the airline, flight number and scheduled arrival time, Detective Trevenar ponders what to do about the sticky wicket of conflicting jurisdictions confronting him. The Vice Squad has enough to get Goossens on a charge of scandalous conduct under state law, but the importation and possession of prohibited material is a customs offence, so takes precedence as a Federal matter.

The following day, Detective Trevenar briefs a Senior Customs Investigator, Nathaniel Craig, suggesting that Federal officers must be at Mascot Airport tomorrow morning, 9 March, to meet, greet and *search* Sir Eugene Goossens.

And once the Federal officers are finished with him? Then it will be Trevenar's turn with the salacious scallywag. The web is woven, the players poised.

•

Well, this is odd.

A garrulous ghoul from the coven by the name of Wally Glover – actually the publisher of Roie's art book – is drunk as *two* lords when he decides to call on the witch ... only to find the door unlocked but the flat empty. What's this though? It is a single piece of paper with the name *George* scrawled upon it, with a phone number. Whoever this George is, he might know their whereabouts.

Wally rings the number, and hears the receiver picked up.

'Is that you, George?' Wally asks in his nuggety way.

'Who's speaking?' an imperious English voice replies.

'Pan, the Horned God,' Wally replies, taking the piss, amused.

'I can't place you,'[7] comes the deadpan response.

And yet no sooner does this anonymous George realise that Wally Glover knows all about the witch's coven, and more importantly *who is in it*, than he insists on a meeting the following morning at a local café where George introduces himself as no less than aristocratic Englishman, George Dovaston, with the most wonderfully rounded vowels and he is – get this – a 'Queen's Messenger'.[8]

As proof, Dovaston opens a small casket in which there is a solid silver greyhound – apparently the secret sign of those doing Her Majesty's work. This, put together with some correspondence from British Intelligence, convinces Glover of his bona fides.

Which brings us to the business at hand.

You must understand, young man, that a Knight of the Realm is about to become involved in some unpleasant publicity. It is very important you do what you can to protect his name – and that means not telling what you might know about this knight's involvement in the witch's coven, as this 'occult connection could be used to harm [him], and damage his reputation.'[9]

Do you understand?

Wally understands.

•

Elsewhere in the naked city, Colonel Charles Moses sleeps soundly.

It is true he had received a strange telephone call from out of the blue, from someone who had not identified himself but spoke quite imperiously.

'Look, if I were you, send a cable to Goossens,' the aristocratic voice had said. 'Tell him to be careful what he brings back in his luggage.'[10]

Charles Moses had given it short shrift. The idea that Sir Eugene would be smuggling anything to Australia was patently 'ludicrous'.[11] The caller was a crank, and Moses had hung up.

8 am, 9 March 1956, Runway One, Sydney Airport, flying into the web

The pools of water on the tarmac of Sydney's longest runway are swished aside as the L-1049 Super Constellation aircraft thumps and bumps down on *terra firma*.

It's Sydney's fortieth day of rain this sodden year and it's not letting up. Gingerly making his way down the slippery portable stairs in the drizzle, droplets bouncing off his black felt homburg hat, Sir Eugene Goossens is exhausted. Yes, the trip has been fairly fast on the 'Kangaroo Route', with only half-a-dozen hops over the last 64 hours, coming all the way from Heathrow. But still, it is no small thing for a 62-year-old, and his only thought at the moment is to get back to his Wahroonga villa and get some horizontal sleep.

Tightly gripping his briefcase, he heads into the International Arrivals shed and straight to the Nothing to Declare queue just as he has every year for the last decade when arriving in Sydney – always to be obsequiously waved through, as befitting a man of his standing – but this time there is a catch.

Him.

From a remarkably large posse of police, customs officers and reporters by the gate, what appears to be the Chief Customs Officer – with gold braid on his peaked cap – steps forward.

A moment, if you would, Sir Eugene.

Ushered to a small room with no windows, where men in ill-fitting suits and pork-pie hats eye him beadily, even as customs officers wheel in six large bags on a trolley – *his* bags.

A bead of sweat appears on Sir Eugene's forehead.

Senior Customs Investigator Nathaniel Craig asks him carefully.

'Do you have anything to declare?'

The question mark at the end of his last sentence is a raised scythe, about to fall.

The conductor nods his pale acquiescence and so it begins.

'What's in that?' the investigator asks, indicating the briefcase, which is dangling from the hand of another customs officer.

'Oh, that's only my musical scores.'

'I've got to have a look at it.'

Oh. Christ.

Vice Squad Detective Bert Trevenar, who at this stage is a mere observer, is standing right behind the conductor, and watches closely as the light blue collar on the conductor's shirt starts changing to an inky blue.

The Sir is sweating. Profusely.

The customs officer swings his arm up and plonks Eugene Goossens' briefcase on the rickety wooden table before him, opening it to reveal many folders of heavy paper, marked with such names as Beethoven, Brahms, Wagner and a new half-written ballet by none other than Eugene Goossens III, the secret score within sealed with heavy tape.

Taking a cold, merciless razor blade, the inspector carefully slices them open, as the stain on Goossens' collar spreads like spilled ink down his back and along his shoulders. Inside the first folder are indeed musical scores . . . and some envelopes. The inspector pulls out the contents of the first envelope to reveal . . . 38 naked images, people in various sexual poses.

Mr Goossens?

The conductor does his best.

'I told Billings my valet not to put them in here,' he says, feigning irritation and disappointment in one. 'It's *his* mania . . . He packed them about a week ago.'[12]

Shame on Billings then. But Inspector Craig is not buying it, and keeps going, opening the rest of the folders with his razor, and then the port – the ineffable sadness of the scene 'strangely heightened by the impassive, plodding tone of the official record',[13] which shows Goossens' excuses falling to silence and then pleas.

> Second Envelope: (Used envelope) . . . 'They're all the same. I suppose they're in [the] package.'
>
> Envelope No. 3: . . . 'All for a stupid private collection . . . there would be nothing left for me to live for if this got into the press . . .'
>
> Envelope No. 7: (275 photos) No comment and no reply.
>
> Envelope No. 8: (234 photos) No comment and no reply.

Envelope with 59 photos: 'Gentlemen, I beg of you not to let this be known; if I could make amends some other way.'[14]

And now come books: *Sharing Their Pleasures, Continental, Flossie and Nancy's Love Life.*

All up, there are over 1000 photographs – of which 837 are found to be obscene – three wicked rubber masks, eight books of prints, which show more of the same and, *oh dear*, a five-foot spool of film which, at first look when the frames are held up against the single naked light bulb hanging overhead, very likely constitute a breach of Section 233 of the *Customs Act* which specifically prohibits 'the possession or importation of blasphemous, indecent or obscene works or articles'.[15]

'I welcome the seizing of them,'[16] Goossens offers, rather pathetically.

These photos and films, they are not declared on your customs form?

'I'm too ashamed about the whole thing,' the conductor murmurs miserably. But he asks the inspector to please not jump to any conclusions, for he must understand that such things are 'not for anybody's use or purposes other than for me'.[17]

And so it goes, with Inspector Craig gathering all information he can on the breaching of the customs laws, before Detective Trevenar of the Vice Squad steps forward to ask Mr Goossens to accompany him down to the Criminal Investigations Branch at Bathurst Street in the city, for an interview.

Yes, of course.

Press photographers start blasting photos the moment they emerge from the shed.

To the shouted questions of the press pack, Goossens says wanly, 'I'm sorry, gentlemen, that I did not see you before, but I have been lying down inside. I have been dizzy and sick, with air sickness.'[18]

This way, Mr Goossens.

Up on the first floor in Detective Trevenar's office, Sir Eugene Goossens is confronted for the first time by – oh, my God – the obscene letters he has written to Rosaleen Norton.

'There is repeated mention of "S.M. Rites" between you and Norton and Greenlees, made in the letters,' offers Detective Trevenar. 'What is that?'[19]

Yes, well.

'Our mutual interest in magic,' the conductor begins, 'led to the occasional practice of certain magic ceremonials. I was distinctly influenced by it and was induced to take part in certain manifestations which might come under the heading of Sex Magick ... which is a ceremony involving sexual stimulation in a minor manner ...'

'How is that rite conducted?'

'We undressed and sat on the floor in a circle. Miss Norton conducted the verbal part of the rite. I then performed the sex stimulation on her.'

'How did you do that?'

'I placed my tongue in her sexual organ and kept moving it until I stimulated her.'[20]

And there you have it.

This is proof positive of 'sex perversion', as specifically banned by the *Crimes Act 1900*.[21]

In for a penny, in for a pound, Goossens even selects one of the Norton/Greenlees photographs the police had confiscated and identifies the one which best shows 'Sex Magick' in full swing.

Trevenar is quite stunned – not by the confirmation, but by Goossens' sheer lack of guile in trying to cover anything up.

Goossens even gives a two-page statement, without asking for a lawyer, and – after punctiliously making a couple of handwritten corrections of spelling errors – signs it, barely blinking.

Such a gentleman!

As he leaves, at 3.10 pm, six hours since he arrived – several hours of lawyer-less confessions and a hearty lunchtime feed – he even shakes Trevenar's hand and says, 'You have been most understanding and sympathetic and I am sorry to have caused you this trouble.'[22]

And on that note, he dons his black homburg hat, wraps himself in his great black coat, putting himself back together, and braces himself for the hungry press. Ever the performer he steps outside, smiling.

•

The front page of *The Sun* that very afternoon shows a photograph of Goossens being taken firmly in hand by Detective Trevenar beside the blaring headlines and story:

GOOSSENS CHECK

PHOTOS SEIZED

VICE MEN ACT

Sir Eugene Goossens, conductor of Sydney Symphony Orchestra, was met by Vice Squad detectives at Sydney Airport today on arrival from London.

He was questioned for 3½ hours, and then he went to CIB head-quarters, where the questioning continued.[23]

•

It is impossible to overstate the shock with which the news is greeted in Sydney circles. In a city that likes pumpkin scones every bit as much as it likes cardigans, that goes to church on Sundays and sometimes wears long socks with sandals, that is still subject to the *British Witchcraft Act* of 1735 (which was repealed in England in 1951), and is not allowed to read James Joyce's *Ulysses*, among many other books on the banned list, for fear of being exposed to impure thoughts, the very *idea* – my dear! – that someone of Sir Eugene Goossens' social stature engages in such activities is beyond shocking.

At an emergency meeting of the governors of the Conservatorium of Music, called so they can be informed of the horrifying details of the charges, it will be recounted that they were so shocked that, 'six pairs of false teeth fell out at once'.[24]

That Welcome Home Party due to be held at the ABC?

It is cancelled.

As for Eugene Goossens' new position on the front pages of the newspapers, it is his for the next five days running as Sydney glories in the stories, devouring every salacious detail:

> The material which the Vice Squad detectives seized on Friday includes more than 1000 photographs and three rubber masks . . . [25]
>
> Sir Eugene Goossens, at his own request, has been 'temporarily' relieved of his duties with Sydney Symphony Orchestra and NSW Conservatorium of Music.[26]

At least an editorial in *The Daily Telegraph* has a kind word for him, even if it reads a little like an obituary:

> Goossens was almost a legend – in the nine years he has been in Sydney he has worked with devotion to advance our city culturally . . . Good music has been brought to tens of thousands of grateful Sydney residents.[27]

In fact, not just good music, but some very good designs for the Sydney Opera House which are being dreamed up by architects from around the world.

This dream [of a Sydney Opera House] he was able, in conjunction with a sympathetic State Government, to move steadily towards the realm of reality.

Australians should remember with gratitude and sadness these credits in the Goossens ledger.[28]

14 March 1956, Sydney, scramble to unscramble

The ABC, on the orders of Colonel Charles Moses, engages one of Sydney's leading criminal barristers, Jack Shand QC – already famous for such things as having somehow achieved the acquittal of blonde bombshell Shirley Beiger, 'a 22-year-old blonde model of Kings Cross',[29] on a charge of murder, despite the fact she had been found holding the gun that had fired and killed the victim at point-blank range, and she had been a tad upset at the time.

He will be the one to defend Goossens and his biblical fall from grace to the outer rings of hell.

For now, Sir Eugene, I would advise you stay in your home and speak only to those you absolutely trust, and even then, please, don't speak any further of the charges levelled against you.

Very well, Mr Shand.

In the distance comes the clink, clank, clunk and grunt of the ravenous journalists and tabloid ghouls who keep digging in the moonlight, hunting for the sordid details that will captivate the imagination of the public.

After inquiries are made, the conductor's wife, Lady Goossens, is found to have taken shelter from the storm behind – oh, *get thee to a nunnery* – 14-foot-high walls in the Convent of the Epiphany at Soisy-sur-Seine, on the outskirts of Paris. 'Rumours of a separation between us are entirely untrue,' she says through a grate. 'I shall be seeing my husband very soon.'[30]

15 March 1956, Sydney, and from all the lands on earth they come

Today marks the deadline to register for Sydney's international architectural competition.

In all, there's an enormous show of interest – about *six* times more architects than they had been expecting – 933 competitors having registered, coming from all over the world.

Stan Haviland summarises for the Committee: 220 architects from the UK, 219 from Europe, 193 from Australia, 113 from the USA, 63 from the Middle East and the Balkans, 32 from South Africa, 28 from the Far East, 25 from Canada, 20 from New Zealand, 10 from Ireland, 6 South Americans and 4 'Other'[31].

•

Before deciding his future course, Eugene Goossens speaks with the sympathetic Charles Moses, who conveys everything to the decidedly unsympathetic ABC Board. After a number of hushed, private conversations, Goossens reads the writing on the wall.

On 20 March 1956, the conductor submits his formal letter of regret and resignation from his positions at the ABC and the NSW State Conservatorium of Music, just two days before his court case is due to take place.

Appearing before the Special Court, the gallery packed with press, Mr J. W. Shand, QC, is eager to have this deeply unfortunate matter put to bed – starting with his plea on behalf of his client.

'Guilty,' says this most unlikely looking and sounding man of the law. (Short, stout and with freckles so marked they are not subsumed by his red face – a face for wireless – and a reedy voice that comes complete with a lisp.)

The press stirs.

No-one had been expecting a guilty plea. But on the other hand, it denies the prosecution the chance to have the 'exhibits' put on public display – as only a small selection is handed to the bench, and even that is wrapped in, what else but, brown paper.

With the plea in, Shand seeks to salvage the shattered shards of his client's reputation.

'Your Worship, it will be revealed the photographs were brought in as the result of threat, the nature of which will become apparent later.'

Threats, Mr Shand?

'I can say,' Mr Shand offers mysteriously, 'the matter is under investigation.'

The important thing for now is that everyone concentrates on the incongruity of such a refined man as this, importing such filthy material.

'One finds it,' the eminent QC notes, 'impossible to reconcile the life led for so long by Goossens – which has been on a high aesthetic plane – with these very bad types of pornographic and salacious pictures.'[32]

This view is fully affirmed by the sole witness called by the defence, Colonel Charles Joseph Alfred Moses, General Manager of the ABC.

Do tell, Colonel Moses?

'The engagement of Sir Eugene from a musical point of view was one of the most fortunate things that could have happened for this country,' the ABC General Manager says firmly.

'What about his reputation up to the time of this incident?'

'The very highest. There has never been a whisper to his discredit from anywhere. It doesn't take very long for rumours about artists who come out here to reach my ears. No artist who has come here has had a higher reputation.'[33]

But let the Crown Prosecutor Mr John Dashwood Holmes QC speak simply.

'The exhibits speak for themselves and I do not propose to use any adjectives to describe them. The nature and the number of photographs make it difficult to imagine a worse case.'[34]

Accordingly, Mr Holmes asks for the maximum penalty, and the presiding magistrate agrees.

As reported in the papers the following day: 'Mr McCauley, S. M., fined Sir Eugene £100, the maximum for having imported indecent films, photographs and literature.'[35]

For Sir Eugene Goossens, it is, frankly, less the fine that counts and far more the ignominy of the guilty verdict – though at least one of the two charges against him has been dealt with.

•

Sergeant Bert Trevenar knows the Federal customs charge is a mere sideshow to the 'scandalous conduct' case he has compiled against the maestro; an organ recital to his grand opera.

All he needs is the formal go-ahead from the NSW Crown Solicitor's office, which is surely why he and his boss in the Vice Squad, Inspector Ron Walden, have been summoned to that very office, in the company of the NSW Police Commissioner, Mr Colin Delaney.

Following protocol, it is the Commissioner who goes in to see the Deputy Crown Solicitor first, while Trevenar and Walden wait in the ante-room. But here comes the Commissioner now, storming out of the office . . . ?

'Sergeant,' he says furiously to Trevenar, 'you've been dudded. They're not going to issue a warrant. You did a good job, now you can go back to your station.'[36]

And that is it. No less than six months of Sergeant Trevenar's patient work is dismissed with no reason given.

Precisely what has happened will never become clear, only that, somehow, someone had made a move at the highest levels of the NSW Government and convinced no less than the Minister of Justice that the charge should not be pursued, despite the overwhelming and irrefutable amount of evidence assembled.

'A couple of people who were involved were pretty high up on the social [ladder] and the government of the day took notice of them,' Trevenar will later insist. 'There's no doubt in my mind. That was the situation.'[37]

Feeling like the fix is in, Trevenar carefully puts all the key documentation in a single file, secretes it in the hubcap of his FJ Holden, and drives home where he puts the file in a back cupboard – where it will remain untouched for the next 40 years.

9 April 1956, Hellebaek, a different take on a high aesthetic plane

Utzon is transfixed from the first.

Oh, what a sight and ohhhh, what a *site*!

It's the best birthday present he could have asked for.

He treats the Brown Book like a holy scripture, leafing through it every chance he gets, staring adoringly at the photographs of Bennelong Point, absorbing the space, trying to squeeze the *feeling* of it, its very nature from the black-and-white images. The tremendous harbour, the great bridge, the box-like buildings on the harbour's foreshore . . .

Such brick boxes are functional certainly, but also dull and uninteresting; the fruits of a practical yet uninspired approach towards architecture. They don't shine, they don't catch the eye, they have no connection at all to the exquisite landscape around them. They don't make you *feel* anything.

What an opportunity!

An opera house built for this uncluttered site need not try to fit in with neighbouring buildings – its only connection need be with nature and the gods themselves!

The gentle muse of inspiration that alights on Jørn's shoulder to whisper in his ear on this day doesn't recognise anything so plebeian as birthdays, cakes and good wishes. It only recognises stunning creativity 'right on the edge of the possible', where he loves it, and Jørn Utzon knows from experience that when she whispers, he must create.

He notices the name of one of the judges in particular – the eminent Finnish–American architect Eero Saarinen, who Utzon had actually visited on his trip to the USA, and who has made his name in recent times by using wafer-thin – just three inches – free-form curved concrete to create remarkable roofs. Utzon has heard talk of Saarinen's design for the terminal building at New York International Airport; it sounds truly pioneering.

It is a good sign, given that Saarinen is as modern as modernists come, an architect free of the stifling stricture that new buildings must always be descendants of old buildings, and a fellow man of Nordic sensibility – creative, progressive.

First things first for Jørn, most urgent is to find out everything he can about Sydney, about its people, about this spot – about what kind of building might look as if it grew naturally from it, that complements the light and textures that surround it. It is information not given in the brief; details not necessarily very easy to come by in Denmark, but he must do his best.

'[The people who wrote the guidelines] could not know the importance of the colour of the sea or about the shades of the light,' he would later note of his approach. 'These were things one had to find for oneself. I studied very carefully everything I could lay my hands on in the way of Australian literature. It was very sparse.'[38]

Journeying to the centre of Copenhagen, just 40 minutes' train ride from his home, he knocks on the door of the Australian consulate, explains the situation and is soon being shown a film about Sydney, which helps . . . a little. Much more helpful are the nautical charts of Sydney Harbour he gets from a marine bookstore in Copenhagen, which not only helps him gauge the scale of the site and its surrounds, the height of the Harbour Bridge's arc, the distance from Bennelong Point to the opposite shore of the harbour and all surrounding points – but gives a *feel* for the place. A man who was reared by a fjord, Utzon immediately recognises Sydney Harbour as precisely that; a small fjord that is the beating heart of Sydney city, every eddy and artery leading towards it.

By pure happenstance, while in Copenhagen he meets a group of young Australian women, on their way to compete in the equestrian events being held in Stockholm for the 1956 Olympics (quarantine regulations prevented the event being held in the main host city of Melbourne).

And they are from Sydney!

Utzon listens closely as they exult about Circular Quay and the old quarter, 'The Rocks', nestled under the south end of the Harbour Bridge; about the beauty of the harbour itself with ferries and sailboats and ships perpetually criss-crossing, even as seagulls and pigeons caterwaul all about; and how right by the booming city centre with its high buildings, just down from Government House and the wonderful Botanic Gardens, there's Bennelong Point, sitting in the centre of it all with its dreadful old tram sheds. Utzon gets a strong impression of a city just coming into itself, a place with a still young and adventurous spirit, a place ready for something daring, not unlike himself. As Utzon will later recount: 'I wanted something that looked like it would grow, as Australia was growing.'[39]

Of the site itself, he comes to understand that it is 'almost a stage in the harbour . . . an open space in the centre of the city seen all around from great areas, in a way as significant to the city as the Acropolis in Athens, which can be seen from all around'.[40]

Utzon returns home, newly impassioned and, as is his wont when seeking inspiration, goes for long walks in the woods and along the beach, sailing his boat around the Øresund, wanting and wishing the whim of whimsy to alight on his shoulders and give whispers from nature about what this new building might look like.

He draws inspiration from one feature in particular . . .

'The sandstone heads at the entrance to Sydney Harbour. These heads slope upwards to the Gap, where they drop abruptly to the sea. The same feature is often seen in Denmark, on a smaller scale, where you walk uphill as you approach the sea to the edge of an escarpment falling away to the beach and sea below. As you approach the edge you look up into the empty sky and only at the very last moment are you able to get a magnificent view of the sea.'[41]

That's it! He can place the entrance to the building atop a high plat-form, so that theatre-goers climb slowly to reveal the magnificence of the entire site to the visitor, like a rousing crescendo of anticipation for the opera-goer, punctuated by a great blast of triumphal trumpets as the sights of the harbour appear all around them – the sea, the sky, the bridge, the city, the harbour with all its coves and inlets – just the way the mighty sandstone cliffs that guard the city reveal their secrets at the very last second.

'It's marvellous,'[42] he says to himself, as he keeps drawing.

26 May 1956, Sydney Airport, the goose flies the coop

This time, there is no adoring press pack, no sailing across the tarmac as a knighted ship of the realm in full regalia, no billowing fur coats, no God Almighty airs and graces. No, this time, Sir Eugene Goossens is little more than a shambling and broken wreck of a man, walking in small steps, head down, travelling under an alias – 'Mr E. Gray' – on a KLM flight to Rome. He turns 63 today, not that anyone appears to know or care.

With his departure, the Sydney Opera House Committee loses their only member with deep experience of musical performance, the only person with intimate knowledge of concert hall dynamics and the many needs of grand opera and ballet. Even more significantly, he had been the only one among them with an expert ear for the prickliest and most polarising of matters in performance hall design – what some call the 'dark arts' . . . acoustics. (Quite. Right now, the great regret is that his love of the 'dark arts' had not been confined to acoustics.) For the moment, they will just have to do without.

'Here was a man who was composing operas,' architect and cartoonist George Molnar will recall, 'he was one of the great conductors of the world, he travelled very widely in America where there were many multipurpose halls . . . And he knew the problem of having a hall that can be used as an opera house *and* a concert hall. All the techniques he used, he performed there, he knew whatever was required to make a change of reverberation time which is necessary.'[43]

Sir Eugene takes solace that with Cahill's Labor government newly returned to power for the sixteenth year in a row, his dream for a Sydney Opera House is emerging as a civic project of great cultural significance.

The nose of the aeroplane lifts, the wheels take flight, rising up and away. This small colonial town he had stooped to conquer, has conquered him.

Northern Summer 1956, Hellebaek, 'New vocabularies from an old culture'[44]

As the sun shines down, the clouds scud past, Jørn Utzon tucks his long legs under his drawing desk and begins to draw – at least in his mind – his own castles in the air.

Bit by bit, Utzon's staggeringly innovative vision of an opera house for this extraordinary site starts to form up under his long artist fingers, as his soft 6B Faber-Castell lead pencil moves back and forth across page after page – using the movement of his wrist, flicking from side to side – before he invariably pauses, carefully returning the pencil to the green holder he always keeps in his pocket against the moment inspiration strikes, and musing some more.

For the building's foundation, its headland-like base – the muse whispers tales of travels gone by. For any structure on such a grand site, built for such a grand purpose must be like an offering to the gods of greatness rather like . . . the Mayan pyramids he had seen on his study trip to Mexico in 1949.

Yes, that's it! Sydneysiders can be like the jungle-dwelling Mayans of the Yucatan, climbing up to enormous stone platforms – like a grand pyramid with its tippy top lopped off – that rise out of the dark jungle.

'I fell in love with [such bases],' Utzon will write of that study trip, 'where I found many variations, both in size and idea, of the platform, and where many of the platforms are alone without anything but the surrounding nature. All the platforms in Mexico were positioned and formed with great sensitivity to the natural surroundings and always with a profound underlying idea. A great strength radiates from them. The feeling under your feet is the same as the firmness you experience when standing on a large rock.'[45]

Consulting the copious photographs he had taken at the time, he finds what he is looking for – the pyramids of the Yucatan and the temple at Monte Alban in Oaxaca, which have a series of terraces joined by wide, grand staircases.

He will recount, 'the trick was actually to get people up – when you come up the steps you see no buildings, you see the sky . . . You get to another world, and that's what you want for your audience, to start already to separate themselves from their daily lives.'[46]

Utzon thus starts drawing what, if built, will be no less than the largest external flight of stairs in the world.

And it's not just a triumphal entrance – in the manner of a Greek procession – that concerns him. A grand podium is a perfect design solution for housing all the functions of an opera house not just atop but *within* it; dressing-rooms, rehearsal rooms, parking spaces and loading docks, and of course, the two multipurpose theatres.

As to how to fit the required two theatres into the designated space – the specifications are 150 yards wide and 250 yards long, for a site covering 51 acres with water on three sides – he comes to a simple conclusion. He will *not* put them end to end to satisfy convention – back-to-back theatres sharing a tall stage tower area – nor on top of each other as – shudder – that would inevitably make it a glorified big box, which summates 98 per cent of modern buildings.

No, on the reckoning that the golden aspect of the site is its view out to the harbour, he places his halls side by side, facing the water, proud.

As to how to house the halls, he concludes it must be 'a "light" sculptural roof, emphasising the heavy mass of the plateau below'.[47]

Yes, that's it, above the podium – so sturdy and resolute with horizontal lines that mirror the earth beneath – shall rise floating roofs as bright and weightless as the clouds. Like two worlds.

'Because the site was rather small,' he will later recall, 'I came to the conclusion that I would have to make one architectural unity out of this whole peninsula.'[48]

Even those crossing the Harbour Bridge will look down upon it from on high so there must be no dusty flat roofs filled with ugly air conditioner vents, it must be exquisite from every angle. As he will later explain, in the true spirit of a sailing man, used to seeing things from all angles: 'I realised that this peninsula popping out in a harbour would mean that it would be looked upon from all sides and even might be looked upon from above,'[49] – a 'fifth façade', to go with the usual four façades on each side of a building – and Utzon wants that to be spectacular, for every angle to offer the viewer something magnificent.

As ever, whenever he is embarked upon solving an exciting design problem, he is transfixed, his mind whirling with possibilities. So that's what he does: he lets his mind and imagination run free, till it finds a path forward. It is the *vision* that captivates Utzon so fiercely, the picture he can see when he closes his eyes. These visions of what could be, what will be, are not unlike those of Goossens, but while the conductor *hears* the orchestra on the wind, Utzon *sees* the orchestra, their stage, the beautiful sight from the site.

'You feel during a work like this that everything you are doing has something to do with this special project. If you go for a walk in the woods or stroll along the beach you look on things with new eyes in relation to your project ... The strange thing was that it was an ideal project for an architect. First, because there was a beautiful site with a good view, and second, there was no detailed program ... In short it had not at all been specified what was wanted. It was left to the competitors, so that they were not handicapped in exploiting the site in a natural way.'[50]

He must, however, house 90-feet stage towers at one end of each hall, but how to do that in a functional and sculptural way?

End 1956, London, falling flat in a filthy flat

'Hello, little one,' Eugene Goossens says, standing from his armchair to hug his youngest daughter, 16-year-old Renée, who has come from her boarding school to visit him in his rented St John's Wood flat.

Renée hesitates before hugging his stooped, sickly, ghostly white form.

'Things are very different for me, little one,'[51] her father says thinly, his eyes empty. The high ceilings in the cold rented room, grubby and poorly furnished – most unlike her father's taste – make the scene even harder to bear for young Renée. 'He looked like a stranger who did not belong.'[52]

She can't manage a single word.

'This is all very strange, isn't it, little one?' Eugene levels with his youngest daughter, his voice reflecting 'his sadness and aloneness'.

'Do you think we will be able to go back to Australia soon?'[53] she asks, the last of her childhood innocence shining through, as if going back to Sydney will make everything great again.

'I've had a really bad time there,' her father admits. 'I loved it and wanted to dedicate myself to the new Opera House, you know the site I wanted was finally chosen, but they were taking so long to organise it . . .'

Eugene Goossens' voice trails off. His wandering mind drops Renée a clue when he mutters, almost imperceptible: 'I had thought people respected me.'[54]

'Daddy, they did!' Renée protests.

Sir Eugene shakes his head.

'Things happened that I don't want to discuss, or to worry you about. But I don't think I am able to go back there. Not for a long time, anyway.'[55]

'I'd like to know what happened, Daddy. It would help me to understand what you are going through.'[56]

Goossens sighs – Gene is banished and Djinn is dead.

•

The fact that Jørn Utzon regularly takes his small sailing boat for jaunts on the Øresund around the small peninsula jutting into it – just like Bennelong Point – is proving useful. For upon it, of course, sits the Castle of Kronborg, which was the basis for Shakespeare's Elsinore in *Hamlet* – the one that had previously impressed Governor Lachlan Macquarie – and it all helps Utzon's thoughts come together as to how a Sydney Opera House might look, rising out of the horizontal plane of the sound, soaring skywards to house the stage towers, all while being visually inspiring.

'If you think of a Gothic church,' he will later say, 'you are closer to what I have been aiming at. Looking at a Gothic church you never get tired, you will never be finished looking at it – when you pass around it to see it against the sky. It is as if something new goes on all the time and it is so important – this interplay is so important that, together with the man, the light and the clouds, it makes a living thing.'[57]

Little by little, a rough form starts to take shape out of his endless doodling, which starts with curving clouds floating weightlessly above the harbour and cloud-like depictions of the curved, floating roofs of ancient China.

'Very simple, really,' he will remark later when called upon to explain the method to his madness, 'I had to cover a rather great stage, even up to a height of 90 feet and a vast auditorium. If you build a normal theatre, it will be like a boot with the stage-house as the top part of the boot, and if you put two boots here you do not use the plateau, you will actually destroy it. I stood looking at clouds over a low coastline, and I had a look at Kronborg castle at Elsinore, and at Gothic churches. There you have forms against a horizontal line like the sea or the clouds without a single vertical line, nothing constituting a weight, and with forms that are different from all angles. Furthermore, the Opera House is to be seen from above, and the city is built on hills. When driving you see a glimpse of it at the inner part of the Harbour – that is you are looking down upon it. So the forms have to be of a sort like a sculpture that can be seen from all sides. You can even sail round the Opera House.'[58]

Yes, the world is full of so-called 'modern' theatres, boxy and rigid and as urban and pedestrian as boots, each one a nod to another.

Slowly Utzon's new, bold idea for an opera house evolves.

Every walk in the open air breathes new creative energy into the young Dane, who picks up his step so he can be home to the drawing desk before the inspiration leaves him . . .

Utzon drops his pencil and stares at what he has just put to the page. *This*.

That's it, the stage towers could be encased inside beautifully curved concrete shells, like sails, weightless and shimmering on the point! A harmony of function and form, not one traded off for the other!

'Normally,' Utzon would explain his philosophy, 'in a modern building you have a cardboard ceiling with all the piping and ducting up there, some columns sticking up, and you stand between these two horizontal planes. You don't know whether you are on the tenth floor or the second floor and it doesn't matter. Here [with the Opera House], I said, the span over your head, is sacred . . .'[59]

But how to build such a span?

Those thin concrete shells that Eero Saarinen, Luigi Nervi and Felix Candela have been successfully building in all manner of free-form, curved shapes would do the job . . . ?

Yes, that's it!

The colour at least is obvious.

'Sydney is a dark harbour,' he will later explain. 'The colours on the waterfront are dull and homes red brick. There is no white to take the sun and make it dazzle the eyes. Not like the Mediterranean or South America and other sunlit countries. So, I had white in mind . . .'[60]

Further inspiration comes from the stunning curved mosque roofs in Morocco and Persia that have shimmered brightly in the sun for centuries, courtesy of ancient ceramic tiles so superbly crafted that they maintain their fine textures and brilliant colours all those years since being fired in the kiln. So, too, can the Sydney Opera House be covered in finely crafted ceramic tiles.

Oh, the sheer *joy* of putting it all together!

With his concept firmly cemented – *ahem* – Jørn begins to build small models of his evolving ideas, in the tradition of his father.

'I tried to shape the things,' Jørn later said of the roof forms that could house the necessary functions of a multipurpose theatre complex. 'I made many models. It came from model work, more than paper work. You couldn't have this on paper because it would not be alive.'[61]

From trial and error, and drawing on the vast visual library that is his mind, it all starts to come together so neatly.

The roof is the key. Functional, simple, beautiful, elegant, innovative, and something else besides . . .

December 1956, Hellebaek, a haul of halls

The Sydney Opera House competition has cast a wide net, but that is now being hauled back in – the deadline looms.

Though hurrying is simply not in his nature when it comes to architecture, Utzon works as hard as he ever has in his life, pouring creativity into his submission from dawn to dusk and on into the night. It has been exhilarating and enriching to dream up his vision for Bennelong Point – turning ancient inspirations from Denmark, Mexico, China, the Mediterranean, Persia, Morocco and more, into something entirely modern. Now is the time for solid plans. He has received some help from his partner Erik Andersson – a Swede he has worked with since 1952 in Andersson's firm, Arton. But Utzon has done the bulk of the work himself.

Truly, there are many technical difficulties in designing an opera house – with the need for strong acoustics, different stage requirements and seating capacities – but in the end, the competition does not ask for technical solutions or technical drawings, just architectural concepts, so he should be fine.

So focused is he on drawing the dream with little concern for earthly matters, it doesn't even matter that his detailed ground plans make way at the end for hastier, sketchier other drawings, nor that his submission is outside the competition guidelines in a few areas, including one rather literal area . . .

A design shall be disqualified if –
(a) It exceeds the limit of the site as outlined on the site plan.[62]

In Utzon's designs, the podium's edge is outside the limit on the west side. But it's too late to change that.

And the Brown Book stipulates:

Drawings shall be in black and white.[63]

Well, that's just too bad. In one of his drawings, he has gilded the underside of his white shell roofs with thin gold leaf, accentuating the beauty of his design. He plans to use it as the opening drawing in his submission – his perspective view – to add a touch of joy. Perhaps they'll appreciate his boldness. Perhaps not. But as this whole exercise is primarily for his own creative pleasure, it doesn't really matter.

Anyway, he worries less about the gold leaf than he does about his take on the 'perspective view' itself, which he has drawn as a close-up view of the entry to the Opera House, and somewhat cropped . . . But they *did* say that 'the perspective drawing may be presented in any medium and any form the competitor may desire'.[64]

So maybe everything will be okay after all?

But does it really matter?

It is not as if his fantastical design will win in any case, and he fully accepts that. At least the panel is made up of architects, and architects are a kind unto their own who speak the same visual language. So, if they *do* get around to looking at it, they'll see Utzon speaking in his native tongue.

'We had in this case,' he will note, 'a jury consisting of all architects, then you do not have to make special efforts to make your project understandable to a layman. You could stress certain things very clearly, and in a very simple way, and leave out certain details, because you knew that the project would be judged by experts.'[65]

It would equally be good to get input from an engineer so as to work out if this dream could actually be built, but Utzon has no time.

Finally dropping his pencil – for he is, if not done, at least as near to done as he can be while still making the deadline – Jørn calls out for Lis. Smart as a whip, her English is so much better than his, and he could not contemplate writing up his submission without her help.

'National Opera House, Sydney, Australia,' he dictates to her in his heavy accent, but no sooner has he said the words than they both start laughing at the absurdity of it all – two country kids from Denmark wandering into the sophisticated world of urban opera house design – but they continue anyway. Lis tap-tap-tapping at the typewriter, suggests a few edits as they go:

> The architecture emphasises the character of the Bennelong Point and takes the greatest advantage of the view.
>
> The approach of the audience is easy and as distinctly pronounced as in Grecian theatres by uncomplicated staircase constructions.

Jørn's report elaborates, explaining the contingency plans in the event of a fire, as well as the functional purposes of the podium.

> The audience is ... led like a festive procession into the respective halls ...
>
> Light, suspended concrete shells accentuate the plateau effect and the character of the staircase constructions.

As for the interiors, Jørn has been doing his research on the latest techniques being used in theatres across continental Europe and has found an inner acoustic shell solution can be used to convert the space from a concert hall one day to an opera hall the next to a ballet theatre for the weekend. With the help of cutting-edge stage towers, the halls will be both multipurpose and beautiful.

> Ceiling and walls of wooden acoustic panels continue in 'overhead' doors closing towards foyers and entrance-areas, which in their turn are closing toward open-air-areas with 'overhead' glass doors.
>
> This construction implies the possibility of a complete opening of halls, foyers and public areas towards open-air during intermission whenever weather permitting and presents to the audience the full sensation of the suspended shells while moving through the foyers commanding the beautiful view of the harbour.
>
> The whole exterior radiates lightness and festivity and is standing as a clear contrast to the square harbour buildings of Sydney.[66]

In the end, he is not remotely at the end of what he wants to do and say when the time comes to send, and in one brief moment of vulnerability, he even contemplates not sending it at all, to spare himself the inevitable disappointment.

But in the end, send it he must – no less than an unfinished masterpiece.

7 January 1957, National Art Gallery of NSW, judge not that ye be judged

Today is the big day.

The judging panel assembled in this room of the NSW Art Gallery – especially cleared of paintings so that promising plans can be put up on the walls – are distinguished. One need only get a whiff of the high-quality pipe tobacco – so distinct from the working-man's 'rollies' of Log Cabin or Drum – to know that this is a room full of important people.

There is Professor Harry Ingham Ashworth, donning his signature bow tie and black-rimmed glasses, together with his dear friend, the famed English architect Dr Leslie Martin, along with the NSW Government Architect, Cobden Parkes. For the moment, the Finnish–American architect Eero Saarinen is yet to arrive in Australia – as the star of the show, the pre-eminent among all this bow tie toting eminence, he is allowed a certain latitude, and a longitude which places him still in America. The others get busy leafing through submission after submission, all piled up on a large table, and hanging up the better drawings and sketches on the empty walls. For the purposes of this exercise no submissions have the names of the architects attached, for it is important that the judges decide on merit alone.

Some of the 233 entries, coming from 32 countries as widely spread as Japan, Ethiopia, Egypt and Switzerland, are easy to eliminate – a mere glance generates three shakes of the head and, just like that, weeks and *months* of work are consigned to oblivion. The same fate awaits those that are too fantastical, those unrecognisable as even being buildings in the first place. One even looks like nuns in a scrum, or maybe they are white sails instead of white habits? Whatever they are, it is not what they are looking for.

All up, they discard over 100 designs on the first day.

What they *are* looking for, is not clear. It is more collective instinct than anything else as the winnowing process goes on for the next four days, until they are down to just 10 finalists and . . .

After a flurry of activity in the corridor, the door opens and the great man arrives. Gentlemen, Eero Saarinen. A well-dressed fellow in his mid-forties, whose red bow tie is surely the cherry on top, enters the room. After a minimum of handshakes and greetings, for they all understand that the time for chat will come later, Saarinen gets to it, scanning the selected designs.

Some show promise, while he strongly disagrees with others. Overall, he has no doubt – none of them make the grade as the outstanding submission that Saarinen is looking for.

Can I see the ones you have rejected?

Reluctantly, the rejected are retrieved and while the others chat a little, even as they keep an eye on the Finnish–American, gauging his reactions, Saarinen turns over, one after another – nearly all of them standard-brand off-the-shelf four back-and-sides shoe-boxes-arranged-as-boots civic statements, many with tangles of stairs, corridors and fire exits onto flat roofs that are perfect for collecting dust . . . the only catch being that *these* roofs are to sit in plain sight of the city buildings and the Sydney Harbour Bridge, which looms like a nosy neighbour, always looking down her magnificent curving nose at the admittedly functional yet filthy and forgotten fifth façade of what is supposed to be Sydney's centrepiece.

Which will hardly do, as Saarinen hints to an audience at a civic reception a few nights hence: 'The Harbour Bridge would play an important part in the choosing of the winning design. The bridge provided a backdrop and the Opera House would have to be chosen with this in mind.'[67]

After all, when he applies his personal design diktat that, 'The only architecture which interests me is architecture as a fine art,'[68] anything that looks like a glorified box of any description immediately suffers the double humiliation of being rejected for a second time, in a time not much longer than that.

Suddenly, the eminent Eero pauses from his endless flipping of flops and now stops entirely and gazes closely.

The soaring lines!

The vision!

'Do you suppose it's possible?'[69] he mumbles to himself. He thinks so.

(After all, he has already used a revolutionary thin concrete shell for his Kresge Auditorium in Boston. And at this very moment he is overseeing the construction of his free-form thin concrete shells for the TWA Passenger Terminal in New York, a cutting-edge design. He is frankly of the view that just about any shape can be built in shell concrete rather cheaply, it is just a matter of working out how to do it.)

The sheer out-of-this-world *imagination* of this design takes his breath away. It is both a work of art . . . and a work of . . . genius.

And it is not just the innovative nature of the silhouette. The soaring, curved form so perfectly houses the halls' soaring stage towers and other functions. More than a building, it is an enormous sculpture – and as one who had himself excelled in his study of sculpture at the *Académie de la Grande Chaumière* in Paris, before studying architecture at Yale University, Saarinen can be counted on to appreciate it more than most.

Holding up the plans so the other judges can see it more clearly for their second look, he says dramatically, 'Gentlemen, here is your opera house!'[70]

•

Truly great architecture is best experienced visually; not explained in words.

To this end, as he will later tell the story, Eero Saarinen is out in a small rowboat, *on* the harbour, about 100 yards off Bennelong Point trying to stay clear of the ferries and yachts, pulling the oars this way and that to get the small vessel into the desired position. At last satisfied, he asks his three fellow judges – caught between bemusement at Eero's unstoppable enthusiasm and fear at the ferry coming too near – to position themselves at the back of the boat, while he manoeuvres up the front.

Right there on the spot he sketches his favoured design on a large piece of paper, and holds it up for them to see what it could one day look like.[71]

As the boat bobs up and down, the other three lean forward, squint, imagine and . . . sure enough . . . start to see it! No, not castles in the air, but something much better, a Sydney Opera House, sparkling in the sunshine, right out there on Bennelong Point, lofty as a cloud, the toast of the city, the champagne structure of the modern world!

It could be *the* antidote to what surrounds the otherwise glorious harbour: dowdy working wharves, belching industrial plants, dull office buildings and myriad red-brick boxes!

It is *precisely* the design they are looking for. A marvel from every angle . . .

Rowing back to the man-o'-war steps, on the eastern side of Bennelong Point, there is little talking, for there is much to reflect on. First and foremost, they wonder – *who* designed it, where is the architect from, is it someone they know?

'People looking at the design must look on it as if looking at a beautiful woman,' Harry Ashworth quips to his fellow judges, 'not as to whether she's a good cook.'[72]

Yes, but . . .

But this opera house is to be a lifelong commitment. Beauty is one thing, but being a good cook is important. Still there is much to discuss.

•

How do you value a dream?

Good question.

'How do I estimate this?' the quantity surveyor whose job it is to put an estimated cost on each of the top contenders asks Eero Saarinen, the only person in the room who seems to have a clue as to how such a structure as this might be built.

'There's nothing in it,' the architect replies blithely. 'These shells might be about three inches thick at the top, and say 12 inches thick at the base.'[73]

Unsure, the quantity surveyor decides to double the figure they come up with, just to err on the side of caution, and using that comes up with an estimated cost of the Opera House at – *dot three, carry one, subtract two* – £3.6 million.

And the good news for the assessors?

They are able to lightly boast in their report: 'We have had approximate estimates made for all the schemes which have been given places and several others in addition. The scheme which we now recommend for the first premium is, in fact, the most economical scheme on the basis of our estimates.'[74]

With their report finalised, the assessors give a taste-teaser interview to the *Sydney Morning Herald*:

> 'The prototype of recent opera houses in the world today was built 70–80 years ago,' said Mr Saarinen. 'The one we've selected won't look anything like these' . . .
>
> Professor Martin added, 'Predominantly, most of the competitors tried to solve the problem in today's techniques. We looked for a monumental work. After all, you don't go to the opera very often. It's a bit of an occasion, and it's nice to go to a magnificent building. That's why we kept in mind that the Opera House had to be an imaginative thing!'

'There'll be criticism, of course,' Mr Saarinen warned. 'But you can't do a good piece of work without criticism.'[75]

Indeed, Eero.

When General Manager of the ABC Charles Moses is confidentially shown the winning design . . . his heart sinks.

How *could* the judges have chosen such an outlandish design? Whatever its architectural merits, who could think that this would ever win the Labor caucus over, let alone the political Opposition and the public at large?

'It was a shock to me when I saw it,' Moses will later recount, 'because I thought, "Look, the government will never accept this. This is so unorthodox . . . so different from any other opera house in the world."'[76]

(Mercifully, he has not heard Premier Joe Cahill's initial muttered response to the winning design: 'It looks like a bloody crocodile!'[77] Thankfully, the Premier knows his place. Architecture is not his area of expertise and so he declines to give his input on the judges' choice. He is of the hoi polloi and proudly so. If this is what the hoity-toity think it should look like, so be it. The point is, it will not be theirs alone.)

Joe Cahill does not believe for one moment that it will be possible to build such a structure for £3.5 million – carefully rounded down for the occasion – but at least the figure won't frighten the horses; at least it is saleable.

It all comes down to getting underway, quickly. He girds his loins for the battle he knows is coming.

FOUR

ENTER THE ARCHITECT AND THE ENGINEER

Architecture is the will of an epoch translated into space.[1]

Mies van de Rohe, one of the fathers of modernist architecture

A Gehry building depends on the taste of Gehry, while with Utzon's, it is as if the site is fulfilling its destiny, as if some other hand had made it.[2]

Richard Weston, architect

The Opera House ... entered the sluggish and provincial context of Australian architecture in the late '50s like some pearly nautilus visiting a mussel bed. Architecture students and leading younger architects were enthralled by it; this was the grand leap of the imagination that Australia badly needed but had not yet made. Some older and more conservative local architects objected to the design as fanciful. And in between, through a barrage of publicity and cross-argument such as no building had ever received from the Australian press, the public realized that it had a myth of sorts on its hands ... Thus, it became a talisman well before it took form as a structure ...[3]

Robert Hughes, art critic, *Time* magazine, 1973

3 pm, 29 January 1957, National Art Gallery of NSW, Yawn's house not so sleepy

The only beings not uncomfortable in this stinking hot room on this day of high summer are the six figures in the florid Italian painting of *The Five Senses*, a mother and her five babes, wrapped up in their own world. Before them in this tight room of the art gallery, just 100 yards or so across the Domain from the NSW Parliament, 150 members of the press and the architectural community are gathered, loosening their ties and removing their jackets as their collective body heat makes things oppressively humid.

The VIPs sit on seats in front of the official dais, while everyone else is well back, behind the thick velvet cords suspended between portable poles of brass. The mood is restless, excited, impatient for the announcement to be underway, for the long wait to be over.

Many in the audience occupy themselves flipping through the official assessors' report, which contains a couple of clues about the winning design. 'The white sail-like forms of the shell vaults relate as naturally to the harbour as the sails of its yachts . . .'[4] while the *Herald*'s photographer, who has been given early access to take photos of the winning submission, whispers to his colleagues: 'There are two French words on the plan.'[5]

Nord, instead of north, and *exterieur* for outside. A Frenchman has won? It *must* be a Frenchman! Could it be the great Le Corbusier?

The gossip spreads till at last, at last, Stan Haviland steps up to welcome everyone, and now hands over to Premier Cahill two things: the dais itself, and an envelope with the winner's name in it. 'I could not give them to you earlier,'[6] Stan explains to the Premier quietly, tapping the envelope. 'They bear the winner's name. It is interesting to know that at all stages of the adjudication, the assessors amused themselves by trying to guess the nationality of the winner – and they were all wrong!'[7]

The Premier adjusts his glasses and peruses his speech notes. The sound of a stuttering television camera starts up and a battery of arc lights flashes on, illuminating the scene to better capture this historic moment.

All is ready.

'But the Premier,' as the *Sydney Morning Herald* will note, 'was in no hurry to open the envelope. He stressed the national importance of an opera house and expressed his confidence that everyone, once having seen the winning design, would think the prize money well spent.'[8]

Yes, Premier. Of course, Premier. Quite right, Premier.

But no-one cares. They are all here for one thing, a thing that lies at the end of such remarks, and all are impatient for him to get on with it. At last, Joe Cahill winds up.

The *Herald* journalist looks at his watch.

Now is the moment. At 3.22 pm the Premier pauses significantly, and a whisper runs through the audience . . .

'Before announcing the name of the person who submitted the winning design,' says Premier Cahill, 'I shall run the risk of trying your patience by making one or two general remarks . . .'[9]

There is an all but audible expulsion of breath as off he goes again for at least another five minutes before again he pauses, and again they lean forward.

'Now, ladies and gentlemen,' says the Premier. 'Before I announce the prize . . .'[10]

Dear God!

'If I can just for a moment take your minds back to a meeting two years ago in the Library building when it was decided this project should be put in hand . . .'[11]

And finally, at 3.29 pm he actually opens the envelope – a real breakthrough! – and draws out a sheet of paper, adjusts his glasses, and slowly reads.

'The design awarded the first premium is Scheme Number 218 . . . The design awarded second premium is Scheme Number 28 . . . And the design awarded third premium is Scheme Number 62.'[12]

Yes, yes, yes, but *who*? Whose scheme is Number 218, Premier?

The only thing for sure is that, as there were 233 entries, it must have been among the last to have been received.

'Those are the numbers,' the Premier says falteringly. 'I'm afraid I haven't the names. Whether somebody will tell us . . .'[13]

Stan Haviland steps forward again and withdraws from the envelope another slip of paper, which he hands to the Premier.

Ah, yes.

'Design awarded first premium,' reads Premier Cahill, 'is Scheme Number 218, submitted by . . . Jørn Utzon – the correct pronunciation is *Yawn Ootson* – of Hellebaek, Denmark, 38 years of age.'[14]

The crowd stirs. It's not a Frenchman.

It's a Dane.

A Dane named Utzon?

Utzon?

Have you heard of him?

Shakes of the head all round. The name rings no bells for anyone. Had Premier Cahill said Walter Bunning or Harry Seidler, most of the press would have known exactly who it was – the local stars – but this name is a complete mystery.

And is his name truly 'Yawn'?

All that they can find out in the short term is what Premier Cahill has already told them – that, yes, they believe his name is pronounced Yawn[15] but spelled Jørn, and that he is 38 years old, lives in Denmark, and . . . that's about it.

Walter Bunning has never heard of this unproven architect from Denmark, and for that matter, he is too busy trying and failing to hide his disappointment to find out. Just a few weeks earlier he had pontificated in the pages of the *Herald*, 'This is the most important competition ever to be held in Australia, because it is for a building of great national prestige, marking the coming-of-age of this country in a cultural sense,'[16] before going on to sing the praises of Eero Saarinen and his revolutionary thin concrete shell designs being built in the USA. Now that the announcement has been made and his hopes dashed against the cruel rocks that line Bennelong Point, he stares at the wall in front of him in disbelief. Not at the splendour and beauty of Utzon's work – thin curved concrete shells, not unlike Saarinen's – but in disbelief that they are not *his* designs that he is looking at.

Not even an Australian's vision?

But a Dane? What could a Dane possibly know about our country?

Colonel Charles Moses has no such reservations and tells the waiting press triumphantly, 'It's something new and exciting. It reminds me of some of the new and modern churches in Scandinavia. It's intended to look exciting from every angle, and it will bring interesting reactions from all over the world. Wherever artists meet they'll discuss this wonderful structure.'[17]

Moses can at least be pleased that one highly regarded architect – though initially disappointed that his own entry has not won – is now waxing lyrical to the press about the Utzon entry:

'The winning design is poetic,' young Harry Seidler gushes to the assembled press. 'It is a piece of *poetry*. It is magnificent. I am quite staggered by it. The jury should be commended for having the courage to award the prize to it.'[18]

Well, that is really something, even if Seidler does now take Moses aside and make the quiet plaint, 'You know, if I'd thought that the Government would take on something so unorthodox, I would've submitted a very different design . . .'[19]

Sure, Harry. We can talk later. For now, Moses looks to the Premier to try to gauge his reaction.

Well, at least the Premier is smiling – even if it is a crocodile smile – which is something. Better still, he is doing so while speaking to the press, declining to get into the merits or otherwise of the judges' decision.

'It is not my intention to enter the lists on that score at any time,' Premier Cahill demurs.

'There has been and doubtless will be some criticism of the project itself, of the site which the government has chosen, of the wisdom of building an opera house at all, and of the community's ability to shoulder the expense of maintaining a National Opera House,' he says smoothly.

'Those are the things that crop up from day to day and are something that the Government and I will have to face.'[20]

And isn't that the truth? While Joe Cahill is indeed resolute in his public comments on the Opera House, he is equally in no doubt that he will have a job ahead of him to bring the Labor caucus with him and, most significantly, the Labor Cabinet, and finally the parliament.

Already thinking far ahead, he adds the need for speed to take the momentum of the excitement over a design having been chosen, and convert it as quickly as possible into a sod being turned, the whole project being underway so the sails of this Opera House can be set to withstand the wildest winds.

The judges, of course, back their selection. True, once the decision had been locked in, Eero Saarinen had flown to London on his own architectural assignment of designing the US Embassy, but before departure he had recorded some crackling if not quite cracking remarks for the press – with his stuttering removed by a clever ABC technician – to help them understand why Utzon's design had been chosen. For the concept is, the press must understand, an 'outstanding piece of art'.[21] And while some of them might be concerned about how hard it will be to build, they shouldn't be. For 'while all gothic cathedrals had used the interlocking shell vault system, they had used stone, this was the same concept in concrete. The system of this winning design is in use in Italy, Brazil, Madrid and America.'[22]

He is also thrilled to find out that the person who designed the winning entry is none other than Jørn Utzon.

'I've seen several competition drawings which he has won,' he tells the press, 'and there is a very fine quality about his work. I've always considered him as one of the really most talented men in Scandinavia.'[23] Such remarks are consistent with remarks the judges have collectively made in the Assessors' Report, which some of the press are now trawling, looking for quotable quotes for late afternoon editions, before racing back to their offices to file copy.

'The great merit of [Jørn Utzon's] building is the unity of its structural expression . . . It is difficult to think of a better silhouette for this peninsular. The dynamic form of this vaulted shape contrasts with the buildings which form its background and gives a special significance to the project in the total landscape of the Harbour.'[24]

It is true, the judges acknowledge, that 'the drawings submitted for this scheme are simple to the point of being diagrammatic. Nevertheless, as we have returned again and again to the study of these drawings, we are convinced that they present a concept of an opera house which is capable of becoming one of the great buildings of the world. We consider this scheme to be the most original and creative submission. Because of its very originality, it is clearly a controversial design. We are, however, absolutely convinced about its merits.'[25]

For now, though, the maddest scramble in Sydney journalism for some time begins – the scramble to get the winner on the phone. Journalist Martin Long, a determined man by nature, races back to the *Herald* offices at Broadway in Jones Street and instantly has the paper's switchboard operator patch him through to international directory assistance, looking for a *J. Utzon* in Hellebaek, Denmark.

29 January 1957, Hellebaek, white horse for a white house

'*Hej?*'

Martin Long hears a young girl's voice crackle down the line.

'*Hej? Hej?*' comes the child's voice again.

This is Sydney Australia calling. We are looking for Yawn Ootson. He has won a competition for Sydney's Opera House!

That is my father. He not here, but I know where he go. You . . . wait?

Her parents have only just left for a long walk in the beech forest on their way to get mail from the post office, but 10-year-old Lin knows where they'll be . . . Leaving the receiver dangling from its spiralling cord, she jumps on her old pushbike and heads out after them. And there they are!

She calls out. '*Far! Du vandt, Far, du vandt!*'[26]

Dad! You won, Dad, you won!

Jørn and Lis Utzon turn around to see her dump the old bike in a ditch, as she covers the last 50 yards on foot.

'Father! Someone from Sydney is on the phone, saying you have won the competition for the Opera House! Now you have no excuse for not buying me the white horse you promised me!'[27]

Jørn's big blue eyes widen in silent disbelief. Lis jumps in delight – you won! – grabbing him by the arm and tugging him back towards the house.

They race home, where Utzon snatches up the dangling phone and is relieved to hear someone still on the other end, who confirms the news in a strange-sounding English: he has won the competition to build an opera house in Sydney! For his part, Martin Long takes down the Dane's remarks in his scrawling shorthand, like the tracks of a spider limping across the page. (For one thing, the Dane's name is not pronounced 'Yawn', but 'Yearn'.)

'So far the Opera House Committee has not contacted me, but [given your news] I am expecting a cable at any moment. It depends on what they can advise me how soon I migrate. But I shouldn't think I would have a great deal of trouble getting a good position in Australia now, do you? It must be a wonderful country with plenty of what we have not been getting lately – sunshine.'

Can you tell us a little more about yourself?

'We have three children,' he happily relates. 'A boy aged twelve, a girl aged ten, and our baby son, who was born on New Year's Day this year. This news from Australia is almost as good as the news of his arrival. My wife is just as thrilled about the win as I am. I have won twenty prizes for architectural design before, in Denmark and Sweden, including six first prizes. But this is far and away the most important.'

How long did you spend on the design?

'I spent about six months from May to December 1956, whenever I could get time off from my other work. I studied hundreds of pictures, photographs, and maps of the site. It is a very lovely position for an opera house and most inspiring to any architect. But from this distance it naturally took a great feat of the imagination to "see" it in its setting.'[28]

If he does say so himself! No sooner has Utzon put the phone down to be heartily embraced by his wife and children than he calls his partner Erik Andersson with the extraordinary news: we have won! Andersson roars his exultation down the phone and tells him he will be on the next ferry across.

The phone rings again. There are knocks on the door. The word is spreading. Jørn has won some competition to design a big building in Australia! Friends arrive with champagne.

By the time the journalist from *The Daily Telegraph*, Emery Barcs, gets through, he can immediately hear the sound of laughter, excited chatter and clinking glasses in the background, interspersed with the regular popping of corks.

'How do you feel about your success?' Emery Barcs near shouts down the crackly line.

'I'm terribly happy,' Utzon replies in much better English than Barcs had been expecting, albeit with a heavy accent.

'You sound as if you are celebrating?'

'Naturally,' the joyous cry comes back. 'We are celebrating. There is plenty of champagne.'

'What inspired your design?'

'The beautiful pictures I have received of Sydney Harbour – all sorts of pictures, not only of Bennelong Point, but also of the whole harbour. It must be one of the most beautiful spots in the world. I have dreamt of it much. Then came the idea with that roof. Do they like it in Sydney?'

Emery Barcs has little hesitation in affirming Sydney's excitement, and leaving out any mention of some of the negative reactions. It is not the time.

'What will you do with the prizemoney?'[29]

The response, first up, is a great sonic boom of laughter, coming from 10,000 miles away.

'Of course, I need all that money to come to Australia, and I'll bring the whole family. It's a long way and it will cost a lot of money. But I hope the fare won't take the lot of it. What do you think?'

'I think you will have some pocket money left out of your five thousand pounds.'[30]

Perhaps enough, in fact, to live in Sydney for good?

'Not sure, depends . . .' Utzon replies. 'At least, I mean, I want to go for a long time. I mean it depends whether they want me permanently. An opera house is not built in a day, you know – not even in Australia. *Au revoir!* Thanks for ringing me. Was a nice thing to do. We are very, very happy . . . *Au revoir* . . . in Sydney . . .'[31]

There is another booming laugh to sign off, and he is gone.

•

The following morning the *Herald*'s front page is ablaze with an image of Utzon's design, above the headline:

DANE'S CONTROVERSIAL DESIGN WINS OPERA HOUSE COMPETITION
'Cheapest to Build'[32]

The inside pages give a fair summation of why the assessors themselves concede it is 'a controversial design'[33], led by the headline:

POETRY OR PASTRY? ARGUMENT ON OPERA HOUSE PLANS[34]

Most Sydney architects commended Jørn Utzon's winning opera house design when the competition entries were displayed at the National Art Gallery yesterday afternoon.

But interested laymen, obviously startled by the original roof,
were less enthusiastic.

One woman said the design looked like 'a piece of Danish pastry.'
An architect said: 'It doesn't thrill me at all, I think it is messy.'[35]

And, of course, he is far from the only one, with even the president
of the influential NSW Town Planning Association, architect Bertram
W. Ford, saying flatly in *The Sun*, that Jørn's Opera House design is
nothing less than 'insane, and would completely disfigure the point'.
Oh yes, these upstart overseas architects seem to have 'gone mad' with
their futuristic designs. For balance, *The Sun* at least reports that Mr
Ford has spotted one good feature: 'I don't think it will ever be built.
They just haven't got the money for it.'[36]

Another bone of contention that caustic commentators focus on are
the submission drawings themselves. The *Herald*, despite its overall
approval, reveals that Utzon's submission is the 'least finished design in
the competition'[37].

The fast-rising art critic Robert Hughes notes the plans are so sketchy
they could be considered 'nothing more than a magnificent doodle'[38].

Of course, the open-ended competition had not called for technical
details or drawings, but, as Joe Cahill reminds the public often – there
will always be critics, no matter what you do.

Now, to fill out said 'magnificent doodle', and let the public have a
better idea of what the building might actually look like *in situ*, the judging
panel organises for Arthur Baldwinson – a lecturer in architecture at the
University of Sydney – to quickly produce a coloured rendition of Utzon's
drawings, as well as a side-elevation drawing. There is no doubt they are
a great success and when they first go on display at the art gallery, just
three days after the announcement of Utzon's triumph – fortuitously, at
the same time as the annual Archibald Prize exhibition, the gallery's biggest
event – some 8000 people crowd through its halls to get a close-up look.
At many times they are 12 deep, crowding around the illustrations and
drawings as if they were Rembrandts at the Rijksmuseum or the *Mona
Lisa* at the Louvre. By the count of *The Daily Telegraph*, 19 out of 20
visitors come away enthused, with one odd man out being Mr W. Shonatus
of Kings Cross, who tells the paper, 'The design is completely European.
I should have liked to have seen something more typically Australian.'[39]
(Alas, alas, such glorified red-box office-blocks as had been submitted had
not done good box office with the judges.) Mr Erik Langker, a trustee of

the National Art Gallery and president of the Opera Guild, is quite fond of its non-Australian quality: 'It is a very imaginative design. It is far in advance of any Australian architecture. I think the plan of the inside is an excellent one. I would like to see a model of the Opera House.'[40]

Another who wishes his scathing assessment be known is none other than Walter Bunning, who – fresh from a bitter debate with Harry Seidler at the home of a mutual friend – unburdens himself of the view that it looks like, 'an insect with a shell on its back which has crawled out from under a log'[41].

Third-place winners, the husband-and-wife team, Paul Boissevain and Barbara Osmond – she had been the only woman to enter – had exhaustively studied the functional aspects of a multipurpose performance hall, sure it would give them the technical edge over the rest; alas, to their disappointment, their two-box building design had not been enough.

But, by and large, the architectural profession comes out on Utzon's side. Even the second-place winners – a group from Philadelphia who had designed a Nautilus shell-inspired building – concede with grace when they see Utzon's design.

'We almost won, but we didn't,' one of the architects, Robert Geddes, will say. 'Why? Because Jørn Utzon's design was a masterpiece.'[42]

Peter Kollar of Cremorne, one member of a Hungarian-born duo who skipped the revolution in the motherland to work on their entry, tells the Sydney press: 'It is a nice concept. He has lifted it up from the sea. He was game to submit the design he did and good on him too.'[43]

And here now is George Molnar, the architect and cartoonist, who feels like a man who has fairly confidently laid down a pair of kings and a couple of queens, only to find himself trumped by a player with four Danish aces. It only takes a glance at the winning design to realise its genius – and how his own design had come up so short.

'[My design] was exactly the opposite of Utzon's,' he would recall. '[The Dane] was inspired by white sails and blue water, I by the lights of the Manly ferry scurrying across the water. The halls [in my plan] were back-to-back, wrapped in blazing foyers. In the centre, like a giant smoke stack, stood the stage tower . . . Steam gave way to sail. Rightly, I thought . . .'[44]

It is a humbling thing for a good practitioner of his art to be confronted by the sheer genius of another, and Molnar is in just such a humble mood when he is asked by his editor at the *Herald*: 'What's Utzon's design like?'

'Marvellous,' says Molnar.

'Explain it to me.'

Molnar explains, and the editor writes his editorial accordingly, exulting about the genius of the winning submission.

Exciting Opera House Design

... the successful Danish entry provides Sydney – and Australia – with the opportunity to possess an opera house of rare distinction ... [Jørn Utzon's] opera house – appropriately for a harbour city – belongs to both sea and land.[45]

Some letters to the editor of the *Sydney Morning Herald* are emblematic of the growing public view – mostly in favour, with still a few nay-sayers.

Sir,

At last! A clean, refreshing breeze has found its way into the musty corridors of Australian architectural thought ...

Although Mr. Utzon's entry may come as an invigorating breath of fresh air to our architectural profession, it will undoubtedly be considered a frightening tornado by a public conditioned for so long to a climate made up of texture bricks and red tile roofs ...

Congratulations to Mr. Utzon for his daring conception and to the four assessors for their equally daring recognition of Australia's capacity to implement such a revolutionary design.

BRUCE LODER
Bankstown[46]

Sir,

All those concerned with the opera house contest deserve unqualified congratulations upon the result.

The prize-winning design is suggestive of some large and lovely ship of the imagination, sailing on the winds of inspiration, that has come to rest in the harbour ...

Our congratulations to Denmark and her artist-architect.

ALAN O. ROBSON
Chatswood[47]

Sir,

On regatta days long pennants could be flown from the peaks, while the whole building could be outlined in varicoloured neon lighting constantly changing to suit the mood of the music being played ...

A. REID
Bexley[48]

Sir,

Faced with the nightmare illustrated in your columns today, some twenty-fifth century Bluebeard's lair, its ominous vanes pointed skywards apparently only for the purpose of discharging guided missiles or some latter-day nuclear Evil Eye, words fail.

It is all very well to chatter about the thing causing an artistic furore, but it is well to remember that the people who have to pay for it will also have to live with it, and, if at some suitably remote period, our descendants regain any sense of taste or proportion, they will be forced to foot the bill for removing it and putting up something less repellent.

Let us therefore cut our losses now, pay the Scandinavian gentleman his prize, and pigeonhole the plans. Better the worst of the Department of Public Works than this armadillo in concrete!

W. H. PETERS
Sydney[49]

Sir,

To me, the winning design suggests some gargantuan monster which may have wandered over the land millions of years ago. It certainly is right out of place beside the dignity of the Harbour Bridge.

M. RATHBONE
Kensington[50]

Sir,

There is one consolation. Although it looks like a disintegrating circus tent in a gale, the building is estimated to cost up to £4,000,000; and that consideration alone will almost certainly ensure that it will not be erected for some considerable time to come, if at all.

The thought that any Government would, in present circumstances, outlay such a sum on a building which, however brilliantly designed in a technical sense, would certainly offend the aesthetic sense of a great body of our citizens, is as fantastic as the exterior design.

HERBERT JOHNSON
Cremorne[51]

Australia's foremost prima donna of the opera, Joan Hammond, says that Utzon's building looks as though it, 'might fly away in the first strong breeze'.[52]

And the list of what the design looks like, according to the people of Sydney, grows exponentially:

'A sink with plates stacked in readiness for washing.'[53]

'A collection of abandoned umbrellas, an unmade bed.'[54]

'Prehistoric pterodactyl with chickens.'[55]

'A haystack covered by several tarpaulins which are being lifted by a strong wind.'[56]

'Is it another plane crash?'[57]

'A cross between an igloo with air ducts and an air terminal . . .'[58]

'A hideous parachute which we cannot fold up and put away.'[59]

'An armadillo with rheumatism.'[60]

'Copulating turtles . . .'[61]

The Australian Women's Weekly plays fortune teller, writing: 'Jørn Utzon . . . with his "White Sails" design for Sydney's National Opera House, has started a controversy which will continue for decades . . .'[62]

(*Ahem.*)

As tough as such commentary is, nothing comes close to the sheer barking force generated by the comment of the great Frank Lloyd Wright.

'God help us all!' he growls to an Australian journalist based in New York.

'Sensationalism! Nothing but sensationalism! This design is not characteristic of Australia, or opera. It's just picture architecture . . . A whim, that's all it is, a whim! . . . A canvas-topped barge trying to make sail out at sea in the wrong direction,'[63] he spits.

And even now, he is only just warming up.

'Tell me, how could you Australians ever fall for it?' he asks the journalist as he stands and begins to pace the room, visibly disturbed, returning to his desk to cast another eye over Jørn Utzon's design.

He begins again . . .

'What is there "Australian" about this opera house you people intend to build? You Australians must develop an architecture of your own.'

The journalist shrinks a little from the famous architect's command, as if the future of Australian architecture has been momentarily placed in her hands.

'There are reports Mr Utzon is one of your pupils,' she offers in return.

'He has never studied with me and I have never heard of him,' Frank Lloyd Wright snaps back. 'Australians are not going to let this abomination happen, are they?'[64]

Despite Frank Lloyd Wright's eminence, Professor Ashworth is not overly concerned, writing to Eero Saarinen:

> I do feel:
>
> a. It is a poor criticism.
>
> b. It is a little unfortunate that a young man producing an imaginative scheme in an international competition should receive such scant support from such a big figure.
>
> c. That the very design itself would appear to meet, at least, to be almost based upon earlier teachings of Wright himself.[65]

Indeed.

Saarinen replies: 'I could have told you that Wright would have said just about that. He has always hated competitions and has very little good to say about anything but work he has done himself, but in spite of that I think he is the greatest living architect. Both *Time Magazine* and *Newsweek* published the Opera House, which is really the best kind of press you can get.'[66]

Quite.

But neither Ashworth or Saarinen themselves escape criticism, with one unnamed 'eminent professor of architecture' apparently holding the view that the choice is the result of 'one bad assessor and three yes men'[67].

Well, as the leading local assessor and member of the Opera House Committee, Professor Ashworth is sure to defend the House, writing in an op-ed to address, 'the inevitable controversy'[68].

> Imaginative and original architecture depends just as much on a sympathetic and understanding public as in its designers – an architect in fact can only be as good as his client allows him to be.
>
> Architecture is the mistress art. We now have the chance to produce a building which could rank among the great buildings of the world. We have a fine site, an imaginative design and a practical solution to the problem, an imaginative architect behind the design who comes from a small country which already possesses world acclaim for its architecture. Let us not make a muff of our opportunity.[69]

In sum?

Pull your heads in! (Particularly those who see this magnificent design as copulating turtles!)

Everything has come together, and all we need is continued public support. It is a theme he warms to in interviews:

'It is easy for people to say the winning design is like a collapsed circus tent. But their criticism does not count unless they argue objectively . . . The four judges spent many days trying to fault the plan on any major issue. But we could not. Its simplicity and magnificence staggered us . . . the design left no dead space, and would call for no costly additions. Construction could be spread over five years at a cost of about £600,000 a year.'[70]

One well-respected architectural voice continues to speak out in blessed, wonderful support:

> Sir,
> Architecture is a language and architects speak it. Most of them just barely manage to speak – very few ever speak eloquent prose, but it happens rarely indeed that any of them create poetry with a few words.
>
> Our proposed opera house is just such a poetry, spoken with exquisite economy of words. But then how many of us appreciate or even understand poetry when we have only ever crude language.
>
> HARRY SEIDLER
> Point Piper[71]

30 January 1957, Dublin, more Great Danes

A giant of a man with eyes of steel and a grip like a vice despite being in his early sixties, the Danish–English engineer Ove Arup CBE first earned his legendary status for his impressive work on bridges and concrete construction – most notably, the playful penguin pool he engineered for London Zoo – and then amplified it through his extraordinary eccentricities.

'He carried a pair of extra-long chopsticks in his top pocket,' his biographer will later write of him, 'to poach enticing dishes from his neighbour's plate; on one occasion he asked the King of Denmark what his name was . . . This endlessly doodling, whimsically rhyming, cigar-waving, chess-obsessed, beret-wearing, accordion squeezing, ceaselessly smiling, foreign sounding, irresistibly charming, mumbling giant: Ove Arup.'[72]

On this day he is having breakfast in his downtown Dublin hotel while on a brief business trip from his London base, when a small article on page five of *The Times* catches his eye.

THE FUTURE SYDNEY OPERA HOUSE

To Cost £A3,500,000.[73]

His pulse quickens, as he reads on.

> The Danish architect Mr Jørn Utzon has been awarded a £5,000
> prize for the winning design for Sydney National Opera House . . .
> The assessors' report described the winning design as 'an original
> and creative submission,' and added 'because of its very originality
> it is clearly a controversial design.'[74]

It is described as 'a magnificent original design that could prove to
be the most beautiful theatre in the world'.[75]

Interesting.

Most fascinating of all though: 'two halls are enclosed with groups of
delicate white shell vaults which, surging upward and outward, reflect
the harbour waters. The form of the design would surprise those who
had come to think that theatre buildings must inevitably follow the
pattern of the opera houses built in the last century.'[76]

The whole thing was rendered by this young Jørn Utzon, a fellow
Dane who 'was a student of the famous Finnish architect Aalto'.[77]

Wonderful! This Mr Utzon will surely be needing some help, especially
with those concrete 'shell vaults'. Looking closely at the accompanying
image, Arup is stunned by the originality and beauty of the design, which
reminds him of an angry swan leaning forward with raised wings.

As it happens, Arup already has more work than he needs, but if he
had to pick a project to work on it would be *precisely* one of this nature.
On the spot, the garrulous Ove Arup decides he will write to this young
architect, Utzon, once he gets back to London.

First week of February 1957, Sydney, operatic gale rising

Calling it the 'National Opera House' seems to have done little to flatter
or entice the Australian Federal Government and its coffer boffins to help
fund the project, and so the NSW Government and the Opera House
Committee quickly drop 'National' in their public announcements as
Joe Cahill strategises on how, exactly, he will convince both sides of
state parliament that the whole endeavour is worthy of their political
commitment and perhaps their financial sponsorship.

A common theme of Opposition is that the money could be better
spent on hospitals, schools and houses people can actually live in: 'To

give the State an opera house at this stage of our economy would be as sensible as giving a grand piano to a homeless family forced to live in a tent,'[78] writes Thelma Bivens from Cessnock.

What is more, a luxury such as opera should hardly be a governmental priority.

'The expenditure of 4 million is inconceivable just to have a few screechy high notes in a foreign language,' argues M. Roberts from Katoomba.[79]

And when it comes to the public purse strings, some of Cahill's own party are beginning to think that the whole operatic operation is well outside the state's budget, one Labor member telling the press of an upcoming Labor caucus meeting, 'Whatever the Opera House outcome, there'll be no sweet music at this caucus meeting, it looks like discord all the way.'[80]

On the subject of where the money will come from, the *Sunday Telegraph* states the case pointedly in an editorial:

On with the Opera!

Must the long-view development of our city's culture and encouragement of its architectural progress always take second place to the utilitarian and pedestrian requirements of the hour? Did the builders of London, Paris, and Rome, in their heyday, take that dull, clod-like view? Of course not.

Well, this is OUR heyday. Sydney's citizens owe thanks to Premier Cahill for his vision and resolution in pressing the Opera House plan.

Through Premier Cahill, youthful, lusty, fast-growing Sydney has a chance to put itself on the world architectural map. Let's take it and snap out of the heavy outmoded Victorianism which has square-cornered our public buildings since Cook and Botany Bay.

The doubters and the carpers are mostly of the same breed which fought against the Harbour Bridge and other advanced projects in the planning stage. They're always around.

But it is to be hoped that Premier Cahill will keep his course to a spectacular goal through which he will be remembered with gratitude.[81]

And so Cahill does just that, sailing his course patiently, tacking and jibing with the shifting winds, intent on seeing the grand concrete sails come to life on Bennelong Point.

It's his biggest political gamble yet – which gives him an idea.

February 1957, London, Ove's opening gambit

A letter for you, Jørn, come from London, from an . . . Ove Arup?

Jørn, who has been inundated with all sorts of offers of help from architects and others in the past weeks, opens this latest note and reads.

> Dear Architect Utzon,
>
> My congratulations on winning the First Prize! I am very pleased that it was a Dane who won it, and after having seen a sketch of your project, I am even more pleased – and also somewhat surprised – that such an imaginative, but unusual design has actually been chosen to be built, instead of merely being praised, as is mostly the case . . .
>
> As far as I can see, it will not be so easy to calculate and detail your design so that your idea is realised in the fullest sense, and for it still to be economically viable. Neither do I think you can count on the Australian workmen and technical resources being of a similar standard to those in Denmark . . .
>
> If my firm can assist you in some or the other, then I shall be very pleased. I have more than thirty years' experience in working with British architects and institutions, and my Partner, Mr Jenkins, is no doubt the leading expert on the calculation of shell structures. No doubt you have your own consulting engineers, but it might be possible for us to give you some good advice. In any case I shall be pleased to meet you – are you passing through London on your way to Australia?
>
> I am visiting Copenhagen next week to interview a few engineers to work in Nigeria, but then you had perhaps already left? Anyhow, the best of luck!
>
> *Ove Arup*
>
> P.S. If you don't know who the hell I am you may think it very odd that I write to you: you may be right![82]

Jørn Utzon is immediately interested, and is in familiar territory.

Between certain things there lies a natural tension: the conductor and the orchestra; the client and the contractor; the architect and the engineer . . .

It is in that exact fault line caused by what is *desired* to be done and what *can* be done, that we see what *is* done.

In his own field of fiercely progressive and radically modern architecture, Jørn Utzon has been aware from the beginning that, while it is one thing for him to conceive extraordinary structures, he needs engineers of enormous ability to help him push the fault line as far forward as possible to allow the *art* of his architecture to see the light of day.

'Kahn described art like this,' he will explain to a reporter, referring to a famed Professor of Architecture at Yale, even as he borrows the reporter's pen and notepad and begins to sketch what he means – a signature Jørn Utzon move, he's far more comfortable with the visual than the verbal. 'On one side of the line is truth – engineering, facts, mathematics, anything like that. On the other side are human aspirations, dreams and feelings. Art is the meeting on the line of truth and human aspirations. In art, the one is meaningless without the other.'[83]

In short, now that he has won the account to build his vision of the Opera House he knows that what he most needs is an engineer not only well versed in the technical and structural matters of architecture – the complex physics and mathematics of it all – but who is also a believer in his own aspirations, dreams and feelings, his *art*.

Could Ove Arup be that man?

At the very least Jørn must fly to London to talk to two of the judges, Dr Leslie Martin and Eero Saarinen, to discuss the way forward, so perhaps he might look up Arup then.

As it happens, when Utzon does meet Leslie and Saarinen three days later, the two highly esteemed architects who had been so charmed by his design are now completely charmed by the man himself.

After the first round of congratulations are over, they get down to business.

To begin with, Martin and Saarinen ask Jørn what he's currently busy with, where he is focusing his immense talent.

As a matter of fact, Jørn is working on a housing scheme in Sweden with his architectural partners Erik and Henry Andersson. It is time consuming, but Jørn is happy to report, 'all the drawings for this work are finished so that it can now be carried on by my staff.'[84]

Jørn flashes his wide smile and can barely contain his excitement as he says, 'I'm ready to start at once on the Sydney scheme.'

Perfect. Absolutely perfect!

But down to the nitty-gritty. How, exactly, precisely speaking, are we going to get the Opera House project actually *done*? Should Utzon have sole responsibility, or should he bring his firm on board, or should he work with an established architectural practice in Sydney?

A pressing question indeed, but the three architects approach it with optimism and wide grins, the three of them happy to share each other's company – it takes an architect to *really* know an architect. The judges settle on telling the Sydney Opera House Committee: 'We are sure that he will be both enthusiastic and helpful in developing the program with the Committee.'[85] They advise that Utzon is 'admirably equipped to deal with all matters of design'[86].

They also determine that the project will only be possible with the help of a serious and respectable structural engineering firm that will be technically capable of realising Utzon's fantastical vision.

Jørn had received a letter from an Ove Arup only days ago. He has a firm here in London. Gentlemen, have you heard of him?

Dr Leslie beams in agreement. Arup is an architect's engineer, a man who wholeheartedly supports architects in bringing their plans to life. He is something of a pioneer among engineers in that sense, a crowd usually intent on telling an architect why their plans *won't* work, Ove is a man who will help an architect make his plans *work*, no matter what. Yes, Arup could be ideal.

Now, what's Sydney like architecturally? Jørn asks.

Saarinen lets out a smug laugh. 'The good thing about Australia is that there's lots to see on the way there!'[87]

The USA and Japan, where they are doing cutting-edge work with shell constructions, China, the Middle East . . . plenty!

And, Jørn, while they are dealing with political and funding matters in Sydney, it would be wise to travel to Europe, to see the latest opera houses and concert halls being built in Vienna, Berlin and elsewhere.

Indeed. He will do just that.

The three men shake hands and part ways, each one with a spring in his step. This is the beginning of something *incredible*.

Utzon makes contact with Ove Arup and is soon staying in Arup's salubrious and superbly designed and built home at Virginia Water, just outside London.

Their connection is instant. For you see, tall and slim Arup, trained not just in engineering but philosophy, too, is a devotee of a particular kind of design which he calls 'Total Design', an approach that sees the divide between the architect and the engineer dissolved, whereby artistic vision pushes the boundaries of technical and structural innovation, and so too the reverse. He believes engineers can be aesthetically creative like architects, and architects can come up with structural solutions like engineers – they must collaborate *closely*. True, it requires a strong bond and unwavering trust between architect and engineer – a rare thing in the construction world, where the headstrong engineers must play second fiddle to the whims of the head architect, which often leads to problems when characters clash and opinions diverge – but with the right people, with the right attitudes, it can be done, and he and Jørn Utzon just might be a case in point! A match made in heaven.

Utzon's fantastical design is what Arup has been looking for his whole career. It will be an ambitious project where the engineer and architect must work in tandem, relying on and playing off each other in perfect harmony, if the design is to ever become reality.

Utzon is in perfect agreement, and smiles warmly at his fellow Dane, a sprightly 62-year-old who looks more like a grandfather than anything else, his tall frame stooped forward, his smile wide and kind. Arup speaks to Utzon mostly in Danish with a smattering of English words thrown in for good measure, and his hands wave about like great bear paws as he tells stories and anecdotes that seem to drag on forever before, eventually, he remembers what he was saying and gets back to the point.

Ah, yes, and, where was I? Oh, yes, the Opera House.

The young Dane takes the pause as his cue, and begins to passionately explain his own design philosophy, his key architectural tenet: the structure must express the architecture, and the architecture must project from the structure. Perfect harmony.

It is like a beautiful melody to Ove Arup's ears. He could not have said it better himself, and given just how good it is, he will steal it and pass it on to everyone he teaches henceforth.

The two Danes speak for hours.

•

Down in Sydney, the letters go on . . .

> Sir,
>
> We should be extremely grateful to the judges of the opera house competition for providing us with the joke of the century . . . May we always regard it as something funny and not build it.
>
> PAUL ALLSOP
> Mascot[88]
>
> Sir,
>
> Nothing of moment has ever been done (in this country, at any rate) without sincere opposition.

Many will remember the controversy we suffered over the building of the Harbour Bridge.

It was stated that a bridge would ruin the harbour, that the cost would be prohibitive and quite beyond our ability to finance, that other works were of more importance, that it would be a 'white elephant'. Many, including at least one well-known engineer predicted that it would never be successfully completed to the design as we see it today . . .

Having allowed the winning opera house design to grow on me I add my meed of praise for its designer, the adjudicators and the State Government, the latter for being big enough and sufficiently farseeing to sponsor the proposal. So let's get to the task and may God prosper our endeavours.

BRUCE GIBSON
Neutral Bay[89]

Congratulations to Mr Jørn Utzon! He has a pioneering spirit! He has contributed an immortal piece of architecture to arouse the latent talent of the Australian people.

NICHOLAS EDWARDS
Forest Lodge[90]

. . . no matter what entry was selected it would have its critics.

When the Eiffel Tower was first proposed it, too, was condemned as a monstrosity, yet today it is spontaneously acknowledged as the symbol of France.

S. STANLEY
Lidcombe[91]

Future generations of Australians, whether they live in Sydney or only visit it, will derive more pleasure from a native park on the site than from the dream stones of 'Goossens Folly'.[92]

And there's one particular feature of Jørn Utzon's design that appears to invite the condemnation of many:

'How is it proposed,' questions Mrs Macquarie of Potts Point, 'to retain the pristine beauty of a glistening white tile roof in the midst of grimy harbour smoke when, with daily attention I cannot keep my light coloured window sill and door free from a grey film of dirt?'[93]

J. R. L. of Beecroft says, 'Its over finished roof with many curved surfaces all covered with white tiles will be a glaring monstrosity.'[94]

A Mrs Coleman of Willoughby is equally concerned: 'I have been a professional colour artist for more than 30 years and consider myself an authority on colour. I am not expressing an opinion on the architecture of the proposed Opera House, but – the suggested white tiles! This will give the impression from the Harbour and foreshores of either an Army camp or a circus. May I say that white can be very ugly if used in a big way.'[95]

FIVE

BENNELONG PUNTERS

When we mean to build,
We first survey the plot,
then draw the model,
And when we see the figure of the house,
Then must we rate the cost of the erection.
Which if we find outweighs ability,
What do we then but draw anew the model
In fewer offices, or at last desist
To build at all? Much more in this great work[1]

William Shakespeare, *Henry IV*, Act I, Scene 3

If the Sydney people want an opera house, let them build it; they
should not expect all the people of New South Wales through the
agency of the Government, to come to their aid.[2]

Geoffrey Crawford, Country Party Member for Barwon, 28 August 1957

10 February 1957, Sydney, a butterfly flaps its wings

Joe Cahill hands the *Sydney Morning Herald* an idea on 10 February, the
tiny seed of a plan to be planted in the soil of the public consciousness.

Lottery Plan for Opera

Special Mammoth lotteries in New South Wales will be suggested
to help finance the building of the State Opera House at Bennelong
Point. Such lotteries could have a record first prize of £100,000
or bigger . . .

The people of NSW would know when they bought a ticket that
they were investing in the future development of culture in their
own State as well as having the knowledge they could win some
money . . .[3]

Take root, wee seed, and grow strong!

106

11 February 1957, Hellebaek, back from the boatyard

Freshly home from the model workshop at his father's shipyard nearby in Helsingør, where he has put the order in for a Perspex model of his design at the request of the Opera House Committee, Jørn sits to write them the news.

> Thank you so much for your letters . . . with the photos enclosed. It was very kind of you to think of sending them . . . I am delighted that my entry was awarded first premium, and I assure you that I shall be happy to do everything to make it possible to carry my concept out to final realisation . . .
>
> I have just returned from a visit to London where I met with Professor Saarinen and Professor Martin who agreed that I am competent to accomplish the building of the Opera House without any partnership, but in co-operation with a structural engineer . . .
>
> With all good wishes for our future co-operation.
>
> Yours sincerely,
> Jørn Utzon, architect m.a.a, Hellebaek, Denmark.[4]

12 February 1957, Sydney, Ben Hall and the bush opera

What's in a name?

It is one of many issues that the Opera House Committee must deal with. Given that the building will be used for opera just two months a year, perhaps the National Concert Hall would be more fitting? Even the Festival Hall, or the National Theatre?

But none have quite the same ring, the same grandeur.

And so, they put it to the populace.

The suggestions flow fast and furious.

John Earnshaw of Lindfield is all for 'Phillip Memorial Hall, as a fitting tribute to the leader of the first of our race who settled in this continent. This name would lift the structure above sectional interest and place it on a national basis. Who then would object to its erection?'[5]

Or perhaps, suggests Mary Grey of Sydney, 'Melba Hall, to commemorate the person who made Australia's name famous in the musical world.'[6]

But over to you, Mr Paul Butz of Strathfield.

Why not, he asks plaintively, call it 'Bennelong Hall', whereupon this could be abbreviated to Ben Hall, as this 'would be in keeping with the bushranger prices that will no doubt be charged for admission'[7].

Other readers like this best of all, suggesting the theatres could be nicknamed 'Big Ben and Little Ben . . . the kind of local wit which gives flavour to a city'.[8]

And yet . . .

'By whatever name it is called,' the *Herald*'s editorial sagely remarks, 'Sydney's "opera house" is too good to lose and it is time to get a move on . . . The site should be cleared. An attempt to raise money must be made while public interest and enthusiasm is at its height. If too long an interval is allowed to elapse with nothing done, there is a danger that the opera house that isn't will be the opera house that never was.'[9]

Oh yes, that most unpleasant of obstacles – securing finances. But though it may be as unpleasant as an English fast bowler on a crumbling pitch, it is precisely what the Opera House Committee must grapple with.

One problem is the entirely unrealistic figure that has been put against the project, and everyone knows it, starting with the architect!

No sooner had Utzon heard the cost estimate of £3,500,000, than he had telephoned Stan Haviland to make clear that his building would likely cost much more.

No problem.

Shortly afterwards, the Danish architect had been cheerfully told by an official, 'We will blind them with paper.'[10]

6 March 1957, NSW Legislative Assembly, time for questions

Order . . . Order . . . *Order!*

The Member for Collaroy, you have the floor.

Stepping forward to the dispatch box, Robin Askin, a veteran of World War II – remarkable for the fact that his pugnaciousness is matched only by his loquaciousness – pauses only a moment before launching in his forceful tones, directly addressing Premier Joe Cahill.

'I ask the Premier whether he has seen reports of the appalling plight of families living in fowl houses in Brookvale and packing sheds at Ryde? If these are facts, will the Premier say whether he thinks that now is the right time to press ahead with this beneficial but lavish venture, and will he inform the House how he proposes to finance its construction?'

It is nothing the Premier can't handle.

'I saw something in the press about this matter,' Joe Cahill replies in a rather off-hand manner. 'If the conditions were as published in the first place it would be a reflection on the Honourable Member for the area.'

Specifically, that would be one Robin Askin.

'However, a later statement in the press showed that the original story was not correct. If the report is not factual, the Honourable Member should not unduly defame his own electorate. The need for housing is urgent, but there should be no political controversy concerning the problem, as the State is concerned with providing houses for its citizens . . .'[11]

For all Cahill's confidence in parliament, condemning the Opposition for condemning the project – 'In a young country like this we ought to be courageous . . . We should pledge the future,'[12] Cahill tells the Assembly later that month, when Robin Askin goes on the attack again – the truth of the matter is that Premier Cahill knows he doesn't have his party behind him when it comes to the Opera House. He must be patient. It is midnight at the Last Chance Saloon, and Cahill can't afford to be the bold and brash cowboy holding his cards in one hand while the other rests under the table on his Smith & Wesson. He must be the quiet stranger on the corner of the table, silently assessing his cards and weighing up his options. He must be patient.

•

There are, true, some doubts about the wisdom and possibility of constructing thin concrete shells of this shape and scale. So, when George Molnar journeys to Mexico City on sabbatical he looks up the world expert in the field, a Spaniard named Felix Candela – an architect, engineer and builder all in one, and the last word in building thin concrete shells.

Just take a look at his own designs!

'He took me to one of his latest structures,' Molnar reports in the *Herald*. 'Huge concrete shells, two inches thick, soared from the ground, intersecting each other, supporting each other, leaning, curling, spreading, like the spray from a frozen fountain. It was a church.'

And Señor Candela doesn't fail to impress upon Molnar that he built it with his own construction company and without engineers. He has no use for engineers.

'In my firm I'm employing only architects. I did have engineers first. It was no good. They always tried to prove that what I want cannot be done.'[13]

As means of proof, Candela gestures behind his shoulder to the cathartic cathedral that stands there, a testimony to the genius of his design and the strength of his willpower. The engineers had told him it was impossible, that it could never be completed and that the design would require cumbersome arches and buttresses to support it all. Candela had considered this dilemma, but came to the conclusion that the problem wasn't insufficient engineering techniques, it was insufficiently imaginative engineers, rigid as their beloved steel. And so, he fired them and did it himself.

Well, with that in mind, Mr Candela, what do you think of this? Molnar hands him Utzon's preliminary sketches as well as a clipping of a newspaper article about the Sydney Opera House.

Candela's brow furrows and crumples.

Interesting.

Still lost deep in his thoughts, Candela mutters something that sounds like:

'But these shells are not self-supporting.'[14]

Molnar has to lean in to make sure he heard right. *Really*, Mr Candela?

The Spaniard equivocates, likely not wanting to sound like one of the nay-saying engineers he delights in ignoring: 'Yes, it *can* be built. Some of the shapes have to be altered. I would like to see the drawings . . . But it can be built. And the shapes can be even more beautiful.'[15]

•

Three long months have passed since Jørn Utzon won the Opera House design competition, but *still* there are no assurances or guarantees that it will actually proceed.

And not for a moment does Utzon take for granted that the NSW Government will go ahead and build his dream.

'He is now preparing a scale model which could be used to raise money for the appeal,' the *Herald* reports. 'He will not come to Sydney to prepare the plans until he knows whether the Government will erect the building.'[16]

27 to 28 April 1957, Sydney Trades Hall, lassoing Labor ladies

Joe Cahill's political prowess is something to behold.

At a time when the Labor Party, federally and in Victoria, has so completely torn itself apart – literally, with one part becoming a party of its own, the DLP – that it will be out of power for well over a generation, ol' Joe has managed to keep his own state party together, and in power.

And rarely is his skill so evident as right now.

Order! *Order!*

No, this is neither a session of parliament, nor a court in session, but there are still some unruly delegates among the 350 in attendance. The annual conference of the Labor Women's Central Organising Committee is notorious for being a rowdy affair. Last year's annual conference had ended in what the press called 'a near-riot'[17].

But the Labor women settle quickly this morning, lifting the belts of their cinch-waisted synthetic dresses so they can breathe a little easier as they take their seats and fold their white-gloved hands in their laps.

Cahill knows he needs to shift the mood of these Labor women, who are the real keys to party approval. Without them, all is lost.

He gets straight to the nub of the issue at hand – whether or not to support the women's motion under debate today: 'Homes should come before the Opera House'[18].

Witness the master politician at work. It starts with *not* being combative.

'I agree with the motion on the agenda, that homes should come before the Opera House,'[19] he says, sombre.

It's quite a turnaround from his previous public tone.

'I had no idea it would cost so much when the project was approved ... We have to be prudent, keep our balance, and have regard to the views of the people.'[20]

The women nod their heads in emphatic agreement. Joe is with them. And he is a *gentleman*, it being noted in the newspapers that, 'He treats women with old-world respect, and gives and demands courtesy among men.'[21]

So, look, while it's too expensive now ...

'If some time in the future it is still possible, the Opera House will be built.'[22]

The mood change among the Labor women is instant. This is the most powerful politician in the state paying them enormous respect in taking their views seriously and making clear that the fate of the Opera House rests in *their* hands. Will it go down in history that *they* were the ones who blocked this great vision, who stood between the working women of this great state and their opportunity to visit the theatre or the symphony come Saturday evening?

There is much discussion, but by day's end, the political winds are blowing from an entirely different direction. Miss M. Walker of Concord stands to do the honours.

'I move that it should be homes as well as Opera House.'

Hear, hear.

'Homes are important, but it is also important that culture-loving Australians should have their own Opera House.'[23]

Hear, hear!

Mrs W. E. Dickinson of Rose Bay now stands and seconds Miss Walker's amendment then offers an addendum: 'We ask the Premier to launch an immediate appeal for funds for the Opera House.'[24]

A riot of applause. The motion is passed easily.

Broadly: this is a good idea, so let's get on with it. 'Old Smoothie' has triumphed again . . .

And yet one notable critic of Cahill's appearance at the women's conference is the fast-rising Deputy Leader of the Opposition, Robin Askin, who, with a curled lip, casts his own paled thoughts about the enterprise over the reporters gathered before him: 'Mr Cahill should make up his mind on the future of the Opera House. Where is the huge amount of money needed going to come from?'[25]

Yes, the current estimate is £3.5 million, but Askin does not believe that for a moment, and says so.

•

As it happens, the subject of where the money is going to come from is the very thing Joe Cahill wishes to address the Labor caucus about, on this, the first day of May, 1957.

He has a three-pronged plan to propose: public money, a public appeal and, most importantly, special mammoth lotteries so there will be no drain on the public purse.

'Special lotteries for financing the State Opera House will return up to £240,000 a year,'[26] he insists to the caucus.

'My proposal is designed to avoid diverting money from housing and public works . . . The lotteries would then continue until the Opera House was cleared of debt.'[27]

But Cahill's plan is not good enough for the irascible Labor Member for Monaro, John Wesley Seiffert, from down Queanbeyan way, who is insistent that not a shilling should be put to such flights of fancy – no matter where the money comes from – until such times as the state has the finest hospitals and schools. For *that* is the business of government, particularly a Labor government, not building places where people can play silly buggers on stage in white tights and it always finishes up with a fat lady singing. A rumbling of approval around the room shows he has good support, some of which is now voiced. And so the issue is deferred to a special caucus meeting the following week.

Meantime, the political Opposition capitalises on the Labor party room conflict, labelling Cahill's government as the 'gambling Government'.[28]

'An opera house financed from the proceeds of gambling will add nothing to the State's cultural life,'[29] the Leader of the Opposition, Pat Morton, insists to the press. 'The hospital shortage today is worse than ever and any proceeds from lotteries should go to them.'[30]

Joe Cahill is not particularly fussed, replying blithely, 'We always get that criticism.'[31]

The State Liberal Party Whip, Mr G. W. Brain, warns the public, 'the State Government is tying its revenues more and more closely to "the betting ring, the one-armed bandit and the lottery marble"'.[32]

Much of the public, and most of the churches, agree though the *Sydney Morning Herald* supports the Premier, editorialising:

'In the light of hard financial facts, it must be admitted that Mr. Cahill's three-pronged proposal for financing the building of the Opera House is shrewd and ingenious . . .'[33]

16 June 1957, Sydney, State Conference of the Labor Party, home and housed

It's the moment of truth.

Premier Cahill puts the Labor Women's motion to the NSW Labor delegates:

'*Homes as well as an Opera House – We appeal to the N.S.W. Government to immediately launch an appeal for funds to commence the building of the Opera House.*'[34]

But the very mention of the Opera House is enough for the delegates to abandon civility and embrace animosity, the debate barely being heard over the constant booing and the Speaker's calls for, '*Oooooorder, Oooorder!*'

Now stands Mr J. W. Thompson, Member for Leichhardt, who moves that the 'section of the women's report dealing with the Opera House be deleted . . . The Opera House proposal was included in the women's report as a "subterfuge" to get it through the conference.'[35]

But Miss Nancy Napper of the Clothing Trades Union shoots back at the Member for Leichhardt: 'Many working women these days have furs, although they may not have diamonds. Are we going to bring up our children in an atmosphere of rock and roll, or of better things?'[36]

Hear, hear. Hear, hear!

This immigrant to Australian shores now brings to the debate ideas from the world beyond, starting with her own island of Malta. Despite being just '16 miles by 11 miles'[37], a place filled with poor people, they have nothing less than the world's third biggest opera house. Do you see? It is possible for poor people to enjoy the finest things in life, too!

It is a line of reasoning not merely in sympathy with the views of the Premier, but in symphony to them.

The President now calls a vote on Mr Thompson's motion that the women's Opera House clause be deleted entirely. The delegates' voices ring out a resounding NO.

And the motion for the adoption of the women's recommendation? HEAR, HEAR!

Cahill's plan, thanks in large part to the Labor women, has won the day.

•

The good Premier wastes not a second, holding a press conference two days later to display the photos of the scale model that the architect Jørn Utzon has sent, along with the Dane's note:

> With all my best compliments on your fine fight for the new Opera House and for a richer life for your people, and with kindest regards.[38]

The Premier lets out a laugh when he notices the little self-portrait Jørn has doodled on the back of his business card.

24 June 1957, London, an opera house for Ove's oeuvre

Ove Arup can barely contain himself, barely able to keep his mouth shut for the sheer *excitement* of the whole thing. He has been boasting and toasting ever since he found out, and waxing lyrical at any opportunity – we are going to 'do the shells'![39]

With anybody else, it would be annoying, but there is no shortage of people who care to listen when the charming Mr Arup has something to say, even if he has said it already. And what's this?

A note from Professor Harry Ashworth of Sydney, yet more to boast about and another boost to his brimming confidence that, yes, he will be a part of engineering history. Eager to keep things moving, Ove Arup does not take long to pen his reply to Ashworth:

> We should certainly be very interested in collaborating with Mr. Utzon on his extremely imaginative project. I have seen Mr. Utzon, and I have seen other work he has done, and I have formed the highest opinion of his ability as an Architect. I am quite sure that he will make a success of the scheme if it goes forward, and I also think

that we can deal with the shells in the spirit in which they have been conceived. As you may know, my partner, Mr R. S. Jenkins, is a world authority on the design of shells, and has just been perfecting methods of dealing with shells of such unusual shapes . . . Mr. Utzon has some excellent but rather costly ideas for internal and external facing of the shells . . . I am quite sure that we shall be able to work very happily with Utzon if the project matures.[40]

Even in the 3 am of the soul, Arup is completely thrilled. This is the project he has been waiting for his entire career.

'[It was] something you know, *special*,' he will say. 'And naturally, from that point of view, I was extremely interested in it because it's the sort of thing I like in a way, you know, it's much more exciting to have to do something which today is a challenge.'[41]

28 June 1957, Hellebaek, something great in the state of Denmark

Hail fellow, well met.

For Ove Arup, having come all this way across the North Sea and along the train tracks from Copenhagen to Hellebaek to meet his young Danish counterpart, it is a delight to step onto the platform and be so heartily embraced by the long, lean and elegant man himself, who has come to greet him. The rest of the station could easily mistake these two for father and son, both of them are taller than any man has a need to be, both of them are beaming to be with the other. The two head off walking through the beech forest towards Utzon's home.

Coming into a clearing, Ove hears the laughter and hurried whispers of children. Lin and Jan run across fallen leaves and over roots to greet their father's new friend, speaking over the top of each other to be heard and noticed. Lis is behind them, smiling and cooing to the baby on her hip, six-month old Kim. This is a picture-perfect family, like something out of a film.

'*Hej*,' says Lis, putting forth her free arm for Ove to shake.

But before Ove can even introduce himself, he is accosted by little Lin and dragged away to the living room, to see her piano. A stooping giant beside Lin's tiny frame, he takes a seat and begins to pick away at the keys, much to the 11-year-old's amusement. It takes some convincing and a bit of effort to settle Lin down, but Jørn is eventually able to drag Ove away from the piano and towards the lunch table, where the family and their guest enjoy a lunch of pickled herring *smørrebrød* – open-faced sandwiches that transport Ove back to his childhood – the adults sipping chilled white wine. So wonderful a reception, so beautiful a family, but Ove and Jørn have work to do, and it isn't long before they must excuse themselves to the studio.

Lis encourages them – go on, she'll look after the kids. She knows they have much to do, much to discuss, and as she goes to sleep that night, the last thing she can hear is the two men down in the studio endlessly discussing complex matters unknown – titans of their blessedly united craft, paddling together towards a distant shore.

Jørn has that electric excitement in his voice whenever he is grappling with something new . . .

And Ove is more rumbling and rambling, the deep timbre of his old man's voice trying to work out *how* to build the shell roofs, while knowing that the solution will lie somewhere within the geometry chosen.

Arup must level with Mr Utzon the architect, and let him know that there are already significant hurdles to overcome.

'Your design,' he tells him, 'is really the wrong shape for the forces that will be in these shells . . . it will be very difficult to make. I am very impressed with the basic simplicity of the planning and I realise the immense architectural potential, but the sails forming the roof will be very difficult to construct because they do not accommodate the basic thrust lines. There [are stresses] which cannot be absorbed by the thin concrete shells you have in mind.'[42]

In sum, as it stands, the building won't . . .

Ah, but Utzon is ready for that, and has kept abreast of developments in this field, including a recent triumph by Luigi Nervi, an Italian architect and engineer whose recent design of a cantilevered curved stadium roof in Rome has begun to attract notice.

'Look at Nervi,' Jørn says. 'Why don't you like Nervi? He makes his things like that. And, well, why can't we do it the same way?'[43]

'Well,' begins Ove, 'you can't do it in the same way because in your design there are not two surfaces which are the same. They are all different.'[44]

But Jørn persists. Nervi has shown how it can be done, to which Ove points out that while using 'spherical geometry'[45] like Nervi did could be cheap – a sphere is uniform in curvature throughout its entire shape so would likely be easier to analyse and build – that is not what Utzon's competition drawings look like.

'If you want this particular shape,' Ove says pointing to Jørn's design, with the peaks of the roofs pointing up to heaven, 'it's . . . quite different really.'[46]

It is, as the engineers will later say, 'one of those cases where the best architectural form is not the best structural form'.[47]

For now, structural engineering consultant Ove Arup has clear advice for the architect Utzon.

'Any major deviation from your proposal,' he says, 'would destroy the essential sculptural quality of the scheme, [and] it will not be the design that won the competition . . . I therefore advise you to retain your basic idea, and we will somehow make it work.'[48]

Jørn heeds the older man's words, and they move on to so many other subjects that beckon, talking late into the night.

Many things about young Jørn Utzon impress the older Ove Arup, but none more than his deep humility, his commitment to his architecture, come what may.

'Architects should be anonymous,' he tells the older man. 'It does not matter [the name] of who does it, as long as it is done rightly.'[49]

Two days later, it is time for Ove to be on his way. They have spent the time going over Jørn's previous work, sharing tales of their time in the industry, telling stories of themselves and their families, their hopes and dreams, all the while circling the huge Perspex model of Jørn's design, discussing how they can make it a reality.

When Ove waves farewell to Jørn from the departing train window, they are not just colleagues but friends – and warm friends at that, each feeling privileged and lucky to know the other, and to be able to work together. They part ways richer for the meeting.

This is going to be wonderful.

•

Premier Cahill meets with the Opera House Committee to go over their ideas on how best to organise a public appeal for funds.

As a first step, the Committee feels that another committee would do the trick, a new 'Appeal Committee'. And so as to avoid confusion, we suggest renaming us, the original committee, the 'Executive Committee'.

Then that is what we shall do, says Premier Cahill. An Executive Committee overseeing an Appeal Committee. Marvellous.

Very good, sir.

Furthermore, while two committees are fine, three committees would be even better, and so the newly formed Opera House Executive Committee recommend: 'A Technical Advisory panel be set up to advise the Executive Committee through Professor H. I. Ashworth, on all architectural questions, including acoustics and decorations.'[50]

And, Premier Cahill, just quickly, while we're at it we advise, 'that a Music and Drama Advisory panel be set up to advise the Committee through Colonel Charles Moses, Sir Bernard Heinze and Mr. Hugh Hunt [Executive Director, Australian Elizabethan Theatre Trust]'.[51]

Now, while the old line that 'a camel is a horse designed by a committee' has likely never had more resonance than when said committee is overseeing a highly technical and artistic endeavour, there is no way around it. This is the way government works. And so . . .

Sounds good to me, says Premier Cahill. But what of the architect?

Well, Premier Cahill, we can do no better than Mr Utzon, and he 'should be informed forthwith of the Government's intention to proceed with the building of the Opera House. He has already prepared a model of the building which he is willing to bring out with him to Sydney at a fortnight's notice. It is proposed that his arrival here be arranged so that it will occur not more than one week before the launching of the public appeal, and that the City Council be asked to agree to the model being placed in the Town Hall vestibule, with the designs, for public exhibition.'[52]

Yes, of course, agrees the Premier, we should have him brought here post-haste.

And on that note, Sir, we think in future, given this project is being run outside the auspices of the government's Public Works Department, that, 'negotiations with the Architect, Jørn Utzon, be carried out by or through the Executive Committee'.[53]

Very reasonable, nods the Premier. The committee will be the architect's client. Keeps it well out of the government's hands and in the hands of non-partisan experts. (As he'd pointed out back in 1954: 'If we merely leave these matters to the Government they do not always go as well as they should.'[54])

Mid-July 1957, Hellebaek, Down Under to Denmark

Knock, knock.

Who's there?

Jørn opens the door to find an Australian, Mr Ralph Symonds, who has arrived armed with a letter of introduction from Cobden Parkes. Well, what a lovely surprise. Jørn and the family are used to Danish architects dropping by, but this is the first Australian!

After a coffee and pleasantries, Mr Symonds comes out with it. He hears Utzon plans to use plywood panels for his interiors, is that so? Smiling, Utzon affirms that to be the idea so far.

So it is that Ralph Symonds offers his services to the architect, explaining that his firm, based in their enormous factory in the Sydney suburb of Homebush Bay, are leading manufacturers of timber in Australia, specialising in plywood panels.

This is promising. For while they will surely be needing plenty of plywood for the formwork that will mould the vast amounts of concrete to be used in the building, Utzon also has in mind a much more refined and permanent use for this most underrated of materials – he wants it to make the acoustic ceilings for the two halls. And it is a delight to find a local craftsman in Symonds who shares Jørn's belief in the unseen potentials of plywood as a structural material – pound for pound it has a higher bending strength than steel, thanks to its unique cross-layered structure and the adhesives used to bond the veneers.

Yes, like Utzon, Symonds *knows* that plywood is not just a cheap cladding as is too widely believed – it has so much more potential! – and has dedicated much of his recent career to pioneering innovative plywood products. He has been experimenting with curved panels, hot-bonding all sorts of plastics and metal sheets to panels – aluminium, lead, stainless steel and bronze – and manufacturing them in a range of sizes, up to 15 × 2.7 metres – not just the standard 2.4 × 1.2 metres.

Such manufacturing know-how could be perfect for Jørn's acoustic ceiling, which he hopes can be self-supporting – standardised, pre-finished panels manufactured en masse at Symonds' Homebush factory could be assembled and bound together in the right way inside the halls, hovering over concert-goers like a cloud.

It would be cheap, efficient and beautiful, the architecture and structure in one.

Yes, there's much to work out, but Ralph Symonds surely has the capabilities that Jørn will need down the road.

In fact, the more they talk, the more Utzon finds in Symonds a man after his own heart and inspiration – an inventor, an innovator, an eager proponent of living and working on the edge of the possible.

'Ralph Symonds,' one commentator would later note, 'was the type of person who appealed to Utzon. He had begun as a furniture maker, but when this bored him he started inventing things. In 1923, Symonds built a surf hydroplane and powered it with a cast-off motor from Bert Hinkler's Avro aircraft. Symonds had anticipated the jet ski by half a century. Skimming over the water, his craft bounced from wave to wave in the surf at Bondi defying dire predictions it would be swamped or battered into small pieces by the rollers. Brilliant and eccentric, Symonds' unconventional ideas were invariably based on logic; however, it was a special kind of logic that others often did not share or understand at first. Symonds was the most energetic and interesting person Utzon had so far met [from] Australia.'[55]

Symonds takes his leave with the pair promising to stay in touch.

Late July 1957, Hellebaek, JOB 1112, fiddler on the roof

Ronald Jenkins is not only cut from a different cloth to the Danish giants he will be working with, they are made of entirely different fabrics.

With echoes of the polar opposite contrast between 'Silent Stan' Haviland and chatty Charles Moses, Bennelong and the London gentry, Eugene Goossens and everyone . . . Ronald Jenkins is just about always the odd man out no matter his company. Shorter, dumpier, and not half as sure of himself as these Danes seem to be, Jenkins is a man with a perpetual look of concern. In fact, so constantly does he churn mathematical models and analytical problems, his face has developed a permanent pronounced wrinkle between the brows. As the brains behind the thin concrete shell domes completed for the Brynmawr Rubber Factory shell roof back in 1951, he will ideally be just the man for this task. Ove has no doubts: Ronald will figure it all out . . . even if Ronald's brow is already looking more furrowed than usual as he contemplates the challenges of the Sydney Opera House.

Speaking of which, it is time to get to grips, for while it is one thing to have drawn the Opera House in such an artistic and inspirational manner that it has captured the global imagination the world over, it is quite another to do the *precise* drawings with mathematical dimensions that the engineers will need to even begin to work out how to make it stand up – or if it even *could* stand up at all? For, as Jenkins knows better than most, once you depart from designing boxes – no more than intersecting straight lines – and start building curves the way God does, everything becomes more complex.

How can we turn Jørn's freehand sketches into something that will stand up straight, if curved?

Jenkins temporarily unfurrows his brow and opens his mouth . . . before closing it again. He's thinking. The silence drags on until he pronounces through pursed lips: *Parabolas.*

Your design is tremendous, Jørn, but each curved shell must be defined geometrically and, ideally, taken from the same geometric source, which would give us the repetition necessary for economic construction.

And with that, the tone is set for a week of long meetings. It ends with Jørn promising to forward his initial drawings of the parabolic roof structure over to London, where they will be analysed by the engineers.

That settled, Ove Arup officially hands the lead position of handling the Sydney Opera House – or Job 1112 as the firm refers to it (even though for Utzon it is effectively Job 1, his first truly big one on his own) – to Ronald Jenkins. The shy maths master will be in charge, but Ove has assured everyone that he will remain closely involved with the entire process, particularly in liaising with Jørn Utzon, the wonderful young architect in whom Ove sees so much of himself.

17 July 1957, Sydney, acrimonious acoustics

Well, the idea of the Sydney Opera House sure sounds wonderful.

But will the Sydney Opera House *sound* wonderful?

After the first explosion of excitement over Utzon's winning design, it is time to dive into the details.

And it seems the Technical Advisory panel will have quite the discordant chorus of opinions to grapple with when it comes to the sensitive subject of sound.

The assessor, Dr Martin, impresses upon his friend, Professor Harry Ashworth, just how opinionated people can be on this topic, writing to him: 'I think you must be prepared for considerable discussions and argument, and you find that a great many people have fixed ideas about what they want . . .'[56]

The rest is . . . complicated.

For yes, people often talk about the acoustics of the Queen's Hall being superior to the Festival Hall, which Martin had designed, but with Adolf Hitler on kettle drums during the crescendo of the London Blitz, Queen's Hall had been blown apart, making comparison rather problematic.

'You have, of course, a special problem in Sydney,' Martin writes. 'The performance of music requires a longish reverberation but, as you will also be using the theatre for opera and drama, it is essential to have good definition [for the human voice]. These requirements are to some extent in conflict with each other . . .'[57]

How to proceed?

You need an expert, and there is a certain symmetry in the fact that one of the world's foremost experts in the field is a Dane, Dr Vilhelm Lassen Jordan, which is one of the names Martin puts forward to Professor Ashworth, before finishing.

'In any case, I am quite certain that we were right to leave all detailed questions of acoustics until the development stage. Utzon's design lends itself to a good acoustic solution, but this involves a considerable amount of scientific work which can only be advanced as design is being developed.'[58]

It is yet one more thing to be resolved as they go along.

Hopefully, in the greatest tradition of show business . . . it will be all right on the night.

•

It is fairly good news. It is a letter from Ove Arup to the Executive Committee responding to their official notice that his global firm is to be appointed as the structural engineers for this project. And he has faithfully promised to 'spare no effort to make the Opera House a success', even if there are one or two qualifications.

'Although the shape of the shells is structurally very sound,' Arup writes from London, 'and indicates that the Architect has a true feeling of structural shapes, the actual calculation by theoretical analysis will be extremely complicated, and will require the use of electronic digital computers . . .

'We do not anticipate any difficulties which we cannot overcome, but it will require considerable effort, and close collaboration with the Architect to achieve the right result.'[59]

29 July 1957, Sydney, the landing of the Utzon

Oh, the sheer *glamour* of it!

Handsome, tall, and adorned in a superb grey suit with suede shoes rarely seen on these shores, Jørn Utzon strides across the tarmac at Sydney Airport with *style*. And that diminutive fellow by his side must be his colleague Erik Andersson, surely Sweden's only red-head, maybe descended from Erik the Red?[60]

They are met by various dignitaries of the Opera House Executive Committee, while a couple of dozen members of Sydney's Danish community wave a large red and white Danish flag to welcome their countryman.

Cameras flash furiously to capture the moment the Dane meets Sydney for the first time, even as the gentlemen of the press press close.

'Mistah Oootson!' . . . 'Yawn! Yawn!' . . . 'Over here!'

Utzon blushes to hear them calling his name. He blinks shyly as the cameras flash. It is surprising that, as he has noted flying in, a city that chooses to cover its superb headlands with so many red boxes should be so excited by an architect who cannot conceive of building such atrocities. Still, on the other hand . . .

His English proves to be fairly strong, and he is more than happy to speak to the press, enthusing about the project in his charming accent.

But say, Mr Utzon, are you really the six-foot nine-inch giant that has been reported?

Laughingly, Utzon stands back-to-back with the six-foot two-inch Danish Consul General in Sydney, while to the great merriment of all, his five-foot five-inch Swedish partner, Mr Erik Andersson, stands on a chair to measure the difference – two-and-a-half inches in Utzon's favour – while the cameras click.

Some in the press think Utzon's tall, rugged athleticism makes him a dead ringer for Sir Edmund Hillary, the conqueror of Everest, which might be useful given the mountain he has to climb himself.

In response to a question about how long the building might take, Utzon estimates the detailed plans would be ready in about 18 months, and presuming an actual start shortly thereafter, the whole thing would not take long!

'Using a lot of men, the Opera House could then be built in two years,'[61] he predicts.

'Your Opera House,' Utzon tells the journalists, 'is the talk of Europe. After I had won the competition, I travelled the continent looking at other opera houses. Everywhere I went architects and music lovers were wildly enthusiastic about the fact that Sydney was going to have an opera house of such an unusual design. Many marvelled at the fact that it would be the same size as the Metropolitan Opera House in New York.'

One journalist is impressed, assuring the *Telegraph*'s readers, 'Sydney will like this brilliant yet reticent young idealist from Copenhagen. He speaks our language.'[62]

And he *looks* the goods!

In the young and easily impressed Sydney city, this fashionable European man is given movie star treatment by the Sydney public, politicians and press.

'Mr Jørn Utzon,' the *Sydney Morning Herald* tells its readers, 'proved to be a personality as outstanding and original as his Opera House design when he arrived in Sydney last night.'[63]

There is, too, for all his sophistication and obvious genius, an engaging humility about him, a down-to-earthedness that resonates with his Australian interlocutors.

You only flew tourist class, Mr Utzon?

'Why not?' he laughs. 'It is cheaper and you get here just as quickly.'

Our kind of man!

As for the unique thin concrete shells he plans to use for the Opera House roof, he couldn't be more definitive.

'The opera house roof will be of concrete several inches thick, and will be covered with ceramic tiles, almost white. This is a very economic method of roofing and is used quite a lot overseas. In Berlin recently, I saw a congress hall with such a roof spanning 240 feet, and it was only three inches thick.'[64]

Who woulda thought?

It is all the more surprising and impressive, however, for the fact that the reporters have before them a newly rich man.

For his winning opera house design, he will receive an extraordinary £5000 for first prize, while the usual architect's fee of 4 per cent of total cost will see him earn another £200,000! (Less, of course, what he must pay his staff, but still, not bad.)

His partner, Mr Andersson seems equally humble.

When Utzon tries to credit him for doing much of the work, the Swede interrupts.

'Jørn did most of the work,' he insists, 'and it is our practice for the one who did most of the work to sign the plan, so he signed it.'[65]

The good news is that such a glamorous presence intends to stay in Sydney for another month or so to survey the site, meet the key people involved in the building, and then return to Denmark to knock up the plans.

•

Always an early bird in want of a worm, Jørn Utzon stretches and wakes to what the locals of Sydney amusingly call a chilly winter morning. The Dane barely notices.

And where else does he want to go but to Bennelong Point, the site where his opera house is actually to be built!

Squired around the site by Mr Stan Haviland and Professor Harry Ashworth, Utzon and Andersson have to brace themselves against a howling wind. A couple of dozen members of the press trail close behind soaking up every detail of this historic moment.

The thing they all note is Utzon's consistently joyous expression. He doesn't care about the inclement weather, he is here on the site he has not only dreamed about, but where he is going to *build* his dream!

It had been one thing to see grainy photos of Bennelong Point, to study rough contours on sea charts, and to hear it be described by the female Australian Olympic equestrian team . . . but quite another to stand here. With great enthusiasm he lifts his Leica camera, hanging from his neck on a black leather strap, and begins to click away, capturing the fine details of the site, for his office wall.

True, the rather dowdy ships unloading cargo on the working wharves that line the western side of Bennelong Point are a little underwhelming, but that is the only downside he can see.

'It's right!' Utzon exults as the gusting north-westerly wind whips up 'white horses' on the harbour, blowing his hair out in a rakish manner and makes his gabardine coat flap as wildly as the fronds of Bennelong Point's palm trees.

'It's okay!' the Dane laughs to the waiting press. 'This is the way they placed the temples in the old days!'[66]

Does he think lotteries are a good way to finance the project?

'Yes, I will buy a ticket in the first lottery if they have them,'[67] he replies. Mostly what he wants to express is his sheer joy.

'It's breathtaking,' he says with enormous feeling. 'There's no Opera House site in the world to compare with it. This site is even more beautiful than in the photographs.'[68]

Not just the site, but its surrounds.

'I'm glad to find the building will have an "intimacy", even though it will be so big. That's because of the closeness of the other points and the Bridge. The Opera House might become a companion landmark with the Bridge.'[69]

(For yes, just as 'the bridge' had become 'the Bridge', just about overnight, so too does the reverence extended for Jørn Utzon see the opera house become ever more often the Opera House, a place worthy of great capitals.)

After tramping all over the site, as the adoring press traipses after him, Utzon must finally take his leave, to have lunch just up the hill at the gracious and plush Australian Club at 165 Macquarie Street – the oldest gentlemen's club in the Southern Hemisphere – with one of the most influential journalists in Sydney, Gavin Souter of the *Herald*.

The most interesting thing for the star journalist is when the Dane expands on his architectural philosophy, the thing he tries to bring to his work that is too often missing in modern architecture and its myriad boxes.

'A little human smile,' says Utzon. 'After all this functionalism, we need a little human smile. You must belong to your surroundings. When we design for Copenhagen, we are Danes. When we made this scheme for the Opera House, we camped on Bennelong Point. We were Bennelong Pointers.'[70] Function must not be a justification in and of itself, it must work in harmony with uplifting *form*.

Erik Andersson, who has been more than happy to play second fiddle to Utzon's role as conductor of the whole affair, chimes in.

'We made it to fit this spot,' the Swede says, 'and no other spot. We don't want Ford cars all over the world. Do you understand that? We don't like standardisation. The tea in America is the same from New York to Los Angeles. It comes out of the same little bags. The bricks in America are the same colour from east to west. But in Denmark and Holland, they treat bricks like fine old wine!'[71]

Souter likes them both enormously. Which brings the journalist to the question of their collaboration on the project. How did it work for you?

The answer, they both agree, is that although both Utzon and Andersson had started working on 'The House',[72] as the Dane calls it – though he sometimes fancies calling it '*Australis*' – the concept had gripped the originator, and Utzon had taken over nearly the whole thing, and that is why it had been submitted under Utzon's name alone. It didn't seem to matter much at the time.

'We didn't dream of winning it,' says Utzon. 'We were inspired to do it. A certain amount of your time you want to devote to clean architecture – without clients or anything like that. That's one of the symptoms of architecture. That's when the architect is closest to the pure artist.'[73]

Describing his first conception of the vaulting concrete shells which will house the tall stage towers so beautifully – of course, the stage towers' function had inspired the tall reaching roofs' form, Utzon tells the journalist: 'I looked at flowers and insects, at organic forms. I wanted something that was growing out.'

Souter interprets such comments for what they are, very much part of the Frank Lloyd Wright ethos of organic architecture, buildings that appear to grow out of the landscape.

And yet, Souter gently raises the subject of Wright bitterly attacking Jørn's Opera House design back in February, calling it 'sensationalism!', a 'whim' and worse.

Utzon winces. In a notably happy time, this had not been a happy memory, and he is still not sure why Wright takes this view.

'But he would not bother attacking it if he were not interested in it,' he says with a smile. 'He also says I have never stayed at [his architectural school, in] Taliesin; but I have. I stayed at Taliesin East in Wisconsin in 1949. I was not a paying student, though, so perhaps that is why he says I have not studied under him.'[74]

Steering the conversation back to what he most loves, Utzon opens his briefcase and extracts photographs of the Opera House model.

'Here!' he says. 'It's a most important thing, in a way. It's what they call sculptural effect. In sculpture, you work with shadow and new lines, new silhouettes. That is how it will be at Bennelong Point. But in a purely functional building you have just a side and then another side. No new sensation!'

Utzon and Andersson know that the final product will need as many facets as a diamond, as wonderful and appreciable from one angle as it is from another, each vantage point a new window into true beauty.

'We will do the best we can,' says Utzon, 'because it is our only interest. I can't say anything to people who say, "modern foolishness". That doesn't interest me. We ride in automobiles and fire rockets. Why should we build in Victorian style today?'

Utzon taps one of the shining, shell-white photographs sitting on his lap. 'This is "Our Time" style,' he says. 'It is our own.'[75]

Afternoon, 30 July 1957, Premier Cahill's office, a meeting of minds

Theirs is a convivial and historic meeting.

It is between the world's newly hailed most dashing architect, Jørn Utzon – the man who dared to dream big, and in revolutionary manner – and the working-class hero, Joe Cahill, who has emerged as Utzon's key champion and protector.

A Scotch, Mr Utzon?

Yes, Mr Premier, don't mind if I do.

In the Premier's spacious office at Parliament House, the two get down to tin tacks and brass bolts, if not yet shells and tiles.

'We want this building,' Cahill says to the Dane, 'because many people in this town have shown that they want [cultural] expressions like opera, theatre, and music in the same way as they have in big cities in Europe. I do not want my people to miss anything that they could get in Europe.'[76]

Utzon couldn't agree more.

One thing that troubles Utzon, however, are the working wharves along Bennelong Point. Could they really have a grand Opera House, right alongside ships unloading crates of canned sardines?

Cahill, in reply, pauses . . .

If you'll excuse him just a second, please, Mr Utzon. The Premier doesn't ask the Dane to leave, but he simply must make this quick call.

Yes, hello, Port Authority? This is Premier Cahill. With the building of the Opera House, we are going to need to shut down the wharves along Bennelong Point. Please see to it, as soon as possible. Thank you.

Utzon, like Charles Moses before him, is stunned.

This is a man like he has never met before. As powerful as he is affable, he gets things done in a hurry, he radiates *possibility*, and will surely provide precisely the kind of back-up Utzon needs.

The Premier gives the Dane to understand that if he has any more such problems with the site, or any particular people, he must come to him and together they will sort it out.

But here is the thing, Mr Utzon.

The Premier himself is under pressure to get the project underway, so it cannot be derailed by political attacks and confected controversy – always a risk for a public exercise of this nature. With that in mind, Cahill needs to turn the first sod within 18 months, before the next election, due around March 1959.

Can that be done, Mr Utzon? Can your plans be ready by that time?

Utzon knows it is a big call – and points out that there is an enormous amount of work to do, to complete the drawings for every aspect of the building and be ready to build the whole – but under the circumstances, what other reply can he make, other than this one?

'All right,' he says, 'we will do it.'[77]

Joe Cahill is very pleased.

The Opera House sails, he knows, are heading out into unknown waters, and there are storm clouds brewing, with even the odd crack of lightning and boom of thunder in the distance.

•

Utzon embarks upon the whole thing with a song in his heart, still scarcely believing the warmth of his reception in Sydney, and that the Australians really do intend to build his dream.

And he has much to say!

'Sydney's proposed Opera House is a symbol for the development of art in an age of technical development,' Utzon says while 'Guest of

Honour' on the ABC. For yes, his work is on the edge of the possible, and will only be possible with the use of digital computers, but it is a mistake to think technological and engineering advances must render architecture soulless or artless. He wants his building – formed using the newest materials, technologies and techniques – to push the frontiers of architecture itself, and *move* people.

This, he says, is why the people of Europe and the United States have shown such interest in this new building.

'They feel happy about it because humanism is very important to us all,' he said. 'We cannot live in a country where it is only technical things that count.'[78]

He is filled with hope that this building will help transform a city and a people, just the way the Ragnar Östberg had transformed Stockholm, 34 years before.

'I really hope and I couldn't be happier if this Opera House would help Australia to have a new musical culture of its own and have its own face of art, together with its own wonderful pioneer spirit,'[79] he says.

He means it.

He also happily agrees to appear on Channel 9's *TV Town Talk* – a chat show hosted by the dashing Robert Kennedy, which will air this evening, following the news bulletin – to promote the whole idea of the public giving money to the construction costs.

And truly?

For Utzon it is not only in the field of architecture that his genius strikes. While on their way to Channel 9's Willoughby studios, he and Erik Andersson stop for coffee and start talking about the appeal. On the spot, Utzon asks the coffee shop boss to bring him a small box. With a quizzical look the fellow disappears into a back room and returns with one that should do the trick, whereupon the Dane uses a sharp knife to make a slit in the top before scrawling '*For the Opera House*' on the top, and puts it on the counter before fishing through his pocket and throwing in a couple of shillings.

'If you can, so can I,'[80] says the proprietor, whereupon he throws in a couple of shillings of his own, quickly joined by another couple of patrons. By the time they leave the café, the Opera House fund is a pound closer to its target.

Bliss was it in that dawn to be alive, but to be young was very heaven.[81]

And to be the celebrated architect of something already considered to be an architectural masterpiece – about to embark on actually designing and building it – is something else again.

'There was this feeling of a new epoch, a new school in architecture, not just among our group but from other learned people in Europe and America,' Utzon will recount. 'We were doing things in our time, in our way as we might have been Romans in their era, or the pyramids in Egypt.'[82]

And Utzon's sheer joy at this endeavour indeed shines through in his every utterance in this city on the other side of the world that is perilously close to making him its favourite adopted son.

Robert Kennedy is clearly entranced just to be in his presence, and exultant about Sydney having such an Opera House.

When, he asks the Dane, do you think it might be completed? In reply, the sparkling Utzon nominates Christmas Eve 1960 as a good goal.

'It depends,' he says, 'on the speed of Australian workers – we'll be fast with the drawings.'[83]

The nitty-gritty, the nuts and bolts of it all, will come.

Meantime, Sydney, and Australia, can't get enough of him.

No less than the bible of Australian women, *The Australian Women's Weekly*, trills that 'lanky Utzon is a young Gary Cooper, only better looking'.[84]

•

Young Stuart Littlemore, just 10 years old, will never forget it. He has come to this reception for Jørn Utzon at the NSW Art Gallery in the company of his father, David, a Bundaberg boy educated at Scots College. David Littlemore is now such a highly accomplished Sydney architect – he'd cut his teeth with the Swedish–Australian architect Emil Sodersten – he has already been sounded out by Utzon over a lunch about the possibility of joining his Sydney staff, when the time inevitably comes that Utzon sets up an office in Sydney. (Littlemore had declined, for the fact that he was far too absorbed by his own industrial projects, and besides, he has his reservations and will say of the winning submission many years later: 'I was shocked to think that such . . . a very sketchy, schematic – would be submitted by any architect for any competition and that any judgement could be made upon it.'[85])

But hush now, for we are at the moment.

Their host, the famous industrial designer Gordon Andrews, is presenting the guest of honour to the crowd, and wants to put one thing to rest straight away. There has been the suggestion that the Dane was such a *foreigner*, he would never fit in with decent Australians.

'But look at this face, ladies and gentlemen,' Mr Andrews says, beaming, as he gestures to the man beside him, 'just look at those wide open spaces.'[86]

And he's right.

The handsome face smiling back at them is as wide open and shining as the Nullarbor, not closed and dark like some Europeans'! (*Sniff.*)

He is all right.

Tall, bronzed and blond, from a distance Utzon could just about pass for an Anzac!

7 August 1957, Sydney Town Hall, a certain appeal

Tonight's the night!

The grand old Victorian building on George Street – itself the result of an architectural competition back in 1868, designed as a symbol of Sydney's wealth and status – is a multipurpose venue with a capacity of 2500 people, which is exactly how many turn up on the night, dressed in their glad rags – ladies' waists as thin as the skirts are puffy, and for the men, dark suits made of textured tweed that would work just fine as acoustic insulation – and things are quickly underway.

As they arrive, the excited guests are thrilled to see Utzon's model of the Opera House set up in the vestibule – and it looks magnificent! Look at the curves, the sculptural shape, the delicate gold leaf detail on the underside of the shells! No-one has any doubt – this will provide the flare, the *grandeur*, Sydney needs.

To set the tone, host for the evening, Lord Mayor Harry Jensen (by happenstance, himself a man of Danish origin) leads the Official Party – Premier Cahill, ABC Chairman Sir Richard Boyer, and more – onto the stage to the flickering of exploding flashbulbs, the loud whir of television cameras, and the *roar* of the crowd. The atmosphere is raw, unfiltered excitement.

Grinning wildly, Utzon and Andersson must delicately extricate themselves from the many well-wishers mobbing them, so they can take their place on stage with the rest of the dignitaries, under an array of Danish, Swedish and Australian flags.

Lord Mayor Jensen steps up to the dark wooden podium.

'The Opera House,' he says, 'will be a symbol of our appreciation of the great cultural efforts of those who have gone before and of our faith in this great city. We must always be on guard to see that purely material needs do not supersede and usurp humanity, the cultural needs, the things for the improvement of our minds.'[87]

Indeed, but as Jørn Utzon now calls out, as the audience cheers, 'It is up to you to pay for it!'[88]

Over to you, briefly, Chairman of the ABC Sir Richard Boyer, to move the motion officially inaugurating the Sydney Opera House Appeal Fund: 'In launching the appeal we should remember that a great deal of its early inspiration came from one who did much to develop our musical life in this city and state. I refer to Sir Eugene Goossens. I hope that not only will the Committee secure money from industrial firms but that every citizen of the State including children will have some part in ownership of the Opera House.'[89]

To get things started, the Lord Mayor announces – over the sound of receding applause – that Sydney City Council will contribute £100,000 over the five-year period of the appeal, before he hands the podium over to Premier Joe Cahill, who commits £100,000 from his government to get the appeal underway, and £50 from his own wallet, which he places with a theatrical flourish into the decorated cardboard funds box. The audience roars. As a politician, Cahill is sufficiently admired to be elected. As a man, he is very close to universally admired. But hark, he speaks.

'We are determined,' Joe Cahill says, his voice breaking with emotion, with sheer gratitude that the crowd feels his excitement, 'that this building shall be finished. We need only a continuance of this present mood to ensure that in the not-too-distant future a mighty Opera House will stand on Bennelong Point, to prove to the world that we Australians have pride in our culture second to none.'[90]

Why, if we can raise enough from this appeal, the Premier has no doubt we can 'lay the foundation stone of the Opera House within 18 months'.[91]

Great applause! Stamping of feet!

And now to Jørn Utzon, whose own speech can only be made over frequent interruption of so much clapping that his words can only just be heard.

'My partner and I . . .' he shouts, 'have difficulty in expressing how welcome we feel here . . . [You have] showed us how much you wanted this Opera House, deep in your hearts . . . The committee has done a lot of great work and I want particularly to congratulate the Premier. We, together with the hundreds of other architects who entered this competition, have done a lot of hard work, too. Now, it's up to you to pay for it – that's the easy part.'[92]

And pay they will!

The big crowd hushes now as Jensen reads the list of initial donors and how much they have committed, to successive rounds of applause.

The Rural Bank commits £15,000!

Australian Consolidated Press is good for another £10,000!

Ampol Petroleum and Hoyts Theatres contribute £1000 apiece.

The whole thing sets exactly the right tone for, in short order, *hundreds* of people stepping up, wildly waving banknotes, carrying on and yelling over the top of each other, every man and woman swarming around the Town Clerk like a flight of bees trying to suffocate a hornet.

Inside the first hour there is no less than £235,000 committed, which is a good foundation for Cahill's goal of raising 'about 1 million'[93] from the appeal overall.

Such is the upbeat mood of the whole affair, so joyous the ambience, that in the after-function party held in the Lord Mayor's reception room, Erik Andersson cries out that he will give £50 for the appeal if he may kiss the famed singer and Sydney beauty, Miss Joan Hammond, who laughingly acquiesces, proffering her cheek as cheering breaks out all around. Not to be outdone, Jørn Utzon donates £50 to kiss the cheek of the flautist Elaine Shaffer and another £50 again to kiss the diminutive wife of the violinist Ruggiero Ricci, who announces as the Danish giant must stoop to kiss her, 'I am reducing the fee. The normal price is £100.'

Oh, how they laugh!

Further getting into the spirit of it all, Mrs Ricci offers £10 to kiss the ABC's Charles Moses, who accepts and now turns the other cheek to donate another £10.

To even more merriment, Lord Mayor Jensen announces that the Leader of the State Opposition Pat Morton has given 15 guineas to kiss him!

'I'll see you later about that, Pat,' the Lord Mayor theatrically whispers.

'Very much later,' Pat Morton laughs.

'The kissing proceeds at the end of the party,' the *Herald* reports, 'amounted to £295/15/.'[94]

And a good time was had by all . . .

•

Even this far from home and hearth, Jørn Utzon has his darling Lis with him, at least in spirit. For even when not by his side, she always writes him letters, sending them to hotels all around the world. As she tells the kids, 'Love is the glue that holds it all together.'[95]

Tired from a long day and night, Utzon hangs his coat in the closet and sits on the squeaky bed of his Bondi hotel room. He unfolds the letter gently, longingly, like it's a precious piece of home.

'*Kærests elskede dreng, Beloved Boy, I find myself pinching my arm, telling myself very slowly and emphatically, "Jørn skal bygge en opera." Jørn is going to build an opera house.*

'*Tears come to my eyes at the very thought of it, my love, and yet I hope and pray that it won't break your heart.*'[96]

16 August 1957, Opera House Committee Meeting, Sydney, sole architect

The gentlemen of the Sydney Opera House Executive Committee sit in the austere anteroom of the Department of Local Government, ready to hear Jørn Utzon's proposal.

It has been explained to the architect that this committee – especially Harry Ashworth and Stan Haviland – are, for all intents and purposes, his client on this project.

'We are here to help you in any way,'[97] insists Harry Ashworth at the meeting's opening. The sentiment echoes Cahill's supportive words; music to an architect's ears.

For now, they will manage the purse strings and liaise with you on all things Opera House design. And they will have their own oversight and assistance, which will come from two sub-committees: the Technical Advisory panel headed by Professor Harry Ashworth will advise on all matters concerning design and construction, while Sir Bernard Heinze, Goossens' successor at the Con, will convene the Music and Drama panel, to guarantee that the people who will perform in the Opera House are satisfied with its design.

(Look, on a bad day they might be mistaken for a bunch of boring bureaucrats bickering with parochial pundits, but Joe Cahill has designed it such that the 'client' is actually better than that. This is in fact a group of *experts*, non-political as possible, dedicated to seeing the project bear fruit.)

Ahem . . . you were saying, Mr Utzon?

The Dane was saying that his preference is for Arton, his firm with Erik Andersson, to be formally contracted as architects to carry out the Opera House project to completion, which would mean that their already-constituted practice of 18 architects could begin at once.

The Committee men pause for a moment and exchange glances.

Well, as it happens, Mr Utzon, we've been discussing this very matter and we have an alternative proposal. For, you see, while you are locked in, we are yet to fully nail down the political and financial support we need to get started – and contracting a foreign firm is a bad look right now, which might threaten the whole thing. Rather than contracting your whole firm, which in any case is unfamiliar with our way of doing things here in New South Wales, it's our preference that you be appointed as 'Sole Architect' at this early stage.

Utzon and Andersson exchange looks. This is a bit odd, and not the way they do things in Europe, but do go on.

So, once you sign on as sole architect, you can develop the design with consultants of your choice as we take care of funds and other issues . . .

Harry Ashworth makes clear to his fellow architect – we are aware this is most unusual but it's touch and go with these politically charged ventures, you understand, Jørn?

But we can work it all out properly once the project is formally going ahead.

Utzon nods thoughtfully, controlled and silent, weighing up what such an unusual arrangement may mean for a huge job like this.

Now, when it comes to payment, Mr Utzon, we cannot give you any formal guarantees at this stage, but we tentatively propose to follow the usual protocol in Australia, the fees payable to you as architect for the work shall be: four per centum of the actual cost of all work, plus 'recoupment of your out-of-pocket-expenses',[98] and of course a percentage on any contracts you administer in the future.

Jørn nods again even as the once jubilant Erik Andersson now positively scowls.

Yes, there is much to discuss, as the architect begins to get to grips with a committee that has real-world needs of pleasing political masters, raising funds and meeting budgets, schedules and expectations from many different groups that have a stake in this building.

Little is decided officially but tentative agreement is made that Utzon shall be appointed as sole architect . . . later.

It's all unusual, but Jørn Utzon doesn't wish to rock the yacht.

Broadly, though?

The Executive Committee could not be warmer.

'[They] were the best client you could think of,' Utzon would recount. 'They were marvellous.'[99]

At meeting's end, Ashworth tells Jørn Utzon once more: 'We are here to help you in any way.'[100]

•

By the time Utzon is making ready for departure from Sydney Airport a fortnight later – after many more meetings, interviews, promotional opportunities and buying toy koalas to take home to the children – the appeal fund is off to a wonderful start, with £450,000 already promised.

The architect is well satisfied with the city, as it is with him. He has become an instant celebrity – television star and public speaker, the project's most important spokesman.

And there is one thing Utzon really is convinced of, and he is happy to declare it: 'No other country in the world would have dared to contemplate'[101] building his Opera House.

As if by a miracle, somehow the stars of the Southern Cross have aligned just right for this country to find sufficient space, money, hunger, need, political will and public support to take a chance on building something extraordinary, something for the ages – his vision. And he is as grateful for that, as Sydney appears to be for him, even as he prepares to head home.

'We will be back next February with a set of large drawings of the Opera House,' Utzon tells the waiting press at the airport with his already familiar wide smile and amused twinkle in his eyes.

'We will be ready for the foundation stone to be laid in 18 months from now.'[102]

So celebrated has Utzon been on this trip that he has already received offers to design numerous buildings, but of course he had declined. He is here for one thing alone – to see the Opera House built.

'We rejected the other work to devote our entire energies to the Opera House project,' he said. 'We will not take on any other work until we have completed the Opera House.'[103]

•

Utzon wastes no time upon his return to Hellebaek getting back to work, his next moves hastened by the letter he receives from the Committee Chairman, Stan Haviland, formally rejecting Jørn's request that his firm, Arton, be engaged and instead appointing him as sole architect. Very well then . . . (Though not so well for Erik Andersson and his brother, who are more than miffed to have had the architectural opportunity of a lifetime abruptly taken away.)

Without the resources of Arton, Jørn now needs to find both a large quiet space and a lot of help, and it is with this in mind that he rents out in the village, 'a big, yellow, two-story villa'.[104]

The ground floor will be for the technical consultants, who are sure to visit often, while the top floor will be for his new design team – half-a-dozen odd architects, young and old, to help him create and produce the design for every part of the Opera House.

They set up their desks in the large, light-filled room, wide windows facing out to a forest of beech trees dotted with lakes, all the way to the Øresund, across which stand the high cliffs of Sweden's west coast.

'When the sun came out,' one writer will describe it, 'yachts with white outstretched butterfly wings fluttered across the sound's grey waters.'[105]

Yes, it is a pleasant spot, with a small gabled porch out the front. Out back, a patio terrace they may take their breaks on, looking onto a yard that runs down to the edge of a pretty lake, where graceful white swans and their baby flappers take their daily constitutionals. What better place to be further inspired by nature? It is exactly the kind of place Utzon likes to work – besides his own home – and his staff feel the same.

'It was most fascinating,' one of his young architects will note, 'to see how the ugly ducklings grew into young swans and how they developed their skill in flying, particularly on the day when the whole swan family could fly for the first time in formation. Everybody who lived around the lake came out of their houses and watched them flying in circles again and again and then breathed a sigh of relief when they alighted, splashing safely on the water.'[106]

Nature, in all its glory, all its superb form coming together in something so extraordinary as flight! But yes, everybody, time to get back to work.

Their job?

Make an Opera House fly.

SIX

THE FOUNDATION STONE

The building when erected will be available for the use of every citizen, that the average working family will be able to afford to go there just as well as people in more favourable economic circumstances, that there will be nothing savouring even remotely of a class-conscious barrier and that the Opera House will, in fact, be a monument to democratic nationhood in its fullest sense.[1]

Premier Joe Cahill in his introduction to 'The Gold Book', March 1959

If the Opera House was designed like a box it would have to be labelled 'This is the Sydney Opera House.' Cathedrals do not have to be labelled. In the same way an Opera House should be distinctive and not like a box.[2]

Jørn Utzon, 5 May 1959

The battle at the start was to extract out of the ether the information required to get the drawings underway. Utzon had received no brief other than the competition conditions, and information about what the Committee required ... only came in dribs and drabs.[3]

David Messent, *Opera House Act One*

Late August 1957, Sydney, difficulties raising funds

It is true that Sydney Town Hall had proved a tremendous launch pad for the Opera House Appeal – the funds had risen up in a fabulous flash – only for it to falter and fizzle and feebly fade back down to earth. What was once a flood of funds has diminished to a choked trickle.

To encourage the good people of Sydney to reach deep, Lord Mayor Harry Jensen announces that everyone who donates to the Sydney Opera House Appeal Fund will have their name recorded in a leather-bound book made of special permanent parchment, which will be on permanent display in a specifically constructed spot inside the completed Opera House. (No matter that for every hundred Sydneysiders, you could count on the fingers of one finger those who had actually been to an opera, and half a finger those who had enjoyed it.)

Sir Bernard Heinze of the Conservatorium suggests an 'opera tax' be imposed on theatre tickets, while one housewife from Roseville, Mrs Blanche Lotz, writes a letter to the *Herald* editor suggesting a 'Vanishing Tea Party'.

'The idea is that eight people are invited to a tea party at which they each contribute 10/ to the Opera House fund. Each of the eight also undertakes to give a tea party and invite seven other people. The people at these parties undertake to give tea parties and invite six people each.'[4]

And so forth.

If no-one breaks the chain, it will involve 109,600 people and £54,800 for the Sydney Opera House Appeal Fund! Forget tea and sympathy – the ladies plan tea, tithes and symphony!

Perhaps the men, particularly, could contribute in another way with the *Sydney Truth* proposing the doubling of licensing fees on the one-armed bandits:

> . . . Why not let poker machines build it? After all, clubs are alleged to be sponsors of culture. The Government is culture minded. Hence the acceptance of an Opera House design that looks like Cape Town's Table Top mountain in eruption. And of course, when the Opera House is built, somewhere high above the roof could stand a huge illuminated poker machine, symbol of culture in this state.[5]

More seriously, a call is even put out by the Sydney Opera House Appeal Fund and Committee to the horse racing authorities to see if they could hold special meetings where the profits of the bookies might go to the Oper . . .

Hello?

Hello . . . ?

One former starting price bookmaker who is willing to speak on the matter, the Opposition's Deputy Leader Robin Askin, makes clear that the Coalition remains implacably opposed to the idea of any public funds going towards the Opera House project. Whatever funds are available, he says, should be going towards such things as building new mental asylums, not monuments to Premier Cahill. 'The Government's apathetic approach to this social problem,' he thunders in parliament, 'contrasts rather strangely with the zeal with which they are pursuing the building of an opera house.'[6]

Premier Cahill does not have the time or energy for such comments – least of all from the ratbag Robin Askin – and is unfazed.

Spring is coming, and Joe Cahill judges the time ripe to throw some fertiliser on the lottery seed he had planted back in February, to make his Opera House bloom – an ingenious plan that will not hit on the public purse, so much as the purse of the public.

In short – if he can't get the bookies on his bandwagon, perhaps the government should join theirs this Spring Carnival season? After all, there is nothing the Australian public loves more than a punt over a pint . . . he knows it's a proven model.

Indeed, New South Wales has had official government lotteries as a fund-raising exercise since 1931, the proceeds used to fund hospitals and schools and housing. But what J. J. Cahill has in mind is a specific lottery for the Opera House, with extra-large prizes on offer – winning the first prize of £100,000 could set you up for life.

For Cahill, the equation is simple: No bloody money, no bloody Opera House.

He is convinced the public at large will embrace the scheme, which will allow Sydney's Opera House to be built debt-free.

Not so fast. As ever, the pugnacious pit-bull Robin Askin is on to the Premier quickly, asking in the NSW Legislative Assembly on the afternoon of 26 September 1957: 'Does the Premier agree that inevitably these special lotteries will result in less support for the ordinary lotteries and consequently less finance for our hospitals?'[7]

Premier Cahill makes smooth reply: 'It is believed that the proceeds from the ordinary lotteries will not be affected to any extent. The field that was exploited by lotteries in other States, until they were restricted by court decisions about newspaper advertisements, will be exploited to the full by the new lottery, and the amount of money that previously went out of New South Wales will now go towards financing this building.'[8]

On 29 September 1957, the State Labor caucus officially gives approval to Cahill's Opera House Lottery plan, and so the wheel begins to turn.

'The Opera House was not to be a project like the pyramids, built on the sweat of the brow of the pharaoh's army of slaves,' the author David Messent would later felicitously put it, 'but on the sweat of the brow of the NSW working public who were slaves to the [pound]. If they must throw their money away, they could throw it away on something constructive like the Opera House. It was to be the ultimate gamble. Utzon had taken a gamble with his design . . . Hoping, against long odds, that his scheme will be the winner. The assessors had taken a gamble choosing it – it was so unusual. Arup had taken a gamble taking the project on as an engineer, he could not immediately see a solution to the shells but he was certain given time he would find one. And now the Australian public were gambling to finance it.'[9]

The usual critics speak out, with one letter to the *Herald* coming straight to the point: 'Gambling and culture are antithesis. We cannot mix the two to form a healthy concoction: they are as fire and water, for gambling destroys culture. If Jack Lang could build the Sydney Harbour Bridge with clean money why cannot Mr Cahill and his Government produce a home of culture, the Opera House, clean and free from the taint of gambling?'[10]

(Of course, the Harbour Bridge is still being paid off, and will continue to be so for the next few decades at least . . .)

For the most part, however, the people – and that is what counts – are right behind the idea, with the first poll showing only 11 per cent opposed. It is a percentage eerily consistent with the numbers who never buy lottery tickets in the first place, as nine out of 10 households in New South Wales regularly do.[11]

Truly the people's house.

Northern autumn 1957, Hellebaek, beside Swan Lake . . .

Just as the cygnets on the lake beside the architects' rented Hellebaek office are growing, so too is Utzon's team of architects and the more detailed plans they are working on for the Opera House. (This is despite the fact Jørn is yet to see a single penny of the £10,000 owed to him by the NSW Government. Though sent back in February, it has been delayed in the London office of the Agent-General, he is told.)

He drives the team onwards, confident they are designing nothing less than one of 'the great buildings of the century',[12] all of them in awe of the man who had first conceived such a building.

As to Utzon himself, he has only a simple desk in the rented premises, as he mostly works from home, where he comes up with design solutions, doing freehand sketches of what he wants in the different parts of the Opera House – an extraordinary building on the other side of the world forming up beneath his flying fingers, his imagination flying as free as those young swans.

Once his sketched solutions are completed to his satisfaction, he takes them to the office and assigns one of his architects to do the technical drawings for specific areas of the complex, frequently lingering to have long discussions on different practical and aesthetic aspects.

For all his casual unorthodoxy as a boss, Jørn Utzon's architects see quickly that he is a tough taskmaster, demanding every drawing 'be properly composed and every piece of information properly arranged on the sheet',[13] always asking his staff to dig deeper – on weekends, if need be, late into the night if you must, whatever it takes.

For the sheer number of drawings that have to be dealt with can look overwhelming – as the team must come up with the integrated detail for two multipurpose halls, a drama theatre and a restaurant, complex cutting-edge stage machinery, backstage space, rehearsal spaces, bathrooms, fire escapes and more, all of it connected by an intricate warren of corridors and stairways – and all of it complete with electrical wiring, air-conditioning ducts, outlets for controls and fire sprinklers, along with the podium itself and, of course, the roof . . . Designing just one of those halls could keep half-a-dozen architects busy for years, and therein lies a problem. For, in the absence of his former firm of 18 or so ready-to-go architects – which the Sydney client has chosen not to employ – half-a-dozen to a dozen new architects is about the maximum number that Utzon feels he can pay and personally guide, like the mother swan. He's not fazed – small firms are common in Scandinavia, and the great Alvar Aalto, who Utzon admires above all else, did the same, preferring a tight team to a sprawling impersonal group, and Utzon had liked it. The core design team will find the design solutions without losing control of the detail, then the technical drawings can be outsourced. Alvar Aalto is a master of the craft, his methods are proven!

Ever and always an optimist, Utzon steers by one star – perfection, the way he has perceived it.

•

On the opening day of sales for the Opera House Lottery, 1250 tickets are snapped up by individuals and syndicates. The latter are frequently groups of workmates who all pitch in a little bit and give themselves names like 'Avago' and 'Free beer', though some stick to the theme and try for a higher cultural plane like 'Mozart' and 'Beethoven'.[14] The clerks at the lottery office have a good laugh at this raw indication that the people are getting into the spirit of the thing.

Equally in the spirit is Jørn Utzon himself, who sends payment for a ticket of his own with a note, 'I seem to be a very lucky fellow, I am sure I have a good chance of winning the lottery.'[15]

Many citizens across the land – and indeed from as far afield as Britain, the USA, Canada, South Africa, New Zealand, Fiji and New Guinea – feel the same, including a quiet family who have just moved to Bondi, the Thornes. They dream – like everyone – just what a glorious vista of life might open before them, if only theirs could be the winning ticket.

4 October 1957, Hellebaek, trajectory tracked

Three, two, one . . . and . . . *lift-off!*

A tiny grey speck lifts off from a pale blue ball in a vast black expanse.

You'd need to be standing on the moon with a mighty telescope to see it that way, but Sputnik has just blasted out of the atmosphere and into orbit around planet Earth.

In the space race, the Russians have narrowly beaten the Americans to lift-off.

At his home in Hellebaek, Jørn is glued to his television set, taking in every detail.

The arc that Sputnik leaves in the sky is a thing of beauty, a blinding white streak gently curving in the cosmos almost like the . . . almost like the ridge of his Opera House?

'It goes forever, and never comes back!'[16] he exclaims to Lis who looks over to see a familiar look in her excitable husband's eyes: inspiration.

Jørn trips over himself like a baby giraffe rushing to his desk, desperate to put pencil to paper. Pulling out a flexible Perspex rod that he normally uses as a ruler, he bends it to mimic Sputnik's trajectory; rapidly up and away before mellowing and flattening as it rises towards the sky. Jørn fiddles with the paper and the Perspex until he finds parabolic perfection.

There. This is not only a new frontier, but a perfectly curved one at that.

Utzon finishes tracing out the arc and sends it to London, where Ronald Jenkins is most happy to receive it. He is a hard marker this mathematician, and is sceptical when he first sees it. But . . . wait. Jørn's crude bent ruler sketch is *almost* a perfect parabola. Truly stunning.

•

Despite the early success of the Opera House Lottery ticket sales, still the attacks go on, both in parliament and in letters to the editor, decrying the government putting such efforts to building such a frippery – and through gambling money! – when in the real world, the people are crying out for homes, better hospitals and schools.

It is a seductive line of political attack, so seductive that even members of Premier Cahill's own family come to believe it, with his daughter Margaret taking her father aside and urging him to consider housing and hospitals first.

But father Joe will not budge. He had said in his maiden speech back in 1925, and he had meant it, that it was time for the finer things in life to be available to everyone, including the workers.

People must *live*, he told the parliament that day. Not merely *exist*. *All people*. In many ways it has been the focus of his political life, and he will not back away from it now.

Everybody has the right to good things, he says to his daughter Margaret gently.

In the face of inevitable dissension, Premier Cahill frequently reminds his caucus that they must stand united lest they be thrown out into the cold, sending a chill through the entire room as they contemplate the horrors of leaving the government benches and heading out into the howling winds found in the wastelands of Opposition, where hungry dingoes hunt in packs and weak politicians die like dogs.

Quite right, quite right.

A dingo growls in the distance, the wind howls from the barren plains of oblivion, and for the most part, things sort themselves out. The easiest way is to trust in the wisdom of Joe Cahill, perhaps even on his strange obsession with this Opera House.

10 January 1958, Sydney, Charlie owns the chocolate factory

It's 8.45 am on the button – and the Executive Producer now presses it.

The giant television camera takes in the poky floodlit scene inside the auditorium of the NSW Lotteries Department on Barrack Street, broadcasting it live to television sets around New South Wales.

The huge wooden lottery barrel – bigger than six 44-gallon drums put together – filled with plastic table-tennis balls, rolls to a noisy stop. An official opens a small trapdoor and Stan Haviland reaches deep into the wooden barrel with a mechanical grabber, plucking out the lucky number . . .

The winner of the £100,000 first prize is . . . Mister Oswald P. Sellers, of Wolseley Road, Point Piper.

Would the 52-year-old Mr Sellers have bet a sheep station on such a result? Of course not, but he actually does own one, as well as a chocolate factory and an advertising agency, not to mention his waterfront Point Piper mansion manned by a housekeeper, chauffeur and gardener whose duties include keeping the brass on his yacht tied to the pier properly polished.

The Opera House Lottery! It can be won by *anyone*!

Northern winter 1958, Hellebaek, total designers

Ove Arup and Jørn Utzon share more than their Danish heritage. Oh yes, they share their native tongue, but that isn't the language they bond over. They share the language of *design*, they speak of light and loads, beams and buttresses, columns and concrete, floor plans, finishes, form and function. They just *get* one another, in a way that is lost on those around them.

If Arup sees in Utzon something of the completely driven young man he used to be – his head filled with magnificent ideas and his energy boundless – so too does Utzon see in Arup the highly accomplished older man he would one day like to be. Neither can get enough of the other.

'Working with this young architect,' Arup writes, 'it actually excites me. I feel that being in his company, and talking over plans with somebody so exciting as Utzon gives me great excitement and great pleasure.'[17]

And Utzon feels the same. If the very nature of genius is an essential loneliness, at least there is solace in being with a fellow genius in an adjacent field to one's own. And when Ove visits for another week-long stay in the Utzon home in the woods, the two work through the days together and talk long into the night, discussing every aspect of the scheme as it stands, how better to refine the plans and how they can – together – better pursue Total Design, where each discipline can lean on the other for ever greater strength.

Take this, for example, Ove. My original plan for the underside of the podium – the concourse area where the cars pull up to drop people off – was for it to be propped up by several columns.

'Would it not be possible,' he asks, 'to do without these columns?'[18]

Funny he should say that. For in this-age-old dynamic between architects and engineers there's one recurring theme: that which is cheapest is often at odds with that which is pretty. 'Of course it is possible,' Ove says. 'But it would cost a lot of money. And as the columns don't obstruct anything, this expenditure might not be justified.'[19]

Jørn Utzon takes a moment before giving his considered response.

'My concept,' he begins softly, 'demands that the architecture is expressed *through* the structure. In fact, the structure in this case *is* the architecture.'[20]

He pauses for Ove's reaction, and seeing nothing but encouragement, he continues.

'It should be bold, simple, on an impressive scale and of a form which combines sculptural quality with a clear expression of the forces acting on it. If we achieve this, finishes could be simple: the concrete itself will speak.'[21]

Taking his pencil from its home in his breast pocket, Utzon starts chatting excitedly, while sketching his idea on a scrap of paper . . . Do you see, Ove?

As is always the case between Ove and Jørn, they warmly agree, and now the older man takes over, explaining a structural engineering trick they may consider so Jørn's vision can be realised. It's all very technical, you see, but in this case, we may be able to fold and twist the great concrete beams along their length in such a manner that they can support themselves . . . then we won't need columns for support.

Jørn looks at Ove with a confused grin. Sorry, *what*? Fold? Twist?

It takes some more explanation and scribbling by Ove – 'a folded slab' he calls the technique – but the engineer is impressed to find that Utzon grasps the idea in no time; no easy feat for a non-engineer. In fact, the architect not only grasps it, he is thrilled at the idea.

Jørn and Lis sense that Ove will be a warm and generous presence in their lives for years to come.

Ove Arup feels the same warmth for the Utzons and, from the first, takes a near paternal approach to Jørn, seeing him as an architectural genius whose precociousness and, yes, preciousness, just needs some gentle guidance. It is true, young Utzon is 'very strong, ascetic and controlled',[22] as Ove will later characterise him, but he is so brilliant and creative and open-minded, and such charming company, he will obviously be a delight to work with.

And yet?

And yet, Ruth Arup, Ove's wife of four decades – and mother of their three cherished children – is concerned.

Having met Utzon when he had visited London, there are a few things that have troubled her since, and she decides to sound a gentle word of warning to her excitable husband in a letter written in early January 1958.

'The trouble with some people,' she writes with the frankness and familiarity of a long-term couple, where sometimes things need to be said straight out, 'is that they have too much of that doubtful commodity. I'm always suspicious of charm, to the extent that when I find it radiating from a person I have only just met I watch very carefully indeed to see if that is all there is, or if it is just a charming addition to something good underneath.'[23]

Listen, Ove, this spousal advice is nothing if not well thought out.

'Best wishes to Mr Utzon,' she writes in another letter, as Ove heads off to Sydney for the first time with Jørn, to meet the prospective client and present the first lot of plans. 'I have terrible forebodings that you will egg each other on to do rash things. It is because you both seem to throw ideas like fireworks, and you are both receptive of new and unusual ideas, so that to pedestrian types like myself there is the ever-present fear that your combined impulses will drive you into rashness – in other words that you will set out for the horizon without the necessary bits of paper.'[24]

And she's not wrong about her husband being swept up in the project.

Like Jørn, it has become Ove's personal obsession.

•

There really is something different about Jørn Utzon.

When his young teenage son, Jan, begs his parents for a dangerous moped, Jørn follows up on a notice in the papers that the Danish air force is selling their World War II training planes for a song, and so buys him a plane instead.

'We went to fetch it,' Jan will recall years later, 'and on the way home I sat in the cockpit, steering the tail wheels through the curves. He was unlike my friends' parents and fathers.'[25]

Such antics can earn a man a reputation, no matter how brilliant he may be in his field. Jørn's is solidifying around not just his whimsy but his fierce independence and his uncompromising approach as a designer. The design must come first.

So it is that when young Danish architect Mogens Prip-Buus hears from his interior designer girlfriend that Utzon is looking for help, it is the advice of some fellow architects that he seek something else. 'It was said that one should avoid this,' Prip-Buus will later write, 'as Utzon was completely mad and impossible to live with. It sounded just the thing for me, so I telephoned and was told to come [over].'[26]

And now, as one of Jørn's latest recruits, Mogens Prip-Buus is over the moon that he made that call. The Sydney Opera House is, with no doubt, the most exciting architecture project in the world. As for the architect, Mogens is nothing less than enamoured with Utzon from the first.

'You couldn't help,' he will say sincerely, 'loving that man.'[27]

Unorthodox, certainly. A demanding, uncompromising perfectionist, to be sure. But a brilliant architect, a generous mentor, and an exceedingly good man.

26 March 1958, Sydney, the devil is in the detail

The Trojans made it very clear that it was important to beware of Greeks bearing gifts, though they never mentioned anything about Danes. For, on this three-week visit to Sydney, Jørn Utzon and Ove Arup come laden down with models of the Opera House as it is currently conceived – including one which, when assembled, will be as large as 30 feet wide and 12 feet high, built to test the House's acoustics – along with the Red Book, the first, official technical articulation of Jørn's competition sketches.

With his Red Book in front of him in his Bondi hotel room, Utzon tells the journalist before him: 'I have been doing nothing but eat, sleep, and work on the House with a lot of people at the office and now we know how it will be built . . . When I was in London, Mr Jenkins, who is Mr Arup's partner, took me to a blackboard in his office. It was covered with mathematical formulas describing the shells of the House. Can't you see the beauty of it?'[28]

They can!

All up, the stylish Red Book goes for 55 pages and is filled with precise drawings, rough sketches and coloured photographs all detailing the progress so far, and including such specialist commentaries by Ove Arup on structures, and Dr Vilhelm Lassen Jordan on acoustics, and so forth.

The most developed of the plans are for the podium and the stage machinery, which is to go in the stage towers of the Major and Minor halls, necessary to change sets quickly between scenes for opera, ballet and drama performances by flying them up and down the 90-foot hollow stage tower using pulleys and ropes.

All the rest of the drawings are more a work in progress, the prime example of which is . . . the roof.

Following Ronald Jenkins' advice – and Sputnik's trajectory – the Red Book explains that the only way to really make the roof stand up, is to give it parabolic curves.

As such, the shells in Utzon's updated drawings appear more drawn back and upright than his competition design.

'By defining the surfaces geometrically, each point of the surfaces can be given spatial coordinates,' Ove Arup details in the Red Book, 'and a basis has been created for the calculation of the forces acting on the shells.'[29]

From here, the engineers will need to calculate those forces on the newly configured shells, which are now to be supported by steel ribs built into the thin concrete structure, to determine if they will indeed stand.

All of which are problems for the future.

For now, things are rosy as the Red Book is accepted by the Executive Committee as proof positive of just how far things have advanced.

Premier Cahill is pleased – he has his eye on the March election next year, acutely aware that having the Opera House underway by that time would not only ensure the project is election-proof – sure to go ahead whatever the result – but might even improve their chances of victory.

On that note, we'd like a word with you, Premier.

Based on decades of experience, Ove Arup is firm: 'It is unwise to start the job before the drawings are made.'[30]

It *never* ends well, Premier.

Which is as may be. But while they are expert in building, he is expert in politics and understands what they do not: if ground is not broken soon and Bennelong Point remains the way it looks right now, the people will lose interest, the Opposition will win, and there will never be an Opera House at all.

And so, over tea and Arrowroot Biscuits, he insists.

But, the Danes want to know, how on earth can you lay proper foundations when you don't know the loads that those foundations must bear?

The short answer is, you can't. But like the old adage of the Wild West that, 'A Smith & Wesson beats four aces every time', so too, when a building project relies on politically contentious money to continue, it means the flaky principles of political expediency outrank rock-solid engineering principles that have foundations going back centuries.

Cahill wins.

Arup at least insists that things are organised so that while the basic work is going on in the first months they can get as much time as possible to keep designing the later work. Let the labour be split into halves.

Stage I. The base of the building, known as the podium.

Stage II. The remainder of the work.

It makes sense, and is quickly agreed to.

(The decision is such a neat echo of Sydney's past it might almost be a tradition. Nearly a century earlier, so keen had Sydney's aldermen been to secure the site for the Sydney Town Hall, they had invited Sydney's first royal visitor, His Royal Highness Prince Alfred, Duke of Edinburgh, to lay a foundation stone on the spot, even though negotiations were still underway for the site and no actual plans for a building had been drawn! In an atmosphere of intense political and personal battles, the design chosen ended up being interpreted, chopped, changed and embellished by successive architects and engineers, as construction stumbled forward in two stages, taking no less than 22 years to finish and costing several times over budget.)

Northern summer 1958, Hellebaek, Ove's invention

And so to Stage I, Act I, of Sydney's dramatic Opera House.

On this day, Ove Arup arrives in Hellebaek ready to unveil his innovative engineering concept for the column-free concourse he and Utzon have been working on, sending the plans back and forth across the North Sea. And so begins yet another of their marathon meetings, day running into . . . day after day, with the pair barely noticing as they tweak, evolve, revolve, devolve and then evolve some more the whole concept, their professional and personal relationship deepening. Yes, there is the cliché of the flighty architect and the rigid engineer ending up at each other's throats as art clashes with science, but both men are aware of how lucky they are to have escaped it.

Early June 1958, Bennelong Point, bored drillers

Sod it. There is no way around it. Before they can turn that first sod to begin building, they need to know precisely how stable said sod *is*. Men from the Maritime Services Board sink 12 'test foundation bores'.[31] It is not a quick process, with only a single drill going down each day, but come July's end, they have ascertained that all 12 bores reached bedrock from five to 20 feet below the top soil.

Joe Cahill is glad to hear it.

Onto the second step.

On 18 August, courtesy of three massive D-9 Caterpillar bulldozers – snarling, beastly behemoths unleashed on a sitting target – demolition commences on Fort Macquarie Tram Depot at Bennelong Point.

July 1958, Hellebaek, a Japanese arrival

A decade earlier, the idea of a young Japanese man being warmly welcomed into the home of a Dane would have been preposterous. Denmark had been under German occupation, and the Japanese their all but equally hated allies.

But things have changed. Japan has shaken off its own militarism and is appreciated as never before by those in the West for many things, including their architectural and engineering skills.

On this sparkling summer's day, upon arrival at Utzon's home in the beech forest, Yuzo Mikami – a young, single architect who Utzon had recruited during his recent trip to Japan – is not only heartily greeted by

Jørn Utzon, but shortly thereafter, despite his complete lack of Danish and dusty grasp of English, is sipping tea and discussing the challenges of building an opera house. (As Prip-Buus will later recall – 'English soon became the in-office language due to all the different nationalities.'[32])

It is a strong beginning for this Japanese man so far from home, and the following day he is introduced by Utzon to the rest of the staff in his office as he begins to grapple with the technical issues at hand.

Drawing boards, lying on simple wooden trestles, are scattered throughout the second-floor rooms, and in the central sunroom sits a large wooden model that Mikami recognises instantly as being the Mayan-inspired podium of the Sydney Opera House.

'The model of the base of the building, which was called the podium, looked like twin Greek amphitheatres made of timber. It looked awesomely impressive even lacking the roofs.'[33]

A more curious 'model' sits close by on a coffee table – a pile of white sugar cubes stacked in such a way as to resemble . . . is it . . . the podium? Mikami looks for assurance from his new boss. Utzon laughs and claps him on the shoulder – Mikami will soon see that Jørn uses whatever is at hand to demonstrate and share ideas with his staff.

And so it begins, the young Japanese man throwing himself into the work and in the meantime doing his best to get a basic grip on the Danish language, helped along by the Utzons' 12-year-old daughter, Lin, who every afternoon after school comes to sit under his drawing board, and helps to teach him Danish, starting with counting.

Try it again, Yuzo.

En . . . to . . . tre . . . fire . . . fem . . . seks . . . syv . . . otte . . .

Ja, godt! Yes, good!

Mikami is not a brilliant student of the Danish language but young Lin is so sweet and patient with him that he continues to make progress, and becomes almost like a member of the family, frequently dining with the Utzons.

Work-life settles into a pleasing rhythm of hard work, starting at 8 am, punctuated by a lunchtime of Danish open sandwiches on the back patio, where everyone sits and talks before getting back to it, and afternoon tea when they do the same around a big yellow teapot and a hard Danish crispbread, *knaekbrød*, often with butter and cheese.

Though usually too busy to take part in the fun and games, occasionally, Mikami will recall, 'Jørn Utzon joined in, telling super jokes and making everyone laugh. He was an excellent talker and everybody enjoyed listening to him.'[34] Late on particularly sunny afternoons, Jørn dispatches the secretary to ride her bicycle to the store and they all wait impatiently for her return, loaded down with smoked salmon and wine, whereupon the world's master architect declares the day's work is done, and they all sit on the back patio to enjoy the afternoon by the swan lake, listening to tales from Jørn's travels, each one designed to deliver a clue to his grand Opera House vision. It is possible that life might get better than this, but nothing comes to mind.

For this is not just another architectural job. They are working on the masterpiece of the age, under the tutelage of an architectural visionary, and all have an enormous sense of privilege to be doing so – a real sense that they are working on something *globally* important, with global and historical influences necessitating the bringing together of people from around the globe to see it through.

'We were a very international crowd at the office,' Prip-Buus will recount, 'all with different upbringings. Each of us spoke his mind and influenced the others. It was very much alive. Anything was possible . . . It was wonderful.'[35]

As for Ove Arup, himself a man of two nations, there is universal respect for the elderly engineer who seems to be watching over all of them like a wise grandfather.

On one of those weeks when Ove Arup visits to consult with Jørn on any number of matters, it happens to be the birthday of one of the junior draughtsmen and, as has become their habit, they all gather round late in the day to share a birthday cake. The presence of Arup means that, including office staff, there are 17 of them and so, for fun, Utzon challenges the esteemed engineer to cut the cake into 17 even parts.

Arup does not hesitate. With smooth dexterity, he takes the knife and cuts the cake into four parts, with just one part a little larger than the rest. And now, after dividing the smaller pieces into four equal pieces, he simply cuts the larger one 'into five, all exactly the same angle, thus completely identical.'[36]

Ove Arup smiles his signature soft smile. 'Well, did I prove myself to be a good engineer?'[37]

Everyone at the tea party explodes in applause, led by the beaming Jørn Utzon.

October 1958, Hellebaek, the October scheme

It's a part of the job that Jørn, frankly, had not anticipated.

The sheer fascination being shown by his fellow professionals, the public and the press from all around the world is overwhelming. People knock at his door, unannounced. The phone never stops ringing. The press have been calling old friends and colleagues, asking for stories on him.

As Mogens Prip-Buus recalls, '. . . after Jørn presented the Red Book in Sydney our numbers quickly grew. Many came without warning and waited on the steps until the master arrived. One said that if there was no other work for him he could always fill the master's pipe, and was very disappointed when I told him Jørn didn't smoke.'[38]

For those who were engaged by the master, they have to learn the ropes. Utzon's office is unorthodox, the man himself an eccentric in many ways. There is no official organisational structure, no titles or grades – all are welcome to contribute if they have something to say.

Jørn takes the entire office for strolls through the forest and along the beach, and on long tours of the shipyard, where Jørn, familiar with all the old hands working there, encourages his architects' 'understanding of how to work with very big and double-curved forms'.[39]

True, Jørn is a man of boundless curiosity, curious quirks and wandering whimsy – childlike, in many ways – but, all jokes aside, when it comes to the Sydney Opera House, he is a man in serious, earnest pursuit of one thing above all: perfect architecture.

One new recruit doesn't know what to make of it when Jørn asks one day, 'Would you care to see the office's most important equipment?'

'Yes!' says the new recruit, with what another recruit describes as 'Christmas candles in his eyes.'

Jørn takes him by the arm and leads him over to one of the many big wastepaper baskets placed in all the rooms. 'We can't work without this one,'[40] he says with a booming laugh.

Among the arrivals are a swathe of Australian architects – Denmark has never hosted so many antipodeans as now – who come for a stickybeak and stay for a smoked salmon sandwich. One reports back to Sydney on Utzon's methods: 'Utzon is in many ways a perfectionist, and does not even consider the time which may be spent in study, trial and error of countless ways of doing a thing – but he must be convinced that whatever is finally done is right.'[41]

Yuzo Mikami will recall: 'The atmosphere in the drawing office was very relaxed and optimistic, although staff were conscious of being watched by the inquisitive and sometimes sceptical outside world. However, they were confident that the building they were working on would become one of the great buildings of the century, and were extremely dedicated to the work and to their boss.'[42]

Ove, too, is now being besieged by the British and Australian press, though their questions tend to be either as pointed or as blunt as a claw hammer, depending on which end they are coming from. When will it be done? Will the roof stand up?

It is all rather strange, but both men have been urged by Harry Ashworth and Stan Haviland to show prudence in their public statements, so as not to accidentally prod any sleeping bears.

But there is no doubt, the Danish architect makes charming copy for the journalists. As to Stage I, the concrete slabs that are to span above the concourse, or 'Ove's Invention' Jørn is sure to tell everyone who asks – the architect simply couldn't be happier with how it is all coming together.

All is well in the State of Denmark as Utzon prepares to fly back to Sydney with the 'October Scheme', the detailed plans for Stage I.

31 October 1958, Hellebaek, the die is cast

Ever and always concentrating on giving theatre-goers the complete experience of his Opera House, Jørn Utzon's energies are going into more than just the roof and interior layout of the Opera House, as he is already turning his muse to possible decorations. It is the Scandinavian way – a holistic concern for the final building's interiors, *including* its furniture, artwork and tapestries.

Leaning on his new-found status – now that his own name is resonating in the highest echelons of the worlds of architecture and art – he gathers his nerve and writes to a man who is globally famous in both: the modernist man of the moment, the Swiss–Frenchman, Le Corbusier, who he'd once met in Paris.

Le Corbusier,
35 Rue de Sevres,
Paris VI,
France

31 October, 1958

Cher Monsieur Le Corbusier,

I have long wanted to write to you to thank you for all that you mean and have meant to me and I allow myself to send you my project for the Opera [House] of Sydney . . . It would be an immense joy if I could be assured of your participation in the decoration, the tapestries and the paintings, of this edifice and I pray to you to let me know if you could make something for it in one form or another.

At the same time I ask if I could obtain permission to buy some of your oil paintings and tapestries . . .[43]

Wonder of all wonders? Joy of all joys?

Le Corbusier replies immediately, saying he would be delighted and even compliments the young architect on his stunning and pioneering design.

November 1958, Sydney, movement at the station

As to Ruth's fear that her husband and Utzon would, 'set out for the horizon without the necessary bits of paper', the good news is that in late November 1958, after more than a full year working on the Sydney Opera House, Ove's firm officially signs the first 'bits of paper' – a 'Memorandum of Agreement' between his firm and the NSW Government.

And a slightly odd one it is, as it happens. The usual way of huge projects of this nature is that only the architect would sign a contract with the client – in this case the NSW Government – making the creator of the design responsible for the whole thing, including hiring and firing the structural engineers and other consultants, while overseeing the whole project.

On this project, the Committee has decided to contract Ove Arup & Partners directly – Arup's is a big firm with the manpower to administer the bulk of contracts. Also, Arup's are familiar with the British system and far more experienced than Utzon in big building projects.

For Ove, taking on so much responsibility is not ideal, but it works. The bright side is, their reward will be a far higher financial share than they are used to, including six per cent of the contracts they are to administer.

For Utzon, so long as he is in full charge of the whole design and directing the consultants' work, he is happy – and given that he has come to trust Ove, as much as his own beloved elder brother, Leif, there should be no problem with co-operation, or the engineers stepping on his toes as lead.

In the final months of 1958, the most pressing need is to determine which firm will build Stage I of Sydney's Opera House.

To get things moving, Arup's representatives in Australia, the Sydney firm MacDonald, Wagner and Priddle have come up with a list of their top five building contractors in New South Wales who should be invited to tender . . .

And sorry, what?

Oh. On the personal insistence of Ove Arup, who has received a visit in London from one of their executives, the name of Civil & Civic is very reluctantly added to the list, despite the fact that Arup's representatives in Sydney advise that 'C&C' are not up to the task and should not be touched with a 10-foot pole.

No matter. In this game, one thumbs up from Ove beats a great hand of rationale every time.

•

On 5 February 1959, the bid of the Australian construction firm Civil & Civic, as the lowest of six tenders, is accepted to build Stage I.

With a quote of just £1,397,929 – well below the second lowest bidder – there is a stirring of serious concern and disbelief among certain players, but who can resist a bargain? Certainly not elected governments!

Cahill gives his pen its final flick as the Sydney Opera House is set in contractual stone. No matter who wins the election come 21 March, little over a month away, the government is bound to honour this contract.

'I've watched brick by brick being taken from the old tram shed that was here,' Cahill tells the bustling reporters. 'And I'm going to watch brick by brick of the Opera House go up.'44

•

To mark the turning of the first sod, Joe Cahill asks Jørn Utzon if some kind of foundation stone can be laid, something that will, you know, really *mark the occasion*, for now and evermore.

Typically, Utzon has no interest in any kind of conventional foundation stone, with a few chiselled bland words into a lump of sandstone. No, he wants something modern, something brilliant, something in keeping with the stunning building that will grow up around it. Still, busy with so many other things, he asks Yuzo Mikami to see what he can come up with.

Serendipitously the Japanese man is currently working on the grid-line system of the plan of the whole building and soon resolves the first issue: where to put it.

'Jørn,' he says, 'why couldn't we put the foundation stone or metal plate at the point of intersection of the hall centre-lines? All the measurement of the halls and the podium are taken and fixed from there. It is a point like the navel in the human body, everything begins to grow from there.'

Utzon beams.

'Good idea, Yuzo. Let's fix the thing on that point and do it in metal. Will you do the design of the plate for me?'45

Done!

He comes up with a two-foot diameter circle of pure bronze. The inscription is composed with the help of the Australian embassy in Copenhagen, and right at the central point there is a cross to mark the exact point where the east–west grid-line intersects with the axes of the two halls.

Who can make it?

Why, who better than the local shipyard, where Utzon's father, Aage, used to be the manager; the place Jørn had grown up running around in. The older workers, particularly, are nearly as proud as Aage is of young Jørn now being a world-famous architect, and, in the words of Mikami, 'wished to show the high standard of Danish craftsmanship to the people of Sydney'.[46]

This being an Utzon operation, there are, of course, several modifications to the original design – no matter, it must be done right – and it is only just finished in time before their departure for Sydney to attend the official ceremony, but just look how good it is! It comes complete with a specially constructed wooden box so Jørn and Lis can carry it to Sydney as part of their personal luggage. It comes, of course, with a screwdriver for the Premier to use to bolt the plaque, engraved with a large 'C' for Cahill.

Well, at least that's what it is meant to be.

But when Mikami shows Utzon the final product in front of the whole staff just prior to departure, it doesn't take Jørn long to put his own spin – exactly 90 degrees – upon it. The 'C' for Cahill suddenly becomes a 'U' for Utzon and as Mikami will recall delightedly: 'We all laughed a great deal at this mischievous idea.'[47]

It is a wonderful thing to be a part of the Utzon team, just to be around him at such a happy and historic time.

2 March 1959, Bennelong Point, 'Oh What a Wonderful Day'

It is the speed that is the most extraordinary.

Just a little over two years after the Cahill government announced the winner of the competition, the great day is here. True, it is hardly an auspicious sign that the burning hot sun that had roasted the guests on arrival has now been covered by a bank of plump dark clouds that look ready to burst. Nor is it encouraging that the whole ceremony is already several minutes behind schedule thanks to the Deputy Leader of the Opposition's vague understanding of punctuality – Robin Askin is late. Pat Morton is busy campaigning, but he could have at least made sure his patsy would arrive on time.

But still, the belting sun and the pelting rain does not quell the spirits of the 400 leading citizens of Sydney invited for the occasion, led by Premier Joe Cahill and his ever-devoted wife, Esmey. And of course, just as Governor Macquarie had been there for the laying of the Foundation Stone for Fort Macquarie, so is NSW Governor Eric Woodward here on this day, representing Her Majesty Queen Elizabeth II.

Joining Cahill on the platform at last is the Deputy Leader of the State Opposition, Robin Askin, who rushes up, waving a hand in silent apology. As to the leader of the Country Party, Davis Hughes, he is . . . indisposed . . . and so represented by his deputy, Mr Charles Cutler. Lord Mayor Harry Jensen is up there, as well as most members of the NSW Cabinet, the Opera House Executive Committee and sundry dignitaries.

Jørn Utzon is dashing in his usual tailored suit, his Ray-Ban sunglasses and stylishly cut hair, longer than the militaristic short back and sides favoured by the Australians, while Lis Utzon clutches a bouquet of white carnations and scarlet nectarine flowers – Denmark's colours – her wide yellow straw hat and white cotton dress elegant and resplendent against the drab grey sky.

The guests gather beneath the dais, muttering to themselves and fidgeting, settling once the long line of gushing speeches start. Even Robin Askin is notably gracious in his remarks.

'The time for controversy is over,' he tells the audience. 'It now remains only for us to work together in a spirit of goodwill to raise the necessary finance to bring this magnificent concept of an Opera House into being. I am sure that the people of this State will meet that challenge.'[48]

It marks the first official endorsement of the project from the Liberal Party.

For Premier Cahill – a man possessed by his passion for seeing the Opera House reach completion, so obsessed that the project has earned the nickname 'Taj Cahill'[49] – this moment is nothing short of a *triumph*.

'I am glad to say,' he says sincerely, 'that the Opera House is purely non-political and I venture to predict that no party will attempt to make an issue of it in the coming election . . . which means that in cultural matters we are all for the advancement of this country of ours and the little things that could divide us at a time like this – the petty things, the small things – will have no place when this magnificent institution begins to be erected. We are not, as some people overseas unfortunately still seem to think, a nation of rough and ready pioneers devoted solely to the needs of self-preservation. Surely we are grown up in the sense that we can turn some portion of our attention to the finer things of life and demonstrate that we are not savages but civilized human beings, capable of contributing our share to world culture and appreciation of the arts.'[50]

At the conclusion of his speech, thanking his Ministers, the Committee men and various individuals who have helped to get the project off the ground – or in the ground, as the case may be – Mr Cahill moves from the official dais to where the bronze 'Inaugural Plaque' has already been put in place.

Jørn Utzon hands over the specially designed bolt and screwdriver to Mr Cahill who – like the old fitter and turner he is – handles it with ease and familiarity. He pauses to admire the elegant 'C' the shipyard workers have placed on the knob in his honour, and of course the inscription on the plaque's bottom half:

> This plaque commemorates the commencement of the
> construction of the SYDNEY OPERA HOUSE.
> All measurements are taken from this basic reference point.
> The plaque was fixed by honourable
> JOHN JOSEPH CAHILL
> Premier of New South Wales on the second day of March 1959

Bending over the plaque, the Premier hesitates. It seems J. J. Cahill's years in parliament have served to blunt his worker's instincts. This is actually a very modern screwdriver, with a very modern screw, *un*familiar to him. He looks at Utzon, puzzled.

Utzon steps forward and demonstrates. Take the bolt, Premier, like so, and place it in the hole. Turn, and then tap down on this thin screwdriver with this special mallet.

The Premier does as bid, there is a distinct *click* of finality as the bolt is set in place, at which point the Premier raises his right hand, rather like a conductor's first gesture at the start of an orchestral concert. In the near distance, the policeman who has been watching for this signal turns on the siren of his car, and on the instant the six workmen with jackhammers who have been standing by, start breaking up the ground even as a large bulldozer roars into action and work begins.

It is not *quite* the sound that Goossens had heard all those years ago when he daydreamed of a Sydney Opera House – there's an awful lot more grunting and yelling and the tempo and key are all over the place – but that matters not to the Premier. To Joe Cahill, it *is* music, the sound of a beginning, the sound of a promise kept, and the first sounds of the grand symphony orchestra to come.

'The stage was set,' one of Arup's key engineers would note, 'for one of the most accidental, random and astonishing acts of architectural patronage of modern times.'[51]

With the ceremony now over, one reporter from the *Sydney Morning Herald* is moved to record his surprise at a notable omission in proceedings: 'There was only one blemish, and that was a very sad one. Mr Jørn Utzon, architect of the whole business, was on the dais – and that's all. Nobody mentioned him and they failed to introduce him to the audience – even failed to mention the charming plaque he made for the occasion. But his reward was the stream of unstinted praise which dominated the messages received from the world's leading architects.'[52]

Jørn Utzon appears unfazed by his lack of mention. Instead, he is particularly gratified when, as he will later recount, all the political leaders shake his hand and repeat the solemn promises that the building of the Opera House would never be a 'political football'.[53]

A what? Lis provides her services as a translator for Jørn, who in turn lets out a great booming laugh to punctuate his understanding. He has never been a man concerned with politics and he never will be. Architecture is his only focus. And the architecture of the Sydney Opera House is the focus of that focus.

Nor has there been any mention of the disgraced Sir Eugene Goossens. But Charles Moses predicted as much, so had been sure to bestow due honour upon his friend by writing of him in the official booklet for the occasion, the Gold Book.

'It is ten years since I first discussed the building of an opera house for Sydney with Sir Eugene Goossens. A Sydney Opera House such as we are going to build at Bennelong Point was Sir Eugene's "vision splendid". Above all else he saw it as a home for his beloved Sydney Symphony Orchestra. As we go along towards the realisation of his dream we should not forget Sir Eugene's early campaigning and his success in persuading people that an opera house was not only desirable but essential to the State's cultural growth.'[54]

Goossens' spirit has been invoked. Djinn lives.

The guests move to a nearby marquee set up for the reception, where the Police Band playing 'With a Little Bit of Luck' can barely be heard above the bulldozer now roaring as it pushes the rubble left over by the destroyed tram depot into a pile.

There is no time to waste. Joe Cahill wants there to be demonstrable construction on site, on the day of the election, now just 19 days away.

As Winston Churchill had famously said of the Battle of El Alamein, 'This is not the end. It is not even the beginning of the end. But it is, perhaps, the end of the beginning.'[55]

The truly hard work starts from now . . .

Let the games begin!

SEVEN

FAREWELL, OLD SMOOTHIE, FAREWELL SMOOTH SAILING

Spring comes to Bennelong Point – A yellow butterfly jittered around piles of broken sandstone; a little patch of clover left by the bulldozers was in bloom; and all over Bennelong Point, like grown buds ready to flower, steel piers were sprouting from the rock. Spring has come to the bare bones of Utzon's idea.

Gavin Souter, *The Sydney Morning Herald*, September 1959

21 March 1959, Sydney, all aboard the Cahill Expressway

It is the ballad of the ballot box, and 2,000,000 New South Welshmen head to schools, churches and country halls to cast their votes and write the final stanza of this bush saga. Within days the results are in, Old Smoothie has done it again – Labor have 18 years on the trot, seven under the 68-year-old Cahill, who the people deem too good a horse to take out the back just yet – he is returned to the Premiership.

21 April 1959, NSW Parliament House, chapfallen chap falling

For Davis Hughes, it is the most humiliating speech of his life. Having been forced to resign from the Country Party leadership early on in the losing election campaign, purportedly for ill-health, the Member for Armidale must now grapple with the 'true position' that had put him in hospital with a nervous condition, and see if he can salvage his political career despite it all.

'I want to make a personal explanation,' he tells his fellow parliamentarians, 'about a matter which affects me personally, which arose during the election campaign, and which I was unable to deal with at that stage because of my health.'[1]

The chamber, as one, leans forward, aware that they are witnessing a man making a speech that is the equivalent of a crippled man attempting to walk again, a disgraced politician trying for redemption.

A deathly hush.

Davis Hughes goes on.

'The question is a personal one of my own academic qualifications,'[2] Hughes says, his voice alternating between wavering and quavering, as the chamber listens in heavy silence.

Despite his previous claims in this very chamber as far back as 1940, and despite the Country Party election advertisements boasting that one in four of their candidates – including Davis Hughes – had university degrees, while Labor, *sniff*, could only manage one in 10 . . . the truth is he . . . uh . . . doesn't actually have a Bachelor of Science degree at all. The election ads had been fact-checked and found false in Hughes' case – now, it's time to pay the Pied Piper.

'I want to say straight out, that is not true. I have seen that in Hansard and I have not taken the necessary steps or action to have that removed.'[3]

'Why didn't you?' the Labor Member for Hartley interjects.[4]

'That was a grave weakness on my part, in not making sure that the title Bachelor of Science was removed from Hansard . . .'

Silence reigns as Davis Hughes, his face pinkish in hue from the awkward public confessions, collects his thoughts.

Ahem.

'I understand,' the Member for Armidale finally goes on, 'that in the Air Force records, the same position occurs . . .'

Soft murmurs bounce around the parliament chamber.

'I regret the position very, very much . . . I believe I still have a part to play in the Government of this State and I hope in Parliament. I will carry out my duties and play my part as a member of a Party that has not been sullied before, to the very best of my ability.'[5]

'Hear! Hear!' the Liberal and Country Party members murmur as Hughes sits down, hoping he has done enough to save himself. (The news soon reaches some of the Air Force officers who trained with Davis Hughes – one of whom appears to expect no less of the man, remarking: 'He has a certain guile that enables him to impress one to an extent beyond the actual value of his actions and, or, words. His efforts are often designed to focus favourable light on himself and to this end he will be quite impervious to the effects or feelings of others. Due to his ego and tendency to understate others' ability and by his actions he loses considerable prestige and status.'[6])

In much better form some weeks later is the former Deputy Leader of the NSW Liberals, Robin Askin, after deposing Pat Morton, and taking over as Opposition Leader.

'My only plan at this moment,' Robin Askin says in the press conference following his victory, 'is to shift heaven and earth to get rid of the Cahill government . . . I believe that Mr Cahill is feeling the weight of his years. When he decides to call it a day what will follow in their ranks will make our recent difficulties look very minor indeed.'[7]

It is a promising start for this, the fourth State Liberal leader in four years and there is a general feeling that Askin – whose father had worked for the NSW railways during World War I, just like Joe Cahill – has the mercilessness and love for a scrap that the likeable Morton lacked. This is something even members of the Cahill government concede.

'Bob knows some tricks in the political game,' a prominent if un-named Labor member tells the *Sydney Morning Herald*, 'and he could make us sit up and take notice of the Opposition for a change.'[8]

And his timing just might be perfect.

May 1959, Hellebaek, a creature of the light

Having promised the people of Sydney that the white tiles on the Opera House roof will reflect 'the mood of the sky by day, mirroring its glimmering lights on the water by nights',[9] Utzon has been working hard to deliver on that promise ever since.

As ever, he takes inspiration from his travels. A trip to the Great Barrier Reef and many long snorkelling sessions in its opalescent waters have shown him that his white sails can reflect more than the celestial lights. As he would later recall of the reef, the most stunning creature of light imaginable, 'white would be good because of the colours it would make and reflect from all the red roofs of the houses around the harbour'.[10]

In the meantime, on his return trips from Sydney to Hellebaek, he has been carefully collecting fascinating handmade tiles from Japan and China, all with different textures, colours and glazes from different centuries and regions, which he lays out on one of the office tables for all to observe and to take inspiration from. With similar zeal he places photographs of his travels in Persia and Morocco. Somewhere within the tiles and photos lying on that table lies the solution he is looking for. He needs to work out the perfect mix of raw materials and glazes so that his Opera House will so shine for centuries to come.

To help his dream become a reality he has already found an ideal tile manufacturer in the Swedish ceramic company, Höganäs Billesholms Aktiebolag, located just over the Øresund and 10 miles up the coast at a spot renowned for its unique clay deposits and, in turn, its world-class ceramics. The architect is particularly taken with one very interesting

Höganäs in-house innovation, that is squarely in the modern tradition of Scandinavian functionalism. The ingenious system sees dozens of tiles attached to prefabricated 'clinker tile panels' on the ground, in the warmth of a factory in the case of long Swedish winters, which can then be quickly bolted straight onto massive concrete walls.

It takes a lot of trial and error, but slowly they move towards the tile that the Dane has been seeing in his mind's eye, until one day . . .

That one there.

Jørn taps one of their several offerings with his long artist's finger.

June 1959, Bennelong Point, rocky rubble; rough rabble

Well, one thing they'll never say about these blokes now turning up in their caravans to set up their homes beside massive derricks on Bennelong Point is that they are smooth . . .

Rough-as-mullet-guts is closer to the mark. They are the drillers, given the task of sinking myriad bores down to bedrock, which will then be lined with steel casings and filled with concrete to construct the piers for the Opera House's foundations.

Looking like refugees from the Geebung Polo Club – coming from *somewhere up the country, in a land of rock and scrub*[11] – these massive, tattooed men in sun-bleached hats, blue singlets, shorts and sockless riding boots are a rough breed more used to drilling water bores for farmers out the back o' Bourke than drilling holes for city-slicker silvertails, but there is a job to be done here and they are the men for it. And what a pleasure, after the dusty, semi-arid country they are usually in, to be right here by breezy Sydney Harbour, which they can use as both their shower and their toilet!

In short order, the drills start going down on the first of what will be 460 holes of nearly one metre diameter for the concrete piers to be built on land, and 160 over water.

And at night, after the day's work is done?

Well, at night, they sit around campfires by their caravans – such open fires being the first at Bennelong Point since the days of Bennelong himself – and, by one contemporary account, 'would spend all their nights celebrating or drinking'.[12]

They really are a special breed.

The profile their drilling starts to build of the land is a bit of a worry, though. It had appeared from the 12 test bores that were sunk last year that Bennelong Point had, bar the odd few fossilised fort fortifications, the same geological makeup as the harbour foreshores – solid Hawkesbury sandstone – but that proves not to be the case. Each new hole unearths loose alluvial deposits, sodden with sea water, as evidenced by the mud-caked drillers, getting ready for a quick dip in the harbour after yet *another* one of their holes collapses around them and fills with dirty, salty water. At times they hit loose rock and manmade debris, obviously thrown here back in colonial days to join the tidal island to the foreshore. The drillers feel a lot more like well-diggers than anything else, and they have the colourful vocabulary to let everyone within earshot know it.

In any case, the science of engineering and the Bible are as one on the principle of the 'wise man who built his house on the rock', which means the concrete piers on which the Opera House will rest are going to have to go a lot deeper than previously thought, and this is going to take a lot longer, and cost a lot more, than they had envisioned.

End July 1959, Hellebaek, under the wave off Kanagawa

Busy, Yuzo?

Never too busy for you, Jørn.

The boss wants to go on a quick excursion to the nearby seashore.

When they arrive on the wet sands, they sit right at the water's edge where Jørn draws Yuzo's attention to the small waves that crest and break onto the shore, every mesmerising detail, as if hypnotising his young charge.

'It was very dynamic and breathtakingly beautiful,' Mikami will recall. 'Every one of the waves showed a different character in its movement.'

It is classic Utzon, who comes quickly to his point, gesturing towards the rising crest of the latest wave about to lap at their feet.

'Yuzo,' he says, 'can't we design the ceiling of the Minor Hall something like that?'[13]

Assembling curved plywood panels, we can create a functional acoustic cocoon of stunning form, like a great wave above the audience.

Not long after returning to the studio, Jørn gives Yuzo a small sketch of his vision, 'no bigger than a postcard',[14] and instructs him to make a start.

Late August 1959, Hellebaek, stepping out, in Utzon fashion

Young architects from around the world continue to seek out *the* most inspirational and revolutionary architect of the modern moment and knock on his door in the hope of breathing in while he is breathing out.

Some make appointments, some don't. He becomes so fatigued by the latter group that he often removes himself upstairs until they have gone, but on occasion, when he's feeling generous, receives the stray knockers, and . . .

And who is this?

Why it is a dapper, olive-skinned young Australian architect by the name of Peter Hall, on his honeymoon with his new bride, Libby. They're from Sydney.

Sydney, you say? Why do come in!

As it happens, Hall – whose tangerine bow tie vibrates with the enthusiasm of his torrent of questions and musings on Jørn's Sydney Opera House – is a font of architectural knowledge! A country boy like Jørn, hailing from a speck on the map called Boggabri, he is well educated from his scholarship at the elite Cranbrook school, and had graduated from Sydney University a year earlier with a double degree in architecture and arts. Having won the Board of Architects Research Bursary and the newly established Hezlet Bequest Travelling Scholarship while there, the runs Peter Hall has on the board are not just from opening the batting and captaining the Sydney University First Grade cricket side.

So impressive is he that when Hall inquires after a short stint of work, Utzon is delighted, offering him a job in the Hellebaek office for . . . 20 months or so? It makes sense having an Australian on the staff to understand immediately the local lie of the land.

Both Peter Hall and his wife are stunned at the great man's generosity of spirit.

'Jørn Utzon has been really wonderful to us,' Libby writes home to her parents, 'greeting us as friends, giving us meals and so much of his precious time.'

But . . . to stop here that long, to work with Utzon in the Hellebaek office?

It is tempting, even though the couple are looking forward to the rest of their honeymoon through Europe – with Hall as eager as Utzon to soak up as much as he can of global architecture.

And the fact is, Hall has a job waiting for him in the Government Architect's office back in Sydney – under his mentor and friend Ted Farmer, who has just taken over from Cobden Parkes. The office paid for his university degree and offered him a handsome salary, so he feels bound to repay them with his continued service. (And this is, by the by, a far more substantial salary than Utzon is offering him, as the Dane's own money is still only coming in small lots from Sydney via the Agent-General, only for the Danish taxman to take huge chunks out of it before passing it on.)

But still, what an opportunity!

'We are both terribly impressed with Utzon,' Libby writes home, 'he is now 39 or so, and just starting really on a remarkable career. He's built very little in Denmark . . . collecting his thoughts, and travelling between times to all parts of the world: now he has suddenly burst out with superb designs, wins huge competitions whenever he likes, and has a large, very competent group of architects working under him in his beautiful office at Hellebaek . . . he is the most likeable, amusing and talented man . . .'[15]

What a model for Peter himself to work from! It is tough to turn the offer down, made easier by the fact that Libby's father, himself an engineer, advises against it.

'This thing will never be built,' he says. 'No-one in the engineering community wants it.'[16] Does Peter really want to spend precious time working on something that will, historically, be no more than a castle in the air?

Best they continue their honeymoon, then young Peter can return to Sydney, working on public buildings that he would otherwise never get a chance to work on in a small private practice.

'[Ideally Peter can progress],' Libby writes, 'with quite rapid rises, and extremely good big work to do, with little problem of fussy little clients and builders. Then later in Utzon fashion, to step out having had greater experience than he would have had struggling as a young experimenting architect on his own.'[17]

Very well then. Mr Utzon accepts the decision, and must get back to work.

Yuzo, could you please show Mr Hall our model for the Minor Hall interior?

Yuzo indeed proudly shows the Australian, and is gratified at Hall's positive comments on the curved profiles of the breaking waves for the interior's plywood acoustic ceiling.

Oh, the sheer glory of it!

•

An indomitable man, Joe Cahill is uncharacteristically ashen-faced during this Labor caucus at Parliament House, and even pauses mid-meeting, wincing in pain and admitting, 'My stomach is playing up.'

But it looks like more than a stomach ache to his colleagues, who *insist* that he go to Sydney Hospital right next door to be checked out.

'No,' he replies gruffly, 'it's nearly over and I'll stay on.'[18]

The meeting continues until Cahill, now white as his dear Taj Cahill, keels over, groaning in pain. Aides help him back to his office where he begins to gurgle – *get a doctor!* – and vomit.

For the first time in years, the decision is taken out of his hands.

The Assistant Superintendent of Sydney Hospital, Dr M. Mishkel rushes over and only has to take one look before he – *get the Premier's car immediately!* – insists Cahill be rushed to hospital.

Still Joe Cahill is not too worried, merely saying, as he gets in the car, ushered by his son Tom, who has rushed to his father's side, 'I think my stomach has caught up with me.'[19]

Alas, no. Examination reveals that the Premier has actually had a couple of heart attacks and will need to stay in hospital, or have bed rest, for at least a couple of weeks before getting back to work.

If only. The Premier continues to sink fast.

And Cahill knows there is some chance – though he still has hope in the power of prayer – that he will soon meet the good Lord he has passionately and devoutly believed in all his life.

At such a time, he wants two fundamental things. The presence of his family – including his daughter the nun, Sister Gemma, who has rushed from the convent to be by his side – provides the first of those things. To simply be with them, his dearly beloved.

But there is also his legacy, the things from his life's work that will outlive him. Of these, there is one thing that stands out in particular.

And yes, Joe, the Minister for Public Works Norm Ryan is here now, the only Cabinet Minister summoned and allowed to the bedside.

'Take care of my baby,'[20] the ailing politician just manages to get out, through what sounds suspiciously like the beginnings of a death rattle.

Ryan, devastated at the vision of his fearless leader brought so low, and deeply moved, promises to do exactly that, that he will keep the Opera House on track come hell or high water, and is ushered out the door.

All of the family stay hovering at Joe's bedside, praying, as their beloved's condition continues to deteriorate through that darkest of nights and all the next day and night, his life hanging by a thread until, the following morning, he has another heart attack.

'He suddenly seemed to realise,' Dr Mishkel would recount, 'he was going to die.'[21]

Which means there is something that must be said.

'I want to thank everyone in the hospital,' he rasps out, Esmey weeping beside him. 'They have done a wonderful job.'[22]

They are the last words he speaks, as his parish priest delivers the last rites and ... This humble son of Sydney breathes with ever more laboured gasps, with his family all around him, 200 yards from where he first entered public life as a union activist, and no more than a hundred yards from the parliament where he has made his fame, before ... with one last gasp ... he is gone.

The news breaks in Parliament House only a short time later when Acting Premier Mr Bob Heffron is handed a slip of paper and then interrupts proceedings to announce, in faltering voice, 'It is with deep regret that I have to announce to the House the sad loss the State has sustained in the passing of the Premier ... It has been agreed that the House adjourn immediately ...'[23]

Members on both sides of the Speaker openly weep at the news that this giant of the House for the last 35 years is no more. In Canberra a short time later the Prime Minister Robert Menzies addresses the House of Representatives, announcing the tragic news and noting: 'Although he was strongly attached to his party and never unwilling to break a lance in the political lists, he died holding the respect and, I think, the affection of everybody in this place. I make only those few remarks. It is difficult to say very much. I have been shocked by the news; so have we all.'[24]

Menzies orders that all the flags on all Commonwealth buildings in both Canberra and New South Wales are to be flown at half-mast both on this day and the day of the funeral.

Much of the public commentary focuses on Cahill's major achievements, with one universal theme.

Charles Moses speaks for many when he says: 'If future citizens sought a memorial to Mr Cahill, they would see it in the Sydney Opera House ... Those of us who have been members of the Opera House Committee from the beginning know well that without the determination and drive of the late Premier the Opera House would not have reached the drawing-board stage.'[25]

The Lord Mayor Harry Jensen asserts that naming the Opera House after him would be the right thing, and for very good reason: 'It would be very fitting, and a wonderful thing to link Mr. Cahill's name with the Opera House because I regard him as its founder. If the Opera House committee decides on another name the main auditorium could be named after Mr. Cahill.'[26]

Jørn Utzon would be happy with that, later noting his own grief at the Premier's death, and observing him as 'a man ahead of his time',[27] which had been precisely what was needed for a building so far ahead of its own time.

And so to the last leg of Joe Cahill's extraordinary life, starting with lying in state at St Mary's Cathedral, where for all day and into the night of 23 October, a continuous procession of an estimated 50,000 Sydneysiders from every walk of life file before the closed casket at the foot of the sanctuary steps, flanked by six flickering candles – the marble altar behind draped with crape – to bow their heads and pay their respects, while two uniformed policemen stand to rigid attention to maintain constant vigil. The mourners include the newly sworn in Premier Bob Heffron, who leads his entire Cabinet to the cathedral to kneel beside the casket – no easy matter for the nigh-on 70-year-old new Premier – and pray. And of course, Mrs Esmey Cahill, flanked by her three sons and two daughters, also comes to attend the first of three masses on the day – each attended by the capacity congregation of 4000 – to weep and pray.

For his final journey from the cathedral to Rookwood Cemetery on 24 October 1959, the crowd outside St Mary's spills into Hyde Park, even as some 300,000 people line the streets all along the route.

As the hearse passes by, men remove their hats and many Sydneysiders weep. Those who cannot see it directly, see it on the ABC News bulletin on television that evening, including a vision of Esmey Cahill at the graveside, weeping and clasping a string of white pearl rosary beads, leaning on her son Tom for strength, as two gravediggers in white dungarees lower the casket, and the heavens themselves now weep as the sun has faded and the clouds of grief have formed.

(Exeunt, Joe Cahill. The stage is bare, as the curtain falls.)

Late 1959, London, the reason things are not going to plan?

Because there *is* no damn plan!

Ronald Jenkins is a solid-gold genius engineer, noted for his extraordinary mathematical ability, his practicality and perseverance.

He's heard of weekends, but never quite liked the sound of them.

But never in all his born days has he worked on a project like this, where he has been asked, essentially, to make a dream . . . come true. And not just come true, but stand up straight and stay standing for years to come. A shy perfectionist who is only truly comfortable when in the deepest and darkest part of a thick forest of numbers – where few others dare to tread and he is the only one with a candle – for the *life* of him he cannot work this one out.

The challenge is to come up with the precise geometrical shapes and the right mix of materials that come together to look like Utzon's sails, capable of withstanding the pressures of their own weight, the extremes of wind pressure, the infinite needs of the networks of rooms and theatres held within. *And*, it has to be buildable and cost-efficient, ideally having enough geometric repetition that it could be built from prefabricated parts.

And so Jenkins adds ever more structural tweaks and adjustments to the parabolic shell design – the latest being a second concrete 'skin', so the proposed roof now consists of two layers of reinforced concrete 15 to 20 centimetres thick and 1.2 metres apart. True, the first run of numbers through the computer doesn't return the desired result, but Jenkins is sure he can make it work, and insists as much to Jørn, who encourages him in return: we have to *make* it possible.

When, sometimes, the friction between Jenkins and Utzon heats up – when engineering needs impinge on architecture, or vice versa – it is usually Ove Arup who works as a coolant. Keep going, Ronald, we will get there.

Ove need not use the same approach to Utzon, whose very nature is to remain a lone wolf happily hunting for the next solution. If anything, Arup must caution Utzon the other way – to settle on *a* solution.

Utzon and Arup, for all their similarities, are liable to bend and lean in opposite directions from time to time. But put side by side, they lean into each other, and stand stronger because of it.

Don't give up! they exhort all.

'It is like when you climb Everest,' Ove tells those who ask him when the shells will be ready. 'You get a glimpse of Everest, and then it disappears. For a long time, all you see are the rows of hills in your way, and you can't imagine that you will ever get there. And then, suddenly, you see Everest again, sparkling in the sunshine.'[28]

For all that . . . just quietly, Arup is shocked at how hard the whole thing is.

In over 30 years of engineering he has himself never come across a project so complex, with so many intractable problems, so many fields of inquiry into possible solutions that prove to be barren.

'I know it is architecturally brilliant and very beautiful, no doubt about that,' he says on one occasion to a pod of architects in the Hellebaek office, his face deeply creased in intense thought. 'But it is a wrong shape structurally. It's damn difficult to make it work.'[29]

Earnestly, they look for a light laugh, a slight smirk, or even just a twinkle in his eyes . . . but Arup is as stone-faced as an Easter Island statue.

He's *serious*.

•

The shells are but one source of grief for Ronald Jenkins.

He is preoccupied with the Stage I building contract, which now appears as though it will drag on well beyond the estimated finish date, March 1961.

Yes, the Opera House is already turning into a sprawling mess of a project, and despite the insistence from pencil-pushers and politicians on keeping a tight schedule and budget, the design side can't help but note that the cause of most of their troubles is that very insistence. Rush over reason. Never mind the logistics or complexity of the feat, we just need it to *look* like we're making progress.

On top of this, Utzon is in Denmark, Jenkins is in London, the Committee is scattered around Sydney, the builders are at the bottom of ever collapsing holes that will likely prove insufficient for the final product, emblematic of the collapsing hole into which the entire project always threatens to fall.

And for all that, things remain busy, as the *Herald*'s Gavin Souter will attest to his readers upon being given a tour of the site, taking down notes as he goes to record some of the more interesting figures:

> Civil & Civic contractors must move 37,000 cubic yards of excavation, including 11,000 cubic yards of rock; sink . . . 500 separate piers in all . . . and pour 120,000 cubic yards of concrete foundations (about ten times as much concrete as contained in the average city building of 12 storeys.)
>
> You won't be able to see Bennelong Point at all; there'll be about five and a half acres of building, and it will extend over the harbour on both sides of the Point. It will look as if it's floating on the harbour.[30]

Exactly as Utzon had planned.

Souter looks out to see three seagulls 'riding in the spring sunshine' about 50 feet away.

'Their folded wings might almost have been made of salt-glazed tiles.'[31]

Late February 1960, Bondi, little big boy

Oh the joys of being a big boy now. He has just turned eight and can do things all by himself.

The wee lad kisses his mother goodbye just before 8.30 am at their Bondi flat, and with his Globite school case in hand – the one marked with his name, G. Thorne, in gold lettering just above the handles – walks the 300 yards down to the grocer's on the corner of Wellington and O'Brien streets, where he leaves the case out on the footpath before heading inside. Always it is the same routine.

'I'll have the same today, Mister,' he says to the proprietor, Michael Mallouk, who hands over a packet of chips for the lad's play-lunch at Scots College Junior School at Bellevue Hill. Sometimes they chat a little before Graeme goes outside to sit patiently on his Globite until a Scots mother, Phyllis Smith, passes by in her station wagon with her own two lads to pick him up and drop them all off at school. It is a pleasant routine, enjoyed by all, played out in a sunny place where the closest thing to darkness is the lightly dappled light beneath the gum trees.

Early 1960, Hellebaek, concerted convertibility

It is the smallest of Jørn's design jobs at the moment, but still a very important one – on his own home. These days so many engineers and consultants from around the world are making their way to his humble home in the woods that he adds a couple of guest bedrooms either side of the back courtyard. Their frequent guests include Professor Walter Unruh of Berlin, his stage technique consultant.

Unruh is a gentle and calm 60-year-old of international repute after decades of working on stages around the world, including the great Metropolitan Opera House in New York. He is advising Jørn on his design of cutting-edge stage machinery for the Major Hall, which is to do far more than any run-of-the-mill stage machinery. For Utzon is not designing a standard multipurpose hall – in which the acoustics or sightlines for secondary functions, like opera, inevitably suffer in the service of the main function of symphony – no, Jørn is pioneering a fully convertible hall that can be transformed from one day to the next with no compromise in quality. To achieve full convertibility, he needs his stage machinery to push the edge of what many believe possible – it needs to do more than just move sets, it must move and remove stages, seats, acoustic ceilings, and more.

When Jørn presents his developing designs and seating layouts to the

Committee, they approve the plans with congratulations on achieving 'such wide variety of uses for the Major Hall'.[32]

22 March 1960, NSW Parliament House, I'm not askin' – I'm tellin'

It is a tough figure to seek parliamentary approval for, but it simply has to be done. In the course of introducing a bill to pay ongoing construction costs at the Opera House, Premier Bob Heffron notes the likely final bill will be ... ... £4,880,000.

A stirring in the House. Interjections. Cat-calls from the backbench of the Opposition.

The Leader of the Opposition, Mr Robin Askin, insists a better estimate would be '10 million pounds'.[33]

Order! *Order!*

But Askin will not be easily ordered around by anyone, noting archly, 'The original cost estimate was three and a half million.'[34]

Make no mistake, Mr Askin notes, the Opposition still supports the Opera House projects – and despite his claim of a year ago that 'the time for controversy is over, it now remains only for us to work together in a spirit of goodwill to raise the necessary finance',[35] which is proving short lived – he roundly condemns the government for their bungled management of costs, coming to the Legislative Assembly after the fact to get approval for funding already spent.

'Treating Parliament like a rubber stamp – almost with contempt,'[36] he charges.

It is unimaginable!

Well, Premier Heffron is having none of it and roundly condemns Mr Askin's estimate as 'ludicrous and absurd'.[37]

The Kiwi-born Heffron is a devout man, though no longer quite in a religious sense. Once an ideological Roman Catholic, his true focus now is socialism, having risen to political power through the union movement in the 1930s, a close ally of the late Joe Cahill.

But unlike his predecessor, Heffron has no particular passion for the Opera House, and makes no particular bones about it. Everyone knows the whole thing had been Old Smoothie's dream.

Still, he will do his best to see it through.

By the following month, the Heffron government is able to pass the legislation it seeks, the *Sydney Opera House Act 1960*, which retrospectively authorises funds for the construction of the Opera House 'at a cost of £4,880,000, such figure not to be exceeded by more than 10 per cent',[38] while also enshrining in law the Minister for Public Works as the constructing authority – effectively, the client – for the project. For practical reasons, the Executive Committee remains the sole body in charge of *representing* the client; continuing to run the day-to-day operations and communications, and retaining authority over approving designs, contracts, costs and payments.

And on that note, Jørn Utzon contacts the Committee about a contract for his cutting-edge stage machinery for the Major Hall. It is the same request Arup had made for the Stage I building contract – there are, 'only a few firms in the world competent to do the work and . . . therefore only such firms nominated by me should be invited to tender'.[39]

Professor Harry Ashworth is typically supportive and Stan Haviland is happy to flout governmental process if the experts advise it. (All standard public project contracts go to tender; but this is no standard public project.)

Jørn is pleased to hear it.

And in terms of getting his way on things, it doesn't hurt that the likes of Professor Ashworth, Stan Haviland and Charles Moses are extremely busy on many other things. Like everyone on the Executive Committee, which has by now expanded to some 20 bureaucrats and interest group representatives, they are unpaid for the work and largely occupied with their full-time professions, and can only oversee the enormously complex, unprecedented design work with whatever hours they can squeeze in. Under such circumstances, saying 'yes' to the architects and engineers, and moving on, makes more sense than losing time making a fuss and saying 'no', as the latter will involve endless correspondence, long meetings and a very annoyed design team – not to mention more costs. (Still, one member – the Government Architect Ted Farmer – has to bite his tongue, his bow tie positively quivering. This is indeed not the way standard government jobs are run. This is all so . . . casual, and to his eyes the Committee seems more prone to bowing to Utzon in reverence rather than overseeing his work with care. On the other hand, his boss Minister Ryan is not asking for his opinion so he decides it really is better to mind his p's and q's for now, and s.h.u.t. u.p.)

•

On another front, Jørn Utzon is not pleased at all.

The architect had had high hopes for Balslevs, the Danish firm contracted to work on the electrical engineering for the stage as well as the stage machinery, only to find their work 'amateurish'[40] and 'unusable',[41] and is so strong in his expression of that view that they resign. (And they are happy to go, as they had formally written to Ove Arup eight months earlier complaining of Utzon's informal method of conducting the work.)

Good riddance. Utzon decides to do it himself and quickly assembles his own team to put together tender documents for the stage machinery's electricals.

It is a tiny piece of burly in all the hurly-burly of design and construction, barely noticed at the time.

1 June 1960, Gunnedah, the ball falls, the ball begins

Today is the day for the tenth draw of the Opera House Lottery, and the press is here in force to see it.

With a pull of the lever, the large barrel starts to turn and 100,000 balls begin to whirl around inside, to jostle, jar and jive, like corn kernels in a hot pot. Each one bears the fate of a family upon it, the question being, which one will emerge first? Ball 3932 bounces with the best of them before the rotation is halted.

An official plucks out the winning ball. The fate of one family is now sealed.

•

Up in Gunnedah an hour later, soft goods salesman Bazil Thorne is talking to buyers in a local store, when – to his amazement – he is told someone from Sydney's *Daily Telegraph* is on the phone wishing to speak to him.

What could this be about?

Mr Thorne? You have won first prize in the Opera House Lottery!

'You're kidding!'[42]

And he first thinks they are. But once the reporter gives him the number of the ticket he has in his wallet – correct – he knows it's true . . . cue, the hullabaloo. Everything becomes a blur as the word spreads, people crowd around, pump his hand, slap his back and even ask for his autograph. What he most wants now is to get back to Sydney, to his wife, Freda, and his wee children, eight-year-old Graeme and three-year-old Belinda. Calls are made and he is soon on the 1 pm flight back to Sydney.

'I believe in the saying "charity begins at home" and I intend to make this my policy,'[43] he tells the gathered press pack at Sydney Airport, before catching a taxi home to the family's humble flat in Bondi.

As ever, the papers cover the win extensively, noting among other things that the newly rich 'Mr Thorne lives with his wife and two children, Graeme 8 and Belinda 3, in a flat in Edward Street.'[44]

Early evening, 14 June 1960, 79 Edward Street, Bondi, a mysterious caller

'Muu-uuum! Someone at the dooo-ooor,' the young boy yells in that slightly sing-song voice that is the mark of the child well raised and well loved, eager for his mother to resolve the knocking that is interrupting his playtime.

Upon young Graeme's call, Freda Thorne walks down the corridor, untying her floral pinny as she goes. She opens the door to find a thickset stranger standing there, asking in heavily accented English if there is a Mr Bognor living at this address?

'No, I know no-one of that name,' Mrs Thorne replies pleasantly. 'But, we have only recently moved to the flat and the previous tenant was a man by the name of Mr. Bailey. Could that be the person you want?'[45] Freda asks, hospitably.

'No,' the stranger replies with an unsettling gruffness, telling her he is a private detective, before consulting a small notebook.

'Is the telephone number here 30 7113?'[46]

Freda flinches. This is odd?

How does this fellow have the number? They have applied for a telephone and have just been told this will be their number, but it is not yet in the telephone directory.

'How did you get that number?'

'We have ways and means,' the stranger replies.

'That happens to *be* my number,' Freda warily affirms, 'but we haven't got the telephone connected yet.'

'I am a private inquiry agent and this is a husband-and-wife affair.'[47]

Well, perhaps inquire with Mrs Lord, who lives upstairs and has been here much longer.

The stranger grunts, and turns on his heel.

EIGHT

PODIUM FINISH

*The start was made in the context of the classical construction
disaster scenario – a well-meaning but dispersed, uncoordinated
and non-professional client, a brilliant, if wilful architect, no cost
plans or limits, no drawings and above all a scheme which was
possibly buildable. Out of these ashes arose the Sydney Opera
House by sheer chance.*[1]

Jack Zunz, principal structural engineer for Sydney
Opera House from September 1961

7 July 1960, Bondi, halcyon days

It has been a wild few weeks for Freda Thorne, what with the windfall
from the Opera House Lottery, the attention from the press, the excited
calls from friends and family. Through it all, first and foremost, Mrs
Thorne is thinking of her children, as she is determined to make sure their
lives remain as stable and regular as they were before this all happened.

So today is no different from any other day. Before heading off to
school, young Graeme needs help tying his shoelaces and his school tie.
She packs his lunch, including his daily Granny Smith apple with the
perfectly peeled back spiral of skin that he can pull off, and kisses him
goodbye as he heads off to school all spick and span in his Scots College
blazer and cap, before she sets about getting her toddler, Belinda, her
breakfast. Things are always a little more frantic when Bazil is away on
business, but there is so much to be thankful for, she would not dream
of complaining.

•

Young Graeme is trotting cheerily down Wellington Street to Mr
Mallouk's shop to buy his morning packet of chippies before waiting
for Mrs Smith to pick him up out the front.

He is about to cross the road at the Francis Street intersection but
pauses when he sees it blocked by a blue car with the passenger door

open. There is a man standing near it with sallow skin, a greasy grin and a funny way of speaking.

'Hello,' the stranger says, 'I am to take you to school.'

'Why?' Graeme asks, a slight tremble in his voice. 'Where is Mrs Smith?'

'I've been sent to pick you up to take you to Scots, because the lady who normally picks you up is sick.'[2]

Disappointed and a little confused, but raised to trust and obey what adults tell him, Graeme climbs inside the car and sits next to the stranger, his little eyes only just peering above the dashboard.

•

Some 10 minutes later, Phyllis Smith is with her two boys in her Holden station wagon when she pulls up outside the Mr Mallouk's grocer on the corner of Wellington and O'Brien streets in Bondi.

Not only is Graeme not there, but neither is his Globite school case on the footpath. It isn't the first time Graeme hasn't been where he should be for pickup time, but whenever he goes into the store the little lad is sure to leave his Globite on the footpath. But today, no Graeme, no Globite.

She sends her eight-year-old son in to get him, only for him to come back to the car . . .

He's not in there, Mum.

Strange.

With some urgency – they'll be late for school – she drives to Edward Street and goes in to see her friend Freda Thorne. Is Graeme here?

Why no. He left 30 minutes ago.

How very . . . odd. And a little alarming. It is so unlike Graeme to be anything other than reliable. Still, surely there must be a logical explanation – and he simply must have got to school another way. Telling Freda not to worry, as she will sort it out, Phyllis and her boys head off to Scots together to, no doubt, quickly get to the bottom of it and locate the sweet little lad . . .

It will be fine, Freda. I'll give you a call, no doubt in 20 minutes or so.

•

It is all a bit odd. Little Graeme knows the way to Scots and asks the stranger why they are going the wrong way.

Mrs Smith never takes me through Centennial Park on the way to school!

'We are going to pick up some other boys,'[3] says the stranger.

Which also seems odd, because what boys live in the park? And now they are going even further into it, and he has stopped the car at a very isolated spot.

Mister . . . ?

But the man doesn't speak, and after pulling something out of a small travel bag he'd had on the back seat, there is a sudden sweet but chemical smell in the car, as the stranger holds a rag in his right hand and looks at Graeme with sudden intent.

Mister . . . ?

•

What is going on?

There is no sign of Graeme at Scots! Not even when the headmaster calls a full-school assembly and asks who has seen Graeme Thorne. They all know who he is – after the Opera House Lottery win, he had been the talk and envy of the school – but not a single hand goes up.

Phyllis Smith goes straight back to the Thornes' in Bondi.

Barely able to stand still, and struggling to put sentences together, Freda Thorne calls the police.

•

Sergeant Larry O'Shea of the Bondi police has only just arrived at the Thorne home, to settle down the crying woman and get to the bottom of this, when the phone rings. It is 9.47 am. Mrs Thorne snatches up the receiver.

'Hello . . . ?'

'Is your husband there?' comes a heavily accented voice.

'What do you want him for?' asks Mrs Thorne tentatively.

'I have your son . . .'[4]

Mrs Thorne, just managing to hold things together, hands the phone to Sergeant O'Shea, who identifies himself to the caller as her husband.

'I have got your boy,' the voice repeats, a little more relaxed now that he is talking to the man of the house. 'I want £25,000 before five o'clock this afternoon.'[5]

'Where would I get money like that?' O'Shea replies, as yet unaware of the Thornes' £100,000 win.

'You have plenty of time before five o'clock,' the caller says, though pausing, realising that anyone who does not know of the big win, is not

Mr Thorne at all, and probably the *police*. 'I am not fooling. If I don't get the money, I will feed him to the sharks.'[6]

'How will we contact you?'

'I will . . . call back at 5 pm.'[7]

The phone goes dead.

As unbelievable as it seems, Graeme Thorne has been *kidnapped*.

•

From a telephone booth on the corner of Spit Road and Medusa Street, just to the south of Mosman's Spit Bridge, the thickset European man walks back to his Ford, glancing nervously at the boot, whence comes a regular thumping. Back in Centennial Park it had been a relatively easy matter to hold the chloroform-soaked rag to the eight-year-old till he was unconscious, bind his hands and feet and gag him, before wrapping him in a blue tartan picnic blanket and then putting him in the boot and shutting it – but clearly, the boy has now awoken.[8]

Winter 1960, Bennelong Point, sodden sod sods it

The seasons change, the drilling goes on, around the clock. The only way the drillers know it is the weekend is because their pay doubles. And with that kind of money and work on offer it is a wonderful thing that, even though they were meant to knock off last November, it looks as if – thanks to the unpredictable bedrock – they're only warming up. Stick with this, Bluey, and we'll all be farting through silk by June!

And so the drillers drill, sinking bores for the piers by pounding sandstone and rocks into a rubbly mush then pumping all the muddy refuse onto the ground next to the rigs, turning Bennelong Point into a ghastly mud-bath, a six-inch deep sea of viscous brown sludge. For look now as Mr Hon Phang, a 22-year-old Malaysian engineering intern, arrives for his first day on site, scarcely believing he has scored such a prestigious job while still studying for his degree here in Australia. Clipboard in hand, hard hat on head, he trots across the muddy site, weaving between steel rods and the rigs, his brand-new gumboots squelching and belching muddy bubbles. He's off to check a newly poured pylon on the western side of the site when . . . with a deep slurp of mud, he disappears, swallowed whole.

Honestly, Bennelong Point doesn't even burp!

One of the engineers who had seen the disappearing act runs over, yelling for others to come.

He went down around here! 'Round here somewhere!

They scan the sea of muck looking for a clue.

Suddenly, one of the men jumps in fright when a hard hat pops up to the mud's surface right at his feet, like a cork in salt water. The hard hat is swiftly followed by the unrecognisable but clearly startled form of Mr Hon Phang, who is writhing about like a confused worm emerging from his earthy hole in a downpour.

He spits and splutters and swears in Malay as he grabs hold of the invisible yet solid edge of the mud-filled hole into which he had fallen.

With a mighty groan he pulls himself up and out, pounds of mud clinging to his clothes.

Without a word, he stalks past the gathered engineers and labourers and away from Bennelong Point, sloughing off his mud-bath as he goes, never to be seen again.

Meliwatnya! Sod this!

•

It has been a tough day for the thickset European man.

So much drama, so many scares, including when the furniture removalist had arrived at the time that a distinct if muffled banging could be heard coming from the garage. Mercifully the removalist had obeyed instructions to take everything in the house but steer clear of the garage, and the banging had stopped soon enough in any case.

Now that the twilight hour has set in and all is quiet, it is time to check on the lad. He opens the boot and, tremulously, he reaches out his hand.

It is every bit as bad as he had feared.

•

Bazil Thorne has just landed at Sydney Airport on his return from a quick business trip to Kempsey and is walking through the terminal when he hears his name being called over the speakers. Winning the lottery has been wonderful news, but Mr Thorne is growing a little tired of all the extra attention it brings him.

He is required urgently at the inquiry desk. A burly policeman awaits.

Oh God, no, please don't say it!

An accident?

'No . . . Your boy is missing from school, he never got to school this morning.'[9]

Bazil Thorne rushes home, to be told even worse news. Someone has rung, demanding a ransom. They have got Graeme!

The rest of the day is a blur of tears, police interviews, visitors and intrusive reporters. Mercifully, friends come to take care of their toddler, Belinda, and a doctor comes to give Freda a sedative, after she has been, according to a family friend, 'sobbing her heart out'.[10]

•

Meanwhile, all police leave across the state is cancelled, and platoons of men and women in blue scour every nook and cranny, every highway and byway, every back alley of every den of ne'er-do-wells, looking for the tiniest sign of the tiny boy. All over Bondi, they go door to door, asking if anyone had seen anything, showing a photo of the smiling lad, and talking of his usual routine. Known criminal haunts in the city and suburbs are raided, and informants in the underworld consulted.

Most of the hardened criminals are offended at the very suggestion they might have anything to do with kidnapping an eight-year-old.

They launch vicious assaults, commit brutal murders, and run illegal prostitution and gambling dens, certainly. But *kidnap* a *child*?

The notorious Kate Leigh, one of the two key figures in Sydney's 'Razor Gang War', is happy to go on the record about her feelings for the kidnappers: 'I've got one of the biggest butcher's knives in Sydney and it would give me the greatest pleasure to use it on the mongrels. I hope I can hear something that will put me on their trail. By the time I finish with them they will make a good meal for the dogs' home.'[11]

At a packed press conference held at Bondi Police Station just after darkness falls, Bazil Thorne makes a public appeal in a croaky, shaky voice.

'All I can say to the person who has got my son, if he's got children of his own, for God's sake, send him back in one piece.'[12]

He buries his face in his hands, unable to say more.

•

At 9.47 pm that evening – 12 hours after the first call by the kidnapper – the phone rings in the Thorne household. Detective Paull of the Bondi Police Station snatches it up.

A male voice says, 'Is that Mr Thorne?'

'Yes.'

'Have you got the money?'

'Yes,' replies Paull.

'Put it in two paper bags,'[13] says the caller.

'Can you just wait a minute?' asks Paull. 'I need to write down these instructions so as not to make a mistake.'[14]

Paull scrambles to find a pen and paper, something to write it all down, to take it all in, if he can just get a . . .

But it's too late.

The line is dead.

•

The search goes on into the night, the police calling it a day at 2 am.

Reports splash the newspaper the next morning – taking up five full pages in *The Daily Telegraph*.

KIDNAPPED BOY

£25,000 RANSOM BID

A man yesterday telephoned the home of a boy kidnapped at Bondi and demanded £25,000 ransom . . . This is the first kidnapping of a child for ransom ever recorded in Australia.[15]

Meanwhile, churches throughout the state offer prayers to the heavens above for Graeme to be found alive, and . . . as to the Opera House Lottery itself, from now on those buying tickets are able to tick a box saying 'Not For Publication', enabling their names to remain secret, should they win.

For much of the population, it feels like the end of the age of innocence on Australian shores.

•

While the rest of Sydney is talking of the shattering news and wondering what the world has come to, a young bloke by the name of Cecil Denmeade turns up at Bondi Police Station with his fiancée Dorothy Warren, and they both affirm to have seen something suspicious the day before, just near where the Thornes are reported to live. It was a swarthy-looking gentleman standing next to a '1955 Ford Customline sedan, iridescent blue in colour, with a distinctive silver chrome strip along each side'.[16]

•

Just a little after midday on this same day, Joe Bell, a 60-year-old bloke from the northern beachside suburb of Collaroy, is walking along that bushy esplanade known as the Wakehurst Parkway looking for refundable bottles to put in the hessian bag he drags with him, when he sees something 10 yards from the road.

Walking over, he picks it up. It looks like a child's school case!

'It had a few scratches on it,' he will recount, 'as if it had been thrown from a car.'[17]

And look here, there is a name above the handles, in gold lettering: '*G. Thorne*'.

Hang on ... ? Isn't that the name of the kid that has gone missing?

'I reckon it is the first decent clue the police have got,' Mr Bell tells the press later that night after he'd taken detectives to the spot he'd found the case. 'And I hope it's a big help in finding the kiddie.'[18]

That remains to be seen, as the Globite case is rushed to the Scientific Bureau laboratories at CIB headquarters for minute examination, including dusting for fingerprints.

•

A swarm of yellow lights bob and weave through the inky night, luminescent butterflies in the blackness. They are the battery-powered torches held by the locals of Wakehurst Parkway where the case was found, all of them banding together to find clues.

In Bondi, meanwhile, Bazil Thorne comes out of his home and, with the red eyes of a man who has been alternately crying and staring at the ceiling in the vain hope of getting some sleep, addresses the press.

'It gives me new heart,' he exclaims. 'It is not knowing anything that is terrible. Somehow the finding of the case ... seems to me ... a sign that the position may be improving. If the person who has him would only let me know that he is all right it wouldn't be so bad. He said he would contact us again. He has not done so. I would be grateful if he rang up. He would not have to discuss money or let us know when we would have Graeme back or anything like that. But just let us know he is all right.'

Pausing, he comes back with a refrain, almost as if he is trying to convince himself.

'I know Graeme is alive. I could not imagine anyone being low enough to harm him. He is a wonderful little boy, good humoured and intelligent and kind. But he is a sentimental boy and very devoted to his mother and his family. I'm sure he must miss his family terribly, particularly at night. It is a nightmare to think of him being somewhere trying to speak to us and wanting us, and we cannot help him.'

Will you go and see the school case tonight?

Bazil shakes his head.

'I understand there is no question that it is my son's, and I have to be near the telephone in case that man rings. I can only pray that he will.'[19]

In preparation for that call, Mr Thorne now has £25,000 on hand, in a briefcase – all of it in £10 notes – guarded by a constable in his home. With one call, he will be on his way. Quietly, to the police, he says, 'Even if we have to pay out the whole 100,000 pounds, we will do so to get our boy back.'[20]

But there is still no call.

•

By 11 am on 11 July, four days since Graeme's kidnapping, much of the rest of the contents of the school case are found nearby the Wakehurst Parkway, about a mile from where the case itself had been found – a Scots College school cap, Graeme's raincoat, a maths textbook and, in a lunchbox, an apple with the skin carefully peeled in a spiral.

Northern Summer 1960, London, getting up to data

Just as Jørn Utzon is a man of his time, so too is the computer – capable of myriad calculations in the blink of an eye – *the* machine of its time, and it is a happy circumstance indeed that the two can come together in the service of a timeless building.

For, as the engineers are finding out, the complexity of the calculations needed to determine the forces that will be acting on Utzon's uniquely shaped concrete shells, is, *ahem*, through the roof. Only computers could hope to do the calculations necessary this side of the millennium, and even then, the task remains huge. The engineers need some of the best in the business to write the programs that see endless spools of one-inch-wide tape punched with eight tracks of holes go in one end, to pass over a bank of photoelectric cells – and come out the other end with the answers.

In London, four young bucks of Arup's – including one long lean Australian by the name of John Nutt, who had been doing his PhD at Manchester University – have been spending long weeks writing their own programs to analyse the forces of each shell, before going down to Northampton Polytechnic, a public research institute in London that happens to have one of the world's best Ferranti Pegasus computers.

Each 'run' – as the lads call the computer's work in running the calculations on a specified dataset – takes about 14 hours, before they must spend further weeks poring over and interpreting the results. It is work as exhausting as it is exacting, analysing every aspect of the roof structure's design as it currently stands.

But the real problem remains: the results keep showing that the roof structure will not stand. At all.

Not even Jenkins' *double* skin design is working. (Sadly, the quip by Australia's foremost prima donna of the opera, Joan Hammond, that Utzon's building looked as though it, 'might fly away in the first strong breeze'[21] will prove as prophetic as those who had said it looked like a 'collapsed circus tent, if they actually build it like that.')[22]

All the dogged Ronald Jenkins and his senior designers can do for the moment is to tweak the weak parts of the roof design then send the young bucks off again to 'run' the latest iteration, hoping they might come back *this* time with a positive result . . .

•

Whoever said 'no news is good news' never had someone they love go missing. Things have gone quiet. Eerily quiet.

It's over a month since little Graeme was taken and there have been no more calls from the kidnapper, no more breakthroughs. The Thornes are starting to despair, to come to the conclusion that . . .

No!

They can't think like that. Graeme *is* alive, he has to be.

16 August 1960, Grandview Grove, Seaforth, hush! – a woven crypt

It is the rite of passage of Australian children in the suburbs. Birds sing, dogs bark, and kids play in the street. It is true that since the kidnapping last month everyone has been just a little more careful, but still the kids of Sydney are largely left to their own devices. See now Phillip Wall, Eric Coughlan Jnr and Andrew McCue, scabby-kneed boys of seven and eight years old, happy as puppies playing in the cubbyhouse they've made in a vacant lot, just over the side fence of Eric's house.

They're playing 'dare', and just as it starts to get dark, young Phillip Wall decides he's brave enough to go over and lift up the lumpy blanket that had turned up in the vacant lot a few weeks ago.

He approaches slowly, the others stand back at a safe distance, knees chattering in excitement.

A fly buzzes by.

His hand shaking, Phillip pulls back a fold of dirty blanket.

Geeeez! It looks like the back of a head! Is that . . . hair? And below it the collar of a shirt?

He screeches and bolts, back to the others.

Knowing they could be in big trouble, they huddle together for a matter of seconds . . . *Are you sure, Phillip? YES!* . . . before running home as fast as their little legs can carry them.

•

It is a good couple of hours before Phillip Wall has thought his way through the whole thing, enough to confide in his older brother Peter what he had seen. Peter immediately goes to see their mother, Lola.

'Phillip says there's a body in the bush.'

Pffft, yeah right.

'Phillip says cross his heart [and hope to die,] there's a body there.'[23]

Get Phillip.

Out of his bath with his jim-jams on, Phillip confirms: 'There's a bundle wrapped up in the bush. There's something like a head in it. I saw a shirt. I did not touch it. It is about my size.'[24]

•

David Wall gets out of his car after a long day and goes inside to find his 11-year-old daughter Diana bursting to tell him a story about the boys having found a dead body on the vacant lot, before his deeply upset wife rushes in with Phillip in tow, indeed telling him a garbled and highly unlikely story about having found a body in a blanket.

'If that's the case,' he says, shaking his head, 'let's go and make sure.'[25]

•

Eric Coughlan Snr – who has heard the same story from Eric Jnr – holds the torch as David Wall kneels and carefully unties one of the blanket's knots to reveal . . . two arms, tied with twine at the wrists, hanging down.

Good Lord!

It is clearly a child, wrapped up snug as a bug in a rug.

But dead.

David Wall gags and reels back.

•

In the small apartment at Edward Street there is a knock on the door.

It's 9.15 pm.

Bazil Thorne snatches the door open – good news, perhaps? – only to see their friend, the Reverend Clive Goodwin, the Rector of St Mark's Church of England, Darling Point, standing there, with a stricken expression on his face.

Oh God, please don't say . . . ?

You haven't . . . ?

They haven't . . . ?

Yes, Bazil, I am desperately sorry to tell you, they have. Three boys found him while playing north of the Spit Bridge, late this afternoon. The police are sure it is Graeme, and he has been dead for weeks.

Bazil Thorne turns pale and wobbles.

Freda Thorne can only just hear the muttered conversation coming from the door but is sure that the tone is entirely different to everything she has heard so far. There is no mistaking what it means. She collapses to the floor in a heap, choking on her own sobs and clutching at the terrible pain in her heart.

August 1960, Hellebaek, model architects

Never has the office at Hellebaek been so busy. And it's not just the podium, the interiors, the technical stage machinery and the soaring roof that occupies their attentions into the wee hours, day after day. It is the knowledge that at much the same time that Professor Ashworth is coming on a visit to inspect the progress of the designs, there will also be many distinguished international architects, who are gathering for a conference of the International Union of Architects in Copenhagen, also dropping by.

'Utzon had a habit of alternative periods of panic and relaxation,' Mikami would recall, 'and naturally the staff at his office were influenced by his mood swings in their work. August 1960 was one of the most traumatic of these periods.'[26]

A large part of the preparations is organising massive models for the interiors of the Major and Minor halls, models big enough for a man to sit inside. Utzon is satisfied with the 'breaking waves' design for the Minor Hall, but needs to refine his concept for the Major Hall's acoustic ceiling.

Yuzo?

This time, instead of heading to the beach for inspiration, they go to the beech forest surrounding Utzon's house, filled with those revered trees that stand well over 15 metres high with large green canopies. In many of those trees the branches grow so wide that the lower tiers inevitably hang down nearly to the ground, forming glorious towering spaces around the trunk 'defined by thousands of delicately coloured leaves fluttering in the breeze'.[27]

This, Yuzo!

Utzon hands his sketches over to the Japanese designer, for him to develop further – 'Yuzo,' he says, 'try to dream up something like this space for the Major Hall ceiling and make a model of it'[28] – before dashing off to join Ashworth on a tour of the great opera houses of Europe, leaving his architects to get on with it.

With that, Yuzo gets going.

'I noticed that most of the branches and twigs formed roughly a triangular pattern,' Mikami will recall. 'So I decided to take up triangles as the main element of the design and arrange them along the vertical radiating planes at equal angles on the plan, similar to what was done in the Minor Hall. They formed zigzag lines in space and were connected to each other to define triangular facets.'[29]

The drawings soon evolve into a small model using thin sticks of balsa wood glued together – he is a quick convert to Jørn's methods – as he works out just how high he can make it, 'in order to secure a large cubic volume and thus achieving a longer reverberation time for concert [sic]'.[30]

Upon Utzon's return, the architect is thrilled with the huge plywood models of the two halls.

Most importantly, when Professor Ashworth arrives at Hellebaek for a four-day visit, and sees the many new models up close – including a 1:60 model of the whole construction – he is quick to see that the interior of the Sydney Opera House will be a thing of true beauty!

In fact, such a thing of beauty, that in his time there, the Professor spends long hours sitting inside the models, gazing at the ceilings, getting a feel for the whole experience of being in such theatres – glorying in it.

Mikami is delighted to personally show him the very twigs and branches of the trees that had been the inspiration for the whole thing!

•

And these tiny twigs, too, are important.

In Sydney, the police have taken fragments of twigs and leaves found on the blanket in which the body of poor Graeme Thorne had been found to Dr Joyce Vickery, a botanist working at the Sydney Botanic Gardens, for analysis – together with samples of shrubs and dirt of that part of Grandview Grove. Under her microscope, she quickly comes to two conclusions.

'We knew the two plants [found on the blanket] were garden plants,' she would recount, 'but they were not present at the site where Graeme Thorne's body was found. Therefore, they must have become attached to the rug somewhere else. In the course of identification, one of my colleagues went out into the Botanic Gardens and brought in a twig of each.'[31]

From now, the police are aware the blanket has spent time on a property that has two kinds of cypress trees, *Chamaecyparis pisifera* and *Cupressus glabra*, and they soon have photos of both.

Further microscopic analysis of the blanket reveals, in the strands of wool, tiny fragments of building material, such as you might find in 'a building, probably a dwelling of high foundation about which was yellowish muddy soil bearing a quantity of pink limestock mortar',[32] three different types of human hair – brown (likely dyed auburn), blonde and grey, the latter of which seems to have been treated with a henna rinse at some point, indicating they belong to a woman. The blanket also contains reddish hairs that are too short and coarse to be human. They are between one and four inches, and fit the characteristics of dog hairs; Pekinese to be precise.

•

Well, this is a bit odd. When the British architect John Carter first visits the Opera House site in September 1960, he is pleased to see how well the foundations and substructure are coming along. But he is more than a little perturbed to hear from one of the building engineers on site that, 'Drawings are arriving from London about a week ahead of construction ... and changes are still being made to the brief.'[33]

Really?

This is, Carter would note, 'not the safest procedure for a conventional building and extremely precarious for a gigantic opera house of unusual design being built on a contract of provisional quantities and schedule of rates'.[34]

And there are other things.

Noting some newly built structures being demolished, he asks why, drawing an amused response from the chatty building engineer.

'The committee has, after protracted debate, at last decided on the size of the stage.'[35]

Seriously? How can the architect put up with this? You're this far advanced in the building, and a committee is deciding on alterations, and altered plans are coming in from London only just in time?

Odd. Very odd. And it seems the people of Sydney are troubled, too, as Carter will later write: 'When the Opera House was discussed, over after-dinner coffee on Sydney verandahs, it was the shells that were talked about: "... they say they can't cope with the wind" ... "is it true they are going to make them in one piece and float them down from Parramatta ... ?"'[36]

When he tries to find the answers to those questions himself, the response comes back: they haven't worked that out yet.

Very odd. He has never come across a major building project with this level of uncertainty and seat-of-its-pants feel about it, and it does not bode well for them being able to get through the whole thing without a major mishap.

30 September 1960, Seaforth, postie on the run

On this sunny day, Detective Sergeant John 'Roy' Coleman returns to Grandview Grove in Seaforth to revisit the Wall family. Despite having a swathe of very specific forensic evidence and a detailed profile of the likely murderer – they've told the public they are looking for a bloke who is around 40, thickset with an accent, driving an iridescent blue 1955 Ford Customline, with a blonde wife and a Pekinese dog, and perhaps a couple of cypress trees in the yard of his brick house with pink mortar – they still have no suspect.

Are there any details, even minor ones, Mr Wall, anything you might remember that you didn't tell us at the time?

In truth, there is nothing fresh.

Disappointed, Detective Coleman is just taking his leave by the front gate and chatting to Mrs Wall when the postie arrives and offers the officer an arresting salutation.

'Did you get a message from my mate, Keith Magor, on the Clontarf run?'

'No,' Coleman replies.

But please, mate, do go on ... ?

'He remembered a new Australian who used to live at number 28 Moore Street, Clontarf. He speaks good English. He fits the description you gave us. He has the blue car, the Pekinese dog and a blonde wife.'[37]

Coleman can barely breathe. He returns to Bondi Police Station and soon establishes that the owner of the house at that address is one Stephen Bradley, a Hungarian immigrant who'd arrived in Australia 10 years before, as István Baranyay. He and his second wife have three children combined from their previous marriages, he is a poker-machine mechanic who ... had already been interviewed at his workplace a fortnight ago, because he was one of thousands of Sydneysiders who owned a Ford Customline like the one described. His alibi for that day had been believed and he'd been excluded as a suspect. His home, however, is yet to be examined.

It takes three days for everything to be in place. On the late afternoon of Monday 3 October 1960, Detective Sergeant Coleman and two of his fellow detectives pull up outside 28 Moore Street, Clontarf.

It is *precisely* as the postman had described. There are the two types of cypress trees, and the garage beneath the house is constructed of bricks held together by . . . pink mortar!

Coleman's heart thumps. His breathing tightens. They knock on the door.

The door swings open and they are . . . greeted by a rather happy-looking urbane fellow, who, clearly bemused at the presence of three detectives on his doorstep, asks can he help them?

If he is the kidnapper, it's a remarkable façade.

Yes, we are looking for Stephen Bradley.

Ah, the man I bought the house from, just a couple of months ago? Mr Bradley has gone. My name is Douglas Palmer. And he shows plenty of identification to prove it.

Could we, uh, have a look at your house, particularly your garage?

Mr Palmer is confused as to what they might want with his garage, but of course the detectives may inspect it. Most certainly.

No sooner has Mr Palmer opened the garage than Detective Sergeant Coleman's breathing again becomes shallow. There is the yellow mud in the corner, which comes from seepage under the house. And, yes, cypress leaves on the garage floor. And there, *right there*, at the end of the garage is a dirt embankment that lies beneath the floorboards. Taking his torch, what does the detective see?

Grains of pink mortar in the dirt. This is the very spot, clearly, that Bradley had stored the body for a while, wrapped in the blanket – which is why it had the yellow mud, the traces of cypress leaves, the pink mortar.

Heading back upstairs, the detectives chat to Mrs Palmer, who mentions in passing that, just a fortnight ago, a vet had knocked on the door, expecting to find the Bradleys, as he had business with them – they were taking their Pekinese dog with them to . . . *England*, and there were certain protocols that had to be observed when taking an animal into the United Kingdom.

The good news is the Pekinese dog.

'Everything,' one of Coleman's fellow detectives would say, 'kept coming back to Bradley, Bradley, Bradley!'[38]

The bad news is the family might be already on their way out of the country. Have the police cracked the case, only to find that the murderer has got away?

Follow-up inquiries confirm that Bradley and his family had left Sydney aboard the *Himalaya* the previous week, and on this day had departed Fremantle heading towards . . . Colombo, as the first port of call.

And not that any more proof is needed, but once Freda Thorne is shown photos of Bradley, her hand flies to her mouth as she identifies the swarthy European man who had knocked on her door and asked her strange questions, in early June.

They have got their man. Now, they just have to *get* their man.

•

In the offices of Ove Arup & Partners on Fitzroy Street, London, Ronald Jenkins and his right-hand man, Hugo Mollman, are worried, as they try to untie a Gordian knot of staggering complexity.

Time and again they point out to Utzon the structural troubles they are facing.

Time and again, on their regular visits to Hellebaek, Utzon the eternal optimist manages to turn them around, encourage them to never give up, with his force of persuasion.

'The co-operation between [Utzon] and us was absolutely marvellous,' one of the Arup engineers, Bob Kelman, will recall, 'he was terrific. And we had a sort of joke that he would suggest the most outrageous things, and one of us would go over to Denmark to try and . . . argue him out of it and we'd all come back saying, "No, it's right. He's got the right idea." It was a case of being brainwashed when you went over there . . . I can remember Ronald Jenkins going over and myself going over and other people going over to talk to him and all coming back with this conviction that we had to try and do what he wanted to do. He was a very persuasive man.'[39]

(For Jørn is in no doubt they will find a way. 'My father,' his son Jan would say, '[as a child] spent a lot of time at the shipyard and saw the magnificent ships on the slipways. He had seen how a small group of people with relatively simple tools could make something big, curved; something that could sail, even. He drew on that for the Opera House, so he wasn't nervous about doing the Opera House. He just knew that he had to find a way of doing it.'[40])

And so Jenkins keeps going, with single-minded focus. His sole respite is to sometimes listen to operas – he is one of the few at Arup's to genuinely enjoy opera and is excited at the idea of being involved in an opera house of this nature.

10 October 1960, Sydney, Uncivil & Civic

The great Australian dictums are crashing head-long into an entirely different approach – Danish perfectionism.

Australia prides itself on the notion that *no problem is so great that it can't be fixed with some fencing wire and elbow grease*, at least in the short term. Why? Because, *she'll be right, mate.* Close enough is good enough, you know, particularly for government work!

But Jørn Utzon doesn't do things like that. He wants things done right, by which he means *perfectly*, and says so with gentle force.

And while Arup's engineers seem to get it . . . the perfection penny hasn't yet dropped for the folks at Civil & Civic.

'It does appear that The Contractor has not yet grasped the full appreciation of the difference in workmanship required between pre-stressed and reinforced concrete [having never worked with pre-stressed concrete before],' writes Arup's man in Sydney. Their original time estimate of 12 months for the complete concourse construction has been rather underestimated . . . 'Consequently, the Contractor and myself are striving for opposite ends: he to complete the structure, at almost any cost within the next 12 months; and myself to guide the construction and pre-stressing. It's a question of "hasten slowly" I think.'[41]

It is true that the original date of completion – Christmas Eve 1960 – is just weeks away, and they haven't even finished Stage I, but, on the other hand, things aren't all bad; the foundations are close to all poured and the concourse beams are getting underway. There is enough optimism that it might be finished by early 1964 that the Sydney Opera House Committee starts to plan ahead for the opening, with Silent Stan Haviland leading the discussion of commissioning a new opera to be written for the occasion, while Charles Moses is insistent it should be a concert, not an opera, reminding the Committee, 'that for most of the year, the main Opera House auditorium will be used by the ABC for concerts'.[42]

•

Detective Sergeants Roy Coleman and Jack Bateman arrive in Colombo and are led down the steps to the dark cell where the Colombo authorities have been holding Bradley, on the cabled request of the Australian authorities – on the suspicion of murder.

The only thing?

This cove just doesn't quite look like what they had been expecting.

'I was prepared for an ogre dripping blood,' Bateman will later recount, 'a man I could loathe on sight. Instead, I met an intelligent, personable, well-spoken man who seemed suave, mild and inoffensive. How could he have done it?'[43]

Well, that is not their problem. He clearly *has* done it, the evidence is overwhelming. Their job, the only one that counts, is to get him back to Australia.

Arrangements for the flight are made, and they get him on the plane, with double cuffs on – his wrists cuffed to each other, and in turn to the safety belt.

9 November 1960, Bennelong Point, Ol' Man River, he just keeps rollin' along

Geez, Bluey, what is this?

Amid the clamouring, hammering and regular shouts and orders in a dozen languages of the busy worksite, there is a sudden pause. Something extraordinary is clearly about to happen, and all the workers can sense it.

Jackhammers stop, the concrete pour ceases and the workers start to gather around a slightly elevated slab of rough concrete, which will have to serve as a stage. For yes, there is an aging but robust black man in a three-piece suit and a fetching black beret stepping up to the makeshift stage – an American, I think, a bloke by the name of Paul Robeson – and they say he is some kind of a singer?

Indeed he is. Robeson is in fact both a very famous singer *and* civil rights leader who has fought the good fight for many decades now, despite at one time being denied his passport and accused of being a communist traitor by white conservatives.

Visiting Sydney as part of a world tour, Robeson has made a special request to be able to 'sing to the workers', and now that he steps up behind the 'broken-down microphone'[44] set up for the occasion, says he would also like to say a few words.

The 250 workers, all bare white muscular torsos and hard hats, take up positions, either standing or sitting on concrete, many types of pipes, or up in the scaffolding that surrounds the spot.

'It is time,' he says in his bass baritone voice, which is surely as deep as Sydney Harbour, 'for peace-loving people to speak out to prevent the warmongers of the world from unleashing a holocaust on humanity. 'And never forget the person in the White House is not always right!'

And now he raises his right hand to cover his ear and starts, his rich, resonant voice rolling out over the workers as they stand around him, transfixed at this first modern performance in the Sydney Opera House, most of them overwhelmed with a sense of great privilege.

The workers stir appreciatively as the opening bars of *Ol' Man River* ring out. This man is singing their language! Robeson goes on, as ever altering a line from the original lyrics at this point to one more respectful of workers.

Just as he also changes the lyrics at this point from some of the original and depressing words with something far more uplifting, with a raised and shaking fist as he sings the word 'fightin''.[45]

Thunderous applause! After another couple of songs, Robeson brings it all to a close, telling the men before him, 'you are working on a project which one day you will be proud of!'[46]

At which point the workers crowd around to give him a higher accolade than a standing ovation with thunderous clapping – which is the much more intimate and appreciative slap on the back, mate, with some even asking him to sign their gloves – before the American must leave, and they all must get back to work.

Among those hugely impressed is one who is not even a worker at all, but a gate-crasher.

A junior pay clerk with the Sydney County Council, just 16 years old, Paul Keating is on his lunch break, and has scurried across from a green double-decker bus that has dropped him at the bottom of George Street to make it just in time.

'He sang the great black spiritual songs that had made him famous and which seemed to come,' Keating will recount, 'not from the bottom of his chest but from the earth underneath him.'[47]

There is no doubt that this, the first performance at the Sydney Opera House, has been a stunning success, not least from the point of view of the singer himself.

'Yesterday,' Robeson tells the press the next day, 'I went down by the Opera House, standing around singing to the workers . . . I could see, you know, we had some differences here and there. But we hummed some songs together . . . These were tough guys and it was a very moving experience.'[48]

8.07 am, 19 November 1960, Kingsford Smith Airport, the one who didn't get away

First off the plane are two stern-faced Sydney detectives with Stephen Bradley between them, all shuffling awkwardly because each of the prisoner's wrists is handcuffed to one of the grim angels of justice.

A gang of press and 200-odd citizens bustle against a wall of police to get a glimpse of the monster.

But this is police business, and Bradley is immediately whisked away to the cells of Central Police Station, where he sits under the watchful eye of two armed detectives before he is taken over the road to Central Court and charged with the murder of Graeme Thorne before being interviewed. (Not for nothing had the detectives escorting Bradley back to Australia instructed him to complete his arrivals form by writing his residential address in Australia as 'care of CIB, Sydney'.[49])

For the most part, Bradley's co-operation with the police is remarkable. He has already confessed to the detectives on the way back that he had in fact committed the crime.

And now he tells all, once again, in a manner remarkable for its candour, even if he does maintain that the boy's actual death was an accident, and he never meant to kill him.

Come the conclusion of the interview, the detectives offer Bradley what they offer all accused persons: a written statement. Most criminals would turn them down cold, but Stephen Bradley is different. He will gladly make a statement, so long as he is allowed to write it himself, thank you very much.

The detectives glance at each other. Odd, but acceptable.

Bradley is given a pen and paper, and so the murderer begins to write.

> I red in the newspaper that Mr. Thorne won the first prise in
> The Operahouse Lottery. So I desided that I would kidnap his
> son. I knew ther adress from the newspaper, and I have got their
> phone number from the telephone exchange. I went to the house
> to see them . . .[50]

The only exception to Bradley's co-operation is when the detectives take him back to 28 Moore Street, Clontarf, where he freezes up.

'I do not want to go into the garage,' he mumbles. 'I don't want to go in. That's where I done it.'[51]

NINE

BACK TO THE DRAWING BOARD

The search for perfection, which Jørn Utzon repeatedly stated as his goal, is no different in principle from his father's yacht designs. Utzon seldom wavered from his conviction that perfection is found in the next solution.[1]

Philip Drew, *The Masterpiece – Jørn Utzon: A Secret Life*

I suppose every Architect is unusual in a sense, but some more than others, and Utzon more than most ... he is certainly unusually gifted, and he is very, very much an Architect, one who masters his architectural media and who is very sensitive to space, form, colour and texture, and to aesthetic logic ... He also has a very good structural sense, and is quick to learn. And he combines a steadfastness of purpose – call it stubbornness if you like – with complete flexibility of mind, by which I mean he is willing to consider any proposal or alternative provided if in his opinion it improves the quality of the scheme, but he will not accept an aesthetically inferior solution if he can help it – he will then rather start all over again and re-open old decisions to try to find a satisfactory answer ... He can cause havoc amongst Engineers who have worked for months on something which is now being improved – but one has to admit it is being improved.[2]

Ove Arup, January 1965

In a century given to architectural sensations and controversy, the most sensational and controversial building ever, anywhere, is the high pointed one on Bennelong Point. While still only half-built, it has already had many seasons: as a glorious vision, as an engineering conundrum, as a political issue, as an economic headache.[3]

Robin Boyd, Australian architect, 18 September 1965

Late 1960 to early 1961, Sydney, high beams

On this hot and sweaty Monday morning, 28 November 1960, the workers from Civil & Civic are just about to pour the first huge concrete beam for the concourse.

A muscular mob mans the mixers and movers that keep the goopy grey concrete flowing down the chutes at either end, all the way along the huge plywood mould, two viscous waves that meet in the middle. The men are a motley crew, some of the Australians as brown, leathery and hairy as the tail of an outback camel, others hailing from all over the United Kingdom. Some of them are those so-called 'new Australians', originating from places like Italy, Malta, Germany and Greece. On Bennelong Point, they're all Sydneysiders, united by their excitement to be building one of the most prestigious projects in the world, and their determination to get this bloody mould filled before lunch!

Like stuffing a cannoli! one of the Sicilians shouts over the sound of the machinery, and the rest of them laugh.

But while the contractors laugh, Arup's man begins to furrow his brow. The northern mixer is not working the way it should, and the concrete all over is 'too stiff',[4] as he will write in his report.

They need a smooth and aesthetically pleasing finish because the underside of the beams will forever be on display in the ceiling of the concourse, the embodiment of Utzon's oft acclaimed goal of having 'the structure express the architecture'.

But they must wait several days to find out if it is up to standard – watching concrete dry has never been quite so nerve-racking – until at last . . .

The workers pull away the formwork like children unwrapping their Christmas presents to see . . .

Oh, Christ!

It may as well be a lump of coal. Arup's man reports back: 'Our worst fears were realised. There was a gaping 3 ft hole beneath the beam, in the *precise* place it really shouldn't be, as well as smaller holes elsewhere and a sizeable area where the concrete hasn't been packed properly.'[5]

Taking that on board, the engineers decide they best hold off pre-stressing the first beam, as they need to see if they can get the second pour right first. A few days later, the second beam has been stripped of formwork, and thankfully it's a vast improvement, as Jørn Utzon has just arrived to inspect.

'I am amazed!'[6] he tells his resident architect, Skipper Nielsen, and the engineers. And he's not joking, as he really is impressed with the sheer size of it. One of the engineers writes back to London to report that Jørn, 'was bubbling over with joy'.[7] But now they brace themselves, for next is the first, far from perfect beam. Over here, Mr Utzon, and let us just tell you what precisely went wrong.

But the Dane is not so upset as they had feared, not even half. If anything, he is thankful for their honesty, 'very sympathetic'[8] to their difficulties, and allays their worry with optimism. Gentlemen, we are in uncharted waters, the only way to go from here is forward!

•

Ronald Jenkins writes to Utzon in late January 1961 with troubling news. The latest iteration of the double skin parabolic roof, the one in development since 1959 ... the one we were sure would work and be completed by April 1961 ... that one, yes, well ...

'It may be that you and Professor Ashworth were under the impression that when we had finished our calculations and the model testing, all that was left was for us to make detailed drawings. Well ... the structure proposed might not be sufficient. Now that we are plotting the stresses and deflections from the model testing we can see that something more has to be done in certain places.'[9]

It is ... troubling, to say the least.

And when major issues remain come March 1961, Jørn becomes worried about the design itself and about the reaction the news may get in Sydney.

Jenkins had already assured Utzon on 21 February 1961: 'I have noted your message to Ove about not spreading any alarm and despondency about the superstructure. In any case I would not do that.'[10]

Meanwhile, Utzon begins to ruminate seriously on the ongoing difficulties with using reinforced concrete shells to build the roof. Is it time, he wonders, to go back to the drawing board?

•

Now look, while it is one thing to have a world-famous cultural venue rising before the world's eyes, it is another to have any culture of note to put in it, and Homer Bigart of the *New York Times* is not too afraid to raise the issue on 19 February 1961, when he gravely advises his readers, 'Mr Utzon's design has been widely praised but doubt persists as to whether Sydney's residents are really ready to take grand opera to their bosoms. This frisky seaport seems to prefer strip tease. Four night clubs in Kings Cross, the local Greenwich Village, feature stripteasers, some imported from the United States. The Lord Mayor of Sydney Henry Frederick Jensen, insists, however, that Australians are marching towards cultural maturity.'[11]

Hopefully.

Ove Arup himself, in British fashion, says the Opera House is 'a civic symbol for a city which seeks to destroy once and for all the suggestion that it is a cultural backwater'.[12]

Yes, a successful Sydney Opera House might go some way to diminishing what some call their 'inferiority complex'[13] and what Australians have begun to call the 'cultural cringe', the belief that the amount of culture most citizens have doubles or triples every time they buy a tub of yoghurt.

29 March 1961, Central Criminal Court, Sydney, shark feed

'Stephen Leslie Bradley, I find you guilty. The sentence of this Court is that you are to be sentenced to penal servitude for life.'[14]

A strangled cry of relief comes from Bazil and Freda Thorne in the gallery and Justice Clancy's gavel comes down hard.

The gallery explodes with jubilant cheers and whistles.

One woman screams, 'Feed him to the sharks.'[15]

Final week of March 1961, Bennelong Point, post-stress beers for the boys

Remember the golden rule, you blokes: stand well clear of the back of those pre-stresser jacks.

The men look blankly at the two unfamiliar machines sitting idle at either end of the massive concrete concourse beam they are about to 'pre-stress'. They've never seen 'jacks' like these. Each one is attached to the thick metal cable that has been threaded through the beam's middle, along its entire length.

The engineer in charge looks stern as he issues a second warning: 'Those jacks may look harmless enough, boys, but they are about to pull so bloody hard on either end of that cable – like mechanical titans in a tug of war – that if the cable or even a single wire in the cable fails, those bastards'll be flinging back at you with the weight of a Sydney ferry behind it. You'll be shot through Sydney Heads like a cannonball with a hole in your middle.'

We read you loud and clear, boss.

Stand clear, and let the dog see the rabbit!

And so the workers of Civil & Civic, having never pre-stressed a block of concrete in their lives, ready themselves, not every man jack

... manning jacks, but certainly plenty of them doing exactly that, while others take readings, and still others observe closely, all care but no responsibility unlike the engineers in their makeshift office, the 'nerve centre'[16] of the operation, who are now the human manifestation of pre-stressed and for good reason.

Easy now ... careful now ... ...

It all happens so quickly.

There is a groan, now a shriek, now ...

SNAP!

With what sounds like a crack of metallic lightning, one of the wires fails under a tension of 46 tons. A 50-foot cable shoots out one end of the beam like the tongue of a steel snake, hissing about and – *get DOWN, youse blokes!* – threatening to decapitate the men as it sends the pre-stressing jack hurtling behind and over the side of the embankment.

Thankfully, the workers really *were* listening, and they have heeded the engineer's warning. The cable and the jack misses them all, and there are no mangled human frames flying through the sky, bound for Botany Bay. But there could have been, and it's not lost on the men. They stand, slack-jawed and wide-eyed at their posts. They've all just seen their own mortality.

The work continues without a hiccup from there, and a week later, on 4 April 1961, one of Arup's men happily reports: 'Well, it's up and standing! It makes all the troubles, all the sweat seem so worthwhile. It's a structure to be mighty proud of ... The beams, now de-propped and completely self-supporting look magnificent ... I have decided to throw a beer party for all those involved.'[17]

An Arup engineer writes back with whole-hearted glee and felicitation, ending with: 'I hope the beer party went off well. That is one activity at which Australians are notoriously successful.'[18]

•

They can be a precious bunch, architects, most particularly those who fancy themselves *artists*. One of the most famous stories illustrating the point – even if of the shaggy dog variety – concerns the English architect W. A. Chambers, who was given the task of building for Bombay a hotel worthy of such a grand city of India. The result was the 'Taj Mahal Palace', designed in the shape of a flat bottomed 'U' with the two upward arms of the U reaching out to the famed 'Gateway of India' standing by Bombay Harbour – a kind of Sub-Continental Arc de Triomphe that King George V had walked through, when first planting his royal foot in India. Glorious! The plans were finished, and Chambers went back to England, returning when it was completed, only . . .

Only to find that the builders had looked at the plans upside down and built it back to front, so that maritime arrivals at the Gateway of India were greeted with a flat bottom, not welcoming arms.

Very well then. Chambers checked in to his backwards masterpiece, went to his room on the fifth floor, put down his bags, and jumped to his death – no longer wishing to live in a world where builders could do that to a man of his sensibilities. They say his ghost can be seen to this day, entering through the side meant to be facing the harbour, the way it was *supposed* to be, dammit!

For it is in the very nature of creative people working on a mass scale, who rely on others to see their creations come to fruition, that they demand a real-world manifestation of their imagination, and nothing less.

And Jørn Utzon feels it much more than most.

But still, a structural solution for his Opera House shells is nowhere to be found. With all the combined genius required – mathematical, architectural and even philosophical – the answer evades them all.

•

Day after day and into ever longer nights, Ronald Jenkins goes through it, and through it again. But come May 1961, the latest design – a 'circular arc rib scheme'[19] – appears to be going the way of its predecessors – into the wastepaper basket. And so again they are back to it, Jenkins and his men teasing and tweaking and twisting, resulting in two new designs before June is even finished! But all for naught, as by July the latest design, involving an ellipsoidal geometry and a steel frame to support the reinforced concrete skin, proves to be just as challenging.

Ronald Jenkins finally decides to utter the unutterable at a partners' meeting.

Gentlemen, is this even *possible*?

Yes, it has always been Utzon's motif to work on the edge of the possible, but what if this roof lies just beyond it? Ronald Jenkins, after much preamble, admits to Ove Arup and the other partners that he is at an impasse with the Opera House roof structure – parabolas, circular arcs, ellipsoids, steel frames, double skins, whatever you like, whatever geometric and architectural framework you want to use – the one consistent thing is that none of them work.

It is a grave moment.

The stark possibility looms that the whole project in its current form will prove impossible to implement.

Ove takes it to heart, feeling it more deeply than the others. Had Ruth been right? Had he and Jørn got ahead of themselves and become overzealous, each one stoking the other's flames until their fire for the job had become out of control a *folie à deux*?

•

The call from Ove Arup comes in late July.

'We give up, we can't do it. The [shells] can't be built.'[20]

They have tried everything, every geometric combination, every kind of technique known to engineering and some not previously known, they have screeds of computer analysis to prove it . . .

Ingen af dem arbejder, Jørn! None of them work, Jørn!

For the engineers, it feels a little as if they have been asked to build a banana but it can't be yellow, or white on the inside, or curved; it has to be round and crisp and red and look like an apple.

In Arup's long and glorious career, he has never faced anything like it. After no fewer than three years, using the best brains in the business, and consulting widely, Utzon's sketched sails just cannot be hauled up to catch the winds of the world's soaring imagination.

But Utzon has other ideas.

Come to Hellebaek, Ove, let's discuss this.

Late July 1961, Hellebaek, two heads are better than one

The Danish duo deliberates.

The two enter a creative flow, an almost trance-like state of chattering in both English and Danish, muttering and mumbling to themselves, pacing and pondering, architectural and engineering symbiosis in action. (True, if you ask Ruth Arup, she will just call it more 'egging each other on'.[21])

But today, they really are making progress. *Practical* progress. Hard as it is for them to accept it, they must – reinforced concrete shells are not the solution. A return to the drawing board is, and an old drawing board it is, a transition and a place that the ever-restless Jørn is more than familiar with.

As ever, Ove finds his now dear friend Utzon, the total architect of his dreams, 'always prepared to consider anything . . . very refreshing . . . without prejudice and preconceived ideas'.[22]

(Jørn's architects find the same, looking on in admiration – Yuzo Mikami later writing that his boss, 'was very fond of having discussions with us. A lot of new ideas were born from these discussions and sometimes led to a solution. He was extremely open-minded and not dogmatic in most cases, if not always.'[23])

Back to the roof . . .

Their conversation lasts three days, both in the office and then back in the Utzon family home, as they approach the problem from all angles, and range from the realms of possibility back to the realities of practicality, before . . . the gleams of a breakthrough?

Utzon is beside himself with joy, practically dancing a jig, knowing they are on to something that will likely work, something fabulous.

While Ove's age and experience tempers his glee, and he encourages young, wilful Jørn Utzon to not get carried away – '*Sælg ikke pelsen før bjørnen er skud, Jørn,*' or 'Don't sell the fur until the bear is shot' – this could well be just another in a long line of potential solutions. Potential does not mean proved, and they would both do well to remember it.

But Utzon has not the time for caution, and implores Ove to have his engineers analyse it, as he begins to do with his architects here in Hellebaek.

•

In London, Ronald Jenkins is shocked to see such a roughly sketched doodle.

This is unprofessional.

Jenkins, a partner of the firm, along with a team of enthusiastic but exhausted engineers, has spent the last three years of his life working tirelessly on a shell solution for the Opera House roof, only to be told that they are now looking at a different solution entirely? It feels like a blow to the gut. Perhaps he was too forthcoming at the partners' meeting? Ultimately though, he has to tell Ove: this new rough sketch of a rib structure? He is not a fan of the fan – it won't work.

But, influenced by Utzon's insistence, Ove Arup pulls rank on Jenkins, and instructs his fellow partner, the nominal head of Job 1112, to have a good gander at the fanned rib structure proposal.

While Jenkins is occupied with that, Ove summons young Jack Zunz, the notably bright spark from Arup's South African office who has just arrived in England, as he has a special job in mind. It must be special, thinks Zunz, as he had only just been placed on a different massive project – the BP building in London – about a week ago.

Jack, I'd like you to have a look with your fresh eyes at the two different schemes we're considering for the Opera House roof.

First up, have a look at Ronald's current solution – elliptical reinforced concrete shells with a steel space-frame. And alternatively, analyse this fanned concrete rib idea, what we call the 'folded solution'.

Zunz sets to work, collaborating with two engineers, one on each design.

All the while, Ronald Jenkins, disrespected and denied but ever a diplomat, goes ahead with his own silent analysis, boiling and brooding as he goes.

29 August to 1 September 1961, London, no need to walk on eggshells

Jørn Utzon strides into Arup headquarters in the English capital, intent on solving the roof problem for good.

Carefully, over four long days – another marathon meeting between the two Danes and their latest recruit, Jack Zunz – Zunz shows Utzon and Ove what his engineers have found with the two latest schemes, the structural challenges involved.

They are certain that both schemes are *viable* and can be made to stand. But, both solutions still require different shapes in different parts of the curve, so for that alone there are still immense practical problems in actually building either of them.

Personally, Zunz warms to Ronald's approach – using a double skin of concrete based on ellipsoids with a steel space-frame – for the fact it could cost less, and may be quicker, given how much work has already been put into it. What's more, it is the scheme that Ronald believes in, so it would cause a lot less strife on the inside of Arup & Partners if we stayed the course rather than tossing it away for a new option. Same goes for the folks in Sydney who believe they are getting shells.

What of the 'folded solution' option, which only a month ago was no more than a doodle on a scrunched-up serviette in Hellebaek?

This one may not be so well received by the aforementioned interested parties, as it could be more difficult to construct – we don't know, it's never been done. Arup himself concedes, 'the fanlike concrete proposal, if possible at all, would require the closest possible integration of design and construction',[24] which would most likely make it much more expensive, don't you see, Jørn?

Is *this* the issue?

Well, that is an easy one to solve.

Pointing at the pile of drawings of the 'folded solution', the Danish architect says clearly, and with such force, that Zunz will remember his words ever afterwards: 'I don't care what it costs. I don't care what scandal it causes. I don't care how long it takes, but this is what I want.'[25]

And that is the end of it. He has spoken.

Don't talk to him about the expense. Think about the *value*.

He is the architect of this masterpiece, Rembrandt before his first sketch of *The Night Watch*, and his final authority is sacrosanct.

'Faced with the choice,' Zunz will recount, 'the architect had no doubt what he wanted – the folded solution. He felt that the integrity of a concrete structure left in its natural state was in keeping with the ideals of his concept for the scheme.'[26] The architecture *is* the structure.

He's the boss, and from an architectural standpoint, Ove Arup sees that Utzon is absolutely right and backs him.

So it is that the tortured eggshell option is dead, and with it all the work put in by Utzon's office and Arup & Partners to make it happen. (It's as Utzon had told his wide-eyed new recruit back in 1958, pointing at the wastepaper basket – 'We can't work without this one.'[27])

As Mikami will write years later of Utzon's bold decision to take this new direction: 'the ribbed fan-like scheme expressed its function of holding up the roof in a natural way, just like the soffit of the Concourse Beams he had admired. It had an honest structural expression which appealed to him. Therefore it was for him an important philosophical choice and was not just a visual matter.'[28]

For Jack Zunz, nothing has been as great a privilege than this four-day marathon meeting masterclass, watching the Danish duo work in perfect harmony, ideas flying and flowing and falling as they come and go. The Danes are greater than the sum of their parts, two minds working as one and becoming more than they could ever hope to be alone. It is as though they have their own language, a wavelength just for them. Zunz would later come to call it the 'Utzon/Arup language'.[29]

Ove frequently reminds Jack and all his engineers, 'Our job is to help the architect express himself,'[30] but no-one understands Utzon's expression better than Ove himself. The job remains, however, *how* to design what the architect has expressed.

As Ove has advocated from the beginning, the ideal way to proceed is to find a singular geometry that will unify the roof structure and simplify the job of the structural engineers and builders.

Utzon nods – he knows this very well by now.

And with that, all three begin examining the potential of applying ellipsoidal geometry to the folded solution, approaching the 'ribs' from every angle to find *the* angle, the shape that will bind it all together.

Jørn walks away from the Arup building with a smile, for while they don't have the solution quite yet, he can see it on the horizon. It's so close that he can practically *taste* it.

•

Ove is not a man prone to ignoring problems or pitfalls. The right thing to do – even if it is a horribly hard thing to do – is inform his partner. Jenkins is at a conference in Holland, it takes a little while for Ove's secretary to get him on the line for a crackly call, but the time is now nigh.

In as delicate terms as he can muster, Ove explains that Arup & Partners will be taking Utzon's directive and they will pursue an alternative approach for the Opera House roof.

Terribly sorry, Ronald, but it's just how things must go ahead from now.

. . .

. . .

The stillness of the quiet on the other end is louder than any shouted reply could be. A simmering silence that sears. Both men know it – this is the moment that Ove has sided with Utzon and bet on genius, and so abandoned normality, caution and his own people.

In the end, Ronald Jenkins has no sooner returned to London than he resigns from the Sydney Opera House project, washing his hands of the whole thing.

'Of course I have to accept your decision on the form of the Sydney superstructures,' he writes to Ove, 'although I regret it . . . I think the conflict of opinion can be detached from personalities.'[31]

But one of Jenkins' head engineers, Hugo Mollman, simply can't take it. He quits not just the job, but the whole firm in disgust.

As one Arup engineer will later tell the author David Messent: '[Mollman and Jenkins] were so heavily committed to that [shell solution], as people do become, that they really weren't able to adapt to the idea of a ribbed solution . . .'[32]

Quite.

'I think it nearly broke Ronald's heart . . .' another Arup engineer will recall, 'because he realised in the long run, that it wasn't possible to design [the roof] as a shell at all.'[33]

Who can take over from the departed Jenkins?

The obvious person is Jack Zunz, that sociable 37-year-old engineer, a fresh arrival at the London office and of no little brilliance. Ove Arup hands him what many engineers would find to be a poisoned chalice – a problem for which no comprehensive solution has been found despite four years of intense effort, and is now starting off on a new direction entirely. The ambitious Zunz doesn't flinch. A pleasure, sir.

Early September 1961, Hellebaek, Jørn has a ball

All their work, all their brainstorming, all the joy of a breakthrough, all the upset with Jenkins, and they still don't have a *complete* solution. Though Jørn Utzon rarely gives in to despair, at the end of this early autumn day in the Hellebaek office, he is close. The staff have gone home and Utzon is the last man left standing.

He walks over to the Opera House model and runs his hands along the smooth eggshell roof.

The ghost of Hamlet at nearby Elsinore whispers close:

> O God, God,
> How weary, stale, flat and unprofitable
> Seem to me all the uses of this world![34]

The long Nordic twilight is just starting to ebb into darkness as he begins to dismantle the Perspex model of the Opera House as he had originally conceived it, taking it apart shell by shell.

He is fitting the shells inside each other when he pauses.

Well, that is very odd.

All of the shells fit remarkably snugly inside each other. But how could that be, when they are all different sizes and shapes?

Unless . . . ?

What was that old saying his father used to tell him?

No, not that one, the other one.

'Here in the dockyard you construct and produce what you can't buy, what is not to be had, what is necessary.'[35]

Could the answer be right here, before his eyes?

'An idea flashed in his head like a lightning in a dark sky,' Yuzo Mikami would later recount it. 'If the [shells] were so similar, why couldn't they be cut out from a common surface? In order to do that the curvature must be the same in all directions. What is a geometrical body with a constant curvature in all directions? A sphere! He jumped up in the air.'[36]

But could it work for *his* design? He now thinks it just might.

It seems counterintuitive. The tall sails look elongated, like they were part of an oval shape, a parabolic geometry, and that is where so many of their problems stemmed from – it's not uniform throughout the entire curve. But now he sees what they have all missed – if the sphere is big enough, and you form the sails from sections of that sphere's surface, everything could be made of uniform parts – precisely as advocated in his cherished Sung-dynasty manual, *Yingzao Fashi* (*Chinese Building Standards*) – all the loads and stresses more easily calculated and . . . all the problems solved, the answer lying precisely within the principle of simplicity that he has always embraced.

Ah, *sing* it, Hamlet's Polonius!

'*This above all: to thine own self be true . . .*'[37]

Excitedly he races home, and runs the bath, animatedly telling Lis that he thinks he might have made a breakthrough.

Now, taking one of Lin's rubber beach balls, he dips it in the bath just so and removes it, immediately examining the light dry parts.

Look!

'He was able to see the shapes of spherical triangles he could cut out from the ball on the parts which were left dry,' Mikami would recount, after Utzon tells him the story. 'After many trials, he realised that the variety of shapes and sizes available was almost limitless, big and small, flat and upright. He could now compose the whole shell complex by the pieces of spherical triangles cut out from just one single sphere. He had found the solution!'[38]

Eureka be thy name.

The following morning, beaming, Utzon arrives at the office, gathers his staff around him and says, with mock fury: 'I have the worst team of architects! Here you have been sitting and you can't see how easy [the solution is]. It simply has to be a sphere!'[39]

At Utzon's behest one of the junior staff members is dispatched to buy an orange from the local shops and, upon his return, Utzon demonstrates, cutting it into alike segments of different sizes – in much the same way, and in the same spirit, that Ove Arup had so cleverly cut up the birthday cake – and arranging them on the plate . . .

He's right!

The orange pieces look just like the famous silhouette of the Sydney Opera House.

It is pure Utzon – shocking in its simplicity.

How had they missed this? It is one of those things where, the instant it is explained, no-one can believe that it had escaped everyone to this point, but there it is. Like all the best inventions.

'Nobody else had thought of the possibility of solving the problem by taking up a sphere . . .' Mikami notes. 'Utzon found the solution quite unaided, all by himself. It was indeed a stroke of genius.'[40]

They will need to do a lot of calculations, and work out the exact radius of the sphere they need, but for now the mood is one of sheer exuberance.

Prip-Buus goes down to the model shop at Helsingør's shipyard with a request to make some large, hollow wooden spheres, cut up into various triangular segments, to show three-dimensionally this new, brilliant principle.

The whole thing takes a matter of mere days. Models put together, taken apart and put together again, and the whole thing is confirmed.

It works!

It *works*!

But through all Jørn's excitement, he can hear a faint whisper. A tiny cry from somewhere inside, a little voice that asks, 'Are you *sure*?'

As one of his young architects, Japanese architect Minoru Takeyama (who had been one of those star-struck young men who had arrived at Jørn's doorstep seeking work), would recall, 'he was full of self-confidence, yet at the same time always self-questioning'.[41]

'Minoru,' Jørn would ask thoughtfully, 'do you think I am doing right?'

Minoru would assure his boss he was doing very right, to which Jørn would simply laugh and quip, 'I am like Prince Hamlet in many ways',[42] as if to shed the weight of his own indecision and bounce back to his usual, optimistic, laughing, self-confidence.

But look, it really *works*!

Utzon puts his staff to work with the technical drawings to send off to the engineers.

After initial analyses, convinced of the spherical solution, Utzon picks up the phone to call Arup in London with the triumphant news. That problem that had defeated the old man and all his best engineers for the last four years? Well, he has personally solved it, even though doing it is not, strictly speaking, in his . . . sphere of operations.

'I have solved the problem – it's a sphere. All the shells can be cut out from a common sphere!'

What?

But it is true.

'It transpired,' Ove Arup will recall, 'that he had changed the whole shape of the shells by cutting each of them out of a sphere.'[43]

'The firm of Arup,' Prip-Buus will recount, 'nearly exploded. His engineers were so, so bloody crazy because they have worked years and years and years on another, on a different geometry, and [Utzon] suddenly changes everything. [No more] parabola. We make a sphere.'[44]

You fucking . . . *what?*

After four years of bent rulers, parabolas, ellipsoids and endless calculations – screeds of papers piled high in storerooms all over England – the architect has now changed his mind and wants a spherical shape?

Jack Zunz, later, would choose his words carefully. 'He had "solved" the problem, yes, but only after radically changing the geometry of the roof surfaces which [the engineers] had painstakingly developed for more than two years.'[45]

We at Arup & Partners surely could have come up with this answer, if we knew it would be considered by the architect, who had seemed hell bent – or at least hell bent ruler – on sticking as close as possible to his original freehand design.

They don't think so.

But Utzon doesn't much mind what some of the disgruntled engineers think. Ove Arup backs him, and that's what's important.

Either way, what counts is there is no denying the brilliance of the solution, allowing every single one of the long ribs required to be built from a single piece of spherical formwork. The breakthrough is so important that Ove now travels to Hellebaek to see the architects' analyses and drawings, allowing Utzon to enthusiastically write to Professor Ashworth of the Committee on 29 September 1961: 'Mr Arup has been with us this week and we have found a very ingenious and marvellous way of producing the shells and they are, finally, as we want them . . .'[46]

Arup later poetically recalled of his visit to Hellebaek and the significant design change, 'We did not want to pull the architect down to hell, but we wanted him to pull us up to heaven.'[47]

Yuzo Mikami would add: 'So it happened, and they started climbing up the ladder to heaven together.'[48]

Fabulous!

•

The Committee men are relieved to hear it – *about bloody time!* – and Ashworth quickly writes back to Utzon and Arup that he assumes Stage II will be good to get underway come March next year, yes?

Well . . . ah, not really.

'I am afraid that this is . . . too optimistic,' Ove tells Harry Ashworth in a private letter on 30 October 1961. 'I think I ought to explain to you what the present position is. I am writing this as a private letter to you, as we are not quite out of the woods yet.'[49]

Ahem, where to start?

'The design of the so-called shells has been beset with difficulties,' he begins, explaining that the last 'fairly definite scheme'[50] didn't turn out so definite.

And so, Utzon and Ove had gone back to first principles and discussed the issues.

'In the course of these very long discussions several old and new ideas were examined and some months ago Utzon made a suggestion which seemed to be a clue to a solution of our difficulties . . . [he] came up with an idea for making all the shells of a uniform curvature throughout in both directions – in other words they are all cut out of the same sphere. He at least is wildly enthusiastic about it. It would also facilitate both construction and calculations. Construction – because all the main shells can be made from identical precast units and calculation – because [it] makes it possible to divide the superstructure into three nearly independent units, a great simplification . . .'[51]

But Arup doesn't want to get bogged down in the technical details in his letter. As is ever his wont, he ends up taking the philosophical view: 'We are therefore very pleased about this development, but it means that we are to some extent starting afresh. This has been a difficult and unprecedented job . . . that some avenues were blind and others almost impenetrable was almost unavoidable. In this case we saw the light through the wood in another direction than the one we were going, and we believe the quickest way out is to change course.'[52]

Utzon will later recall of this tumultuous summer, when the Opera House threatened to drift away, unmanned: 'We were up against a wall more or less in May 1961. We had arrived at a shell complex which was completely structurally forced. It took some months to persuade the engineer to start all over again, and in September he accepted my new shell geometry, which is clean and as beautiful as anything in nature . . .'[53]

Sail on!

TEN

ALL THE WORLD'S
A STAGE...

An opera house is not built in a day, you know – not even in Australia.[1]

Jørn Utzon, January 1957

All the opera houses in the world are different, but this is a kind of temple for Sydney – there's the question of civic pride. It is a monument that will provide uplift and a sense of the spiritual ... Why is this opera house being built? Because it's the most marvellous thing that's been built this century.[2]

Ove Arup, November 1962

16 November 1961, Bennelong Point, the end of the beginning

Just as the sun throws the last of the shadows of the Harbour Bridge over the Opera House building site on this day in late spring, so too is the final concrete pier foundation at long last *finished*.

Slated to take just eight months – maybe as many as nine months, they said, if things didn't go to plan, but there would always be plenty of change left over from a year – the job has actually taken two and a half years. At long last, the drillers pack up their caravans, say goodbye to the passing parade of stickybeaks, the water all around, their regular trips up the hill to Kings Cross, their fires by the harbour and the most lucrative job they've known, and head back on the track winding back o' Bourke way, and see what work awaits them for the coming summer.

27 November 1961, Hellebaek, this magnificent solution

As plans for the roof progress, and issues are worked out, detail by detail, Utzon writes exultantly to Professor Harry Ashworth: 'Back from London at last with a feeling that we have overcome the shells and you will get the most marvellous solution you can dream of. We were riding two horses for a long time. The last six months the real solution for everything technically and aesthetically was developed and it was even the cheapest way of making it you could dream of . . . Of course, all the work during the past three years has been the background for arriving at this magnificent solution.'[3]

•

Ashworth writes to Ove to congratulate him: 'I am looking forward to meeting you and Utzon in early March . . . although some feel it is a nuisance having the architect and engineer 10,000 miles away, in my view it has considerable merit in this particular job as it allows you to both get on with the real job of work and avoids you wasting time in all manner of local arguments, usually of a political origin.'[4]

•

Wither the great engineer? Almost before our eyes. The fainting attacks that start to hit Ove in January 1962 are of indeterminate cause, though stress and sheer exhaustion are likely suspects.

'Since the change of the design,' Arup writes back to Ashworth, 'we and Jørn had to telescope what would normally be a year or more of work into a relatively few months.'[5]

Sixty-six-year-old Ove becomes so rundown that in February he is hospitalised for a few days. One way or another, he is starting to feel older and colder, and simply incapable of returning to his previous workload, or any environment of high stress. (Just quietly? Ever since Ove unilaterally backed Jørn's design changes last summer, to completely change the firm's course on the Opera House roof, the upper echelons of Arup & Partners have been fighting like cats in a sack. Ove still has his supporters, but the detractors in the partnership are the worry, and as an executive body they not only take serious exception to the way the whole matter was dealt with, but say so loudly. The senior partners wonder – is this a partnership at all?)

The feeling starts to grow within Ove: does he really need the endless problems associated with the Sydney Opera House in his life? He does not. Let the younger more ambitious men deal with it. Utzon and Jack Zunz can go to Australia in a fortnight without him.

Mid-March 1962, Sydney, neither civil nor civic

Yes, you heard us right, if you don't cough up more money, we'll walk.

Civil & Civic mean business. The venerable Committee offers the builders another £15,000 for their troubles.

The offer is sneered at and immediately rejected, for sound reasons – the job has taken four times longer than expected and has put the builders between the Devil and the deep blue sea; they will need many multiples of that absurd amount just to keep their heads above water.

Industrial arbitration looks certain.

Roll out the barrel? Precisely. Because that is what they have the government over.

'This might mean some political uproar, which from the Committee's point of view might be undesirable up towards the election,' one of Arup's men writes to London. 'Even if Civil & Civic were paid extra, we could still not get a satisfactory job ... We all feel like suggesting them to finish the course and pack up.'[6]

The animosity on Bennelong Point is palpable, with Civil & Civic at the throats of Everyone & Everything.

March 1962, NYC to LAX, of blessings and curses

Apologies, Jørn!

Jack Zunz means it. He hadn't meant to be so late for their flight from New York to LA, en route to Sydney, but the structural drawings for the roof took longer than expected.

No problem, Jack. Utzon, of all people, knows how this project is – everything takes *quadruple* the time that it should.

And as it happens, it had been a fortunate flight to miss. For no sooner have they landed in Los Angeles than they hear the news: the flight they were meant to catch had gone careening into the waters just off Long Island, killing everybody on board.

The tragedy and their narrow escape from it brings these two professionals – from opposite parts of the world – even closer. There is an easy rapport between them, that consciousness that grows between many on this project that they are likely engaged in the work of their lives.

Not for nothing had Utzon, after he and Zunz had solved a particularly knotty problem, put his arm around the South African and said with some feeling, 'Jack, it's good to work with you, we force the best out of each other.'[7]

So what now?

Going for a life-affirming walk in Beverly Hills during their 24-hour stopover, they pass an enormous gated house, with sure pretensions that it is a handsome abode, defended by two massive gargoyles poised atop the stone pillar gateposts.

The playful prankster in Utzon, one of the most famous architects in the world – certain that they have before them an architectural monstrosity – stuffs a dollar bill in the mouth of each gargoyle, turning them into grotesque clowns at a carnival sideshow, and they both run off in the night, grown men giggling like children.

There goes the creator of the built masterpiece of our times . . .

This childish side of Utzon pleases Zunz enormously. It is so unexpected and refreshing in such a serious architect. Zunz's own four young children adore Jørn, too, as the Dane had no sooner entered his London home for dinner than he had been down on all fours pretending to be an elephant, giving them rides on his back. There are no airs and graces with this man.

Life is good, and gets even better when, on 14 March – as his plane is approaching Sydney Airport – Utzon is invited up the front by the Qantas captain as the jet does not one but two circles right above the Opera House site.

They hit the tarmac running, Utzon soon presenting the Yellow Book to the Executive Committee and the Technical Advisory panel – essentially the updated Red Book showing the newly spherical 'shells' and their tiling, together with the latest designs of the interiors – while Zunz presents the engineers' drawings compiled in the Black Book.

This is the first of many times Jørn Utzon will explain the novel roof design to all who ask him over the years: 'It is really very simple, strangely enough. But it is always rather simple when you have been working for a long time with such things. These curved planes which were once formed by curves, parabolas and ellipses are formed now by the same spherical surface.'[8]

It really is a magnificent solution, everyone must concede.

The fact that the shells are spherical means that every part of them can be prefabricated from a handful of standard moulds, and the uniform shape makes tiling the exterior surface vastly simpler, too.

'You have here the precision of mass production, with the freedom you normally have only from handmade things.'[9] Utzon beams.

This solution really does give the whole structure a single unifying principle – a central sun around which every other part of the building can revolve, and evolve from there.

The Committee men beam back at Jørn.

The presentations go well, with Zunz later recalling, 'Jørn was a magician . . . first off his visual and verbal presentations were so superb that he really carried all before him. And he had these people eating out of his hand . . .'[10]

Yes, the architect is clearly enjoying it all. You can tell by the constant glints in his eye, a harbinger of the brilliant plans to come for what the committee designates as 'Stage III' – the interiors. (The roof design and construction is 'Stage II'.) When will that be, by the way?

Utzon is a little vague on that subject, but makes it clear it will be soon.

•

All up, with this part of the design challenge seemingly solved, it is time to talk about how we will actually *build* the thing . . .

Heading out to Ashfield, Utzon and Zunz are introduced by Sir Manuel Hornibrook to his best Construction Manager, a great big lug of a man by the name of Corbet Gore, who will – should all go smoothly, and the NSW Government agree to contract Hornibrook – be in charge of Stage II.

Gore has a touch of the eponymous about him, a good man, but not one to mess with. He is a tall, beer-bellied bull of a man, a highly trained engineer with big blue eyes and a friendly gaze – albeit with fingers always cocked to either prod chests of recalcitrant staff, or clench if necessary. His engineering studies at the University of Queensland had been interrupted by the need to serve with the RAAF in Europe, and he had no sooner gained his degree on his return than, when Hornibrook had needed to send a hard man into New Guinea to run operations there and build bridges, airfields, houses, oil installations and roads all over that wild country, they had sent Gore. He has only just returned – inevitably harder than ever. He has the air about him of a man who will get things done, who has a notable penchant for innovation. Speaking of which, Gore now bids Utzon and Zunz to follow him into a room down the hall, so he may show them the large plastic model of a revolutionary piece of equipment they've been developing to make the sails soar . . .

Ta-DAAAA!

Gentlemen, the erection arch.

The . . . *what*?

Gore laughs his booming laugh.

The 'erection arch'.

Jørn and Zunz begin to circle the extraordinary model, fascinated, while Gore explains.

Instead of complex, costly scaffolding, we have devised this moveable and adjustable erection arch that can move both laterally *and* vertically while supporting the heavy concrete rib segments, allowing them to be fixed into precise position, mid-air!

Storslået, thinks Utzon to himself, but 'Magnificent,' he mutters. His thoughts are still organised in Danish, despite how well he has taken to Australian English.

And it really is *storslået*, even if Utzon has never seen an innovative idea he didn't like the look of.

Zunz feels much the same; this fellow Mr Gore is just what the London team needs to help them engineer the shells. It is decided Gore will fly there next month to finesse and finalise the construction scheme for the roof.

18 April 1962, Sydney, the old rumour mill

Although the new roof design has been kept quiet during Utzon's visit for fear of setting the papers off into a frenzy and starting a political punching match, these things have a way of getting out.

After Silent Stan asks the site office in Sydney for, 'some material for a statement regarding the changes in the shape and method of construction of the shells',[11] one of the engineers endeavours to get some advice from Utzon.

Engineer: 'I wish to dictate an overseas cable to Denmark.'

Office girl: 'Name and address, please?'

Engineer: 'To Jørn, J-O-R-N.'

Office girl: 'Utzon, U-T-Z-O-N?'

Engineer: 'That's right – Hellebaek, Denmark!'

Office girl: 'Yes! And the text?'

Engineer: 'Haviland, H-A-V-I-L-A-N-D, Haviland requests for press statement next week reasons and extent of alteration to shells . . .'

Office girl: 'Golly, they are not going to alter them *again*, are they . . . ?'[12]

•

On the last day of April 1962, Silent Stan Haviland steps up to the microphones held out by bustling reporters to happily put the rumours to rest: 'The problem of how to construct the sail-like roof of the Opera House has been solved.'[13]

The reporters bustle closer.

'The cluster of shells forming the roof will be precast on the site, then lifted into position . . . to great precision,'[14] he says in his precise way.

The reporters call out their most burning question: *And what about the shape?*

'Statements that the shells have been radically altered are not true.'[15]

The only difference Haviland says calmly is that, 'all the shells are now defined as separate portions of a single theoretical sphere giving a consistent and very satisfactory solution architecturally as well as structurally'.[16]

Mid-1962, Europe, Herculean task upon Herculean task

Back in Hellebaek, Jørn Utzon turns his attention back to the interiors, where the issue pushing in from all sides is seats – there aren't enough of them in the Major Hall. The client has specified 2800 seats for orchestral concerts and 1700 for opera, but now that they have gone from a thin roof to a thick roof – from a matter of inches to six feet – the walls have closed in, leaving him with less volume to work with and . . . less space for seats.

With the help of his architects, Utzon comes up with 'eight alternative scenarios'[17] for the hall layout, placing more seats at the side and rear of the stage for symphony concerts than originally planned.

It should do the trick.

Onwards.

•

Well, this is awkward.

One of the world experts on the production of opera, ballet and the like – Mr Martin Carr, Stage Director of the Royal Ballet, Covent Garden – is visiting Sydney to stage-direct operas for the Australian Elizabethan Theatre Trust and has not only taken the opportunity to look over an old set of Sydney Opera House plans, but has also vented his views.

As reported in the *Herald*, he believes that what's proposed 'is unsuitable for opera because of limited stage facilities'.[18]

Worse, he says the building is a 'white elephant for opera',[19] not to mention 'the most costly building for opera in the world'.[20]

In response, Jørn Utzon takes a dim view.

'Mr Carr,' he tells the *Herald*, 'does not know details of the stage or how it will operate . . . We will have a lot of criticism because the whole plan is rather fantastic. Most of the criticism will be because of lack of knowledge.'[21]

Silent Stan Haviland is another who is distinctly underwhelmed by Mr Carr's comments. For the moment, he feels he must do what he can to counter the criticism circulating Sydney. He has a meeting with Mr Carr, to hear his stated views . . . and the *Herald* reports the upshot.

> Mr Carr said last night that Mr Haviland declined to show him
> plans that could have cleared up some points of criticism and did
> not supply him with any information to contradict his arguments.[22]

George Molnar for one thinks Mr Carr is rather off the mark in his comparisons, opening his own editorial on the flare-up by writing, 'recent criticism of the Sydney Opera House has started a controversy which, for lack of facts, has reached an emotional stage'.[23]

In the meantime, at least the form of the Opera House continues to so capture the public imagination that it is becoming iconic, as witness the new hat that is all the rage among ladies going to the races – the Opera House hat, as featured on the front page of the vanguard of popular fashion, *The Australian Women's Weekly*.

13 June 1962, London, in the distance, the fat lady warbles

Eugene?

The times since being discovered by Eugene Goossens have been more than good to Joan Sutherland. On her Italian debut, in Venice – singing the title role of *Alcina* in February 1960 – the hardest-to-please critics in the world, the Italian reviewers, had christened her *La Stupenda*, meaning 'the stupendous one'. Just last year, she had made her debut at New York's Metropolitan Opera in Donizetti's *Lucia di Lammermoor* and received 'a 12-minute ovation'.[24]

And it is all because the man on the other side of this door had recognised her talent, believed that a Sydney stenographer could become an international star, and nurtured her thereafter.

When Sir Eugene opens the door of his nondescript London flat, Richard Bonynge and Joan Sutherland – who had married in 1954 and now have a six-year-old son – can barely believe it.

Where once there had been style, swagger and a suave *savoir faire*, there is now little more than a broken, shrunken, wan old man – the phantom of the opera, blinking in the light and the unaccustomed interruption of visitors.

'It was tragic to see him,' Richard Bonynge will later recall. 'Tragic. It seemed he'd become half his size. He was absolutely destroyed physically. I believe that Australia destroyed him. Definitely. He was pilloried by a very insular society.'[25]

Not long after their visit, on 13 June 1962, 69-year-old Sir Eugene Goossens III breathes his ragged last as rheumatic heart disease and a

View of Bennelong Point from Dawes Point, circa 1804.
Courtesy Mitchell Library, State Library of New South Wales

Bennelong Point, from the Harbour Bridge during its
construction, circa 1930. *Wikimedia Commons*

The Fort Macquarie Tram Depot, demolished in 1958.
City of Sydney Archives

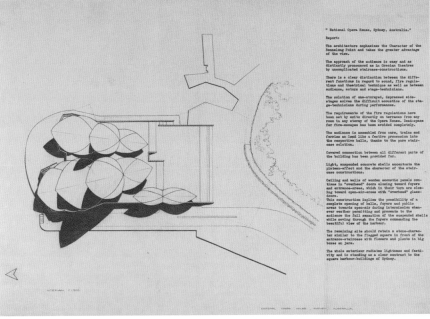

Original competition drawings submitted by Jørn Utzon, 1957.
NSW State Archives

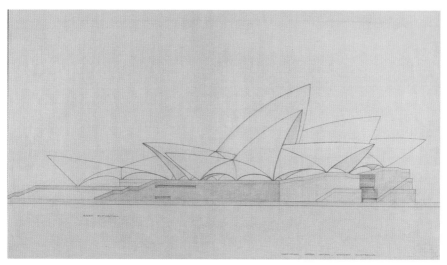

Original competition drawing submitted by Jørn Utzon, 1957.
NSW State Archives

Model of Utzon's design for the Opera House, 1958. *Collection: Museum of Applied Arts and Sciences. Gift of Ove Arup and Partners, 2003. Photographer Jean-Francois Lanzarone. Courtesy ARUP and the Sydney Opera House.*

Eugene Goossens, the first to lobby for an opera house in Sydney, *The ABC Weekly*, 1946. *Reproduced by permission of the Australian Broadcasting Corporation – Library Sales. The ABC Weekly © 1946 ABC*

Eugene Goossens, circa 1950. *Courtesy Mitchell Library, State Library of New South Wales*

Joseph Cahill, circa 1952. *Newspix*

'Sculpture in architecture, idiot! Not architecture in sculpture.' One of George Molnar's earliest cartoons on the Opera House, 1957. *George Molnar (1957) sourced from National Library of Australia*

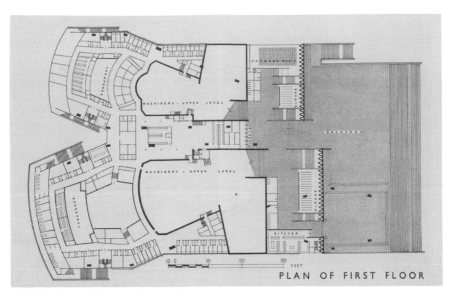

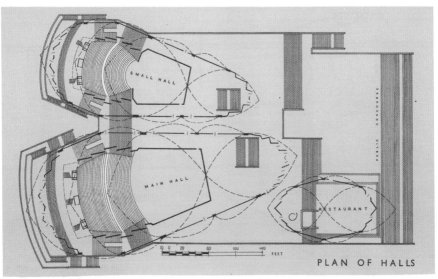

The Gold Book, 1959, plans of first floor and halls. *NSW State Archives*

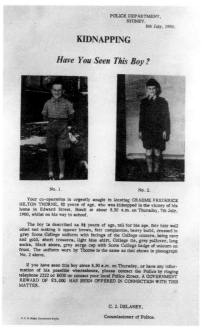

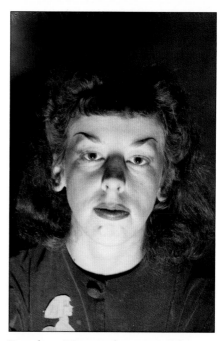

The kidnapping of schoolboy Graeme Thorne, police poster, 1960. *NSW Police Forensic Photography Archive*

Rosaleen Norton, known as 'the witch of Kings Cross'. *Wikimedia Commons*

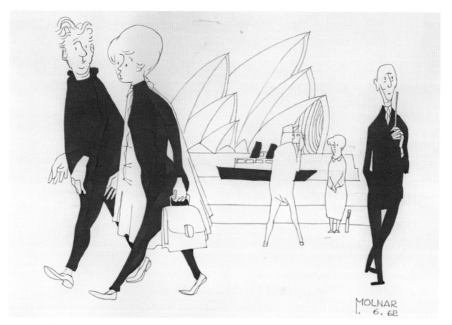

'But where did Mr Carr get his quaint idea that an Opera House is meant to produce operas in?' George Molnar cartoon, 1962. *George Molnar (1962) sourced from National Library of Australia*

Cover, *The Australian Women's Weekly*, 1962. *Are Media Pty Limited/ The Australian Women's Weekly/'The Opera House hat'*

Utzon and Minister for Public Works Norman Ryan on-site, 1964. *Courtesy Mitchell Library, State Library of New South Wales*

From left: Jack Zunz, Mick Lewis and Ove Arup on-site, 1964. *Courtesy Mitchell Library, State Library of New South Wales*

Harry Ashworth, Professor of Architecture, University of Sydney. *NSW State Archives*

Charles Moses, ABC General
Manager, 1935–1965.
*Courtesy Mitchell Library,
State Library of New South Wales*

Opera House construction workers,
1964. *Courtesy Mitchell Library, State
Library of New South Wales*

Ove Arup, circa 1965.
*Central Press/Hulton Archive via Getty
Images*

Robin Askin, 1967.
*Fairfax Media/The Sydney Morning Herald
and The Age Photos*

haemorrhaging gastric ulcer combine in basso profundo to drain the last of his life away and the curtain closes.

Though survived by his five daughters, they are mostly estranged and his small estate is left to 'my faithful companion and assistant Miss Linda Main'.[26]

(In Sydney, the news is met with sadness by those one-time students of the Conservatorium and members of the Sydney Symphony Orchestra who had so prospered under his tutelage. Though it will take some agitation, some musicians from the SSO will eventually perform a well-attended 'Sir Eugene Goossens Memorial Concert' at the Conservatorium in his memory, playing various chamber pieces composed by the maestro. There will be no mention of matters that are as unpleasant as they are unmentionable.)

•

Zunz, Gore and the engineers are making great progress on their plans for building the roof. All of which is good news.

The bad news is that the changed design – while, yes, it will stand – has changed the overall weight of the roof, which will now be . . . an extraordinary 30,000 tons, *twice* the weight of the original design!

And the problem? The foundation piers that have been designed to hold the wafer-thin granny are going to crumple under the weight of the thickset rugby forward, and so some of those piers will have to be replaced, while the remainder will need to be significantly beefed up.

10 July 1962, Melbourne, send a man to watch all night, my fair lady

It all happens so quickly.

One moment a 47-ton semi-trailer carrying a 38-ton power-shovel into Melbourne is making its way over the city's brand spanking new King Street Bridge and the next moment there is a clunk, a screeching of metal, a lurch and – *oh my Godddddddddd* – an entire span starts to give way under it! From as far as a mile away people can hear the piercing shriek of the metal tearing, as the terrified driver – *feeling* the bridge giving way under him – puts his foot down before his rig tumbles into the river.

Horrified passers-by see a large jagged crack appear in the pylon at the city end, even as several fractures open in the concrete wall beneath the overpass.

Fortunately, the driver and the truck make it to the other side, but the waves of panic made by the crashing span reach all the way to Sydney.

For the NSW Public Works Minister Norm Ryan, the possibility of the collapse of a new structure is real and, given it will be his responsibility if it occurs, it focuses his mind more than somewhat on the forecast difficulties with building the Sydney Opera House. He had been a humble electrician before joining the Labor Party so understanding complex matters of physics and structural engineering does not come easily. In fact, he still can't grasp exactly how they are going to get the roof to stand up, if not with 'invisible sky hooks',[27] as he has been heard to remark.

And it's not the only danger that stalks the Minister . . .

3 August 1962, Sydney, money is a good soldier

The bull sharks gliding hungrily about the Opera House project are not just the ones occasionally spotted off Bennelong Point by the workers fishing on their lunch hour. For the newly invigorated Opposition under the leadership of Robin Askin – who has everything but a dorsal fin – are also getting stronger by the month, in no small part because they manage to foment public unease about the cost and endless delays and potential problems in the building of the Opera House.

On this day, Askin happily releases a report, written by three members of the State Parliamentary Liberal Party, condemning the government for 'misleading Parliament and the public on the cost of the Opera House', for 'sheer maladministration',[28] and claiming the 'astronomical increase'[29] in costs might go as high as an extraordinary £15 million – three times more than the previous estimate of £4,880,000 made public in April 1960 – allowing the press to have that thing that it enjoys most of all: a field day.[30]

The Committee's explanation that, 'the Opera House is a unique construction involving much trial and error'[31] gets no sympathy from Askin.

'This has been known to the government, but the facts have either been suppressed or ignored, presumably for political reasons.'[32]

The same day the report is made public, Corbet Gore writes to Zunz in London: 'I have a sickening feeling that the whole thing is grinding to a political stop.'[33]

The sharks circle closer and closer.

15 August 1962, London, 'To sleep, perchance to dream – ay, there's the rub'[34]

Is it the school bell signalling the end of the day, back in his Johannesburg alma mater, on a day when the sun has completely disappeared?

No.

Christ.

It is the middle of the bloody night, and the phone is ringing in Jack Zunz's London home. Scrabbling for the receiver, the engineer brings it to his ear to hear someone who introduces himself as 'Minister Norm Ryan' from Sydney.

What can I do for you, Minister?

'Mr Zunz,' Norm Ryan says down a line that's as crackly as dead gum tree twigs underfoot, 'we would like you to come to Australia immediately to attend a Cabinet sub-committee meeting, and would you please bring Mr Utzon along, because the whole project is in jeopardy.'[35]

Zunz hides his bemusement as the Minister explains between regular long-distance phone beeps just what has happened. A bridge collapsed, you see, *(beeeep . . .)* in Melbourne *(beeeep . . .)* some 'new welding technology'[36] *(beeeep . . .)* all checked by the engineers *(beeeep . . .)* we can't have that *(beeeep . . .)* with the Opera House . . .

Zunz does his best to settle the rattled politician.

No trouble, Minister, our design will stand up. No, there is no chance it will collapse. But yes, I will come to Sydney with Mr Utzon as soon as possible. Thank you for the call, Minister. Not at all.

Zunz has worked on some strange jobs in his time, but this is the strangest.

He is on an aeroplane in the company of Messrs Utzon and Arup, the latter there because the firm's managing partner, Peter Dunican, has insisted that the still unwell Ove go to lend 'grey hair'[37] to the discussions.

18 August 1962, Bennelong Point, Sydney summons

Skipper Nielsen, Utzon's representative in Sydney, has no sooner sat down at his desk with his morning coffee, and spread the *Sydney Morning Herald* before him than he learns his boss is coming for an unexpected visit . . .

CABINET CALLS UTZON TO TALKS ON OPERA HOUSE COST.

Premier Heffron's statement reads: 'Certain engineering matters and the costs involved in the building of the Opera House will be discussed.'[38]

Some Labor members are reported as forecasting that, 'the Opera House cost could become a major issue against the government at the next elections in 1965, if allowed to climb higher'.[39]

22 August 1962, Sydney, crisis or custom?

It is a strange circumstance when the designer of a global architectural masterpiece presumptive has only time for a fleeting glimpse of his growing creation in the distance before rushing to a meeting, but such is the case for Jørn Utzon on this day. Having just landed at Sydney Airport, Utzon, Arup and Zunz must first hold a press conference.

'Is it a crisis meeting?' a journalist asks Utzon.

'It looks like it from the newspapers, but I don't think so,'[40] Utzon replies calmly.

(In truth, and in private, all three know that this is a crisis politically and Zunz will write much later, 'the whole project was in the balance',[41] while Utzon confided to the South African on the way over, 'I don't care if they cancel the project, I have solved all the problems.'[42] The younger Zunz had been shocked at his fatalism, but is at least content with the efforts the architect makes now to settle down the press.)

And what about the cost rise? Yes, Utzon says, the politicians are bandying about such figures, but what must be appreciated is that this figure includes 'associated works'.

'The final cost will be a serious problem,' Utzon acknowledges with his ever charming frankness. 'But not as serious as in other buildings. We are willing to spend more money to achieve a perfect result.'[43]

So, settle down. Ove Arup beats much the same drum in his own remarks before, at last, the three jetlagged men wave polite farewells to the press mob and head to the Astra Hotel at Bondi to rest but . . .

But it is not just Utzon who is feeling the pressure. While he goes to his room, Arup and Zunz settle into their adjoining rooms, whereupon Arup remarks mildly, 'Your room is nicer than my room.'

Zunz will never quite know what got him to reply as he does: 'Go and f*** off!' he explodes. 'Get out of my room and out of my life!'

Arup reels back.

'The trouble with you,' the much older man says, clearly very hurt, 'is you are just like my wife. You take everything I say seriously.'

Coming to his senses, Zunz apologises, later noting: 'What could I do except to go on loving him?'[44]

Meanwhile, Opposition Leader Robin Askin is not letting up. He has already read the transcripts from Utzon's doorstop interview at Kingsford Smith Airport that morning, and is sure to thunder about it to the press that very day.

'We have every respect for Mr. Utzon, but we are concerned about the total cost to the public of the whole project, not how it is divided between the Opera House and associated works.'[45]

23 August 1962, Premier Heffron's Office, bored into submission

The last time Jørn was here, he had been greeted by the warm and welcoming smile of Joe Cahill. The office looks the same as it did back then, but the man behind the desk is different – not Joe, with his easy smile and his open air. *How can I be of help?*

Soon, suited men are filing in, shaking hands, slapping shoulders and assembling around the large conference table – a group that Jack Zunz later describes as, 'a very formidable array of ministers and officials, headed by the Premier'[46] – where discussion gets underway, led by Premier Heffron.

In short, they want reassurance that Humpty Dumpty won't have a great fall. Utzon and Zunz are trying to find the right words to respond, when Ove Arup jumps in first: 'Oh well, I'd better deal with this.'

(The three men had agreed over dinner during their stopover in Hawaii that Ove was in no condition to expend any energy on the conversation. Better to let him exert influence through his presence alone. And yet, when it comes to his firm's most important project, he simply cannot stay quiet, he must speak!)

'And then he rambled,' Zunz will recall of Ove's speech this day.[47]

On and on and on.

'Unfinished sentence followed unfinished sentence.'

There was an array of trained stenographers on hand to record the proceedings. They do their best, but the occasional glance between them says they have recorded some incoherent gibberish in their time, but this is on a whole new level.

Still, while it might not have made sense on the page, and although he didn't finish a single sentence . . .

'If one listened carefully, one could get a picture of what he was saying – rather like an impressionist painting.'[48]

Yes, like a Monet, one must take a step back and take it in as a whole for the picture to come into focus.

After 40 minutes, it is over, whereupon Zunz and Utzon also have their say.

After five full hours, the meeting is over, and the NSW Government again has confidence in the structural integrity of the Opera House, though they request the plans be double-checked and verified by another engineering firm of repute. Ove Arup accedes.

(Later, very quietly, Utzon is asked if Arup and his partners still enjoy his confidence? The architect nary blinks. He supports Arup & Partners all the way, and will not consider working with anyone else.)

•

The issue of cost blow-outs is less easy to deal with. It's *the* issue the Opposition and the press have been pursuing from the first.

The Premier can obfuscate no longer.

Read it and weep, Sydney. (Tears of joy for the Askin Opposition.)

OPERA HOUSE NOW £12.5 M
Heffron Tells of Big Increase[49]

Premier Heffron explains that the original estimate, 'had not included items which would now cost an extra £2.6 million . . . "Heavy" extra payments had arisen from difficult site conditions; the stage machinery cost had risen from £470,000 to £1.6 million; and the estimate for the construction of the roof was now £1 million higher than before.'[50]

Despite all this, he tells the pressing journalists: 'The Government has decided to proceed with the work, and the completion date is expected to be about the end of 1965.'[51]

Robin Askin scoffs to hear the new estimate. He tells the press immediately the increase is a 'public scandal . . . the final cost could still be closer to £15 million'.[52]

The *Herald*, too, has had enough

'The Government's approach to this undertaking has been grossly complacent,' it thunders in an editorial responding to Heffron's latest cost estimate. 'Its supervision of the project has been casual. It is intolerable that for more than two years costs and estimates should have been soaring without a word being said to Parliament which authorised that the estimate of £4,880,000 "shall not in any circumstances be exceeded by more than 10 per cent".'[53]

Well, this cannot go on.

'From now on the public will expect to be kept much more closely informed of the progress of the building and its cost, and it will need excellent reasons for any further delays.'[54]

Jørn Utzon himself comes under personal attack on the reckoning that his fees are guaranteed to be not less than 5 per cent of the total cost. Stan Haviland provides exact details of payments to the architect – as of 30 June 1962, Utzon has been paid £224,000 which covered fees and expenses from 1957.

Yes, to the public it looks like a King's ransom. But the truth is, so far he has been paid less than 1.7 per cent of the overall cost estimate, and nearly all of it has been put towards running his office, paying his staff, paying the architectural consultants, paying his taxes in Denmark and expensive trips to Sydney, just like this one he's on now . . .

•

After several more meetings, the trio prepares to fly home, and the Danish architect is as upbeat as ever.

'There will be no compromise,' he says flatly to the journalist from the *Sun-Herald*. 'I promise the people of Sydney, they will have the most marvellous . . . yes, the most wonderful building in the world.'[55]

'But the cost blow-outs?' the journalist returns to the theme *du jour*.

'The price was given for a dream – the sketch, of an idea,' Utzon says softly. 'But now we are getting there, and I am most impatient to see it up. I don't think I'll ever get another chance like this in my lifetime . . . I regard it as the proudest work of my life.'[56]

Leaning in, Ove Arup also marks it down as the work of a lifetime, but in a different manner.

'I think it is the most complicated, the most difficult building structure ever attempted anywhere,' he says flatly. 'We knew we would build it, but when we began, we didn't know how.'[57]

Jørn Utzon approves of the sentiment.

'And *that's* where costs come in,' he says. 'Everything about its construction is unprecedented . . . This estimate is really the first one for which we say there is foundation.'[58]

In the course of his remarks, the Dane mentions his recent trip to Moscow where he had noticed a particularly beautiful building of rare and odd design, erected in the time of the Czars. Upon inquiry, his Russian hosts had told him something of the history of the building, including the fact that the building had so impressed the Czar, that he had said, 'How wonderful. I don't want any other buildings made like this.'

But that was not enough for him.

'To make sure of this,' Utzon says, pausing for effect to the assembled press, 'the Czar ordered the architect shot. And *that* is why we are making the Opera House so difficult to build. We do not want to be shot.'[59]

•

The political turmoil they leave behind only worsens as State parliament begins its spring session.

'It is making this State a laughing-stock, not only throughout Australia but throughout the world,' the Libs cry.

'If the Government has any sense of decency or responsibility it should resign.'[60]

HEAR, HEAR!

Order! ORDER!

Premier Heffron does his best, maintaining the party line that everything is under control and that the project, 'has not cost the State one solitary penny'.[61]

'Even though most of the finance is being obtained through lotteries,' Robin Askin replies rather acidly, 'it is still *public* money, which otherwise could have been available for *hospitals*.'[62]

That evening, Minister Ryan releases a statement equally insisting that, 'The Government has complete control over expenditure on the Opera House.'[63]

Premier Heffron meanwhile sends a stern note to Stan Haviland and the Executive Committee, insisting they 'ensure that the Minister is at all times kept fully apprised of all developments as they occur'.[64]

Fortunately, Utzon still enjoys the broad support of the press.

'On the face of it, the recent estimate of £12.5 million seems a reasonable figure,' *The Daily Telegraph* happily opines. 'Since it is being painlessly financed by lotteries and the fund is comfortably on the black side of the ledger there is no reason to cavil . . . It is a project that will bring Sydney worldwide prestige as well as providing a splendid centre for all the performing arts.'[65]

Frederick Hewitt, though a Member of the Liberal Party, couldn't agree more and though a man rare to side with the Labor Party, publicly praises the Heffron government for its 'loyalty and steadfastness of purpose' in going ahead with the project.

'We have to accept the Opera House as it is, with all the errors that have gone into it,' he insists. 'It will be a beautiful structure – probably one of the greatest monuments built in the world in the last 50 or even 100 years – and it even may attract tourists as the Taj Mahal does.'[66]

The Taj Cahill lives!

•

Given how stressful the trip to Australia has been, it is a rare pleasure for Jack Zunz to be able to have a quiet dinner with Jørn Utzon in Honolulu, so he can bring up a few things about . . . work . . .

Jørn, I need a better flow of detailed plans and information from your office . . .

'You have all the information you require,' Utzon snaps, tired.

Zunz is stunned.

'Utzon's response was unexpected, unfriendly and sharp,' Zunz will later write.

This brief exchange sees young Jack Zunz begin to sour on the architect, developing an attitude that Jørn has 'no concept of the demands of a project of this magnitude, that it required the production of a steady stream of information for others to process'.[67]

•

In Sydney, there is good news and bad news out of all the recent trouble.

The good news is that, after personal pleas from both Jørn Utzon and Ove Arup, Minister Norm Ryan has finally acceded to their request to negotiate the Stage II contract directly with Hornibrook, instead of tendering the job.

RAH!

The bad news is that the Civil & Civic mob call the engineer's site office just after lunch, to lower the boom.

'We have served notice this morning on the Attorney-General that our claims should be resolved by arbitration.'[68]

And how much might these claims be?

The engineer on the other end of the line almost drops his lunch to hear it.

£3,055,000![69]

It's no wonder Civil & Civic had said no to the £15,000 they had been offered back in March!

Not surprisingly, shortly after arriving back in Hellebaek, Jørn decides with so many crises cascading, he needs to be closer to the action, and the problems, and informs Harry Ashworth and Stan Haviland that he will move his family to Sydney in the new year, to open an office on site.

•

The two men sitting side by side in the heated passenger cabin of the Denmark–Sweden ferry are in deep consultation, clearly discussing something of the utmost importance.

And it *is* important, Corbet Gore!

Jørn Utzon leans in.

With every rise and fall of the sun and moon, the Opera House must be *alive* out there on its harbour stage.

And regular tiles, like the ones we use in a bathroom, won't do it – they lend no texture, no variance in light and shadow: they make a surface appear two dimensional.

Jørn explains he has settled on 'a type of clay and glaze which produces the silvery effect you get when the sun shines on water'.[70]

They're 'manufactured from an off-white clay body and intermixed with a white rather coarse chamotte',[71] he explains, which gives them a slightly rippled surface which creates the luminous effect.

I saw first the technique in Japan. The white element that I've chosen comes from the Carmen stone, mined right here in Sweden.

More than that, using a mixture of glazed and unglazed tiles arranged on precast lightweight concrete panels, or the 'tile lids', which Höganäs have created to efficiently tile large surfaces, we can arrange the tiles on the ground then simply bolt the panels to the roof structure once it is done, leaving the roof textured and magnificent from every angle under every light.

At the Höganäs headquarters, Gore is more than impressed to see two huge models of the Sydney Opera House shells, upon which sit an impressive range of tiles. He places the first order – 5000 of Utzon's chosen tiles, the 'Sydney tile' the boys from Höganäs call it – for the trial rib sections that Gore plans to erect in Sydney.

18 October 1962, Sydney, Hornibrook struts the stage

The construction folk of M. R. Hornibrook Pty Ltd are pleased. It is no small thing to have secured a 'cost plus fixed fee'[72] contract to build Stage II – the sails themselves, with their tile claddings – of the highly prestigious Opera House.

Hornibrook has confidence. Having prospered from their base in Queensland for their noted ability in building bridges – including Brissie's famed Story Bridge – a part of their pitch to get the contract without public tender has been that because the roof vault more resembles a bridge than a traditional roof, they will be well suited to build it, and are sure they can do it within the two years and three months that have been estimated.

Their no-nonsense irascible founder, Sir Manuel Hornibrook – who'd got his start in the building trade as a carpenter's apprentice who'd belted the boss's son in a bareknuckle biffo then gone off to start his own building firm – makes no apology for it.

'It would sound egotistical to say we were the ONLY company who could do the job,' Sir Manuel tells the *Sunday Telegraph*. 'But off-hand, I can't think of anyone else.'[73]

Yes, these shells will be a hard nut to crack, but these ball-breaking builders with their tattoos, blue singlets and hairy chests – and that's just the bosses – have an air about them of being up to anything, pass the hammer will ya.

'We don't underestimate the many problems to be faced and overcome once the work has begun,' Hornibrook's project manager, Corbet Gore, tells the *Telegraph* with a laugh. 'It will either take a few years off or put a few years on my life. To me this is the most fascinating engineering job in the world today.'[74]

And he means it.

One of the Goondiwindi Gores, Corbet has already earned the respect of the entire Opera House team – he's practically an Arup staff member and a favourite among the architects, too. Who wouldn't like this quintessentially Australian bloke? A bloke who has not only been around the block, but built half of it – and if you dispute it, he just might knock *your* block off.

•

Things are starting to come together, at last. From London, Jack Zunz writes on 12 October 1962 to Stan Haviland, saying that Arup's will follow Utzon's lead and open an office in Sydney. They are sending an Associate Partner, Mick Lewis, a fellow South African who had studied engineering with Zunz, to head up the office, together with four assistants – all men who have been working on the project for years, 'our leading lights',[75] as Zunz calls them – to look after the engineering from right on site.

For his part, Mick Lewis is a no-nonsense sort of engineer, straight-down-the-line-with-a-T-square just like father used to make, and is pleased to get out of a deteriorating situation in South Africa.

True, he knows nothing of the Sydney project and had to look up on the map exactly where Australia *is*, but the key thing is it *isn't* South Africa, and, besides that, the job looks interesting. He has been hearing about all kinds of angst about the technical difficulties of building this structure, but even so, on arrival in the London office in October, he is shocked to find 50-odd engineers working on this one project. The Johannesburg office had a staff of 30 total, working on various projects!

'I [thought],' he would recount, 'there is no job in the world that justifies that number of people, it's just these lazy Poms. They can't do it properly.'[76]

Early November 1962, Sydney, 'I'm crazy to build it'[77]

It is something of the rule of life: more often than not, right up to the point that infirmity takes it the other way, the older . . . the bolder. With decades of experience under the belt and a growing awareness that time is now a finite resource, many a soul takes whatever opportunity comes along to say what needs to be said and let the Devil take the hindmost.

Ove Arup is such a man. So when, on a visit to his London office a journalist from the *Sydney Morning Herald* keeps returning to the theme of the mounting costs, Arup, resplendent in a fashionable wide red tie that stands in bright contrast to his shock of white hair – and surrounded by the baubles of his glorious career and his endless quirks, including Picasso pottery, an ancient Chinese sculpture, a beloved chess set – lets loose.

'This petty criticism,' Mr Arup says strongly, 'just what type of mentality does it take? You know, personally I feel very virtuous and very good about this job. I don't care a damn. It's so ludicrous.'

But let's make no bones about it.

'There is no doubt that this is one of the most difficult jobs ever attempted in the world, [and] speaking for us, I would say we are quite crazy to take this job . . . I never realised it would be so hard . . . It's taken two or three years off my life. I think Utzon and I are possibly to blame in being too idealistic or too stubborn. Maybe we are a bit silly in refusing to compromise. But my excuse, if I need an excuse, is that in this particular concept, if you don't get the whole idea in the building, it could be disastrous. I don't know how you could do anything to cheapen it without spoiling the idea.'

What has caused most of the problems?

'It's the kind of job we could design for ten years. But we didn't have half a year before the foundations went in.'

As to the absurdity of those first figures that were bandied around: 'As soon as that figure of £3,600,000 came out people took it as gospel,' he notes. 'I know what the shells contain in steel and tile, but I don't know what it will cost to put these big units a couple of hundred feet up in the air, it's never been done before. We are always struggling to get an economical result. We are trying to save half a million on the shells by avoiding scaffolding, but this is involving us in design work that could cost thousands. It's better to do a good job – it's your reputation in the long run.'

Speaking of which, with continued cost blow-outs, there have been whispers about Utzon's earnings. Arup is aware.

People are saying that the Danish architect wants such blow-outs – for he is on 5 per cent of all money spent! Why wouldn't he want to increase costs? (In fact, Arup's is on 4.5 per cent, and taking 6 per cent for all the building contracts they manage for the architect, so they're getting an even bigger cut, but they're not the ones making the news.)

Anyway, Ove will not *hear* of it.

'Utzon cares less about financial gain than principles,' he insists. 'In fact, I'm worried about him. He's spent a lot of his own money on this. It's quite amazing that such a young architect has been able to master such a thing. I've worked with hundreds of architects but not one of them would compare with Utzon.'[78]

Would Arup tackle the job again?

'I'm not so sure. I'll give my answer on the day it's opened – that is, if I live so long.'[79]

Mid-December 1962, Hellebaek, so long, Swan Lake

It is a singular circumstance which has seen this humble yellow house beside the swan lake in the tiny Danish village of Hellebaek give birth to the mighty Sydney Opera House on the other side of the planet, but the time has come for Utzon to close the heavy wooden front door one last time, turn the key and walk out from under the gabled front porch.

Unfortunately for Jørn, his whole team won't be coming with him to Sydney. Four of his most experienced architects, the core of his A-team, who have been with the Opera House project from the start, always counselling him wisely 'on matters of management and design',[80] have declined to uproot their lives, and will stay in Denmark instead. It means Jørn is taking with him his younger, more intrepid but less experienced lot, with the gap to be bridged by local recruits in Sydney. But he will design that bridge when he comes to it.

Before leaving, Jørn, Lis and the kids spend some wonderful time with his father Aage and brother, Leif, and his family – Jørn will miss having their counsel close by.

December 1962, London, a many-headed monster

Ever afterwards, Corbet Gore, in London to continue planning the construction of the Opera House roof, will regard this episode as his best insight into the mind of Ove Arup.

Gore has been to Christmas parties before, but never one like this, attended by some 700 people at the Napoleon Suite of the Café Royal in London, as the string quartet in the corner competes with the happy babble of ambitious and successful people at the end of a prosperous year and the regular popping of corks.

But hush now, as Ove steps to the microphone to say a few words of welcome and to deliver his annual homily, which, this year of all years, touches on the serious, noting that, 'As I am getting older and see this firm of mine grow into a many-headed monster, I feel a certain urge to talk to the monster and remind it what it was created for and how it ought to behave in future – in short – the sort of moral uplift which parents and old people are fond of inflicting on the young, and which possibly benefits no-one . . .'

The room goes quiet. This is, clearly, the father of the firm preparing to leave the stage. He goes on to speak of the virtues of individualism, of not allowing 'big brother' into the firm, where power is wielded for its own sake to the detriment of real people and creativity and higher principles . . .

'Loyalty to a group,' he tells the room earnestly, 'is good only if it transcends the group, if it is loyal to something greater, to certain principles and attitudes, if it is based on a common endeavour.'[81]

To that end: 'Let us remain a collection of oddities, if you like . . . We must not strive to produce or take on yes-men.'

That's it.

'. . . I've nearly finished now – I will only mention that we have tonight broken a rule which we have stuck to all along, that of not inviting any guests to the party . . . However, tonight we have as our first and only guest Mr Gore from Hornibrook of Australia, the contractors for the Sydney superstructure. But Mr Gore is actually a very important member of the team working on Sydney, so it is natural that he should be invited. And anyhow, it is nice to break the rules sometimes . . .'[82]

ELEVEN

THE EDGE OF THE POSSIBLE

It is no good coming along with cost planning, scientific programming or modern management methods – they don't apply to masterpieces.[1]

Ove Arup, January 1965

26 December 1962, London, the Boxing Day meeting

Jack Zunz is uneasy.

It had been one thing for Utzon to announce after the crisis trip to Sydney in August that he was relocating to Sydney in the New Year – indeed, Arup's had decided to follow suit – but closing up shop entirely for a matter of *weeks* to make that move? That concerns the eager Jack Zunz, who wishes to work out the final details for the tiles *now*, holiday season or not. He's off skiing with his good friend Mick Lewis and their families soon and, despite the week he has just spent in Denmark with Utzon and the Höganäs lads working out details for the tiles, crucial architectural decisions on the tile lid arrangements remain.

'At the time,' Zunz will recount, 'I had more than 60 people working on analytical studies . . . We faced a situation where there would be no way to consult the architect about these problems . . . I would like to think that he simply did not understand the magnitude of the task we all faced. Otherwise, I can only describe it as one of the most irresponsible acts I have experienced in my professional career.'[2]

Jack decides to say as much to Jørn.

'I had one or two fairly sharp exchanges with Utzon,' he will later recall, 'because I just felt we weren't getting the right kind of leadership on that front.'[3]

For all Zunz's stress, Jørn, as head of the project, takes a longer-term view – having worked on the Opera House full pelt for six years, compared to Zunz's 15-odd months, a break won't hurt – the tiles are well ahead of schedule, and with the Stage I contractors still on site, there is no real rush. In short, he does not share Zunz's anxiety. Rather, he

239

brims with optimism, sure the tiles will be a punctual success. It is vintage Jørn. As Zunz would later say: 'Utzon never complained. I mean . . . he had things to say about the quality at times, and he made criticisms, which we took on board, but generally, it was all very positive.'[4]

In the end, Zunz manages to persuade Jørn to stop in London on his way to the US and Sydney, to meet with the full Arup's team including Ove himself, even if the only way they can manage it is on Boxing Day afternoon at the Ariel Hotel, just next to Heathrow.

It is the coldest day in England in *a decade*, and the thick blanket of snow enveloping London proves difficult to move through, either on foot or by cab. By 3 pm the men have reached Utzon's small room at the hotel, all of them exhausted and all of them *still* freezing – the heating in the hotel has failed.

One by one, Zunz goes through his list of handwritten notes entitled *Matters Affecting Utzon* with 63 items on it requiring the Dane's attention . . .

> A7. Inclination of Shell 1 – new position . . .
> A12. Ridge detail tiles? . . .
> A17. Jointing in ridge member either radial or parallel between ribs (when seen from below) . . .
> A22. Backstage wall – pattern of formwork and quality . . .
> A29. Depth of joint in tile surface . . .
> A35. Details at bottom edge of tile lids . . .[5]

Utzon, in turn, gives firm directions on the first matters, with occasional input from the others – all of it interrupted, alas, when the ill Ove Arup decides the room is so cold that the only way he can stay warm enough is to run a hot bath and continue the meeting while – with an engineer's penchant for practicality, focusing a little more on the outcome than the look – he sets up his chair next to the bath, rolls up his pants and keeps speaking with his feet in the hot water, his grumpy voice floating ethereally through the bathroom door.

Various other decisions are reached until, nearing midnight, another delicate matter arises – the fact that Utzon will not be easily contactable over the coming weeks, meaning no further firm decisions can be made, unless . . .

Unless Utzon hereby gives written permission for Ove Arup & Partners to make decisions independent of him.

Jørn, his teeth still chattering in the chill, agrees on strict condition that all of Arup, Jack Zunz and Yuzo Mikami are in unanimous agreement.

There is great relief, as there remains an unbelievable workload to get through – 800 working drawings for the shells and tiles alone – and unresolved issues needlessly complicate things.

At last it is done, and while the others struggle to straggle off into the frozen night, Ove struggles to get his socks on over his toes, which have gone puffy and wrinkly in the warm bath. Rarely has he felt so old.

January 1963, London, fighting founding fathers

There is trouble at the mill, as the fallout continues from Ove Arup's executive choice to back Utzon's changes to the Opera House roof design, back in the summer of '61.

In January 1963, the firm's Managing Partner, Peter Dunican, writes a memo to fellow partners that takes aim at Ove himself:

'This is supposed to be a partnership and I think the time has come for some plain speaking. There is far too much concerned with "I" and not enough "we". Sydney highlights this. Ever since the summer of 1961 the interests of the job and the firm have been clouded by an undercurrent of conflict. In my mind there is no doubt that the basic decision taken with respect to Sydney in September 1961 was correct though I think the way it was implemented could be argued about . . .'

Not to be too blunt about it, but that's *you*, Ove. You will recall how you backed the architect over your own men? Because we do.

'So let us stop indulging in the cult of personality and all that . . . May I remind you of the Battersea Coat of Arms. It is a shield surmounted by a dove carrying an olive branch, and it has the superscription "Not mine, not thine, but ours". It is with this in mind we should try to move forward.'[6]

Ove has no choice but to acquiesce, the hydra he has created has too many heads to be controlled.

Challenges aside, with talented architects being added to the firm's fold this year – Arup's are set to open their own architectural branch and have even managed to recruit Yuzo Mikami – the ultimate goal of Total Design may still be reached.

•

A soon-to-be key member of the team, the question has to be asked: what if Mick Lewis fell under a bus?

The Arup's team can now find out, as on a stopover in Tel Aviv, on his way to Australia to take up his new post as head of the Sydney office, Lewis has no sooner looked the wrong way when crossing the road, than – LOOK OUT! – a bus collects him, in the worst sense of the word. He finishes in the gutter with a very badly broken leg, and pelvic injuries.

True, the old saying goes, 'Break a leg', but this is ridiculous.

Lewis sees only the endless mountain of work that looms over him as he lies helpless in his hospital bed. London showed him that the great number of men working on the Sydney Opera House project was not, as he had expected, because they were a gaggle of 'lazy Poms'.[7]

To the contrary, 'by the time I left [London]', he will later recall, 'I thought we didn't have enough staff to do it . . . so, it was quite a conversion course that I had to undertake to get to know the job'.[8]

Alas, instead of being in Sydney, it looks like he'll be stuck for months in this hospital room in Tel Aviv – not so far from Damascus in the scheme of things – in a plaster from the chest down.

3 March 1963, Bennelong Point, an unlikely enthusiast

Her Majesty Queen Elizabeth II is not known for spontaneity. But on this occasion, after a scheduled luncheon at Government House, she and the Duke of Edinburgh have decided, on a whim – one of the rare whims of her decade-long reign – that they would like to have a closer look at the Sydney Opera House site.

Phone calls are made, ties are tightened, scuffed shoes are roughly 'polished' of their dust by being spat on and rubbed on the backs of pants. Most importantly, by the time the Sovereign and her Consort alight from their white Daimler at 3 pm, Stan Haviland and Professor Harry Ashworth are there to bow.

Now, as the day is whistling wind, cloying clouds and a darkness in the distance, lesser Royals might baulk and turn away from the weather. But these two are veterans of the cold and windy moors around Balmoral Castle, and Her Majesty will not be cowed. Rather, she climbs the 30-foot-wide processional staircase without pause to explore the structures in various stages of completion, paying no mind to the rubble or the open holes. In the absence of photographers and journalists to document the moment, Her Majesty seems more relaxed than ever, walking around gaily with a wry smile, stopping to place her hands on her hips, one foot in front of the other, gazing about, clearly impressed, and asking architect Skipper Nielsen a barrage of technical questions.

'We walked right round the project from underneath the podium to the top,' Professor Ashworth tells the press, 'as far as the seats in the main concert hall. The Queen and the Duke obviously knew quite a lot about the scheme. They were most impressed and interested, and I think they both realised it was unique.'[9]

4 March 1963, Royal Yacht *Britannia*, Your Majesty, there is nothing like a Dane

It is an odd thing to be freezing while travelling just south of the tropics, but such is the situation for the Utzon family as they travel on their last leg to Australia, from Tahiti to Sydney, aboard this *Transports Aériens Intercontinentaux* airliner, now at 20,000 feet. Noticing that some of the passengers up the pointy end are being handed out woollen socks, Utzon – who has been seriously ill with pneumonia the past weeks – politely asks the hostess if he might have five pairs, too, for his wife and three children travelling with him?

'Socks, sir, are only for first-class passengers,' he is informed with that brusqueness reserved for lowly tourist-class passengers who do not know their station, and so must be told where to get off – and take their poxy luggage with them. Utzon defers to her authority and squeezes back into these singularly ill-designed seats, his mind turning to the challenges ahead. It had been a great thing, and so exciting to visit Australia almost six years before, just after winning the competition, but there have been so many challenges since, most of them exhausting, and he is all too aware that still the greatest challenges are to come – proceeding with Stage II, the design and construction of the roof – and Stage III from on site.

For one thing, they will have to keep troubleshooting issues as they build it, designing and tweaking as it is assembled, even as they must keep feeding the insatiable hunger of the press who follow him around like hungry cats, and . . .

And what now?

The same hostess has returned to Utzon, this time laden down with as many socks as she can carry.

Sir, it's about my former mistaken reluctance to offer you socks. I am hoping you and your fine family might be so kind as to take some now?

Why yes, yes, we would . . . ?

Thank you. Here they are. And oh, by the way, the Captain has just received a message over the radio. Her Majesty the Queen of England is currently visiting Sydney on the Royal yacht *Britannia*, and she would be delighted if you would join her for lunch when we arrive in Sydney.

Sure enough, the moment they land in Sydney it is to find an official car waiting for them on the tarmac, complete with a police escort.

After sorting out the children to be looked after – they don't have time to change clothes, and although Lis feels a little uncomfortable going without stockings, Jørn insists it doesn't matter. So it is, they are whisked away to *Britannia*, anchored across from Bennelong Point at the Overseas Passenger Terminal, where they are greeted and treated as *architectural* royalty. As they wait to go aboard, they find themselves next to a man who is apparently Australia's most famous and accomplished writer – Patrick White, I think he said his name is, Lis? White certainly knows Jørn Utzon, the most famous architect in Australia, who he later remarked was 'the most important guest' on board, and a 'tall man as handsome as they come, but handicapped by the English he spoke, which was boneless, and to me as unintelligible as his native Danish'.[10]

There is a blur of other people to whom Jørn is introduced, including a rear-admiral, a newspaper proprietor by the name of Fairfax, a former Governor-General in Sir William McKell and an Olympic swimmer by the name of Murray Rose.

As to Her Majesty, she makes her entrance once everyone is settled in the saloon with a refreshment. The first moment that Utzon himself is aware that the star of this production is about to arrive is when he sees some toe peepers coming down the stairs in his direct eye-line, followed by ankles, calves, thighs, hips, torso and shoulders and finally ... the English Queen! Quietly, to Jørn, it feels more comical than regal as entrances go, and he instinctively starts to contemplate how he would re-design *Britannia*'s interior, if only he could, to ensure that the Queen could make her grand entrances genuinely *grand*, 'seen in her entirety from the first, not bit by bit like a print-out emerging from a telex machine'.[11]

At lunch, though Jørn sits directly across from Her Majesty, a large vase of flowers partially blocks his view of her, meaning he can only see an arm here, an ear there, and yes, a smooth hand reaches out to claim sovereignty over a fluffy bread roll: 'small and without character – the soft hand of privilege unmarked by labour'.[12]

Eventually her actual face appears from behind the vase, and she greets Jørn, evincing an enormous interest in the Opera House just a few hundred yards from where they are anchored, and questions the architect closely as to what the contours of the emerging building will lead to.

As enthusiastic as the sovereign is, however, even her enthusiasm likely pales against that of Patrick White who, after lunch, drifts back over to join the Utzons.

A curmudgeon like they don't make them anymore, White not only doesn't make friends easily, he barely makes *acquaintances*. But today? Today he looks cheerful, genuinely charmed to be sitting so near to the architect he is so struck by.

'At least I enjoyed talking to Utzon,' he later remarked of the day's events. 'And I think we both enjoyed standing together uneasily at one end of the saloon.'[13] White is less charmed by Lis, who he later serves a backhanded compliment saying she is like 'The Little Mermaid . . . that plain, dank-haired mermaid kind one sees in Denmark, very pleasant.'[14]

But White could not be more thrilled as, once they leave the Royal Yacht and set foot upon Bennelong Point, Utzon leads him on a personal tour of the whole site. For White, it feels like being present for the building of the Parthenon or the Pyramids, and he will later recount: 'it has made me feel glad I am alive in Australia today. At last we are going to have something worth having.'[15]

Alas, it's not quite all that to Jack Zunz, who is on site when they arrive, and takes issue with the whole – glory, glory, hallelujah! – *thing* around Jørn.

'And lo and behold,' Zunz pens to a London colleague. 'God appears from Heaven. He flies into Sydney from Tahiti. And his plane lands at nine or ten o'clock and then of course he's wheeled into lunch with the Queen . . .'[16]

For his part, Jørn Utzon remains blissfully unaware of Zunz's envy, taking no notice of the Total Design ideal crumbling around him.

Instead, at the end of a long and extraordinary day, it is time for Jørn and Lis to collect their children and head to that part of Sydney they have decided to make their home, on the far northern beaches, about an hour's drive from the Opera House site, away from the harsh and sharp lines of concrete and steel, back to the sea and the flowing shapes of the natural world – where he can sail, where he is at his most comfortable.

Wide-eyed, the children gaze out at the passing scenery, the hilly greenery of what will be their new home, 16-year-old Lin later recalling that it felt like they were 'in a kind of quaint English county. The airport was small and rather ordinary, the houses all red brick, and the Newport Arms Hotel was little more than a run-down public bar with dozens of sweaty, singlet-clad men swilling beer – a bit different from the Royal Yacht.'[17]

But, all up?

'As a family,' Lis Utzon will recount, 'we were very excited and very happy.'[18]

•

The slow tide of progressive change that has brought the Utzons to these shores, of course extends well beyond Bennelong Point. As Patrick White himself will happily note, Australia is experiencing an opening of 'the country of the mind'.[19] The civil rights movement of the USA is trickling across the Pacific and entering the antipodean polemic, even as the *Commonwealth Electoral Act* of 1962 is about to grant, at long last, all Aboriginal and Torres Strait Islander people the option to enrol and vote in federal elections. To the horror of the Christian establishment, *the* musical sensation of the world, The Beatles – with those haircuts! – has just announced their tour 'Down Under' for the coming year.

The horrors of World War II are now a whole generation ago, as the Japanese Prime Minister Hayato Ikeda announces his own forthcoming 'goodwill visit' to Sydney in order to sign a new trade pact. Things that were unthinkable, are now established fact. Just a year ago, the AMP 'Sydney Cove' Building had been opened – its 26 storeys soaring to nearly 400 feet tall, it is now nearly twice the height of anything else in Sydney!

Yes, all things considered, Sydneysiders feel more connected to the world than ever before, as new ideas and new people keep flooding forth, even while the close-minded and materialistic provincialism of White's satirical white suburb of Sarsaparilla slowly recedes.

Out with the old, in with the new, with the Sydney Opera House to the forefront.

7 March 1963, NSW Legislative Assembly, awkward acts

Minister Ryan steps forward to present the amended *Sydney Opera House Act 1960*, lifting the approved cost from £4.88 million to £12.5 million.

'The Government is confident on the advice of the consultants, that the Opera House can be built within the amount of expenditure authorised.'[20]

(The truth is, Ryan was given an estimate of £13.75 million back in August 1962, so he is bluffing . . .)

Ryan reminds parliament that 'the whole of this amount can be financed from the proceeds of the Opera House lotteries'[21] and, for a comparison, that the Lincoln Center in New York is costing US$142 million . . .

Be that as it may, Robin Askin isn't buying it. He knows the government is weak on the Opera House accounting flank and attacks accordingly.

'Speaking in the purely political sense, we members of this House have been the victims of a gigantic confidence trick. We were led to believe that on a certain basis the Opera House would cost a certain sum of money, whereas from the outset it has cost three times as much ... It seems to me we are not out of it yet.'[22]

But down at the Lottery Office, the ticket sales keep coming and, as it stands, Stan Haviland and Harry Ashworth know that the Opera House account remains in surplus of £3.7 million.

For all the furore in parliament, the Opera House purse is brimming over.

On this day, the first big order for tiles has been sent to Höganäs in Sweden for no less than 1,044,250 tiles of the highest standard. The 'Sydney Tile', which Jørn proudly announces to the public through the pages of the *Sydney Morning Herald*.

Opera House Roof to be Two-Tone

The sail roof of the Opera House will be two-tone white, a combination of glossy and matt tiles, the Opera House designer, Jørn Utzon, said last night. 'From a distance you will get a pattern of glossy tiles shining like fingernails against the flesh-like texture of matt tiles,' he said.

'No matter from what angle you look at the Opera House it will stand out very clearly – as clear as the Snowy Mountains.'

Mr Utzon described as a misconception reports last year that the Opera House would have black stripes.[23]

But Jørn, a quiet word if you please. Sir Charles Moses – now knighted for his service to Australian industry – takes the architect to the side and raises a small concern.

'I'm worried about the fierce Australian sun dancing on the thousands of white and cream glazed tiles, Jørn. The effect could be dazzling to the point of being blinding.'

I hear you, Sir Charles, you aren't the first to raise such a worry, but, I've used an old Japanese technique ... 'We've designed the tiles to be manufactured with a wavy surface. This almost imperceptible ripple has the effect of deflecting the sun's rays and preventing blinding dazzle.'[24]

Sir Charles furrows his brow, not entirely convinced, but for now he'll have to trust the Dane.

•

Civil & Civic pack up and leave the site on Monday, 11 March 1963 ... the day the arbitration hearing resumes with Arup's new barrister – a notably red-faced legal veteran by the name of John Kerr QC, who has arrived from Melbourne the day before, and only had a chance to look at the brief this very morning, though he is ably assisted by his junior, Anthony Mason.

'Mr Leavey,' Kerr says to Civil & Civic's Managing Director, Bill Leavey, theatrically tossing back his admittedly magnificent silver mane. 'When you tendered for this project, did you make allowance for shipjacking these beams?'

Mr Leavey looks at him curiously, but makes no reply.

'I repeat my question, Mr Leavey,' the QC says with a mane-toss that this time is a little impatient and a lot imperious. 'When you were tendering for this project, did you make allowance for shipjacking these beams?'

'Mr Kerr,' Leavey replies carefully, 'I don't understand the question.'

Got him now!

'Mr Leavey, I will repeat my question for a third time. When you tendered for this project, *did you* allow for shipjacking these beams?'

'Mr Kerr, I don't know what you are talking about – I don't know what you mean by shipjacking these beams.'

Ah. With this, John Kerr QC turns to the presiding arbitrator, and says, with the air of a man revealing his four aces to a man with no more than a pair: 'Mr Arbitrator, would you please explain to Mr Leavey what shipjacking these beams means.'

'Sorry, Mr Kerr,' the arbitrator replies, 'I don't know what you are talking about.'[25]

. . .

Ah.

'Mr Arbitrator,' Kerr says, with now rather limp mien, 'if you don't know what shipjacking means, and Mr Leavey doesn't know what shipjacking means, how do you expect me to know what shipjacking means?'[26]

Good question. Like the Opera House itself, the complexities are many and this is going to take some time. Are they really going to do this for another 12 months, the estimated time it might take for the arbitration to conclude? No-one can bear the thought of it, and after an unruly session where the bosses of Civil & Civic and Ove Arup – who has flown in for the occasion – and Jack Zunz hurl insults at each other, the Director of Public Works, Alan Johnson, is sent in by Minister Ryan to see if a settlement can be reached, which would spare the government embarrassment.

•

Before Stage II can get underway, the first thing Hornibrook needs to do is to augment the foundations, which will see a delay of four months, maybe more, another increase in costs, and more embarrassment for the political masters.

Which is why the architects, engineers and the Committee men have kept their discussions of the issue under tight wraps, and . . .

And, oh Christ.

Look at the news . . .

PLANS RUSHED FOR POLITICS.

A major blunder revealed yesterday in the construction of the Sydney Opera House will add a fortune to its cost. Twenty reinforced concrete columns built to carry the roof cannot support the load. This is because the roof design has changed last year, after work on the base of the roof had begun.[27]

Ah, but that is just for warm-ups.

Mr Ove Arup is quoted, saying: 'It is only one of a million troubles. The Opera House is being built on a trial-and-error basis. If the planner had been given five years to design the building, instead of being rushed into it for political reasons, about £2 million might have been saved on the ultimate cost . . .'[28]

There is more, much more, including two unnamed engineers working on site who reportedly tell the paper the problem with the columns is, 'only one of many secret changes in the Opera House plans . . .'.[29]

Christ alive, these anonymous engineers are just making it worse!

'It was, of course, a complete distortion,' Jack Zunz writes privately of the report '. . . at the moment we are dreaming up ways of building a few nameless newspaper reporters into the pedestals'.[30]

25 March 1963, Bennelong Point, raising the roof

Despite the deluge that pours on Sydney town, whole battalions of Hornibrook's workers crash upon the rocks of Bennelong Point to storm ashore and swarm all over the nascent building. As one, they are united in their resolve to tackle what the *Sydney Morning Herald* describes as, 'the greatest architectural adventure in Australian history'[31] and what their engineer cum builder boss, Corbet Gore tells them 'is something out of the ionosphere. We have never seen anything like it in this country before.'[32]

If you say so, boss.

The foreman rounds up the rabble and begins explaining the state-of-the-art machinery and specialised tools they'll have to master. Most crucial of all are the red tower cranes bought from the French, now brought on site as the priority, even though they can't be tested until they are assembled and the rail tracks they'll rest on are finished.

And that's just scratching the surface of what lies before them.

Strewth! Merde! Govno! Σκατά! Christ, she's a tough one!

Weathered hands of varying tones from 20 different countries are all united in rolling cigarettes and pulling sandwiches, *Panini*, *Pita* and *Pane*, brimming with continental splendour, out of their lunchboxes. There is plenty to do, an endless litany of trials and tribulations, but right now . . . it's smoko.

The rain is pouring, and that means the concrete isn't.

Late March 1963, Sydney, Bennelong-Pointer to Sydney-Sider
Laughing in the near distance.

Jørn Utzon doesn't know their name yet, but they're kookaburras. What a unique thrill it is for him to wake to such a sound early on a warm and drizzly Sydney morning, drink coffee with his Lis, and then head off down Pittwater Road and over the Spit Bridge, along Military Road before opening up to the mighty Sydney Harbour Bridge, from where he can see . . . well, not much. But Jørn is certain that before his time here is done, through the harbour mists and drizzling wet will appear his treasured fifth façade, a series of resplendent sails that strain credulity as they stretch up to the sky, greeting any commuter who cares to look to their left on their way into the city.

The raw potential of it all still takes his breath away, pushing the boundaries of the possible.

But for now, to work! He walks into the new office, a simple wooden house at Farm Cove, tucked away on the eastern edge of the building site, just a short stroll from the gorgeous Botanic Gardens. The windows out back look straight towards Mrs Macquarie's Chair and beyond, providing a clean view of the harbour at eye level, as if they are working from a houseboat. The endless roar of machinery is just far enough away that it doesn't disturb either the architects or the engineers – the latter occupying the other half of the Farm Cove house, joined by a door in the middle, known as the 'back door'.

Jørn is happy to see the drawing office already set up with several white drawing tables, each with its own chair and adjustable lamp, scattered with the architect's quiver of tools – paper, rulers, pencils. Some tables are already manned by busy members of his team brought from Hellebaek, including Mogens Prip-Buus, and Oktay Nayman, a Turkish architect who Utzon calls 'the fastest drawer in the West'.[33]

They look up and give their boss a welcoming cheer. Like all of Utzon's coterie of designers, they are more than just employees, and more than mere colleagues. Really, they are something a little closer to disciples.

'I learned from him to be a decent man,' Oktay Nayman would say. 'That's very important. When you talk about Jørn, he's a great architect, he's a genius of an architect, but he was a very decent human being. Without being that kind of a man, he couldn't achieve that intense human touch in his architecture.'[34]

As to local recruits, Utzon's key Australian appointment is one Bill Wheatland, who fits firmly into the team like the missing piece of local Lego: a lanky, blond, blue-eyed rowing champion from down Geelong way who could easily pass as a Dane himself. Had things worked out differently Bill might well have rowed for Australia at the Helsinki Olympics of 1952, but he had dropped his oars and taken up a pencil instead. He had so excelled in his subsequent architecture studies at the University of Melbourne that he had been able to cut his professional teeth over in Sweden during the 1950s, learning architecture the Scandinavian way, and admiring it greatly. Jørn hires him as an associate concerned with managing documentation for the project.

Mogens Prip-Buus is the third handsome Dane to grace Australian shores as part of the Opera House team, his svelte frame and impeccable fashion second only to Jørn himself. A junior back in Hellebaek, here in Sydney he will be Utzon's Chief Assistant and, having already been a month here with his young family, writes home to his beloved parents:

'Sydney is a lovely city, mostly because of its position. The houses are dreadful, but when all is said and done, that's what houses look like over most of the world . . .'[35]

And while he misses his parents and the beauty of the French Riviera he likes to visit, he relishes the idea of contributing to the beauty of this tremendous harbour city, leaving his mark.

'I don't regret anything and am now completely convinced that the Opera House here is the greatest piece of architecture of our time . . . entirely different from anything else and yet so simple and natural.'[36]

And as for the people in his new hometown, he is most impressed: 'Our neighbours are just as nice . . . their daughter with six children has offered to babysit in the evenings, so stories about the kindly Australians are not exaggerated.'[37]

Utzon's experience is no different, being greeted everywhere he goes by well-wishers and admirers, all of them wanting to thank him for 'The House'. Most grateful of these fans are their neighbours up Palm Beach way, an exotic collection of bohemians, boat-builders and beach bums.

'It was a fabulous friendliness,' Utzon would later recall, 'and we – as a family coming to Australia, as immigrants, when you compare what immigrants normally felt when they'd left their own country for a new country, and the problems they had with the language and with the work and so on, how terrible it can be – we were on the sunny side all the time. It was fabulous. We met this Australian openness which Australians don't know of themselves, because if . . . you've been in Europe and you come to any country in Europe, you'll feel a difference.'[38]

26 March 1963, Sydney, Ove's declaration of independence

Jack Zunz – now himself an associate partner of Arup & Partners – is growing evermore fed up with the unusual contractual arrangements Ove Arup had signed the firm up for back in 1958, and has been urging Ove to take a stand ever since their crisis trip to Sydney the previous August. He wants less responsibility for the firm, or, if that's not possible, he feels they should be given formal recognition of their considerable input – working drawings and all.

Zunz would later write of the firm's extra responsibilities on the Opera House project, and his own growing reluctance to remain committed to the arrangement: 'This was work, I kept reminding myself, that should strictly speaking have been carried out by the architect. This increasing burden . . . became another cloud forming on the horizon.'[39]

Ove has so far refused to meddle with the setup, as stepping back from their commitment amounts to effectively withdrawing the firm's full support of the architect, which he had pledged at the beginning in light of Utzon being appointed sole architect without his firm in the very early days. On the flip-side, asking to be made co-principals is equally fraught.

But the winds are shifting in Zunz's favour as the headache of arbitration and the infighting at Arup's combine to force Ove's hand. On this day in Sydney, Zunz and Ove sit down to write not to Utzon, nor the Committee, nor even to the Minister, but to the Premier of the NSW Government himself, addressing the fact that while Utzon as architect has, 'the overriding responsibility for the whole of the scheme . . .' which is fair, Arup's are lumped with administering many of the specialist consultant contracts. So, although we do get paid for the work, we are somewhat caught in the middle, you see?

'It amounts to this,' they write, 'that we have responsibility without power, we are simply a convenient victim, scapegoat or stooge who can be blamed and made to pay if anything goes wrong, but cannot possibly get any credit or financial reward if all goes well.'[40]

They explain – there were no complaints when Ove signed up for this arrangement all those years ago because, 'it was felt to be desirable that Utzon who was a young and comparatively unknown Architect, not it was thought, experienced in the execution of jobs on this scale, [and] should have the support of a firm who could supply what might be missing in experience of resources'.[41]

Please, don't get us wrong, Premier, we do not wish to be seen as seeking to be co-principals with the architect – though they are sure to qualify this by adding 'there would be some justice in such an arrangement'[42] – nor do we wish to abandon the project entirely. But the current arrangement is untenable to the firm.

'By this time,' they insist, 'it is pretty well established that Utzon is well able to look after himself and the job.'[43]

Truthfully, Jack Zunz has serious reservations on that front, but the Premier doesn't know that. And Ove does not agree with the young South African, as Arup now puts his personal touch to the memo: 'He is a brilliant designer – one of the best, and probably the best of any I have come across in my long experience of working with architects . . . This Opera House could become the world's foremost contemporary masterpiece if Utzon is given his head, and if it is not spoilt by an attempt to squeeze it into established patterns.'[44]

But for us?

Let us out of the current arrangements and we will act as consultants only – 'the present agreement should be amended by deleting from it all reference to services other than those of structural and civil engineering'.[45]

•

But what about that arbitration that's buzzing like a bevy of bees in the collective Opera House bonnet?

The short answer is . . . nothing will spare the government the embarrassment of this drawn-out shemozzle, and on this day, they agree to pay an extra – *gulp* – £1.383 million to Civil & Civic. Yes, the original contract sum of £1.197 million has now been increased to £2.58 million.[46]

For now, it's kept quiet, but it's another dark cloud looming for the Labor government.

April 1963, Bennelong Point, Gore goes Guy Fawkes

Corbet Gore is a man with no time for nonsense, so when facing a task like demolishing the existing foundations – heavily reinforced concrete columns below the ground – he can only let two men with jackhammers go so far – and two weeks is enough! At that rate, the construction would be lucky to be finished by the year 2000, and good luck telling the brass something like that.

No. Remember: *When in doubt get a bigger hammer, and if still in doubt try dynamite.*

Precisely.

On 1 May 1963, Jack Zunz, back home in London, can barely believe the opener of the latest dispatch from Bennelong Point.

'Hornibrook are investigating the possible use of explosives to trim back some of the existing shell columns. Before you have a fit as I did . . .'

Too late! He reads on.

'We tried it out last night. While the immediate visible effect was not very remarkable, it does appear greatly to reduce the hours spent on the jack picks . . .'[47]

Well . . .

Well, whatever explosive Gore is considering using, it'd be cheaper to just stick a fuse in a bottle of what Zunz is feeling right now – an ounce of the South African's rage would reduce a skyscraper to rubble.

He bellows to his secretary to get some bastard on the phone this instant!

The conversation is loud enough to be heard through walls, and the Arup engineer who fields the call writes to Zunz once the waters calm a little.

'What better way to be awakened . . . than your dulcet tones over the international phones . . . gabbling away like an enraged Chinaman. I will instruct Hornibrook to desist from the use of explosives. So far, apart from making the Commanders of two Manly ferries wonder if they were being fired on from the Point, no damage is done . . .'[48]

May 1963, Sydney, a shift in the wind

The Australian expression, apparently is to be, 'busier than a one-legged man in a bum-kicking competition', and right now the South African, Mick Lewis – still on crutches from his accident in Tel Aviv – is pretty much exactly that.

As Ove Arup is moving towards semi-retirement and Zunz is 10,000 miles away in London, the responsibility for managing the day-to-day engineering side of the Sydney project and co-operating with the architects falls to him. In his view, engineering is a matter of mathematics, physics, business and the sweat off your brow. He understands the first three intimately, and intends to deliver pints of the latter.

Of the site itself, Lewis is nothing if not impressed.

'It was rather marvellous, there was just a sort of open podium like a Greek amphitheatre . . . just this podium and the water.'[49]

Slightly less marvellous, however, are Utzon's endless exultations about it, how he found inspiration for the podium, by travelling through Mexico and seeing the ancient Mayan structures that lifted people out from the sweaty jungles and into the rarefied godly air above, just as there will be echoes here of Greece and Morocco with their dazzling bright white buildings sparkling in sunshine. The tiled roof will do much the same, it's so wonderful, don't you see?

Yes . . .

Quite.

But Lewis is wary. Utzon is really talking poetry, when he is a physics man. His old friend Jack Zunz has already told him of Utzon's unorthodox ways, and Lewis intends to brings some orthodoxy to the place.

For at the end of the day, Mick Lewis is an engineers' engineer from his own once-British colony, a land that breeds ruthless pragmatism into the blood of every man.

He understands that Utzon is impressive.

'He's a very inspirational sort of guy,' he will allow, 'and, I suppose, in many ways he seduced everybody in this firm . . . I mean, he's a very, very charismatic personality. And if he wants to charm you, I mean you would be very hard pressed not to be charmed. And if he wants to impress you, you would be very hard pressed not to be impressed.'[50]

The problem is, Mick doesn't want to be either charmed or impressed. He wants proof of *action*, black on white down a straight track that's been properly surveyed.

'I don't seduce easily,'[51] he will note.

But he can see that many others are already long gone.

Even his own men, among them the talented Australian John Nutt, fresh from London and leading the design team for the side shells, who tells *The Daily Telegraph* in late May: 'I can see the building giving the Harbour a feeling of unity because the roof arch describes the same curve as the Harbour Bridge.'[52]

Lewis is wary of all this architectural speak coming from the engineers.

'That romantic view,' he will recall, 'is . . . a very real view, and that's what I walked in on. I said – please, in what way are [the architects] gods? Why is everyone seduced around here? And I suppose that also affected my approach.'[53]

Utzon worship is fine as far as it goes, but it cannot be allowed to disrupt the flow of technical drawings and time schedules and budgets, matters that Mick Lewis intends to manage with a stick, not a carrot.

•

Speaking of sticks, Jack Zunz concedes the battle over using sticks of dynamite.[54]

But seriously, lads, keep the racket to a minimum, you hear?

Yes, Jack. Yes.

But how?

Perhaps we can detonate the explosives so the blasts coincide with the loud hum of morning rush hour?

Yes, that might help.

And so it is done: holes are drilled into the columns, dynamite placed, and then detonated each day at around 8 am, when the noisiest buses and trucks can be counted on to be on the roads.

Nothing to see here folks, please just keep moving.

All goes well, right up until the moment when, one fine morning, a piece of blasted concrete soars from a shattered column and – *incommmming!* – hits a passing Sydney ferry.

•

Unsurprisingly, those who take the grimmest view about proceedings are the ferry captains. Mick Lewis is taking a ferry harbour cruise with a couple of international visitors when he hears the driver announcing over the intercom, 'On your right, you have our . . . our *Opera* House, or so it's called.'[55]

Letting out a farcical laugh, the ferry captain proceeds to 'tear the Opera House to shreds'.[56]

They've been at it for years and now they're blowing it up to start again. Why, not long ago, some of the debris hit a ferry! The whole monstrosity is little more than a white elephant and a dangerous one at that!

Lewis, anonymous on the ferry, nevertheless shrinks in his seat. He is appalled and takes it upon himself to have a meeting with Minister Ryan.

'You know,' Lewis tells the Minister in his very direct, unabashed way, 'you must do something about your public relations. I mean ... the ferries are run by the NSW Government, for goodness sake. Tell these chaps what to say about the Opera House. There are some good things to say.'[57]

Minister Ryan promises to look into it immediately and clearly is as good as his word.

A short time later, Lewis has another visitor who he takes out on the same cruise. As they pass by the Opera House construction site, the South African leans in, to take in every word.

'On our right is the Opera House,' burbles the ferry captain, before lowering his voice conspiratorially. 'I'm not supposed to say this to you, but ...'[58]

The whole monstrosity is little more than a white elephant and a dangerous one at that! Why, not long ago ...

●

Like fish to water, or more particularly, lizards finding sunshine, the Utzons' 18-year-old son Jan and now 17-year-old daughter Lin quickly take to their new life in Australia, falling in love with the beaches, the harbour, the sailing mecca of Pittwater and all-around warmth and sweetness of the Southern Hemisphere. Only their younger brother, Kim, is not quite so sure – English just about beats him in the first months, but not as badly as he is actually beaten with a cane at his Anglican prep school.[59] He won't return under any circumstances, he informs his mother through a mist of tears. But altogether, the family finds a lot to like in their new home.

'We lived in a marvellous place and we liked to swim and sail and everything,' Utzon *pater* will recount. 'We were just happy people like anybody else who loved nature and did our job and went to school. Our children loved it very much. We did not feel like foreigners ... It did not feel as if once this job was finished, we would be away. We had found our place in the world. We had settled there. We made very many friends. This was our home, much more even than Denmark, and we felt like this as a family.'[60]

Lis Utzon will go one step further.

'Our children felt very much this way. They were Australians.'[61]

To be truthful about it, in some ways Jørn himself is like her fourth child. And the Jørn Utzon brand of humour, all pranks and whimsy, makes him an instant hit with many he meets. To the dismay of Lis – part embarrassment, part amusement – he begins to offer pretty Sydney girls the Faber-Castell pencil he happens to have on hand, telling them with a wink, 'This is the pencil that made the Opera House.'[62]

It's as his son Jan would say years later: 'He was more on the same wavelength as us teenagers.'[63]

When the project's stage technique consultant, Willi Ulmer, goes to a meeting at a nearby café with the Dane, and in passing expresses admiration for the voluptuous nature of the waitress, Utzon takes swift action. Reaching over, he firmly grasps Ulmer's white cuff and with a flick of the wrist, dashes off a quick sketch of her line, calling on his own specialty in drawing curves.

'Now you take her home on your arm,'[64] Utzon tells him, as all in attendance fall about laughing.

Bliss was it in that dawn . . .

13 May 1963, London, potentially pulling the plug

It was a bold move, Ove Arup's statement to the NSW Premier back in March. Some of the lads in London are calling it, 'Ove's Declaration of Independence', while Utzon had been startled and not a little disgruntled to hear after the fact of his consultants going direct to the Premier to rearrange the project, and yet the end result . . . is naught. Or at least, there has been no official change to the contractual arrangements.

But in the meantime, Mick Lewis lets Jack Zunz know that there appears to be a growing chasm between the Public Works Department and the Committee men. The Premier has ordered Minister Ryan, as the official constructing authority, to take more control of the project . . . which means that Ove's statement *has* had some impact?

Either way, Jack Zunz needs a new angle.

Trying again, he writes a formal memorandum – signed under Ove's name for additional weight – and sends it to Mick Lewis, asking for him to broach the topic of reorganisation with Utzon.

> It appears that during recent meetings in Sydney this matter has come up for more detailed consideration. The time has now come for us to face facts and reality so that our own obligations for the completion of the job are clearly understood.[65]

In other words, we must act to reposition ourselves now.

The memorandum outlines the choices available to the architect and client, from the engineers' perspective.

First option: we complete Stage II and then hand all administration over to Utzon.

Second option: we stay the course, allowing ourselves to drift into *de facto* administration of Stage III.

Third option: we backoff [sic] now and hand Stage II over to Utzon.

Fourth option: we stay the course but do so as co-principals with the Architect.[66]

'This choice,' the memo goes on, 'is mainly a choice for Utzon, because he is at the moment the principal consultant . . . The question is, however, whether he will in fact be willing and able to set up the necessary organisation on the site to run Stages II and III. This organisation need, of course, not take over from us immediately . . . I am afraid we will need to insist, therefore, on a choice between 3 and 4 . . . This matter should be discussed immediately with Utzon because when the Minister comes here on the 27th May, it is sure to come up, and we must know Utzon's views beforehand.

(Signed)

OVE ARUP[67]

27 May 1963, Sydney, Over Arup

On receipt of the memo, handed to him by Mick Lewis, Jørn Utzon is deeply shocked. This is the second time in a few months that Ove Arup has employed such a cold, corporate and unilateral method of manoeuvring. Where was the man he used to know, the one who stayed at his home, played with his children, talked with him into the night? What *happened* to that man?

There seems only one conclusion, and as much as Utzon keeps trying to escape it, it keeps stalking him, most particularly hovering close in the quiet watch of the night: it looks like Arup's are appealing directly to the political client – the Premier and the Minister – brutally isolating the architect in order to secure their own nest.

27 May 1963, London, Norm's new norms

When the Minister for Public Works, Norm Ryan, comes to Arup's Fitzroy Street office in stylish central London for detailed meetings about the Opera House . . . he comes like a rather cool wind blowing through the corridors.

It seems so to both Ove Arup and Jack Zunz, at least.

In his manner – a manner they have not seen before in this otherwise affable and even rather docile man – Minister Ryan starts to lay down the law.

Very broadly, the Heffron government is already on the run-in to the next election, just two years away, and one issue that is starting to become just that – a real issue – is the cost blow-outs and endless delays with the construction of the Opera House, not to mention this messy arbitration fire we have just put out. You've raised with us the concerns of your firm, so let me be firm, from now, make no mistake, you engineers will deal with me, Minister Ryan, and not just the Committee which has been way too much of a rubber stamp for whatever you and Utzon want to do.

As Zunz writes to Lewis: 'He [Ryan] is quite adamant about his assumption of power . . . there is no doubt that all major decisions will flow from his department.'[68]

Which is one thing. For the most part, Arup's the engineers get it, and start conferring more with the Department of Public Works.

One important player not in attendance, who never receives a similar visit from the Minister, rather misses the point, for Jørn Utzon continues to see the Executive Committee and the Technical Advisory panel as his primary contacts, as Joe Cahill had set it up. Crucially, they have always been supportive of the overall aim – to create a masterpiece; they understand that architecture is as much in the world of *art* as building, and is not a purely corporate exercise.

As to the so-called 'cost blow-outs', the Dane is not concerned, on two counts.

Firstly, as he will rightly explain, 'It was started with a false estimate [of £3.5 million], which I had nothing to do with.'[69]

And secondly, it is 'nonsense to speak about cost to the voter, because it was being paid for by the Opera House Lottery, which was a very good scheme'.[70]

The upshot? It's a barely perceptible fork in the road for Total Design: the engineers under their new manager, Mick Lewis, heading off one way with the Department of Public Works; the architects another way with the Committee men, all sure they are on the right track.

March to July 1963, Sydney, stopped before started

The storm clouds on high, which seem to never dissipate, are at least matched by those on site as the grumbling and rumbling of the workers starts to build. Led by members of the Building Workers' Industrial Union and the Builders' Labourers' Federation, they have taken to walking off the job in support of claims for improved wages and conditions. Right now, they want 'a site allowance of £2/15 a week, payment for public holidays and cumulative sick leave',[71] the beginning of a months'-long dispute.

Between the strikes and the historic rainfall – 'Sunny Sydney' is now called the 'Saturated City' – Bennelong Point remains at a standstill.

•

Despite his initial misgivings, and a few terse words with the architect over the May memo, Mick Lewis is starting to feel the same pull of seduction that everyone else has already given in to. He insists it's a grounded state of seduction – he shan't be getting ahead of himself – but tells *The Sun-Herald* in early June, 'We are building a dream here. Our job is to make that dream – the roof – come true.'[72]

(He has been spending a little time with Utzon lately.)

With such progress, morale is good in the architects' office.

'We get on fine together in the studio,' Mogens Prip-Buus writes home.

'There is a positive atmosphere that makes the hard work we have at the moment proceed incredibly easily.'[73]

•

On his own trip to London, the NSW Premier Robert Heffron visits the offices of Ove Arup & Partners to see up close the work being done on the Opera House and to discuss the myriad problems that have seen so many delays and cost increases. He hears much the same as Minister Ryan had a month earlier – Zunz's concerns about the tight administration of the project, which troubles the Premier.

Emerging, he says to a waiting journalist, 'I hope it will be finished in my lifetime.'[74]

In the scheme of things, it is only a passing comment, but it certainly adds to the growing unease.

July 1963, Bennelong Point, measure twice, cut once

Once a fort; now a factory.

Or a 'casting yard' as it's known to the boys on site, for making the House's huge concrete ribs for the roof.

With the rain subsided, Bennelong Point is now home to various 'casting beds' – 75-foot-long arcing steel-framed, plywood-lined moulds,

10 feet high at the centre and all lying next to each other. Each of the beds can mould five segments at once.

On these mid-winter mornings, bright and early – *Buongiorno a tutti!* – the men of Hornibrook stream like ants around the mixers and the forklifts and the moulds, preparing for a new day of construction. They pour top-grade concrete from the mixer to the casting beds, the stony grey sludge sliding down chutes with vibrators to expel any air and keep it flowing into every part of the mould to gain maximum density and therefore strength, and of course a smooth finish.

But, as with the concourse beams, they won't know quite how well everything has worked until they peel away the plywood casing and peek at the finished product beneath. Will it be free of blemishes? Will the colour be uniform? Will they reach the high bar the architect has set for them?

High bar? High bar! Funny you should say so, as the architect wouldn't mind a word with everyone right now actually.

On 17 July 1963, Mick Lewis and all his staff, the Hornibrook foremen and engineers, Utzon's architects and all the king's men gather in the Dane's office for a quick talk. The long and short of it? Utzon will not have a repeat of Stage I. The project simply can't handle 3-foot gaping holes that get patched up post-pour. Stage II must be an improvement, he says, and begins by highlighting the point.

'Standing under a rib,' he begins, looking up dreamily, as if he is indeed gazing upon his creation, 'the soffit lines can be lined up by eye from almost any position and therefore any inaccuracy will be very noticeable.'[75]

He pauses to shuffle through the papers on his desk until he finds a sketch hidden among the drawings and the dross. Pulling a faded green Faber-Castell pencil from his shirt pocket – worn down to the nub and in need of a sharpener – he begins to illustrate his thoughts: 'These areas of rib . . . as well as the edges, will be exposed, so that's where a first-class quality of work will be mandatory. It would be best if we get sample segments set up on the site so that these edges and surfaces can be clearly marked.'[76]

As for the walls and slabs and beams . . .

'I do not consider it possible to obtain a perfect off-form finish on the walls, but all slabs and beams must show the same standard of workmanship as the ribs. My aim is to convey to the patrons a feeling of consistency when they move through the building and therefore, the character of materials must be the same throughout.'[77]

The discussion proceeds, before they all head out behind the Dane for an inspection of the site, with Utzon pointing to anything he fears needs improvement. By the end, the foremen return to the casting yard – they've been read the Riot Act, and wouldn't mind just, uh, quickly double-checking that casting bed they just assembled, just to be sure . . .

Meanwhile, the French contractors are busy assembling the huge red cranes that will move the segments around the site, but there is a long way to go. For the moment, they're no more than piles of red trusses, rails and nuts and bolts and girders.

Bennelong Point is a metallic hive of industrial life, and the workers move to a deafening buzz of cursing and casting and blasting and building.

•

The mood is all at once tense, impatient, expectant, fearful and . . . hopeful.

After much experimentation with the plywood moulds, and endless consultation with the skilled Italian workmen who have constructed them, the concrete on the first rib segments has by now sufficiently cured to examine the result. The plywood is popped off using a hydraulic ram to reveal . . .

Perfection!

'The edges were pure,' one of Utzon's new Australian recruits, Peter Myers, will recall, 'there wasn't a blemish'.[78]

It really is the moment.

As Myers looks up, it is not just that he sees the tears of joy running down Jørn Utzon's face. It is that the swarthy tough Italian workers are crying, too! They are proud *artisans*, the latest and greatest heirs to centuries of evolving skill, and it is a wonderful thing for them all that the scheme works and that their know-how is being so warmly acknowledged by this sophisticated Danish architect, a European just like them.

And Utzon's joy is not simply because of the look of the thing. The whole scheme is working beautifully! For if each casting bed makes five rib segments in one pour, they should have the 2194 precast elements required to make the 224 ribs needed in no time.

Question is, with demolition of the foundations still going on, where to store all the precast elements on this narrow, busy point, until such time as the cranes can begin to move them into place? That has been thought of. They are loaded onto barges and transported out through Sydney's headlands, and around to Long Bay, to be stacked in the courtyard of Long Bay Gaol where, ideally, there will be no chance for anyone to daub vulgar graffiti on them – *Ban the Bomb* and *End the War in Viet Nam* are appearing around Sydney lately.

For now, the success of the process puts Utzon in spectacularly good spirits, and his new recruits are inspired, coming to see he's unlike any boss they've had before.

There is a sophistication to him, a sleekness, a *savoir faire* uncommon in the Australian realms. And yet, while he drives a superb and rare Citroën, has a chrome piano in his living room and always dresses well enough that he could strut down a cat-walk . . . he affects no superior airs with his staff. In fact, his expectations of them are nothing if not relaxed. He is confident, calm and collected. While architects in other firms are expected to turn up to work in a suit and a tie, and not even remove the suit-coat on a hot day, Utzon's young architects are encouraged to wear that which will make them most comfortable – which to an Australian, is *significantly* less formal than the Dane is accustomed to. Many of them have grown up on the coast and arrive without ties or jackets, and some even dare to wear sandals. It is perfect attire as many of them are invited back to the Utzon family beach house for beers and barbecues, something the Utzon family has learned to love here in Australia.

'We, as a team who worked with him, we really came to love him,' one of his architects, Richard Leplastrier, would say. 'We would have gone to the ends of the earth for him.'[79]

Keeping to the schedule? Well, not really.

When it comes to deadlines, it's not quite that Utzon loves the 'whooshing sound they make as they fly by',[80] but certainly he is not remotely alarmed by them. He sees them come and go with little more interest than he might see a train come and go on the platform over yonder, a train he is not catching.

Far more important is to strive for *perfection*, to do the finest work possible, no matter how long it takes.

Did I ever tell you about the great Danish furniture designer Kaare Klint?

Yes, Jørn, but tell it again.

'Someone comes to Klint's studio and asks him, "What are you working on?" Klint replies, "I'm working on a chair." Eighteen months later, the same man visits and again asks Klint what he is working on. "I told you," Klint says, "I'm working on a chair."'[81]

They get it. Forget the calendar. Keep going until it is *perfect*.

•

Once a closely held secret, the explosive project taking place on Bennelong Point to rectify the foundations has now leaked out to the public. The story breaks in the *Sunday Mirror* with the title 'COMIC OPERA HOUSE'[82] and it is snapped up by the political Opposition, fresh ammunition to bring down the House.

The Country Party member for Armidale, one Mr Davis Hughes – the same man who was absent at the laying of the Opera House's foundation stone on account of faking his university qualifications – rises in parliament and clears his throat to speak out.

'I ask the Minister for Public Works,' he begins with a mix of wry amusement and dry sarcasm, 'whether he can explain how erecting columns and then pulling them down, instead of doing the right thing in the first place, can cheapen the cost?'

Minister Ryan replies: 'It should have occurred to the Honourable Member for Armidale that it is possible, by modification in design and an alteration in procedure, to make an economy. That is normal practice and frequently occurs on big projects. It might not be obvious to the Honourable Member, but anyone engaged in building or has any knowledge of building practices and procedures understands that this is possible and frequently happens.'[83]

September 1963, Sydney, Moses parts the sea but not the seats

Sir Charles Moses is not happy.

As General Manager of the ABC, broadcaster and promoter of the Sydney Symphony Orchestra – which, by the way, is absolutely booming as demand outstrips the supply of seats – he would like to raise his concerns, also shared by the Sydney Symphony's conductor, Sir Bernard Heinze – about Utzon's seating arrangements in the Major Hall.

Namely, that the architect wants to place 900 seats *behind* the stage for orchestral concerts.

But, Sir Charles, have you forgotten that Utzon made his seating plan known in his Red Book of 1958, and you had seen and approved it in plans back in January of 1960, and again in 1962, when he presented his convertible hall scheme?

Well, be that as it may, Colonel Sir Charles Moses is a man of many commitments and can't be expected to remember *every* single detail from those endless and arduous Opera House meetings.

The seating arrangement must change, so that all of the audience in the Major Hall be in *front* of the orchestra as is traditional. Who would buy seats looking on the *backs* of the musicians?

But Charles knows not what the architect is privy to, which is that the *Concertgebouw* in Amsterdam and the *Philharmonie* in Berlin are designed with a similar seating plan, and neither have had any trouble selling tickets. Now, true, the ABC has no direct authority over Utzon at all, for they are not the client. Yet Sir Charles is a founding father of the Executive Committee, which remains ostensibly in charge, running the show and remaining the paymaster and so of course the ABC is the major tenant of the Opera House to be. What's more, Moses has come to know Utzon well over the years, so has no trouble in getting him to come to lunch.

Broaching the subject delicately, Sir Charles points out the need to move *all* the seats in front of the stage. That is, the need for the Dane to make significant changes to plans he has been developing since the start.

To Sir Charles' surprise, his dining companion takes it very well. Calling for the waitress to bring him a piece of paper, please, he takes out his pencil and starts to do some illustrative sketches.

'I think we can do this,' he says, indicating his solution at first blush.

'You know, Jørn,' Sir Charles says, 'you surprise me. I thought you would have been annoyed – you've done a lot of work on this. Now you've got to start again.'

Extraordinarily, Utzon does not seem overly fussed.

'Architecture is a very exciting art,' he says, continuing to draw. 'Always there are problems; and for every problem there is a solution. For me, it's exciting to find solutions to problems.'[84]

September 1963, Bennelong Point, back door politics

Speaking of problems, Mick Lewis has one. And it's not so much an architectural problem as it is an *architect* problem – one with the exact form and function of Jørn Utzon. The Dane had been generous enough to offer Mick Lewis a newly designed house on the plot of land Mick has purchased at Middle Cove, but he confides in a note to Jack Zunz:

'I am not at all sure whether I should be sad or happy, but Jørn is far too preoccupied with the Opera House to design my house – he is even having difficulty in producing the drawings for his own.'[85]

But like any good joke, there's a seed of truth, and Lewis's scepticism about Jørn Utzon is growing, just as a rift between architects and engineers is widening in turn.

The Minister's been on the phone again, asking questions, and a frustrated Jack Zunz writes to Lewis in September 1963: 'There is no doubt in our minds where the real power lies and I think if Utzon persists in bluffing himself that it lies with the Committee, it will merely complicate his, and unfortunately, our lives.'[86]

Also on 24 September 1963, Arup writes to Lewis: 'I am very fond of Jørn, he is inspiring company and I consider him to be just about the best architect I have come across. But he also has some defects which his genius and lively imagination probably make unavoidable. Being an aesthete and an aristocrat, he is inclined to value inspiring vision more than pedantic truth.'[87]

And the pedantic truth for Arup & Partners is – they want to show the pushy political client plans for Stage III as soon as possible, lest there be any blame cast their way about yet more delays or cost rises . . .

•

For Jørn Utzon, the antipathy, the anger, coming from the adjoining office is palpable and it is becoming ever more difficult to deal with. After all, with all the other growing problems, the endless political storms, the ever-changing brief, the supremely difficult problems of design, the last thing he needs is a brooding and critical consulting engineer like Mick Lewis. But the South African seems to be coming at them from all angles, starting with endlessly marching through the 'back door' uninvited demanding to see drawings for Stage III . . . even as Stage II is yet to get underway proper. Utzon is confused. If the engineers were sincere in desiring to stand back, as they had said back in May, why are they being ever more managerial and pushy? Why are they meeting with Minister Ryan and Premier Heffron without him or one of his representatives?

Fed up with the barely articulated argy-bargy, in September 1963, Jørn writes to Jack Zunz over in London, to make a few things clear.

> Only I, I am sure, can possibly visualise the final picture of the Opera House . . . No matter how difficult and heavy it is for all of us, I cannot leave any detail to other hands, and especially in this building.[88]

So to be clear . . .

Après moi, le déluge.

As to Arup & Partner's new arrangement, in which Utzon is dealing with an entirely new partner in Mick Lewis:

> I think my mistake has been that every time you have had new people coming into this scheme, as now for instance Mr Lewis

... I have not been able, even if I have tried hard, to make them understand what great danger there lies in side-tracking and not even the smallest detail, which, in the newcomer's mind has no importance, could from the architect's point of view, be left over or taken carelessly, because a number of details always add up to a total picture ... I would be very glad if you and Ove would write a stimulating letter to Mick and the staff here stating that the reason for our fine collaboration has been a mutual respect and that this mutual respect must be our main base for our relations in the future for Stage II.[89]

On the subject of design, Jørn Utzon will not be rushed into making poor decisions.

Give us *time*, Mick. Hasten not.

October 1963, Sydney, Utzon enters the labyrinth

Sir Charles Moses' eleventh hour direction that there be no seats behind the stage in the Major Hall has the distinct feel about it of the old line that a camel is a horse designed by a committee. For, as ever with Utzon's Opera House, solving problems in one field creates problems in other fields. In this case, an awkward lump of a hump has been plonked right in the middle of Utzon's original convertible Major Hall plans – a steep hump that Jørn is labouring hard to surmount.

Jørn and the architects are scrambling to figure out how 2800 seats can fit in a space only designed for 1800?

The Farm Cove office is a mad blur of brainstorming, every last man looking at the problem from every angle, but no matter which way they cut it, it just won't work.

Yuzo Mikami will later reflect on the dilemma Moses handed to Utzon: 'If you appreciated the severe limitation of the space available for the Major Hall auditorium under the new spherical roof which had been fixed by 1963 properly, it would become quite clear that what Moses requested of Utzon was in fact asking for the moon.'[90]

Nevertheless, Utzon remains remarkably calm and collected, controlled and composed.

All he knows is that he must go back to his natural home – not Hellebaek, but the old drawing board. The solution is there somewhere, he knows it. They simply must find it.

•

Two months after Sir Charles Moses casually changed the brief for the Major Hall interiors, Jørn Utzon sits down with the Opera House Technical Advisory panel under Harry Ashworth to present not just a new seating arrangement but a completely new scheme.

The solution turns on shifting from a convertible hall to a multipurpose hall and eliminating the passageway running down the centre of the hall – which will, after all, give them back the best seats in the House, right in front of the stage – and even narrowing the passageways down both sides.

Harry Ashworth and the rest of the Committee are satisfied for the moment, knowing that for all the challenges so far overcome, Utzon is the man for the job, and they retain their faith in him.

'I think we can accept the architect's suggestions,'[91] says the optimistic Harry Ashworth without analysing the sketchy new proposals. Thank you, Jørn, meeting adjourned.

●

One keen observer of such interactions between the architect and the Committee client is the NSW Government Architect Ted Farmer, employed in Minister Ryan's Department of Public Works, whose bow tie remains a'quiver with his ever-growing worries about what he sees as a lack of correct supervision over the project.

'It got to the point,' he would recount, 'that whenever [Utzon] made some suggestion or other, Ashworth would say – "I think we can accept the architect's suggestions." And that was that, there was no discussion . . . I sat there biting my tongue.'[92]

Things are done very differently in his office.

22 November 1963, Bennelong Point, triumphal arches

In Houston on his penultimate swing through Texas, President John F. Kennedy is preparing to fly to Dallas – which will stage the last act of an extraordinary story.

In Sydney, the great day has come, for the first of the giant red cranes has finally been assembled and swings into action, a three-man crew manning it, its arm operating on a radius of 30 metres to carry the 10-ton blocks, and in short order the first precast rib segment of the first shell is carefully lowered into position atop its concrete pedestal and secured – the first act of another extraordinary story.

Immediately the first segment is in position, the second one is placed on it. Finally, when all segments from base to apex are in position, cables are threaded through and tightened using massive jacks developed in Canada, tying the individual segments into one unified and immensely strong whole. Sure enough, over succeeding days and weeks, slowly but perceptibly as Sydney ferry commuters note with interest, magnificent arches start to reach out towards each other – the older passengers noting it is just as it was back in the 1920s when work started on building the Sydney Harbour Bridge.

'There the proud arch, Colossus-like, bestride
'Yon glittering streams, and bound the chasing tide . . .'[93]

Now, ensuring the curved ribs are exactly where they need to be in mid-air, is proving a whole different challenge due to all the stresses and strains, and the heating and cooling of the materials from day to night, making it easy for the arches to move out of alignment and beyond the inch-perfect precision required. Again, innovation is required and one of Arup's finest young minds, the Irishman Peter Rice, is put on the task. First, 'surveying pins' are placed on each arch to determine exactly how the erection arch should be positioned so that the next arch will re-align perfectly. As for the calculations required to perfectly position the segments in mid-air, they are extraordinary in their complexity, each one taking so many days it is estimated – *dot three, carry one, subtract two* – it will be well into the new century before the ribs could be completed, unless . . .

Unless, a computer could do the job?

Thankfully, General Electric on York Street has computers powerful enough for the task and agrees to lend a hand.

So it is that late each weeknight a humble surveyor and a shy computer programmer clock on, gather the relevant documentation waiting for them at the Farm Cove office and head off to the dark and empty General Electric building to use their computer – the whole thing so much on the dark side of the street and so much in the wee hours, it actually feels more like Cold War spy work than a construction job. They keep going to that point of the night when very, very late starts to meet very early, and just as Sydney's bakers are clocking on, this unlikely pair are clocking off, delivering the night's numbers down to Bennelong Point on their way home, so the builders have precise placement data each morning, ready for the day ahead.

(In fact, this is not the only computer in use. After Hornibrook's resident mathematical genius, Joe Bertony, works out the stresses and deflections for each rib by hand, a younger man by the name of David Evans is sent, for a week each month, to the only computer in the land powerful enough to check the calculations – the IBM 7090 at 'the Woomera Rocket Range' as it's known in South Australia. Though the computer is more often used to track the trajectories of long-range missiles, the Defence Research Centre has allowed young Evans use of the computer from sun-down to sun-up.)

Such use of computers for construction purposes has rarely, if ever, been done before and certainly not in Australia.

All of it is right at the edge of the possible. Precisely – within a half-inch – as Utzon wants it.

As for the men doing the construction work, they are a bold lot, working right on the edge of a bloody freefall, folks brave enough to strike out from the Old World and emigrate to an unknown land at the end of the earth. So, the nous needed is in them already.

And broadly, they like what they find down on Bennelong Point – conditions here in the 'workingman's paradise' could not be better as unions are strong in this land and particularly active on this most famous building site in the country to ensure that the pay is as high as the compensation for injury. Any resistance, and we strike! The unions are even able to insist that the bosses pay for translators to be on site to better inform the workers of all relevant issues.

Assured safety in the workplace, however? It is an admired concept, but not yet born in this historical moment.

Without anything that even resembles a 'safety harness' – few of the workers have even heard of such a thing – the men spit on their palms and scramble over and under the massive ribs of exposed concrete, 'riding the hook' that swings from the red giants, hundreds of feet up into the open air with nothing but a hard hat to protect them. One wrong move, one poorly placed foot or loose grip, and they will fall to certain death. Theirs is a brazen display of reckless confidence that would become unthinkable in the years to come.

At day's end, many of them sling a line in to the harbour in the hope of taking home a big fish for dinner.

•

Utzon's senior architect, Mogens Prip-Buus, is appalled.

'As for Arup's comments to the newspapers,' he writes home to his parents in Denmark, 'of course they're all lies and slander. They have been out to steal the honour and haven't exactly behaved properly over the last year . . . The point is that they are establishing a firm of architects including Yuzo among others, and they have been wanting to smother us so as to come out on top themselves. The way Jørn is being treated is incredible, and I think I am one of the few who can say where the truth lies, as I am up to my eyes in it.'[94]

Yes, the arches of the Opera House roof are reaching out to each other, and it is indeed glorious, but the same cannot be said for the professionals working on the project, as they lean on each other less and less.

On hearing the news of major design changes to the Major Hall interiors, Ove Arup in London is aghast at the compromise the ABC's request will force upon Jørn and the building – a complete departure from the convertible hall scheme that the architect and consultants have been working on for years. Although relations with the architect are not quite what they used to be, Ove writes to Jørn on the matter in early 1964:

> I imagine you would not have agreed to this unless it was abso-
> lutely necessary, for I do not think you would have agreed to a
> solution which bears the mark of compromise, and which seems
> to destroy some of the wonderful clarity and simplicity which
> characterised the original idea.[95]

Ove even brings up the freeze in relations that has come after Arup's move to restructure the contractual relationship with the Premier and Minister the previous year, saying:

> I must admit I was deeply affected by your attitude to my suggestion
> that clear lines were needed as regards the other engineering work. It
> had nothing to do with avarice, but on the contrary with the sound
> principle that responsibility and the right to make decisions must
> follow each other. Our people in Sydney are despondent, they do
> not feel there is progress with Stage III, and they are fighting with
> problems on Stage II. I do not know whether you have thought of
> getting other engineers to help you with Stage III – that would in a
> way take quite a weight off our shoulders, but I do not think it is a
> realistic solution even if I would welcome the idea of someone else
> solving the problems and experiencing your method of working. And
> it would be a calamity politically – it is my opinion that it is unthink-
> able. We must therefore work together, there is no alternative.[96]

For Jørn's part, Ove's note hardly helps him to solve the enormous design issues he faces with his Major Hall and is a sign that the feelings of their once warm and productive collaboration are cooling further, reduced as it is to resentments and arrow slinging.

Utzon replies:

Dear Ove, please desist from your criticism! Be secure in the knowledge that I am the only one who can manage Stage III of the project.

Your criticism of me and your letter to M Lewis with your suggestion for the management of Stage III is wide of the mark. You have confused your staff and removed some of the respect for me on the part of M Lewis which is a precondition for us working together. Without knowing me or my staff he has indicated that he has doubts about our management skills. That I can only regard as being the result of the attitude of his boss, which is you. Management is in a way the easiest part of the job, something which most people can learn. The difficult part, the real problem, is to create the possibility of achieving what you want, and that, you must admit, I have shown myself able to master.[97]

In the words of the famous folk song . . .

The old grey mare, she ain't what she used to be,
Many long years ago

TWELVE

STORM APPROACHING

It started life as a fine, free soaring of the human spirit in the architecturally optimistic 1950s, and it developed into an intense intellectual exercise in the soberer 60s.[1]

Robin Boyd, Australian architect, 18 September 1965

I sometimes wonder whether those future architectural historians who will write about the Sydney Opera House will understand how largely its fate was influenced by the politics of the State of New South Wales – straight, knock-down, drag-out party politics.[2]

John Yeomans, *The Other Taj Mahal*

I am not an actor who is used to working in the limelight all the time, and this can be distracting. It would be well if we could cover the whole site with canvas and reveal the product when it is finished. But you cannot ask for that.[3]

Jørn Utzon, 1 July 1964

[Jørn] is of course completely dedicated to this job – one can almost say that he gives his life to it. But geniuses are of course difficult to work with. Utzon is a very charming and genial genius, but uncompromising and very demanding when the quality of the job as he sees it is at stake.[4]

Ove Arup, January 1965

Early 1964, Sydney, it never rains but it pours

The first months of this year, 1964, have been among the toughest of Jørn Utzon's life. He's swimming in a sea of troubles.

First, there's troubles with the plywood manufacturer, Ralph Symonds, whose builders and engineers he has been working with, developing the designs for his acoustic ceilings, among other things. After Ralph had suddenly died a couple of years ago, the firm was left with its affairs so out of order that it has just been placed in receivership. Utzon *knows* the company has precisely the expertise he needs, but there are already signs that the government is distinctly underwhelmed by the notion of giving a contract to a company submerged in the red sea, with no sign of Moses.

Also troubling the Dane is that sound solutions for the seating of the Major Hall remain so elusive that both Arup's engineers and the acoustics consultants are none too happy about the ABC's eleventh-hour change of heart, which is pushing them all back onto the now well-worn but jammed path that leads back to – yes – the old drawing board. Utzon will later write of the ABC's late-1963 directive for no seats behind the stage: 'I accepted this blindly because of my respect for my client and his demands, although I immediately found my consultants against me. Nobody wanted to collaborate on this, neither the structural engineers nor the acoustical specialists . . .'[5]

Even the uncritical Utzon admits to his architects that, after all the alterations of design and brief over the years, the Major Hall 'has some very ugly proportions'.[6]

Then there's the ever mounting pressure on the architect coming from the Public Works Department. With an election one year away, Minister Norm Ryan begins breathing so hot and heavy down the architect's neck that, at the beginning of March, he even appoints an old South African architect from Ted Farmer's Government Architect's office, Bill Wood, as 'a liaison' between Utzon's office and the department. Many years later Ted Farmer would admit that his department had put in one of his staff, 'as a sort of spy down there to see if he could find out what was going on'.[7]

Utzon and his architects know it, too, Mogens Prip-Buus writing home to his parents: 'an old architect from Public Works has been foisted on us to keep check on us'.[8]

Not that the appointment in any way calms Minister Ryan's nerves, as the hits keep on coming. Sadly, it is not an April Fool's joke when, on 1 April 1964, the quantity surveyors send over the latest estimate from London . . . £17.4 million! For the moment, the Minister keeps that shocking figure out of the public domain, hoping to find a way to get such new expenditure approved by the parliament without Robin Askin biting the government's head off – perhaps the architect could shoulder the blame this time?

For Utzon, troubles with the Opera House take a back seat when in mid-April, his beloved eldest brother, Leif, suffers a heart attack and drops dead at the age of just 49. Leif's grief-stricken widow and three children are stranded in Paris, where they have been living, so it's up to

Jørn to take the first plane, help to arrange the funeral and escort them back to Copenhagen and settle them.

He is only able to return to Australia and his own family six weeks later in early June, to find that things at the Opera House have become even more grim in his absence. For by now the goodwill engendered by the Queen's visit a year before, which Utzon will later say gave him breathing space – 'she has great influence in Australia. I had no trouble for a year after that'[9] – is gone.

While he was overseas, Minister Ryan had sought to open negotiations to lower the architect's fee, for all the world as if the lottery proceeds are not right now £4.68 million in surplus! The Minister cares not. In politics, perception is all, and right now Utzon, the project's figurehead, is perceived as expensive, which means the Opposition Leader is gaining traction on the subject, and Ryan is trying to head him off at the pass. What's worse, for the first time, Utzon does not have the NSW Premier in his corner as on 30 April, Premier Heffron had handed the Premiership over to one Jack Renshaw, a younger man from Labor's right faction with an axe to grind on many matters, but not one to swing in the service of the Opera House and its architect. He simply doesn't care that much.

For the Opposition, Labor's disarray is perfect, and Robin Askin pounces: 'The hidden strategists who control Labor politics have decided on a top-level reshuffle in a desperate effort to avert annihilation at the coming elections.'[10]

As much as possible, Jørn Utzon tries to steer clear of the politics and simply takes solace that Stage II is moving forward nicely. The casting yard down on Bennelong Point is as busy as an ant's nest, while the red giants that have become the symbol of the harbourside worksite are nearly always in full swing, their great arms lifting and swinging and lowering, one by one, the huge concrete segments on the lengthening ribs.

Stage III, too, is coming along, with the Minor Hall scheme ready to be model tested out at Symonds' factory.

Fine. But what concerns Minister Ryan is handing money over for the prototypes without it going to tender, not to mention the *lack* of progress in tender documents, schedules and cost planning for the Major Hall, for which there are few working drawings (according to old Bill Wood), and – when mixed with public reports of blow-outs in the bills – it is becoming ever more a live political issue as the election looms. Ryan must tread carefully.

Then there's the trouble with Arup's leading man on site, Mick Lewis, who continues to be a source of stress for Utzon in private, making no secret of his disdain for the Dane to a number of colleagues.

For nine months now, Lewis writes to Jack Zunz, Utzon has been promising the drawings for the acoustic ceilings in 'three weeks' time',[11] but he might as well have promised it on the 12th of Never. Because they bloody well *never* appear!

He adds sardonically: 'I leave it to your judgement whether you think he can produce the documents . . .'[12]

Frankly, Lewis doesn't. So what the hell can a consultant engineer do? An engineer can get very angry is what an engineer can do, and that exactly describes the mood of the surly South African.

Matters are made infinitely worse when the news breaks that Utzon has not only entered another architectural competition, this one in Zurich to build a theatre, but he has won it!

Lewis has been screaming for drawings for Stage III and Utzon's mob has been working on *other* pie-in-the-sky projects? For the South African, it is *outrageous*.

(Lewis is not the only one distinctly underwhelmed. 'It isn't every architect who,' the *Herald* notes with sarcasm, 'with a mammoth project like the Opera House in hand, could turn his spare time to such constructive and rewarding account.'[13])

Utzon makes no apology whatsoever. He is an architect, Mick, running a business. And it is the very nature of a business to go out after new work, even while overseeing the final stages of a previous work. It is with that in mind, he and his team have *also* submitted a plan to win an architectural competition to design the Madrid opera house. (Yes, he had said in 1957 that he'd 'not take on any other work until we have completed the Opera House'[14] . . . but that had been seven years ago, before the sod was even turned.)

Lewis's simmer turns to a boil, and he is now barely managing to keep a lid on himself.

Finally, Utzon makes a key response to Lewis's frequent unannounced visits into the architects' office through the back door, to curtly demand drawings and peer over their shoulders as they work – and does in fact oversee one key bit of building without so much as a preliminary drawing. In this chilly winter of 1964, the 'back door' between the engineers' and the architects' offices is bricked up. The Total Design principles that once guided the close collaboration between Jørn Utzon and Ove Arup – those halcyon days now seem so long ago – have now, officially, hit a brick wall.

Meanwhile, Minister Ryan calls a press conference to address the many issues that are buzzing around.

17 June 1964, Sydney, another architect?

The day before The Beatles are set to touch down at Kingsford Smith Airport in Sydney, on their first tour of Australia – oh, how the older generations flare angrily to see the teen girls swoon – and just as Prime Minister Robert Menzies prepares to take off to the US and then London to discuss the communist threat sweeping South-East Asia – 'the Red Terror' – Premier Jack Renshaw's NSW Government announces the latest, damning Opera House estimate.

Minister Ryan steps to the dais and chooses his words purposefully.

'The architect of the Sydney Opera House, Mr Jørn Utzon, now estimates that it will cost £17.4 million – £4.9 million more than the last official estimate in 1962.'

The press pack gasp as one.

'We are very concerned and surprised,' says the Minister. 'I have requested the architect to carefully examine all possible economies that might be effected to reduce the estimated cost.'

'What will happen,' a journalist presses, 'if Mr Utzon's revised estimate is not acceptable?'[15]

'We will have to examine that when he gives his report. I would not expect that there would be any thought of abandoning the project.'

Another pressman steps forward.

'Has the government considered employing another architect?'

'Mr Utzon's contract is ratified by parliament,' Mr Ryan replies, then reiterates: 'We are very concerned and surprised that the cost has reached the estimate submitted by Mr Utzon. I don't think anyone thought the cost would reach this figure.'

'Mr Askin did!'[16] calls out one of the press crowd.

Quite. And, in fact, the Leader of the Opposition will have plenty more to say, starting by calling the government's handling of the project, 'one of Australia's most notorious financial bungles'.[17]

According to Askin, the key ingredients which have contributed to the Opera House 'scandal' include 'mismanagement, deceit, Communist-inspired strikes, and shameful waste of public funds by a government no longer fitted to be entrusted with the State's affairs'[18] ...

On top of it all, the *Herald* prints another article focused on the views of arguably the Opera House's longest-time architectural critic, the lugubrious Walter Bunning, who thinks it's time to call in – *don't hold your horses* – all the King's men.

'A Sydney architect, Mr Walter Bunning, last night called for the appointment of a Royal Commission to investigate the steeply rising cost of the Sydney Opera House.'[19]

As to what should be done about it, Bunning says: 'The State Government should halt work on the project and set up a Royal Commission' to ascertain among other things, 'Why has the accommodation been changed, reducing the number of seats?' and 'Why has the roof form and construction been radically changed from the original design; that is, from a revolutionary shell dome construction to conventional beam and slab?'[20]

All this controversy, and that bloke Utzon is making a fortune?

'Architect Gets £389,000,'[21] reads a report in the *Herald* the following day.

The situation for Labor will be summed up by film-maker John Weiley, as narrated by Bob Ellis: 'Faced now by a growing number of administrative scandals and holding power by a perilously small majority, the Labor government were only too happy to let some of the blame fall on Utzon. He was an artist, after all, and probably therefore irresponsible.'[22]

One letter to the editor is emblematic of the dozens that are published in all Sydney papers:

> Sir,
> Rather than continue this solid gold Opera House it would be better to roof it with corrugated iron for a bus depot, so that it will be a constant reminder to us of the many blunders of our present State Government.
> B. Schumacher, Rose Bay[23]

Utzon, still grieving the death of his brother, is more embattled than ever. He can't pick up a paper without feeling pilloried, can't answer the office telephone without being distracted from the work in hand, can't go to a café without being asked pointed questions by doubt-filled passers-by. To make things worse, Utzon is under strict new orders from the Premier and Minister Ryan to never talk costs or design specifics in public, but he can talk about other things ... A talk with the first journalist he ever sat down with might help allay the public anxiety?

•

The *Herald*'s Gavin Souter cannot help but quietly note just how much older Jørn Utzon looks now, since their first meeting at the Australian Club years before. The Dane's hair has turned a white grey, his skin slack, dark bags under the eyes. Yes, he is still handsome and has his child-like charm as he stands up from his chair at the site office – impossibly tall and lanky, smiling broadly to greet the veteran journalist in his Danish lilt – but Souter notices a dull edge on the architect's once overflowing joy. There is a weariness to him now that looks to go clear to the bone.

'Does public criticism worry you?' Souter asks softly.

'No,' the Dane replies. 'What worries me are problems arising from the job, most of the criticism has no sound basis. I see much bigger problems in the job than people who are not working with us can see.'

'Have you yourself at any stage in the last seven years been surprised at the way cost estimates have increased?'

'I cannot say anything about costs until after I have seen the Premier. On the latest estimates, though, our Opera House with its three stages is still relatively cheaper than the corresponding facilities at New York's Lincoln Center, and it is no more expensive than the latest new theatre in Germany . . .'

'Would it have been feasible for you to have demanded more time for planning before the building began?'

'This was not possible, because Mr Cahill's program was for political reasons fixed in time, and if we could not fulfil the program the building would not have been started . . .'[24]

Opposition Leader Robin Askin pounces again, describing as '*start-ling*' Mr Utzon's recent remark that Joe Cahill had rushed the start for political reasons, and he demands a frank public explanation from the Premier. Now make no mistake. The Liberal Party will complete the project upon taking office, but will no longer condone 'the shocking waste of millions of pounds that has occurred'.[25]

The Premier cannot go into an election defending the figures on the table – get me the architect!

23 July 1964, Macquarie Street, Sydney, Utzon goes through a bad stage

Well, this is uncomfortable.

No, not just the freezing winds whipping off Pittwater that turn Jørn's hands to ice blocks as he hops in the car and drives into the city.

Jørn Utzon has been summarily summoned – and that is very much the right phrase – to a meeting with the Premier and a cabinet sub-committee of five senior Ministers now assigned to look into the Opera House.

Prip-Buus meets him outside and they make their way into the austere meeting room in silence. Mick Lewis is already seated when they arrive. Now, back in August of '62, when Utzon, Arup and Zunz had been called to Sydney for a similar meeting about the engineering of the roof structure, things had been convivial and collegiate. But this is not like that. The mood is hostile towards Utzon from the first, and after an exchange of pleasantries that is neither pleasant nor even much of an exchange, the discussion begins by focusing on the *outrageous* increase in costs, and what can be done to curtail them. And what of these Stage III drawings you have shown us, which our Government Architect, Ted Farmer, has looked over? Deputy Premier Pat Hills places a stack of drawings onto the table.

'Mr Utzon, are these your working drawings for Stage III? Because as far as we are concerned, *these* –' Hills picks up three drawings from the piles and waves them in Utzon's direction, '– are the *only* working drawings. And how are we to place a contract if that's the extent of the work you have done?'[26]

And he's not done there.

'I see you've been putting forward suggestions for the carpark,' Hills continues with a snarl. 'If we want a competent architect to design that carpark, we will engage him to do so. But you are not engaged to design that carpark!'[27]

And so goes the tenor of the meeting – what Mick Lewis will describe as 'pretty abusive'[28] treatment of Utzon who receives nothing less than 'a mauling'.[29]

It is all so nakedly aggressive, so adversarial, as if instead of being the architect, responsible for the greatest masterpiece on earth, Utzon and his men are the enemy!

'I . . . received,' Prip-Buus writes home, 'the biggest shock I have so far had in this country.'[30]

Utzon, himself profoundly shocked, begins citing figures and details.

Pat Hills again – 'Stop, stop, stop. We don't want figures and details, only facts.'[31]

Utzon takes pause, grins ever so slightly at the absurdity of the Deputy Premier's statement, and starts again, asking: 'How can you get facts when you refuse to listen to figures?'[32]

More bluster follows, but the political men are not backing off.

When Utzon notes calmly that things were running well under the Committee – who fully understand the technical issues – he is firmly told that those days are gone, and he must now deal with *this* committee.

'We had to bring him down to earth with a jolt,' one Minister will later comment, 'and we did it in record time.'[33]

Utzon and Prip-Buus, along with Mick Lewis – who has been shocked into a rare state of sympathy for the architects – amble back down to the site office together. Walking up the poky wooden steps to the shared office verandah, Jørn invites Mick to, 'Come and have a drink.'

Inside the architect's office, before the first bite of the sandwich Jørn has rustled up for them, Lewis blurts out what's on his mind.

'You know, Jørn,' he says, according to his recollection many years later, 'you've got to do something about this. You've got to get some-body to produce the documents for Stage III. You haven't got in your staff the sort of people you need, and you're never going to get there.'

'Oh, I don't know,' Utzon replies mildly. 'I don't believe you should employ another architect for that. All the architects, like Mies van der Rohe and Le Corbusier and a few of the other greats have tried that, and it doesn't work. I must do everything myself. That's the only way this Opera House can be built.'[34]

'Well, if they're prepared to give you fifty years to build it, it's just a possibility you might finish it then. But otherwise, you haven't got a chance.'[35]

Jørn Utzon sighs. It's been a long day. A long year.

'Anyway,' Jørn says, 'I think I'm going to resign.'

'Oh, I don't think that's a very good idea,' says Lewis, aghast. 'You were appointed by an Act of Parliament. I've got an old-fashioned view about resigning. You never resign. Because you don't solve problems by resigning.'

'Oh, no,' Utzon replies. 'If I resign, they'll come back to me . . . and I'll get it exactly the way I want it to be.'[36]

He tells Lewis the story of his Swedish architectural hero, Gunnar Asplund, for whom the resignation tactic worked a treat with complaining political clients – they always realised they *needed* him, and backed down right away.

Well, that may fly in Sweden, but the South African Lewis – party to many back-room governmental chats of late with the leading figures of the Public Works Department – is far from sure: 'Well, I think that's a pious hope.'[37]

But there is no way around it.

The heated political meeting is reported the next day.

CHALLENGE BY RENSHAW ON OPERA HOUSE COST . . .
'Plain talking' at meeting[38]

As for Mr R. W. Askin, he's a having a ball, telling the press that Mr Renshaw is simply flexing, anxious to, 'get the Waratah by-election over before more bad news about the Opera House cost spiral hits the startled public'.[39]

Jørn Utzon meanwhile assures a reporter over the phone – after Lewis has left by the front door – that, 'Sydney people are getting value for their money. It is a shame that people are getting so unhappy about it because of so much propaganda. I have given myself to it body and soul for the last seven and a half years.'[40]

From where architect Mogens Prip-Buus sits, the meeting was pure political bluster. 'To be perfectly honest, [the Ministers] were scared,' he tells his parents. 'Jørn is to be turned into a scapegoat for both the government and the engineers and has been denied a right to defend himself.'[41]

Though his years on the job have helped Utzon learn, hands-on, about managing a project of this size – before that, he'd never managed a job even a hundredth this size – he has *no* experience with politics, let alone NSW State politics, and no idea of what it takes to deal with bare-knuckle political infighting before a close election. Under Joe Cahill, Old Smoothie, everything had been . . . smooth and supportive. Now every-thing is rough, jagged and filled with back-stabbing and blame-shifting.

The press, who had usually swung between praise that is either lavish or slavish, is now attacking him personally.

'In the mounting controversy over the cost of the Opera House,' the State Political Correspondent from the *Herald* had recently noted with tightly pursed lips, 'Mr Utzon has not helped the public to understand his cause. In his dealings with the press he has been courteously vague, as if a sensitive musician were being interrogated by someone who was obviously tone deaf.'[42]

The public know not of Minister Ryan's order that the architect never publicly speak on the details of costs or design . . .

'The situation here is approaching the limit of what we can tolerate,' Prip-Buus writes home to his parents. 'Because of politics and approaching elections, the entire Opera House affair is now caught up in a network of lies, and we have no chance of defending ourselves, partly because the Government forbids us to make statements; and then the newspapers won't write the truth even if we do try to defend ourselves, as the truth that is good for us is not such good copy as the scandalous lies . . .'[43]

And the engineers have a hand in it, too! Aside from the fact they earn more than the architects, and have just themselves advised the government that it remains 'impossible to estimate the final cost of the [Stage II] construction until one of the "roof sails" had been erected'[44] – likely after Christmas some time – their reputation is rosy. Prip-Buus tells his parents of a visit to the site by two prominent English architects, Basil Spence and William Holford, who 'warned us against Arup whom they knew only too well in England, as he always seeks the honour for the architect's work'.[45]

It is all so *unfair*!

So grim is the mood that Prip-Buus even writes: 'We are just on the point of calling a halt, so now we will finish the designs and then if they won't build on the basis of them, we must leave, as we have no intention of ruining the Opera House by going along with compromises.'[46]

He and Utzon are agreed: no compromises.

•

All put together, the pressure starts to tell on the normally good-humoured Utzon.

That much is evident when, in August 1964, the Dane visits both Zurich for the Schauspielhaus project – the architecture competition he had won – and Berlin to consult his acoustic experts, and on his way back to Australia drops in to London where, in a fierce meeting with Jack Zunz and Ove Arup, there is nothing less than the 'banging of fists'[47] upon the table as Utzon unleashes on what he sees as the lack of support coming from Arup's Sydney office this past year.

Utzon asks them for support in his shaky relationship with Lewis, and Jack Zunz is surprisingly swayed by what he hears, writing to Mick: '[Jørn] is nettled at the thought of our not supporting him in handling Stage III. He put up very powerful arguments to support his case and insists . . . we support him loyally as he has supported us in Stages I and II. We should do this.'[48]

Apparently Zunz has come back to the notion that it is important they show a united front. But still, he tells Lewis to keep one eye on the panicking Minister for Public Works.

•

Upon his return to Australia in September 1964, Utzon opens a second design office up Palm Beach way – in Goddard's boatshed, out the back of the general provision store on Snapperman Beach. For the Dane it feels a lot like home, positioned with its own slipway jetty and reminding him of his grandmother's house on Øresund. A refreshing change from the high-pressure atmosphere down at the site office, it fits better with his preferred calm demeanour.

In fact, such a place of peace is this he chooses *not* to install a telephone. He doesn't want to stay on top of endless messages and calls from Bennelong Point, the press, the many-headed client, he wants to get to the *bottom* of his interior designs – specifically the plywood acoustic ceiling and the frustratingly complex glass walls he is designing to close up the open end of the shells that look over the harbour, not to mention the issue of seat arrangements in the Major Hall.

There is, mind you, one image of a phone apparent . . . after a fashion. It comes in the form of an enormous poster he plasters on the wall showing a disassembled telephone, its hundreds of components strewn across a table. The caption reads: 'Put them together and dial anywhere.'

For Jørn, the poster is a reminder of the extraordinary things that can be accomplished by putting disparate components together in the right way. On their own, they are inanimate lumps. Assembled together you can speak to someone on the other side of the world!

So, too, with the Opera House. They just have to find the right way to put the disparate components together and it will be something *extraordinary*.

(Which might be fine for Utzon and his closest designers. But Mick Lewis is beside himself with barely contained rage. On a project of this complexity – and in the history of the world there has never been a building of equal complexity – to have an architect who is unreachable on the telephone a few days a week creates deep frustration, as he tries to keep the engineering on schedule.)

With some relief, Utzon settles into a new rhythm, working a few days a week close to home at Palm Beach, and the rest at Bennelong Point, with occasional forays out to Homebush with Ralph Symonds' boys, sorting out the details of the plywood designs for the acoustic ceiling.

September 1964, Sydney, Renshaw reins the Dane . . . again

The time has come for the Dane to be addressed firmly, to be spoken to frankly, for pragmatism to trump perfection, and so on 23 September 1964, six months out from the election, Premier Renshaw seats himself to write to Utzon, mincing no words when it comes to what must happen:

> The work will not proceed on Stage III until the architect has:
> 1. Provided a comprehensive detailed report . . . in regard to each section of Stage III.
> 2. Satisfied the Minister for Public Works that the whole of Stage III has been fully designed and that there can be no doubts as to construction procedures.
> 3. Prepared working drawings and specifications and all other documents required to enable the calling of competitive tenders.[49]

These prove to be merely his opening remarks . . .

Utzon receives the letter, and replies without addressing the request for a detailed report on all of Stage III. What he does want to talk about, to get Stage III humming along, is to get moving with making models to test the plywood acoustic ceiling designs.

'The co-operation with Ralph Symonds together with the fact that the design is based on their know-how and the machinery in their factory, makes it possible to reduce the number of components to a minimum, and allows the simplest possible solution [for the acoustic ceilings] and thereby the cheapest manufacture.'[50]

The fact is, Premier, the plywood ceilings for both theatres are to be assembled from huge, pre-finished plywood panels with bronze hot-bonded on one side. If it all works out, the design will appear to the theatre-goer as if 'hanging like a cloud in the sky'.[51]

Now, to turn the Minor Hall drawings into prototypes should require £60,000, and this is crucial expenditure, to check the structural, acoustic and architectural details.

Then I can do the final working drawings, Premier. You must understand that Symonds is the only company in the world equipped to do the work . . . or did I mention that?

Well, in one letter to Minister Norm Ryan he mentions it 11 times: 'produced only by Symonds' – 'Only Ralph Symonds' factory is capable . . .' – 'Vitally important to let Ralph Symonds participate . . .'[52]

After all, Utzon points out – not unreasonably – this is precisely the way he had done things with the tiles. And not only had they been completely successful in the product they had come up with, the final costs had been lower than any of the other quotes tendered, and they had finished the whole thing ahead of schedule. This is the European way of doing things. And as he is architect of this project, it is the way Utzon wants to do things.

•

Through it all, the ribs of the majestic first shell – one of the smaller ones – is now complete, and, for the first time, tourists and Sydneysiders alike start to have their photos taken in front of it. Old-timers tell the story of the days of the Harbour Bridge being built, and watching the great steel fingers reaching out to meet each other. Well, this is like that, but they're fingers of concrete reaching out, and it is *mesmerising*.

On the opposite side of the harbour, the priests of St Aloysius' College must pull the blinds of the classroom to prevent their students from staring out the window all day. Artists begin to set up their easels in the Botanic Gardens to better capture the majestic shell from on high, even as such famous Australian photographers as Max Dupain, David Moore and Harry Sowden start clicking it from every angle imaginable.

Meanwhile, Government Architect Ted Farmer stares down at the site each weekday from his office on high, in the Public Works Department on Phillip Street – and is something less than mesmerised.

Mostly, he feels frustrated, at just how *slowly* they rise, at how it's all being run.

In an effort to speed things up, and to attempt to smooth the growing tensions, both Ove Arup and Jack Zunz arrive in Sydney in September 1964. A round of meetings ensue, but the bottom line remains: Utzon needs those prototypes before he can produce the drawings.

'Unfortunately,' Prip-Buus writes home, 'the shells have been much delayed; even though they are starting to get a move on, the building will scarcely be ready for opening before the beginning of '68 when we take into consideration the time for testing the machinery. Unfortunately, we can't start on the interior until the shells are up.'[53]

•

One major item that is way ahead of schedule is the innovative stage machinery that Utzon's team and consultants have designed for the Major Hall, which is now being packed up and sent on its way by sea from Europe – no less than 1200 tons of it – so sophisticated, so capable of seamlessly moving stages and sets up and down the stage tower, it will reportedly put Sydney's Opera House ahead of its famous forebears like London's Covent Garden and New York's Metropolitan.

'When *Das Rheingold* is staged,' one of the consultants in Vienna boasts to the *Herald*, 'the Rhine maidens will swim across the stage, apparently in real water. We will be able to create on stage in a moment, a great vista of scenery, and to elevate or lower the stage to create mountains and plains and caverns. Picture the last act of *Aida*, when the lovers go hand in hand to their death in an underground tomb! On your stage, they will appear to walk deep into a mountain, while the crowd gathers above.'[54]

In the current lull in public support for the House (and Utzon), the news is a boon.

Not that it really matters what the public and the government think.

'They can do very little against us,' Prip-Buus notes, 'as they realise that no-one else can manage the job.'[55]

After all, who else but the original creators, the people who have been working on the design for years, could deal with these unique and huge performance spaces?

25 November 1964, NSW Parliament House, 'Why not sack him?'

In the wake of the Premier's remarks, Mr Speaker, to the effect that Mr Utzon has recently affirmed that the final estimate of the cost of the Opera House remains at £17.4 million, irrespective of what the government's opinion might be, the Leader of the Opposition, Robin Askin, seeks to confirm one matter.

'Does the Government already know that no matter how much the figures are adjusted and rearranged it will get no change out of £20,000,000? Is it true that this represents the greatest financial bungling in the history of this State?' he asks.[56]

'Though Mr. Utzon and his associates are highly qualified people,' Premier Renshaw replies, as he carefully lies the architect down in front of an oncoming electoral campaign bus, 'they were unable to give an estimate of cost that I, as Premier, my officers and the Minister for Public Works and his officers, regarded as satisfactory . . .'

'Why not sack him?'[57] interjects, most unpleasantly, the Country Party Member for Barwon, Geoffrey Crawford.

'Order!' calls Mr Speaker.

But it's all right, the Premier is happy to answer.

'With due respect to the Honourable Member for Barwon, sacking would not resolve the problem. I am sure that all Honourable Members accept the Opera House as a unique building and a prototype in design.'[58]

There are bound to be problems with something so unique. We will get through this.

(But one 'prototype in design' the government rejects are the plywood prototypes for the Minor Hall that Utzon is seeking funding for.

No, the reply comes back to the architect. Not now. Not with a company in receivership right before an election. Instead, we want a full report on the state of the project . . . that should buy us time.)

•

With the announcement by the Prime Minister of Australia of the *National Service Act* – essentially conscription, requiring 20-year-old males to serve in the army – in response to what Menzies describes as the 'aggressive communism'[59] in Asia, the Opera House drops a rank or two back in public concern. Only the state politicians maintain their fierce focus, with constant clashes and public calls for Utzon's head . . . which are all starting to wear on the impossibly optimistic Jørn Utzon.

At the forefront of his mind is that his brother Leif had died an overworked man, and Jørn often tells himself that he must not do the same, must not leave Lis and the kids for the sake of a building. No, he doesn't work less because of it, but he does try to get more exercise, eat better and at least occasionally go sailing on Pittwater.

'We were quite unprepared for the media attention we received,' Lis Utzon will recount. 'We were just normal people, a normal family, not the urban sophisticates we had been made out to be by the press. It was quite a strain on our family . . . totally unexpected and at times overwhelming.'[60]

All up though, they couldn't love their Australian lives more and, in the quiet of the night, Jørn and Lis even start to talk of the possibility of staying here permanently, and putting down forever roots. The strong and vibrant community on the northern peninsula is beginning to feel like home.

By now their son Jan is studying Architecture at the University of New South Wales and to save him travel time, the Utzons have bought a terrace house in Paddington for him to share with friends, which Jørn and Lis also often use as a southern base. In the meantime, down at the south end of Palm Beach, where the Utzons go to the ocean pool every Saturday morning for a swim, they have befriended an interesting woman. Her name is Margaret Fulton, the cooking editor for the popular magazine *Woman's Day*, no less than the first 'food writer' in the country who will one day be credited as one of the writers who 'began serving up Chinese recipes to Menzies' Australia',[61] trying to steer Australians away from meat and three veg and explore other cuisines from around the globe. She's a pioneer, like Jørn, and their families become fast friends.

And his boatshed office is helping him concentrate. Sometimes, after working all morning in the boatshed at Snapperman Beach, he takes the design team for a picnic lunch at a nearby oceanside cave he had discovered on one of his walks, a beautiful, acoustically original home, carved into the rippling sandstone cliffs, nature again achieving finer craftsmanship and design than a human could possibly aspire to. It's inspiring. And he needs inspiration.

Around this time, Utzon and one of his young Australian assistants, Richard Leplastrier, happen to be walking in bush near Palm Beach when they hear a strange avian cry. And there it is! A glorious peacock, a strutting rainbow of delight, up around the bend.

'Colour, Ricardo!' Utzon exclaimed. 'If you really want to understand colour, we must do studies of the birds!'[62]

Yes, that is the effect he wants.

Theatre-goers will arrive at a warm, glittering, visually rich performance space that envelops them from the moment they step inside the theatre. For here they will be hit by 'a climax in colour' – red the guiding light – to 'uplift you in that festive mood, away from daily life, that you expect when you go to the theatre', as the halls would have that glorious rainbow 'like a big exotic bird'.[63]

Which is as may be.

Utzon has repeated his previous pleas to the Secretary of Public Works, reiterating his request for Ralph Symonds to be approved for the plywood contract, and funding approved for the test models he needs to check his ideas structurally: 'I wish to reiterate my earlier requests for approval of these matters and I'm afraid that if it is not forthcoming immediately serious delays to Stage III of the works will be incurred . . .'[64] But the response remains less than encouraging, thanks to Symonds being in receivership, not to mention the government's desire to follow protocol and open all contracts for private tender as, not unreasonably, they want to minimise their political risk.

Oh, and it certainly doesn't help that Mick Lewis voices vague concerns to the department about using huge plywood panels in the ceiling as a structural element. And although Lewis's advice might not be the straw that actually breaks the camel's back, it's close.

For, it's like this. While Vegemite and toast, football and Holden cars, meat pies and sauce, cricket balls and willow bats are all matches made in heaven, meant to prosper 'neath the Australian sun, no-one ever said that about Jørn Utzon and Mick Lewis.

As Christmas 1964 approaches, Utzon attempts to stave off what feels like the encroaching influence of Arup's engineers with his client – they are now taking Opposition politicians around the site without his knowledge and speaking with Minister Ryan about Stage III contracts in Utzon's absence.

'It must be made clear,' Jørn writes to Zunz, 'that Michael Lewis keeps out of any negotiations, discussions or remarks regarding Stage III with the Public Works Department, the Trust or Constructors.'[65]

If Utzon can't get approval for his prototypes soon, the problem will compound and even more delays are certain.

26 January 1965, Sydney, report back

With Utzon's return from Christmas holidays, the increasingly frustrated Minister for Public Works, Norm Ryan again gives his architect the rounds of the kitchen.

'I find it very embarrassing as Minister in charge and as the constituted constructing authority,' he begins, 'not to be adequately informed as to what is happening . . .'[66]

He goes on at some length, before getting to the nub of it.

I expect a full report on the state of play!

Jørn flinches to hear it. Another report.

'We have no completed drawings for Stage III. We agreed that we would have bi-monthly reports on all these matters . . . This matter is now most urgent and must be attended to promptly. Have you any doubt in your mind as to what is required?'

Reeling, Utzon gathers himself and makes reply.

'No,' he says carefully. 'I have complete confidence that I can carry out this job to your satisfaction. There is nothing wrong. You and your Government should be very happy and proud of what takes place down there. This is because we have strived to make this building perfect on all points . . .'

Jørn explains how the change in the roof design changed the dimensions of the halls – in fact, they still don't have final dimensions for the interiors – and how changes to the brief have also set back the work, concluding calmly, 'As yet we are just not able to present you with a final set of working drawings.'[67]

But the Minister will not be easily calmed.

'We appreciate the problems you have. The Government's concern here . . . is for details of Stage III.'

'These details cannot be given before we get the last sizes and shapes of Stages I and II.'

'A letter was sent to you setting out in the clearest possible terms what was required. We are awaiting that information from you. Why haven't you supplied it?'

'I cannot give you the final estimate because there are some things which have to be cleared up.'

'How could you truthfully give me that last report and claim it to be a final estimate when it was based on information you didn't have?'

'You asked for an estimate at that stage.'

'What working drawings for Stage III do you have completed?'

'I have working drawings for several parts for Stage III.'

'Why haven't you submitted that detail to me?'

'Because I haven't got the *final* working drawings.'

'This is a serious situation something that can't be brushed aside. I think I have been as sympathetic as I can be. We have reached the stage where there must be some straight talking and some positive action!'[68]

January 1965, London, Ove speaks for himself

Speaking before the, ahem, 'Pre-stressed Concrete Development Group' – on what else but the Sydney Opera House project? – Ove Arup figuratively takes off his hard hat and dons a personal hat to speak candidly.

'My first contact with the scheme was when Utzon came to see me at our office some time in 1957, after he had won the competition and been to Sydney to receive the prize, and, incidentally, had charmed clients and public alike by his enthusiasm and personality and had been enrolled as public speaker and television star in the fight against the vicious and noisy opposition to the winning scheme.'

His audience leans forward, fascinated to get an insight into what it is like to work with the world's most famous architect.

'What struck me . . . was that this was a most unusual and exciting project. And that is what I first of all want to impress on you. This is no ordinary job; in fact there is nothing ordinary or normal about it, and one cannot apply normal standards to it.'[69]

He goes on, ticking off a list of factors that make the project the most . . . *unusual* and exciting job in the world, explaining each as he goes.

'The site is unusual'[70] . . . 'The brief is unusual'[71] . . . 'The solution submitted by Utzon was a very unusual one'[72] . . . 'The assessors . . . very unusual' . . . and then he comes to his old friend Jørn, 'The architect is very unusual,' he says.[73]

Poking an old engineers' joke, he says, 'I suppose every architect is unusual in a sense, but some more than others and Utzon more than most . . . he is certainly unusually gifted, and he is very, very much an architect . . .'[74]

Ove goes on, coming to his pet philosophy – Total Design.

'For thirty years or more architects and engineers have talked and talked about collaboration between our two professions . . . But, as I have frequently pointed out – it rarely happens . . . Well, it has happened in this case. It has happened because Utzon is a creator, ideas pour forth from him, he is not cramped by an ideological straitjacket or bound by any style. And of course, this is a case where it should happen, where it must happen if the scheme is to be a success, because the structure here is the architecture . . .'[75]

But for all the good, Ove tells the audience, 'It is not a complete portrait – I wouldn't attempt that – but just what is relevant to this situation.'[76]

Ove looks out at the ocean of engineers seated before him and almost smiles as he says, 'He can cause havoc amongst engineers who have worked for months on something which is now being improved – but one has to admit it is being improved. However, I should perhaps add here' – to be fair – 'that most of the alterations which have occurred on this job, and they are numerous, are due to . . . Client's wishes, unforeseen difficulties and especially the work of other specialists . . . the briefs for each have to be gradually developed through a process of trial and error. This is the central difficulty.'

One change in any area, affects all the rest, Ove explains, adding: 'Sometimes the only really satisfactory answer is to start all over again . . . incorporating the new requirement. Few architects and engineers would face up to that possibility, and that is why so much architecture is a botch up . . . Well, Utzon does face up to this possibility. He may also let you wait for many months to make a decision, because he has not found the right answer yet or has been occupied with more urgent things. And only he can make decisions. It is no good coming along with cost planning, scientific programming or modern management methods – they don't apply to masterpieces.'[77]

And that is all Ove wishes to say on the matter of the architect, his once close yet now somewhat distant friend.

Overall, there is no playbook for the Sydney Opera House. 'Rarely in the history of architecture has a job of this size and intricacy been controlled in such detail by one man. This is both a cause of the greatness of this job and of some of the hold ups on design decisions.'[78]

In his words lies an unspoken warning – we need patience from all parties, to see the job through to its best possible conclusion.

In his perspicacious, paternal way, Ove Arup has summed up the current state of play effortlessly.

His wisdom would work wonders down under, but his words are lost to antipodean ears, and Ove has not the energy or inclination to jump back onto the job. He's too old for it, now. He must leave it to the firm's ambitious youngsters.

•

Utzon and his architects draft the latest report requested by the government – he can't make final working drawings of Stage III till he has the scheme fully worked out, as he has tried to explain to the Minister.

In lieu of them, Jørn writes a descriptive narrative with the skill of a master storyteller – 'When completed, the Sydney Opera House will serve as a home for the cultural activities of the city and will inspire artists and technicians to present to the public the highest quality performance for many years to come.'[79]

Fine. But such blandishments get them no closer to resolving the issue that the Minister has decided to home in on with fierce focus: Stage III drawings so they can get to cost planning and time programming . . . he wants modern management methods that he can defend in parliament! Like those used in the department's Government Architect's branch. Speaking of which . . . Ted Farmer is given a copy by the Minister and smirks. Farmer would later describe it as 'a curious document completely misleading and much of it untrue . . . He also wrote a similar report on the acoustics which contained so much fantastic verbiage that, to me, it was laughable. It came out later that he wrote it without the knowledge of his three excellent acoustic consultants.'[80]

The report states Utzon's case again. Just as he had ensured a negotiated contract to work intimately with Hornibrook in working out the roof construction, he must work tightly with Symonds on Stage III, and he must get those prototypes before he can do the drawings . . . he's starting to hear himself like a broken record.

Alas, with the election just weeks away, a stubborn Minister Ryan concedes no ground to his insistent architect and the stalemate over

Symonds remains ... nobody can agree what must come first – the chicken or the egg?

1 March 1965, Sydney, Crisis? What crisis, officer?

If the situation is not yet a full-blown crisis, it could at least get into a fancy-dress 'Come As Your Worst Nightmare' party without being kicked out. For it is not just the engineers who are frustrated by a lack of plans for Stage III – the Government Architect Ted Farmer is now getting directly involved, liaising with the Minister via his man in Utzon's office, Bill Wood.

A confidential report from Ted Farmer to the Minister lists what remains to be resolved:

Major Hall – ceilings – information awaited from architect

Minor Hall – balconies – architect's drawings awaited

Major Hall – galleries – The engineer stated a clear preference for precast seating – architect's opinion awaited

Levels – awaited from architect

Major Hall – seating – engineer's scheme under consideration by the architect

Ceiling suspension – engineer's scheme under consideration by the architect

Thickness of plywood web members – engineer's scheme under consideration by the architect

Finish on the rear walls of Major Hall – information required from the architect[81]

•

It is just a small item in the *Herald*, true, but under the circumstances it is perfect innuendo, sure to raise a few eyebrows among Ministers, Mandarins and media. Any information about Utzon is being lapped up by sleepy Sydney town, so the *Herald* runs the otherwise humdrum story:

'Jørn Utzon's house at Bayview, is still a "dream home". Warringah Shire, which refused to pass his original design, is happier about the revised plans which provide for a house and a studio. But council can't give formal approval until working drawings are available. Utzon's office says the whole thing "is still in the embryonic stage".'[82]

What *is* it about this man and completed plans?

•

In these grim times, the rumours about Utzon in Sydney's architectural and engineering communities continue to swirl. The Dane is out of his depth. He doesn't know what he's doing; it won't be done for decades; the costs will blow out by a factor of 10. *Didn't you hear? He is totally incapable of taking his wild concepts and turning them into working drawings that the engineers can actually use!*

Harry Seidler has heard them all and is disgusted at the glee with which they are usually passed on. Somehow or other, Sydney has a chance to boast an architectural wonder of the world, and they are happy to hear of its possible complete failure? Like taking an axe to the tallest poppy. Against that, the rumours are so persistent, he feels honour-bound to investigate. As Utzon's most public supporter from the Sydney architectural fraternity, he and Jørn have become friends, and there is a strong bond of trust between them.

And so Seidler asks. Can he have a look at some of the drawings?

Of course, Harry, Utzon replies in his soft Danish lilt.

As good as his word, Utzon first gives Seidler a complete tour of the whole worksite and the building as it stands, before taking him back to the site office by the water's edge at Farm Cove, where he shows him the enormous volume of drawings on work that had already been done, and that which is projected for the second and third stage.[83]

Page after page after page of it, which altogether are many feet thick!

And so many different fields too, one affecting another.

Acoustic Plaster
Air conditioning and mechanical ventilation
Asphalt to floors
Balustrading
Basement brickwork
Brick and block walls above +4 level
Bronze doors and gates
Boardwalk paving . . .[84]

And so on and on and on!

Seidler gasps to look at it all, to see the numbers, the details, the calculations, the sheer unbelievable scope and complexity of it all. His primary emotion is one that he feels rarely – humility. Certainly he is coming into a whole new level of architectural complexity himself for the fact that he is currently immersed in the design of Australia's 'first skyscraper', the 50-storey 'Australia Square' building in downtown Sydney, something he is managing with the help of none other than the world-renowned engineer Pier Luigi Nervi – and it really is difficult. But after seeing Utzon's drawings and evolving schemes, Seidler has the self-awareness to recognise that the far simpler 'curtain wall' construction of his own project is as nothing to the moon shot being attempted by Utzon.

'I can only remember,' he will recount, 'the sort of feeling of genuinely being humbled at looking at this unbelievable complexity – and the audacity almost with which man can deal with forms and shapes and translate them into technical terms. It defies description . . .'[85]

THIRTEEN

MALICE IN BLUNDERLAND

The Opera House could become the world's foremost contemporary masterpiece if Utzon is given his head and if it is not spoilt by an attempt to squeeze it into the established patterns. What is required is that everybody, Public, Press and Politicians should want this to happen.[1]

Ove Arup, memo to Premier Heffron, 26 March 1963

Labor was in charge from the conception of an Opera House competition in 1956 to May 1965. This was nine years of sheer incompetence, great confusion and a total loss of control. To say that the whole project was in a state of suspended animation would be generous ... To say that it was in a state of inanimate chaos would also be generous but closer to the truth. It was near disaster.[2]

Davis Hughes, 'Twenty Years at the Sydney Opera House', 1993

1 May 1965, Sydney, the symphony's third movement

After 10 days of counting, the last prayers are uttered, the last curses are muttered and ... the last ballots counted ... the Coalition of the Liberal Party and Country Party wins the NSW election with a slim majority of 47 to 45, to form their first government in 24 years.

The newly crowned Premier, Robin Askin, is exultant.

'We're in the tart shop now, boys!'[3] he is overheard to say to some of his fellow Ministers when the victory is announced.

In the words of *The Daily Telegraph*, 'The message of this is that the majority of the people of this State have finally revolted against being pushed around by a Government grown arrogant and indifferent to public opinion. After 24 years they are saying: "We've had enough".'[4]

(Which is quite possibly true. But certainly, helping fill their electoral sails is the fact that the 'red terror' sweeping the globe, even as Australian boys are being shipped off to Vietnam to stop it, has seen an overall swing towards both conservative press and politics.)

The first thing on the Coalition's agenda is sorting out the Opera House mess.

Premier Askin, knowing he needs a no-nonsense hard nut to take over Public Works, the most politically contentious Ministry of the day, hands the job to the Country Party's former leader and the member for Armidale, William Davis Hughes, a man looking for redemption – after that unfortunate matter of faking his academic credentials had nearly wrecked him.

From the first, it is recognised he will have his work cut out for him.

'I have not yet seen the file on the Opera House,' the newly installed Premier Askin quips to a journalist from the *Herald*, 'but I wouldn't be surprised if . . . the Minister for Public Works, Mr Davis Hughes, doesn't turn up to Tuesday's Cabinet meeting with it under his arm – if he can carry it; he might need a wheelbarrow.'[5]

For his part, Davis Hughes is sure he has the grit to take it on and resolves to take the Ministry in general and the Sydney Opera House, in particular, by the horns.

Of course, the choice of Davis Hughes in the Public Works role is not obvious to everyone, even in his own family. When Hughes' appointment is confirmed with a phone call from the Premier, Hughes' wife, Joan, roars with laughter, 'For God's sake – *you're* Minister for Public Works? You can't drive a nail!'[6]

As for the new Minister's interest in the performing arts and design? Well, Sir Charles Moses would address that very question when it came to Hughes and his colleagues some years later.

'Did they have backgrounds of being patrons of the arts, interested in the arts, interested in opera houses?' he said, roaring with laughter. 'I would say no, absolutely not. None at all.'[7]

•

Jørn Utzon cannot help but be a little relieved with the election result. After his recent testy relations with Norman Ryan, Utzon is certain his relationship with the incoming Minister Davis Hughes will surely be better, especially with the campaigning over.

And yet the pleasure of meeting the incoming Minister must wait, as Utzon is in Germany working with his acoustics consultants, leaving his staff in charge. Some of them, at least, are all too aware that the situation, in fact, is more fraught than ever and on 3 May, Jørn's secretary, Shirley Colless, writes in a letter, 'feeling down here at the Opera House is that nothing could be worse, and most of the chaps seem to think there will be an inquiry or a Royal Commission, so the Liberals can start off with a clean sheet . . .'[8] But at least, with Utzon at their helm, they remain somewhat optimistic.

'The Government lost the election,' Mogens Prip-Buus writes to his parents, 'so now we are saddled with a new lot of idiots. I suppose we'll find peace some time, but first the new lot have to have it all explained to them, and then I think they will be better for us than the last crowd was. That would be a relief.'[9]

As for Skipper Nielsen, in the thick of it in Sydney since 1960, he is wary: 'If there is going to be more fuss with the new Government, God only knows how many chronological reports and narrative descriptions they are going to ask for. I just could not bear to write another one.'[10]

For now, not to worry too much. They simply knuckle down and get on with the job, and keep going as Jørn has instructed, designing the theatre interiors and being as careful as always to get the details right, a priority that comes a long way ahead of submitting it before some arbitrary deadline made by people who simply do not understand.

Late May 1965, Sydney, tide comes in; tide goes out

So much to do, so little time to do it.

No sooner has Davis Hughes settled down behind his big Ministerial desk than he is trawling through every report he can get his hands on concerning those wasteful culprits down on Bennelong Point, who he is intent on bringing to heel.

And what's this?

It is a report from the Arup engineers about the roof which is . . . not very easy to understand. Talk about *complex*. All those calculations, diagrams and technical language. He does note two things, however: firstly, that the Arup engineers have done a LOT of work, and secondly – curiously – they make no mention of the architect at all?

Interesting. Moving on, Hughes works his way through the available documents for Stage III and is shocked to find Utzon is asking him to do away with the usual system of public tenders and approve a contract to a company in receivership? This is more than merely troubling to Hughes. He may know little about architecture, engineering and construction, and *nothing* about the virtues of plywood for acoustics, but he knows the governmental way of doing things and this is not it.

What is going *on*, Ted Farmer?

Well, Minister. It is fair to say that things were a little on the casual side of things when it came to the arrangements between the architect and his committee client. The architect was nearly always deferred to, and his invoices signed without question. Your predecessor, Minister Ryan, changed things a little, and was well . . .

Well, Minister Hughes is *not* fine with it. First things first, he calls a meeting of the Opera House Executive Committee and is soon sitting at the top of the table – in his well-tailored three-piece suit, his eyes alert under dark wide-set brows, his hair slick with pomade – as before him sits expectantly an array of the original Committee men since 1954, led by Moses, Ashworth and Haviland – all of whom have devoted enormous chunks of their lives to the Opera House project, and all for no pay. Yes, their power has been slowly whittled away under Minister Ryan, but perhaps things will change now, and they lean forward to get a feel for whether there might be a new approach?

There is.

Minister Hughes leans forward in turn, and begins . . .

'There is going to be no more waste on the Opera House,' he says, stern, eyeballing the men before him.

Goodness!

'I remember our first meeting with the new Minister, Mr Davis Hughes,' Sir Charles Moses will recall, 'and he spoke so – I hesitate to use the word – arrogantly – about what he was going to do, how he was going to stop this wasteful expenditure . . . and looking at us as if we were responsible for wasting public money.'

The Opera House Committee men walk away from this latest political meeting certain of one thing – Davis Hughes has donned his Ministerial crown and given these dedicated public servants an unequivocal private scolding. The Premier might be in the tart shop, but he, Davis Hughes, is king of his own castle – the nascent Opera House.

'Well,' Moses thinks to himself, 'I'm glad Utzon isn't here to hear this.'[11]

5 June 1965, Sydney, raise the main!

It is a great day. After straining for two years now, the concrete ribs of the Opera House's main sail finally . . . touch!

And there she is!

The tallest shell, which is to house the Major Hall auditorium with its towering stage machinery, is taking magnificent form.

'Sails unfurl on Harbour foreshore,'[12] the *Sydney Morning Herald* leads on its front page.

The Farm Cove office is filled once more as the Palm Beach office is closed for the winter, on the grounds it is far too chilly to work in a boatshed, even in sunny Australia, and . . .

And, hang on, who is this who has suddenly flung open the door, to stride in?

Why, it is none other than the boss himself!

After flashing his broad smile at the early-bird architects and secretaries who are sipping at their instant coffee and eating their Vegemite on toast, Jørn Utzon does something extraordinary. To their amazement, he flips himself head over heels into a handstand and walks across the room on his hands!

Finally losing his balance by a drawing table, Jørn quickly gets his feet back on the ground to right himself and, his face red and plump from the rush of blood, but still beaming, announces the cause for his unorthodox victory lap . . .

Did he mention? The new hollow plywood mullion design for the gigantic glass walls they are designing to close up the shells? You know, yet another innovative use of plywood that the architects are working on for Stage III? Well . . . the prototypes made up at Symonds' factory show they will work!

Hurrah! Hurrah! Hurrah!

It's an important breakthrough, even if Utzon still lacks formal approval for the acoustic ceiling prototypes he needs for the theatres' interiors . . . maybe the new Minister can help.

16 June 1965, Ministerial office, Sydney, it ain't over till the fat lady serenades one of them off his mortal coil

Utzon answers the rather crisp summons to the office of the newly installed Minister for Public Works, Davis Hughes, by loping up the sandstone steps two at a time before disappearing into the shade of the portico labelled 'Secretary for Works' at the Phillip Street entrance of the Chief Secretary's Building, a vestige of times past, designed by Colonial Architect James Barnet.

After taking the stale smoky lift up to the first floor, he walks down the echoing marble corridor to the heavily carpeted headquarters of the Armidale member and . . .

And this is a good sign!

Inside Minister Hughes' inner sanctum, beside the mahogany desk where the Minister sits expectantly, Jørn sees two large easels supporting grand photographs of the Opera House building site!

'This is the right man,' Utzon will record his thoughts, 'he likes the Opera House.'[13]

Splendid!

Utzon's expert eyes take in the room, its ceiling no less than 20 feet high, and coming complete with a cornice in gold paint and an enormous marble fireplace with the date 1876 carved into it, above which is an oil painting of Queen Victoria's Diamond Jubilee procession. It's a striking contrast to Jørn's cutting-edge designs shown on the easels, which leading architectural critic and historian Siegfried Giedion has recently hailed in the latest, illustrious Milan-based *Zodiac* magazine as the forerunner in a new, 'third generation' of modernist architecture.

Minister Hughes knows nothing of *Zodiac* or architectural epochs, but nevertheless the painting lends the office a certain grandness that Norm Ryan never had.

Quietly, Utzon tries to get a feel for the man before him. With his firm handshake, slicked-back streaks of silver and black hair, his stern expression and deep voice, Hughes seems both engaged and authoritative, in a manner perhaps a little reminiscent of the late Joseph Cahill? Might he be the ally Utzon needs to get things done, starting with getting the plywood prototypes and contract moving forward? A curl of white smoke wafts upward from the Minister's omnipresent cigarette. Utzon notices the dark yellow stains between the tips of Hughes' forefinger and middle finger.

A broad discussion ensues while the scratching of a pencil off to the side never stops as Hughes' discreet secretary, Dorothy, chronicles proceedings in shorthand. Utzon begins talking, as Hughes would characterise it years later, 'about this wonderful design, its place in the area, in the harbour and its relation to the sails and everything like this, and it was very interesting . . .'[14]

To a point.

Well, that's good, Mr Utzon, very good.

But the Minister must make it clear that, from now, things will be done a little differently. Drawing deeply on his cigarette, Davis Hughes peers through the curtain of smoke at the list of points he had prepared earlier with the help of his departmental officers and Government Architect Ted Farmer, before going through them one by one, and telling Mr Utzon precisely what his and the new government's expectations are. The Dane leans in, interested.

Firstly, Mr Utzon, the Minister insists that hereafter, there will be 'monthly consultations' between the two to check progress. Now on that subject. The Minister would also like to see, within a week, 'a summary of the acoustics Report [for the Minor Hall]' and 'a list . . . of all works in Stage III for sub-contracting'.[15] Furthermore, from now on, there will need to be public tenders for *every* aspect of the work, as is protocol here in the department. No exceptions.

Utzon nods but brings up the key thing *he* wants out of this meeting. He still desires to sub-contract Ralph Symonds without going to tender – just as had happened with Hornibrook for Stage II to great success, as you may know, Minister?

Hughes raises a gruff eyebrow, and emits a rough sigh. Yes, he knows all about the Symonds issue, having been fully briefed. He knows how Minister Ryan had refused to engage them – in Hughes' view, one of the few things his predecessor had got right. And it's Hughes' strong instinct – his only instinct – to follow Ryan's lead and insist on a public tender no matter what.

Again, Utzon pleads his case.

We need that contract to progress so we can then make the final drawings – much as it was with the roof, which is still being finalised as we go along.

For you must understand, Minister, he says in his soft lilt, Symonds is the only company in the *world* doing the precise kind of work we need now. And it's right here in Sydney; we've already worked with them extensively in Stages I and II!

Hughes seems non-committal and informs Utzon he will give it consideration, however . . .

'As I see the position at present, a case has not been made for dispensing with competitive tenders for this work.'[16]

(Jørn sighs inwardly. He can do no more than he has already done, pointing out the obvious and self-explanatory.)

It is all friendly enough, but also no-nonsense. In the end, Hughes hardly asks questions of Utzon, so much as he issues orders – please get to work with the quantity surveyors, and have a new estimate report to me within a month.

The man has a strange urgency about him that the Dane finds . . . odd. A little funny[17] even, as the Minister seems to think the Opera House is a regular box house, easily planned, drawn up and put to tender for the lowest bidder, voila. He will see.

Oh, and one last thing, Mr Utzon, 'Is any of your work being delayed by the Department of Public Works?'[18]

Well, Utzon doesn't want to start off on the wrong foot, and in the hope that this new Minister will take a longer view, and come to appreciate the many design challenges that the architects are working on, answers, 'No.'[19]

Very well then. Hughes likes the answer, and records it in his minutes. If there are no hold-ups our end, we are hoping for the same from you.

Ah, and one more thing. The Minister has money on his mind, and exhorts Utzon to be less like a drunken sailor and more like a careful accountant when it comes to spending public monies.

After all, the broad-accented Australian notes, in his own electorate of New England, the farmers are suffering severe drought and their cattle are dying in droves – they need low-interest loans to save their businesses; opera in the big smoke is the furthest thing from their minds. And you know, Mr Utzon, up there just '£15,000 . . . could make a lot of culture.'[20]

Utzon nods cordially.

Standing and extending his hand to show the meeting is over, Mr Hughes says, and Mr Utzon will never forget it, 'This story doesn't end before one of us dies.'[21]

What?

A curious thing to say – *what, like this is a fight to the death?* – and he is slightly discomforted by it, but no more than that.

The main thing for Jørn, ever the optimist, is that the new government has new energy. As he takes his leave, back down the stale smoky elevator and out into the winter sunshine, Davis Hughes lights another cigarette and writes at the bottom of the minutes that his secretary, Dorothy, hands him: 'It will be interesting to see how far these undertakings are carried out . . . General tenor of the interview was satisfactory.'[22]

Yes, Davis Hughes doesn't seduce easily, and if he is to be running this show, he needs obedient soldiers, including his architect.

So far, Jørn is satisfactory.

•

Back in the office, Jørn fills in his senior architects.

All up, Utzon and his staff feel positive enough about the political change – and the fact they tend to be now dealing with more sophisticated and worldly types than in the previous administration.

'There are now people in office who seem to have had a little more than 6 years education at elementary school,' Prip-Buus tells his parents. 'There is even a slight chance that some of them have heard that over on the other side of the globe there are countries where people have theatres and something called operas, things that have nothing to do with football.'[23]

Ah, yes, they had laughed in the office over that observation.

'Perhaps we can believe that the new people will appreciate our work and help us to get it finished instead of opposing us and putting spokes in our wheels like the last lot did.'[24]

Almost as an afterthought, the Dane adds.

'We'll see, but everything suggests a change that in our eyes is almost a miracle after the experiences of the last three years.'[25]

The only thing that is a real worry is this new Minister's singular focus on costs, deadlines and the insistence that every single Stage III contract go to public tender *now* – which conflicts with the realities under which the project has always run. Utzon, and all his consultants, have been playing catch-up from the start (final drawings and estimates for Stage II are still being produced!) – and this new focus jars with the Utzon approach, where the aim of the game is to design something *new* and finish it *perfectly*.

Well, with the rising roof as testament, the Utzon camp is not to be so easily put off on its path to pioneering perfection. And as a matter of fact, on the day that Utzon is having his first meeting with the incoming Minister, Mogens Prip-Buus has to ask the engineers to redo two entire rib sections, and he takes some wry pleasure in doing so.

'Arup's are still swindlers,' he tells his parents, 'but today I've had the great pleasure of going out and rejecting two whole shell ribs, which correspond to something over 100 tons of concrete, and at the same time there was the loss of two months' production of special tile elements which they had insisted on making without first testing them as we had asked, but they knew so well at that time, so now I hope that they will know rather more as a result of this little lesson. Oh, how I enjoyed it.'

Prip-Buus admits. 'Jørn is a little shocked at how devilish I have become.'[26]

7 July 1965, Public Works Department, Sydney, a two kings in the castle problem

Minister Hughes reads the final line of Jørn Utzon's latest letter one more time:

> It is therefore desirous that you approve of the nomination of Ralph Symonds as a nominated sub-contractor for all the plywood work.[27]

He groans.

What will it take for the architect to understand that this option is off the table?

Hughes wants things run by the departmental book, and here is uppity Utzon trying to rewrite that very book as he sees fit.

Dorothy, Hughes calls to his secretary. *I need to dictate a letter.*

> 7 July 1965 – Letter from Hughes to Utzon
> I explained to you that as I see the position at present, a case has not been established for dispensing with competitive tenders for [the plywood] work. My Department's previous instructions in respect of this work are to be carried out, and the necessary proto-types, drawings, specifications and approximate quantities should now be made available on the site so that any other firms wishing to tender may examine them and submit their names for selection . . .[28]

Also, please note:

> You gave dates on which certain sections of the work will be ready for tendering. I assume that this letter is not intended to satisfy my request . . .
>   I require a firm schedule supported by your unqualified assurance that you will adhere to it . . .[29]

To show he's not mucking around, Mr Hughes would like to remind Mr Utzon:

> In view of the number of years which have been available to bring the project to the final planning stage and the advance made with construction, it is no longer possible to accept uncertainties as to planning schedules or costs . . .[30]

(Or, as he will later quip with casual exaggeration, he is determined that finishing it will 'not take another 15 years'.[31])

And make no mistake, it is not just time that is at issue, it is money.

> The major part of the work to be performed under Stage III of the project cannot proceed until the additional expenditure involved has received Parliamentary approval and I am not prepared to make a recommendation for a further financial appropriation until I have a final and reliable estimate of cost upon which the recommendation can be based. Such an estimate necessarily depends upon completion of final and detailed planning . . .[32]

And so it goes on. Four pages, detailing all the actions that are required by the Minister before he personally approves . . . well, anything at all that Jørn Utzon has planned.

Hughes ends the letter with a list of 44 items for which he demands a schedule of work and accompanying tender documents, forthwith. Not yet two months in the role as Minister, and with a slew of actual public works on his desk – hospitals, schools, roads, funded by state revenue – Davis Hughes wishes to make clear to the architect that, of all that comes across his desk, he is homing in on the details of the Sydney Opera House most particularly.

·

Utzon puts the letter down and groans. They simply refuse to listen to him, to accept that he knows what he is doing. Even more curious is the new Minister's overbearing confidence that he knows better than the architect, despite the fact he has been the Minister less than two months and not once visited the architect's office, nor even asked any questions about the design problems Utzon is tackling. All he does is make unreasonable demands in the name of efficiency which, contrarily, slow everything down.

Just replying to this letter *alone*, with all its attendant demands for information will take hours of his time that he is not devoting to the design of the Opera House itself.

Shirley! Utzon calls to his secretary. *I need to dictate a letter.*

12 July 1965

He begins by addressing the Minister's points one by one, eventually getting to Hughes' statement: 'It was gratifying to receive your assurance that none of your work was being delayed by officers of this Department.'[33]

Well, Jørn would like to correct the record, if he may:

> It is difficult for me to criticize your department in any way. I want to collaborate with the Department and I respect the Department's reasons . . . but you must understand that the never-ending stream of correspondence which has not led to a decision on the appointment of Symonds has put me in a very difficult situation with regard to the preparation of final drawings for Stage III . . . I must stress, and have already said so in our discussions, that it is essential that we now receive the final decision to nominate Ralph Symonds Ltd

for the plywood contract, in order that we may move ahead on this facet of the work.[34]

The letter goes on for many pages as Utzon continues to labour the point of how difficult the government has made it for him by refusing to embrace his desired consultants, burying him in paperwork and reports, continuing to make modifications to their original specifications – as recently as September 1963, years after the work was in hand – and, as to your mention of Arup's report on Stage II (which had failed to name Utzon at all), 'you might have been misled'[35] insofar as I am the one who has overseen every last detail of the design.

> I have not at any stage complained about the almost impossible situation with which I have been constantly faced . . . I have shown to you and to everybody by now a satisfactory result from my work in the form of a partly-built building which is already world famous for its architectural qualities.[36]

So, Minister, to that end:

> It is absolutely vital that, in order to prevent the building being destroyed, I must remain in full command of every detail that comes into the building.

And to end, Utzon writes:

> It is obviously very important for the whole project that you and your officers visit me in my office as soon as possible and spend at least two hours here, because by then you will, I am sure, after having seen a few examples, fully understand the situation and gain the necessary confidence in me which your department obviously does not have.[37]

Davis Hughes puts the letter down and groans. He lights another cigarette and calls through the doorway:

Dorothy!

And so continues the back and forth between Jørn Utzon and Davis Hughes, their exchanges reflecting their positions on diverging tracks, and, with each letter, a growing tension.

Mogens Prip-Buus, a man inclined to pessimism, unlike his boss, writes to his parents on 13 July 1965: 'The new minister also turns out to be a Politician, i.e. doesn't care a damn about the truth.'[38]

•

The men of the Executive Committee are coming to feel much the same, and are shocked by the new Minister's near-immediate adversarial approach to the architect.

Sir Charles Moses, for one, has dealt with all manner of politicians in his decades running the ABC, and sees the writing on the wall.

'I've got to say his arrival on the scene was a tragedy,'[39] Sir Charles will later say.

When it comes to Hughes himself, as the back and forth drags on, he is increasingly frustrated that his position as client is not being fully respected by the architect, Mr Utzon.

'[We would meet and] that afternoon I would send him a letter,' he would later say of his exchanges with Utzon. 'And without fail in two days, I'd get one back denying everything we'd ever said. The fact that there'd been a girl there taking it all down was quite beside the point. And that went on and on.'[40]

Well, that won't do. The Minister decides a tougher approach is needed and changes tack.

The nub of it?

That cold wind that blows through the Opera House site as July falls and August rises?

At least a good part of each southerly buster is actually southerly bluster coming from Macquarie Street in general and the Ministerial office of Davis Hughes in particular.

•

Jørn Utzon is feeling the kind of fatigue that goes clear to the bones, a kind of tiredness that not even sleeping day and night could fix.

'Before Mr Davis Hughes, the Opera House Committee were the best client you could think of,' he will recount some years later. 'Then Mr Davis Hughes came and it was nothing.'[41]

On top of that, two or three years ago, Jørn could easily have turned to Ove Arup for counsel and support, but now, after all that has happened, with Ove standing back from the project entirely, what energy Ove does give to Utzon seems to be mostly in expressing the frustrations of his staff.

Lately, Arup has been disturbed to hear from Mick Lewis that, after asking Utzon to see the drawings in development . . .

'No,' Utzon had replied. 'It is necessary to work undisturbed during the development of my ideas and systems as the scheme could suffer by side-tracking at this stage.'[42]

After the firm's blow-up over the roof in '61, Ove Arup has to defend his staff, and instead of sending Jørn an encouraging note, or visiting to help resolve matters – as he may have done earlier, when Total Design was in full swing – he writes to let the architect know that . . . *Something is rotten in the state of Denmark* . . . and from where Ove sits, far removed from Sydney politics in his palace in London, and from what his little birdies say, that something smells distinctly like . . . Jørn.

'I wonder whether you really are master of the situation,' Arup writes to Utzon in July 1965, abrasively, 'and can manage without help except from sycophantic admirers. I have often said that I think you are wonderful, but are you all that wonderful? You will probably dismiss my doubts with contempt. You have clearly indicated that our role is to do what we are told and leave you to manage your affairs. And believe me, that suits me . . . You have killed the joy of collaboration – but I want to see the job finished all the same.'[43]

Charmed, he is sure.

Jørn Utzon is shattered to read the words of his colleague and once close friend, and his sense of isolation grows.

At least, however, one notable Sydney figure stands as Utzon's friend.

'I hope all this fuss is not getting you down,' Harry Seidler writes to him. 'I went over the Opera House recently. It is utterly magnificent and really impressive. You must experience great satisfaction and fulfillment which, I hope, is not marred by all the bickering. If there is any serious suggestion to stand in your way, I will scream out publicly. Whenever you feel like a talk come to lunch at the office . . .'[44]

If only others could understand the challenges, and the sheer magnificence of what they are working on, as dear Harry does!

For his part, very quietly, Utzon finds it hard to take Davis Hughes seriously.

'Ministers for public works,' he will later note, 'are usually concerned with housing developments, fire stations and sewers. Davis Hughes wanted to identify himself with an opera house.'[45]

And he, an internationally renowned architect, is meant to take design directives from the Member for Armidale? No.

After all, this same man who has never built so much as a chicken coop, had recently had the *presumption* to give his opinion on the way the Opera House should look.

'The insides of the shells, all the ribs,' he had said gruffly, 'should be covered in some way . . .'[46]

As gently as he could, Utzon had tried to explain the development of the roof, virtues of the ribs – he will not bore the impatient Hughes with the whole sordid tale – but could make no headway on the Minister's view that the inside should be as smooth as the outside.

'He couldn't figure it in his mind,' Utzon would later recount with amazement, 'he couldn't get it.'[47]

As to the Minister's current impatience with Stage III, and his insinuations that Utzon is out of his depth, the Minister doesn't seem to realise how absurd such a plaint is.

'If we could make these shells,' Utzon will later say, 'how could it be that we would not be able to make the interior?'[48]

To add to Jørn's troubles, there is a rumour coming 'from so many quarters'[49] – one of many disturbing rumours going around – to the effect that '[Public Works] had appointed two architects to take over'.[50]

Which is absolute madness. Imagine being a couple of new architects and starting this project from scratch, taking up a complex edifice and fierce struggle not of your making, nor even of your understanding, and having to push it forward without the creative brains behind the entire scheme, Utzon himself?

It is unimaginable – certainly unethical, and very close to undoable. It would send a man mad.

11 August 1965, Public Works Department, Sydney, looking for a path out of the wood

Come in Mr Wood, please, take a seat.

Look, it's not the 'fog of war', but it's close. So thickly does the sickly sweet stench of tobacco fill the Minister's office in the Public Works Department, and such are the circumstances of this meeting that it not only feels like a Council of War, but it is all Bill Wood can do to find his way to his seat in front of the Minister's dark mahogany desk.

Now, Bill. You have been in Utzon's office as our man on site for a year now.

The Minister would like a candid report on how that office runs, what you've seen? Just between us, of course.

And so, the discussion begins, all of it reflected in a strictly confidential memo from Wood to Davis Hughes the following day, on ways to take better control over the project.

Wood proposes four measures, the most important of which is: signing no more cheques addressed to Mr J. Utzon, until such times as he does what he is asked!

'This I have always termed "cheque book control" and no other method is equally efficacious . . .'[51]

Another measure that Wood proposes in light of the Minister's desire to have final working drawings as fast as possible, is: 'the establishment of a Drawing Office or the letting out to sub-contract of the preparation of working drawings. Some 25 Architects, Assistant Architects . . . together with a senior Departmental architect, would be needed.'[52]

Wood just adds one rider to all his advice – the Minister must be careful to ensure that the Dane does not resign. (Of course, the Minister cannot dismiss Utzon as he is appointed by an Act of Parliament.)

'To replace him as the designer would present serious difficulties and would cause a scandal with worldwide reverberations,'[53] Wood advises.

Well, the Minister will burn that bridge when he comes to it.

•

Just quietly, Hughes has been speaking confidentially with a range of people, including his Government Architect, Ted Farmer, as well as the consultant engineer, Mick Lewis.

Utzon says he *needs* the plywood ceiling prototypes made first, to make sure his scheme is workable structurally and constructionally, and *then* do the final drawings, but Hughes' talks with Mick Lewis suggest – instead of large, plywood panels, as Utzon is planning – a steel framework may be preferable for holding up the interior plywood acoustic shell.

The engineer's word is proof enough for Davis Hughes that Utzon's way is not necessarily the only way, and may not be the easiest way to get the bloody thing *done*. (In fact, Utzon has already tested a steel-frame design back in 1962, well before Lewis or Hughes were around, but it was rejected by his acoustics consultants – too many gaps between the standard plywood panels for sound to leak out.)

Besides, Davis Hughes likes Mick Lewis, the no-nonsense man's man from South Africa who is so much more relatable than the artsy Scandinavian Utzon.

So it is that Davis Hughes has the department secretary officially write to Mick Lewis at Ove Arup & Partners on 20 August 1965, pursuing this promising alternative: 'It is understood that it is the Architect's intention to support the plywood superstructure of the Major and Minor Halls by means of laminated timber trusses. This would appear to present certain constructional difficulties, inasmuch as it would necessitate making the auditoria watertight before the trusses could be installed. If, on the other hand, steel trusses were used, this difficulty would not arise and the plywood cladding could be added after the glass walls were completed. Your views on this suggestion are invited and will be appreciated.'[54]

By any measure it is an extraordinary move: Hughes is asking the engineers to design something other than what the architect is planning, and without telling the architect!

What's more? From his discussions, Hughes is forming a belief that, as he will later say, 'Utzon knew next to nothing about theatres. The result was that he set up a structure for the architectural demands of this enormous project which was far too small – a personal fiefdom. Out of a tiny office with a tiny staff was supposed to flow a torrent of working drawings to keep a vast construction team busy. It simply didn't produce such a flow.'[55]

Enough with the airy-fairy, the arty-farty. It is time for the argy-bargy!

It will all aptly be summed up by one Joseph Skrzynski, a later Chair of the Sydney Opera House Trust.

'Utzon wanted the best possible idea,' the prominent businessman will recall, '[Hughes] wanted the best idea you can have by Friday.'[56]

In his bid to get all his ducks in a row NOW, with or without the co-operation of the architect, Minister Hughes arranges a key meeting.

23 August 1965, Pioneer Club, Sydney, unwilling Gilling gets roped in

Of course the NSW President of the Royal Australian Institute of Architects, Ron Gilling, is happy to have lunch with Minister Davis Hughes and the new Director of Public Works, Col Humphrey, at the swish Pioneer Club in the sandstone-colonnaded Royal Automobile Club of Australia building on Macquarie Street. The meeting is arranged at Hughes' personal invitation over the phone – no reason is given but it seems routine enough to Ron Gilling. When you are the Minister for Public Works, whose department is the number one client of private architects in the state, one would naturally wish to speak with the president of the profession's representative body, the Royal Institute's state chapter.

And a pleasant meeting it appears to be, at least initially, over a drink, before the conversation moves to the nub of why they are really there.

Without naming Utzon, the Minister now speaks up.

'As a client, am I entitled to know how long a project will take?'

'Am I entitled to know how much it will cost?'

'Am I entitled to ask my architect to meet me on a regular basis?'

'Am I entitled to receive the working drawings?'[57]

The length of the answers varies, but the essence of the response does not, for it is 'Yes,' to all of the above.

'Only a fool,' Gilling will recount, 'would not have guessed what the Minister was driving at.'[58]

Obviously, his relationship with Utzon is not going well, and the Minister needs to know just where he stands on his rights, before making any moves, pass the pepper.

But now what Gilling will call, ever afterwards, the 'king hit'.[59]

Leaning in, the Minister narrows his eyes, and delivers it.

'What would you say,' he says, 'if I told you that there are no working drawings for Stage III of the Sydney Opera House?'

'I don't believe it,' Gilling replies, stunned.

Col Humphrey now says icily, 'Mr Gilling, the Minister does not tell lies.'

'My reply,' Gilling returns serve, 'was an expression of surprised disbelief and not intended to imply that I do not believe the Minister.'[60]

As they move on to lunch proper, there is no more pretext, and the Minister and his Director spill all the tea over steak and peas.

As Gilling will later recall: 'The Minister told me of the problems encountered by the previous Labor Government in dealing with Mr Utzon and the difficulties he himself was encountering. It was only mentioned in very broad terms that there were problems between Utzon and his engineer, Ove Arup and Partners, in particular over the matters relating to the use of plywood.'[61]

Gilling sits silently, surprised by the extent of problems the Minister paints.

Not to worry, Minister, Gilling assures him.

'Good staff are difficult to get, but I feel sure that if Mr Utzon makes an appeal to the profession for assistance in this direction we can help him.'[62]

Still, once back in his office, over the bridge in North Sydney, Gilling puts in a call to Bob Maclurcan, one of Utzon's architects and an executive member of the Institute's NSW Chapter Council, to give him the lie of the land and to warn that the Minister is getting restless.

Maclurcan promptly and sincerely assures Gilling there is nothing to worry about.

'Drawings for Stage III *are* available and only need some amendments which are in hand . . .'[63]

Excellent. Gilling is *most* relieved.

Perhaps then, Bob, you could personally meet with Minister Hughes to give him a briefing?

He will have to 'speak to Mr Utzon first',[64] but yes, he is happy to come. Honoured, even.

Gilling quickly telephones the Minister to arrange a meeting.

•

The following day, the Askin government's first day in the Legislative Assembly, one indication of just how concerned Mr Hughes is about the Opera House is clear in his short statement:

'I have had a close examination made of this project,' he begins, before ominously adding, 'and I want to say first that the present government will continue with the construction of the Opera House. And second, that it will ensure that the building as envisaged . . . will be completed to the original plan. However, I would add that the Government is extremely concerned at the question of cost control at the Opera House . . . under the previous regime, it got completely out of hand. Next Tuesday I will make several submissions to Cabinet.'[65]

The Daily Telegraph reports it to the public – including the latest estimate from the quantity surveyors, which has been leaked to the press – the article headlined, **HALT TO BUILDING POSSIBLE.**

> The State Government next Tuesday will consider the action it will take on the Opera House, including even a possible halting of work. A new estimate of its cost, [is] about £25 million . . . Cabinet will decide on Tuesday whether or not to accept that estimate as final.
>
> . . . Mr Hughes is known to be worried . . . A cost of £25 million, if really final, would be more than five times [the estimate in 1959] . . . On this basis its designer, Mr Jørn Utzon, must receive at least £1.25 million in architect's fees.
>
> He could receive more.[66]

25 August 1965, Bennelong Point, Maclurcan found workin' on two fronts

He's nervous. He *knows* it's not normal. Nor a good look.

Still, what can he do?

Bob Maclurcan comes into Jørn's office and announces, 'I am to have a meeting with the Minister Davis Hughes together with the chairman of the association of architects, to discuss the Opera House question.'[67]

The Opera House question, Bob?

Jørn is blindsided.

A meeting between the Institute, the Minister and one of his architects? And he is not invited?

No, says Bob.

It is very strange, indeed, and Utzon tells Bob as much. The client appears to be consulting and actually listening to everyone except the architect himself.

In any case, off Bob goes, to meet with the Minister.

•

Thank you for seeing us, Minister.

'I do feel,' Ron Gilling says to the Minister, 'you will be much happier once you hear what Mr Maclurcan has to say.'[68]

(Among other things, he will say it in Australian English, which the Minister much prefers.)

Over to you, Mr Maclurcan.

And the architect does his best.

But there is no way around it. The forceful presentation of two days ago over the phone now comes across as uncomfortable, awkward and . . . forced. To begin with, the Australian architect is, according to Gilling, 'ill at ease with the Minister',[69] and in terms of his presentation, it is like all of his tyres have gone flat at once.

Hughes starts peppering Utzon's architect – *we have captured us a live one!* – with probing questions and, at least by Gilling's account, 'one question in particular was about the number of staff Utzon had available and the answer clearly indicated that the number stated confirmed that the project was seriously understaffed'.[70]

The Minister closes down the meeting more convinced than ever that what they are facing is less a problem and more like a crisis.

The Minister calls Ron Gilling that very evening and says plainly, 'the answers to my questions were unsatisfactory'.[71]

•

It is pitch dark and nearing 6 pm when Bob Maclurcan returns to find the front door locked. Prip-Buus comes to open it. Clearly, Bob is shocked to see them still there, turning red with embarrassment and heading straight to his office without looking them in the eye.

Utzon and Mogens exchange looks and follow him to his desk, asking him to recount what he had been talking to the Minister about.

'We were discussing,' Maclurcan says, somewhat sheepishly, 'what could be done to help us get the work drawings finished – possibly by means of help from outside. I cannot tell you everything, as the conversation was confidential, but I think you can believe my good intentions as I told the Minister that Jørn last year had been so fed up with the situation under the *previous* Minister that the entire office had worked on Zurich and only one man had taken care of the Opera House, but that I can assure you that there are now eleven men engaged on it.'[72]

What?

'There are 15 of us in the office here and three overseas,' Prip-Buus declares, frustrated. 'That is what you ought to have said.'[73]

Prip-Buus records in his diary: 'Bob was not happy with the situation, was pretty aggressive – a sign of bad conscience.'[74]

•

It's been a long day for Minister Davis Hughes.

> CABINET MINUTE
> CONFIDENTIAL
> ... I proceed with the various actions outlined above in the full knowledge that they could lead to a dispute with the Architect.
> Davis Hughes
> Minister for Public Works

I need to dictate another letter, Hughes tells Dorothy.
She slides the paper down into the typewriter.

> Mr Utzon ...
> I do not believe that I have yet been successful in having your acceptance of some basic principles which must govern the construction of this project ... your wish to build the 'perfect' Opera House is understood, but it must be accepted that all proposals must be considered in relation to cost.

He goes on:

> I shall be glad always to give full weight to your views, but in this project as in all cases, it must be accepted that it is the client's responsibility to make the decision ... that my approval be obtained in all cases except where I have made some delegation of authority to you. This is normal procedure as between client

and architect and there is every reason why it should be followed strictly in the present situation.

One of the matters causing me great concern at present . . . is the amount of work remaining to be done in preparing plans and specifications for calling tenders for Stage III . . . I am not able to accept the view which you appear to hold that detailed planning of the works should be deferred . . . I must ask therefore that you give me an assurance that this will be put in hand immediately and its completion expedited.[75]

•

Jørn Utzon puts down the letter. A throb behind his eyes betrays his fatigue.

Hughes says he is 'glad to give full weight' to Utzon's views, only to discard his views entirely.

A maudlin gloom hangs over the whole office, the mood nearly as dark as the circles under Jørn Utzon's eyes.

In a letter to his parents Prip-Buus makes clear: 'The whole thing can fall about our ears at any time . . . The New Government . . . are seeking information from everywhere except us . . .'[76]

Jørn Utzon is frankly not sure where to turn. Yes, of course, to Lis, as ever for love and solace. But to whom can he turn for help with this whole looming disaster of the Opera House? Ove is in London and semi-retired these days. The new Minister won't listen to his position, and even two of his own architects have now met with the Minister confidentially without him, even as Arup's engineers are in communications with the Minister about alternative solutions. Even the Institute of Architects, which by its very constitution is meant to be on his side, is . . . meeting with his client without him! Everywhere, people are authoritatively discussing the Opera House design despite the fact that *none* of them are privy to the extremely complex design dynamic at its core!

It's frustrating. And exhausting.

But Jørn Utzon is not easily defeated. He fought the Nazis as a lad, and certainly feels he is up to handling a State Minister in Mr Davis Hughes.

After stewing on it, Jørn consults another Australian architect in his office, the lanky rower from down Geelong way, Bill Wheatland, who agrees 'that the behaviour of both the Association and Bob is unethical'.[77]

Exactly as the Dane thought.

Very well then, Utzon tells Maclurcan the following morning, given he chose to wear the Institute's hat with the Minister and keep the details confidential from Utzon: 'You can no longer represent us.'[78]

And yes, he is tempted to fire him on the spot, but on the reckoning that would bring more grief than it is worth, tells him he can simply work out his contract over the next two months.

Shirley, I need to write some letters!

First, Utzon sends a letter to the Royal Australian Institute of Architects, seeking an explanation for their unethical behaviour and requesting it be discussed at the next meeting, before dashing off a note to Mick Lewis:

> I would appreciate that, in your reply to the Secretary concerning [the design of the structure for the auditoria], you inform him that you have submitted your report concerning this matter to the Architect and that the Architect will comment on the suggestion made to use steel trusses in lieu of plywood in the design of the auditoria ceilings.
>
> I seek your full co-operation and in future will you please refer the client directly to me on all matters of design and construction of the Sydney Opera House.[79]

And finally . . . Minister Hughes.

Utzon – feeling besieged from without, and betrayed from within – writes to him with some feeling.

> It is obvious to me that there exists a great misunderstanding on your behalf of my position in this scheme . . . You obviously do not realise that everything that exists at Bennelong Point today I have been doing personally in my office . . . I see that the reason for your misunderstanding . . . [is] clearly being caused by the fact that I have actually in this case had two Clients, who have never collaborated.
>
> During the past seven years, the Committee, my first Client, and I have worked together in complete harmony and with confidence in each other, to create the Opera House, and I have given full consideration also to the costs of each aspect of the design which was agreed upon between my Client and me. Every time I mention this fact to you or your officers to help you understand my position in this scheme it has not been accepted.
>
> I would much like you to hold a meeting with the full Committee and inform you of my qualifications as seen from the Client who has actually been creating the Opera House . . .[80]

Now, Jørn Utzon tries a new tactic.

I also want to warn you that I do not want to participate in this scheme if it is to be a compromise and thus destroy the concept of the Opera House.[81]

If he won't be listened to, he will do what his mentor, Gunnar Asplund, had done – if they don't appreciate you, walk away and see how they like *that!*

30 August 1965, Bennelong Point, the plot thickens

Jørn picks up the phone.

Colin Humphrey here, Mr Utzon, Director of the Public Works Department.

Yes, Mr Humphrey?

He clears his throat ... ah ... You see, Jørn, 'there will be discussions in Parliament tomorrow on the Sydney Opera House, and your future position, but whatever you do, you must not react to what the press might write, for we will soon be having a meeting to discuss the matter'.[82]

Curious.

31 August 1965, NSW Parliament House, scaring the horses

Goodness!

Members of the NSW Cabinet peruse the document before them with rising alarm.

What's going on down there at Bennelong Point? The revised estimate is now at a staggering £24.7 million, and much of what the architect proposes for the remains of Stage III, including engaging the Ralph Symonds firm (which is in *receivership*, for God's sake!), 'must be fully examined'.[83]

All eyes turn to Minister Hughes, who outlines his plans to rein Utzon in by taking 'personal control'[84] of all payments to the architect, but he gives his colleagues fair warning.

'It's possible that the action outlined could lead to friction with the Architect ... It may be that the Government will be faced with the Architect not co-operating, or ultimately wishing to withdraw from the project.'[85]

Fair enough. But this is Hughes' bailiwick and he seems to have the situation in hand. They give their permission for him to proceed.

1 September 1965, Palm Beach, there is such a thing as bad publicity

The Australians, bizarrely, call this time of day 'sparrow's fart'. Utzon will never grasp the scatological humour that passes even among adults in this country, but that is certainly the time of day. He rises to find Lis is up before him and has already collected the rolled up *Herald* thrown over the fence, and laid it out on the kitchen table for him, while she makes the coffee. The front page brings a chill. It is far worse than Col Humphrey had made out.

'Govt. bid to hold Opera House cost talks with Utzon' reads the headline.

> The Government will hold talks soon with the Opera House architect, Mr Jørn Utzon, as part of a policy to ensure that the increasing costs of the project are contained. The Premier, Mr Askin, announced a new estimate of £24.7m for the Opera House yesterday, an increase of £7.3 on the . . . estimate made last year.[86]

Referring to rumoured administrative changes, Mr Hughes said:

> The architect, Mr Utzon, is in charge and will remain in charge . . . A Cabinet Sub-Committee on the Opera House comprising [three Coalition ministers] . . . was set up to hold negotiations with Mr Utzon in the next fortnight . . .[87]

Utzon's head feels like it's in a vice.

> Mr Hughes said . . . negotiations with Mr Utzon would have a 'non-political atmosphere . . . We must ensure a ceiling is placed on expenditure because indications are that the Opera House lottery funds will reach only £26.3m by June, 1969, the date of completion'.[88]

Utzon sighs heavily – at least Hughes wants to help him put a ceiling on *something*. Is there no respite from this?

Yes. As ever, his respite is Lis, blessed Lis. For she has no sooner heard his sighs than she has wrapped her arms around him. They read the rest together, as the *Herald* subtly makes clear where the blame for all the cost blow-outs lie – the accused is Jørn Utzon, foreign architect.

Even the *Herald* editorial – usually speaking out in favour of the Opera House project, and its architect – has altered course.

'Judged by the criteria of careful planning, efficient administration and sound costing, the building of the Opera House has become one of the most disastrous projects in the history of Australia . . . There are two [questions] especially: Who is to blame? And, should we continue?'[89]

Enough.

These days, if Jørn read every negative thing about him he would barely do anything else. He has to get to the office and, after kissing him, Lis watches through the kitchen window as he backs out of the driveway past a few pressmen on the kerb who wave to him, as if friends.

Wolves in sheep's clothing, Lis thinks, and she is glad that her husband doesn't stop. It is all so different from how it had been when they had been greeted by the fawning press on arrival less than three years ago.

For his part, though exhausted, Jørn soldiers on, still hopeful that, as he gets on with the Minor Hall, the whole thing will blow over.

But Utzon's confidence in that field is troubled by a strange event the next day. He is in a meeting with Arup's – after all the brouhaha being kicked up over Stage III, Stage II is still very much underway, likely years from completion, and yet another matter taking his time – when an urgent, if mysterious, phone call tells him: 'Go to the gate. A man in a green car will be waiting for you.'[90]

Curious, Utzon does exactly that and finds, huddled low in the back seat, and clearly afraid of being recognised . . . Norm Ryan!

The conversation is brief, but the former Minister says what he has come to say: 'The Government is going to try to make a scapegoat of you, Jørn, but my party and I will support you. Ring me on Sunday at home. I am afraid my phone at the office is being tapped.'[91]

With which, he says his goodbyes, and drives off!

How very, very *odd*.

Why is Norm Ryan endeavouring to be his friend now, after so recently having thrown him to the wolves? No doubt it is a matter of politics, but it is confusing.

For the moment, Jørn tries to push it all aside and get back to work, on this day writing urgently to his acoustics consultants in Germany, urging them to push harder and faster: 'Our problem is more to finish our scheme off in time as I am being pressed very hard by the client for final working drawings.'[92]

Oh, another odd thing in all of this?

One of the office secretaries, Elsa Atkin, would recount of her boss: 'He never showed nastiness. Even when Utzon was having such a horrible time with Davis Hughes, he was still a nice person. He never showed bitterness. That's why he was so adorable. He was a beautiful, beautiful human being.'[93]

But it is exhausting for all that.

13 September 1965, Sydney, dismissive missives

Another day, another letter.

> ... I can finish the drawings for Stage III within a year, but this does not include drawings for loose furniture, curtains, illumination and colour and other details of that nature, and also it does not include the drawings for glass walls and the halls as these are held up until your permission is given to start mock-up at Symonds' shop. When the mock-ups are started I will very soon be able to give you information on the time it takes to produce drawings for those two items ...[94]

14 September 1965, letter from Hughes to Utzon

As a man representing his 'bush' electorate, Minister Hughes is not inclined to beat about it when dealing with a big city fella.

Writing back to Utzon – perhaps even a feisty cattle dog barking at a Great Dane and nipping at his heels – he tries again to pin him down, while still being careful to put his intent in formal and professional language. Yes, Mr Utzon, it had been good to meet with you, but I write to you now 'to clarify the position considerably and to establish quite clearly the relationship which must exist between you, as Architect, and myself, the Minister for Public Works, as Client'.[95]

So, make no mistake, sport:

> I, Minister for Public Works, am your client and accept as your responsibility the obligations to meet my reasonable requirements in respect of the work.[96]

Now, concerning the lack of working drawings for the next stage, he must be clear. He looks forward to the near future, 'when you provide a programme showing when you propose to have contract documents available for the various sections of the work'.[97]

Davis Hughes is running this show, and don't you forget it.

Thank you and good day, I said *good day*.

(Hughes will later recall of this time, that while he kept insisting that Utzon get on with 'planning Stage III ... Everything on this front was at a standstill, and the construction authorities were being driven to distraction ... Utzon would not be pinned down.'[98])

22 September 1965, Ministerial office, Sydney, no more mock-ups, no more muck-ups

He is of one mind. And right now, the Honourable Member for Armidale lets Committee Chairman Stan Haviland have a large piece of it.

'The Government's intention is to complete the Opera House to Utzon's concept, Stan,' he says in his thick Tassie accent. 'BUT subject to unified control and due regard to cost.'[99]

Stan nods, silent.

'The normal relationship of Client and Architect must be established between myself and Utzon,'[100] Hughes says, exasperated by his own point.

By 'normal', he means *his* way, the way things run in his department.

From this point forward, Hughes will personally exercise Bill Wood's key recommendation – 'cheque book control'. No more rubber stamp by the Committee, no more blank cheque to the architect; Hughes will use his own magnifying glass, and that of his Government Architect, Ted Farmer, before approving any contract or invoice, *anything*.

And we will see how Mr Utzon copes with that . . .

But that leaves the Committee – all 30 members representing various performing arts organisations – and its primary functions where, exactly?

Exactly.

Hughes moves quickly, assuring Haviland the Committee will remain useful as an advisory body, when and if he needs them. You gentlemen will function now as the 'Opera House Trust', and will come to manage the building once it opens.

'We need the co-operation of the Trust, Stan,'[101] Hughes says, his bushy grey brows raised, expectant.

'The Trust will be forthcoming,'[102] Haviland assures the Minister.

Hughes, guarding himself, even holds a party for all the Committee members where . . . with champagne glass in hand . . . he thanks them for their service . . . Which is no longer required, and don't forget your coats on the way out.

'Some of them were very bitter,' Hughes would recall many years later. 'One man still won't speak to me. He felt very hostile about it . . .'[103]

Though not recorded, that one man could very well have been Sir Charles Moses, who continues to tell friends his private views on the matter – 'this building will be known as Davis Hughes's folly . . .'[104]

FOURTEEN

'SINGLE LINE OF CONTROL'

When sorrows come, they come not single spies. But in battalions . . .[1]
William Shakespeare, *Hamlet*, Act IV, Scene V

Australia has rarely before experimented, or pointed a new way, or taken a dare in matters of art. It was high time we did. The only disaster or tragedy that could happen now would be a last-minute collapse of faith in the outcome of the Opera House, followed by some action that might stop the full realisation of the idea.[2]
Robin Boyd, Australian architect, 21 September 1965

There was something happening I didn't know anything of. Davis Hughes had obviously his ideas and he would make this Opera House cheap and correct and he wanted more people in it and so on. And this is the authority of a Minister. An architect cannot do anything about it . . .[3]
Jørn Utzon, speaking with Daryl Dellora in 1998

Late September 1965, Bennelong Point, the pursed purser

Jørn looks up to see Stan Haviland enter the Farm Cove office. His brow is furrowed and there's so little spring in his step it's more like autumn. Once the door is closed, Stan gives the architect the news.

'You now have to get your money from the Minister of Public Works, Mr Davis Hughes.'[4]

But what about the Technical Advisory panel? Surely Professor Ashworth and the others still have some control over design matters, and can help me with the Minister?

No. It's been disbanded.

Jørn Utzon's heart sinks to the cold depths of Sydney Harbour. Staring out the window, he watches as the water does what he cannot: flow around all the obstacles placed in its way – a ferry, a hydrofoil, the building site, a rock and a hard place.

It's official. Jørn's every interaction with Minister Hughes is now an agony as Hughes is only concerned with deadlines and drawings, costings and calculations, with no appreciation for the complex design challenges faced by the architects, who are trying to ensure that a Masterpiece for the Ages does not come out stilted and acoustically lacking because bureaucrats and buffoons insist on their petty parameters of political performance being observed. All this management speak sounds impressive, but misses *and* obscures the point.

(Utzon had said some time ago now, 'I would not dare to build this Opera House before seeing a successful full-scale mock-up of almost everything,'[5] and he had meant it.

Australian architect Robin Boyd commented: 'That is indeed the only correct way to build something as original and complicated as this, although no architect before in Australia has ever been lucky enough to be able to do it.'[6])

All up, it really seems that the luck of the Irish bestowed upon Utzon by the late Joe Cahill is doing what luck so often does – it's running out, and he has no Danish luck to rely on in lieu.

The real problem, though, nearly bigger than all the others put together?

Utzon is starting to run out of money.

While the politicians, the press and the public decry the amount of money he is paid and debate whether he should be paid even less, they have little idea of not just his office expenses but the big income tax bills he is being hit with from both Denmark and Australia. There's no tax agreement between the two countries, so Jørn must pay both. And given Denmark has the highest tax rate in Europe – up to 70 per cent for top income earners – once he has paid that bill, there's not enough left over for the Australian bill! In short, he's being taxed more than he is paid.

'The rest of us didn't know about it,' Prip-Buus will later note. 'Jørn didn't let it interfere with work.'[7]

Right now, the account from which his staff is paid sounds like the bottom of a 44-gallon drum when a nut is dropped in it – it echoes.

23 September 1965, Sydney, paralysis

Again, it is just a snatch of conversation with Jørn Utzon, but Ron Gilling finds it troubling. After having lunch together at Gilling's behest, as the Australian tries to help the Dane navigate his way through his difficulties with Davis Hughes, Gilling is then given a guided tour of the site.

Surely, Jørn, he suggests, it is time to produce the final drawings.

Utzon demurs.

'It cannot be documented in the conventional manner.'

'[But] surely a stage has to be reached when you must say "build it".'

'You are so naïve,' Utzon replies, half-jokingly, half-seriously.

But the answer jars with Gilling, as does Utzon's response when he raises the Dane's reluctance to attend site meetings.

'Site meetings,' he says blithely in his soft Danish lilt with a smile, 'are for the birds.'[8]

Gilling feels it in his bones: this is not going to end well.

27 September 1965, Ministerial office, Sydney, a liberal dose of Australian practicality

Jørn Utzon can barely make sense of it.

It is one thing to have a meeting with Minister Hughes, together with Stan Haviland and Professor Ashworth. It is quite another, however, to find that the Committee men have now positioned themselves on the Minister's side of things on every issue.

Professor Ashworth insists at one point, 'Jørn, you cannot have *everything* just as you want, but will have to compromise, for instance, on plywood.'[9]

It feels like the wind has changed, and maybe even the whole tide has turned. And it doesn't look as if the Minister will be giving way any time soon on the matter of the plywood.

As much is confirmed a couple of days later with a stiff note from Minister Hughes to Utzon: 'a decision in accordance with your recommendation can only be made after it is established that there are no reasonable alternatives available'.[10]

What follows is a long list of all the technical problems as Hughes sees them, and it all boils down to one thing when it comes to Utzon's insistence that they proceed with the services of Symonds: NO.

Oh, and the whole thing comes with a demand for several detailed reports from Utzon of the work remaining to be done, how he intends to do it, the resources he has, how these resources are to be applied in production of the drawings, both for contract documents and for the information of other consultants, and the production of bills of quantities, schedules, specifications, etc., and all of it as early as possible.[11]

No doubt.

Utzon says little at the time, but the architects have a laugh the next day, when another two letters arrive from the Minister, and the boss, with a twinkle in his eyes, throws them into the wastepaper basket, for a joke.

Prip-Buus fishes the letters out to find . . . more of the same, one seeking assurances that Utzon's drawings are not only underway but would be soon *on their way*, while the other asks why he needs 50-foot plywood panels anyway?

It feels like standing beneath a Dutch windmill in a stiffening blow of ill-wind as successive blows come ever faster to send them reeling, and they are only trying to right themselves when inevitably the next one comes ever faster.

•

In early October word comes that Mick Lewis is heading back to London, where he will discuss with Ove Arup whether the time has come to leave the job.

'We imagine,' Prip-Buus records, 'that this must be seen as an ultimatum to the Minister: that they will only stay on if he gets rid of us.'[12]

Utzon can scarcely fathom that such a man as Arup would do that to him, and to the building, but at lunch with Norm Ryan the next day, the former Minister repeats an old rumour: 'The Government already has two other architects they want to associate with the project.'[13]

•

In some ways, the life of aspiring young film-maker John Weiley is like the constant drives he takes in his sports car back and forth through the famous S-bends of Bilgola on Sydney's Northern Beaches. On the one hand, he is very close friends with 19-year-old Lin Utzon and frequently goes over to the Utzons' house with Lin's boyfriend, Alex Popov, for lunch, before they hit the beach in the afternoon – he adores their whole vibrant family life, and listening to Jørn's views on the world in general and matters artistic in particular . . . including his problems with the government in realising the Opera House exactly the way he wants it.

And on the other hand, at night-time John frequently dines with his father, the Country Party parliamentarian for Clarence, Bill Weiley, where a frequent guest is his father's close colleague, none other than Davis Hughes – and a frequent subject of conversation is how long and how much bloody money the Opera House is taking to construct, mostly because Jørn Utzon is being too bloody precious in wanting everything his way! We could build 10 theatres in Armidale for that price!

'I lobbied furiously,' young John will later recall of his support of the Dane, 'but it didn't help. The politics of the clash of values was totally intractable.'[14]

The one thing he does know from the first: whatever they say, whatever the politics of it, the Utzons are *wonderful* people, and the Opera House itself is a cosmic work of wonder, somehow come to earth in his home city, and he is privileged to have such extraordinary access to this masterpiece in the making.

'That whole family is very important to me,' he will later recount. 'It had a vast impact on my personal life. As did the building itself. I've sat on top of the [highest] shell with my legs dangling off the top of it, drunk with the marvellousness of it all.'[15]

•

Despite Utzon having gone from being the toast of the city to a sly tipple behind the wood shed, still he does what he can to withstand the blows, and keep the whole project moving. To Hughes, the Dane continues to argue his case, and for that of Ralph Symonds Ltd, and the virtues of full-size mock-ups.

> These mock-ups are necessary and urgent. These halls, or any other structure of an entirely new design, could not be built without mock-ups. I would never embark upon any structure in the Opera House without having a Structural Engineer's support, whether this would be either Ove Arup & Partners or another expert, or both.[16]

Why the massive plywood panels? This has been the plan for several years, approved in principle by the Technical Advisory panel *and* the Committee, your liaisons.

> The existing schemes cannot be built with anything else but sheets of plywood of these dimensions. If you stop me from pushing ahead with these schemes, and require me to make alternatives, then I can foresee complications and delays which would lead to the production of an unsuccessful project.[17]

Mid-October 1965, Sydney, blonde bombshell

Yes, it is all of eight years since Peter and Libby Hall had visited and been so graciously received by the Utzons in Hellebaek, and they have not seen them since, but Libby has an idea. Surely, they will remember us, Peter?

For Libby, who is now importing a new line of clothing from Finland – Marimekko – is looking for a model and decides that the young and gorgeous Scandinavian girl Lin, who she has seen photos of from time to time in the papers, would be perfect. Tracking down the Utzons' address takes no time, and no sooner has she written to Lin, inviting her to come down to her studio to do some modelling for her, than she receives a reply saying she'd be delighted!

Her picture appears in the *Sunday Mirror*, 23 October 1965 – 'Not so much a fashion . . . more a way of life' reads the slogan.

Lin looks radiant with her bright blonde hair and wide smile.

•

What is going on? Utzon's latest invoice for fees hasn't been paid?

Yes, the Minister now controls the purse strings, but it appears he isn't opening that purse at all?

So how is Utzon meant to hire more people and move faster, if Hughes is refusing to pay him for the staff he has?

After dashing off a note of polite complaint, a reminder of the bill previously submitted and still unpaid, he gives fair warning to Professor Ashworth, and Silent Stan Haviland: 'We must close the office on the 1st of the month, if we do not receive the money.'[18]

Of course, they are powerless to help.

• ·

Days go by without a single word from the Minister, much less a single dollar of the much-needed finances.

Hopefully, things can be sorted out.

In the meantime, given how tight things have become, Jørn has another invoice he wishes to present, one that has been on his mind for some years, for work done but never paid for.

28 October 1965, Ministerial office, Sydney, invoices from the past

Davis Hughes is sure there must have been some kind of mistake. The invoice he has before him from Utzon, to the amount of £51,626, is for work done . . . in 1960?

Is 1960 a misprint?

He looks closer still.

The following is a claim, with account, for the fee for the engineering part of the Stage Technique . . . Briefly, Balslev & Partners
were not able to cope with the technical problem and I engaged
other consultants and developed in my office a team of specialists,
and, together with these, I provided the full tender documents on
the Stage Technique.[19]

Taking up his pen, Hughes writes a note, *What happened about payment
to Balslev & Partners?*[20]

In the Minister's mind, Utzon is as serious as cancer.

Further investigation shows that Utzon's figures at least add up, but
the Minister wants more information.

If this bill is dinkum, why on earth didn't Utzon present it *at the time*?

If only all of Davis Hughes' decisions could be so easy:

NO.

That invoice will remain unpaid until a full and sufficient explanation
is provided. So too will the request for fees, until he has fully investigated
it *personally*.

And if that puts the architect in dire financial straits? Well, that is
a shame, but it is a problem for Utzon, not for Davis Hughes and the
NSW Government. And no, he doesn't bother replying formally – the
claim is too preposterous to take seriously.

•

It is a phone call from out of the blue to Ron Gilling, from his elderly
mother who lives on the Northern Beaches not far from the Utzons.

'Did you know Utzon was preparing to leave the country?'[21]

No.

No, Ron has not heard that, and does not take it seriously, but thanks,
Mum.

1 November 1965, Sydney, who's the boss?

Word arrives to Utzon's office that Davis Hughes has requested, once
again, alternative design work and information directly from Arup's
engineers.

It is outrageous.

'I remind you,' Utzon writes to his client, 'that it is not professionally
correct for you to seek advice direct from any of my consultants on Stage
III, which I am administering. You cannot achieve anything by going

directly to any of the consultants. On the contrary, this might give you an incorrect picture and thereby lead you to make a wrong decision.'[22]

Davis Hughes is not cowed – *he* employs the engineers directly, not Utzon – and his broad view is that with this kind of carry-on the Opera House has clearly found its first prima donna and his name is Jørn Utzon.

•

It is time. After months of rumours about the critical problems down at the Opera House, and mounting speculation that Utzon is to be sacked, things are coming to a head.

On this day, 3 November 1965, seeking to establish firstly that the situation is not just in hand, but better still in his own hands, Davis Hughes steps up to the microphone in the stuffy Legislative Assembly chamber to make his long-awaited 'Ministerial Statement' on the Sydney Opera House.

'Since this Government took office last May,' he begins, Mr Speaker, 'I have had a full investigation made of the future of the Opera House. I have made a number of decisions . . .'

But before that, can I just say once again:

'The whole history of the Opera House is one of the grossest misman-agement by the previous Government. In its attempt to keep the truth from Parliament and the public, it resorted to devices which ranged from the illegal to the improper.'[23]

'Rubbish!' cries the Leader of the Opposition Jack Renshaw, but Davis Hughes will not be quelled.

'We have learnt more about the Opera House in five months than you did in eight years,'[24] Mr Hughes retorts. Let this Assembly be told, things are going to change. From now on, he, and he alone, as the Minister for Public Works will be the sole person holding the purse strings.

'We have stressed that the architect is responsible to me, as Minister . . . There was complete agreement from the Committee on the establishment of this single line of control which makes it possible for the Minister to be clearly known and recognised as the client for this project.'[25]

'If he does not approve,' reports *The Daily Telegraph* the next day, 'there will be no pay forthcoming.'[26]

Such dictatorial measures arouse the inevitable interjection – Jack Renshaw, a bare-knuckle political fighter like Grandpa used to make, puts Davis Hughes on notice: 'You have been found out before, and you did not like it.'[27]

Minister Hughes does not back off. 'You got into deep water on this,' he shouts at those Labor interjectors, 'and we are now reaping the harvest.'[28]

He goes on . . .

'The Committee was responsible for payment of the fees of the architect without reference to the Minister, together with so-called "out of pocket" expenses,' Mr Hughes says. 'These were of considerable magnitude. Indeed, fees and expenses paid and approved to the end of August 1965 to the architect amounted to £547,553. Total fees and expenses paid in this way, to all consultants, to the end of August amounted to £1,495,422.'[29]

'Shame!' 'Shame!' 'Shame!' cry the government members.

The situation with Stage III, Hughes thunders, is 'most unsatisfactory. If proper control of costs and programming of the work are to be achieved these plans must be prepared, and until all necessary documents are available, construction of Stage III should not commence.'[30]

There will be no more building by trial and error, no more money for models, but Davis Hughes is at pains to affirm that the building *will* be finished.

> We recognise that it would be quite improper, and indeed unthinkable, to leave unfinished a building of this nature where £9,000,000 has been spent already, and where further quite big sums of money have been committed . . . We believe also that when the building is completed it will be a truly magnificent one – one which this country may well be proud. We must ensure that it is completed to a high standard, in complete harmony with the conceptions of the architect who designed it.[31]

The speech takes nearly an hour, but at its conclusion, as he resumes his seat, Davis Hughes is confident that he has demonstrated that he is indeed the strong man needed to clean up the Opera House mess the new government has inherited from the Labor Party.

Opposition Leader Jack Renshaw does not agree – and at some length. He speaks for over two hours in response and looks Davis Hughes right in the eyes at one point as he utters with complete contempt: 'You are acting like a shyster, not like a minister.'[32]

Order! *Order!*

Hughes barely blinks. Sticks and stones. He has the backing of this parliament.

•

And so it goes.

Hughes talks, the press publishes and Utzon – who with his wife, Lis, has started declining social invitations for fear of the grilling that will inevitably take place – remains under the client's instructions to stay silent. Hughes' speech occupies the front page of the *Sydney Morning Herald* the following day and two full pages inside, with the usual focus on how much the architect is being paid: '£547,553 for architect' reads one subheading.

The report mentions neither that Utzon's invoice of a month earlier has still not been paid, nor that Utzon's office is near running on empty, nor that the greatest budget blow-outs have been in engineering, nor even that the sum total of his taxes in two countries now comes to more than his salary.

The *Sydney Morning Herald*'s editorial comes out swinging for Minister Hughes:

> The language of accusation used by Mr Davis Hughes in the first
> candid account we have had of the construction of the Opera
> House was unusually strong; but it is justified by the sorry series
> of blunders and waste, deceptions and self-deceptions which he
> described ... The major blunder, long known, was Mr Cahill's
> decisions to begin operations before detailed working plans, even
> for Stage I, had been prepared. Another earlier blunder ... was the
> decision to accept a prize-winning design which nobody, including
> the architect himself, knew exactly how to build ...[33]

Jørn Utzon is tired. Most nights are spent sleepless these days.

Lis Utzon's concern for her husband grows, as he seems to age before her very eyes, day by day.

19 November 1965, Ministerial office, Sydney, enough with the politics, apparently

The good news is that the two large easels displaying the photos of the Opera House building site are still there in the Minister's office.

The bad news is that, looking through the window over his right shoulder at the site itself, Utzon is all too aware the growing of the shells hides the problems shortly to come: approvals for Stage III are still where they had been more than a year ago. Hence why this meeting has been called for the key players in the whole affair, with the Minister himself,

Jørn Utzon, Stan Haviland, Harry Ashworth, the Minister's director Col Humphrey and his secretary Mr Walker.

'Welcome everyone,' says Davis Hughes, unusually rosy, stubbing out his cigarette.

'With my recent statement to parliament, the political aspect of the project has for the moment been cleared up,'[34] he announces happily, presumably referring to the fact that now he has seized control, he is about to exert it.

But please, Mr Utzon, there is something you wish to discuss first?

Indeed. After addressing a few remaining issues of Stage II construction, the Dane moves on to carefully let out some of the bees from . . . under his hood . . . no, *bonnet* . . . I think you Australians say?

Firstly, that of fees.

'Regular payments are essential,' he tells Hughes with surprising force, and the Minister suddenly, miraculously, seems to understand and even agree.

'The Department will work along similar lines to those adopted by the Committee as regards regular payments,' the Minister assures him.

And what of Minister Hughes consulting directly with the engineers about alternative designs for the interiors of the House, without going first to me, the architect? That must stop, Utzon insists.

Ah, no. Must the Minister remind Mr Utzon that, 'Ove Arup and Partners are consultants to *me*, the Minister. This led to my requesting a report [on the plywood ceiling] from them.'[35]

At least Utzon has the support of Harry Ashworth, who delicately reminds the Minister of professional practice: 'the Architect is the responsible authority for all work and consequently communication should be channelled through the Architect'.[36]

Jørn nods. Exactly what he has been saying for months now.

And for the first time, the Minister seems to understand, too, as he sits and nods back at the Professor.

The minutes of the discussion record the upshot: 'All agreed that in Stage III at any discussion between the Minister and any of the Specialist Consultants the Architect should be present . . .'[37]

It is also agreed that, as there has been much confusion, the architect will make one detailed submission on the plywood proposal before leaving for overseas in mid-December, and, 'Mr. Utzon agreed that he would confer with Mr. Lewis on structural matters.'[38]

9 December 1965, Sydney, as you don't like it

At first it seemed like just another request from the troublesome liaison architect, Mr Bill Wood, this time asking if Mr Utzon could attend a meeting at 3.30 this afternoon in the office of the Director of the Public Works Department, Col Humphrey. Mick Lewis and Corbet Gore will also be there, and together they will try to resolve the plywood question.

'No,' as Jørn has another meeting already scheduled at 4.30 pm, that meeting will have to wait.

But Wood won't quite take no for an answer. At 2 pm, he comes into Jørn's room and emphasises how important the meeting is, how it will, 'enable Humphrey to decide whether or not he should continue with pushing the plywood option, or ask Arup's to work out an alternative'.[39]

Yes, Utzon is normally slow to anger, but the Dane is now a man under extreme pressure, and there is a growing sense he might explode.

Arup's to work out an alternative? They are not the architects! He, Jørn Utzon, is, and as a matter of fact, in the contract, the 'Sole Architect'! He had thought this matter had been put to bed in the November meeting, but now it is obvious the department are *still* trying to design the interiors with the help of the engineers . . .

'What is the meaning of this activity behind my back?'[40] he asks Wood. 'You could very easily soon find yourselves in the situation where we simply go and you would then just be left with a building you are not capable of mastering. And you, Mr Wood, as an architect, you ought to support us instead of opposing us. I have had enough of the fabric of lies that the Department is spreading about us.'[41]

Wood says nothing.

'And why is Gore invited?'[42]

'To discuss the erection of the hall,' Wood replies sheepishly.

'Symonds will naturally put this work out to tender,' Prip-Buus says, dryly. 'It is far from certain that Hornibrook will get it.'

'Hornibrook are involved as the general contractor . . .' Wood offers.

The double standard irks Utzon.

'How on earth do the Public Works Department dare propose *them* for Stage III without tender when everything else is to be put out to tender?' he challenges old Bill Wood. 'Under Hornibrook, the estimate [for Stage II] went from £1.8 to £5.2 million over three years. Are *they* not afraid of criticism?'

'Wood,' at least in Prip-Buus's estimation, 'was finally completely flattened.'[43]

All up, Christmas can't come quickly enough. All of Utzon's office look forward to it with relief, so exhausting are the times – and getting more exhausting all the time as the previous stiffening breeze has turned into a raging and buffeting headwind, even as the tide has now definitively turned.

'The situation,' Prip-Buus tells his parents, 'can be compared to reefing the sails in a storm, trying to avoid the worst waves and meanwhile planning the journey ahead, so there is plenty to see to.'[44]

But they need a break!

The storm over the plywood issue, however, will simply not abate.

At a subsequent meeting, which Utzon can't attend thanks to a nasty head cold, Mick Lewis insists he will present an alternative acoustic ceiling proposal in his upcoming report – Arup's preference is for a steel-framed ceiling system – despite the architect not having instructed him to do so. He explains, among other things, that one of the problems with Utzon's current plywood ceiling design is that it's too heavy to be hung from the roof as proposed.

What's more, Lewis says coldly to Mogens Prip-Buus, 'The minister cannot permit more experiments such as the shells, so if it is possible to find ordinary tried and tested methods, they should be used and the architect's plywood proposals abandoned.'[45]

Oh, really? Plywood abandoned on the say-so of the engineers who surely have never engineered a piece of plywood in their lives, and who never saw a steel-based solution they didn't like? Need Prip-Buus remind those present that such a steel proposal has already been investigated, found wanting acoustically and shelved way back in 1962?

Well, he does so remind them anyway!

Humphrey, looking worried and eager to avoid open conflict, tries to soothe Utzon's man, saying this is just Arup's way of examining the construction.

But this is not good enough for Prip-Buus.

'We have received a report from Symonds' engineer, Mr Peter Miller, to whom Symonds have shown our proposal, and his report is favourable.'

Christ! Mick Lewis blanches. Peter Miller is a well-known Sydney structural engineer, a capable leader in the field and partner in the consulting firm, Miller Milston & Ferris, and his word carries a lot of weight . . .

Lewis is now trembling with anger as he near bursts: 'I am *not* interested in hearing what *other* engineers have to say about the Sydney Opera House. I WON'T TOLERATE IT! I know many architects in Sydney and they all have their opinions about the Opera House, but I do not listen to *them*, and I do not believe that *others*, especially not Miller, are competent to express opinions on it.'[46]

Lewis's remarks in fact go on for some time, and Prip-Buus must wait for him to pause for breath before jumping in, to explain to Humphrey that, 'the idea had *originally* been that the hall should be supported by the concrete structures in the base . . .'.

Turning to Lewis and Arup's Australian engineer John Nutt he asks frankly how much weight the base could stand.

'We do not have this information,' John Nutt replies glumly, 'and have not taken note.'

An extremely technical conversation now ensues with, as ever, no satisfactory resolution. As they take their leave, Prip-Buus takes Humphrey aside to get something off his chest that has been bothering him.

'Can you get the pedestal with the bust behind your desk fixed, as it is difficult to concentrate when you look at it and have to be ready to rush over and catch it.'[47]

As a matter of fact, it feels like *everything* is on the point of collapse, not least the relationship between the architects and engineers. Jørn can only hope, but has little confidence, that Arup's engineers will do as he has asked and put their energy and expertise into the requested structural work for his plywood scheme as it stands. But his confidence wanes further when in a final meeting with Minister Hughes on 17 December, before the Utzons head off on the Christmas break, the Minister most wishes to discuss . . . he should have known . . . plywood and fees.

On the fees front, the Minister has unilaterally decided Utzon is worth less than the standard 5 per cent and is now paying him 4 per cent. Utzon wishes to know why, but gets no adequate response.

The discussion meanders aimlessly on about plywood, as usual, with the Minister at one point repeating himself several times, as if caught in a loop: 'If I don't like plywood, I won't have plywood.'[48]

Those words echo in Utzon's ears as he flies to Hawaii with his family for the Christmas break.

If I don't like plywood, I won't have plywood.

Over and over!

Kristus den Almægtige. Christ Almighty.

There are sound reasons architecture is called 'the mistress art' – Harry Ashworth had warned of it back in 1957, writing in the *Herald* 'an architect in fact can only be as good as his client allows him to be',[49] – and lately, Utzon feels like a scorned mistress, indeed.

If I don't like plywood, I won't have plywood.
Well perhaps if you don't like me, you won't have me!

•

Usually, when the family goes away on holidays it takes Jørn at least a few days to leave his work-life behind and fully relax. But even after three weeks of the surf, sun and sand of Hawaii, Lis can see that her beloved husband is still desperately stressed and with, more often than not, a faraway look in his eyes – as if he is always gazing back to the Opera House. And as she gathers from him, it is not just problems with construction. It is the ongoing problem of invoices going unpaid, of being crushed by taxes.

Without telling her husband, Lis quietly writes, woman to woman, to Jørn's secretary back in Sydney, Shirley Colless, asking her for copies of all the 1965 accounts so she can get to the bottom of their financial situation. *Please don't send it here, Shirley . . . I don't wish to add to Jørn's stress.*

Lis will look at them when they get home.

23 January 1966, Castlereagh Street, Sydney, tats for the sheilas
Some light relief, anyone?

Bob Hammond, the tattooist on Castlereagh Street, is pleased.

For decades he has been doing tattoos for tourists who have wanted an image of the Harbour Bridge on their skin, which has been a real problem.

'I can't do it properly. All those criss-cross struts when they're scaled down just look like a blur.'

'Is there nothing else in tattoo designs to typify Sydney?' the junior reporter asks.

'Well, there will be,' says Mr Hammond happily, 'Can't you guess? The Opera House!'

He beams at the thought.

'All those sails at different angles . . . it'll be a beauty. It'll go all over the world. It's got everything! I can't wait until they get the roof on the Sydney Opera House: only eight quid. Beauty!'[50]

The *true* wonder and glory of this Opera House, slowly growing before Sydney's eyes?

It is the global nature of this extraordinary building, as it draws from influences around the world, from ages past and from the edge of the possible on the day it is built. Designed by a Dane, engineered by a

Danish Englishman, built by Australians, the podium would fit neatly beneath a Mayan temple of the first millennium AD, its rising staircase welcoming guests to another world, like the beginning of an ancient Greek procession or the grand ceremonial entrance of imperial Rome. The shells are neatly Gothic from the middle centuries of the second millennium with a nod to the curves of ancient Chinese floating roofs; the tiles owe no little to Islamic mosques and Japanese ceramics, while even the relationship between the exterior and interior as Utzon plans it, is inspired by the Japanese, who he has studied minutely – and the whole thing is put together using the Scandinavian design revolution from the early part of the century, which in turn echoes ancient Chinese building codes *and* relies on the cutting-edge world of twentieth century computing. And there is also a parallel for which the architect had not planned and few are aware. These enormous white shells on Bennelong Point pay accidental homage to the middens of pearly shells built up on this long-ago tidal island by the original custodians of this land, the Eora people. Yes, this jewel on Sydney's harbour is both timeless and ultramodern – sprung from the ancient land yet appearing to be from the future.

And if the Sydney Opera House then is the full bloom of a dozen historical and global movements at once, who better to nurture it and build it than this same bloom of multicultural workers, come from all over the world in the post-war immigration boom, bringing with them the skills from their homelands that, in many ways, go back centuries.

See the Italians, always tight with each other, a real tribe, earnestly stooped over the tile lids, doing the finicky work of filling the joints between the steam-cured tiles with a special epoxy resin. As Corbet Gore would later put it – 'that was a very tedious task . . . Very patient little Italians pouring epoxy resin into the joints. They took a great pride in it and caught a lot of fish off the wharf at lunchtime. They were very enthusiastic.'[51]

Another problem that Gore and his team are struggling with is how to stop the mortar from bleeding through the joints of the tiles – Utzon has given strict orders – and therein lies a story.

Gore and his boys have been trying everything to stop the mortar flowing as it passes through the cracks between each tile – a layer of sand on the bottom of the grid, an aluminium barrier, but nothing is working. They kept ending up with misshaped joints, broken tiles and, overall, a quality that Utzon rejects, over and over.

Until one day, when Gore and Mick Lewis are on site discussing this very problem, a big shirtless bloke, one of the assistant carpenters, walks over and says, 'Gidday.' He has a broad Australian accent that clearly comes from south of the Black Stump and just a little way north of Woop Woop.

'Did yers want to solve that problem?'[52] he asks the big brass, thrusting his calloused finger down at another failed tile lid.

'Typical Australian,' notes Lewis, amused by the matter-of-factness of the man before them.

'Yes, we do,' they reply.

'Well, I can solve it for ya,' 'e sez.

All right, mate, let's see then – 'How do you do it?'

To which the young man replies warily, a tone that suggests he wasn't born yesterday: 'Now, ya gotta pay me.'

'Okay. How much do you want?' asks Gore.

'Fifty quid,' the man says.

'Okay, you've got it.'[53]

The bloke grins, like he's won the Opera House Lottery.

'Well, whatcha do is, ya use animal glue. As ya put the tiles down, ya run animal glue along the joints, which sets. You can cast the concrete on it and ya steam-cure it and the steam melts the animal glue and nothing penetrates past it, you see.'[54]

Bloody hell.

Corbet Gore tests the carpenter's solution and, sure enough, it works.

Bob's your uncle and the carpenter is a richer man by the tune of 50 quid.

24 January 1966, Bennelong Point, a house divided cannot stand

What can John Nutt do?

He likes Jørn Utzon. He admires the Opera House, and feels privileged to be working on such a project. But he is also a professional, with professional duties and obligations. Right now, the client has asked Ove Arup & Partners to write a report on the efficacy of Utzon's pure plywood solution for the acoustic ceiling, *and*, despite Utzon's protests, to look into a steel alternative. Diligently, he has done the numbers, crunched the figures and come to a conclusion.

He prefers steel, because the final structure is lighter and, likely, easier to build.

And he says so, all of it neatly stapled together under the heading:

Report on the Structural Details of the Proposed Scheme for the
Minor Hall Auditorium Ceiling

It is only after finishing it that he has, if not a crisis of conscience –
because he stands by every well-considered word – at least a crisis of
loyalty, as he is all too aware of how his words might be used.

Perhaps the least he can do is explain to the architects why he has
written what he has?

Now, as both Jørn Utzon and Mick Lewis are away, the most senior
person that Nutt can talk to is Mogens Prip-Buus and their meeting
takes place at the architect's office, at Nutt's request, for a quiet chat.

Yes, John?

'I want,' Nutt begins carefully, 'to express my regret that the collaboration between the two firms has turned out like this . . .'

'Such things arise,' the Dane replies with caustic demeanour, 'for
instance, when the engineer collaborates with the client behind the back
of the architect . . .'[55]

Which is as may be. Nutt is at peace in the fact he personally has
nothing to do with all that.

But Prip-Buus has not heard the worst of it, and Nutt now must tell him.

'The report . . . goes against you. What do you have to say about
us providing the Government with ammunition in this way, when they
want to put you up against a wall?'

'As you have been asked by the minister to write a report on the
ceiling in the auditorium and the use of plywood, you simply have to
write what you believe . . . The only objection that we could raise would
be about your brains, which is beyond discussion. In any case, we are
used to being shot at and are almost immune.'[56]

There is little left to discuss.

Nutt takes his leave, and the report is sent to Utzon's office a few days
later, saying the engineers feared 'that the proposed plywood ceilings,
through the sheer weight of the suspended forms, might bring the roof
vaults down'.[57]

That is, as the engineers see it, Utzon's plywood scheme weighs more
than the maximum the roof could tolerate, in contrast to a potentially
lighter steel solution.

Prip-Buus is not worried.

'Luckily, this will be very easy to rebut purely logically and
constructively, as they have shown themselves to be very bad engineers

in the report, and we can receive full support from a local engineer [Peter Miller], but is it all politics or based on facts? As expected, Bill [Wheatland] and I have managed fine, and we expect Jørn home this evening so that the guns are in position, and we are ready for battle.'[58]

•

Even before opening the report, Jørn Utzon has a letter from Minister Hughes insisting it be forwarded to his department by 14 February, ahead of their first meeting of the year, to be held on 18 February.

Yes, yes, yes, but let him look at it first.

Utzon is most interested to see what the engineers have pronounced on his plywood scheme in its latest iteration, and so turns the pages quickly waiting for the word plywood to leap out at him, for they have barely mentioned it – just enough to dismiss it, all so they can present an alternative steel proposal . . .

'Arup's came into the open . . . with a report directly contesting our design and point by point saying what we all know the Minister wants,'[59] Mogens Prip-Buus tells his parents.

Going into their alternative, Utzon is convinced their analyses are off on a number of fronts, starting with the fact that their proposal is *hopeless* acoustically.

His first day back and already he is tired.

Jørn Utzon, desperate, writes to the only man left who can help him.

> 10 February 1966.
>
> Dear Ove . . .
> I want your personal assistance in the development of the ceilings of the halls . . .
>
> The situation is very bad, not unlike the situation when the first scheme for the shells was about to be scrapped. I have a perfect and ingenious scheme which takes care of every aspect of the problems in building the ceilings of the halls. I want that to be built and it needs your support and brilliant engineering because your partners here do not deal with the scheme and present an absolutely hopeless [alternative] idea in a very amateurish way.
>
> I would also like to inform you that the behaviour of your partners here is not professional. They are dealing directly with my client behind my back in spite of my telling them not to do so. This leads us all into trouble . . .[60]

•

On 14 February, as requested by Minister Hughes, and yet to hear back from Ove Arup, Jørn Utzon forwards the engineers' report but puts with it a strong rebuttal of its ideas, asking them to defer scrutiny of the report.

'The engineers, Messrs Ove Arup and Partners have not put forward a full report on the structural aspects of my scheme,' he explains. 'Firstly, they have not, as agreed between me and their staff, worked on a refinement of the structure on my plywood scheme, and, secondly, the engineer's report deals with some of the problems and overlooks others completely and so presents a false picture of the situation.'[61]

Further, Jørn sends his own report of the Minor Hall ceiling, and justification for those prototypes he still needs . . .

> It details the manufacture and erection of three full-scale ceiling rib [prototypes] by Ralph Symonds at a cost of around £60,000. The benefits – integrates all the mechanical, electrical, fire and other services into the prefabricated segments, besides which it made a higher standard possible because 'the geometrical system inherent in the design of these elements [which] lends itself to decoration being applied in the factory and not on the site.'[62]

•

Loyal chronicler of his times, Mogens Prip-Buus writes to his parents: 'Lewis came back on the 17th, came into our office and announced that now he would collaborate and believed that the report should not have been sent (honest?). He promised to send a letter withdrawing the report.'[63]

But, whatever Mogens hears, Lewis does *not* withdraw his report. Instead, he writes to the Minister and requests that consideration of the report be delayed.

'As a result of the discussion with [Utzon] we consider it is advisable that scrutiny by you of the report should be deferred until we are able to reach complete agreement with the architect on the technical matters concerned . . . We feel sure agreement can be reached soon.'[64]

Despite Lewis's letter, Davis Hughes is not at all inclined to defer scrutiny of the report.

And nor is his view changed by Utzon's views on the subject. Instead, he recognises the engineers' report as proof positive that Utzon is not competent as an architect. The Dane is proposing an enormous amount of money be spent on something that the engineers say cannot be built!

His own position is unchanged from the previous year: 'If I don't like plywood, I won't have plywood.'[65]

Report in hand, he *really* doesn't like plywood.

18 February 1966, Ministerial office, Sydney, happiness is a warm gun

After working their way through a range of minor matters, the Minister moves on to what this meeting is actually all about.

'The engineers,' Davis Hughes says, 'disagree with Mr Utzon on the plywood proposals.'[66]

Utzon jumps in: 'I have spoken to them, and they said they would withdraw the report pending re-investigation by them.'

'I refuse to believe that,'[67] Hughes retorts, stern.

Utzon: 'The steel scheme has been proposed by the engineers because it is less complicated. The prime consideration in my opinion, is that of acoustics . . . the plywood proposal was recommended by the Technical Panel 18 months ago.'[68]

Ultimately, after a long, heated discussion, the Minister declines yet again to approve the prototypes for the Minor Hall's plywood ceiling, saying he can grant no such approval until he has a joint recommendation from both the architect *and* the engineer.

'How can you alter *everything*,' Utzon asks Hughes, 'against my advice?'

'Here in Australia,' Hughes says gruffly, glaring at the Dane, 'you do what your *client* says . . .'[69]

That part of Utzon which has had it up to *here*, has now had it up to *there*.

February 1966, Bennelong Point, silver linings

It has been a long haul for Utzon and his team over the last week, but at last, it is done, and here are the 1:50 scale drawings of Utzon's latest scheme for the Minor Hall ceiling. After looking them over, at meeting's end, Mick Lewis scribbles a note on SOH Drawing 1408 – he accepts that the third alternative could, indeed, work.[70]

Could it be the beginnings of rapprochement?

•

Jørn Utzon is a man in the midst of a hurricane, looking to the sky in search of a silver lining . . .

Because yes, there is one. He has spent *years* on the tiles, more time than any sane man should spend thinking about tiles – just as a drunk on the tiles spends more time thinking about booze than is humanly healthy – and finally, here it is: the very first of the chevron-shaped tile lids has just been bolted to the roof.

He writes to Höganäs in Sweden, ecstatic to have made this crucial piece of progress a reality.

'We have some six [lids] already sitting on the shell and they look fantastic in the sun. I think it is the best publicity for Höganäs you could dream of . . . I hope you are well and selling a lot of tiles. My warmest greetings to all my friends in Höganäs.'[71]

Indeed, everyone is ecstatic.

It is just as Utzon had described it – 'The fine lines defining the form of the curve like the seams in a billowing sail'[72] – and Sydneysiders momentarily forget about the cost of the Opera House to marvel at the growing patch of glistening white, creeping up the mighty sails. Even the engineers, mostly at loggerheads with the architects, admit that it is a spectacle to behold, one noting, 'Utzon was right about the tiles. He said they would gleam like an Islamic mosque, and they do.'[73]

(Personally, Corbet Gore is so taken with them that when there prove to be some tiles left over it is not long before . . . the pathway around the side of his house in Avalon suddenly has a rather white translucent look in the day, and a certain gleaming in the gloaming as the sun goes down!)

The shells, mind you, do not please everyone, despite the engineering triumph in making them stand to take on all comers – wind, rain and critics – who had said they shouldn't and *couldn't* be done, and wouldn't even look good if they *were* done.

One *Daily Mirror* columnist notes of the final vision: 'I think it looks like an untidily sliced apple, or perhaps a bunch of toenails clipped from some large albino dog.'[74]

25 February 1966, Palm Beach, taxing times

Shirley Colless drives up to Palm Beach – through the S-bends of Bilgola – with the wheezing accounts book.

Though greeted as warmly as ever by the Utzons into their home, both of the Danes become uncharacteristically grave once they get down to tin tacks and look at Jørn's personal financial situation.

'The combined tax would have come to something like 131.7 to 136.7 per cent, exceeding by more than a third his actual earnings,'[75] one writer later calculates of the Utzons' situation.

It is obvious that if the Australian tax authorities don't reach the common-sense solution to give Jørn relief via credits for the tax he has already paid in Denmark – despite there being no reciprocal tax agreement between the countries – Jørn will face a choice of being bankrupted, or having to leave.

Shirley Colless's Milk Arrowroot biscuit suddenly seems sour.

27 February 1965, London, the death of a dream

Ove Arup has been thinking long and hard about the letter from Jørn, appealing for his help.

It is high time he responds, and it's not an easy letter to write.

'In your letter you appeal for my assistance. This pleases me, because I want nothing better than to help you and the job. But you do it in a most peculiar way, by insulting my trusted friends and collaborators.'[76]

He goes on, getting to the nub of the matter quickly.

'If you find Mick's scheme and Nutt's scheme absolutely hopeless and amateurish, at least you could tell me what is wrong with it. I have not seen the drawings of our scheme except for the cross-section shown in our report, but as far as I understand it, it gives exactly the same outward appearance as your scheme. But it weighs much less and can be built and costs less. So, what is so frightfully wrong?'

He keeps a channel open, however, writing: 'I have not seen your complete scheme yet, so I keep an open mind.'

As to other pointed matters, Ove says, 'I repeat what I said before: it is absolutely essential that we stick together. If we don't, we could end up with a very nasty situation . . .'[77]

The old man warns: 'As I see it, if you resign all is lost. It would be a most dangerous thing even to hint at it. If you want to just use it as a threat, you must be quite sure that it will not be accepted. And can you be absolutely sure? If you first have resigned you cannot prevent your building from being messed up. You have poured your life blood into this building and it must not fail.'[78]

FIFTEEN

EXIT, WITH A STAGE LEFT . . . TO GO

It is not I but the Sydney Opera House that creates all the enor-mous difficulties.[1]

Jørn Utzon, 1966

It is terrible and unbearable to an artist . . . Through all the world there goes one long cry from the artist: Give me leave to do my utmost![2]

Karen Blixen, Danish writer, *Babette's Feast*, 1953

In the profession, the architect–engineer joke is like the mother-in-law joke – it can turn serious.[3]

Philip Parsons, theatre academic, February 1967

28 February 1966, Ministerial office, Sydney, though this be madness, yet there is method in't

What other time could be better for such a showdown?

It is just before high noon.

On the powerful side of the Ministerial desk sits he who must be obeyed, Minister Davis Hughes, flanked by his loyal director, Col Humphrey, and his Government Architect, Ted Farmer.

On the other side, flanked by his loyal Australian assistant, Bill Wheatland, is Jørn Utzon, who has obeyed to the best of his abilities but is – what is that strange thing the labourers on the site say? – 'bloody well jack of the whole thing'.

As it tends to go in meetings between this pair, things get off on the wrong foot, with Minister Hughes saying he will pay Utzon every month an advance on fees of 20,000 'Australian dollars' – the new currency that had been introduced a fortnight before – which the Dane calculates at about £10,000 in the old money – less than the architect is entitled according to the Royal Institute guidelines, but the look in the Minister's eyes shows he won't budge.

Jørn Utzon seethes.

Now, on the rather delicate subject of your bill for £51,626 for the work you say you did back in 1960, and which you wanted paid by 15 February.

'I still cannot accept that bill,'[4] the Minister says.

'We are giving this claim of yours every consideration and by the end of this week you will have a definite reply.'[5]

The Danish architect will not be so dismissed, and returns to his main point of angst.

'You are always putting me off,' he says, frustrated. 'I need the money.'[6]

Hughes makes no reply, instead offering up something like the stare and glare of a grizzly bear by way of response.

Well, for his part, Utzon can bear no more.

'Very well,' he says. 'I go. I resign.'[7]

'You are always threatening to quit,' Hughes says dismissively. Oh, and Mr Utzon – 'This is no way to address a Minister of the Crown.'[8]

Utzon leaps to his feet in frustration, barely able to contain his anger.

'Well, goodbye, Mr Minister,' he says. 'That's it, I *go*.'[9]

He means it.

'It is impossible to continue.'[10]

Almost before Minister Hughes realises what is happening, Jørn Utzon is moving towards the door so fast that Bill Wheatland can barely keep up, and they only just get through the door before Wheatland turns back to the Minister and pronounces theatrically, 'Finita la musica!'[11]

Exit, stage left.

He *slams* the door shut behind them.

Minister Hughes is . . . a little surprised, but also bemused. Such carry-on! It is not the first time the Dane has threatened resignation, though admittedly the threat seems to have reached another level today. Well, enough. This time, if Utzon follows through, he will accept his resignation, as simple as that! The Public Works Department is filled with capable architects already on the public purse, and they are led by an enormously competent leader in Ted Farmer, with whom Hughes happens to get along very well. Do they really need Utzon and his carry-on, his endless delays, his absurd invoices?

He thinks not. Better to get some of our own lads to do it, actual Australians who know how to get things run and done.

The Minister must make some calls.

•

From first to last, the whole meeting has not lasted 15 minutes.

This time the storm heading down Macquarie Street – the southerly buster to beat them all – is Jørn Utzon himself, with Bill Wheatland trailing in his magnificent wake. Recognising the wizard of Bennelong Point, a passing motorist pulls over and asks him if he'd like a ride, but with uncharacteristic abruptness Utzon brushes him off, and continues to roll and rumble down the hill towards his unfinished masterpiece.

How has it come to this?

(Truly? Jørn is following in the footsteps of the great Gunnar Asplund, who had forced his client's hand several times with theatrical threats to resign. As Utzon himself will acknowledge, there had been more than a touch of attempted method in his seeming madness: 'I resigned to show them I could not go on like this. This was the only way to get my client to understand the situation.'[12])

But deep inside, Jørn feels he has *no* hand to play against Minister Hughes, let alone the upper hand.

Surely it can't be over. Can it? *Can* it?

No, surely the government will come to its senses and realise that, without him, the project will be even more delayed, and expensive – if it is even possible at all.

He'll get back to the office and Shirley will be waiting with a message begging them to return to the Minister's office, as he awaits and is eager to get through this momentary misunderstanding.

Strangely though, no, there is nothing – no message, nothing but the tense faces of his ever loyal staff, wondering if the Dane had finally felt the blade of Damocles' sword. In a few miserable words he tells them that is exactly the case – at least for the moment.

Very well then, he must write his letter of resignation and set out the reasons for his action – as much for posterity, as legality; as much for form, as to formalise things. Knowing he must get the tone absolutely right, he gets through five drafts over the next two hours, a process that would have been even quicker had Bill Wheatland not kept interrupting, insisting he should get legal advice, so as to know his rights. He will not hear of such a thing.

For, truly?

Truly, the Dane still does not believe it can actually be happening.

Committed, Utzon calls out to one of the secretaries – 'Elsa, come here!'[13]

He dictates his letter.

Elsa, quietly, is shattered.

After finishing the letter, Utzon goes out to see his beloved staff and tells them simply, 'It's all over.'[14]

They sit there, completely stunned. Utzon sits with them.

Silence.

•

In response to urgent calls from the Minister's office, Stan Haviland proves to be away on business in Katoomba and so can't come. Professor Harry Ashworth is urgently summoned and told the detail of what has happened.

Ashworth's face turns ashen. 'No, no,' he thinks to himself. 'One never resigns.'[15]

(George Molnar is soon brought into the fold, as he will recall years on: 'Crisis. Utzon's resignation. Long telephone conversations with Palm Beach . . . The voice of Professor Ashworth over the waters: "One does not resign. One never resigns."'[16])

And a moment, please, Professor. Yes, Dorothy?

Minister, a letter has arrived from Mr Utzon, delivered by his secretary, a somewhat flustered Shirley Colless.

Good God.

Professor Ashworth reels as he reads Utzon's letter. (*Why didn't he call me?*)

After summing up the essence of their meeting – Utzon had requested and set a final date for payment of a legitimate invoice and Hughes had once again declined – the Dane gets to the point.

For the record:

> As you could not at this date, February 28, 1966, satisfy me on this, you have forced me to leave the job. As I explained to you and as you know also from meetings and discussions, there has been no collaboration on the most vital items in the job the last many months from your Department's side, and this also forces me to leave the job as I see clearly that you do not respect me as the architect.
>
> I have therefore given my staff notice of dismissal. I will notify the Consultants and Contractors and I will have cleared the office of my belongings and you will receive my final account before the 14th March, 1966.
>
> Yours faithfully,
> Jørn Utzon[17]

Utzon *is* serious!

Davis Hughes is more relieved than anything. It had been one thing for Mr Utzon to say he resigned, but that meant nothing without written confirmation – and here it is.

Well, that's it then.

Dorothy, I need to dictate a letter.

•

Professor Ashworth takes his leave of the resolute Minister. He is alarmed. Losing Utzon is unthinkable. Why, it will take *years* for whoever takes over to apprise themselves of all the myriad issues involved, let alone resolve them.

He does his best to reach Utzon to talk him out of this madness but, wherever Jørn actually is, he is either not answering or having the people who do answer insist that he is not there and the Professor should try elsewhere.

Very well then, the Professor will drive up to Palm Beach and try his luck.

Alas, Utzon is not home.

•

Excuse me, Minister, I have Premier Askin's secretary on line one.

After Hughes briefs Premier Askin, he makes several more calls, starting with Mick Lewis and Corbet Gore, to seek assurances that the engineers and builders will continue on the project even without Utzon. The answers come back: yes, they likely will.

Many such phone calls are made with a similar theme.

An associate of Utzon's will later recall one such breathless communication from one of Davis Hughes' staff, well known for speaking only in short sentences, which he then repeats to get full price on the dollar.

'Utzon resigned! Utzon resigned!' he yells down the phone. 'Will you stay? Will you stay?'[18]

The associate agrees. He has a family; he needs the money.

•

Shirley has only just arrived back from delivering Jørn's letter to the Minister than the Minister's reply is heralded by a timid knock on the door.

Utzon tears at the envelope.

Dear Mr Utzon,
I have received your letter of resignation which I deeply regret ...

I have referred your letter to my officers to initiate discussions as to the proper proceedings to follow your actions.

Again, I am extremely sorry that this unhappy position has arisen.

Minister Davis Hughes[19]

A dagger to the heart would have been kinder, but Utzon must remain as composed as possible, to give his staff the shocking and unexpected news: the Minister appears to have accepted the resignation.

'The whole office was absolutely, absolutely saddened, upset, not knowing what to do,' one of the secretaries will recall. 'We never expected this sort of response from the Minister.'[20]

With everything caving in, his Opera House starting to sink into the harbour, Jørn taps Mogens on the shoulder. Let's get some air. Strangely, given that inside the office it felt like the world had stopped, it is odd to walk down the poky front steps and soon be on the site itself, to the red giants swinging overhead, the hum and rattle of workers all around, some of whom greet them warmly.

Hello.

Continuing on their way, talking tightly, they head up rough-hewn sandstone steps into the Botanic Gardens, below Government House, before plonking themselves down on, yes, a grassy knoll, where they stare glumly through the jail-like bars of a metal fence, down to Bennelong Point.

After a long silence, Jørn says quietly . . .

'One thing I know – we can handle technical, artistic and such problems. The only thing we can't overcome is human stupidity. Human stupidity defeated us.'[21]

Mogens sighs to hear it.

They sit in sad silence as Utzon's roof rises before them.

What a piece of work is man!

•

Night is falling and the press are calling.

Davis Hughes has called them here to announce Utzon's resignation, so *he* can have the first word – surely not the final one – and hopefully minimise any damaging accounts that too often leak out of governments at times of high drama. It is important that he get his version out first.

In fact, there are so many members of the press wanting to hear his words that Minister Hughes has no space for them in his office, and must descend to the street, where they can all gather around him.

Choosing his words carefully, while having to lift his voice above the swish of the passing traffic *and* trying to appear at least a little mournful is no easy thing, but he'll do his best. The Minister reads from a prepared statement, announcing firstly, 'Mr Utzon will be leaving the project by 14 March.'[22]

'The Government,' he says, 'finds the resignation of Mr Utzon is a matter of regret and pays tribute to the whole conception of the Opera House, which has gained recognition throughout the world.'[23]

Yes, regret. But if the greatest tradition of show-biz is that the show must go on, so must the building of the venue in which the show-biz will take place.

'It is the Government's intention,' he continues, 'to complete the Opera House, ensuring that the spirit of the original conception is fulfilled. Arrangements will be made for the completion of the Opera House on this basis. There is no reason why the changeover should affect work on the construction of Stage II, the roof shells currently being erected on the site. I will report to Cabinet tomorrow and in due course make a statement on proposals for completion of the project.'[24]

The reporters bustle forward and call questions to the Minister but he's said what he came to say. He turns on his heel and walks back inside.

•

Late that night in his Palm Beach home, as the concerned Lis hovers close, Jørn Utzon begins jotting down a list of conditions that the government must meet before he will even consider finishing the Opera House.

As a family, they are tense. Can this *really* be happening? It wasn't long ago that the family *pater* was the most celebrated man in Sydney, and now he is one of the most controversial.

Trying to muster strength in the face of it, Jørn tells his kids what he has said many times in the years since Uncle Leif suddenly died.

'I will not give my life for a building.'[25]

They have never seen their fine father like this.

And it is not just him who is affected, of course.

All five of them in the family – Jørn, Lis, Lin, Jan and Kim – have lived through the project with him; the Opera House is practically a family member. Not to mention, they have come to love the city, and the nation, so much so they have recently got the papers to become naturalised, to become full Australian citizens.

•

When the phone rings just before midnight, it is rarely good news.

And Ron Gilling, the President of the NSW Chapter of the Royal Institute of Architects, is tired. Having returned from a fishing trip all the way down in the Snowy Mountains just a few hours before, he had packed his stuff away in the garage and is having a well-deserved nightcap when it rings.

What is wrong?

Something with one of the children?

Snatching the phone up he is at first relieved. It is a journalist from *The Daily Telegraph*, and he wants to know about *what* . . . ?

'Did you know that Utzon has resigned from the Opera House?'

'God, what a bloody disaster.'

Will you make a statement?

'No. Not on behalf of the Institute until some of the circumstances surrounding the resignation are known.'[26]

The following morning's papers, of course, are full of the story – the *Sydney Morning Herald* leading with blaring headlines . . .

UTZON QUITS OPERA HOUSE

Angry Clash on Fees Reported

Danish architect Jørn Utzon resigned yesterday as designer of the $50m Sydney Opera House . . . The collision between Mr Utzon and Mr Hughes, both strong-minded men, followed months of mounting tension between them . . . The precise nature of the conflict . . . is not yet clear, but it is claimed Mr Hughes foresaw the possibility of yesterday's showdown. He was determined not to give ground, nor was Mr Utzon. Government authorities said last night they expected no major problems in completing the Opera House in Mr Utzon's absence.[27]

The *Telegraph* also gives it an acid splash all over its front page.

Opera House 'Bombshell'
UTZON RESIGNS HIS JOB[28]

And phone calls have been flying around the world from Sydney journalists.

Contacted in London, and asked for his views, Ove Arup is typically blunt without being bellicose.

'The atmosphere has been very strained lately,' he tells the *Herald*. 'But I do not know what caused the latest difficulty. Mr Utzon has been very inaccessible lately. We have found it very hard to get any information from him. We have sent him a cable today at the Opera House site asking him to phone us without delay.'[29]

And what of your firm, Mr Arup? Will you continue working on the Opera House without Mr Utzon as the architect?

'Obviously it is too early to say whether our position will be affected,' Arup says with a combination of great fatigue and sorrow down the line. 'We are waiting further advice about what is happening.'[30]

Ronald Gilling is quoted in a personal capacity by *The Daily Telegraph* reporter who had called late the night before: 'Mr. Utzon's resignation is a disaster for the whole Opera House project. I doubt if anyone else can finish the Opera House in its original idiom.'[31]

Of course, Mr Gilling is privy to the fact that the Stage III drawings are still in a preliminary stage – it is the crux of the trouble, so far as he understands – and warns, 'If final details have not been completed, a very difficult situation could occur.'[32]

As for who will be asked to finish the job?

Davis Hughes stays mum but the *Tele* reports, 'Government observers believe that . . . the Government Architect, Mr E. H. Farmer, will be asked to supervise the completion of the work. Government authorities believe the project has reached a sufficiently advanced stage to reduce the impact of Mr Utzon's resignation, particularly if a man with Mr Farmer's recognised ability agrees to take the job.'[33]

Whether anyone can or can't is not the concern of the Grand Old Man of Danish architecture, Professor Arne Jacobsen, who had visited Jørn's Hellebaek house years earlier and been so impressed by his architectural talent. He is of the view that it should not even be *attempted*, as it is directly contrary to the ethics of the architectural profession.

'The remark that the building will be continued in Utzon's spirit is sheer nonsense,' he says. 'It just cannot be done.'[34]

•

Order!

ORDER!

But there is none.

Parliament explodes, as Labor goes over the top with all guns blazing, targeting the Askin government's mismanagement of the whole affair. Such incompetence! They had been handed a project in progress, with a contented maestro, and now? Now the architect of the whole masterpiece is intending to head home, rather than continuing to work with the architect of the whole debacle, Minister Davis Hughes!

'Was the relevant action taken by the Minister for Public Works taken after consultation with the Cabinet, the Premier, or both parties, or was it taken entirely on his own? If the latter ... Will the Premier inform the House whether a clash of personalities occurred, resulting in the architect's resignation which may, in turn, cause an appreciable escalation of the cost of this multimillion dollar project?'[35]

Government members laugh. Hughes stares across the chamber and asks mockingly, 'You are joking, surely?'[36]

Davis Hughes is completely unrepentant, to the point of being exultant at Utzon's resignation. The *Herald* reporter describes the Minister's remarks as an 'aggressive address'.[37]

'I believe,' he roars, over constant interjections, 'that we as the Government and I, the Minister, had a very real responsibility when it came to whether we should proceed with the building of a structure which was going to cost more than $2 million. This structure was largely experimental and required me as Minister to approve the construction of prototypes at a cost of $120,000 [£60,000] to see whether in fact they worked.'

He went on to detail Arup's report that the weight of the plywood was not practical within the structural limits of the shells. 'Would any Minister on that advice have said, "Go ahead and spend $120,000 on prototypes?" If any Minister did so he would be recreant to his duty.'[38]

But fie! Hear Hughes now and hear him clearly; he is not only not sorry for his actions he is proud to have done so.

Asked about Utzon's charge over a lack of co-operation from Hughes' department, Hughes seethes and spits, 'If co-operation means that one person in the setup has the whole say and dictates everything that is to take place, and that the Minister and his Government are to be completely left out of consideration then that is not my idea of co-operation.'[39]

But have no fear. Everything will proceed under new management, most likely a panel of Sydney architects. 'The Opera House will one day be a magnificent edifice.'[40]

'Not the way you are going about it!' the former Minister for Local Government, the irascible Pat Hills, interjects.

Minister Hughes tries to resume, only to be interrupted by a visitor in the public gallery, who roars at the Armidale member: 'What would you know about it?'[41]

While attendants eject the visitor, Minister Hughes resumes, only to again be interrupted, though at least this time it is from an elected member, not an ejected member of the public.

'Why did the architect resign?' Norm Ryan yells.

'For two reasons –'

'Number one,' Bob Kelly, Member for East Hills, interjects, 'was because you would not pay him!'[42]

Order! ORDER!

For his part, the Premier, also under attack, is more than happy to defend his Minister: 'The Government regrets the architect's decision to *resign* of his *own free will* . . .'

Of course! Tell us another one!

Mr Speaker looks as if he might explode, but the Premier goes on, undaunted, nor remotely haunted by what has occurred.

'I want to say without equivocation that the Minister for Public Works has discussed the matter with Cabinet today. Cabinet unanimously supports Mr. Hughes in the attitude he has taken. We regret what has happened – but the initiative was taken by Mr. Utzon . . . We regret the matter has been handled in a slapdash fashion in the past.'[43]

The heated debate goes on in what is another long afternoon for Minister Davis Hughes, as no sooner does he make it back to his office to have quick meetings with Mick Lewis and Corbet Gore – batten down the hatches, and full steam ahead, or something like that – than he must contact all the consultants, to confirm they are all still on board.

They all agree, for now and . . .

And now Professor Harry Ashworth is on the blower, to ask if the Minister will at least meet Utzon? You will? Your office, 6 pm? Thank you, Minister!

In the meantime, Hughes has his director call Ronald Gilling. Have him come see us this evening, Col.

1 March 1966, Paddington, conditions set, to be met – or else

Mogens arrives last, pushing open the filigree-style cast-iron gate with a tortured squeak, before walking up the narrow path, through the whitewashed wooden doorway of the Utzons' Victorian terrace house on Windsor Street, Paddington. Jørn appears at the end of the narrow, polished timber hallway and waves him in.

Again and again, Utzon, Prip-Buus and Wheatland go over it, before the meeting set for this evening with Minister Hughes. Now that Utzon has called the Minister's bluff by actually resigning, how best to set the conditions for his triumphant return?

Just what should the Dane insist upon?

It turns out to be very easy.

Before Utzon will deign to come back, he wants his authority as *the* architect in charge of the whole operation to be acknowledged. He must be paid for his work from 1960. And Bill Wood – who Utzon always knew to be the worst kind of spy, one who contributed little actual work that could be used – must be removed from the Utzon office because, as Prip-Buus notes, they now have 'evidence of his sabotage'.[44]

If these conditions aren't met, the Minister can *beg*, but Utzon won't come back.

•

Where is he?

Besieged at home by a belligerent and braying press, Lis Utzon tells them her husband is, 'somewhere in the country'.[45]

But have no fear. Yes, she tells reporters, she will try and persuade her husband to give some kind of comment to the press when next he gets in touch.

•

Of the many phone calls Ron Gilling receives on this most difficult day – enraged architects in the main, carpet-biting mad at the treatment meted out to Utzon and telling Gilling he must intervene to save Australia's lone architectural masterpiece – the most benign is from the Director of Public Works, Col Humphrey.

'The Minister requests to see you at 8 pm,'[46] Humphrey tells Gilling.

Yes, of course.

Gilling tells the Institute's NSW Chapter's Public Relations Committee, who are itching to release a public statement unequivocally supporting Jørn Utzon: 'No press statement until we can investigate the matter further.'[47]

1 March 1966, Ministerial office, Sydney, to be, or not to be, that is the question

Professor Harry Ashworth has worked miracles to get this far, only because he has retained respect for, and the respect of, both Jørn Utzon and Davis Hughes. But, yes, on this, the day after the big blow-up, the aggrieved Minister has agreed to see the aggravated architect in the Minister's office at 6 pm, and the agitated latter does indeed turn up, accompanied by the ever-glowering Mogens Prip-Buus and Bill Wheatland.

The atmosphere is . . . tense.

On the one side, as ever, sits the Minister for Public Works. His authority rests on his party's victory in the recent election, the purse strings he holds in his right hand, the leading bureaucrats of the Public Works Department and the Government Architect he is flanked by, and the resignation letter from Jørn Utzon, which lies on the table before him.

And there is Mr Utzon himself, with no legal power at all, with no path open bar making the ethical case that he should be reinstated. But on that subject, and *despite having resigned the day before*, the Dane now presents nine conditions which he insists must be met, conditions which prompt Director Col Humphrey to jot down on his notepad – Mr Utzon did not come to the meeting in the spirit of conciliation . . .[48]

That much is evident from the fact that one of the first conditions he puts upon his return is a restoration of his monthly payment of $30,000 – the rate approved by the Institute of Architects – instead of the $20,000 that the Minister spoke of the day before.

Utzon has barely cleared his throat, as there is more.

Approve payment of the 1960 bill for the Stage Technique; plus the Minister must affirm that Jørn Utzon is the final arbiter of what will and won't be built in his Opera House, while the Minister must also advise all, 'Consultants that the Architect is in charge and that the Client will not go directly to the Consultants or the Contractor'[49]. Oh, and the 'mock-up proposal for plywood structures which was delivered to the Minister be accepted immediately', while Mr Wood must be replaced by 'one or two experienced architects and that the Architect will have the right to interview'.[50]

In sum, Mr Utzon, Minister Hughes addresses him shortly, you want exactly what you wanted before – but also the dismissal of the government architect you don't like in your office – and we of the government are supposed to accede and beg you to come back?

Ahem.

Humphrey jots it down – Mr Utzon was told by the Minister that his terms were entirely unacceptable.[51]

Two hours later, meeting over, and the two men have finished further apart in their positions than they began.

As Hughes will chronicle with a handwritten note, 'I believe that I now have no alternative but to implement this programme without his services.'[52]

Jørn Utzon stalks out of the Minister's office, missing the incoming Ron Gilling by a matter of minutes.

The Minister and his men watch him go in silence. Door closed, they exchange a heady cocktail of looks – smirking amusement and shocked disbelief being the main ingredients. Get a load of the bloke, would you?

Farmer pours them all a stiff drink.

•

Ron Gilling has come as summoned and finds the Minister in deep discussion with his leading men – his War Council, if you will – Col Humphrey, Ted Farmer and Farmer's assistant, Charles Weatherburn.

There is little time or appetite for pleasantries.

'My architect has resigned,' Minister Hughes begins, 'what should I do?'

'Get him back,'[53] Ronald Gilling replies.

It's not that simple.

'I do not expect Utzon to be on the site after 14 March,'[54] Hughes says.

The Minister has personally had a gutful and, Mr Gilling, let me be clear – 'Henceforward the Government Architect will be personally in charge of the project. If under any circumstances Utzon returns, he will not be in sole charge.'[55]

Never, you hear?

And so the Minister asks Mr Gilling, quite pointedly . . .

'In the event of Utzon not returning, how best can architectural services be provided to finish the project?'

Gilling's reply is equally pointed: 'Having a consortium of architectural firms as mentioned in the press today is quite impractical and inadvisable, and furthermore it is not the function of the Institute to provide names of architects in circumstances such as this.'[56]

What Gilling does want to do, however, in his role as President of the Institute is clear.

'I will give you all the assistance I can to achieve a reconciliation with Utzon,' says Gilling carefully, knowing that there are architects all around Sydney planning to rally around Utzon. 'And failing that, will help when called upon, but I will never suggest names.'[57]

Very well. The meeting rambles on, Hughes and his men filling Gilling in on the details of the resignation and all that remains to be done, which

Gilling will later put in something of a laundry list: 'Unresolved seating numbers, untenable solutions offered which give a seating arrangement no more commodious than the Sydney buses ... disagreement over the acoustics, plywood ceilings which could not be carried on the shell structure, the architect and the engineer at loggerheads, a construction team far from happy with the delays now costing them dearly and threatening to stop the project because of the lack of information and forward planning . . .'[58]

Leaving Parliament House around 10.30 pm, Gilling is far more informed on the many problems of the Opera House, which he later described as, 'a rudderless ship heading for potential disaster'.[59]

•

On the late evening of 1 March, Hughes calls a press conference in front of Parliament House and confirms rumours that the government's intention is to, 'engage a consortium of private architects from NSW whose activities would be directed through the Government Architect, Mr. E. H. Farmer'.[60]

But, Mr Hughes, the journalists ask, how can you stay faithful to the original conception by employing architects other than Mr Utzon – creator of the concept?

Hughes does not hesitate.

'The spirit of the conception is so well known that the incorporation of it into the building,' he says, 'while posing tremendous technical problems, can be achieved.'[61]

Any chance of a reconciliation between yourself and Mr Utzon?

'No comment,' he says on the record.[62]

Off the record, he and other insiders express their views strongly enough that the *Herald* can report: 'Government authorities said later a reconciliation was out of the question.'[63]

•

Sitting at his desk in the Government Architect office, architect Peter Hall is tidying up the last of his work, having just given his notice ahead of his planned move to private practice, when a colleague breaks the news.

Farmer is taking over the Opera House project. They need new architects.

You should do it, Peter!

The colleague is amused at the idea of it, but Hall is not.

For one thing his high regard, his *awe*, for Utzon has not wavered since the days when he and his bride Libby had visited him in Hellebaek. Taking over from him? *No*.

Utzon is a genius. He has come up with a masterpiece design. He should be allowed to finish it. Simple as that.

'I thought,' Hall will recount, 'it was potentially one of the world's most exciting buildings.'[64]

But it is obvious that potential can only be reached with Utzon himself *finishing* it.

He makes no bones about it.

'I was appalled. I didn't think anyone should replace Utzon as architect.'[65]

Which is fine. But even while he had been batting off his colleague's suggestion, others had been coming to the same conclusion. Their numbers include the *Sydney Morning Herald* journalist Gavin Souter, who has covered the saga from its beginnings and – copy-boy! – now sends to 'the stone' a small piece he has edited for the following day's paper, lauding the fact that the best operators in the Government Architect's department 'are still on the young side of 35'[66] and he leads his list with . . . Peter Hall.

•

Yes, it's all engines firing at the *Sydney Morning Herald* building in Ultimo this evening. The printing presses containing tomorrow's scathing editorial by John Pringle are just beginning to roll.

EXIT MR UTZON

MR. UTZON'S RESIGNATION is the most disappointing develop-ment yet in the daunting history of the building of the Opera House. It is sad for Mr. Utzon, and it is sad for New South Wales. With the end of his work in sight, and with the most difficult of its problems solved, he will now be unable to complete to his own satisfaction the majestic concept which, from the beginning, has been his alone. Stage III, the interior – literally the heart of the project – will be the responsibility of another.

As for New South Wales, it must now accept a compromise: the integrity of the unique aesthetic concept of one man to which, grumblingly but doggedly, it committed some fifty million dollars is now unattainable.

This blow to the idealism of a brilliant artist and to that of the society which backed him is the harder to accept because its immediate cause is petty in the extreme. The immediate cause is a demand by Mr. Utzon for payment of $102,000 for special fees which he claimed last October for work done before 1960 . . .

Such a display of petulance, the *Herald* declares, has shocked Australia. After all, let's not forget . . .

Each rise on the cost of the Opera House has added substantially to his fees from the undertaking. He has never, in his costly search for perfection, felt it necessary to renegotiate his contract in favour of the increasingly embarrassed Governments who employed him . . .

No architect in the world has enjoyed greater freedom than Mr. Utzon. Few clients have been more patient or more generous than the people and Governments of New South Wales. One would not like history to record that this partnership was brought to an end by a fit of temper on the one side or by a fit of meanness on the other.[67]

And yet, as is the way of the *Herald*, while the staff might reluctantly acknowledge that the editor John Pringle is entitled to his opinion, that does not mean it has to be their own opinion, and long-time *Herald* cartoonist George Molnar is a case in point . . . with an entirely different point of view. In his cartoon, published right by the *Herald* editorial he shows Davis Hughes asking a room of architects for the plans of the old tram-shed.[68]

The cartoon chorus soon has *The Daily Telegraph* as lead soprano, showing the half-built construction being hawked in a fire sale for warplanes and a carton of ciggies – a country spiritually closer to the war effort and the perpetual hunt for fags than the absurd and wasteful artistic crusade of the uppity Dane. In the pub and around the dinner table, debate around the issue heats up – a battle of cultural values is underway.

One of the first letters to the *Herald* editor, from Norman Edwards, sums up the mood of the disappointed side – 'Architects who produce good work are venerated in Utzon's home country . . . In Australia the opposite occurs – it is because Utzon is producing a building of outstanding quality that he suffers. The attitude of mediocrity prevails . . . The Opera House is about to suffer the fate of previous architectural competitions . . . Le Corbusier's League of Nations building, Walter Burley Griffin's Canberra. Frustration, bureaucratic bloody-mindedness, and ultimately the great compromise.'[69]

Many artists and architects feel the same, none more than Harry Seidler who is so ropable he sets to work amassing other outraged members of the profession to . . . *do something*. What, specifically? Well, for the moment it is decided that the first is to get the Institute back on side and representing Utzon's interests in the public domain. Yes, that's a start. Tomorrow, 40 of them will arrive as deputation at the office of President Ron Gilling, demanding that he and the Institute support the reinstatement of Utzon. As to the rising generation, many architectural students send around a petition and begin to draw up plans for a street march complete with placards and bull-horns, so can you nip out and get some fresh batteries while I look for the paint and cardboard?

For his part John Weiley, the aspiring film-maker and good friend of Lin Utzon, is livid. How can he pursue his own art of making important and creative films in a country with so little regard for the arts that it can treat a genius like Utzon in such a barbaric manner?

Another friend of Lin's, Martin Sharp, the iconoclastic Sydney painter, has no doubt where the blame lies and in a cartoon lampoons Hughes, delivering a stream-of-consciousness rant, congratulating himself: 'Brilliant move forcing that Danish prima donna to resign, he'd want to sing his own bloody operas if we'd let him stay.'[70]

Yes, charges of 'philistinism' begin to be slung in Davis Hughes' general direction. Well, the Minister, just quietly, does not take kindly to the accusations. Beyond Ministerial machismo, demonstrating that he is the master of his domain even with explosions all around, Minister Davis Hughes is personally hurt at the bitter criticism being hurled his way. Oh yes, he hears the slurs, the sneers from the coffee-shop-sitting, inner-city elites – who, all right, are perhaps better educated than him – that he is a philistine, the country bumpkin from Tassie and tiny Armidale who the political winds have blown way above his station to be in charge of a genius like Utzon. But he knows he is just not like that. For one thing, as he begins to tell people in self-defence, as a young man he had been quite the thespian, both acting and producing, and had particularly cherished a starring role in Chekhov's *The Cherry Orchard*. Beyond that, he is widely read, and when it comes to the world of musical theatre, well, he doesn't like to boast, but, as he will write some two decades later, still irked by the charges against him: 'I think I could say I know every classical ballet intimately.'[71]

But now, somehow, he is the barbarian, trashing and thrashing his big clod-hoppers through the sophisticated Dane's finely manicured rose garden?

What the hell else did they want him to do? It was pretty simple. The Liberal–Country Party Coalition had come to government promising to get the Opera House finished, on a firm schedule, and with an agreed budget. He had taken steps to do that, hoping Mr Utzon would fit in with the new plans. But Mr Utzon had proven incapable of executing what he had been contracted to do.

So be it.

But he, Minister Hughes, had *not* dismissed him.

Utzon had resigned.

•

The uproar that explodes in the architectural profession has two focuses: getting Utzon back, and stopping any of their own from stabbing him in the back by attempting to replace him.

An editorial in *Cross-Section*, the journal of the University of Melbourne Architecture School, puts it neatly: 'Every architect who believes in the ethics of his profession, in the cause of good architecture, in the principles of justice, must support Utzon. The Royal Australian Institute of Architects is challenged to declare participation in the Minister's proposed "team of architects" as an unethical act.'[72]

•

Even as the shouting over Utzon's resignation goes on in parliament, just down the hill at the Opera House site, a besieged Ron Gilling is meeting with a shattered Jørn Utzon.

No, the NSW Chapter of the Royal Australian Institute of Architects has no official standing in this dispute between client and architect, but as president, Ron has been inundated by communications all morning and into the afternoon: Support Utzon! This is a matter of *principle*!

'Tempers were running hot,' Gilling would recount. 'I had a call from my own office to say that I would not be welcome back if I did not support Utzon!'[73]

And Gilling does broadly support him. But it is not easy as he equally has no doubt that Minister Hughes has legitimate plaints that Utzon had never addressed.

'I was privy to much information damaging to the Architect . . .'[74]

As it turns out, so, too, are many other architects, who have their own strong opinions, and the truth of it is that, despite public proclamations to the contrary, some in the architectural profession are very quietly behind Minister Hughes. Walter Bunning is among them.

But Ron Gilling's meeting with Utzon, Wheatland and Mogens Prip-Buus is brief. There is an exchange of views, with the Utzon camp insisting that Minister Hughes had been outrageously unreasonable on all fronts – denying payment and imposing impossible schedules – but Gilling will no more budge than a Caterpillar D-9 out of fuel, which is what he is starting to feel like.

'The Institute,' he says with infinite fatigue, 'considers that an architect has a moral duty, no matter how difficult the circumstances, to stay with his client and not resign.'

'This is too big for moral issues,' Bill Wheatland remarks.

But here is the key.

'The door is not shut on reconciliation, Jørn?'[75]

'It is not.'[76]

Gilling comes away hopeful.

The view of the Utzon camp is likely expressed in the recorded view of Prip-Buus, that Gilling is 'a swine'.[77]

After all, how can this head of the professional body of architects in New South Wales, of which Jørn is a fellow, *not* take their side, when the situation is so clear-cut, and Utzon is so clearly being railroaded out of town by politicians?

Utzon, personally, is gutted at what he sees as the lack of support from the Institute, later noting, 'It is a tragedy for Australian architects that the Public Works was their biggest client.'[78]

Back at Gilling's office in North Sydney he is met by a deputation of 30 to 40 architects, led by Harry Seidler, seeking an assurance that Utzon would be supported and that the Institute would not help to facilitate the government getting a panel of architects to replace him.

'I was able to assure them on both counts – we would support Utzon to the best of our ability and we had not taken part in any discussions relating to a consortium or panel of architects.'[79]

But, as it happens, there is something that Gilling seeks from them. There is talk of a protest march the following day, and that many architects would take part. Gilling makes his view clear: 'This action was considered unprofessional and I expressed my personal disapproval of this type of public demonstration.'[80]

To Gilling's satisfaction it seems that most of them, including Harry Seidler, agree.

'Far from demurring,' Gilling will note of Seidler's position, '[he] agreed with our deliberations.'[81]

Even more than that, Gilling insists, 'Mr Seidler stated he would not be marching and said that the march was ill-advised!'[82]

At length, Gilling agrees to place Seidler himself on a seven-architect 'Select Committee' that is being formed to examine ways in which the Royal Australian Institute of Architects (RAIA) can help the government find a solution to keeping the construction of the Opera House going. But it is to be understood that the Select Committee takes no position itself on the rights or wrongs of the Utzon saga.

Meeting closed.

On the footpath outside, Harry Seidler talks to the gathered reporters.

'It is the fervent hope of everyone,' he says, 'that Mr. Utzon, somehow, will be able to finish the Opera House. If anyone replaces Mr. Utzon, it will be to the detriment of the project. No-one except Mr. Utzon could finish the Opera House in the spirit in which it was designed.'[83]

In the meantime, the entirety of Utzon's staff – 15 architects and two secretaries – announce they will work for no-one but Utzon.

'The vote was unanimous,' a secretary tells *The Daily Telegraph*. 'We work for Mr. Utzon on this project, and for no-one else. The only definite instruction we've had from Mr. Utzon is that we are not to say anything to anyone.'[84]

•

It is only a small episode, but somehow feels emblematic of the crumbling of the whole Opera House project. Just before the final shift ends on this tumultuous day in the history of Bennelong Point, six workers are standing on the scaffolding around the steel erection arch positioned on the highest reaches of Shell A2 on the western side – the Everest of these Opera House Himalayas – when something gives ... waaaaaay!

JUMP FOR YOUR LIVES!

And so they do, throwing themselves as flat as they can onto the shells to slow their slither and mercifully come to rest on more secure scaffolding 20 feet below. Luckily, there are bruises only, but one way or another it really does feel like the Opera House – the whole building program, and the building itself – is falling apart.

3 March 1966, Sydney to London, Lewis pulls no punches

And what of the firm Arup's in the midst of this whole intractable imbroglio?

Well, there is no little chatter within the firm that 'the old man', Ove, wishes to pull out. But Arup's key man on site, and Associate Partner,

Mick Lewis, does not agree and has assured the Minister from the beginning that the firm will observe the terms of its contract which is, after all, with the NSW Government, not Utzon. Ove Arup can think whatever he likes, this is not his call. And personally, Mick Lewis has no doubt where the blame lies, as he makes clear in a confidential memo to all the partners.

'It is not possible for us to go through a rational process attempting to understand [Utzon's] behaviour,' he tells the partners. 'By definition, his behaviour is irrational and we must accept it as one of his artistic foibles.'[85]

And he has no confidence that anything will change on this any time soon.

'Reports . . . seem to indicate that he is becoming more autocratic and increasing his demands rather than reducing them. In light of all this, it seems hardly likely that the government will retain his services under any circumstances . . . I think he has done everything he possibly could to have us removed from the job. It has been extremely difficult for him because of the magnitude and quality of work we have done . . .'[86]

For the moment, Jack Zunz and Ove Arup – following events from afar and alarmed at how quickly things have deteriorated – decide to make no official statement, and see if things can sort themselves out. But, certainly, if they don't, a trip to Sydney may be in order to see if they can help bring about a reconciliation.

3 March 1966, Parliament House, Sydney, the lady doth protest too much, methinks

Does the spirit of Joe Cahill hover in this drama fit for an opera of its own?

Some 50 years earlier, he had been part of the mob that had marched up Macquarie Street and on to Parliament House, screaming into a megaphone, pursuing better conditions for workers, the everyday citizen.

But this protest is rather different.

For in the country of 'she'll be right, mate', where, as a general rule, apathy rules unless laziness falls off a log at the right moment, there is nevertheless an exception – when people feel that something *is just not right*. And what is seen as the sacking of Jørn Utzon is a case in point, forget the technicality that he had resigned.

They've done what?

They've sacked the architect that gave us the Opera House?

How dare they?

Sydney is not particularly known for its protest marches, but this one attracts hundreds – and they're not railway workers either, or blue collars of any sort, who are usually the ones making a public noise . . . like the never-ending strikes down at the Opera House, ahem . . .

Rather, it is hundreds of architects and architecture students, straight out of the city's private schools and sandstone universities, led by the likes of Harry Seidler, who has decided overnight to ignore Gilling's request to have nothing to do with it. He is accompanied by no less than the Dean of the Faculty of Architecture at Sydney University, Mr Denis Winston; the novelist and playwright Patrick White, and the President of the Society of Sculptors, Mr M. Nicholson.

'Utzon Only,' it will be reported of the group, 'is a group of citizens who are determined to ensure that Sydney *does* gain one of the great buildings of our century. This can only be done if Jørn Utzon is retained as the Architect of the Sydney Opera House.'[87]

These people, united by the idea that 'a committee cannot finish a Rembrandt',[88] march from their gathering point at the gates of the Opera House building site, up Macquarie Street to the seat of government to protest against those who would destroy the architectural integrity of this shining masterpiece – the Sydney Opera House.

Their hand-painted signs tell much of their angst.

Will Australia never learn?
Sydney's Loss!
Save our Opera House
POLITICS CANNOT CREATE ARCHITECTURE
FREE HAND FOR UTZON
Art before politics – JUST FOR ONCE
Utzon started. Utzon must finish.
Griffin now Utzon.[89]

What do we want? Jørn Utzon back as the architect in charge.

When do we want it?

As soon as the Minister comes to his senses!

Right near the front of the pack, enjoying the whole thing, is Peter Hall, whose anger at what has been done to Utzon has only risen in the last couple of days.

'I was appalled,' Hall will recall. 'I didn't think anyone should replace Utzon as architect . . . It was a very personal concept he had and I think as a principle the man who conceives of a building ought to direct it straight through.'[90]

At the conclusion of the march, the leadership group, the newly formed 'Utzon-in-Charge Committee' is granted an audience with Premier Robin Askin, where they present him with a petition – 'We the undersigned express the strong belief that the only architect who can finish the Opera House in the spirit in which it was conceived is the existing architect, Jørn Utzon,'[91] – bearing 3000 signatures as proof positive of the level of angst over the very *idea* that Utzon would not be allowed to complete his masterpiece.

After 90 minutes, Askin agrees to meet with Mr Utzon the following day.

'Mr. Askin,' the *Herald* reports, 'would not confirm a report that the Government, while wanting a reconciliation, will not give Mr Utzon a "blank cheque".'[92]

The fact that the government is not budging comes in the same article, quoting Davis Hughes to the effect that he 'hoped to make a recommendation to Cabinet on Tuesday for the appointment of a panel of architects to complete the Opera House'.[93]

So runs the *Herald*'s front page, covering the saga for the fourth day running.

As for the letters page inside, it has been turned into a full-page article of its own, under the headline THE GREAT OPERA HOUSE CONTROVERSY, with the letters editor introducing the missives by way of a note that betrays a certain surprise at the zeal coming forth from a usually docile population.

'The many letters we have received about Mr Utzon's resignation as architect of the Sydney Opera House reflect a fervent, even passionate, public reaction.'[94]

There is indeed a mix of support and derision for Utzon.

One writer dismisses entirely the notion that a brilliant set of plans needed the original architect on board the whole way through. After all, A. S. Carter of Earlwood notes:

> The plans for the Taj Mahal were proposed by a council of architects from India, Persia, Central Asia and beyond, and many of these were dead before the structure was completed, but that did not prevent it from being a very fine and successful building.[95]

Lorna Nemmo from Waverley, on the other hand, wishes her views to be known:

> SIR. – The possibility that the Opera House will be finished by other architects recalls to my mind something Ruskin once wrote:

'There is hardly anything in the world that some man cannot make
a little worse and sell a little cheaper, and the people who consider
price only are this man's lawful prey.'[96]

Eva Buchrich decries that the fate of Utzon appears to be going the way
of Walter Burley Griffin, but predicts:

No doubt in 20 years, when a lot of water will have washed past
the Opera House and today's politicians will have been forgotten,
we will make amends and, as with Griffin, honour Utzon on one
of our posting stamps. For such is the size of our vision.[97]

Which remains to be seen.

One correspondent wishes to recall the evils the whole thing has
brought upon their fine city, starting with that damned lottery: 'The
method of raising the money, £100,000 lotteries, is morally doubtful
and already has been responsible for one murder that we know of.'[98]

How many more lives and livelihoods must be sacrificed for this
tragedy-riddled edifice?

In the here and now, the first result of the protest march is not Utzon's
reinstatement, but Seidler's dismissal by Ron Gilling from the Select
Committee for having addressed the marchers at Bennelong Point – you
can be an Utzon agitator, or on the RAIA Select Committee trying to
resolve the situation, but you cannot be both.

Seidler does not care, and has completely thrown in his lot with Utzon;
penny and pound, publicly and privately. In his view, and the view of
many in the profession, it would behove the Royal Australian Institute
of Architects to do the same.

After meeting with the tired Dane following the protest march, Seidler
tells the press: 'I think we will know something definite tomorrow. I am
very optimistic that Mr. Utzon will complete the Opera House.'[99]

Others feel even more strongly, one of them, George Berger, even
writing to Jørn:

Dear Mr Utzon, Your forced withdrawal from the Sydney Opera
House has upset me more than the assassination of President
Kennedy. He was murdered by one or more madmen, while your
withdrawal was arranged by the 'Government' of the State where
I am living ...[100]

Some architects, however, take the completely opposite view, and hold
it with great passion. One of them, Douglas Snelling, feels so strongly

about it he composes a several-page letter to the *Herald* editor, putting enormous efforts into every paragraph.

> Dear Sir,
> . . . In the first place, the Sydney Opera House is largely only famous abroad for its fantastic cost in relation to our national product. Many intelligent foreigners, and even Architects, have only vaguely studied the sculptural form of this building, which form has often been admired – but only for its elegant form. Many world-famous Architects who have taken time to study the Plans in detail see this building as sculpture with an Opera House stuffed inside it.[101]

Davis Hughes?

Douglas Snelling has no doubt. '[He] is to be congratulated for his firm stand . . .'[102]

Yes.

The person to blame for all this, and again Snelling has no doubt, is the man they are now making a martyr of, Jørn Utzon.

> A designer of anything must surely know within reasonable limits how to build what he commits to paper. The cart-before-the-horse attitude of a pretty picture first is a negative approach to design and today is the ace card of the charlatan.[103]

After long consideration, Snelling decides not to send his letter, and instead files it away, but still he feels much better for having got it all off his chest. In many ways, he feels as if he put down a truth that dare not speak its name.

Evening, 4 March 1966, Sydney, up against the wall

The pack of journalists who have been staking out the Premier's office are growing bored; some dash off to get another packet of cigarettes, some toss pebbles into the gutter to pass the time, others have left, after waiting all day in the hope of . . . precisely this . . . just after 6 pm, one of them catches sight of Jørn Utzon *himself* leaving through a side door and coming out onto Bridge Street!

Mr Utzon! *Mr Utzon!*

As the press pack closes in, the Dane turns with a pained smile and pretends to try and hide behind Bill Wheatland, even as he is forced to shuffle backwards and backwards by the pushing throng calling out endless questions, until he is, as the *Herald* will report, 'cornered against a brick wall at the entrance to a parking lot'.[104]

In the face of it, Jørn is cheerful. Yes, he is happy to confirm he had met with the Premier.

'We had a good and friendly meeting,' he says, even as he reaches out to playfully straighten a reporter's tie, so it is just so. The journalist smiles, amused. Classic Jørn – everything can be made to look at least a little better, if you first *care*.

'We are in the middle of discussions to narrow the gap between us,' Jørn goes on. 'Today's meeting was a good one, and there will be a final meeting [with Mr Hughes] on Monday.'

The reporters, straining to hear him due to the heavy traffic of peak hour roaring past, lean in close to capture his softly accented answers to their questions.

'Will the architects on your staff go back now?' one reporter calls out.

'You will get the answer to that on Monday [after I speak to Minister Hughes]. I am in the middle of a dispute, you must understand that. All of us are trying our best to narrow the gap.'

'Are there any personal differences between you and Mr. Hughes?'

'I think this building is completely above personal disruptions. Everyone involved would say that. It has nothing to do with personal feelings.'

Mr Utzon notes how pleased he is with the demonstrations as they, 'show there was a deep feeling in the community for the building'.[105]

'Do you think the building could be finished if you do not go back?'

'I can say what I can do myself, but I can say nothing for anyone else.'

All he will say about the specifics of the meeting with the Premier, is ... pretty general: 'Mr. Askin was very helpful. The political football which it has been, should not exist any more. There has been a lot of public discussion, as well as at the political level, about costs. Yes, I admit that, but this has nothing to do with this situation. I have only one desire. That is to build an Opera House you will enjoy.'[106]

And what, Mr Utzon, did you think of the protest rally to reinstate you?

'This demonstration was marvellous for me,' he says, again smiling broadly. 'It was good to see this demonstration. I am very glad people seemed so enthusiastic for me.'[107]

For his part, Premier Askin tells the press, 'There [were] no heated words in today's talk. There were very frank exchanges of points of view.'[108]

Will you allow Utzon back?

'I hope the [differences] can be settled so that Mr Utzon can return to the project.'[109]

Mr Askin makes it clear, however, that he had spoken only as Premier and on policy.

'He had left technical matters,' *The Daily Telegraph* reports, 'to Mr Hughes in whom he had full confidence.'[110]

And Mr Hughes?

Now up in Armidale, he tells a *Herald* reporter on a trunk call of his upcoming meeting with Utzon: 'I hope that the proposals I will put to him on Monday will be accepted.'[111]

Up in Palm Beach, Lis Utzon receives a *Sun-Herald* journalist graciously and tells him, while lounging tanned and fit, in a monochrome swimming costume by the family pool, 'Of course we all enjoyed it here. And we want to stay if we can. But we will not try to influence my husband's decision. That is his own responsibility and we will not interfere.'

But not to rush on this.

'The final decision will be made after the meeting on Monday. Until then, my husband has gone away and he will make no comment. We all hope this matter can be settled happily.'[112]

Indeed.

The phone calls fly. What should Arup's do?

Mick Lewis is certain: the firm *must* stay on the job, he implores the partnership. Jack Zunz is not so sure.

'I felt too, at the time when Utzon resigned,' Zunz would say, 'a very strong emotional pull to walking off the job as well. Because, in a way, Jørn had woven his magic spell on us and we were – we had that same dream of this extraordinarily perfect conception building. And we knew that without him, it would come to – our dream would not be fulfilled. Not in the perfect way in that we had first thought it might be.'[113]

Ove Arup?

Mostly, he is saddened that it has come to this.

'The fundamental thing behind it all is a clash of personalities,' he tells a Sydney reporter who phones him in London. 'This Government came into office with a sort of mandate, having always criticised the other Government on the handling of the scheme. There would be business methods introduced and the whole thing would be in a proper business footing. That is all very well, but the nature of this scheme is so extraordinary and different from anything built before that you cannot apply ordinary standards.'[114]

But at the same time, Ove is sick to death of Utzon's antics and typically candid about it.

'Mr. Utzon has been far too stubborn and unyielding on his part,' he says, 'and the Government is insisting on things which make it difficult.'

Oh, but he is not done yet.

'Mr. Utzon has been saying for years that he has solved all the problems but there are still some enormous difficulties to overcome . . .'[115]

In sum, when it comes to picking sides in this unfortunate clash, Ove Arup worries he will have no choice but to side with the client. Jørn Utzon is exactly where he has been for some time – way out there, and on his own.

SIXTEEN

'THIS STORY DOESN'T END . . .'

Unfinished, it'll cost £50 million. It was hailed by world architects as a turning point. A new dimension. The most unified big work of art ever designed. And yet it's a failure. An appalling fiasco. A four and a half acre, 220-foot high scandal, an antipodean tower of Babel. The centre of a nation's debate on how much art is worth and the greatest continuing local joke on record . . . The Sydney Opera House is the product of a people who had a genial bash at culture. And then went back to their beer. But oh, what a lovely bash.[1]

Bob Ellis, Autopsy on a Dream, 1968

That Jørn Utzon was viciously slandered and subjected to press trial by rumour and inspired 'leak' now seems deplorably clear. At the time of his resignation the press was practically unanimous in presenting Utzon as the man solely responsible for intolerable delays and absurdly increasing costs at the Sydney Opera House. Whatever Utzon's actual part in the trouble of the Sydney Opera House, the publicity attending his departure was a humiliating affront to justice.[2]

Philip Parsons, Meanjin, September 1967

3 pm, 7 March 1966, Ministerial office, Sydney, this above all: to thine own self be true

Once again, Minister Hughes and Jørn Utzon are glowering at each other from opposite sides of the Ministerial desk, flanked by their loyal lieutenants. The difference being that, this time, Utzon is the *former* architect of the Opera House. In No Man's Land sit two men: a harried Harry Ashworth and a silent Stan Haviland.

The purpose of this meeting is to determine whether there is any scope for reinstatement, if Mr Utzon's position has changed in the last week, if he has climbed down from what Minister Hughes views as his *absurd* demands.

In the end?

In the end, despite there being no mulberry bush, they do go round and round the same sticking points for the next three and a half hours, with no real progress made until it is obvious to all there is no more point in continuing. The Minister and the Architect remain uncompromising.

It leaves the Dane with the last card he has in his deck. He must see the Premier, Mr Askin.

And no, he doesn't have an appointment, but this can't wait. Taking their hats, their coats, and their umbrage, Utzon and his team leave the office of Minister Hughes, make their way downstairs, through the solid wall of wary-eyed reporters and photographers outside – 'I have nothing to say. I am going to see the Premier'[3] – before crossing Bridge Street and indeed making their way to the Premier's office.

. . .

Which all turns out to be . . . a tad on the awkward side of things.

For only five minutes later, the architects are back.

'The Premier has gone. We missed him by 10 minutes,' Utzon says. 'We will meet tomorrow.'

Is there any chance of breaking the deadlock?

'They will be important conversations.'[4]

For his part, Minister Hughes, when asked the same question, at first declines to answer. Pressed further, he offers a small glimmer of hope to Utzon supporters, who are a larger and noisier group than he had bargained for.

'Under the conditions I laid down,' he says carefully, 'I would like to see him back.'

But, make no mistake, because it is an important point against all those saying the Dane had been dismissed: 'Mr. Utzon resigned, let us face the fact.'[5]

Ove Arup, on vacation in Portugal, to rest after all the hubbub hit the London office, has still not heard from Jørn, which is starting to upset him.

'Utzon *had* resigned,' the old engineer will later note, with no little bitterness. 'I mean he had resigned – without telling us about it, or without consulting us. He even refused [contact with us]. So, I mean, I couldn't do anything about that.'[6]

One thing Ove does do is write to Lis Utzon. Surely, through Lis, he can get through to Jørn and help fix this situation.

Tuesday, 8 March 1966, Sydney, now cracks a noble heart

If not quite the final blow for Utzon, it is close. The Dane is trying to catch his breath, leaning back on the ropes. First, he has a meeting with Premier Askin, where the NSW political supremo makes it clear that he supports Minister Hughes. Then, afterwards, he hears that the NSW Cabinet feels the same way.

Utzon is devastated, and, in a meeting with reporters in his office on the Opera House site, is variously described as 'worked up' . . . 'the very exemplar of artistic frustration bubbling out of him'.[7]

He simply cannot hold it in.

'[The Opera House is] dying,' he says dramatically, 'sick on the bed now.'[8]

The reporters call questions but Jørn rambles, as if clearing his own mind.

'For some months I have not been able to find any respect for my ideas . . . No architect can compromise [that much]. I can try to do what the client wants, but the whole idea of the final details is on the architect. This decision is difficult to make but it is impossible to accept the suggestion of a big team of architects controlling the work. Cabinet has confirmed this suggestion. I am out of it.'[9]

To a slew of further shouted questions from the journalist collective, the architect is short.

'It is finito and there is nothing I can do about it.' Utzon says flatly. 'I dare not go on. I can't accept his conditions.'[10]

To a television reporter, camera whirring, Utzon says: 'I've got a lot of patience after nine years. An architect can only stay on a job with full collaboration from his client. If my client doesn't want me, I can't stay. Then it's all over. It's not my wish, but I have to yield.'[11]

And the state of the project now, and the suggestion that a panel of architects is to replace him?

'I said to the Premier, "I am sorry for you because it will be very difficult to get this together . . . I am not saying I am the only architect who could get the Opera House together, but it may be that the architects in this city who come and finish the job will never be able to get it as I want it. We want to get the spirit and they have cut the spirit out."'[12]

What has gone wrong, Mr Utzon?

'What is behind this, we do not know,' he says, sadly. 'Mr. Hughes hasn't listened to me. The Government wouldn't go down to the site and investigate what was happening there. One of my great problems was to get Mr. Hughes to collaborate with me . . . Mr. Hughes's liaison with us has been hopeless.'[13]

Some of the journalists look at him quizzically because the way they hear it, Mr Hughes and his people had been complaining bitterly that the heart of the problem is the refusal of the Dane to produce any drawings for Stage Bloody III!

In parliament this very day, Hughes had stated his overall position on the subject, and does not wish to budge from his central parliamentary point: 'If complete control of the Opera House is left in Mr Utzon's hands, the building will never be completed.'[14]

Another problem Utzon has?

'You must have confidence and only by having confidence can you help the architect, and that is what I ask for, confidence.'[15]

And there is an interruption.

Lis Utzon has suddenly appeared at the site office and now quietly asks her husband to finish the interview and come home because '[You] look so tired.'[16]

And maybe something more than just tired.

Utzon looks like he is close to having some kind of breakdown – something in part confirmed when Lis Utzon calls Ron Gilling not long afterwards to say, 'Please do not try to keep Jørn here, he is not a well man.'[17]

But Jørn simply can't go home just now.

Ron Gilling, himself physically and emotionally exhausted by all that is happening, has just arrived at the office, and now here is a bustling and emotional Harry Seidler, shattered that it has come to this. Together, they file into the back room of the office, where starts another extended parley with the broken Utzon. The strain on all the men is evident when, some several hours later, Gilling puts in a call to Minister Hughes' office and, first up, tells the Minister, who is still there burning his own midnight oils – 'I think you are being badly and wrongly advised in many respects,'[18] before asking the politician would he come down and talk to the architect?

The Minister declines, but says Gilling can come and see him – despite the owls of Hyde Park and the heavy mechanical ticking of the GPO clock tower marking the approach of midnight.

On my way.

When he arrives, Gilling is not long in getting to the point.

'We believe Utzon is competent to finish the project,' he begins before going into the complexity of the project, the need for a 'full and proper investigation'[19] . . . but the conversation comes back to Hughes' immediate demand for a full program of works and costings.

As one who had passed End of My Tether Station about three stops back, Gilling frankly suggests that Hughes should, in that case, take the gloves off and 'make public reasons why you would not re-engage Utzon as Sole Architect'[20] – namely, a lack of working drawings for Stage III.

'I will not be a party,' Minister Hughes says, 'to ruining that man's reputation.'

Gilling explodes, and thumps the table as he does so: 'What about *my* reputation?'[21]

Don't you understand, Minister? Right now, the public and press think you just shot Rembrandt, and I am the president of the Painters Guild who did nothing to defend him. You need to make clear just how reasonable you were, and how unreasonable he was!

'Calm down,' Hughes says. 'Time will heal your problem.'

Well, Gilling *never*.

'He was not behaving,' Gilling will later claim, when time had indeed healed some wounds, 'as someone hell bent on the destruction of Utzon as the architect, but was trying desperately to find some way to get some control over how the job was to be completed.'[22]

At meeting's end, Gilling asks the Minister, 'Will you see Utzon again?'

Davis Hughes gives him an imperturbable look that would pass muster as an Easter Island statue at a fancy dress party. 'I will not seek a meeting,' Hughes says. 'If Utzon approaches me, I will see him. But in each meeting so far, Utzon has always insisted on being Sole Architect.'[23]

Gilling leaves in the wee hours. He must convince Utzon to see Hughes again and to accept at least part of Hughes' proposals.

Wednesday, 9 March 1966, RAIA Chapter Office, Sydney, they bleed on both sides

Looking over a dark cup of coffee – he's just peeled himself off the office couch where he slept, not for the first time this week – Ron Gilling scans the morning papers.

The Daily Telegraph brings the bareknuckle drama – 'Utzon bows out of Opera House – "It is finito"'.[24]

The *Herald* is more measured – 'Day of talks confirms Utzon's resignation'.[25]

Inside, the *Herald* editor stands more or less in Minister Hughes' corner: 'Architects and artists abroad, who have studied the design of the Opera House but who do not, of course, have to pay for it, will immediately assume that here is another case of a great artist dragged down by petty bureaucrats and politicians . . . This is an argument which will win much support from generous-minded people, but is it fair?'

The *Herald* quickly comes to the conclusion it is *not* fair and that as 'Mr. Utzon seems to have lost the confidence of all his partners,'[26] he had to go.

As ever, however, George Molnar brings his own wry perspective, poking gentle fun at the whole mess and providing balance to the editor's now shoulder-to-shoulder four-square support of the Minister.

•

Reading the reports, it seems very terminal, but still Ron Gilling doesn't give up hope. At least he finally gets the Minister to agree to one final, secret meeting. Alas, just as it takes two to tango, it needs at least that many of the key protagonists to mend a schism, and for the life of him Gilling cannot get Jørn on the telephone. His strong suspicion is that Harry Seidler and other NSW Chapter members have been in Utzon's ear and are, 'adopting an antagonistic attitude towards me and the Council', advising Utzon to, 'avoid contact with the Institute'.[27]

But perhaps that is Utzon now?

Gilling snatches up the phone, to hear the commanding tones of . . . Minister Hughes, asking if the meeting has been arranged yet.

Advised that that is not yet the case, but he should soon have it sorted out, the Minister restates his position to make it absolutely clear: 'I will agree to discuss the matter just once more on the basis that it be within the framework of the proposal, call it a partnership, or whatever you like . . .'

Yes, yes, Minister, Gilling replies.

And Gilling? 'Ensure there's no publicity about this meeting.'[28]

Yes, Minister.

Hanging up the phone, Ron Gilling dashes off a note to the Dane –

> In the face of the Minister's stand in the matter I must make this personal plea to you not to close the door on negotiating with the government's proposal to accede to some form of partnership agreement. I make this plea for the sake of the Opera House. To complete this project without you is unthinkable.
>
> I sincerely hope you will give this your most serious thoughts for I believe that in this way it is possible to vindicate you . . .
>
> Please, Jørn, think most carefully before this tragedy becomes a catastrophe.

With kindest regards, sincerely yours,
(Sgd) Ronald[29]

•

Wounded and brooding, Jørn Utzon has cause to bitterly reflect on how everything has changed. Right at the beginning he had wanted the NSW Government to contract his firm to deal with the workload, only for them to insist he be engaged as 'Sole Architect' – their title, not his.

And yet all these years on, after the ever-changing client has changed the brief ad nauseum, and as the shells rise despite the challenges, sure testament of his capabilities, this latest client in Minister Hughes is now insisting he be demoted to a mere cog in the Government Architect's department. Worse still, he is doing so with the seeming connivance of the Institute of Architects' Ron Gilling!

Despite it all, Jack Zunz writes to Utzon, urging him to swallow his pride and return under the client's conditions.

'Why don't you put the Opera House first?' he pens, pleading with him to reconsider, while also asking him to focus on the real problem. 'Can you not see that the problem arises out of your uncompromising and proud attitudes? One wonders whether you really want to finish the job.'[30]

Utzon makes no reply.

Thursday, 10 March 1966, Sydney Town, simmer in autumn

Another day, more of the same. *The Daily Telegraph* sets a fatalistic it's-all-over tone:

> 'FINITO' – Mr. Jørn Utzon's own word has ended once and for all his connection with Sydney's Opera House. After ten days of emotional argument, this is the plain fact which must be accepted. The die having been cast, the State Government now has no further choice but to go ahead immediately with the task of finding someone to finish the job.[31]

The paper quotes Davis Hughes' vision of 'a team of local architects' working under the Government Architect Mr Ted Farmer, for whom such a role would be quite a satisfaction. (Farmer has been dubious of Utzon's project from the beginning, and has watched its unravelling with a gimlet eye. 'There is no doubt that the assessors made their decision solely on aesthetic grounds,' he will note, 'without cognisance of the shortcomings of the plan . . . Future historians will marvel that so many distinguished and presumably competent people acted in the foolish and extraordinary way they did.'[32])

Late in the morning, Gilling's phone rings, and he instantly recognises the soft Danish lilt of Jørn Utzon, sounding strained.

'Your letter has moved me to have a further discussion with the Minister,'[33] Utzon says.

Excellent! Like a scene out of a spy novel, Gilling quickly makes the arrangements, with the Minister, along with Ted Farmer and their entourage, to meet with Gilling and Utzon in their own cars near North Sydney Oval, at the corner of Falcon and Miller Street. The entourage follows tightly behind Gilling's car – his arm occasionally appearing out the driver-side window, indicating for them to go this way or that. After a circuitous route through quiet Willoughby streets, designed to ensure that they are not being followed, Gilling leads them to the ground floor suite of a Lane Cove motel he is a director of – and then the President of the NSW Institute of Architects bows out. His job has been to get them in the one room at the one time, and that is now done.

(Before he goes, he hands Minister Hughes a letter, for him to read now, please, Minister: 'I know that you must be near the end of your patience in these protracted negotiations, but I now make this further plea for a compromise solution ... It has become increasingly apparent to me that it will be extremely difficult to find a competent substitute to what Mr Utzon has achieved. We cannot discard his contribution already made ... as negligible.'[34]

At the letter's end, Ron Gilling offers that the Institute be given leave to handle the matter of Utzon's re-engagement in terms that will suit both parties.

Hughes peruses the note, and makes no comment.)

Once the door is closed, Jørn Utzon begins, presenting a letter which sets out his central point.

'It is not I but the Sydney Opera House that creates all the enormous difficulties,' he insists. 'The Minister will be faced with exactly the same problems as he is now when he starts the new group of architects but they will be handicapped because of lack of nine years knowledge and also will not have our strength and enthusiasm that comes from the fact that I and my staff of collaborating architects, as I call them, have been benefiting from the creative process that has built the Opera House to date. Your new architects will start from zero. They will be coming to you as soon as they realise the difficulties and they will be seeking the same support and the same permissions that I have for a long time tried to obtain . . .'[35]

In person, however, he is at least a little softer, and sounds like he might consider a compromise.

'I would like to look at the settlement before I enter into it,' he begins. 'This would mean another month for my staff. Could you make an advance payment to them?'[36]

Hughes responds in moderate fashion, 'if we can reach agreement . . . There is no problem with finances, the problem is one of agreement.'[37]

What would that agreement look like?

Hughes pushes a piece of paper towards the Dane.

The new organisation, we have in mind:

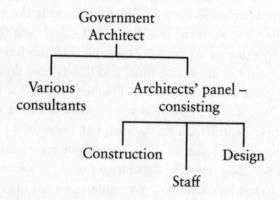

'Farmer will be completely in charge.'[38]

But, do you see there, Mr Utzon? You will be in charge of the design team, exclusively devoted to producing the drawings we need. 'We will provide you with any staff you may require,'[39] Hughes says, almost triumphantly.

Utzon leans forward and looks closely at the chart.

Yes, there he would be. Not on the top tier, as 'Sole Architect' as he was appointed back in 1957. Nor even on the second tier. No, he would be one part of the third tier, down there, to the right, on purely the design side of things. A draughtsman; a sketch boy.

From being a Field Marshal in charge of his own battle plan, he is to be busted down to the rank of Captain, in charge of a single battalion.

And now Ted Farmer, the new Field Marshal, is speaking up.

'I'm terribly sympathetic,' he says, though Jørn is not so sure he is. 'You have not been properly instructed by the client before now.'[40]

For the moment, Jørn plays along, entertaining the idea of accepting the Minister's proposal.

'It seems under the scheme,' he says to Farmer, 'you will take care of programming and the consultant. Will Arup be responsible to you?'

'There is no distinction between Mr Farmer and Hughes,' Col Humphrey now speaks up. 'Arup will be responsible to the client in accordance with the present arrangement.'

'There is no worry with Arup,' Hughes says, looking plainly at the architect.

Utzon doesn't skip a beat. 'The setting up of the panel [of architects] will take time . . . You don't know who is on the panel?'

'No,' says Col Humphrey.[41]

Even as Hughes sighs and reveals: 'This position is not easy for me. It has been a heavy strain.'

'We are sure as reasonable persons,' Farmer adds, 'we could make this proposal work.'

'There should be no press statement,' Utzon says.

'I will have to say something,' Hughes demurs, 'they know of the meeting already.'

'Then say we need more time.'

'We must have *a* time,' Hughes insists. 'We must put a day at the end of it, by Tuesday.'

'I want another fortnight. I want to ring Germany and set up things. It's complex – there are many things involved . . . Don't say to press "Tuesday" or they will press me every day till Tuesday. Leave out the day. I can't say yes or no straight away. We will have to have meetings with Farmer . . .'

Hughes and Humphrey exchange looks, with the former giving an all but imperceptible nod. Tell him . . .

'I am not clear what you will be doing over the fortnight you have asked,' Mr Humphrey says. Pushing the organisational chart towards Utzon again, he says, 'You should say whether the Minister's organisation chart is acceptable to you . . . We will do this. Why do we have to get in touch with others?'

But Utzon will not be moved.

'We must take up everything on technical matters. I have been required to enter into a partnership with people I don't know. I can't answer by Tuesday.'

Jørn is growing flustered, and begins to ramble: 'You will not put my enemies there, such as Bunning . . .'

'No,' Farmer tries to assure him.

'You must give us time. If no time there is no possibility for me to accept it.'

But Davis Hughes will have none of it.

'There is no room for compromise within that proposal of mine,'[42] he says in the manner of a man who will not, will not, will not be moved.

In the usual way of things, conditions are laid down by the man who has the upper hand. And Jørn Utzon's hand is filled with no more than low clubs, and a two of spades.

'Yes,' Utzon says carefully. 'But I want to talk to my staff and consultants and let them know where they stand. Give me a *fortnight*. This is a new contract I am going to embark into.'[43]

'Do you think some of the consultants will object to this?' Ted Farmer asks.

'I would not like this [if I was them],' Utzon replies to the Minister. 'They don't know Farmer or who he is.'

'Will you give us an okay by Tuesday, in principle, subject to consulting the consultants?'

'No,' says Utzon, not budging. 'I want a fortnight.'[44]

The Minister demurs ... with some force. Allowing this to drag on for another fortnight is out of the question. We will have your answer by Tuesday, and that is our last word. Good day, Mr Utzon, I said good day.

Good day, Minister Hughes.

Ah, but Ted Farmer is not done.

Even as one of Hughes' off-siders takes a whisky bottle in hand and pours those remaining a generous dram, starting with the Minister himself, Ted Farmer, with pipe in hand goes over to Utzon and, with a twinkle in his eye, taps him on the chest with his pipe and says, 'I'm sure we'll get on well together, old boy.'[45]

•

The press and public feel like they're on a wild goose chase ...

'Utzon is not yet "finito",'[46] reads *The Daily Tele* the morning after the 'secret' Lane Cove meeting, a dramatic reversal of the days before, and the latest inexplicable twist in the thick Opera House plot that has reporters back at their desk writing more pages, and the readers at home turning them ... there is no conclusion ...

The show must go on!

In the hurly-burly of the tug o' war to get public opinion on their side of the argument, the NSW Government has the ongoing, impassioned support of architect Walter Bunning, who pens a piece with a told-you-so tone, laying the blame for the debacle on the Danish architect Jørn Utzon and, 'many well-meaning but romantically minded people who have believed that a mystique had developed about the building which took it out of the good common-sense practices of the work-a-day world into the realm of cloud-cuckoo land'.[47]

He, Walter Bunning, had tried to warn you all. So, much as it pains him, let him reiterate now that reason appears to have stormed the cloud-cuckoo land's castle's gates ... 'The many failures of the project are world-shattering. Contrary to much that has been written, Sydney Opera House, from a functional point of view, will be a second-rate building ...'[48]

The following day, Sydney architect Don Gazzard makes reply.

'A countryman of Jørn Utzon's called Hans Andersen once wrote a story about an ugly duckling who was supported by nobody. Have patience, Mr. Bunning – remember that the ugly duckling ended up as the most beautiful swan.'[49]

In Denmark, Utzon's architecture professor, Steen Eiler Rasmussen, writes in an article for Sydney's *Sun-Herald* newspaper, 'If you imagine that you had asked the violin-maker Stradivarius to make the best violin in the world, and he had been promised that it was to be built according to his design, but not from the wood which he knew to be the only suitable one, and not by the craftsmen whom he knew to be competent, wouldn't he then have to say, "no"?'[50]

Among the tents in the Sydney-based Utzon camp, there is a stirring. A plan is afoot ...[51]

Monday, 14 March 1966, Sydney Town Hall, hungerstruck

Look, it's true. It's kinda what started this whole thing. The acoustics in the cavernous Sydney Town Hall are not ideal for this 1000-strong 'Utzon-in-Charge' protest meeting. Then again, it is less about hearing every word spoken than understanding their sentiment and appreciating the sheer number of people who have turned up.

Speakers include such leading luminaries of Sydney – from ranks of architects, artists, sculptors, writers and academics – as Harry Seidler, Patrick White, architectural Professor George Molnar and the legendary headmistress of the prestigious all-girls Abbotsleigh School, Miss Betty Archdale.

Oddly, the best received words from the podium are not the many thunderous orations but rather a poem delivered by 50-year-old sculptor

Michael Nicholson where, after several verses about the glory of the Opera House and the horror of what has happened to her architect, he promises . . .

> Before you all
> To take no food for three
>   days from now.[52]

The simmering and bubbling among the crowd *erupts*, threatening to spill out onto the street in a wave of passion and rage and excitement.

Just quietly, though, a journalist takes Nicholson aside as he comes off stage and asks, are you really going on a hunger strike?

The answer is Australian gold.

'This is dinky di,' he says. 'I have embarked on a fast unto death.'[53]

(Mind you, that death might be a while yet, given that his level of commitment to the cause so far has meant that he has 'not eaten since breakfast . . .'[54] It is a very Sydney kind of hunger strike, and the first recorded in the country.)

Patrick White is up next, Australia's leading literary light, who had famously remarked that Utzon's Opera House made him, 'feel glad I am alive in Australia today. At last we are going to have something worth having.'[55]

On this day, his views are equally unequivocal: 'How shocking to think of those miserable little aldermanish devils attacking such a magnificent conception from their suburban underworld.'[56]

Harry Seidler delivers the key speech, attacking the government for having carried out a premeditated campaign, 'perpetrated with all the viciousness of a military operation'[57] and made 'Mr Utzon . . . the scape-goat for its own bungling.'[58]

And make no mistake!

'The apostles of mediocrity are about to take over! If they are allowed to step into Jørn Utzon's shoes, they will make the greatest mess of all time out of the building!'[59]

Mr Utzon has *not* resigned! Rather, the Sydney architect roars, he has been, 'Thrown out of office!'[60]

After 90 minutes the meeting is over, the audience filing out into the intoxicating evening, ready to hold this government to account, and see Jørn Utzon restored to his rightful position, in charge of building the Sydney Opera House!

•

As for the press, they are not without sympathy for the Dane or his defenders, but an editorial in *The Daily Telegraph* the day after the Town Hall protest shows they are going to continue holding the government line:

> Mr. Utzon must realise that public money cannot be spent without firm and sensible controls ... Mr. Utzon has been paid on a percentage of cost basis ... The more it costs the more he gets.
>
> To suggest that there are no architects in the country capable of completing the Opera House is so much bunkum. For every person who attended the protest meeting yesterday, there are probably 1000 who disapprove of the lavish, careless and unplanned manner in which the whole Opera House conception has been developed.[61]

15 March 1966, Sydney, the rest is silence

Christ Almighty, what now?

Ron Gilling is listening to the 6 am ABC news bulletin when Harry Seidler's voice sails over the airwaves: 'Utzon has rejected the Minister's terms.'[62]

Gilling is furious.

Why on earth would Seidler pre-empt Utzon's official reply? Seidler must know something.

In an effort to head this whole disaster off – it is unthinkable that Utzon will actually leave – Gilling dashes off a note to the Minister.

> Dear Mr Davis Hughes,
>
> Before you close the door on further negotiations this morning, may I please have the privilege of a further discussion with you.
>
> Yours sincerely,
> (Sgd) R A Gilling[63]

Too late.

Minister Hughes is reading Utzon's letter aloud to a meeting of the NSW Cabinet ...

'Having designed the Opera House and having worked on this great project for the past nine years, I have naturally been anxious to see it through to completion and without going into detail I think it should be assumed in my favour that I would not lightly have resigned ... Having regard to the intricate nature of the design and the infinite problems associated with its execution, I feel – and I am sure any experienced architect would confirm – that it would be virtually impossible for any architect or panel of architects, however eminent, to take over at this stage and produce a building which would be in accordance with the original concept . . . Naturally I am anxious to assist in avoiding such a calamity.'⁶⁴

And make no mistake.

'A change of architectural control at this stage would not only result in great delays but also add immeasurably and unpredictably to the ultimate cost of the Opera House. This too I would wish to assist in avoiding.'

As to the proposals that he cede control, and allow himself to 'be relegated to the subordinate role of "design architect"' . . . well, the Dane never.

'It would seem . . . that I am merely to prepare designs in accordance with instructions and leave it to others to supervise construction.'

Well, think again.

'Such a proposal is not only unpractical but quite unacceptable to me. If I am to prepare all designs, plans and specifications necessary to continue the building operations, then if efficiency is to be achieved it must be done by me . . . in an intricate and complex building such as the Opera House I must, as a matter of common sense, supervise construction.'⁶⁵

At a press conference held shortly after the Cabinet meeting concludes, Hughes tries to be diplomatic.

'I am extremely sorry that this has happened,' he says. 'For one thing, it really does bring a whole new set of problems, in terms of getting a new team up to speed and taking over from scratch. We do not underestimate the problem, which is a big one.'

But, Minister, is that problem intensified or simplified by the departure of Mr Utzon? Hughes' face twists to an uneasy smile as he turns to a different reporter. The question goes unacknowledged.

Can you at least tell us how much the Opera House will be estimated to cost from now?

'I believe the new team, through their preparation of plans, and specifications and their calling of tenders, will enable us to arrive at a reasonably accurate estimate of the cost of the building. We will have full control over the cost.'⁶⁶

It's over. So over, in fact, he hopes to name the panel of architects to replace Utzon by next Tuesday.

Do you mean, Mr Hughes, there is no more possibility of negotiations? The Minister is unequivocal: 'Yes. To all intents and purposes negotiations are closed. He resigned and he has told us he could not accept the Government's proposals for his return to the Opera House.'⁶⁷

Finitissimo.

What they need to do now is find Utzon's replacements.

•

The following morning, Peter Hall comes to see his mentor, Ted Farmer, about another matter, when Farmer turns the conversation to more pressing issues.

'Utzon is resigning from the Opera House ... I'd like you to do the design work on it.'

'Nothing doing, that's Utzon's job.'[68]

The very *idea*! And Farmer should know that Hall feels so strongly about it – he had engaged in the protest march up Macquarie Street, and chanted with the best of them. He is now even the proud owner of an 'UTZON ONLY' t-shirt.

Farmer doesn't mind any of that. You are a younger man, and younger men are prone to be swept along by all kinds of things before they can take mature pause to look at things more closely.

Think about this, Peter.

'He was a ... very fine designer, and a man of many parts,' Farmer would affirm many years later of Peter Hall. 'I had enormous respect for him.'[69]

So *do* think about it.

No, Peter won't.

After all, as the *Herald* points out this day:

> It is far from certain that any panel of architects can do this more quickly or more cheaply than Mr. Utzon and by no means certain that they can do it at all. And Mr. Hughes must now be haunted by the knowledge that if anything goes wrong with the final stage – if, for instance, the acoustics of the concert hall are faulty – it will not be Mr. Utzon who will be blamed.[70]

It will be Mr Hughes, and the architects who replace Utzon.

In terms of more immediate problems, the *Herald* notes that the 'Utzon-in-Charge Committee', as Harry Seidler's group have now called themselves, have asked their solicitors to take out an injunction seeking to restrain the government from proceeding with the Opera House without Mr Utzon as architect.

When Hughes is told of the report, he, for the first time, appears comfortable over the matter of Opera House finances, telling the press:

'Parliament has authorised expenditure of $27.5 million and so far, only $20 million has been spent . . .'[71]

Hughes adds: 'Government authorities have estimated that expenditure of $30 million more will be necessary to complete the project.'[72]

Yes, Minister.

•

Ted Farmer is hunched over his desk, pen in hand, madly scribbling along the paper as he completes his report for the Minister, entitled, 'Sydney Opera House: Matters to be considered if the Government Architect is to Take Responsibility' . . .

Among those is the matter of just who should sit on the panel. Hughes wants Australians, and Farmer agrees.

So, Farmer offers up the name of David Littlemore.

The choice of Littlemore, a highly regarded architect of industrial bent, is obvious. He is experienced, hardworking and, most importantly, he doesn't reject it out of hand, as a couple of others – leading architects like Ken Woolley and Col Madigan – had. Littlemore could manage the construction angle, and liaise with the engineers.

'I knew nothing about the Opera House at that time,' Littlemore will later recount. 'I passed it every day and thought it was a magnificent sculptural shape, and I was familiar with the controversy. But the offer to help finish it came like a bolt from the blue. I didn't know what to reply. It was an exciting prospect, but it was also a daunting one. I finally asked for 48 hours to think it over.'[73]

Later, Littlemore will characterise his reaction to the offer as 'one of sheer terror'.[74]

Hughes, meanwhile, puts forward the name of Lionel Todd – founding partner of Hanson, Todd and Partners, and a highly regarded operator in the field of sorting out contracts.

17 March 1966, Bennelong Point, Ted Farmer takes over

If it is not quite the last supper, it's at least the last afternoon tea.

Just a day after Hughes' announcement in Cabinet, there's a conference at the Opera House site office. Jørn Utzon is there, along with the faithful Prip-Buus and Wheatland, all sitting to one side as Jørn's lawyers meet with the smiling Ted Farmer, the Assistant Crown Solicitor Mr C. Lewis and other government officials to oversee the very outcome that so many feared.

Against the express wish of the building's first political champion, Joe Cahill, the hulking Public Works Department and its Minister and Government Architect are now ... taking over.

It is not as simple as that, though. There will be more negotiations to work out just how much money is still owed, and how many documents and drawings will be handed over and under what circumstances – it is announced on this day that 'Mr. Jørn Utzon's solicitors, Messrs. Nicholl and Nicholl, have retained counsel, Mr. J. W. Smythe QC and Mr. Neville Wran, to advise generally as to his rights and the appropriate legal action to be taken by him in connection with the Opera House dispute'[75] – but today feels a lot like the end in terms of being on site, with a right to be there.

At the conclusion of the meeting, Utzon gathers the last of his belongings in a box and starts to make his way to his car.

'Is this the last chapter?' a photographer with *The Daily Telegraph* calls to him.

'Who knows?'[76] Utzon calls back cheerily, before pausing a moment and then gazing back to his half-built dream. 'Look at the Opera House. Isn't it magnificent?'[77]

It is that. And in many ways that is the final answer, actually and metaphorically, to all of his critics, for now and forevermore.

And yet still, the regret that it has come to this is palpable.

'After all this,' he says, gesturing towards the building, before, with some theatricality, he snaps his fingers, '... just like that.'[78]

•

Despite their differences, and despite Mick Lewis's chronic stream of complaints about the architect to colleagues and the client since taking on the job as head of Arup's Sydney office less than three years ago, he is, somehow, personally saddened that it has come to this.

'It seems now that the break between Utzon and the Government is beyond repair and Davis Hughes has closed the door to further negotiation,' Lewis writes to Ove Arup and Jack Zunz the next day. 'I have the feeling that Utzon wanted to accept their terms but was too proud to say it directly ... In spite of my previous distrust and misgivings concerning Utzon, I feel terribly sad for his sake at having to give up this project after so many years.'[79]

•

In his bed at his Wollstonecraft home, David Littlemore stares at the cracks in the ceiling, well into the silent watch of the night. There is no doubt, Hughes' offer for him to be on the panel of architects to take over from Utzon is an extraordinary one.

And Hughes is persuasive, going so far as to tell him, 'David, if you don't do this, it *won't* be built.'[80]

It really feels like he means it. And there is talk that it really might not be built.

What an embarrassment that would mean for Sydney and Australia. It is unthinkable.

Against that, for him personally, he must factor in his health, which has been fickle of late, including the discovery that he has a 'dicky ticker'.

'This job might kill me,' he says to his wife, Nancy, as they discuss it late that night.[81]

It is her answer that helps convince him.

'Better you die building the Opera House,' she says, 'than while working on some factory's leaking roof.'[82]

And she is right. (Little do they know about the problems to be faced with waterproofing the Opera House's roof . . .)

Very well then, Minister, David Littlemore will be on your panel. There will be some criticism from his fellow architects of course, for breaking ranks with the Utzon-in-Charge camp, but the old architect doesn't care.

He is his own man, and strong enough to cope with whatever criticism comes his way.

But what of the key role, the one to do the remaining designs? Littlemore is convinced that they need somebody 'young, who is filled with vigour, who is perhaps *avant-garde*, and who would be excited, and who would perhaps excite all of us'.[83]

And Ted Farmer might have just the man – he just needs to work on him.

The 34-year-old Hall has, after all, recently won one of architecture's most prized gongs, the Sulman award for his design for Goldstein Hall at the University of New South Wales.

And the third on the panel? Lionel Todd has agreed to oversee the contract documentation of the project.

Now, the Government Architect must do what he can to convince Peter Hall . . .

18 March 1966, Public Works Department, Sydney, mutiny in the air

For Peter Hall, it is not a difficult decision. Of course, he supports Jørn Utzon, and – though he is now in his final weeks working at the department, himself having recently resigned – is happy to add his name to a petition that circulates among the Government Architect's staff of 82 architects, which makes no bones about it:

> Mr Davis Hughes / Minister for Public Works
>
> The undersigned members of the Government Architect's Branch of the Department of Public Works, N.S.W. believe that, on the facts presented publicly, Mr Jørn Utzon is the only Architect technically and ethically able to complete the Opera House as it should be completed.[84]

Put together by one of the staff architects, a fellow by the name of Ted Mack, the petition gathers no fewer than 75 signatures, an overwhelming majority.

21 March 1966, Sydney, soap opera

Through it all, the press remains camped before the Utzons' house, while at their elder offspring's Paddington terrace, one outrageously intrusive reporter breaks all journalistic protocols by trespassing into the courtyard! Lin wakes at 6 am to find him standing outside the door to her bedroom, pen and notebook in hand.

Excuse me, excuse me . . .

'Are you happy to be going home?' he asks.

As Lin will later recall, 'I think I just replied "yes". What else could I say? The next day, the headline read: "Utzon's daughter hates Australia. She's looking forward to leaving." All I said was, "yes". Our words were twisted and came out wrong, laden and ugly.'[85]

So it is that all the Utzon family come back to the Palm Beach nest.

'It was not a nice time at all,' Lin will recall. 'Dad had lost his brother 18 months earlier . . . [The project] had gone haywire. Dad was hounded by the press and it was very unpleasant. I was heartbroken to leave because I loved living there . . . The press was like a pack of wolves, hungry for a chunk.'[86]

Well, Lis Utzon will be giving no more chunks of her family's happiness. The phone will go unanswered and knocks at the door will go unmet – this is time for privacy, to care for the devastated Jørn.

And he needs it.

'He was under a lot of stress,' his oldest son would recall of these darkest of days in their family home. 'At one point he collapsed in the bathroom, and blacked out, and the doctor told him to wind down, and take good care of himself . . . [It] put a strain on him. No doubt about it.'[87]

(Back in 1962, Ove Arup had collapsed in the shower, in no small part due to immense pressure brought to bear on his aging pins by the Opera House. He had had the luxury to be able to stand back from the job entirely, with no criticism from any quarters. Jørn Utzon does not have such a luxury.)

Some of Jørn's architects worry about their usually unflappable boss.

'I had friends who lived in Palm Beach,' young Australian architect Richard Leplastrier would later say, 'and they told me that they had seen him walking with Lis around the streets at two and three in the morning. Not sleeping. And because of his humility and his sensibilities, that must have been just the most horrendous time for him. I don't think he would have lived without Lis.'[88]

For those who are close to the Utzons, to see the usually cheerful and smiling Jørn Utzon like this is a deep concern, and finally one of them can bear it no longer and leaps to his defence in the public domain. It is true that writing about matters architectural is not the usual realm of *Woman's Day*'s legendary cookery editor Margaret Fulton, and nor is it usual fare for the magazine itself, but such is her clout that when she tells the editor that her next piece for the magazine will be defending the Dane, it is run no questions asked.

'The Opera House, dream of his professional life, has become the nightmare of his social life . . . a couple who have almost been sacrificed in the cause of a great architectural achievement.'[89]

She even tells her readers the appalling story of how a cab driver had picked the Danish couple up one evening to take them home, only to launch into an ugly tirade about the highway robbery Jørn is pulling off in broad daylight. For shame.

'They, being quiet and courteous people, said little in reply . . . But the hurt was there. And it makes my blood boil to think of such ignorant and malicious attacks going unanswered.'[90]

Jørn continues to do his best to remain calm and on top of things in the office and when in front of the cameras and talking to the press, but at home with Lis, where he can let it all out, he is precisely as she had once feared he would become.

Almost a decade ago when Jørn had been on his way to Sydney for the first time, his giddy inner child excited to show the city the model of his grand vision, she had written, *'Tears come to my eyes at the very thought of [you] building an opera house, my love, and yet I hope and pray that it won't break your heart.'*[91]

And here they are. Jørn's heart and soul crushed, and so is hers.

The family ache as one.

Meanwhile, Mogens Prip-Buus chronicles the situation for his parents in his now-entrenched sardonic tone: 'According to the newspapers, the Government Architect has taken over, but we are still in our office and have all the designs, and our solicitors are very busy. We receive letters from Ove Arup to the effect that Jørn must be ill and that it is scandalous that he should want to sabotage the Opera House in this way and prevent them from finishing it. Ove is a psychopath.

'We are living in an environment of hatred and malicious gossip – as these are the only means they can find against us, as there is nothing professional to criticise. The Association of Architects is openly split over this. I call this show: "MALICE IN BLUNDERLAND".

'Now we'll see; we are alive and the Opera House is still standing and otherwise – well they jolly well don't deserve it either.

'ADVANCE AUSTRALIA FAIR.'[92]

•

It takes a lot to rile Lis Utzon, a placid and caring soul by nature, not given to flights of anger. But disrespect her family in some way? Give her the sledge-hammer at the fair, and she will win you a grizzly bear.

A case in point is a letter she receives from Ove Arup, imploring her to get Jørn to see reason, and *find* a way to stay!

Oh, really?

After everything Arup's have done to isolate her husband on the job in recent years, and more particularly in recent months, *now* he wants to step back in and help? Well, she won't have it and writes a letter back, telling him in no uncertain terms.

28 March 1966, Sydney Town Hall, anarchy in architecture

The extraordinary meeting of the NSW Chapter of the Royal Australian Institute of Architects, held in the Lower Town Hall, is as fierce as it is frantic.

At issue before the 750 architects in attendance: a motion of No Confidence in the Chapter Council over their lack of support for Jørn

Utzon, who is not only in attendance, but clearly aggrieved. (As is Harry Seidler, who shouts 'Liar!'[93] at one speaker who seeks to support Ron Gilling and attack Utzon.)

Also in attendance is Peter Hall. But hush now, as Utzon speaks from the stage, and makes one thing perfectly clear. He will *not* be returning to work on the Opera House unless he is the architect in sole control of the project.

'If I can't go and see my consultants and my contractors and have full control of this, I give up. I don't care,' Mr Utzon says. When it comes to the actions of the President and Council of the NSW RAIA, he recalls the first secret meetings Gilling had with Hughes the previous August, and the several since, and says, 'No council in the world would make comment [on such sensitive issues], without going to the architect to check the facts with him. But this had never been done in this case.'[94]

And now to a direct *j'accuse*.

'You should have,' he says, turning to glare at Ron Gilling, who is also up on the stage, 'come straight to us for the facts'.[95]

And yet, his speech and other speeches notwithstanding, when the votes come back Ron Gilling has carried the day, winning a vote of confidence, 369 votes to 283 – though some 100 abstained.

(Prip-Buus is disgusted by proceedings, certain that the many Sydney firms dependent on government work, 'had threatened their employees with dismissal if they voted against it, hence the large number remaining passive'.[96])

Upon hearing the results read out, the Dane feels his shoulders slump and his brows droop. Something has gone out of him, the last bit of energy he had to keep fighting the machine.

'I knew then,' Utzon will recount, 'I was completely out.'[97]

As he leaves the Town Hall, many of the architects who had supported him come up to shake his hand, and give him a consolatory pat on the back. One of them is Peter Hall, who grips Utzon by the hand, looks him in the eye and tells him straight: 'I am appalled.'[98]

•

Say what you will about Jørn Utzon, but his charm is extraordinary. It is not even that the wife of Harry Seidler, Penelope, knows him that well. But in the middle of everything that he is going through, for him to take the trouble to write to her, and say such lovely things about her husband is extraordinary.

Dear Penelope!

A good man fights for his ideas!

But a great man is a man who fights for other people and for ideals.

Such a man is your Harry and I have come to respect him deeply – he has taught me a lot because I have never been able to do what he has done in the last month.

To experience this – his marvellous friendship – outweighs completely any disappointment and bitterness in me.

Love from Jørn.[99]

1 April 1966, Sydney, who is the April Fool?

Minister Davis Hughes blanches to read Ted Farmer's report:

I have been able to make some investigations on site to estimate what we are faced with. It is not a fine picture.

(a) After 9 years there are still no working drawings or general arrangement drawings.
(b) Our first job will be to measure up the work before we can get a start.

And so begins the list of problems as seen by the new head of the Opera House project. Less anyone miss the point, Farmer is sure to chronicle where the blame for this mess lies ...

(h) Much of the complicated ceiling construction could not be carried out and all requirements for cabling, fire sprinklers, air conditioning ducts outlets for controls, are dismissed seemingly as irrelevant by the architect.[100]

Jesus wept! It is going to need a lot of manpower, a lot of energy to get things under control. They need brilliance, and a lot of it.

Early April, Sydney, 'If not me, who? If not now, when?'

It is urgent, Peter Hall.

Director of Public Works Col Humphrey wants to see you immediately. It's about the Opera House.

Courtesy and curiosity drive Hall to the meeting.

Though he'd been honoured to be sounded out by Ted Farmer, he has no interest in being on this panel they are talking about. After all, how could anyone take over from Utzon? It is *his* work. Hall wishes to create his own 'visions splendid'.

So, his answer is ready when Humphrey indeed makes him the offer to be the panel's design architect.

'Look, it's Utzon's job,' Hall replies, 'in fact, I've signed the petition of architects and interested people seeking to influence the Government to keep Utzon on the job.'[101]

Yes, Humphrey shakes his head, disappointed. He knows about that petition – a scourge on his department, but he shall come to that. For now, Humphrey will not leave it alone.

At least consider it. And go chat to David Littlemore, who wants to talk to you about it.

Which is why, with his wife, Libby, beside him, Peter Hall is soon tossing and turning in the night, going over and over the whole thing: the offer, the *opportunity*, the ... *risks* ... the poison that fills this architectural chalice ... the DISDAIN ... from architectural colleagues.

For already the word is starting to get out in confined architectural circles, and he has been getting strong phone calls and messages from friends.

'Don't touch it! Don't touch it!' they say. 'If you do it, Utzon will never come back.'[102]

What's worse, Libby agrees with them.

Theirs has not been an easy marriage as they have faced many challenges, from issues of Libby's mental health dating all the way back to their honeymoon, to Peter's penchant for pretty younger women, to raising two young children while leading busy lives. But on this issue, Libby sees things clearly, and tells him straight.

'This is the wrong thing to do, to have any part of it.'[103]

(For Libby, it has not been six months since she had photographed young Lin Utzon, who had happily modelled her imported clothing line at no charge ... it wouldn't feel right ...)

And yet?

And yet, the more Peter Hall thinks it over, the more he sees it really is an extraordinary opportunity to have control of such a major and lucrative project, so young.

'It was a very difficult decision for me ...' Hall will later recount, 'to take on that immense and complicated thing ... to be put in the position of not actually supplanting somebody else but taking on the design of something which was so individual was really a very worrying decision to have to make ...'[104]

But here's the thing.

Someone really is going to have to do it. So, just as it had been back in the days captaining the Sydney University First XI, even on a sticky wicket, and having to face mad fast bowlers from Randwick and Gordon and do his best, Hall plays the ball with a straight bat.

'Without any false humility, I thought of myself as better than quite a lot of my co-practitioners in the city.'[105]

Such are the things Libby can hear him turning over as he mutters to himself, pacing back and forth in his home at 12 Bray Street, North Sydney, before coming back to bed, and giving his developing view.

'If I don't take it on, they'll get someone worse than me.'[106]

Which is as may be. But Libby remains firmly against it. Their entire professional and personal milieu are artistic people – many, like Libby herself, have a fondness for the creative arts from weaving baskets to hand-making artefacts and doing all kinds of painting – and there is only one thing that could outrage them more than sacking an artistic genius of Utzon's ilk. That would be for one of their own, Peter, to replace him. They will turn against you, Peter. I am against you doing this.

Hall listens, but the temptation is just too great – he is warming to the idea, so long as he can put one issue to bed.

'I wanted to get the ethical ramifications of Utzon's resignation cleared up first, and I also wanted to talk to the other members of the team.'[107]

Which is why, on this evening of early April, two men sit huddled in the corner of the bar at the University Club on Bent Street.

It is David Littlemore and Peter Hall, the older man exhorting the younger man – who he has just met for the first time – to *commit*, to come on board, to get this job done! Yes, there are difficulties with the project but they can be resolved. It will mostly be a matter of taking Utzon's plans, such as they are, finishing them off, and getting the job done – finishing the masterpiece in his spirit. All else being equal, they could finish the whole thing in under two years!

Bit by bit, almost against his better judgement, the young, brilliant architect begins to imagine himself as the architect who finished the Sydney Opera House . . .

7 April 1966, Sydney, no show

Another day, another meeting.

This one has been requested by Jørn Utzon himself, and organised by Professor Ashworth, to allow the Dane to say goodbye to the Technical Advisory panel.

And they wait for two hours, and engage in small talk but, sadly, Mr Utzon does not show up.

No phone call.

No message.

Nothing.

He does not show up.

•

For most of the workers on the Opera House site, all the carry-on is neither here nor there. For the moment, there is enough work to go on with to guarantee the weekly pay-packet for the foreseeable future, and that is the main thing.

Still, here and there a few of them do speak to the press, most particularly when an enterprising journalist from *The Sun-Herald* stands outside the gates with a pencil and notepad and talks to a few of them as they leave at the end of the day.

'My views on the subject are too left-wing for you,' one says. 'You couldn't print them.'

'With all those architects on the job,' says another, 'it's going to be a case of too many chiefs and not enough Indians. They will be getting in one another's way.'

Another labourer couldn't agree more, though manages to put a distinctly Australian flavour on it, taking aim at the whole idea of a panel of three architects replacing the Dane: 'You can only have one "gun" shearer in a shed.'[108]

And the public at large?

Broadly, as evinced in many letters to the editor, their natural sympathy lies with the men with rolled-up sleeves and the engineers, over the fancy-pants architects, particularly (*sniff*) foreign ones.

Tuesday morning, 19 April 1966, ask not for whom the bell tolls

And so, all is set.

Peter Hall has decided to become the design architect on the Opera House, taking over from Jørn Utzon.

And it has come with the expected jeers and sneers, not all of them *sotto voce*.

Like Paul on the road to Damascus, they say – a turnaround so fast it would give you whiplash. *Traitor*, others say. *Farmer's favourite . . .* the teacher's pet turning into Benedict Arnold before our very eyes.

True, there are those who publicly support Hall, like Walter Bunning, who insist Hall is *brave and bold*, doing what must be done. But even his supporters worry that he has taken up a *poisoned chalice*.

Hall, the best he can, tries to ignore the bluster and stay his *own* course. But there is one doubt that he must lay to rest before signing on the dotted line.

After a little finagling, he gets Utzon's personal number and . . .

'Hello?'

It's him!

'Mr Utzon . . .' the young Australian begins falteringly, 'my name is Peter Hall and I've been asked to take on the design part of your job.'

'You're a brave man, but I don't think you can do it.'

'I can't do it as well as you. You're cleverer than I am. That's why I'd prefer you to do it. Will you go and see the Minister again?'[109]

'No,' says Jørn in his soft voice. 'It is best that I go away now. But I will always be ready to come back any time the Government is willing to let me return in sole charge.'[110]

The bottom line remains.

Peter Hall is satisfied that he is not taking another man's job, and there is no prospect of Utzon returning.

And that settles it. From Boggabri to Bellevue Hill, Peter Hall is now bound for Bennelong Point.

Very ambitious of you, Peter? Are you driven by it?

'No, I don't think so,' he tells an old school colleague who poses the question. 'Though I am selfish, which I suppose is one of the ingredients of ambition. I've just taken situations as they've come – a sort of Scott Fitzgerald approach to life. It all shows a shocking lack of self-knowledge.'[111]

Could it be that Sydney has traded its Hamlet, the tragic Prince of Denmark, for its own Gatsby? There are hallmarks of the mysterious and striving Jay Gatsby in Peter Hall, as his friend will subsequently write in the *Herald*: 'Hall continues to be better at his job than at personal relationships. He depends far more on reason than emotion and never really becomes involved with people; he has no really close friends, doesn't warm to people easily and doesn't see much of his parents even though they have moved to Sydney . . . like most self-sufficient people, he puts himself first in most things.'[112]

Above all, Peter Hall is a man of iron will and persistence.

'His cricket shows a lot about Peter,' his friend continues in the *Herald*. 'He was pretty hopeless when he started out. He became good at it by intensive study of the theory and technique of the batsmanship, and by practicing hard. Peter likes to be good at everything . . .'[113]

He *will* do this.

Later that morning, Peter Hall signs the contract proffered, and in the early afternoon Minister Hughes announces the news, which is reported in the *Herald* the next day.

OPERA HOUSE PANEL ANNOUNCED

A 34-year-old Sydney architect, Mr Peter Hall, will complete the Opera House design . . . Mr Hughes said yesterday that in all matters of design, supervision and administration, Mr Farmer would be senior partner.[114]

Just quietly, to some observers it is more than passing odd that Minister Hughes – who has no experience in design or construction – has done such an extraordinary thing. On the advice of Ted Farmer – who also has no experience in opera house design – the Minister has appointed three architects who *also* have no experience in building concert halls or drama theatres, let alone a state-of-the-art multipurpose theatre with the most cutting-edge stage machinery of the twentieth century.

Some comment that it's like Michelangelo leaving David's statue for someone else to complete – unfathomable.

For all the uncertainty that a new panel brings, both Hughes and Farmer seem remarkably calm, perhaps for having left their most pressing concern by the wayside.

For their part, after Utzon's infuriating flights of fancy, what they want from the new team is compliance, a willingness to *work the department's way*. Right now, creativity takes second place to *compliance*.

Asked afresh whether the selected team would be able to translate Utzon's concepts to reality, Mr Hughes' former assurances on that front appear diluted: 'I don't think it would be necessarily right to say the panel will translate Mr Utzon's ideas into practice, but it does not mean that it will be any less than perfect . . . no man would produce exactly the same building . . .'[115]

•

For the new triumvirate, the first signs about how their appointments will be received down on Bennelong Point are good.

On the morning of the announcement, David Littlemore picks up the phone to hear the voice of Corbet Gore, the leading Hornibrook man on the Opera House, who had concerns it would all fall about their ears any moment. He utters just ten words.

'I just rang up to say one thing – thank Christ.'[116]

Littlemore does not have time to muster a response before he hears a click and dial tone.

20 April 1966, Sydney, doubt truth to be a liar

Surely, even this late in the day, Ove Arup might be able to make Jørn see reason?

Kaere Jørn,

I don't know whether this will reach you, or whether you will read it if it does. But I should like you to consider what I say in the following. I realise that nothing I can say will alter your distrust of me or my motives. Lis's letter shattered me and showed me how completely you have misunderstood me. But forget about me.

It must be frightful for you to give up the job for which you have worked 10 years, and which has made you famous all over the world. You can of course easily get other work, and you are still young enough to create a body of work which will consolidate and extend your position as one of the world's leading architects. But how can you leave this child of yours to be messed up by other people? Can you see this will hurt you immensely? It is a disservice to architecture and it will always be held against you. You will be known as the architect who didn't finish the Opera House. You will say that you were forced into this situation, I will not dispute this, but this is not the point. The question is whether something cannot still be done to save the situation, or at least to make it better.

I feel that I am the man who is in the best position to bring about a compromise solution which will at least prevent that the Opera House is spoilt by others, even if it does not satisfy you entirely . . .

It would of course be easier if you trusted me, but I am content to be judged by my actions. Distrust me if you must, but consider my arguments. Is it not the most important thing, that the Opera House is saved? Is it not more important than what happens to you and me . . . ?

I am afraid a little humility is needed on your part in this case if there shall be any hope of moving the government from their position.

I can almost feel your distrust of me rising in you, as you read this. But what can I do? I am only stating a fact. I do not want to humiliate you, but humility coming from within, from respect for architecture, for your mission, and from gratefulness of the divine spark in you – such humility will do no harm.

I am of course not suggesting that you should compromise on design or architectural matters – that should not be necessary if you have good structural and other advisers. I am coming to Sydney on the 27th of April. Could you not see me then? I am staying at the Belvedere. Even if you don't trust me – it couldn't do any harm could it? The situation can't get any worse so why not try?

Yours,
Ove[117]

Utzon replies almost immediately.

Dear Ove
You say in your letters several times, that the Opera House will be destroyed without me.

Act accordingly:

Tell the Minister for Public Works that Utzon must be in charge ... I want you to sincerely understand that I do not dare to take the enormous responsibilities of being attached to the scheme without being in charge as the Sole Architect. As little as you – as structural engineer – would ever dare to take on the responsibility for the structure of a bridge without being fully in charge of all phases of its construction ...
Jørn[118]

Ove had always thought Jørn's design looked like an angry swan leaning forward with raised wings, defending its nest. Now, it seems, Jørn has become that swan.

23 April 1966, Sydney, drawing drama drags

It's a small piece in the *Herald*. On the face of it, a dry legal detail ...

'Payment to Utzon Hinges on Drawings', the unassuming headline reads.

In the article, Hughes says the matter of paying Utzon for his Stage III drawings is under consideration.

'The drawings were not included with the account for fees,' Hughes explains to the reporter.

'First, [Farmer] and his team must determine which drawings will be of use to them, and will make a counter-offer for the drawings on that basis.

'Mr Hughes would not discuss the extent of Mr Utzon's claims, but they are believed to total about $500,000.'[119]

•

For Jørn Utzon, there remains one thing left to do before departure, and after gathering up in the encroaching twilight some sticks, dry driftwood and the newspapers reporting his humiliation, Utzon puts a match to the pile. When the blaze is sufficiently high, he starts feeding into it his hopes, dreams and wildest fancies. Among other things, those working models of the Opera House he and his people had so painstakingly constructed back in Hellebaek and so carefully brought to Australia, are broken up and fed into the hungry flames, his whole dream going up in smoke together with their lives in this country.

As to the drawings, arrangements have been made, his lawyers are taking care of it now. Some of the 5000-odd will be bought by the government for the use of the incoming panel of architects. One full set will come with him in his luggage. The rest, those the government don't want, will be placed in storage under the care of Bill Wheatland, in the white terrace house in Windsor Street, Paddington.

Utzon is not sure of their fate, only that such drawings are leverage, and who controls them has a serious lever to pull for his own advantage.

Who knows what the future holds?

Right now, after selling the Bayview plot, his boat and other assets, he has paid his staff members for the next six months, feeling it only fair, as they will need time to find new jobs. It is nothing if not generous but it also means the Utzons themselves can no longer pay their bills and are living on hand-outs from friends. Silently, Utzon stares into the fire, his Nordic face lit by the flickering light. How *has* it come to this?[120]

And how *could* that trio who presume to replace him, manage to look after his masterpiece?

'The architect's creation is largely in his own mind,' he tells a Danish journalist. 'No person can copy it.'[121]

And it is never truer than for a man like Utzon, whose mental filing cabinet of images is encyclopaedic. And that filing cabinet is about to leave the country, taking with it all of the knowledge of the Opera House built up over the last *decade*.

End of April 1966, Sydney, autumn leaves . . . and so does Utzon

And now for one last hoorah at the Utzons' Palm Beach home, for the architects formerly employed down on Bennelong Point.

'We all filed in there,' Richard Leplastrier will recall, 'pretty shell shocked about what had happened.'[122]

Should auld acquaintance be forgot, and never brought to mind, they drink cups of kindness and more, talking of the rich and wonderful times they have known together, the things they had achieved, and how sad it is that it has all come to such an end.

Finally though, at a point where most of them have a good load of wine and beer on board, Utzon ding-ding-*dings* his glass.

'I have a film to show you,' he tells them triumphantly, flashing his grin.

As his former staff find seats facing the white screen arranged for the occasion, Jørn switches the light off and soon the machine whirs into action, its flickering lighthouse beam cutting the dusty darkness and showing these images for the ages.

'It started with the platform of the Opera House being there, and then slowly in this film, like a flower opening, all the shells of the Opera House came into being.'[123]

It is extraordinary. Yes, they had seen Jørn over the years taking photos of the building site – from the neighbouring Botanic Gardens, from the water, and of course from the Harbour Bridge, capturing the famous fifth façade that had inspired the sculptural effect of the roof in the first place – but they had no idea this was *his* endgame.

The wonder of it all! The platform with its grand stairway! The red giants! The growing of the shells!

They had always known they had had the privilege of working on a masterpiece, but never before had they realised just *how* masterful it was, and how blessed they are to have been a part of it.

The party goes on to the midnight hours, reminiscences ending in promises to remain in touch once all this blows over. Jørn and Lis show every last guest to the door, where Jørn gives them a strong hug and farewell.

'So,' recalls Leplastrier, 'that was the last time that we saw him . . . It was a sad affair and I think this wonderful man was very, very seriously misunderstood . . . I think it broke his heart for a while. Ultimately, it didn't break him. But then, you know, I think that Lis and his family were behind him, and as we all know, who have kids, that, family is the strongest element of all, and the most important thing of all.'[124]

27 April 1966, Sydney, too little, too late

Hopefully, they are just in time.

After two months of writing letters, making calls and leaving messages, Jack Zunz and Ove Arup arrive at Sydney Airport this morning in the hope of seeing Jørn and maybe even persuading him to change his mind at this, the eleventh hour.

Alas, alas, Jørn Utzon cannot be reached.

Who *is* eager to see the engineers is Minister Davis Hughes, and while the much older Arup stays in his Bondi hotel room to get some sleep, the sprightlier Zunz is ushered into the Minister's presence not long after having put his bags down.

There is no time for small talk, so the Minister gets to it.

'What are your intentions in working with me and my department in order to help complete the Opera House?'[125]

Zunz pleads ignorance about why the question is even being asked. What makes you think, Minister, that anything might have changed in our regard?

'From information I have received from my staff,' the Minister replies lugubriously, 'I have been led to understand that Mr Arup had been suggesting that his firm might resign from the project, as a consequence of Utzon leaving the job.'[126]

'No such decision has been taken,' Zunz assures him, 'and to my mind there is no question of our not fulfilling our commitments to you and your government.'[127]

In fact, the Minister's sources are not far off the money. 'Ove felt and I felt too,' Zunz will recount, 'at the time when Utzon resigned, a very strong emotional pull to walking off the job as well. Because, in a way, Jørn had woven his magic spell on us and we were – we had that same dream of this extraordinarily perfect conception building. And we knew that without him . . . our dream would not be fulfilled. Not in the perfect way in that we had first thought it might be . . . And so, there was a strong emotional pull to walk away.'

But . . .

'This partnership wouldn't have let us.'[128]

Herein, the nub of the rub. Whatever the founding partner might think, the firm's partnership don't wish to leave such a lucrative patch.

The Minister is reassured, a bit, but cannot help making clear to the South African just what is riding on this decision.

'You realise,' Hughes says, looking Jack deep in the eye. A pause. 'If you resign, I will have to leave Government and my political career will be finished.'[129]

Zunz is startled by the admission.

Hughes is playing for his political life here.

Within 48 hours of touching down in Sydney, talking everything over with Lewis and others, Jack Zunz's view falls into line with that of the partnership: Arup's *must* stay.

Ove remains unsure. Maybe it is the right move for the firm – and even if he had tried, there is little he can do to stop it. But still, how can it be? The Sydney Opera House without Jørn?

28 April 1966, Palm Beach, good night, sweet prince

Jørn, still unable to sleep through the nights, has risen early with his daughter, Lin, to pay a final visit to his favourite sandstone cave at Palm Beach.

Though late in the autumn and a little chilly, they go for what the Australians call a 'quick dip' in the ocean at the south end of Palm Beach. Afterwards, father and daughter sit on the sand to dry in the morning sun, gazing out at the cresting and crashing waves on the shoreline – reminding Jørn of the very waves that long ago inspired his interior ceilings for the Opera House, taking him back to the day he'd sat with Yuzo Mikami by the Øresund, watching small waves lap at the beach. 'Yuzo,' he'd said, 'can't we design the ceiling of the Minor Hall something like that?'[130] He shakes off the nostalgia and stands, then heads back to the house.

And within only an hour or two, it's just like the newly released John Denver song . . .

All their bags are packed, they're ready to go.

There's no taxi waiting, blowing its horn, but Jørn and Lis will drive the two family Citroens, both heavily laden, to the airport, before a couple of friends drive them from there to their new owners. In Jørn's largest suitcase, he has the boomerang given to him by Harry and Penelope Seidler at the farewell party they had thrown for him, to encourage his return. And yet, truly, right now – almost 10 years to the day after Eugene Goossens slipped out of the country – Jørn feels like he is being, 'driven from the country like the worst possible criminal'.[131]

And just like Sir Eugene, it has been a dramatic fall from grace, at the behest of a singularly ungracious government. Welcomed like a Royal, indeed by the Royals, and now removed like a convict caught with the governor's wife. From toast of the town to the town's toast, he is seen by many as the disgraced wastrel who couldn't get the job done, the flighty artist whose plane had crashed into Reality Mountain. Yes, here is the tragedy of Jørn Utzon, the former Prince of Denmark, showing himself out.

That notwithstanding, he does intend to return and had even written a note to Norm Ryan that very morning, thanking him for his support and writing: 'I am looking forward to meeting you again when I come back because I feel absolutely sure that I will come back.'[132]

Onwards.

The sparkling sunshine of the morning has disappeared in a sudden, moody change that takes hold of the city. There's a chill in the air that belongs more to Aalborg than it does Sydney. Kim's teeth chatter as his mother herds him into the back seat of the car where his big sister is already sitting, staring sadly out the faintly foggy window at her boyfriend, Alex Popov, who has skateboarded over with a friend to wave the Utzons a sad farewell. (Smitten with Lin, Alex has been dreading this day, as has she, though they already have plans to reunite.)

The only sound is the rustle of autumn leaves and the grumbling of the freshly started engines. Nobody speaks as they reverse – Lin waves madly – pulling away from their happy life.

Of course, crossing the Harbour Bridge, Jørn's eyes are drawn to the inevitable, his Opera House . . . Nearly a decade ago his vision of this masterpiece had started with imagining clouds over a headland. And right now, searching, he sees a cruel twist of fate: a dark cloud of fog, so low and heavy it obscures his site from his sight.

Who could ever have thought it would end like this?

His heart is breaking.

In the cars, still neither Utzon, nor Lis, nor any of their three children – all of whom have been plucked from their schools mid-term – utter a word.

As arranged, to avoid the press pack, the cars head straight out onto the tarmac to the foot of the Qantas plane, QF588, bound for Nadi, Honolulu and San Francisco – under false names.

'Only prime ministers and dangerous prisoners usually get this VIP treatment,' one airport official dryly remarks.[133]

Up, up and away. Leaving on a jet plane indeed.

As the plane flies north, out to the port side Utzon can see his nascent masterpiece and keeps gazing until it is no more than a speck over his left shoulder and now . . . nothing.

In short order his feet are cold, but this time there will be no socks.

•

414 • THE OPERA HOUSE

Back on the stage that is Bennelong Point, the show must go on, and while Minister Davis Hughes indeed expresses surprise to the press at the 'sudden and unexpected departure'[134] of the Danish architect – he'd had no idea until informed by a journalist – he is pleased to assure everyone that the three Sydney architects he has appointed to take over will get the job done.

Hopefully.

At least the Minister is satisfied to have the press on his side. So poisoned have the Sydney waters become for Utzon that most of the press seems happy to see him go, with one editorial writer noting that Utzon, 'did not only want to be the conductor – he wanted to be the whole orchestra as well'.[135]

•

There is another departure on this same day, with a lot less fanfare for the common man. Young John Weiley, Lin's friend and former flatmate in their Paddington house, the aspiring film-maker, is jack of it all here in Sydney. He cannot bear even one more self-congratulatory lunch with his father and Davis Hughes, can't stomach seeing what they have done to Mr Utzon, can't cope with watching young men being conscripted and sent off to the useless war in Vietnam. Most of all, how can he make art in a country that doesn't give a stuff about film, about the arts?

Weiley's off to London, where he at least has a shot at making something of himself, or, at least, making something artistic.

•

Even in the absence of Utzon, the agitation for his return goes on and it includes a gathering of several hundred of his supporters, which Ove Arup, Mick Lewis and Jack Zunz are invited to attend.

For Lewis and Zunz, the response is obvious. No, we have better things to do.

But Ove Arup, a diplomat at heart, is sure that everyone will be reasonable and insists that all three of them go.

Alas, alas, *alas* . . .

Though invited to sit on the podium, every time Arup tries to speak, he is rudely interrupted by the chairman.

On the sixth occasion it happens, Arup has had enough. Taking up his hat, and not forgetting his briefcase, he stands and says to the chairman, 'I think you are a very disagreeable fellow,'[136] before walking out, closely followed by Zunz and Lewis in his magnificent trail.

Zunz will later note, 'We [were] of course, relieved that at least we were not assaulted. We should of course have declined the invitation to attend in the first place.'[137]

Yes, such are the times.

So fraught is the whole Opera House situation right now that 'not being assaulted' can be counted as the good news.

But Arup is badly shaken by the whole thing.

'They called me a liar,' he tells *The Bulletin*'s Financial Editor, Michael Baume, who is writing a book on the Opera House saga. 'What can you do when you're telling people exactly what happened and they keep shouting that you are a liar?'[138]

And yet, despite the agony of it all, the angst, the harsh words, the commitment to go it alone without Utzon, he is grieving most the loss of his friendship with this man he so admires.

'He told me,' Baume will recount, 'what the break with Utzon had meant to him, of the deep affection he had for Jørn and his wife, of how he hoped for a reconciliation.'[139]

Arup is completely gutted by the whole thing, as he further makes clear in a letter he writes to Jørn's former teacher, Danish Professor of Architecture Steen Eiler Rasmussen, who in Denmark has spoken out for Utzon in the whole affair. For the professor must understand: 'It is Jørn who inexplicably has withdrawn from co-operation with me. I am deeply saddened and bitter over what has happened.'[140]

If only Rasmussen could know of the indignities that Utzon had heaped upon him, including the ludicrous claim he has heard on this latest trip to Sydney, that the architect had single-handedly done the engineer's work for them.

'It was not,' Arup claims, 'Utzon who told us how to "solve" the superstructure.'[141]

On the other hand?

On the other hand, and this is what keeps him awake at night, they had both been outspoken and even self-congratulatory champions of the whole architect–engineer relationship, only to have seen that relationship waver, buckle and then crash to the ground on the world stage. Was it perhaps his responsibility to have stood by Utzon despite everything?

He had said as much just the year before in a speech.

When it comes to Utzon and his work, he had said, 'It is no good coming along with cost planning, scientific programming or modern management methods – they don't apply to masterpieces.'[142]

Yes, some days he leans towards the notion that they must walk out in support of the architect.

Other days, no – why tear the whole house down for the sake of Jørn's stubborn pride?

Jack Zunz will recall of Ove at this time, 'All his emotions were involved with this Danish architect, genius friend, really – or ex-friend – and all his reason also told him, as my reason told me, that the thing would never be what we'd all dreamt it would be . . . But then he went into it and he convinced himself, eventually, that Utzon couldn't be brought back.'[143]

It is as simple as that. And yet it is not that so convincing himself brings Arup any peace.

'I mean,' he says, 'I've been trying to search my own soul, searching for . . . what we are doing if we're not resigning? Is it cowardice? Is it not getting into trouble, not getting into fights, not fighting the government or anything like that . . . I don't think we ought to do that. And that's the result I've come to.'[144]

The bottom line remains: despite all the angst, Arup & Partners will stay on the job – Sydney Opera House, Job 1112.

•

Sure. Utzon professes to no longer care.

Stopping off in Mexico on the way back to Denmark, to show the kids the structures that once inspired his masterwork, Utzon sends a postcard to one of his Sydney loyalists.

'Went to Yucatán. The ruins are wonderful, so why worry? Sydney Opera House becomes a ruin one day.'[145]

In the end, it's just like he'd said to his daughter, Lin, that last morning on Palm Beach, just before they left Australia. He'd said it out loud, half to his daughter, half to himself, but he'd meant it.

'Well, you know. This chapter is finished.'[146]

Site from East Circular Quay, with casting yards in foreground, 1964. *Courtesy Mitchell Library, State Library of New South Wales*

Shell construction, 1964. *Courtesy Mitchell Library, State Library of New South Wales*

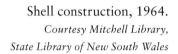

Rib segments, 1964. *Courtesy Mitchell Library, State Library of New South Wales*

Craning rib segments into place, 1965. *Courtesy Mitchell Library, State Library of New South Wales*

Tile lid storage under great staircase. *Courtesy Mitchell Library, State Library of New South Wales*

Construction of Major Hall. *Courtesy Mitchell Library, State Library of New South Wales*

Shell base construction. *Courtesy Mitchell Library, State Library of New South Wales*

Site view from Mrs Macquarie's Point. *Courtesy Mitchell Library, State Library of New South Wales*

Site view from Circular Quay. *Courtesy Mitchell Library, State Library of New South Wales*

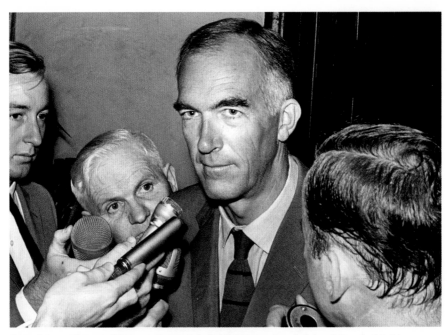

Jørn Utzon leaves his meeting with NSW Premier Askin, March 1966.
Fairfax Media

Jørn Utzon after meeting
the press, March 1966.
Fairfax Media

Protestors gather in support of Utzon, 3 March 1966. *Fairfax Media*

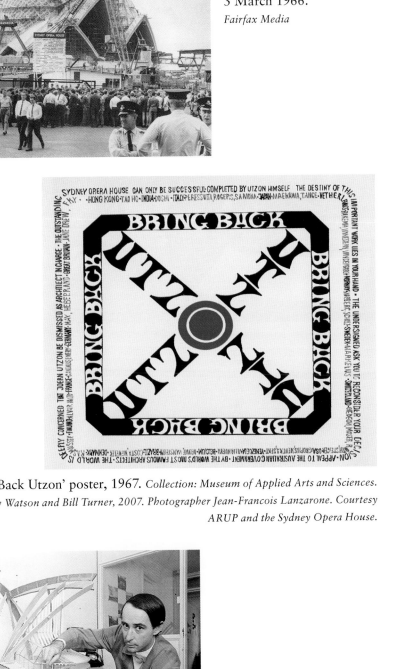

'Bring Back Utzon' poster, 1967. *Collection: Museum of Applied Arts and Sciences. Gift of May Watson and Bill Turner, 2007. Photographer Jean-Francois Lanzarone. Courtesy ARUP and the Sydney Opera House.*

Peter Hall, 1968. *Fairfax Media*

Davis Hughes, NSW Minister for Public Works, in his office, 1968. *Fairfax Media*

From left: David Littlemore, Lionel Todd and Peter Hall, 1973. *Courtesy Mitchell Library, State Library of New South Wales*

Indigenous actor Ben Blakeney portrays the spirit of Bennelong, October 1973.
Fairfax Media

The Sydney Opera House. *Alamy*

SEVENTEEN

A TALE OF TWO HALLS

I'm overwhelmed – but I think I can finish the Opera House.[1]

Peter Hall, 20 April 1966

We were abused for daring to change Utzon's design, on the ground that Utzon's working drawings were complete. When I asked if they had checked the documents, I received no answer. To this day, it is an absolute waste of time trying to explain the results of our studies. They don't want to accept them. The sincere conviction is that Utzon had designed and documented the perfect solution for a dual-purpose [Major] Hall.[2]

Lionel Todd, architect on Sydney Opera House, 1986

Early May 1966, Farm Cove, 'Nessun Dorma'

With Utzon gone, maybe they should just abandon ship? Stop the whole bloody thing?

This view, once the minority opinion of a minor minority, is now widespread.

'When Utzon resigned . . .' Lewis will recount, 'I was firmly of the view that the Government should stop the job now . . . keep this as a kind of an object on the sea-shore and just let's see how it's use would emerge – as an open-air theatre, if you like . . . like the Pantheon.'[3]

For many, architects and artists in particular, a political nobody appointing a panel of architectural nobodies trying to finish Jørn Utzon's masterpiece is reminiscent of what happened when the great composer Giacomo Puccini died in 1924, right at the point when he was about to start work on the last act of his opera *Turandot*. A contemporary, Franco Alfano, was hired to finish the job, fleshing out the rough sketches left by Puccini, which was strictly against the views held by many in the musical world. Alfano was never forgiven for it, either. In fact, for the opera's premiere in Milan in 1926, the famed conductor Arturo Toscanini had laid down his baton at the exact point the ailing maestro Puccini had laid down his pen, announcing, '*Qui finisce l'opera*'[4] and refusing point blank to conduct that which had been composed by Alfano.

Exactly.

In the words of the Dane's former valued colleague, Yuzo Mikami, who still works at Arup's in London, where the staff, if not the partnership, remains divided on the question: to be or not to be on the Opera House job? – 'No-one who had worked directly with Utzon could believe that it was technically possible or ethically justifiable for anyone other than Jørn Utzon himself to do the design of the Sydney Opera House as long as he was alive and active.'[5]

Which is one view.

Another view is the one taken by the three men making their way towards Utzon's former site office at Farm Cove on this chilly day of early May, as the wind whips the 'white horses' to gallop across the harbour.

The symphony must be saved. The Opera House must be completed. Inevitably, the quest for perfection must fall behind the need for completion of this strange architectural project which, as Peter Hall will later characterise it to his children, was 'designed from the outside in, not the inside out like most buildings'.[6]

Together, they are an unlikely trio. The short, young and 'hip' Hall has fashionably long hair curled to sit on the collar of his striped blazer, his 'eccentric dark half-glasses'[7] on the tip of his nose and a penchant for flamboyant bow ties, sports cars and fancy cigars – 'more like a rather raffish vaudeville comedian than an architect'[8] an old school friend and journalist writes of him, while another relates him to 'dandyism'.[9]

David Littlemore is a good two decades older, conservatively dressed with an avuncular nature, a tremendous moustache and what he describes as 'catholic tastes in music'.[10]

Thirty-six-year-old Lionel Todd, the Minister's pick, is simply a very quiet fellow who is instantly lost in the sea of office workers the moment he leaves the Opera House site.

These three men are under orders from Minister Hughes and Ted Farmer to get things going fast, which means all of them have to throw their work lives into high gear, from now until . . . God only knows when.

'When Utzon threw in the towel,' Davis Hughes would write some 30 years later, 'the whole project was in a state of chaos with a total loss of direction and morale at its lowest ebb throughout all the contractors and workers on the site.'[11]

His new team is here to shock that stalled system back into working order. But what shocks are there to their system, now that they have taken on this colossal responsibility, and must get to grips with the lie of the land?

Of these there will be plenty.

'When I first walked into Utzon's huts beside Farm Cove,' Littlemore will recall, 'I was staggered to find them lit by paper Japanese lantern spheres with minimum watt globes in them. I had expected to find a well-lit drawing office fitted for day and night work, which a project of that size and complexity cried out for.'[12]

And the working drawings?

What working drawings, officer?

For here comes the *real* shock . . .

3 pm, 17 May 1966, Opera House site, pass the parcel

The deal is done between the NSW Government and Jørn Utzon's lawyer.

In return for some $150,000, Utzon's team hands over 117 of the 5000 unfinished drawings of the Opera House that the Government Architect feels are of use. It is not the $480,000 that Utzon believes the whole lot is worth, but if the Minister doesn't like plywood, the Minister won't have plywood, and he won't be needing all Utzon's plywood acoustic ceiling drawings, for starters.

The whole exchange is conducted amid great secrecy as, with grim countenance, a representative of the NSW Crown Solicitor hands over a cheque made out for that amount to Mr Utzon's solicitor, Mr R. W. Nicholl, who in turn hands over the chosen drawings to Ted Farmer's Assistant Government Architect and new representative on site at Bennelong Point, Mr Charles Weatherburn.

Done. There is no bonhomie. No sense of a deal well done. No celebratory cigars. This is an unpleasant business, and it is indeed *business* with little space for the personal.

Mr Nicholl is soon on his way with the cheque, and in short order Hall, Littlemore and Todd – none of whom had met either of the others just a month earlier – are in the Farm Cove office, eager to look over the scheme they are tasked with fleshing out and finishing, all of it taking place in what Littlemore will describe as 'an atmosphere of suspense and fear'.[13]

Hall tears open the surprisingly thin package as soon as it arrives and they begin to go through the drawings one by one . . .

Only to be . . .

Staggered.

For one thing, there is not roll after roll of plans stacked to the ceiling as they had been expecting. It's just this small pile of prints, not even originals! And even those are as sparse as the Nullarbor in a hot summer.

'There were no drawings which we would regard in the profession as working drawings,' Peter Hall will later say. 'There were not even fully resolved design drawings. Not one drawing identified a material, dimensioned a room or described a building component. They didn't even represent a worked-out sketch scheme.'[14]

How *can* this be?

'They have only been given prints of old drawings relating to what has been built,' Prip-Buus tells his parents of the drawings bought by the Minister. 'And nothing on all the new parts . . .'[15]

(And so it goes. As with everything in the Sydney Opera House story, everyone has a different version. Ron Gilling will relay a rumour many decades later: 'It has recently been told to me that when Utzon was due to hand over his papers and drawings to the Government, he went through them and there were various files which he pulled out, saying that "they're not having this, they're not having that".'[16] Sir Charles Moses, on the other hand, will assert, 'Utzon was prepared to sell [his drawings] to the State Government and they refused to buy them all . . . the Panel had to start *de novo*.'[17] As for Davis Hughes and Ted Farmer, a lack of working drawings for Stage III had always been their gripe – they just hadn't made that known to the public, or the replacement architects.)

Whatever the means of arriving at this mess, Peter Hall and his colleagues are charged to take it to an unmessy end.

Hall had hoped to be given near completed plans which he could merely tweak and then oversee the construction of. That, at least, would make it easy to fulfil the mission to construct the Opera House in the spirit of Utzon. What is more, he had been hoping that, with the near completed plans, he could finish it within 18 months or so – even faster than the two years David Littlemore had reckoned on – and return to his previous private practice plans.

But *this*?

If this is all there is to work with, years of his life have just disappeared before his very eyes.

Peter Hall looks over the drawings for hours that turn to days.

Going through each drawing, he records that, generally, critical items, seating and ceiling, are either not shown or not in the set, and makes specific notes on particular drawings, ranging from useful to design idea to practically useless.[18]

'The drawings did not show for a builder or architect what he wanted to do with the rest of Stage III,'[19] Hall will recount flatly.

How is he to honour the spirit of Utzon when the man has left them practically a blank canvas?

'One of the accusations made against the Minister and ourselves in 1966,' Hall would recount years later, 'was that we would reduce the quality of the job. We had no such intention. The big question, though, was what were we supposed to build?'[20]

(Another curious thing? The next day's *Herald* reports, 'the drawings include working plans for interior finishes, cladding and paving, glass walls, major and minor auditoria, rehearsal rooms and windows'. Bill Wheatland is quoted: 'They are the result of many years of work by a highly skilled team of architects working under Mr Utzon's direction and from his inspiration . . .'[21])

Peter Hall scoffs at the optimism of such a statement.

For the far from triumphant triumvirate of architects, this won't be merely starting from scratch, it will be starting blind. Hall quickly moves to address the first and most obvious problem – grasping the fundamentals – how does one design a functional, multipurpose hall for symphony, opera, ballet, drama and more?

TAXIIIII!

He is soon on his way to the airport, embarking on a months-long world tour to immerse himself in the subject – just as Utzon had done over the years – visiting concert halls in all Europe and America while visiting and consulting with the likes of Jack Zunz in London, and the acoustics consultants, Professor Lothar Cremer and Professor Werner Gabler in Germany, and Dr Vilhelm Lassen Jordan in Denmark.

•

David Littlemore is nothing if not busy, dealing with the builders and engineers, while corralling the new architects.

His cheery presence is already familiar to the workers, thanks to his daily sweeps around the building site.

'Good morning, Mister Carpenter!' he calls, lifting his Homburg hat.

'G'day, Dave,'[22] many of them greet him back.

'You must walk on that site so every man knows you, and every man knows where you are and what you can do,' Littlemore will say. 'And you're not there as a slave driver, you're there as a friend and helper.'[23]

The building managers, however, are not nearly so cheery.

'When I went on to the job,' Littlemore would recount, 'I found the construction team on the verge of chucking it in. Utzon never held a site meeting or conference with them [upon leaving]. He had left them in the dark.'[24]

Littlemore is entirely different. And Mick Lewis is more than grateful, now, to be able to pick up the phone any time and talk to him.

'I saw the job of supervising architect,' Littlemore will recount, 'as one which commenced in the drawing office. What are you drawing? Do we understand the materials we are going to use? How can we co-ordinate all the various disciplines – structural engineers, civil engineers, hydraulic people, mechanical people, air-conditioning people, electrical? You know, it's an awfully long list and it must dovetail. It must be co-ordinated. That's supervision.'[25]

Such are the initial questions, and soon enough there is strong follow-up as he continues to co-ordinate the drive forward.

•

Lionel Todd, too, is not long in getting to grips with the many tenders and contracts already underway, and the drawings bought from Utzon.

One drawing and attached report is of particular interest – Utzon's attempt to rearrange the Major Hall so all seats are in front of the stage, as had been requested by Sir Charles Moses back in 1963. In two reports from January and June of last year, the Dane had said the hall would be designed to seat 2800.

'I decided to do a routine check,' Todd will recount. 'To my astonishment I found the space Utzon had provided would only allow for seating of 1800 by acceptable standards. Utzon had been trying to squeeze in extra seats by reducing the spacing between the seats to 2 ft 7 ins, [and some as little as 2 ft 5 ins] against a minimum 3 ft required for reasonable comfort, and shoving some seats in the orchestra pit.'[26]

Peter Hall would later say, 'The auditorium on which Utzon was working was plain illegal and would never have been accepted by the client.'[27]

Alerted to the problems, Littlemore goes deeper into the plans such as they are.

'We found,' the older man would recount of the drawings they'd been given, 'that he provided for a rehearsal room that could take no more than 30 players, and had made no provision, as required, for a grand organ, electrical wiring, or sewer pipes, or adequate air conditioning . . .'[28]

One issue that proves fairly easy to resolve is whether or not to pursue Utzon's insistence on the plywood-only acoustic ceiling.

As Todd would recount of a meeting called by Symonds, 'They told me they were withdrawing from all commitments . . . They gave no reasons.'[29]

Besides, the new trio has no hesitation in pursuing the engineer's steel-framed scheme with plywood cladding, as the Minister and Government Architect request.

•

Davis Hughes informs the Sydney press in early June 1966 that 'examination of Mr Utzon's plans for the interior of the [Major] hall have revealed serious deficiencies in the seating accommodation'.[30]

But never fear, the *Herald* informs the public, for, 'the Minister . . . has authorised the complete redesigning, if necessary, of the major Opera House hall'.[31]

'The whole thing is most upsetting,' Silent Stan Haviland tells the *Herald*. 'It is a very severe jolt.'[32]

•

Over in England, things are at least a little rosier for the still-downhearted Ove Arup, now able to make light jokes about the open wound that *was* Total Design.

'There is such a lot of humbug in architects, but there is such a lot of stodginess in engineers,' he quips. 'I am almost in favour of humbug, temperamentally.'[33]

Right now, charting a path forward, he views his role as being at least a symbolic mediator between the stodge and the humbug.

The London *Financial Times* announces the news in early June 1966:

> It is a timely gesture to award this year's Royal Gold Medal for Architecture to the British engineer Ove Arup, for architecture and engineering have for too long been out of sympathy with each other . . . Arup has provided a fine practical example towards bringing the two professions more closely together, if only because he is himself a designer in his own right. Within this partnership he has gathered around him a coterie of engineers and architects of great talent, each of whom possesses that creative spark which is necessary to a maintenance of the functional tradition. In pursuing his insistence

on the one-ness of structural engineering and architecture, Arup has recently formed his own architectural firm of Arup Associates.[34]

Ove is the second engineer in 120 years to be awarded the prize; the first to receive it was Pier Luigi Nervi in 1960.

In Sydney, journalist Michael Baume writes in his growing manuscript of the central irony of the award: 'The finest example of this combination in Arup's life, his aesthetic union with Utzon ... had already been broken.'[35]

Arup's feelings on his former friend, meantime, are hardening, and he writes in a letter to Professor Steen Eiler Rasmussen, in August 1966: 'I find that my feelings toward Jørn Utzon are gradually undergoing a change – the spell is wearing off. As I gradually discover what Utzon has left behind in the way of drawings for Stage III and when I see all the problems that were supposed to be completely solved are in fact not solved at all ... then I almost feel as if we have been the victims of a confidence trick ... It is quite clear to me that there is no hope of bringing Utzon back.'[36]

For all his anger, Arup remains conflicted at his core, as he tells ABC television around the same time that he regards Utzon as, 'just about the greatest living architect there is'.[37] (Utzon is not there to see it, or hear it. He does hear about Ove's prestigious architecture prize, though, and it stings like salt in his wound.)

Overall, Arup has had a gutful of the whole project, and Jack Zunz feels much the same, later noting: 'I had a long-lasting hangover following Utzon's departure'[38] and 'My personal involvement – and that of our London Office – in the design and execution of Stage III was minimal ...'[39]

In the whole imbroglio there seems only one positive thing.

Through it all, slowly, slowly, the shells continue to grow, the sculptural form on Bennelong Point taking ever stronger shape.

•

That man down on his hands and knees, crawling over New York's magnificently modern Lincoln Center? It is, of course, Peter Hall, measuring seating dimensions, just as he is soon on his knees in London's Covent Garden and Royal Festival Hall, pausing only to mark down the numbers in his notebook and occasionally take photos of features that please him with his ubiquitous Rolleiflex camera.

Bit by bit, he is building up his knowledge of state-of-the art theatre design.

In particular, Peter Hall is struggling with the complex issue of how to design the whole structure of the Major Hall so there can be orchestral and operatic *and* ballet performances there. Draining the brains of the experts helps a great deal.

'In New York I learned a lot,' Hall writes to Minister Hughes from New York on 7 July 1966. 'You will remember that [Dr Jordan] . . . recommended that we engage Ben Schlanger to work on our seating and circulation generally in both halls. I know Ted [Farmer] doubted the use of this and I did too. However, after meeting Schlanger, I have changed my views completely . . .'[40]

The man is so experienced, so knowledgeable!

After a good look at the plans for Sydney's Major Hall, Schlanger had declared: 'It's too skinny where it should be fat, and it's too fat where it should be skinny.'[41] (What Utzon had dubbed its 'ugly proportions'[42] after thin concrete shells were abandoned back in '61.)

The upshot, Minister?

Schlanger doesn't think 2800 seats can be put in front of the stage, as the ABC demands . . . 'If Schlanger were to say that the ABC seating requirements cannot be done in the space available, I doubt if there would be anybody, competent or insane, who would argue with him.'[43]

So, what to do, *what to do?*

•

It is Jørn, pacing the floors at midnight.

Back in their Hellebaek home, things have been tough for the Utzons, particularly for the one responsible for both moves, to and *from* Sydney.

The key problem for Jørn when he had arrived home is easy to summate: no work.

Jørn's architecture student son, Jan, remembers the Danish architectural establishment giving his father a cold reception. 'We have no use for architects who say no to clients,' they'd said. 'The client is always right. You have harmed your profession – so we will see to it you will never get a public job in Denmark.'[44]

And he doesn't.

'Not a nice thing to come home to,'[45] Jan adds.

Perhaps the unkindest cut of all, back in his home country, is the chair of the Danish Association of Architects – the rough equivalent of Ron Gilling in Sydney – telling him that, given he had walked away from such a major government job in Sydney, the Danish Government could not trust him enough to give him their own projects and he was on his own.

Even his old projects, like the one to build the theatre in Zurich, have stalled. He has bills to pay – starting with his Australian and Danish tax bills – and no work coming down the pipes.

Yes, he is now a world-famous architect, but his reputation as one who had been sent packing from Sydney, as uncompromising, costly and impractical, is now entrenched and no new projects are forthcoming. Cautious clients have no desire to be caught in the same morass as had occurred in Sydney.

Sydney . . . Sydney . . . Sydney . . . as much as Jørn tries, as fatalist a philosophy as he can muster on the good days, reminders of his half-finished masterpiece on the other side of the world are omnipresent. Even in his own home, the tapestry that the late great giant of modern art, Le Corbusier, had done to hang in the Opera house – '*Les Dés Sont Jetés*', 'The Die is Cast' – now hangs on the wall of his family home, 2.18 metres by 3.55 metres of heartbreaking beauty.

And if the sting of his former close collaborator, Ove Arup, receiving the Royal Gold Medal for lifetime achievement in architecture from the Royal Institute of Architects in Britain isn't enough, Arup also receives a knighthood from the Danish Royal family . . .

His one hope?

'For a while afterwards,' his son Jan will recount, 'he thought: "When they find out how hard it is, they'll call me".'[46]

That, however, will not pay the bills in the meantime.

'That building, the Sydney Opera House, was his great piece of luck,' architect Oktay Nayman will say. 'But, at the same time, it turned out to be a curse on his career. After we returned from Sydney, I was his only assistant. We didn't have any work and those were hard days.'[47]

Jørn's accountant advises he leave Denmark with his family and become an expatriate to avoid taxation. For now, the family heads to a seaside shack that his family owns in Sweden – to regroup.

•

And now it is Peter, pacing the floors at midnight.

Having recently returned from his six-months-long overseas sojourn, Libby's husband is restless, even in the wee hours, pacing, a fat Schimmelpenninck cigar between his teeth and a Campari soda in hand, the ice tinkling against the glass with each footfall. As if it is not enough to have taken on this whole catastrophe, he has the author of it – Jørn Utzon – attacking the project in the press.

Libby had saved all the newspaper clippings while he was away.

'They can tear the Opera House down as far as I'm concerned,' Utzon was quoted as saying in the Danish press back in June. 'The finished project won't be mine and I don't want my name associated with it in any way.'[48]

And what is worse, from this architect of his own demise?

Reuters had reported: 'If he had stayed, drawings would have been completed by late this year.'[49]

Oh really, Mr Utzon! Hall doubts that very much.

And the deepest cut of all is that Utzon talks of coming back.

'If the Labor Government regains power and sends for me, I will most certainly come,' he had said. 'If nothing has been ruined.'[50]

Mighty big of you, Tex.

The one solace for Peter Hall and the new panel in such troubled, pressured times is the atmosphere of collegiality between everyone on site. 'Every single one of those people,' David Littlemore will chronicle, 'not only pulled his weight, but gave of his best. It was magic ... We didn't have any outbursts of egos and battles on the site ... We were brothers in arms. We were all humbled before the task.'[51]

Davis Hughes would profess himself thrilled.

'Within three months, the new team had created a new atmosphere. The change was electric.'[52]

•

And so to grips.

In the site office at Farm Cove – no matter that it is now wired for large fluorescent lights – Hall, Littlemore and Todd burn the midnight oil with an ever-expanding cast. For such is the complexity of what is required, so overwhelming is the workload, that it really does require almost 10 times the number of people Utzon had; and inevitably Peter Hall has to do what the Dane could not: cede control over every minor detail.

'The Opera House was too complicated for any one man,' Hall will say. 'What was needed was a large expert team. Utzon was marvellously talented, but he never had the kind of organisation needed for the job.'[53]

True, there is a certain reluctance from some designers to get involved in doing anything for Sydney's most famous white elephant standing on the harbour foreshores, but that is overcome by giving them salaries well over the odds. This is no problem from the government as even more important than cost now is proving it had been no mistake to do it without Utzon.

The first major things built under the direct directives of the new regime, thus, are more huts lining Farm Cove to house them all.

What else can be done, after all, when you are putting the detail in a building that will have over 1000 rooms; an air-conditioning system comprising 28 plant rooms, circulating, every hour, 60 million cubic feet of filtered air that is both temperature and humidity-controlled; no less than 120,000 feet of pipe taking water to fire sprinklers; 400 miles of electrical cable; and 7500 square yards of glass . . . Then there's electricals, carpet, cladding, tiles . . . it's endless.

What had started as Utzon's dreamy designing, and transformed to Utzon and Arup nutting things out together at the Utzon dining room table, before being polished by a dozen people who knew each other's birthdays . . . has now morphed into an impersonal endeavour aimed at completion, not perfection; an intellectual exercise conducted by dozens of professionals all over the world, and all of it overseen by powerful institutional grunt that has no time or space for experiment and idealism.

20 October 1966, Sydney, they're really here

Premier Askin is pleased. Minister Hughes has a firm grip on the Opera House project, and that in itself is a fulfilment of their election promise, whatever happens from here. It gives Askin the distinct pleasure of being seen as both the building's most powerful backer and its saviour, one of many offerings to which he is helping himself in the tart shop.

On this day, 20 October 1966, there's certainly no humble pie on the menu, as this working-class boy from Glebe finds himself sitting beside no less than the President of the United States, Lyndon B. Johnson, the first US president to visit Australian shores, and he has come with his wife, the petite and drawling 'Lady Bird'. Ah yes, and they are joined by Australian Prime Minister Harold Holt, but Holt is not the host. He, Robin Askin, is and he can barely believe he has the honour of showing the President his home city, and, of course, the magnificent Sydney Opera House.

(Even more extraordinary, even though neither Askin nor Holt know it? They are sitting in the Lincoln Continental in which John F. Kennedy had been assassinated by Lee Harvey Oswald three years earlier in Dallas – the famous, stretched 1961 four-door convertible, which has now been substantially rebuilt with a permanent roof, bulletproof glass, titanium armour plating and solid tyres to prevent them being shot or blown out, the whole thing repainted from midnight blue to black and is now – all the way with LBJ – flying around the world with Kennedy's successor.)

As they make their way from Kingsford Smith airport to a state reception at the Art Gallery of New South Wales in the largest motorcade ever seen in Sydney, a million people line the streets, throwing streamers from where they stand behind police cordons chanting loudly: 'All the way with LBJ!'

And yet others, mostly long-haired youngsters, and many of them holding placards, are here to protest against the Vietnam War.

'Hey! Hey! LBJ! How many kids did you kill today?'

When the presidential limo heads down Liverpool Street, there is sudden drama. A group of young protesters have broken through the police cordon and are now throwing themselves in front of the car, prostrating themselves on the road and forcing it to stop! The horses on either side of the car rear up, the car comes to a halt as secret servicemen rush forward.

Bob Askin, being Bob Askin, says it without thinking – 'Run the bastards over!'[54] he grumbles, unamused as ever by the commie rabble-rousers he disdains.

President Johnson grins. 'A man after my own heart,'[55] he quips.

Mercifully, there is no need. With little ceremony, the protesters are dragged away – some by their hair, which serves them right! – across the asphalt and into police custody, while the motorcade moves on.

•

The idea has taken hold of young John Weiley's soul.

Why not do a film, a documentary, chronicling the Opera House saga? Yes, that would be it. Utzon had said that the House was dying – 'sick on the bed'[56] – and now Weiley will perform the autopsy, following its story from dream to death, a *j'accuse* that would nail the actual killer: the politics that giveth and taketh away, politics as usual.

'I was very committed to the ideals that drove Utzon and a cohort of my contemporaries in Australia at the time,'[57] Weiley will later recall.

Alas, alas, the ABC won't touch it. It is all very well to *accuse* the political entity of murder, but much more problematic when you depend on that entity for funding, as the ABC does. What's more, the ABC will be the Opera House's primary user.

Unbowed, in London, Weiley takes the idea to the most respected broadcaster in the world, the mighty BBC.

He manages to secure an audience with the controller of the newly formed and highly adventurous BBC2. It's a man by the name of David Attenborough, a natural scientist by training but a mover and shaker at heart, with grand ambitions.

Immediately taken with the idea, Attenborough sends a cable to the sister organisation, the ABC, asking that it lend him a film crew for a week – under the usual arrangement whereby the ABC and the BBC share resources in each other's countries. The answer is cabled back from Australia with remarkable speed – and right from the top, personally, from Charles Moses' successor at the ABC, the General Manager Talbot Duckmanton.

Attenborough calls Weiley back in to the office to personally give him the news.

So yes, Mr Duckmanton has sent a lengthy reply by telex, and allow Mr Attenborough to read it to you. It is very long, but boils down to one word repeated many times over: *no*, a thousand times *no*, such a film, by John Weiley, is never to be made, the head of the ABC makes absolutely clear.

Finishing, Attenborough summates the BBC's stand on the matter.

'We are flatly told that we must not let you make this film,'[58] he says.

Weiley's heart sinks.

Going on with that perfect diction that will become famous the world over, for decades to come, David Attenborough concludes with a grin: 'Well, they can get fucked.'[59]

The BBC will send their own film crew.

'They handed me a wad of cash,' Weiley will recount, 'and said, "Go make the film".'[60]

Production of the 24-year-old's documentary, *Autopsy on a Dream*, will begin in the new year.

17 January 1967, Bennelong Point, a full rack o' ribs

It is perhaps the best use of ribs since God made Eve.

For on this day, to the cheers of the workers, one of the giant red cranes swings its arm high above them and lowers the 2194th, and *last*, precast segment of the last rib into place.

It has been one small haul for the crane, and the end of a very long haul for the workers, lasting no less than three years and two months from when they had placed the first segment.

And of course, they equally 'plant' a tree, using the crane to place a small tree at the peak.

'The tree is an ancient construction tradition,' one writer will later explain, 'associated with the raising of a building's highest beam or structural element. Hence the name of the rite: the topping-out ceremony. It's a sign that a construction project has reached its literal apogee, its most auspicious point.'[61]

It is not finished, of course. For they still must finishing attaching the tile lids.

At the vision of those magnificent shells now in place by Sydney Harbour – no dazzling reflection to blind the weary driver – the city begins to fall in love.

29 January 1967, Sydney, the Peter principle

Peter Hall can barely bear it.

He's trying to relax on this sunny Sydney Sunday morning, only to be greeted with tales of his own inadequacy, under the *Sun-Herald* headline of **'HOW WE GOT STUCK WITH SECOND BEST'**.

He's barely bloody started!

But the *Sun-Herald* is already well ahead of him.

'A few weeks ago in a four-page illustrated article, America's *Life* magazine told its many millions of readers the Sydney Opera House was a "beautiful concrete camel."'[62]

Do tell?

'Who can wonder at the world laughing at us?' the journalist muses. 'It seems that whatever we get now will be second best.'[63]

Well, not if Peter Hall can help it. Persistence is his forte – as an old friend writes of him in the *Herald*, 'I remember Peter as a disciplinarian . . . a believer in rules ("buildings should be finished on time and cost what they are supposed to") . . . marked by the habit of persistence . . . He adapted perfectly to the hierarchical system which characterises a private school [like Cranbrook], leant upon it to reinforce his authority, worked within the rules . . .'[64]

Yes, the hissing hurts – *traitors* to architecture – but he will persist, if only to prove them wrong.

And look, no matter that it's Sunday, he has work to do – just as he works pretty much every day of the year. He stands up from the desk in his home office to pace the room, cigar in clenched teeth, and is still doing precisely that, into the wee hours.

'[I was] very, very anxious,'[65] Hall will recall of the entire time.

The follow morning, early, after too little sleep, Hall is back at it again.

February 1967, Sydney, Can't find an answer? Change the question!

It's been almost a year since the trio has taken over, and it is now time to submit to the Minister and other important Opera House personages the panel's *Review of Program*.

The triumvirate's first proposal is to abandon the multipurpose Major Hall altogether and design it for symphony concerts only.

'In 1957 people believed in the very large multipurpose hall,' Hall will say. 'By 1966 . . . all those large multipurpose halls in North America were built and tried. And they were hopeless . . . there are now very few 3000-seat auditoria [that] are musically any good.'[66]

If they try for the best of both worlds, Hall argues to Davis Hughes and Ted Farmer, they risk spending a lot of money on a complex design and ending up with two half-worlds, and that is not good enough for the Sydney Opera House.

Speaking of which, what about the opera?

Easy. The opera can be staged in the Minor Hall.

It does seem a bit odd – like putting the most important news of the day on page 2 of the *Herald*, or calling a spade . . . a hammer – but ABC General Manager Talbot Duckmanton for one supports it. After all, from the beginning, his primary concern is to have a world-class concert hall with 2800 seats, which is achievable in a single-purpose hall, Peter Hall insists, once all the stage machinery is removed and they will have to put seats behind the stage. It was Duckmanton's predecessor, Sir Charles Moses, who had come up with that number of 2800 – and if the seats absolutely must be behind the stage, well, the current management of ABC can roll over on that point, Beethoven, and tell Tchaikovsky the news.

But the Elizabethan Theatre Trust – the managing body for ballet, drama and the country's fledgling opera company, all of it under the chairmanship of the redoubtable H. C. 'Nugget' Coombs, the famous Mandarin – is nothing less than furious at opera's relegation to the back stalls, and says so with some fury.

In a public letter printed in all the papers, Coombs makes a diplomatic plea to Minister Hughes to delay making any rash decision.

The decision to use the large hall for symphony concerts only, he insists, 'poses a serious limitation on the possibilities of developing musical theatre, in particular, opera and ballet, which being confined to the Minor Hall would have to accept serious limitations on repertoire and scale of representation . . .'.[67] Don't you understand? This move kills off the staging of all grand operas! You can forget all the Wagnerian operas, and *Aida* is out of the question – we won't have the space. The only thing operatic about the Opera House will be the name! All the rest will be a sham.

As for the acoustics consultant, Professor Cremer, head of the Institute for Technical Acoustics in Berlin, he leaves the project over the matter, reportedly because the 'Opera House is now not good enough to hold their interest.'[68]

For the outraged opera buffs and appalled architects, their hope is for there to be enough of an outcry that Minister Hughes will reject the radical rewrite of the brief and tell them to go ahead as it was conceived.

Architecturally, Peter Hall knows the move will be seen as a tragic loss. 'Of course there's the architectural question of taking the stage tower out,' he will later say, 'and I couldn't possibly argue that that is not an artistic loss, that in a way the unity of the architecture suffers.'[69]

For now, Davis Hughes takes the proposal into consideration.

•

As predicted, controversy erupts over what many see as the craven cave-in to mediocrity represented by the proposal to abandon the multipurpose Major Hall and build a plain Concert Hall in its stead.

The broad camps are Minister Hughes, the new Architect Panel and the ABC vs. the Opera House Trust and the Elizabethan Theatre Trust.

Then, there's the architectural profession and its supporters in the arts, for whom this fresh insult to architecture in general and Utzon's concept in particular, inflames the Utzon-Only mob as never before.

The well-known university drama lecturer and influential member of the Elizabethan Theatre Trust, Dr Philip Parsons, comes up with a plan. Clearly, the only way forward is-to convince Davis Hughes of the need to get Utzon back to complete his multipurpose Major Hall. How best to do that?

Parsons writes a long letter to Utzon that details his strategy for bringing Minister Hughes to the table, and includes in it the draft of a letter he would like Utzon to sign so it may be sent to *The Australian* newspaper, making it clear that the Dane is available to come back.

The important thing, Jørn, is to be humble, to sound as if you could work within the structure proposed by the government, the one you previously rejected.

The point right now is to show you are open to discussion.

Utzon agrees it may be worth a shot.

Energised, Dr Parsons and *The Australian*'s drama critic, Francis Evers, launch nothing less than a campaign to bring back Utzon, jointly penning a series of articles calling for the Dane's recall.

'Events since Utzon's withdrawal,' they write, 'suggest an increase in cost rather than the reverse.'[70]

They explore the history of the project, opening fresh wounds yet again, including the breakdown with Arup's Sydney office, quoting a defensive Mick Lewis – 'Throughout the project, Utzon never produced a drawing I could give to a rough foreman which he could understand and proceed from.'[71] (It's rather beside the point, given the working drawings for Stage II were Arup's responsibility, but it's Lewis's way of battening down the hatches, to survive the latest cloud of controversy over Bennelong Point.)

One of *The Australian* newspaper's leading writers, Mungo MacCallum, pens a piece entitled 'Utzon: Let Me Complete the Job' on the first anniversary of Utzon's resignation, 28 February, in which Utzon insists that he can solve both the seating and acoustic problems that Hall et al are struggling with, and the *Sydney Morning Herald* soon joins the fray.

'We had already solved this major problem, as it is called,' Utzon is quoted in the *Herald* on 1 March, the same day a conference is held between Minister Hughes and the various interest groups on the question of the Opera House brief. 'It is very detailed and not something I can explain over the phone, but you can be assured it was solved.'[72]

Same thing with the seating.

'For concerts in the Major Hall there would be seating for from 2600 to 2800 and for opera a similar number, depending on the size of the opera.'[73]

And what of Mr Hall's plans to abandon the dual purpose hall, and confine opera to the Minor Hall only?

'Ah,' he says dismissively. 'That is the easy way out, anybody could do that. But they are taking out all the stage machinery that they cannot use in the Major Hall and thus throwing away its very purpose. It is ridiculous. It is not necessary to do that. When I left we were in the final stages and we had a perfect scheme.'[74]

Return to finish the work he began?

'I have not made any move to get in touch with Mr Hughes,' Utzon tells the journalist. 'Does he feel it necessary for me to come back?' he asks. 'If he does then I would. In the long run what is best for the

Opera House is what should happen. It is my wish and everyone else's, I'm sure . . . We must ignore personal matters, and think more about the Opera House.'[75]

Peter Hall is beside himself.

Think more about the Opera House? If he thought any more about it, his head would explode! Solved all the problems? He hasn't seen any sign that Utzon had done any such thing.

'Mr Utzon,' the *Herald* reports further, 'said two professors in acoustics from Germany . . . had pronounced the acoustics of the halls as splendid.'[76]

A small parenthesis here. Alas, they never told the skipper of the massive ocean liner the SS *Canberra*. For it is when the Danish acoustics man, Dr Jordan, is in Sydney to test the new cladding in the Major Hall with the help of some students from the Conservatorium playing some classical music, that he is stunned to hear the long blare from a ship's horn! Can it really be? After everything they have done, that a sound as strong as that can penetrate with such volume?

Yes. When he plays it back it is even more shattering than in real time. 'There it was on the tape,' he would recount. 'At 50 to 100 feet it had a noise level of 100 decibels, about the same as a jet plane at an altitude of from 500 to 1000 feet.'[77] Close parenthesis.

Anyway, Peter Hall need not worry too much – the Minister and government are on his side, as in the same article Premier Robin Askin himself is quoted: 'The government regards the combination of Mr Utzon and the previous Labor Government as responsible for the mess which we inherited. Mr Hughes has dedicated himself to straightening out the whole matter . . .'[78]

Mr Hughes, meanwhile, smirks at the suggestion Utzon would be brought back. 'The question of his return does not arise,' he says. 'There is no situation which requires the attention of Mr Utzon. The panel is very competent to deal with any requirement of the client for the completion of the Opera House.'[79]

Peter Hall is happy to read as much.

•

Now, to up the ante on pressing Hall and Hughes to sue for peace. Again, in a move organised by Dr Philip Parsons, no fewer than 50 architects from Hall's old workplace at the office of the Government Architect – half the staff, it's a mutiny! – write Peter Hall a letter, leaked to the *Herald*:

> We understand that you are deeply committed to the principles of
> Jørn Utzon's design for the Opera House and that you accepted your
> present position in good faith believing that he could not return to
> the project. Utzon is willing to return, and only your negotiations
> with the Minister can bring this about.[80]

Meanwhile, a more secretive resistance movement springs up behind
enemy lines, and these fifth columnists suddenly make their move. For
from the Government Architect's office itself – where the employees are
sure their phones are being tapped by the department, ever since Utzon's
departure – these architects of the public service spread out one evening
to wreak their havoc. The following morning, the Sydney CBD is plastered with 3000 'Bring Utzon Back' posters! And the 3001st is on the
wall inside their own office! (It is quickly ripped down by a shocked
Mandarin, but the point has been made.)

'Those who have sided openly with Mr Utzon,' one anonymous
Government Architect tells a journalist, 'have been blocked from
promotion . . . We haven't forgotten Utzon. The Opera House will be
a disaster if he isn't in charge. We wanted the public to know this and
the poster idea came up spontaneously.'[81]

For his part, Harry Seidler, the original leader of the 'Utzon-in-Charge'
protest a year earlier, busies himself endeavouring to harness the prestige of the international architectural community to the cause, seeking
20 of the most highly regarded architects in the world to sign an open
letter to the NSW Government calling on it to retain Utzon's original
vision. He even suggests a draft of the letter: 'This is the first time in
our period that the architect's intentions – based on the explicit demands
of the former client – are changed by another political government . . .
something that should deeply offend the architectural profession. The
architect has to be regarded as an artist!'[82]

George Molnar, meanwhile, vehemently opposes the changes in the
Herald, ending up in a sparring match with his former student, Peter
Hall himself.

'There we were,' Molnar will recall. 'Peter Hall and I arguing in newspaper columns on reverberation times, raising the level of journalism to
an unprecedented level.'[83]

For all the agitation, it is for naught, as the *Herald* reports, all remains
much as it is: 'Hall has his supporters, Utzon has his. Both sides have
sincere convictions in this fight so wounding to architecture in Australia.
The letter sent by those 50 architects to Hall shows the feeling. Has

Mr Farmer, the Government Architect seen it? This we don't know, but one thing seems certain. That letter will never be answered.'[84]

Friday, 17 March 1967, Sydney, orta recens quam pura nites, 'newly risen, how brightly you shine'

Could the official motto of New South Wales have any greater physical manifestation than this? Just *look* at it, as the last of the 4253 tile lids, representing the last of 1,056,006 tiles in total, is bolted to the mighty sails of the Sydney Opera House.

Newly risen, how brightly you shine.

Not for nothing will the famed American architect Louis I. Kahn note: 'The sun did not know how beautiful its light was, until it was reflected off this building.'[85]

On this, the first day of its completion, as the newly preening sun finally starts to fade, in preparation for giving way to a delighted and impatient moon to have a go, a man who has devoted a decade of his life to the Opera House picks up his briefcase without fanfare or ceremony and walks in silence out of the site office back to his car. John Nutt is lost in his thoughts, but quickly comes back to earth as he reaches the open air. He looks up. And what does he see, if not one of the finest architectural achievements of the century? The white sails soar skyward above him, the precise curved angles of its shape cutting neat lines against a pink and purple sky, mirroring the bridge in the background. The hues of the autumn sky are beautiful by themselves, but never so stunning as when their soft colours dance along the white tiles of the Opera House.

'The final effect will at times resemble what we call Alpengluhen (literally, alpenglow),' Jørn had said all those years ago. 'The colour you get on snow-capped mountains when the sun is setting, the beautiful pink and violet reflections from the combination of mat snow and shiny ice.'[86]

Nutt feels a tug in his gut, a weight of regret that for all their achievements, for those years of exhilarating collaboration, Utzon is not here to share this moment.

'The great architectural strength of this building,' John Nutt will say, 'is the sure hand of the one architect through the roof structure. He wanted to do most of the things himself and took that right through to the detail. When you see this building, you see Utzon.'[87]

No-one doubts it!

For, oh the wonder, Utzon's original stunning vision of a cloud-like roof floating atop Sydney Harbour, elegant from every angle, indeed now shines brightly in the last of the day's sunlight on Bennelong Point, just as it will glow in the moonlight.

The hordes of surveyors, builders and engineers who have poured their own blood, sweat and tears into making the tiles a success over the last year can now stand back and soak it all in.

Could it possibly be more glorious?

For here is the final answer to all those ludicrous attacks on Utzon's choice of colour.

Somewhere in the naked city, J. R. L. of Beecroft is surely lying low, hoping no-one will remember his letter to the editor in 1957: 'Its over finished roof with many curved surfaces all covered with white tiles will be a glaring monstrosity.'[88]

And Mrs Coleman of Willoughby is surely, too, hiding behind the couch, having similarly written: 'I have been a professional colour artist for more than 30 years and consider myself an authority on colour. I [write concerning] the suggested white tiles! This will give the impression from the Harbour and foreshores of either an Army camp or a circus. May I say that white can be very ugly if used in a big way.'[89]

Nothing, clearly, could be further from this glorious reality.

Utzon himself might take some satisfaction when the overall reaction is reported to him, but not for long – busy as he is filling out the last of the affidavits needed for the legal action he is about to embark on in the NSW Supreme Court against the NSW Government seeking, via his lawyer Neville Wran, a further $349,000 for work done that he insists he has not been paid for.

21 March 1967, Sydney, reverse-engineering the brief

It is done.

On this day, the NSW Cabinet approves the proposal by Hall, Todd and Littlemore to abandon the multipurpose hall, and design the Major Hall for concerts only, while the Minor Hall will be for operas and drama.

For the moment, the decision is kept under wraps, as Minister Hughes needs time to work out how to get around too much public protest from the Elizabethan Theatre Trust and the Opera House Trust, but all key insiders are informed nonetheless.

The fact is, Hughes has decided to follow Hall's suggestion, no matter what – 'This was already cut and dried,'[90] says Sir Charles Moses of the deliberations. Or, as Hall will later recall: 'Davis Hughes' response was simply magnificent. And he hasn't been given the credit he deserves. He didn't flinch. He agreed to back us to the hilt. At no stage did he try to get us to cut corners or skimp on the finished product.'[91]

In response, after cables fly between Sydney and London, Ove Arup is not long in expressing his dismay.

'I understand,' Arup writes to Davis Hughes on 28 March, 'that your Government has now finally decided to abandon the idea of using the Major Hall for opera. It is a very dramatic – almost one might say, tragic – decision because it makes a nonsense of the whole form of the shells, which were meant to house the stage tower.'[92]

Ah . . . yes. Most architects must agree. The move is, indeed, a dagger to the heart of architecture and Utzon's beautiful, lonely idea. Don't you understand? The whole wonder of the design had been that it had been beautiful *and* as functional as nature itself – the greatest, functional piece of artwork ever built. By removing the stage machinery, you will be left with little more than an . . . empty shell of Utzon's vision. Or, as Yuzo Mikami puts it, 'a skull without a brain'.[93]

Well, Davis Hughes doesn't quite believe in all that humbug – tragedy in architecture? It's a bit much – nor does he have time for a history lesson.

This is the plan, and this is what is being done.

(Jack Zunz, still heading Job 1112, comes to agree with the move, claiming: 'I hadn't realised, not until very late in the day: – a) that the brief for the Client for the whole scheme was fatally flawed, and b) that Utzon's response to the brief was equally flawed.'[94] He will further claim: 'To this day, there is no precedent for a performance hall to fulfill both the operatic and orchestral function and to be designed to the highest international standards – and to seat the numbers required in the brief . . . The need for a home for Australia's major orchestra was such that, despite the advanced state of construction of the backstage structure, the Government decided to wipe the slate clean and instruct Peter Hall to proceed with a single purpose hall.'[95])

Either way, it's Hall's hall now.

•

Good God.

Peter Hall can barely stand it.

Utzon, *again*!

This time the Dane has signed a prepared statement to the press:

> My only interest in the Sydney Opera House, is, and always has
> been, to finish the building in the perfect way and to the complete

satisfaction of the client. While I cannot retract any of my decisions or actions in the past, I am concerned now only with the present circumstances and what is best for the Opera House.

I am therefore willing to discuss with the present architectural panel possible forms of association, co-operation or partnership by which we might all provide architectural services to complete the Sydney Opera House in such a way as to ensure the best possible building for the people of Australia.

Jørn Utzon[96]
4/4-67

In short?

He is *still* available. Give him a call.

Minister Hughes doesn't blink, and refuses to take it seriously. But Hall is troubled by it, and never more so than when he finds out from a friend, a few days later, that bloody Philip Parsons had written it, as part of the whole Bring Back Utzon push, which *still* goes on! A few days later again he finds out that another friend – an artist by the name of Owen Tooth, who had given Hall the Utzon family's number at Palm Beach a year ago, and has been pushing him lately on the subject of Utzon, wanting him to talk to Minister Hughes about bringing him back – is also in on the whole thing!

Can he trust *no-one*? Is *everyone* against him?

Hall is far from happy about it, recording in his diary: *O Tooth rang and [I] was very rude to him.*[97]

All this, even as the first book comes out detailing what is seen as the crucifixion of the Dane – *Utzon And the Sydney Opera House* by Elias Duek-Cohen – to be sold in bookstores, on the streets and at the gates of the Opera House itself. (Well, at least Hall knows that Michael Baume, a journalist who had shadowed Minister Hughes after the resignation, will soon be releasing his own book – a version of the story which will surely at least provide balance to the mythology that has grown up around Utzon.)

Anyway, what can the likes of Hall, Todd and Littlemore do in the face of such continuing noise, continued assertions that it is all so simple, if only the government had the brains to get Utzon back?

Exactly what they have been doing: persist.

The pressure is inexorable, and the problems sometimes seem insuperable.

'Always,' Peter Hall would say, 'you come back to this thing that it's not *your* building and you can't be ... an arrogant, unpleasant person, an architect often is about a building ...'[98]

No, you just have to get it done.

14 September 1967, Sydney, humble pie

Peter Hall? It is Jørn ...

It is indeed, but a very different Jørn from the one Hall had dealt with 18 months earlier. This is an almost meek Jørn, taking an entirely different approach. No longer is he imperial and imperious. And he is calling – at the behest of Philip Parsons, who is still driving the whole move for a rapprochement – with a serious proposal. Maybe this whole chapter of his life isn't over after all. He wants to come back and ... collaborate.

(Perhaps the reason for Utzon's change in tone is that Parsons had sent him a psychological profile of Hall, which, among other things, makes clear that the new Opera House architect is best dealt with gently: 'Because Hall wants not only to "succeed" but also to be liked, his position at the Opera House has been pretty painful. Ambition made him accept the job but he is not tough enough to ignore the hostility of your supporters ... As you probably know, he has been under medical treatment for nervous exhaustion.'[99])

Peter Hall groans inwardly but is at least courteous.

'Philip Parsons,' Hall tells Utzon, 'has already suggested somebody talk to Davis Hughes and the Government about these possibilities.'[100]

One thing, though, and Utzon insists on it.

'If I do come back, the question of who the client is, must be made quite clear.'[101]

He had loved working with the Committee, had hated working with politicians.

Well, then. That is a real problem.

But, of course, as Utzon also knows, it is not just the Minister who he needs to get on side.

'Would Mick Lewis be all right?' the Dane asks of Arup's Sydney boss.

Hall chooses his words carefully.

'If the Government agrees that you should work with us, I am sure Mick would accept that ...'

'That is good news! What I would like would be for you to talk to the Minister and tell him that the Minister should settle my fees, invite me to come out and pay my fare, and a fee for a period of discussion.

And you could let me know what the Minister's reaction is – if he was in favour of it, that would be fine.'[102]

Hall's view is that Utzon is hardly in a position to be making demands, but he promises to pass on the message . . .

Goodbye then.

Hall must get back to work, always back to work. There is much to do.

•

As promised, the next week, on 20 September 1967, Peter Hall lays before Minister Hughes the record of the conversation he had with Utzon.

Hughes reads it through, slowly, carefully, allowing himself the odd harrumph, as he goes, and never greater than when he gets to the paragraph – 'if the Minister would have him back, then the question of the Client would have to be quite clear and we would have to be able to work without any publicity at all and just quietly resolve the problems'[103] – which seems to seal it for him.

'Well,' Davis Hughes says, 'the last paragraph really makes it absolutely impossible . . . I don't believe his return would be in the best interests of the job. I have already heard these sorts of Utzon statements for hours on end and I really don't think there seems to be any significant change in Utzon's attitude. I don't think Ove Arup himself will really be interested in having Utzon back. I know that Mick Lewis doesn't want him back, nor does Jack Zunz.'[104]

As a matter of fact, when Hall had shown Mick the same copy of the telephone conversation notes he was now showing to the Minister, Mick had snorted most unpleasantly: '"Would Mick be all right?" I tell you he bloody well wouldn't be "all right".'[105]

(On that subject, Lewis has already put his views in the public domain, telling *The Australian*: 'If you spoke to Ove Arup himself in London, he would agree that Utzon should return. He and I have agreed to differ about that. However, if the architect wished to return and this was desired by the client, then we would happily resign for the sake of the project, should this be a pre-requisite.'[106] In short, the project can have Utzon or Lewis, but it can't have both. And what Ove Arup thinks about it is neither here nor there anymore.)

Still, for now, Hall feels obliged to push the case for an Utzon return, just as he had promised the maestro of the Opera House he would do.

'Parsons,' he begins, 'believes there is political advantage for you in the magnanimity you would show if you agreed to what Utzon wanted.'

'Absolute nonsense!' Hughes snorts. 'The Labor Party would say that I had made a complete mess of it, that the architects I'd hired had been unable to do it and that I had to get Utzon back. I can see nothing but disaster for me and for you and your fellow architects and I don't think there is any political advantage in it whatsoever.'[107]

And in the end, this is the star by which Minister Davis Hughes unfailingly steers – where lies the most political advantage?

Hall persists the best he can, but doesn't truly have his heart in it. In fact, when Hughes now asks him directly does *he* really want to work with Utzon, he can't help be anything other than frank.

'At some stage I thought it might be possible to work out a way of collaborating, but the more these discussions with Utzon have developed and the more I learnt about the job, the less interested I became . . . Todd and Littlemore have never been interested in the possibility, nor the Government Architect, and I feel that the thing shouldn't be raised again. I will ring Wheatland and tell him that this is my feeling after talking with the Minister, and I will also ring Utzon.'[108]

Done. One last thing though.

'You shouldn't allow this to worry you and distract you from your job,' the Minister says, lighting another cigarette.

'It really isn't worrying me any more,' Peter Hall says, numb in the moment. 'And I propose to put it right out of my mind.'[109]

Back at the desk, Hall takes off his tangerine bow tie, pours a Campari soda, lights a cigar, picks up his pencil and gets to work.

Persistent Pete.

It's his hallmark.

26 October 1967, Sydney, no grand opera for Sydney's grand Opera House

It's now gone 18 months since Jørn Utzon left, and on this day Davis Hughes stands triumphant before the press pack at Bennelong Point, eager to show just how brilliantly things are working out without the Dane – with Peter Hall standing proudly by his side to make the point, while Dr Jordan's latest acoustic model of the interiors is on display.

'I estimate the job will be finished within four years,'[110] Minister Hughes is happy to declare to the press and public at last.

As the *Herald* reports, 'Mr Hughes' decision confirms that the Major Hall will be reserved for orchestral concerts, conventions and "pop" performers. The Minor Hall will be used primarily for opera and ballet.'[111]

'The architects are now briefed to carry out final planning.'[112]

Once all is explained, Hall and Hughes take a photo opportunity, posing inside the giant model.

Gavin Souter is in the press pack and announces to his readers the next day that it is a 'red-letter day for the man who presided over the change [in architects] – the Minister for Public Works, Mr Davis Hughes'.[113]

Exit the old guard, stage left.

'The Opera House sailed away under the new team,'[114] George Molnar will recall.

•

What now? The young Australian film-maker working for the BBC, John Weiley, approaches Ove Arup and Jack Zunz in London, seeking their co-operation for a documentary he is making on the building of the Opera House.

'We were not keen,' Zunz will recount, perpetually grumpy about nearly all things Sydney Opera House, 'but he was a very plausible young man, seeking our collaboration. He was at pains to explain that he wanted to present a factual account of the Sydney Opera House story so far and avoid any contentious issues at all costs . . . Ove and I were impressed by Weiley's . . . sincerity and agreed to cooperate in making the film.'[115] (Weiley later said Zunz's claim that he promised to 'avoid any contentious issues' was 'patently ridiculous'.[116])

At Ove's suggestion, Weiley interviews him at home. The cameras are set up in Ove's home office by none other than Director of Photography, Bill Constable, the friend of Sir Eugene Goossens who long ago had first put to paper the conductor's Grecian vision for the Sydney Opera House!

The lights are positioned, the microphones placed, and the crew roll tape.

Weiley sits across from Ove, out of the shot, and begins: *What drew you to the Sydney Opera House project?*

'This was obviously something quite unusual,' Ove begins. 'Something, you know, spatial, and from that point of view I was extremely interested in it because that's the sort of thing I like. It's much more exciting. We've alone had over 200 engineers working on this scheme . . .'

Now, Ove being Ove, he is candid – most particularly when it comes to his one-time great friend Jørn Utzon.

'The fact is that the collaboration deteriorated, to a degree that simply stopped.'[117]

Talking about it all puts Ove in a philosophical mood, so when Weiley asks why he had chosen not to resign in support of Utzon, the old engineer follows his meandering mental track: 'It would be so much nicer to resign. I would have much preferred it. It is a very muddled thing, complicated thing . . . this has been such a deep question for me, and I have been trying to search my own soul . . . is what we are doing, if we are not resigning, is it cowardice? Is it not getting into trouble? Is it not getting into fights, not fighting the government? . . . but I don't really think it is. I don't think we ought to resign. That's the result I have come to . . . I don't know.'

It's Arup's Hamlet moment, on camera.

He goes on, at some length and with no little frankness.

Other interviews are conducted with players like Jack Zunz, while, over in Sydney, Weiley sits down with all those who agree to meet him – Norm Ryan, Mick Lewis, Harry Seidler, and even a nervous-looking Peter Hall. He also meets such outspoken boffins as young Harry M. Miller, the rising impresario of Sydney and member of the Elizabethan Theatre Trust, who is bitterly critical of the decision by Davis Hughes to switch to a single-purpose main hall, based on what he sees as the Minister's 'infinite wisdom that orchestral concert attendance are the things that are going to remain constant in the serious music scene for the next 50 or 80 years. He's chosen to ignore the fact that those audiences for those concerts all over the world are in fact, diminishing.'[118]

Miller, for one, is already dreaming of bringing theatrical extravaganzas to Sydney, far removed from stuffy, outdated orchestral performances, and has done his best to dissuade the Minister, but he won't be told.

'It's a staggering, staggering decision to make and very ill informed. I really don't believe that the information is collected properly from anywhere. Quite strange. I mean, but the Minister saying to me, oh, yes, but I've seen *Swan Lake* in somewhere or another . . . But he saw it somewhere in a small theatre with eighteen swans. What about *Swan Lake* with thirty-two swans? It's to give them grand opera, grand ballet, grand spectacle.'[119]

Oh, but he's not done yet, and others too have a word to say, one architect in Sydney pointing out – 'Utzon may be a very great architect, but he's not particularly adept at administrative and political manoeuvring . . . his lack of skill at what we might call "bureaukarate" tended to be disastrous' – while a punter on the street says in a thick Australian drawl, 'If they'd been honest about it, they could of [sic] built a sports stadium instead – in fact, one's promised but we probably won't see that for another forty years either.'[120]

With such a surfeit of material, Weiley moves on to the next issue, that of providing the voice-over narrative to the field. Initially he thinks of the Australian actor with the deep voice, Ray Barrett, who happens to be in London at the time. But then again, there's the big lump who has been sleeping on Weiley's couch for the last few weeks, a friend from home. His name is Bob Ellis and there are three things that commend him for the task. Firstly, he is a brilliant writer and could help to polish the script. Secondly, his naturally stentorian tones would be perfect for giving the documentary gravitas. And thirdly, with the money that BBC would pay him, he would have enough money to get off Weiley's couch and into his own digs!

Bob Ellis it is.

•

The likes of Arup, Ashworth, Moses and Molnar are certainly not the only ones upset with the cancellation of opera in the Major Hall and the extraction and destruction of the cutting-edge stage machinery Utzon had designed. Who wouldn't be appalled at $3.2 million worth of state-of-the-art technology, now consigned to the scrap heap ... and all in the name of *thriftiness*?

The demolition expert charged with supervising breaking it up is visibly moved by the scene of jump-suited thugs climbing and dismantling what he has been told is some of the most modern stage machinery ever designed. As he remarks afterwards, it feels like 'cutting up a live deer'.[121]

EIGHTEEN

OF JACOBITES AND PHILISTINES

VIKINGS AND VANDALS – A Loss of Integrity ... Although the standard of its design may be regarded well above average, the interior of the House is nevertheless a result of political expediency and architectural compromises made during the construction period, and can hardly be evaluated as excellent ... To put it quite bluntly, the Sydney Opera House is a curious mixture of magnificent architecture and ordinary utilitarian building ... Despite the well-meaning endeavour of Peter Hall and other architects in charge of the design, it is hard not to describe all these acts as an architectural vandalism. Alas the Vandals were stronger than the Vikings. They were under the patronage of the State Government and could re-arrange the whole interior as they wished.[1]

Yuzo Mikami, architect on the Sydney Opera House, 2001

February 1968, Sydney, let the works begin! ... Again

Just a week before the election, and nearly two years after Utzon's departure, Davis Hughes sits comfortably in front of the press microphones at his desk, 31 storeys high in the new State Government office building (designed by one Ken Woolley, who was one of those who turned down an offer to replace Utzon).

As always, a cigarette butt smoulders in the ashtray beside him. And not only is he master of all he surveys, but also everything over his left shoulder, as through the huge window the gleaming white sails of the Sydney Opera House seem to be reflecting his hubris.

Speaking of which, he now leans into the mics to speak. 'Work on the final stage of the Sydney Opera House will start in six weeks and the building will be completed by the end of 1971.'

Great. But the press still hasten to ask the ever-present, haunting question.

There is a public meeting to be held on Monday, Minister, to discuss bringing back Jørn Utzon. Are you going, Minister? (After all, Opposition Leader Jack Renshaw had recently stated, 'Davis Hughes has adopted a dog in the manger attitude on the question of Mr Utzon's possible return.'[2] It is clear to all that if Labor win the next election, they would certainly consider his reinstatement.)

But Hughes ain't biting.

'The question of any terms for the return of Mr Utzon does not arise,' Minister Hughes says evenly. 'I do not agree that there are large numbers of people who want Mr Utzon to return. Most people realise we have taken control of the Opera House and have an orderly program for completion . . .

'No costly mistakes have been made while we have been in charge.' A pause as he looks, steel-eyed at the reporters: 'We inherited costly mistakes.'[3]

All the king's horses and all the king's men are trying to put Humpty Dumpty together again . . . we need no more distractions, you hear?

Mr Hall himself reiterates the sentiment, telling the press that Utzon's presence would serve 'no useful purpose'.[4]

As to the cost, the Minister says they do not yet have a final estimate.

The *Herald* editorial sums it up:

> On the whole Mr Hughes was able to persuade us that the Opera House is at last moving towards completion in a sensible and orderly fashion. He will not, of course, satisfy the Utzonites who believe that nothing can possibly go right since their hero's resignation. He will not satisfy the opera buffs who are convinced that the Government decision to make the Major Hall into a Concert Hall was a major disaster. There will, however, be general relief that work on the final stage . . . is to start in six weeks' time . . . though Mr Hughes could tell us nothing about the final cost. One would like to be equally confident about the design. Here a great burden falls on Peter Hall . . . It is absolutely essential that Mr Hughes should not press him to accept second-rate solutions for the sake either of economy or speed . . .[5]

As those final words are uttered, a faint groan can be heard on the wind, wafting down from somewhere in the far north.

It sounds just a little like Jørn Utzon.

19 February 1968, Sydney, Hughes is the King of the Castle and Jørn's the Dirty Rascal

The Utzon camp plays its last card.

On this Monday lunch hour, just five days before the State election, some 1500 people gather at Sydney Town Hall, where they are addressed by the likes of Norman Ryan, Elias Duek-Cohen, Harry Seidler and others. As they build to the climax, they play a taped address by Jørn Utzon himself.

His introduction is like a distant Danish echo of that long-ago call from Sydney's GPO – 'This is the Australian Broadcasting Commission . . .' only this time:

'This is Jørn Utzon . . .'

'I stretch my hand forward to you, Mr Davis Hughes. I appeal to you to have faith in me, to have faith in my methods and ideas . . . I have proof for my idea and my ability. The proof lies there in front of you in the form of a marvellous building, the proof that I can carry out my ideas to the last detail from the very beginning.'[6]

Utzon's voice, 'like some ghost of Bennelong Point', says, 'It is not possible to consider the existing building as an empty shell under which you can do what you like. I must come back and follow up what is begun . . .'[7]

At the end of the meeting, Elias Duek-Cohen, speaking of Hughes' refusal to ask Utzon back, defiantly calls out – 'It's not his building!'[8] The crowd rise in unanimous agreement.

'It was rather like a gathering of Jacobites toasting an absent Stuart,'[9] writes the *Herald* reporter.

And, like a spark hitting the pool of petrol in the corner of the workshop, the debate over art and architecture, culture and values, flares up once more.

Under pressure, Hughes speaks out, rejecting the biblical reference being thrown his way in this unceasing debate – 'The thing that hurts me most in the Opera House row,' he tells the *Herald*, 'is being called a Philistine. It's unfair and untrue.'[10]

He's seen *Swan Lake*, did he mention?

The sides are entrenched, there is to be NO rapprochement.

And it doesn't matter much, as the Askin government easily winning the election, expanding their majority by six seats, makes the point of it all rather beside the point. The last words on the Utzon push are left for Ove Arup when, on a flying visit soon after the election, he tells the press: 'Constantly what he said he had solved, he had not solved. If he would see that he acted rather foolishly and . . . now try just to help the job, then the situation would be different. But the Utzon which we knew from the latter part of the job would be absolutely no use here. The Utzon we collaborated with in the beginning would be welcome with open arms. But which Utzon? That's the question.'[11]

No Utzon, is the Minister's firm answer.

•

For his part, Peter Hall quite understands the motivation of the Utzonites as, after all, he used to be one. He does not hold it against them, even if most of them bitterly resent him. As a matter of fact, he so little resents those who want Utzon back that when one remarkably beautiful 21-year-old woman from Roseville, Penelope McDonnell, comes to visit him at the Farm Cove site office in the company of a Finnish film director, he not only notices how voluptuously she fills out her t-shirt bearing the slogan 'BRING BACK UTZON'[12] but ends up contacting her again to see if she can perhaps arrange to bring him a t-shirt just like that for himself. For fun. And so he can see her again.

•

It is time for Hall, Todd and Littlemore to . . . take their time. For, whatever else, they really are now granted the key things that Utzon was not in his final years on the project – unpressured space away from politics and press to solve the problems that remain *and* whatever resources they need to get the job done.

The trio get on with the eternal struggle, endeavouring to solve the remaining problems, even empathising with the long-departed architect at times. For never has Utzon's line 'It is not I but the Sydney Opera House that creates all the enormous difficulties,'[13] had more resonance. Even after abandoning the multipurpose hall concept, there are technical problems in designing the building that would still kill a brown dog.

At least there is some progress with the acoustic ceiling . . .

In a nutshell, the solution is . . . a nutshell.

The same rough idea Jørn was planning but with steel to hold up the plywood panels, as Hughes wants.

They will need money for prototypes, Minister?

Of course.

The Minister agrees in principle, only insisting they finish their designs first.

At least some lessons have been learned.

Late 1968, London, results of a cultural autopsy

John Weiley can't stop fidgeting. Tiny droplets of sweat bead on his brow while he chews at his lip. All those interviews. All that work. All that editing, cutting and splicing, working out what to include from the massive amount of material he had, how to put it together into a coherent narrative. But it has been done, and now tonight is the *premiere* for a gathering of Australian expats living in London, many of them Weiley's friends, and friends of his friends, all of them squeezed into a BBC studio.

The lights go down, and within seconds the screen is filled with the image of the half-built Sydney Opera House, even as the stentorian tones of the narrator, Bob Ellis, roll out.

'It's an object like no other object. Not so much a building as a thing and a thing like a pyramid or a Druid altar. An object of almost ancient reverence. A gesture towards the infinite like St Peter's. Yet its Gothic arches point up to no God, only to an ideal of functional excellence . . .'

Weiley hears a few chuckles in the audience, and he breathes a short sigh of relief, but the scene has already moved on, as a montage of Sydney Town comes on screen, filled with images of the Randwick races, Anzac Day marches, car sale lots that have come to dominate the urban environment, and of course red-brick boxes perched on cliffs above the ocean, where Australians surf and sunbake; another shot of the horse races, punters sipping on frothy beers.

'In a land where . . . noble headlands submerge under seas of red bungalows, seems a bit odd that the people should perform a cultural act of faith and build an opera house,' Ellis goes on, 'and they had nothing to put in it. How did it happen here?'

So, the stage is set, and Weiley's film unfolds, covering the whole saga, the conception, the staggering technical challenges that had been overcome, the political interference, the schism that had developed between architects and engineers and the final with Utzon vs. Hughes playing out in the main arena.

'In a country where apathy is a watch word . . . 1000 people marched on Parliament House, a lot of them fearing the Opera House would turn into one of the great Australian anticlimaxes, like Gallipoli or the messed-up capital city of Canberra. Angrily they compared the Minister's plan to have a committee finish off the Opera House with a committee to finish a Rembrandt . . .'

And so it goes for some 56 minutes, building to the final scene – an aerial shot of the great white shells on Bennelong Point, resplendent yet empty.

'And now, after it all, the building proceeds apace of whatever it is, whatever cenotaph of whatever hopes, whatever great utopian prank that laughs over the water. And Utzon lurks overseas and threatens like King Arthur to return, and Hughes sits at home and says he can't think of any possible circumstances in which Utzon might be needed ...

'Hallelujah, we guess. Hosanna, to whatever's possible in the best of all possible climates. She'll do mate. Or, will she?'[14]

John Weiley looks about him as the lights come up, and is stunned by the reaction. On the one hand there is raucous applause and cheering, for a job well done, a real glimpse behind the scenes of this whole extraordinary saga and a powerful airing of artistic discontent; a pointed and timely critique of culture and its worth in the land down under. On the other hand, some are in tears at what has been done, how Australia had been handed a work of genius, only to have connived to bring the genius down and accept the stilted form of the masterpiece it might have been.

Four days later, Jack Zunz sees it, just by chance. The words 'Opera House' leap out at him from his BBC television program.

Oh.

Odd.

Weiley's documentary is screening tonight at 10 pm on BBC2. Strange that they had received no warning. Anyway, Zunz looks forward to it, and is sure it will be interesting right up to the moment that ... he actually watches it.

For, far from being uncontroversial, as he felt that Weiley had promised, the film-maker has, in part, cast Arup & Partners as handmaiden to a misguided Minister Hughes, and – to his eyes – opens old wounds. No, more than that, he is opening new ones.

Ove is quoted as saying before the resignation crisis – 'To destroy what may be a work of genius is a serious business. And the verdict of history will not be kind to those who could be named for it.'[15]

Zunz leans forward as he sees himself come on screen, sitting at his desk.

'The whole idea, this extraordinary dream, this poetic thing which Utzon created became a vision for all of us because it was so unusual in this day and age to embark on a project of this nature ... One's imagination had been fired and we pulled out all the stops. We turned the whole firm virtually upside down, inside out, to try and meet this challenge.'[16]

Here now is an interesting claim.

'In September 1961,' the narrator intones, 'Utzon had an idea. He saw that if he started with a sphere, he could make all the shapes he needed from its regular surface ... This gave the shell a unifying geometry, made calculations simpler and it was in line with his personal belief that the structure should be the form and the form should be the structure.'

Over to Harry Seidler, who Zunz had met a couple of times while in Sydney.

'In one stroke, almost like a Gordian Knot solution, he found not only a way for engineers to compute the thing structurally, but he also found a way of building quite unbelievably complex shapes and forms with virtually industrialised means ... it made this building a great thing, by world standards.'[17]

Jack Zunz reels. The way it is told, it is like Arup's had done nothing but drop the ball. (Five decades later, Zunz will answer the question of who came up with the spherical solution with a singularly pithy answer: 'The short answer is Utzon, the long answer is Arup's.'[18])

Bob Ellis goes on.

'They tried different sorts of concrete and double skins of concrete with spaces in between ... but the roof would not be moved. No amount of hundreds of thousands of formulas fed into gnashing computers would make the stone wings fly. The years passed and the very shape of the Opera House that had made the idea so exciting now, it seemed, was making the real thing impossible. They kept trying ...'

There is no doubt Utzon had been the prime mover, but by God, it had not been done *alone*.

Oh, wait ... they get a nod.

'The problems weren't over. The fiercely committed engineers now had to place 2194 15-ton segments in their exact theoretical position in space to within an inch. On a structure of that shape the normal scaffolding method would be slow and expensive, so they invented a new construction technique altogether.'

The documentary goes on, one man admitting its beauty but saying the whole thing should be scrapped, now coming back to the narrator.

'Public criticism wasn't the only problem. Utzon was beginning to make enemies. Some of them among his colleagues. The engineers had tried for years to design his parabolas. But then he had changed the problem to spheres and solved it himself. Some of the engineers were annoyed at his intrusion ...'

Ove comes on screen, speaking of Stage III – 'The fact is that the collaboration had deteriorated to a degree where it simply stopped.'

'This put Utzon in a very precarious position,' posits one Sydney academic. 'Because most Australians, I think, pride themselves on being intensely practical people and if there's a dispute between an engineer who is, more or less by definition practical, and an architect, who's always suspected as being somewhat airy-fairy, they will tend to side with the engineer . . . When the Government came into office in 1965, they were presented with a very easy way of making Utzon the scapegoat for what had gone wrong. It was almost, prima facie evidence that he was impractical and woolly and airy-fairy simply because he had fallen out with the engineers.'

Zunz is furious.

'The final argument was over Utzon's plans for the ceiling. The disagreement was trivial and in happier days could have been resolved. But now the engineers rejected Utzon's scheme and submitted two alternatives of their own. Intentionally or not. They gave the Minister evidence with which to challenge Utzon's competence as an architect.'

Zunz shakes his head. This is not a good look for the firm.

'Some of Utzon's unswerving and myopic supporters even accused us of positively undermining his position,' he will record in his memoirs. 'It was also said that he had to solve our technical problems . . . It would be risible were it not so insulting, and so far removed from the truth . . .'[19]

In his home, Ove Arup, who had been called by Zunz and told that the documentary was on, sits silently as Bob Ellis, after noting the breakdown in the friendship between the Danes, builds to the climax . . .

'Arup wasn't prepared anymore to put his neck nobly in the noose for the man who'd accused his engineers of plotting against him and suspected Arup himself. And though he knew it was his support alone that made the government look respectable, and now he realised that the infuriating Utzon was indispensable, if the building was to be the master work he himself had already sacrificed so much for, Arup . . . decided with some pain *not* to resign.'

It's not quite what he says, it is the way he says it, almost casting Arup as Brutus to Utzon's Caesar, complete with an *Et tu, Brute?* moment.

And all this before Mick Lewis comes on screen and seems to acknowledge that real compromises have had to be made in Utzon's absence. It is the truth, but far from helpful in terms of arming the Arup critics.

To Zunz's eyes, the documentary is a disaster for his rapidly growing, ambitious firm; a poisonous piece of publicity.

'The film Weiley made,' Zunz will insist bitterly, 'was not only libellous, full of factual errors and falsehoods, but was also a very poor piece of film-making. We felt badly let down. Weiley had been charming and persuasive and we felt we had been conned into collaborating.'[20]

Well, that just won't do. What follows, exactly, is lost to history in more than one way.

'I asked . . .' Zunz will recount in his memoirs, 'Ove to write to the Controller of Programmes at the BBC advising him that we considered much of the film's content untrue and damaging.'[21]

John Weiley knows nothing about it . . . until one day, a short time later, he is urged by colleagues and friends to hold another screening of his now notorious film. Upon going to the BBC archives to retrieve the film rolls, he is told the film has been . . . destroyed.

'What do you mean "destroyed"?' Weiley asks, exasperated, his blood rising, in tandem with his panic.

'Well,' says the librarian, trying to be helpful and not too patronising to this young Australian, 'when we get a "destroy" notice we put the rolls on that chopping block and we chop them up so there's no possibility of an accidental re-run when the rights have run out . . .'

In a fever, Weiley calls David Attenborough.

'Impossible,' says Attenborough, 'there must be some mistake – it could not be destroyed without my approval and I have authorised no such thing. I'll call you back.'

Several days later, Attenborough calls back, only to say, 'I'm sorry but it's true.'[22]

Crushed, Weiley heads to the isles of Greece to lie in the sun, lick his wounds and think about just what it is he wants to do with his life. Like Utzon before him, he feels the weight of the establishment – undefeatable. Does he really want to be a documentary-maker when this is the treatment you receive, when anyone who disagrees can use their power to silence, when this is the thanks you get?

1968 to 1969, Sydney, sailing on becalmed seas

At least, things are calm.

In June 1968, the *Herald* editorial celebrates the armistice: 'For a time it was almost impossible to mention the Opera House without stirring up the whole debate. But those days are now over. A happier spirit is noticeable. The formation of the Opera House Society, with Utzonites and Hughes men sitting amicably together is an excellent portent. But this does not mean that all the problems are solved.'[23]

Come September 1968, the estimate is finalised to Minister Hughes' satisfaction.

The Opera House will cost $85 million.

'Fortunately,' the *Herald* reports, 'Mr Hughes is confident it can be financed out of lottery receipts.'[24]

(Out at Rookwood, Joe Cahill rolls over in his grave to hear Hughes finally admit it.)

'All that can be done now is to get on with the job with a sigh for Mr Utzon, a prayer for Mr Hall and his colleagues, and a sense of gratitude to the gambling spirit of the people of New South Wales whose buoyant hopes alone have made it possible and whose dreams of wealth fortunately match the follies of politicians and the extravagance of architects and planners!'[25]

The truth? The issue largely passes the entirely uninterested public by, a big white upside-down ship in the night sailing off to a port unknown. If Sydney thinks about it at all, it is in the sure knowledge that the Battle of Bennelong Point is over.

June 1969, Sydney, nightmare remains

A year later, and it seems to Peter Hall that while most of the architectural problems they have faced have been either solved satisfactorily . . . or unsatisfactorily, but sort of solved all the same . . . there is one problem with which they are struggling to make any headway at all.

It's the glass walls that are to enclose the enormous shell openings, known as 'the curtain wall', as it hangs off the roof.

The *Herald* reports: 'Sydney Opera House architects and engineers are wrestling with the last major problem of the $85 million project – the building of the glass walls. They see the problem as nearly equal to that of the revolutionary "sail shells" which sent the cost of the Opera House soaring . . . A panel of Australian and international glass manufacturers has been invited to study the problem before the Department of Public Works issues specifications and calls for tenders.'[26]

Most challengingly they must be able to 'hang' these tons of glass like a curtain with 'no intermediary means of support between the roofs and the foyer-lounge base',[27] as anything looking like a support beam would destroy the whole look of the Opera House.

Despite many disagreeing, including his own panel, Peter Hall is stubbornly sticking to Utzon's original concept in this case – so they have to look clean and be soundproof while still being strong enough to withstand occasional gusts of winds off the harbour of 160 kilometres per hour.

And so it goes, as these Australian architects, who have never worked on anything more technical than a ten-storey curtain-wall building, are now out on the very ledge that Utzon had been on for so long – right on the edge of the possible. And they are making it come together!

It's exhilarating, and exhausting.

But . . . back to work. Always, back to work.

1969 to 1970, Sydney, Hall's glass walls got 'im by the balls

Something is wrong with Dad.

In the Hall household at North Sydney, they had noticed.

Libby, for one, is worried. Mostly her husband is never at home, and even when he is, he's still not quite with them. He seems rarely to sleep, the fuse on his temper has now burnt down to practically nothing and he goes off in a rant at the slightest provocation. It feels like he has entirely withdrawn from the family, his brow perpetually knotted up like a tangled fishing line that the rest of them can neither untie, nor cut through. His once clear dark eyes are now forever glassy, the stink of booze ever-present, the man they knew . . . a near empty shell, though always with a bit of grog in the bottom.

'He did have a very serious collapse at one stage,' his son Willy would recount. 'That was a bit of a fright for all of us. It was kept very quiet.'[28]

(A definite pattern is forming. First Ove Arup, then Utzon, had suffered collapses and breakdowns while immersed in the Opera House work, so Hall's collapse is perilously close to being a tradition – and even Davis Hughes has taken to sleeping pills for the first time in his life.)

Fortunately, after a brief stint in hospital, Hall emerges. He has survived to work again. Alas, his marriage has not. Libby Hall can only take so much and while it is one thing to support him through tough times, she has just about had enough. Oh, and she knows there's been another woman, maybe more than one, for years now. Peter Hall is obliged to move out of the family house . . . and not long afterwards is in a serious relationship with the young woman who had visited him wearing the 'BRING BACK UTZON' t-shirt, Penelope McDonnell.

Not that the intensity of his work on the Opera House will diminish one jot.

'Sometimes,' Penelope Hall will recount, 'the only way I could get his attention late at night when he was working – which was every night – was to lie down naked on the Opera House plans he was working on.'[29]

Which works, for a bit. But then he is right back at it, his head in the drawings all day and into long nights that stretch into weeks and months.

April 1972, Sydney, a gift

Jørn will not be returning to the Sydney Opera House. Not only is the chapter *really* over, but the book is closed.

It's been a long, tough road to acceptance. And some days he still can't accept it. Most days, the mail arrives with some letter concerning the Opera House but Lis has started to simply toss them out – 'Otherwise we would have to maintain a full-time staff',[30] she quips some years later, half sad to watch her husband continue to be haunted by his own creation.

But, there are silver linings.

At the moment, he is building a church he has designed – Bagsvaerd Church, just north of Copenhagen – with the help of his architect son, Jan, and his son-in-law, Australian Alex Popov, who is now married to Lin.

Jørn hadn't wanted to take the job and initially declined it. But his devout Lis had needled him gently – *you must do it*. And so, he had.

The church council wanted a modern church and had given him a free hand on a modest budget.

'Jørn,' Mogens Prip-Buus will recall, 'was inspired by Lis's childhood prayer. *Thank you for the light, for life and for all you have given*. Jørn didn't delve into philosophical or religious notions – but he said that the church is light. Bagsvaerd church soaks up light from all sources, and it gives it back. It's brilliant.'[31]

At least it is keeping him busy and paid, for these days he must take whatever work he can find. This includes lecturing in Hawaii, and it is while there in 1972 that he wins an invite-only competition to design Kuwait's National Assembly building. It stands on the seafront with, in Utzon's words, 'haze and white light and an untidy town behind'.[32]

Yes, Jørn Utzon, both as man and as architect is moving on with his life and career. Tidying up loose ends, he instructs Bill Wheatland to donate the 5000 Stage III architectural drawings, still in storage in Sydney, to the State Library of New South Wales, on the understanding that the material is to be restricted for 10 years from the date of the gift.

Any applications thereafter are to be made to Jørn Utzon personally.

17 December 1972, Sydney Opera House, if only Cahill were here

Positions everyone.

Yes, they say that the Opera House will have more openings than Dame Nellie Melba had farewells but, let the record show, this is the first and most egalitarian of the lot.

It has been more than 10 years since Paul Robeson had sung for the workers on the nascent building site, effectively the first performance for the new venue. So, who better than the workers again, many of them with their wives, to sit 'neath the roof they have built, upon the seats they have bolted in – a relatively comfortable 36 inches apart – for the first big acoustic test of the nearly completed Opera House.

For this has been much more than just another job for most of them. Yes, there has been a fair bit of industrial strife along the way, but as the secretary of the NSW Builders' Labourers' Federation, Mr Jack Mundey, notes, 'Workers identified themselves with the Opera House ... Building workers normally change jobs about five times a year. But many builders and labourers worked at the Opera House for eight to ten years and some for the whole fourteen years.'[33]

They'll sure miss fishing on their lunch break.

No fewer than 2490 of them file in on this afternoon to take their seats before and behind the stage, the culmination of Joe Cahill's hope of nearly two decades earlier that this Opera House would not be exclusively for ladies with mink coats and men in tuxes, but also for the *workers* and common people. Because, as Joe always said, 'Everybody has the right to good things, and ...'

And now what?

No sooner have they settled in than a slim bloke in a dark suit – clearly not one of their own – walks out onto the stage and takes from his pocket a ... pistol?

Yes, a pistol!

With no ceremony whatsoever he holds it above his head and fires!

'When do we die?'[34] someone quips from the stalls.

But no, it must be a blank – for nothing falls from the ceiling, and there are no ricochets. Every minute for the next five minutes this fellow – one of the big bosses of Hornibrook, they reckon – continues to fire. Apparently, it is some kind of acoustics test.

Up on the concert stage, no less than the Sydney Symphony Orchestra settles, before its conductor, Sir Bernard Heinze – strides with appropriate elan onto the stage and taps lightly on his lectern.

Drum roll, please.

As it commences, the official party, presided over by Premier Sir Robert Askin – who with his knighthood in 1972 had decided to be Sir Robert rather than Sir Robin – and the Minister for Public Works, Davis Hughes, along with the Governor, Sir Roden Cutler, and all their merry wives, enter what is now officially called the Concert Hall.

In the front rows are the architects and engineers, executives of the ABC and other dignitaries, along with members and former members of the Opera House Trust. (Sadly, Silent Stan Haviland is not with them, having died just a few months before.)

And . . . now.

With a wave of Sir Bernard's baton, the SSO bursts into life and the melodic tones of 'God Save the Queen' fill the Concert Hall, the first symphonic sounds in the Sydney Opera House. It has been a long haul, but surely worth it. The SSO moves into several classical pieces, including Ravel's *Bolero*, Mozart's *Eine Kleine Nachtmusik*, and Beethoven's *Coriolan Overture*.

The workers, many of them from cultural backgrounds where they had taken classical music with their mother's milk, smile, some of them closing their eyes and clearly being swept away by it all, remembering their young times in those old countries where they had first heard this music.

At the back of the hall, the Danish acoustics expert Dr Vilhelm Lassen Jordan uses not only his own ears to determine the success or otherwise of the performance, but also 10 recording instruments to test the quality of the sound in various parts of the auditorium.

Minister Hughes is more than usually nervous. Not long before, Cabinet had approved his appointment as the NSW Agent-General in London, meaning his job here is done. He will leave politics and the job of overseeing the Opera House next month. There is no doubt that today his legacy is on the line.

'To me,' Hughes would recount, 'it was an occasion of high expectations and great emotion. If it was a failure almost all of our work would have been in vain.'[35]

At the conclusion of the performance there is a momentary pause, as the orchestra looks to the workers, and the workers to the orchestra, and then it starts. The clapping from the front row sweeps to the back and rolls back again. It is applause for the orchestra certainly, but also for the entire Opera House community that has been involved in this project, that has made this possible, made this happen.

The Opera House, *our* Opera House – it works!

'The concert and tests,' Hughes would exult, 'were a triumph!'[36]

To mark the occasion, he walks on stage and thanks the workers for 'giving life [to a] wonderful dream',[37] before particularly acknowledging the outstanding work of Australian architects Peter Hall, David Littlemore and Lionel Todd. As to mentions of Jørn Utzon, you could count them on the fingers of a closed fist. (A reporter from *The Australian* notes,

'Apparently it slipped Mr Hughes' mind that a fourth architect, a Dane named Jørn Utzon, had something to do with making yesterday's concert possible, too.'[38])

So be it. Heading into the conductor's room, Hughes warmly shakes the hand of Sir Bernard, who, with tears in his eyes, says to the former Minister, with great emotion: 'This is the first time I have heard my orchestra.'[39]

For the most part, the press feels the same.

'This hall compares to Sydney Town Hall as quadraphonic stereo compares to the scratchy old 78,' writes *The Australian* reporter. 'You may think you've heard the SSO before but you'll discover new things you never dreamed of in its aural storehouse. In that marvellous closing climax of the *Bolero*, you could actually differentiate between the pitches of the kettle drums, hear the bass drum as well as feel it, observe the precision of the snare drums as they pounded out their mesmerising rhythm.'[40]

Roger Covell, *Herald* music critic, agrees.

'We may have a first-class concert hall, or something very close to it, on our hands,' he writes. 'I was present at the introductory concerts given in the Royal Festival Hall, London, when that building opened in 1951. On yesterday's evidence I would say without hesitation that the acoustics for orchestral music in the Sydney Opera House concert hall are already – 10 months or so before the official opening – far more satisfying than they were in the Festival Hall in its first phase of actual operation . . . The booming murk familiar to audiences at orchestral concerts in the Town Hall was magically lifted at this happy and momentous occasion.'[41]

There will be other moments of great encouragement, as Peter Hall's team build towards the official opening, due to take place late the following year.

At one point, the greatest violinist in the world, Yehudi Menuhin, comes on a visit to the Opera House with his glamorous wife, the ballerina Diana Gould. Of course the new Minister for Public Works, Leon Punch, and the General Manager of the Opera House, Frank Barnes, are delighted to show them around. As they come into the Concert Hall, Menuhin – a veteran of most of the more famous performance spaces in the world – looks around and says appreciatively, 'This hall I think is perfect.'[42]

Whereupon he takes from its case the violin he always has with him and plays, unaccompanied, the famous prelude from Bach's Partita No.

3 E Major for solo violin. Concluding, he lowers his violin and says: 'I was indeed right, it is superb.'[43]

So superb, as a matter of fact, that he makes a comment that has a surprising resonance with a rhetorical question previously put by Utzon's former professor, Steen Eiler Rasmussen, whereby he had compared Utzon to Stradivarius being asked 'to make the best violin in the world ... according to his design',[44] and therefore having the right to choose his own materials. Utzon had lost that argument. But now, playing in Peter Hall's Concert Hall, Menuhin remarks, 'It's like playing inside a beautiful violin.'[45]

For his part, Peter Hall himself is ... relatively ... satisfied with how the whole thing has turned out, always recognising that what they had done would be judged against what others felt Utzon would have done had he remained.

'Whether it stands up as a complete unified work of architecture,' Hall would say of the final result, 'that I don't know.'[46]

For all the highbrow banter that attends the crescendo of excitement leading up to the official opening, due at the end of 1973, Joe Cahill's original notion that it should be a house of the people continues to be sounded, again and again.

'It's a great place,' one fellow tells *The Australian*. 'When they get the wrestling put on there, I'll be going at least twice a week.'[47]

Sir Asher Joel, who is organising the festivities for the opening day, on behalf of the Sydney Opera House Official Opening Committee, agrees.

'We don't want only stuffed shirts and diamond tiaras,' he says with unbridled enthusiasm. 'If they want to see a strip-tease dance there, or a pop show, or professional wrestling, then they *should* see it.'[48]

For both Hall and Farmer, such pronouncements are a salve for the soul, as so many critics still abound all around, despite their achievement of bringing this extraordinary project to its conclusion.

The true test, of course, will come with the official opening.

•

Personally, Jørn Utzon is a republican, and sees the Sydney Opera House as almost an adornment to that republicanism. To his mind, as he will later recount, the building represents 'a time which is at the end of the colony [of] Australia and at the beginning of republican Australia. The spirit of the building is independent of anything from anywhere, it is one hundred per cent Australian. It could be the best example for what you are going to do, because you are going to do that – be an independent republic, with all respect for the Royals – so I think this fits beautifully together.'[49]

Which is fine.

Many others in Australia take a similar view.

But when it comes to who should open this building, there is little discussion and, besides, the invitation had been sent long ago – January 1972 to be precise, for 'our gracious Queen' is busy. Wonderfully, Her Majesty graciously accepts.

Now, even though all contact between the NSW Government and Utzon had ceased from June 1970, when their legal dispute had been settled with a final $46,000 payment to the Dane for work done, the decision is taken to at least invite him to the opening, for the sake of decency, if nothing else.

Utzon, however, would clearly sooner put hot knitting needles in his ears. 'It has been turned into a horrible mess,' he tells the *Sun-Herald* frankly.[50]

Even now, he is only clearing his throat.

'Why should I be humiliated and attend their ceremonies? Why should I go down there? My concept has been changed and ruined. They have made something which is lousy . . . Famous architects have called and said they are destroying it.'[51]

Hall, Todd and Littlemore are distinctly unimpressed – and hurt. In a conversation with a reporter from the *Herald*, Lionel Todd says he will, 'consult his colleagues on the possibility of protesting to the NSW Chapter of the Royal Australian Institute of Architects'.[52]

But the Institute has other plans . . .

28 March 1973, Circular Quay, a blast from the past is stopped

As the mighty P&O liner *Oriana* leaves the Sydney Passenger Terminal on its way to England, the captain waits until it is just a little more than a stone's throw off Bennelong Point, before, as he has been asked to do, he presses the button to emit the opening salvo of what will be nine 'test-toots'. The first of the shattering blasts, 96 decibels, rattles office windows at Circular Quay. Inside the Concert Hall, where an orchestra is in full flight, Dr Jordan looks at his instruments. Just 50 decibels – the level of an intimate conversation. It disturbs neither the orchestra, nor the audience. From that close, to cut the sound in half is judged a triumph. The nutshell, in a nutshell, works!

Winter 1973, Bennelong Point, the conspicuous absence of Jørn Utzon

The Sydney Opera House Press Officer, Ava Hubble, at least has a clear goal, as the whole building moves towards its grand opening.

'The building's board of directors and the Askin Government,' she would recall, 'were keen to see the media and the public forget the controversies.'[53]

One such controversy is Jørn Utzon's decision to decline the invitation to the opening ceremony.

But many Sydneysiders remember only too well.

'The establishment may have expressed shock and disapproval when Utzon "snubbed the queen" by turning down his invitation to the official opening,' Ava Hubble records, 'but many ordinary people said they would have done the same in the architect's place.'[54]

But the truly amazing thing?

'There was just one photograph of him in our files in the publicity department,' she will recount. 'It had been taken soon after he won the design contest. There he was, blond and handsome, pictured with a model of the Opera House. How happy he looked in that photo – and what a contrast to the "bitter recluse" portrayed in the newspaper stories.'[55]

Well, the House will soon be open and all that will be forgotten. Including the 'bitter recluse', Jørn Utzon.

•

If one didn't know better, this looks like another very calculated snub, this time from the Royal Australian Institute of Architects (RAIA) to the conservative establishment. Just months before the opening of the Sydney Opera House, the RAIA award their annual gold medal to the most accomplished architect on their books to ... wait for it ... *wait for it, I said* ... a Danish man by the name of Jørn Utzon!

Now, just the year before, Ted Farmer had received the gold medal for his work, but make no mistake: the establishment in general, and Davis Hughes in particular, take the award as an insult to Hall, Todd and Littlemore, who had achieved the mammoth task of finishing the Opera House and done so with distinction, especially Hall.

Too bad. With the opening approaching, feelings are warming up, and with so many Australian architects still feeling the acute sting of Utzon's departure at the hands of the barbarian politician, the desecration of what may have been Australia's first architectural masterpiece must be answered ... and the gold medal is their final slap, given they never managed to get Utzon back.

Peter Hall is used to it. Still, it really does sting.

19 October 1973, Sydney, closing credits of the soap opera

All is near readiness for the Opening by Her Majesty tomorrow. To help make for a gala atmosphere, five of the state's grandest buildings on Macquarie Street have been illuminated with 25,000 light bulbs, even while the eastern face of the Esso building on Macquarie Street has been especially lit with horizontal stripes, and all of the major department stores of David Jones, Farmers and Mark Foy's have Opera House–themed window displays. On the northern shore of the harbour, opposite the House, each and every household has been asked to turn on every light they have so the waters will gleam and the newly completed masterpiece will glow. Tomorrow, extra train services will be provided, just as there will be 1600 police on duty for the occasion. And tonight?

The Opera House Opening Ball is tonight, and it is being hosted at Fairwater, the residence of Sir Warwick and Lady Fairfax, and right now the house looks as though it is on fire, lit by *thousands* of individual candles, stretching from their garden lawn down to Seven Shillings Beach.

An extraordinary thousand guests, including Premier Sir Robert Askin and Lady Askin, the First Lady of the Philippines Mrs Imelda Marcos, the former Prime Minister Mr McMahon and Mrs McMahon, the Duke and Duchess of Bedford, and Cristina Ford, wife of motorcar magnate Henry Ford II, are being welcomed by the Sydney Thistle Highland Pipe Band.

Shortly they will dine on 'Taramasalata, spatchcock with chestnut stuffing and white grape sauce with wild rice, Italian salad, New Zealand strawberries and cream', washed down by 'Australian rieslings and clarets and nearly 400 bottles of champagne',[56] before dancing the night away among the family's collection of sculptures by Rodin and Degas.

A rather more mute gathering is taking place at the Sydney Conservatorium, that rarest of concerts: by musicians, for musicians, in protest. Having heard that nothing in the following day's proceedings – not even an acknowledgement, let alone a celebration – will dip the lid to Sir Eugene Goossens, who they regard as the 'father of the building',[57] they are doing it themselves.

2.30 pm, 20 October 1973, Sydney Opera House, the sunlit city's glory

I *told* you – positions, everyone, and get your Leicas and Kodak Instamatic cameras ready!

You know who you are – you, the 300,000 people lining the harbour foreshores within line of sight of our mighty beauty – the ones already getting through the 96,000 meat pies and ten tons of hot dogs brought in for the occasion, and the thousands thronging the harbour in boats bedecked with flags and coloured ribbons. The fire-boats sending massive jets of water skywards might as well be giant champagne bottles, releasing the celebratory fizz over one and all. We've done it!

For yes, the grand day is really upon us, the day of the opening of the Sydney Opera House – what travelogue producer, James A. Fitzpatrick, has called the 'Eighth Wonder of the World'[58] and *Time* magazine has called 'Australia's own Taj Mahal'.[59] One of the many visitors to our shores, Mrs Goodie Oberoi, wife of Biki Oberoi, the globally famous hotelier from India agrees, telling the *Herald* on the day, 'it is absolutely stunning. Not only is it the most beautiful building in Australia, it is the most beautiful of the century. You will be flooded with tourists to see the Opera House, just as they come to India to see the Taj Mahal.'[60]

This is, make no mistake, a *global* event, with over 300 million people watching live or on delay on television sets around the planet.

And we are now getting close to formal proceedings beginning, as Jørn Utzon's grand processional staircase leading up to the Opera House is a heaving mass of Sydneysiders, who cheer all new arrivals including the procession of marching bands and servicemen from Australia and nearby Pacific countries in their colourful 'native dress'.[61] Of course, being Australians, still with the spirit of the irreverent larrikins, some of the greatest cheers go to the arriving toffs who suddenly lose their hats in the wind. Don't look so smart now, doya, mate? All is good humoured though, as all share a sense of privilege just being here, with the only cloud on proceedings being the dark ones overhead that may yet conspire to ruin the elaborate schedule.

The formalities are to be presided over by no less than Her Majesty the Queen, newly installed as the 'Queen of Australia' by the equally newly installed government of Gough Whitlam. She has returned with the Duke of Edinburgh some 10 years after they had been first shown over the building site, trudging around mud-filled holes in the drizzling rain.

But *now* look at it. Where there had been cranes, scaffolding and hundreds of workers, there are now soaring white sails. Where there had been riggers and electricians, there are now guides and officials.

And here she is!

Right on schedule, of course – for punctuality is the courtesy of kings and queens alike, not to mention dukes – the gleaming black Rolls-Royce with the Union Jack fluttering gaily on the bonnet and the symbol of the Crown for a numberplate, sweeps through the roaring crowds, passes by the Australian Armed Services now playing a fanfare of trumpets to greet the visitors, and right up to the forecourt of the Opera House. In a twist so perfect it would make the absent Utzon cry, the clouds part and the sun shines down.

As underlings rush forward to open the doors, Her Majesty Queen Elizabeth II and Philip, the Duke of Edinburgh, alight. After obsequious greetings, mixed with much bowing and curtsying, the Royal pair are ushered to some of the only sheltered seats of the day on a small, covered platform that has been set up for them on the forecourt, while the bulk of the 15,000 invited guests stand on the Opera House steps facing them, clapping their arrival and eventually resuming their seats. Among them, incognito, but stiff and ready, are dozens of plain-clothes security men. There will be *no* reprise of Francis de Groot charging forth with silver sword in hand to precede proceedings with an act of insurrection, as the thought of upstaging Her Majesty is *unthinkable*.

Meanwhile, though there is a place on the official dais for the Premier, there is none for Prime Minister Gough Whitlam and his wife, Margaret, who are in attendance, but as guests only. In the first place, this is an affair of the NSW Government, not the Federal Government. In the second place, Mr Whitlam is on the opposite side of politics, the mob that nearly mucked this whole thing up. And in the third place, Premier Askin is aware that Gough had even dipped his oar into trying to get Utzon back, cabling Askin back and forth as Opposition Leader to see what he could do to help. The Whitlams sit among other dignitaries so important they are marked down not as 'VIPs', but 'VVIPs' and include such people as the First Lady of the Philippines, Mrs Imelda Marcos (who had also been at the ball the night before); the Chief Minister of Papua New Guinea, Mr Somare; the Prime Minister of Fiji, Ratu Sir Kamisese Mara; and the Deputy Prime Minister of New Zealand, Mr Watt. And, of course, the inordinately proud Davis Hughes, back from London for the occasion, and his former Government Architect, the newly retired Ted Farmer, are both here, along with their wives.

Right beside them is Sir Charles Moses, who had long ago established the Sydney Symphony Orchestra and attracted Goossens to Australia, which had started this whole thing. And there's Peter Hall, David Littlemore and Lionel Todd, along with Ove Arup, Jack Zunz, Mick Lewis and Corbet Gore, all barely able to believe the day has finally come.

As the final bars of 'God Save the Queen' are played and everyone retakes their seats, proceedings truly begin, starting with a nod to the ancient and sacred past of this site, *Tubowgule*, and that long-ago corroboree staged for the Governor by Woollarawarre Bennelong, performed amidst a far more humble arrangement of white shells.

Atop the highest shell of the Opera House, while the haunting and wonderful sounds of a didgeridoo come through the speakers, the rhythm laid down by the clapping of two *bilmi*, the cameras close in on a descendant of Bennelong himself, an Indigenous actor and former soldier by the name of Ben Blakeney – whose job it is to play 'the Spirit of Bennelong' – hanging on for dear life.

'It was so windy up there,' he will recall. 'I started off with five feathers on my head and ended up with two.'[62]

But hark. Speak to us, oh Spirit of Bennelong, speak to us!

'I am Bennelong,' Blakeney intones, his voice being carried over the loud-speakers, 'and my spirit and the spirit of my people lives, and their dance and their music, their drama and their laughter also remains.'[63]

This is not just another acting job. This is real, and even if he is likely the only member of his race here, the fact that he *is* here is really something and he feels it.

'Here my people chanted,' he will later recount his feeling, 'their stories of the Dreamtime – of the spirit heroes – and of Earth's creation – and our painted bodies flowed in ceremony.'[64]

He is acutely aware of the significance of the moment.

'I represented a race, a country and a historical building,'[65] he will later say.

And so from this nod to the past to an embrace of the present.

Premier Sir Robert Askin now steps to the dais to welcome the Sovereign in the name of the people of New South Wales, and indeed Australia, and notes the importance of the occasion.

Beyond everything else . . .

'It is fit and proper that we should pay tribute to the many men and women, from other countries as well as our own, whose talents, skills and dedication have brought about the realisation of Jørn Utzon's original and imaginative design.'[66]

After not even having his name mentioned during the ceremony to lay the foundation plaque or the sound test concert for the workers, at least the Dane has a passing reference this time. In Hellebaek, Utzon is just waking, and knows today is the day, but is not watching.

The Premier continues, noting the historical significance of the site, and including the fact that it was on this spot in a small hut that the nascent colony witnessed its first dramatic performance by white men, 'a production of John [sic] Farquhar's *The Recruiting Officer*'.[67]

And now here we are. After all this time, the opening of this masterpiece is no less than 'one of the great architectural adventures of modern times'.[68]

And beyond its designers, engineers and builders, there is one entity in particular that must be thanked.

'This is indeed the people's Opera House. They have built it, they have financed it, and their continued support will ensure that here there will be performances which will bring that artistic and cultural satisfaction which must be a part of truly rounded community life.'[69]

And now to the moment that everyone has been waiting for as, clutching her hat against what is indeed a howling gale, the Sovereign composes herself. Her dress for the occasion has been cleverly chosen: a slim-fitting, pale-powder-blue sleeveless silk frock with weights sewn into the hemline to prevent an unfortunate gust revealing too much, and a silk tie at the waist – the only part of her outfit that moves. One white-gloved hand clutches her speech as she makes her way to the microphone, while the other holds down her hat. As, even now, the wind threatens to blow away her notes, the Duke himself leaps to his feet and so chivalrously offers to help – bringing an appreciative roar from the crowd for the great man – but she is a gracious Queen, and graciously indicates she can rise to the occasion herself.

For what an occasion!

The setting is supremely difficult, but her words are strong.

'The Sydney Opera House has captured the imagination of the world,' she begins.

'I understand that its construction has not been totally without problems.'[70]

There is a small stirring in the front row. Her Majesty understands quite correctly.

Peter Hall, sitting beside his second wife, Penny – who he had married in the chapel of Wesley College three years earlier – could only agree that the project had been not without problems or personal cost.

'I got asked to do something which, on reflection, was close to imposs-ible,' he will note. 'And I'm certainly not sure that if I were offered it again now, I would take it on.'[71]

Seated just to Hall's right, Sir Ove Arup – yes, Ove too has been knighted by the British, back in 1971, for services to engineering – feels the same. Back in 1962, when the engineers were in hot water with the political client over the much-delayed roof, Arup had been asked, 'Would you tackle the job again?' He'd said: 'I'm not so sure. I'll give my answer on the day it's opened – that is, if I live so long.'[72] Well, here he sits, enormously proud that the building is complete, that the final result is a triumph for his firm. And yet, the cost really has been staggering.

'The full realisation of Utzon's departure and the accompanying acri-mony were a devastating blow to him,' Zunz will note of his boss, 'one which I believe stayed with him for the rest of his life.'[73]

For his part, David Littlemore is sure of his overall feelings: 'I have neglected my practice and my home life for the past seven years, but it has been worth every moment.'[74]

As for Harry Ashworth, he is a happy cynic – happy to attend the opening along with, in his words, 'all the knockers, the argumentative politicians and the people who said it could never and should never be built. And if I had my say, I should be watching something large and magnificent, such as the opera *Aida*. That's what Utzon would have wanted.'[75]

Cobden Parkes, one of the original judges who had selected this design, is, nearly two decades later, beyond thrilled with the result.

'Seeing the Opera House on its site today, it is almost trite to talk in terms of money. It is there, a *fait accompli*, and that is what is important. The Opera House is one of the wonders of the world. Time and money and acrimonious bickering are irrelevant.'[76]

It had been worth it.

Harry Seidler, watching on the television at home, doesn't think so.

As fine as the Opera House looks from the outside, 'Davis Hughes and all those who supported him are the culprits in what we have to put up with for the rest of our days. It falls far short of what we had expected from what we had seen of the Utzon design for the interior; his design would have put us on the international map architecturally.'[77]

And all those reasons given for why Utzon couldn't continue? That he was taking too long? That had been over seven years ago! But the cost, you say? Please.

When Utzon left, he had spent $20 million.

'Mr Hughes at the time said it would cost less than $50 million,' says Harry Seidler. 'Yet it has cost double this to complete.'[78]

In fact, over four-fifths of the overall cost has been spent on the Askin government's watch of more than seven years, and in that time, the lottery never abated . . .

But sorry, Your Majesty, you were saying?

'But every great imaginative venture has had to be tempered by the fire of controversy. Controversy of the most extreme kind attended the building of the Pyramids, yet, they stand today – 4000 years later – acknowledged as one of the wonders of the world.

'So, I hope and believe it will be with the Sydney Opera House. And the Opera House will have something the Pyramids never had: it will have life. They were built as tombs, but, *this* building is built to give happiness and refreshment to millions. To express itself fully, the human spirit must sometimes take wings – or sails – and create something which is not just utilitarian and commonplace . . .

'I join with you, Mr Premier, in paying tribute to the many people whose devoted efforts and inspiration over more than a decade has combined to bring this unique conception to fruition, and I congratulate the people of Sydney, and, indeed, of Australia, on this remarkable addition to its cultural and community life.

'I have much pleasure in declaring the Sydney Opera House open.'[79]

A tour of the grand building ensues, climaxing in a rough antipodean equivalent of appearing on the balcony of Buckingham Palace before the roaring crowds. For as Her Majesty appears on the northern balcony, the code-words 'Anchors Aweigh' are uttered by the Opera House Opening impresario, Sir Asher Joel, to an Army communications officer, who relays them to the Maritime Services Board HQ at Circular Quay, who fires off their own signals from there to begin what is nothing less than, 'a land, air and sea exercise, the likes of which Sydney has never seen before'.[80]

Within 30 seconds, nine F-111 jets of the RAAF come in from the sea and fly low across the harbour and Opera House, followed by a squadron of Royal Australian Navy helicopters flying past and going under the Bridge, an odd show of military might to go with this flowering of a cultural leap forward. No fewer than 60,000 multicoloured balloons are released from five off-shore barges, 12,000 streamers are let go from the

Opera House's twin peaks, while hundreds of racing pigeons are released from their cages to be instantly swept away by the wind, and the 2000 vessels on the harbour sound their horns and sirens in a cacophonous riot of colour and sound.

•

After a long and glorious day, things are at last starting to quieten down.

The festive crowds have dissipated around the foreshores, the fireworks have been let off from Cockatoo Island, and Her Majesty the Queen and the Duke of Edinburgh have finished their personal tour. They leave the reception held in the Major Hall to return to Government House, with the cheers of the last of Her Majesty's loyal royal subjects still ringing in their ears.

Thrilled at how the whole thing has gone, the General Manager of the Opera House Trust, Frank Barnes, starts to do the final rounds with his wife, Jenny, making sure everything is secure, and all is in order. Their course takes them through a throng of musicians from the Sydney Symphony Orchestra, who have been enjoying a post-show party of their own, backstage. Knowing a few of them personally, he stops for a chat with one or two when he becomes aware of something as surprising as it is awkward, as it is disappointing. He is being booed. And it is getting stronger.

It's about Eugene Goossens.

All those speeches, all those program notes, all those thanks and acknowledgements, and not a single mention of Sir Eugene Goossens the Third.

For shame.

For *shame*![81]

But the musicians themselves, in this now sacred temple of music, have put it right. Sir Eugene, the phantom of the Opera, has been remembered.

EPILOGUE

A building that changed the image of an entire country.[1]

Frank Gehry, American architect, 2003

It has not aged. The Sydney Opera House will outlive all of us.[2]

David Littlemore on the 10th anniversary of the Opera House opening, 1983

Jørn Utzon's rage over his treatment by the NSW Government does not fade quickly, and he is not the only one to decline to move on.

'Utzon got a shock,' the Chairman of the Sydney Opera House Trust, Sir Philip Baxter, sneers to the BBC's John Amis in 1974, demonstrating the dismissive attitude to the Dane that dominates in the years immediately after the opening. 'He thought he would be begged to stay. Well, he wasn't.'[3]

More shocking still is that, after the triumph of his Opera House design, serious work only ever comes to him in dribs and drabs – the only thing ever drab about any of Utzon's work.

Perhaps his most well-known contribution to architecture after the Opera House is the National Assembly of Kuwait, completed in 1982. However, the critics' pick is his Bagsvaerd church, completed in 1976. Noted architectural author and critic Ada Louise Huxtable describes it as 'a church that remains a masterwork today'.[4] It is indeed unlike any constructed before, filled with glowing light and a ceiling like a rising wave – or is it a bank of clouds? One commentator remarks that while the Opera House is Utzon's extroverted masterpiece – for which he was never able to execute his ideas for the interior – Bagsvaerd is his introverted masterpiece. The latter's exterior is boxy and unremarkable, set on a suburban street, while the interior is what architect Carlos Jimenez describes as 'sublime',[5] designed the way Utzon envisioned down to every last detail – including the furniture and the artwork, just as he was planning for Sydney.

The Turkish architect Oktay Nayman would say of Bagsvaerd Church: 'I think this is one of the finest buildings of twentieth-century architecture. When I first saw it, inside . . . I was blown over. The simple beauty and the dignity and the sort of majesty, and the light filtering through, it was just incredible. Tears came to my eyes, it was so beautiful.'[6]

Nevertheless, despite that and Utzon's many, lauded humane housing projects, the fact that he designs a furniture store in Copenhagen because he needs work is testament that he has come a long way down from such iconic structures as Sydney's pride.

Equally emblematic of this time in his life is that sometimes his musings about his masterpiece lead him to an unexpected place – dreaming of dressing as a woman. Yes, he could, 'wear some lipstick and a wig and go back to Australia as a woman',[7] he is to muse, just so he could see the whole thing up close, without being troubled by the press, without making any fuss whatsoever. Just so he could see it. Be with it, up close.

But the time is never right. Maybe later.

Sigh.

He is no little haunted by what might have been.

'I still wonder,' he is quoted in the *Herald*, 'I still ask myself just what I should have done, perhaps could have done, that I didn't do. Any man would say that when he is kicked out. I questioned myself, what could I have done to prevent this terrible situation, like there is always a way to solve a problem.'[8]

Alas, he can find no answers.

'The Opera House was always there,' his daughter, Lin, will note. 'Throughout Dad's life. There was a time when all the negative things dominated . . . he felt scorned everywhere, that grieved him.'[9]

His rift with Ove Arup never mends.

In 1978, Utzon is in London to receive the Royal Gold Medal for Architecture – the award Ove had won the very year Utzon left the Sydney Opera House.

At the reception afterwards, Jørn and Ove actually shake hands before Jørn says – effectively sitting astride the elephant in the room – 'Well, it's all in the past and forgotten.'[10]

But, as both are devastated by what they had lost – with memories of those long-ago days talking into the night right on the edge of the possible, advancing Total Design – it is too painful for either man to go further.

Years later, a mutual friend, a senior Danish engineer from Arup's, Povl Ahm, decides to try and move heaven and earth – Utzon and Arup, if you will – to bring the two together, and succeeds in getting Arup to accompany him to Hellebaek.

Now, stay in the hotel room, Ove, while I go and see Jørn and tell him you are here.

Alas, alas, Utzon declines to see Arup.

•

Around this time, Ava Hubble, in her role as Sydney Opera House Press Officer, spends three weeks trying to track down Utzon and get him on the phone to interview him for the fifth anniversary of the opening, to publish it in the *Sydney Opera House Monthly Diary*.

As it has become clearer by this time just what a stunning master-piece the building is – hailed around the world and a booming cash cow – antipathy to Utzon is fading and Hubble is even authorised by the Trust to invite him to Sydney for the celebrations, and give a talk.

When she finally gets him on the phone, he politely declines her invitation and affirms that the reason he had not attended the opening was because his presence there with the likes of Davis Hughes, 'would have increased the likelihood of controversial issues overshadowing the celebrations and embarrassing people who had not been involved in those issues. I did what I could to prevent that happening.'[11]

Was he upset, perhaps, that there was no plaque or the like honouring him as the architect responsible for this masterpiece?

Not at all.

'Everyone knows I designed the building,' he replies. 'I don't want a sign set up there to say I did.'[12]

It is a warm chat, and the first real contact between Jørn Utzon and the people running the Opera House in over a decade. Ava Hubble even begins to send him the monthly Opera House publication – it seems right.

Utzon himself is pleased enough that, three years later, Hubble receives a note in the mail.

21 November 1981
Hellebaek

Dear Ava Hubble!
My daughter Lin will come and visit you . . .
    It would be marvellous for her if you would show her the great house inside and out . . .

1000 greetings from Jørn Utzon.
Thanks a lot for keeping me in contact with S.O.H.[13]

Hubble obliges and personally takes Lin on a tour of the building – she is the first Utzon to visit, though at Lin's request it is kept strictly secret from the press. When they walk into the empty Concert Hall, Lin gasps and her jaw gapes as tears begin to roll down her cheeks. 'What has been done inside,' she says between sobs. She cheers up as the day goes on, however, smiling backstage after the evening performance as she is approached and charmed by none other than Richard Bonynge, Australia's most famous conductor.[14]

By the time the 10th anniversary of the House rolls around, things have warmed up further as the first Labor Premier in a couple of decades takes over, in the form of Neville Wran – the man who had represented Utzon against the Askin government as he pursued payment for work done. Wran announces on Channel 9's *Sunday* program a $500 million plan to call back Utzon and redo the Major Hall to host opera, which sees all of Peter Hall, David Littlemore and the then Trust Chairman, David Block, come out against it.

Again Hubble contacts Utzon for his reaction, only to be told by his daughter, Lin, that her father has been besieged by the media seeking his reaction, and is declining to make comment until he is told officially of the Wran plan.

'He thinks it's all political,'[15] Lin tells Hubble.

Which is a fair assessment.

Nothing comes of the Wran announcement in the short term, but the iconic stature of the building is now extraordinary – its silhouette is nothing less than the symbol of Australia.

'Celebrating its tenth anniversary this year,' the *Sydney Morning Herald* intones in an editorial on its front page, 'the Sydney Opera House has insinuated itself totally into Sydney's way of life, has become Australia's biggest tourist attraction and, somewhat remarkably, has already found itself to be the Grand Old Lady of the nation's performing arts venues.'[16]

In October that year, after the celebrations, Ava Hubble heads to Europe to, hopefully, meet Utzon in person – at an address in Majorca, where the Utzons are now living. (They had moved to Majorca a few years earlier, in part because the life is so much like Australia and in part because of ongoing tax liabilities – 'His accountant told him he had to become an expat,' Hubble will explain, 'or he'd have to sell the [Hellebaek] house because he couldn't afford it. So he had to move abroad . . . until they moved back home in 2004. That saved them from going broke.'[17]

Besides, as Jørn always tells people, his desire is to live 'where Lis is'.[18]

Well, Lis thinks Majorca is the best place, and he is happy with that – sunshine, sailing and serenity.

Hubble comes with a letter from the State Librarian, Mr Russell Doust, to pass on to the architect, asking him to lift access restrictions to his papers in the Mitchell Library.

Alas, no sooner has Hubble arrived in Stuttgart than she is handed a cable from Lis asking her to cancel the trip as Jørn has gone sailing. Having already come so far, she decides to ignore Lis. She has nothing to lose by continuing on her march on Majorca – apart from being thought rude and intrusive – and presses on regardless.

A few days later she arrives at Utzon's clifftop home in the pouring rain early on a Sunday morning, and knocks on the door. Lis opens it, surprise on her face.

'Mrs Utzon?' the Australian says sheepishly. 'My name is Ava Hubble.'

'You are persistent, aren't you?' Lin snaps, furious at the intrusion.

But now, here is the man himself, Jørn Utzon, appearing in the doorframe beside his wife.

Hubble breaks down crying, apologising for her unannounced visit, not to mention her dishevelled appearance.

Jørn Utzon is gentility itself.

'I told my children not to send anyone to me,' he says softly. 'I did not realise it meant so much to you.'[19]

Lis Utzon, too, immediately softens, and offers Hubble a hot drink, returning with a light meal of toast, cheese, cakes and tea.

'Every so often,' Jørn tells Hubble as they sit down, 'something blows up about the Opera House. I did not want to see anyone. I cannot spend my life discussing the Opera House with journalists.'[20]

But no, seeing as you ask, there had been no official invitation from Neville Wran to resume his duties, to fulfil his original vision. But let us talk more over lunch.

Utzon drives them to a fine restaurant in the family station wagon where Lis orders for them in Spanish, one of the six languages she speaks.

In passing, Utzon mentions that he simply cannot get through all the correspondence he receives about the Opera House and reluctantly has to throw most of it away.

Looking at her husband, Lis says ruminatively, 'The Opera House won't let you go.'[21]

In the late afternoon, they enjoy the Utzons' home, the remarkable *Can Lis*, a stunning and innovative structure of Jørn's design, set on the clifftop above the Mediterranean, looking as if it had naturally *grown* there – made of local sandstone and open to sky and sea. The sun deck extends to the cliff's edge where, on a fine day, the Utzons 'sun bake naked'.[22]

'The rounded room where they spent their evenings,' Hubble writes, 'admiring the seascape bathed in moonlight, reminded me of an immaculate cave.'[23]

This is precisely Utzon's inspiration – his beloved sandstone cave at Palm Beach.

In a reflective mood, as the sun sets, Utzon covers a lot of ground while Hubble takes notes.

'No other country in the world,' he says, speaking of Australia, 'would have dared to contemplate [building my Opera House].'[24]

As for Davis Hughes, the pain is still there and Lis's eyes narrow as her husband speaks.

'Ministers for public works – they are usually concerned with housing developments, fire stations – and sewers. Davis Hughes wanted to identify himself with an opera house.'[25]

Clearly, Jørn still doesn't quite understand how it had come to that – but not for want of pondering the question at great length.

Before Ava leaves, Utzon signs the form lifting restrictions on his papers at the NSW State Library, adding as an aside, 'You mustn't go back and say I did this for you. I would have done it anyway.'[26]

There is time for one last kindness.

When the taxi arrives only for Hubble to realise she has no local money left, the Utzons arrange to charge it to their account and give her some pesetas as travel money. When Hubble promises to reimburse them via mail, Utzon replies sincerely, 'Buy a meal for one of the poor people in Singapore.'[27]

Finally, he takes down one of the plaster Christmas reindeers Lis has put up for decorations, and gives it to her as a gift.

'Criticism never put one brick on top of another,' he says as his parting words. 'But it has pulled many down.'[28]

These are, she is certain as she is driven away, beyond wonderful people who she has been privileged to spend time with.

•

A decade later, leading Australian journalist Eric Ellis also journeys to Majorca to interview Utzon at *Can Lis*. Here, he finds Utzon 'retired but not tired'[29] as he playfully puts it.

By this time the Dane has apparently mellowed and the ill-will is gone, leaving mostly pride at the enduring glory of his building all these decades on.

'I am not bitter about anything,' Utzon says. 'I have had a marvellous career, more than I could have imagined. I have nothing but sincere love and warmth for a fabulous country and marvellous people.'[30] (His daughter, Lin, would say – 'Dad had another quality that's also a great strength. He didn't hold a grudge. His mother always called him a forgiver. He didn't let the negative gnaw away at him.'[31])

And yet there is a certain regret at what might have been if things had turned out differently.

'Sydney could have been an architectural laboratory,' he tells Ellis, 'there would have been 10 or 15 buildings just as fabulous as this if we had stayed there. Of this I feel sure.'

Why is he talking now to Fairfax's *Good Weekend* magazine, after so many years of declining all requests? Well, Utzon explains – while photographer Jack Picone sets up his camera – it feels like the right time.

In Ellis's view, 'The climate of philistinism in Australia which spurned him "like a common criminal" 26 years ago has changed.'[32]

Despite being an older man, Utzon's playful spirit is intact.

'He grabs Picone's Nikon,' Ellis chronicles, 'and starts snapping him. The frustrated Picone complains it's like shooting "an enthusiastic puppy", to which Lis replies, "Yes, a 74-year-old, nine-year-old boy".'[33]

Most happily, the Dane's sense of wonder over his own creation has not faded.

'This was the most brilliant building any architect could wish to work on. When I see my models and all the sails on the harbour, I simply soar into paradise. It is my idea of perfection.'[34]

Which begs the obvious question.

Surely, Mr Utzon, you must want to see your masterpiece in all its glory, now that it is finished?

'Of course, I would love to go back but I cannot,' he says. 'I have been wanting to go back many times before but if I go back, it will be crazy, I will be torn to pieces. I suffer from high blood pressure. My health would not stand it. I have declined many invitations.'[35]

•

The publication of Ellis's profile in *Good Weekend* helps with the long overdue rapprochement between Utzon and institutional Australia. Not long after the piece is published, the NSW Chapter of the Royal

Australian Institute of Architects offers Utzon the prestigious Sulman Medal, which had been given to all of Walter Bunning, Peter Hall and to the Government Architect, Ted Farmer, twice, while Utzon had been resident in Sydney . . . but no need to get back into that again . . . Bygones be bygones, they also offer 'an apology' for not having come directly to his assistance back in 1966. Both are gratefully accepted by the distant Utzon. 'I am grateful for this award because these are my people,' Utzon writes in his acceptance note. 'The honour is sincerely felt.'[36]

He had already accepted a previous honour by the Hawke government in 1985, the awarding of an Honorary Companion of the Order of Australia, making him Jørn Utzon AC.

Utzon's renaissance with the Sydney Opera House itself, however, really started in 1998, not long after the City of Sydney presents to him the keys to the city, in recognition of his extraordinary contribution to the metropolis that has come so far from being Manchester by the Sea. When the Sydney Opera House Trust request permission to display a bronze bust in his likeness, Utzon asks that instead they display a bronze model of the spherical solution – an exact reproduction of the wooden models he had made in 1961.

•

On one of Lin Utzon's many continuing visits to the city, the newly installed Chair of the Sydney Opera House Trust, Joseph Skrzynski, arranges a meeting where he voices his key concern.

You see, the thing is, Lin, now that some parts of the building are 40 years old, all kinds of maintenance work and refurbishments are being done, but it is all *ad hoc*. What it needs is one architectural mind behind it, and who better than . . . your father?

It is a compelling argument.

'I was eager for him to go back,' Lin will recount, 'because I felt all the positive vibes. But Mum told me he wouldn't be able to bear it.'[37]

Between Lin Utzon and Joseph Skrzynski they work out in subsequent exchanges that the best way to proceed will be for the request to Jørn Utzon to come from a fellow architect, and who better than the award-winning Sydney supremo, Richard Johnson? That year, as was later revealed by Geraldine Brooks for a piece in *The New Yorker*, Johnson had got Skrzynski's attention at a meeting of the Trust by taking a proposed master conservation plan of the Opera House and throwing it on the floor.

'The architect is still alive,' he'd said. 'The most "conservative" thing is to go back and reinforce his ideas.'

Rembrandt is still available!

Puccini can finish Turandot!

Why on earth would we go to anyone else?

Later in the year, visiting Utzon in Majorca for three days, Johnson gently puts the question to the old man on the final day.

'We have no right to ask any more of you,' he says, 'but there are now many experts on the Sydney Opera House, and you are not one of them. But if you write down the design principles, then *you* are the authority.'[38]

To Johnson's amazement, Utzon agrees and it is arranged that his accomplished architect son, Jan, will visit Sydney and act as liaison between Utzon the Elder and the Trust, translating his father's ideas into detailed drawings.

Hallelujah!

When the news breaks, Davis Hughes calls from his retirement home and gives Skrzynski the rounds of the Opera House kitchen, insisting that as Utzon had proved himself incapable of finishing the job the first time, there is no way he should be given another shot at it.

'I did Utzon a favor. I put him out of his misery like you put down a dog.'[39]

Despite that, the changes go through and Utzon indeed begins by contributing his 'Design Principles' of the Opera House in 2002 – the ideas that guided his original design and those that future changes to the Opera House must fit within. When Utzon's document is formally submitted to the NSW Government, cognoscenti of the entire saga are pleased, and surprised, to see a generous comment from Utzon about one who most had thought he regarded as his nemesis: 'Luckily Ove Arup stayed on the job; otherwise it would never have been completed.'[40] He is gracious to the replacement architects, too, writing: 'The Opera House today is of course not my or our building, it is as much a building made by Hall, Todd and Littlemore.'[41]

In tight sum, the principles are a reiteration of what Utzon has always said – draw 'inspiration from nature for organic form' and create 'an architecture that is predominantly experiential in character'[42] – something that people can *feel*; put people first. Oh, and looking to the future, build for *now*. The original brief and the building techniques of the '50s and '60s are long gone; be true to what the building is *now* – 'Our Time style'[43] as he once called his embrace of progressive design and modern technologies, on the edge of the possible.

'Dad made his peace with the Opera House through this reconciliation process,' Lin Utzon will recount. 'He had an extreme personality and he took things on his own shoulders. So he also took on his own shoulders to an extreme degree, that maybe he could have acted differently to realise [the Opera House]. Now he was able to make his peace with it.'[44]

In 2003, Jørn Utzon is awarded the illustrious Pritzker Prize, architecture's highest accolade.

•

Finally, after all the to-ing and fro-ing with Jørn and Jan Utzon over the planned modifications – attended by the now traditional burst of outrage and controversy which always come with Opera House construction – in May 2005 scaffolding starts to appear before certain parts of the building, upon which is placed a sign.

Western Loggia Project
Architect Jørn Utzon

The budget for the renovation is $350 million (equivalent to £30,500,000 in 1957, when Utzon's original budget was set at £3,500,000).

At the age of 87, Utzon is once again involved, fighting the good fight to see his visions become a built reality.

And it feels good.

'I have the building in my head,' he tells the press, 'like a composer has his symphony.'[45]

True, at his age, his input into the redesign is more symbolic than substantial, but just his presence, his inspiration, is thrilling for all involved. Among the renovations is the addition of 45-metre long, 5-metre wide loggia on the building's western side, where large windows are built into the previously closed-off podium wall to allow patrons in the Drama Theatre foyer to have the panoramic vision splendid of the harbour and Harbour Bridge – it transforms the previously dark space on the inside and the unused space on the outside into functional and ambient environments.

A multipurpose room on the eastern side of the podium, looking out over the harbour towards the Botanic Gardens, receives such particular

Utzonian attention, with new timber flooring and panelling, together with a tapestry designed by Jørn himself, it is renamed the 'Utzon Room'.

Utzon is thrilled with the whole thing, but still will not consider coming to see his masterpiece. As noted by Geraldine Brooks in *The New Yorker*, 'Perhaps for the first time in history, an architect is designing spaces he will never see for a building in which he will never set foot.'[46]

•

In his deep twilight years, at the age of 88 in 2006, Utzon wrote the foreword to the book *Building a Masterpiece*, edited by Anne Watson, where he set down some of his thoughts on his master work:

'The Sydney Opera House has been an important part of most of my life, and of the life of my family . . .' he wrote. 'The sensation I felt when it was announced that my scheme had been selected for the first prize was one of elation beyond comparison . . . I would like to take this opportunity to thank Australia for giving me this opportunity. Unfortunately, it was not in my cards to be able to complete this marvellous work.'

But, this was no time for bitterness, and Utzon rose to the occasion.

'My successors, who completed the building, did a tremendous job. They virtually had to start from scratch, learning all the disciplines and absorbing all the complicated information my team and I had spent nine years developing.'[47]

Others would be less forgiving.

•

As for Utzon's architectural legacy, it is hard to pin down.

On one hand, his work is universally admired and has influenced an entire generation of Scandinavian designers, in the manner of Utzon's own hero, Alvar Aalto.

The young Danish architect Bjarke Ingels, one of the most famous of the current generation, says, 'to me, the Sydney Opera [House] is probably the ultimate building . . . It's extremely unique . . . synonymous with an entire continent, Australia. It's actually the most recognisable building in the world.'[48]

On the other hand, Utzon remains an enigma in the profession. His name is not found on any university syllabus. As another young Danish architect, Louis Becker, says of what he learned while studying at Utzon's old university, 'Utzon was introduced at the School of Architecture, but very much as a mystic . . . he was sacrosanct, but also unapproachable.

The lectures where he was mentioned were not dedicated to him, but he was a reference . . .'[49]

Such was Jørn Utzon. A vastly complex original. No fan of boxes and never to be boxed in.

•

Sir Ove Arup never stopped admiring Utzon the architect. It was Utzon the man he was troubled by.

In one of his final interviews on the subject of the Sydney Opera House, Arup said, 'I think that [Jørn] was a very, very great architect . . . I think he is the best architect in some ways or other. But as a person, I'm afraid, you cannot be friends with Utzon . . . he's full count obsessed with his own importance.'[50]

In his later years, the old engineer lived quietly, playing chess, delivering the occasional lecture at universities – most particularly on his new passion, the need for engineering to honour ecology and deal with the many problems of environmental destruction – and dining with friends and family, always with chopsticks in his top pocket to snatch morsels from fellow diners' plates. And of course, he watched with some satisfaction as Arup's continued to grow, well on its way to being the global colossus it is today, with over 16,000 staff in no fewer than 33 countries. His reputation for ingenuity lives on in the philosophy of the firm, all the staff made well aware that they sit on the shoulders of that singular, gentle giant of a man.

On 5 February 1988 Ove Arup died in London, aged 92, having spoken to Utzon just that once, at the Royal Gold Medal for Architecture ceremony, in his last two decades.

•

Sir Jack Zunz was knighted for his services to engineering in 1989. He remained rightly proud of his work on the Opera House – he is the engineers' and builders' pick for the Most Valuable Player of Stage II, his drive ensuring the roof was successfully built at all – though troubled by the breakdown of his relationship with its architect, and he remained convinced the blame for the pain lay mainly with the Dane in Spain.

'Why did Utzon resign,' he wrote rhetorically in the *Arup Journal* Special Edition on the Opera House in 1973, 'did he jump or was he pushed? My guess is that he jumped. His behaviour, his letters, his interviews, all point to a path of self-destruction. He ditched his friends and collaborators for footling or no reasons at all and literally overnight left Australia . . .'[51]

For all that, Zunz said, 'You can't quantify the extent to which the human spirit has been lifted by the Sydney Opera House.'[52]

Though, after his work on the Opera House, Zunz would say life became 'dull',[53] his career continued to flourish as he moved on to other prestigious projects of global fame, including the HSBC headquarters in Hong Kong. In 1977, he was made chairman of Ove Arup and Partners, and then co-chairman of the Arup Partnership, a position he held from 1984 to 1989, the year he retired.

One morning in 2003, Zunz received a call from an unknown number, the voice on the other end sounded like an elderly Danish man.

'Is this Jack Zunz?'

'Yes.'

'This is Jørn Utzon, calling from Majorca, how are you?'[54]

Silence since 1966 and now here is the great man on the blower!

'We spoke for a long time about the project,' Zunz would recount, 'and the work we did and the fun we had together. He had met my family, and my children still remembered him crawling on all fours giving them a ride on his back . . . I believe he wanted to draw a line and bring closure to the unpleasantness which had soured our relationship . . . I was sorry that Ove wasn't alive – his disappointment and anger might have been assuaged, at least partially.'[55]

Jack Zunz shuffled off this mortal coil on 11 December 2018, two weeks before his 95th birthday.

Utzon's softening of attitudes towards those he had worked most closely with on the Opera House and fallen out with had other extra-ordinary parallels . . .

•

Sir Davis Hughes received a knighthood for public service in 1975, which was quite the comeback for one whose entire career had been threatened for lying about his academic qualifications just 15 years earlier. In 1978, Sir Davis retired as Agent-General in London and moved back to Australia, taking up a position as a director with the French bank *Société Générale*. Little was heard from him over the next couple of decades, bar the odd pronouncement one way or the other on Utzon and the Opera House, the former which he decried and the latter of which he remained inordinately proud.

Occasionally he could bring the two together and be almost generous in regards to Utzon, as when he noted in 1993, in an essay written on the 20th anniversary of the building: 'Mr Utzon has been recognised as an artist and a sculptor of great merit. His imaginative proposal has been translated into the most striking building of the century.'[56]

But mostly he was dismissive of Utzon having any merit as an architect, to the point of being vituperative, with various quotes over the years.

'Jørn Utzon's initial concept which caught the attention of the committee made a beautiful contribution to a lovely external shape,' he allowed in his 20th anniversary narrative. 'It was his sole contribution.'[57]

Utzon's 'idea', Hughes told forever more, 'was translated into the reality . . . by Ove Arup and his Engineering Staff'.[58]

As for Utzon's demonstration with the orange back in 1961, which his architects corroborated, Davis Hughes forever dismissed it as a fib, a myth – 'Mr Utzon has made reference to his orange concept as a key to the final design. It is a pleasing thought. I leave it as that.'[59]

On another occasion, he grudgingly conceded to the ABC, 'You could say that he produced the shells, [but] he was a sculptor. He was not an architect.'[60]

Such statements went on for *years*.

'It was a great day when the Utzon designs were accepted for the creation of the Sydney Opera House. Sadly, it was an even greater day when he resigned.'[61]

In the same breath, Hughes maintained, 'neither during that period nor since have I attempted to denigrate Mr Utzon'.[62]

And so it went.

As Premier Bob Carr would later say in parliament: 'To his credit, Sir Davis never resiled from the decisions of those years; his self-defence was courageous and consistent.'[63]

On 16 March 2003, when he was 92, Sir Davis died in his retirement home at Erina on the NSW Central Coast.

'This story doesn't end,' Sir Davis had said to Utzon on the occasion of their meeting four decades earlier, 'before one of us dies.'[64]

True, but there really was an extremely surprising final twist to that story.

The day after her husband's death, Lady Hughes rang David Messent, who was writing *Opera House Act One* at the time, to inform him.

After expressing his deepest condolences, a thought came to Messent.

'I've got Utzon's number,' he gently said to the widow. 'Would you like me to tell him?'

'Yes,' she replied, 'that would be all right.'[65]

Utzon's response 'nearly floored'[66] Messent.

After all, not a word had passed between the two men since the day the Dane had stormed away from the attempted peace deal at the Lane Cove motel.

But now what Utzon most wanted was to express his gratitude that Davis Hughes had pushed through to get the building completed! Realising the historical significance of what Utzon was saying, Messent took copious notes to report the conversation to Lady Hughes in a letter he sent the following day.

'Please believe me,' Utzon told Messent, to pass on to the widow, Joan Hughes. 'I'm very sorry I didn't get to talk to him. Please tell her that I'm very lucky that the building was finished at all. Sydney got that building because of him and his support of Peter Hall and the Hall, Todd and Littlemore architects. He gave them all the best support. I'm sorry I didn't get time to tell him.

'How can a man who has never built anything follow in the same way I was intending? The architecture wasn't the same but you can't repair Beethoven's symphony by asking Mozart to repair the second half. I'm very sorry I had difficulties in meeting him, he was completely sincere in his dealing with me and what he said about the costs and what kind of theatre he could build in Armidale for 25 million pounds.

'Say to [Lady Hughes] she must have my kisses and my comfort for his passing. I'm so grateful the building had his enormous force behind the project and he finished it. It was because of him that the complicated building was finished at all.'[67]

Two days later, upon receiving the letter, Lady Hughes rings Messent to tell him, as he would recount, 'that she and her daughter had both been in tears, and she said Utzon must be a great man to have said what he did'.[68]

Lady Hughes was also deeply touched to receive, a couple of weeks later, a personal note of condolence from Lis Utzon.

•

Sir Robert Askin resigned as New South Wales Premier and retired from politics in January 1975. In June that year he was elevated to Knight Grand Cross for his service as Premier. His time in the role was marked by a significant increase in public works, which some felt came at the expense of Sydney's architectural heritage. This culminated in the union-led 'green ban' movement in the 1970s, which sought to conserve the heritage of the city.

Despite Askin's legacy being marred by allegations of widespread corruption and links to organised crime during his time as Premier, at the time of his death in September 1981 he held claim to being the second longest serving premier of NSW after Henry Parkes (his record has since been overtaken by Neville Wran and Bob Carr). He remains the longest serving leader of the NSW Liberal Party and the state party's first premier.

•

Following the opening of the Opera House, **Peter Hall** struggled to find his niche, to achieve professional and personal satisfaction.

'It was not at all clear what I should do next,' he would recount. 'The Opera House was so enormously complex, that the work [seemed] almost too easy.'[69]

After a brief stint in Canberra as the head of the Department of Housing and Construction, in 1980 he went back into private practice, but – in broad terms – as the 'man who had replaced Utzon', he did not prosper. What reflected glory there was from the Opera House tended, over time, to go to Utzon, while the enduring angst over what was seen as architecture's answer to 'The Dismissal' of Gough Whitlam gravitated to Hall.

'It is impossible to understand how hurtful the disdain of the profession must have been,' the author Philip Drew would comment. 'He was the man who buggered up the Opera House, who deprived us of the vision that Utzon so desperately wanted to give us.'[70]

All the public criticism and retrospective speculation weighed on Peter Hall heavily, a constant cause for self-doubt amidst his rightful pride at having finished the job with distinction. He told the *Herald* in 1986 of one key regret: 'I was knocked out by a performance of *Aida* staged in the concert hall [recently] using clever improvisation. I now wish we had left [the stage machinery] there . . . Unfortunately, it's impracticable to do it now.'[71] Hindsight can be cruel.

In the autumn of 2021, while I was chatting to Peter Hall's youngest daughter, Antigone, she mentioned that she had just come back from a walk down to Kirribilli Point, on the opposite side of Sydney Harbour to the Opera House.

'When others look at the Opera House, they see a masterpiece,' she told me. 'But when I look at it, I see the destruction of my father's life.'[72]

Yes, Peter Hall's career continued after a fashion, and his new architectural firm, Hall Bowe & Webber, in fact won the contract for the new forecourts for the Opera House, for which they won the RAIA's Lloyd Rees award in 1988.[73]

But while the early 1990s delivered Australia a deep recession, Peter Hall went into a deep depression, both economically and psychologically. Work dried up, bills went unpaid, the firm fell apart at much the same time as his second marriage. Antigone would later describe this time as, 'a disaster in the sense that we had debt collectors banging on our door and trying to jump the fence and cut the electricity and water and stuff, we didn't have a phone for about a year or two, 'cause we couldn't pay'.[74]

One night, Peter Hall's youngest son, Henry, told me, they woke to the sound of their roller-door being broken down, as the family car was repossessed.[75]

Finally the house itself was repossessed, the final blow for a man who, though his relationship with his second wife, Penelope, was ruptured, still cared for her and his family.

'He always had beautiful, dark, clear eyes,' Penelope Hall would tell me, 'until the final crushing blow when the bank repossessed the house.'[76]

This man who had shown such promise, who had taken on the poisoned chalice of the Opera House and finished the job, finally ended up bankrupt, living in a small, rented apartment in Cammeray, over the harbour but well over the hill from the Opera House. By now all his famous flamboyance, his panache, his *savoir faire* was long gone, leaving not even an echo on his persona. When his eldest son, Willy, took him out to dinner, Peter Hall became so distraught over how everything had turned out, the younger man had to take him straight home.

'It was like watching a slow death,'[77]Antigone would later say. 'It was like watching someone that just had had enough. I can't imagine how demolished his pride was. To be living the life and to just [finish up with] five-dollar bottles of sherry.'[78]

It was never worse than when, in December 1994, an architectural student, Philip Nobis – who for his architectural thesis for the Sydney University of Technology intensely studied the 5000-odd drawings that Utzon had left behind and were now in the Mitchell Library – put together a magnificent digital approximation of what could have been, had Utzon stayed. His work was put on display in the Opera House Exhibition Hall and served to breathe new life into the Utzonite crowd, reviving the popular myth that Utzon had all the solutions for the interiors; solutions that Hall had struggled and failed to find, and so asked the Minister to change the brief – the ones for which he was said to have 'compromised' his professionalism, his ethics, his reputation, you name it.

Peter Hall said nothing in the public domain, and very little privately as he had few real friends, a handful of professional colleagues and strained familial relations. But Davis Hughes could not contain himself, putting out a four-page press release, describing the video[79] that went with the exhibition as 'a delightful form of self-deception', while its maker must have 'a great future on stage as an illusionist'.[80]

'No matter how spectacular the designs may look to the uninitiated,' he growled, 'they failed to solve the problems they were meant to address, mainly the acoustics and the seating capacity.'[81]

Yet surely, the *Canberra Times* journalist asked Hughes as he attended the exhibition, he has to believe evidence before his own eyes, that some of these designs really look remarkably complete? And magnificent? Is this really the first evidence you've seen of Utzon's ideas?

'I wanted him to produce something, I would have loved him to do it,'[82] the old man shrugged in reply. 'We can't continue to accommodate the mythical part of the Utzon legend at the cost of robbing the real creators of what lies under the roof of their due. Utzon was out of his depth and could never have finished the job.'[83]

None of which assuaged the angst, the aggravations and the many ailments of Peter Hall, as he continued to deteriorate mentally and physically, though still only in his mid-sixties. His son Willy would later be told by a member of the Salvation Army that on occasion they had to retrieve Peter Hall off the street. It was that bad.

His first wife, Libby, would later observe: 'To say it destroyed him is a very strong thing, but yes I think so, and it destroyed his relationship with his children.'[84]

On 19 May 1995, Peter Hall died, with barely a penny to his name, three days after his 64th birthday. His biographer, Anne Watson, would be clear: 'Hall's premature death . . . was, I believe, partly precipitated by the rekindling of old prejudices in the highly partisan, and uninformed, response by the media to the "Unseen Utzon" exhibition at the Opera House in 1994–95. I recall the exhibition well: the beguiling drawings of Utzon's final schemes for the halls, the captivating models, the underlying thesis that Utzon's designs were "ready to go", as one journalist put it.'[85]

'I would like him [my father] to be remembered,' Willy says, 'as just that – a tragic victim of that incredible building.'[86]

Antigone Hall agrees, but more so: 'His heart had enough. It was a lifetime of no recognition for his contribution on what is undeniably the most famous building in Australia. Instead of being applauded and hailed as its saviour he was shunned. My dad copped a lifetime of not being known and I want the world to know that he is the man who took over the Opera House when no-one else had the balls to do it. And he did a bloody great job. But I feel it led to his premature death and broke my heart.'[87]

Ted Farmer, delivering the eulogy at Hall's funeral at Sydney's Northern Suburbs Crematorium, agreed, saying: 'I had to choose a design architect who would replace Utzon. I then asked Peter if he would do this but warned him that the project would always be mixed up with politics. That it could lead to fame for him or the reverse . . . After a great deal of thought he accepted. He succeeded beyond doubt but there is no doubt he sacrificed his career in loyalty to his profession . . .'[88]

At least in the years following his death, Hall's contributions, along with those of Todd and Littlemore, became more publicly acknowledged alongside that of Utzon's. In 2006, the NSW Chapter of the RAIA officially recognised the architectural quality of the Concert Hall and Opera Theatre, assessing Hall's interior designs as 'among the major achievements of Australian architects of the 1960s and 1970s' and considered that they combined with Utzon's 'great vision and magnificent exterior' to form 'one of the world's great working buildings'.[89] In 2015, the opusSOH group was established to promote wider historical awareness and appreciation of the contribution of Peter Hall and others to the completion of the Sydney Opera House.

Vale Peter Hall, a major unsung figure in the completion of that magnificent building.

•

Harry Ashworth, who Sir Charles Moses called as a close second 'unsung hero of the Sydney Opera House',[90] retired as Emeritus Professor of the University of New South Wales in 1972, and according to his obituary 'he had achieved many of his goals for the UNSW'.[91] Thereafter, he rarely spoke publicly of the Sydney Opera House, or his old friend Utzon, with whom he lost contact. In all the Opera House story, it must be said that Ashworth – who despite being a key player from the beginning, and who was unpaid for his troubles – was a dedicated servant to the building and all it represented. He left a vast slew of papers from the project in the Mitchell Library. In his later life he would continue in some professional activities, such as acting as a consultant for the Reserve Bank in Sydney and the Australian Jockey Club in Randwick. He died of lung cancer on 26 November 1991, aged 84.

•

After leaving Sydney, **Mogens Prip-Buus** worked in Denmark before becoming an academic. In 2000, he published his letters and diary from his time in Sydney, following it up in 2011 with his book, *Tiden med Utzon (My Time with Utzon)*. In his own words, 'The text of the book is deliberately not intellectual but is held in the simple manner of speaking we used at the studio, and which I later used with students. There are no theories, no dogma, no final conclusions, only the indications of a working method.'[92]

Prip-Buus remained bitter ever afterwards towards all those who would insist that Utzon and his team of architects just weren't up to finishing the job, though Utzon himself, his lifelong friend who he kept in touch with and visited from time to time, would always counsel calm to his excitable former assistant whenever the subject arose.

•

Yuzo Mikami continued to work at Arup's before returning to Japan in 1968 and, in 1973, set up his own practice: MIDI Architects. In 1984 he was commissioned to design a performance hall in Tokyo which could accommodate symphony concerts, opera and ballet – in other words, a hall much like that originally intended for Sydney. The resulting Orchard Hall, opened in 1989, is a successful example of the convertible hall concept Utzon was developing for Sydney, which Mikami had so admired. 'In Mikami's mind, the world now had the convertible hall envisioned by Utzon: not at Bennelong Point but in the Shibuya district of Tokyo.'[93]

In 2001, Mikami published his account of working with Utzon on the Sydney Opera House, *Utzon's Sphere: Sydney Opera House – How It Was Designed and Built*. He died on 27 August 2020. 'Yuzo passed away peacefully in an aged care home in the Mount Tateshina area of Nagano. His wife of 57 years, Karin, had died in January 2019. Yuzo and Karin are survived by two daughters, a son and eight grandchildren.'[94]

•

After Utzon's resignation, **Bill Wheatland** spent the next few years sorting out the documents and drawings from the project, and securing adequate terms of severance with the help of Utzon's lawyers. 'A settlement was eventually reached, but for Wheatland it was an exhausting and disheartening process.'[95]

In 1976, he became architect for the Albury-Wodonga Development Corporation. He moved with his family to Yackandandah, a small town south of Albury-Wodonga, where he lived for the rest of his life.

'The Opera House years remained with him,' the *Herald* would report, 'sources both of pride and regret. He had unfaltering admiration for Utzon's European approach to both architecture and life. The two men stayed in contact for years.'[96]

Bill Wheatland died in September 2013.

•

Corbet Gore stayed on at Hornibrook until it was taken over in the early 1980s and he decided he'd had enough. Gore got in touch with his old friend **Dr John Nutt**, at that time a director at Arup's Hong Kong office, who gave him work as a construction consultant.

Come 1984, when all of Gore, Nutt, Zunz and another Arup engineer from the Opera House days, Malcolm Nicklin, were in Sydney at the same time, they arranged a golf match. On the eighteenth green, with Nutt and Gore the winners, Zunz was about to hand over the customary golf ball when they offered – 'No, no. Losers pay for an Opera House Lottery ticket' – to be split four ways on the one in a hundred thousand chance they would win the First Prize.

The ticket was bought under the name Job 1112, for nostalgia's sake.

A few weeks later, another early morning phone call from Sydney . . .

Jack?

Yes . . .

John Nutt, here.

Jack, we won!

Won what?

The Sydney Opera House Lottery! Job No. 1112!

The four men could barely believe it, but it is true. From the proceeds all of Gore's children will be able to put down deposits on houses of their own.

John Nutt bought a sailing boat with his winnings, calling it *Come by Chance*, sailing at the Friday night twilight races at the Royal Sydney Yacht Squadron. Of the Opera House, Nutt wrote, 'It was undoubtedly the first computer-designed building of significant scale which could not have been built without the use of computers . . . It is a magnificent tribute to the collaboration of architect and engineer, to art and technology.'[97]

Nutt continued to work at Arup's, where his role and stature only grew, heading the Australasian arm and opening the firm's first North

American office in New York. In 1998, he was made a Member of the Order of Australia for his services to engineering. He continues to live in the northern suburbs of Sydney.

As for Corbet Gore, in 1998, he received an Order of Australia for his 'service to civil engineering, particularly as project director for the construction of the Sydney Opera House'[98]. He died on 29 September 2004, aged 83.

For his epitaph, on his work on the Opera House, let Jack Zunz have the last word: 'For sheer skill, coupled with an ability to manage people and for getting the Opera House shells built, he deserves all the credit.'[99]

•

After 11 years as head of Arup's Sydney office, **Mick Lewis** returned to London in 1974. As a full partner at Arup's, he led major projects which developed the firm's expertise in high-rise buildings, such as the OCBC Centre in Singapore, while also doing such things as running the design team which came up with the alternative route for the Channel Tunnel Rail Link, named the 'Arup Alignment'. For the rest of his life he was dogged by pain from that terrible accident in Tel Aviv on the way to Australia, and died in 2011 at the age of 81.

•

David Littlemore would keep a fairly low profile in his last years, while still heavily involved in the architectural community. In 1979 he was made an Officer of the Order of Australia.[100]

Littlemore died in Longueville on 10 September 1989, aged 79. His son, Stuart, recently told me that, when it came to the Opera House, while his father remained sad about the fate of Jørn Utzon, personally he was glad that he had overcome his personal reluctance to take over another man's vision, and was nothing but satisfied that they had solved the problems and got the job done.

•

At the completion of the Opera House **Lionel Todd** resumed private practice as chair of his own company, while also lecturing at the University of New South Wales and being an examiner for the Board of Architects.

By the 1990s, Todd had mostly retired from architecture. He died on 21 February 1998, six days before his 68th birthday, following a long battle with cancer. He was the last surviving of Hughes' appointed team assigned to finish the Opera House.

•

Ted Farmer retired from his post as Government Architect in December 1973. By that time, he had been honoured with all the highest accolades of Australian architecture, recipient of three Sulman Medals and the Royal Australian Institute of Architect's highest honour, the Gold Medal in 1972.

In an address to his staff shortly before retirement Farmer said, 'I flatter myself that the Branch has achieved an aim that was always before me, and that is to lead the profession both in aesthetic and practical aspects. The public recognition that we have received both in Australia and overseas is proof of this. I think our status was never higher.'[101]

Ted Farmer died in his sleep early on 17 June 2001, aged 91.

•

Ronald Gilling, President of the NSW Chapter of the RAIA from 1964 to 1966, documented an account of his role in the Utzon affair, a record of which was deposited with the State Library. Among his many respected positions, he went on to be National President of the Royal Australian Institute of Architects and was later elected President of the Commonwealth Association of Architects. He died on 27 March 2005, aged 87.

•

Harry Seidler's career continued to prosper in Australia, also achieving all of the highest honours the profession has on offer. In 1976 he received the Gold Medal from the Royal Australian Institute of Architects and a decade later he was awarded the Gold Medal of its British counterpart. Over his career, he won the prestigious Sulman Medal for five different buildings and, among other honours, was made a Companion of the Order of Australia and an Officer of the Order of the British Empire.

When he died in 2006 aged 82, his beloved Penny by his side, no fewer than 180 major buildings in Australia and around the world had his signature in the bottom right-hand corner.

•

In Opposition, **Norm Ryan** continued to serve his community in Marrickville, as well as contributing further through his trusteeship at the Art Gallery of New South Wales. In 1973, he retired from politics after 20 years in parliament. He died at Killarney Vale, on the NSW Central Coast – not far from Sir Davis Hughes' retirement home at Erina – on 25 March 1997, aged 86.

•

The name of **Sir Eugene Goossens** lives on in Sydney, most prominently at the Eugene Goossens Hall at the ABC's Ultimo Centre, which is their key performance and recording theatre. In the Opera House itself, a picture of the famous music man was hung in the conductor's room of the Concert Hall in 1973.

•

Sir Charles Moses, pioneer of live radio cricket commentary, founder of the ABC's six symphony orchestras, and the bridge between Eugene Goossens and Premier Joe Cahill, attended the opening of the ABC's Ultimo premises in early 1988, where his late friend was finally recognised in the form of the Eugene Goossens Hall. This 88-year-old veteran of two world wars appeared gaunt, walking stooped with a stick, but his presence was as upright and commanding as ever. Three weeks later, he died.

•

Following the Goossens scandal in the 1950s, **Rosaleen Norton**'s life began to slowly unravel. Due to the sheer coverage of the salacious happenings inside her Kings Cross flat, tourists interested in the story began searching for Norton, turning her into a local identity, who, from a derelict Darlinghurst squat was able to scratch a living by – illegally, if you can believe it – practising 'witchcraft' through such things as casting hexes and making charms.[102]

Late in November 1979, Roie Norton, aged 62, took a turn from ailments unknown and was rushed to the Roman Catholic Sacred Heart Hospice for the Dying at St Vincent's Hospital. With her last gasps she told a friend, 'I came into this world bravely. I'll go out bravely.'[103]

And so she did.

Though entirely surrounded by crucifixes and nuns, she died worshipping Pan to the end, on 5 December 1979.

•

Bazil and Freda Thorne never recovered from Graeme's murder and actively mourned their son ever afterwards. Bazil died on 5 December 1978, aged just 56, only a fortnight before what would have been Graeme's 27th birthday.[104] Freda lived the rest of her life as quietly as ever, declining all interviews, and died on 30 July 2012, aged 86.

•

Stephen Leslie Bradley was divorced by his wife Magda in 1965. He had a difficult life behind bars, and was detested by his fellow prisoners for his un-Australian crime – kidnapping an actual *kid*. The only two obvious joys he had was being conductor of the Goulburn Gaol band – yes, I know – and playing regular games of singles tennis in the Goulburn Gaol tennis comp. It was while playing the latter that he died of a heart attack, at the age of 42.

In 2015, the then NSW Crown Prosecutor Mark Tedeschi, while writing a book on the whole case, closely studied all of the evidence that had been assembled to convict Stephen Bradley, and came to one strong conclusion: Bradley, as evil a man as he was, had not actually intended to kill Graeme Thorne.

•

In 2012, ABC creative director Sam Doust was looking for some old film in a stock room when he stumbled across something a little odd. It was a 16-millimetre rough cut of a documentary called . . . what is it? . . . *Autopsy on a Dream*.

Completely stripped of sound, it ran 56 minutes and opened with a panning shot across a construction site on Sydney's Bennelong Point. The building under construction? The Sydney Opera House. He watches, absorbed, as a series of famous faces talk about it, and he immediately recognises many of them, including Jørn Utzon, Premier Robert Askin, Harry M. Miller, Harry Seidler and Donald Horne. There's a name at the end, crediting one **John Weiley** as the writer and director. No doubt Mr Weiley has his own copies, but on a whim, Doust googles a contact for him, and sends an email.

'I looked at who was involved,' Doust would recount, 'and saw John Weiley. I googled him and found his email . . . And then on Saturday morning I got this ecstatic, euphoric response. He couldn't believe it. He thought the film had been completely destroyed. He said that "we'd found his lost child".'[105]

The loss of sound proved to be no problem. Bob Ellis, by now a famous writer in his own right, was still around and happily agreed to put the voice down one more time for the road.

The long-lost film was given its second public screening on none other than the ABC – who had once refused it to be made at all – for the Opera House's 40th anniversary in 2013, including a special screening at the Opera House itself. Both Jack Zunz and the family of Ove Arup were told of the forthcoming screening by the BBC, and expressed their desire that it not be broadcast in Britain, but this time, there was no stopping it.

John Weiley had gone on to have his own strong career in documentary-making as a writer and director, before becoming a producer and was particularly pioneering – in a manner to do Utzon proud! – in the world of 3D filming, and was heavily involved setting up the Sydney Imax Theatre at Darling Harbour. He is now retired and living up on the NSW North Coast.

•

The grave of **Bennelong** was discovered in the backyard of a house in the Sydney suburb of Putney in 2011. He is, nevertheless, at least partially memorialised on the point that bears his name, with eight paintings by the distinguished Australian artist Donald Friend telling the story of the great Indigenous figure's life hanging in the General Manager's office at the Opera House – including a scene where he has his hands over his ears while he is 'suffering Handel'[106] during his trip to England.

•

Joe Cahill is mostly forgotten by the people of New South Wales, his name truly only enduring in the Cahill Expressway. For his work on the Opera House, among many other things, he deserves much better. He was an unlikely man to be Goossens' and Utzon's key ally in creating such a cultural masterpiece for the Ages – from opposite sides of the planet, inhabiting completely different worlds – but without him, there would be no Opera House.

Sir Charles Moses told Ava Hubble in an interview in 1986: '[Joe Cahill] was a man of extraordinary vision . . . It was his vision that readily accepted such an unorthodox building, and kept pressing, that if there was any obstacle, anything holding us up, he wanted to see if he could help us in any way. And I would say the unsung hero [of the Sydney Opera House] would be Joe Cahill.'[107]

And Cahill's extraordinary vision became extraordinary reality. 'Surely it is proper in establishing an opera house that it not be a "shandy gaff" place,' he had said in 1954, well before Utzon's submission had won, 'but will be an edifice that will be a credit to the State not only today but for hundreds of years.'[108]

As for his lottery plan, it worked a treat – the Opera House was paid for and profitable long before the Sydney Harbour Bridge was finally paid off in 1988.

Bravo, Mr Cahill. And I, for one, think that at the very least there should be a bust of you, somewhere on site.

Perhaps right by the foundation stone?

•

'The shells in Sydney Harbour have placed Australia on the global map like nothing else,' wrote Professor Bent Flyvbjerg, Danish planning and management academic, in *Harvard Design Magazine* in 2005. 'But given the costs involved – the destruction of the career and oeuvre of an undisputed master of twentieth-century architecture – Sydney provides a lesson in what not to do.'[109]

Even in her generally positive piece in the *New Yorker*, looking at the whole history of the Opera House, Geraldine Brooks did not pull her punches when it came to flaws she perceived in the finished building.

'Costs soared as Hall struggled to find solutions for the interiors,' she noted of the period after Utzon departed. 'The concert hall became a pedestrian, Lincoln Center-style venue, the opera theatre an aesthetic and practical disaster. Instead of the festive climax Utzon had envisioned, its walls are a stark and forbidding black, with tiers of boxes in Brutalist concrete, many of which have limited sight lines.'[110]

It was a view with much support.

'It would be unfair to call Hall's work on the Opera House a failure,' internationally famous art critic Robert Hughes wrote. 'But, in aesthetic terms, the passage from Utzon's exterior to Hall's interior is a wrenching drop from poetry to grandiloquent decor.'[111]

What's more, Sir Leslie's long-ago warning to Harry Ashworth about the acrimony acoustics can cause – 'I think you must be prepared for considerable discussions and argument, and you find that a great many people have fixed ideas . . .'[112] has proved all too true.

Conductor Sir Simon Rattle, the music director of the London Symphony Orchestra, 'complained that the sound in the Concert Hall lacked richness and clarity, and came "from all sides"'.[113]

'Music insiders have been grumbling about the building for years,' wrote Marina Kamenev in an article entitled 'Easy on the eyes, not the ears' for *Time* magazine in 2011, 'Matt Ockenden, an Australian bassoonist, has likened listening to a performance in the Concert Hall to watching it on a 1980s-era television.'[114]

For all the bellyaching, it must be observed that when an already contentious topic like acoustics is placed in the cradle of controversy that is the Sydney Opera House, well ... criticism, complaint and conflict becomes part of the established tradition.

With the notable exception of Sir Davis Hughes, no-one ever doubted Utzon's genius. But sober appraisal in some expert quarters did come to the conclusion that the Dane's managerial and political skills – to oversee such a labour-intensive project in the midst of internecine warfare over budgets and production schedules – were not the equal of his architectural skills.

Anne Watson, a shrewd observer of the saga of the Opera House and changing perceptions of events and its architects, observed in her book on Peter Hall that even 'Philip Drew, a widely published defender of Utzon in the past, has in recent years undergone something of a revision of opinion.'[115]

Drew posited, rather less than positively, in an academic article in 2008 – 'Romanticism Revisited: Jørn Utzon's Sydney Opera House' – that the collision between Utzon's romantic and modernist orientations, 'resulted in a powerful, but ultimately flawed outcome to the extent that Utzon failed to fuse the emotional with the rational dimensions ... This is the great drama we experience at Bennelong Point, which is made all the more poignant by our sympathy with his aims and the unconscious recognition that in some fundamental way, the goal was unattainable.'[116]

Back to Watson – 'Drew concluded that Utzon's reluctance to confront or supply the facts that might have dispelled the mythmaking was a tactic, whether conscious or otherwise, to perpetuate the image of the persecuted genius, and that the Romantic baggage attached to Utzon and the Opera House obstructs attempts to write a factual account of its history, which would be more fascinating than the myth because it is true ...'[117] In all humility – and obviously for you, the reader, to be the judge – that is precisely what my researchers and I have tried to do with this book.

Whatever its enduring flaws, however, the Opera House itself has become no less than the symbol of Sydney, and in many ways Australia. Before it, we were known internationally as 'the nation that rides on the sheep's back'. Our symbols were such things as our fauna, but no more.

Writing in 1973, Robert Naur, the music editor of the Danish newspaper *Politiken*, put his finger on it.

'If you discuss the cost of these things, ask people in the advertising world what they have to pay for a symbol. Well, you've got one and it's more interesting than a kangaroo.'[118]

Now, we have a building that can look the Empire State Building and the Eiffel Tower and even the Pyramids in the eyes without blinking. 'As an icon,' Richard Weston, Professor of Architecture at Cardiff University wrote, 'its profile must be almost as familiar as Muhammad Ali's face or a Coca-Cola bottle.'[119]

Bernard Levin, writing in the London *Times*, wrote a piece emblematic of the impact the building had as an international destination: 'I must tell you, as I told you of the Taj Mahal, that no picture, no description, no effort of the imagination, can prepare the visitor for what he sees when he first sees Sydney Harbour and the billowing sails of the Opera House. The first reaction is exactly the same, word for word, as that prompted by the first glimpse of the Taj Mahal . . .'[120]

Sydney is no longer 'Manchester by the Sea', but a global city of renowned beauty, and the Opera House is no small part of that. Utzon's original vision, to come up with a building that would change a city and indeed a country just as Ragnar Östberg's Stockholm City Hall had done half a century earlier has been more than fulfilled.

In Utzon's words, 'You could actually say, and this is very rare, that the building itself forced the people on it, everybody, to live up to an extraordinary standard . . . The fact that it was in Australia, a new country, a young country with the potential for limitless imagination, made us all absolutely selective and perfect in what we did.'[121] For me, the whole thing has been reminiscent of the first famous line from Oscar Wilde, during his days at Oxford University, after buying two superb vases for the mantlepiece of his room at Magdalen College: 'I find it harder and harder every day to live up to my blue china.'[122]

For having such a stunning theatrical space, Sydney, too, had to live up to it and a proliferation of theatrical and dramatic institutions were established to fill this nursery for the arts with world-class performances. At the time that it was conceived, Sydney's passions were confined principally to sport. And yet, as the years rolled by, so too came into existence such now revered institutions as the Australian Ballet Company, Bangarra Dance Theatre, the Sydney Dance Company and the Sydney Theatre Company, all of them staging regular productions in the iconic building of their birth.

Paul Robeson now merely stands as the first of hundreds of world-class musicians, performers, conductors and global figures who have appeared there, including the maestros Lorin Maazel, Daniel Barenboim, Edo de Waart and Simone Young. The Berlin Philharmonic, the London Symphony Orchestra, and more. Then there is Joan Sutherland, Ludovico Einaudi,

Yuja Wang, Stuart Skelton, Steven Isserlis and Vladimir Ashkenazy; Ella Fitzgerald, Leonard Bernstein, Iggy Pop, Patti Smith and Lizzo; Billy Connolly, Hugh Jackman, Oprah Winfrey, Arnold Schwarzenegger, Nelson Mandela, the Pope and Prince, to name just a few.

Among world-class performers, to have 'played the Sydney Opera House' is up there with having 'played Carnegie Hall . . .' 'played Royal Albert Hall . . .' and 'played Madison Square Garden . . .'

Oh, and the grand tapestry Utzon commissioned from Swiss-French master Le Corbusier way back in 1958 – *Les Dés Sont Jetés* (The Dice Are Cast) – as part of his vision to fill the House with the work of great contemporary artists? After hanging in the Utzons' Hellebaek home for over five decades – Jørn had paid for it, after all – it was purchased in 2015 by a generous group of Sydney Opera House donors, led by the late Peter Weiss AO and facilitated by the NSW Government. The tapestry hangs in the Western Foyer and is what the current Sydney Opera House CEO, Louise Herron AM, calls 'an extraordinary piece of original DNA back [in] the Opera House . . . a daily reminder of the standard of excellence which we must meet in all we do'.[123]

As for Joe Cahill's dream that the Opera House be as much for the hoi polloi as the hoity-toity, and Sir Asher Joel's admonition that if the people wanted to see anything from a pop show to professional wrestling at the Opera House they should be able to – that, too, has at least partially been achieved.

As opposed to some of the aforementioned grand theatres of London, New York et al, at the Sydney Opera House there is no dress code *per se*, tickets sell at a price within reach of most, and the Sydney Opera House regularly holds free events, rock concerts on the steps, charity events like the Winter Sleepout, and such things as 'Opera in the Park'. It's a long story, but back in the late '80s in my Wallaby days, your humble author even appeared on stage in the Concert Hall taking on a tadpole Sumo wrestler. (Australia 1, Japan 0, thanks for asking.)

And, in the grand tradition of operatic-level melodrama on Bennelong Point, it is fitting that in 1995, an opera about the Opera House saga, *The Eighth Wonder*, was premiered by Opera Australia at the Sydney Opera House, in the presence of its Australian composers, Alan John and Dennis Watkins. Eugene Goossens couldn't have made it up!

The Opera House sails themselves have become ever more iconic as the years have passed, not just for how they gleam in the light of the sun and moon, but in recent times often used as *the* banner of the city to express – via images projected on to the sails at night – our identity, our mood, and even our solidarity. They are the centrepiece screens for the Vivid festival of light; on Australia Day we show things Indigenous and iconic; on Anzac Day, images of the Diggers are front and centre; we displayed the red, white and blue of the French flag to show solidarity when they suffered a terrorist attack. And Sydneysiders treasure the Opera House. When, recently, the radio shock-jock Alan Jones led the charge to use the sails to promote a horse race – backed by both Premier Berejiklian and Prime Minister Morrison, the latter of whom described the sails as the 'biggest billboard Sydney has'[124] – so many people turned out to protest the Riot Squad had to be called in, and the government backed down.

(Let me hear you say, RAH!)

As a tourist destination it is without peer in the entire Southern Hemisphere, no less than the best-known modern building in the world, with the World Heritage judging committee describing the Sydney Opera House as 'one of the indisputable masterpieces of human creativity, not only in the 20th century but in the history of humankind'.[125]

The listing allowed it to join other such iconic sites around the world as the Statue of Liberty, the Great Wall of China, Egypt's pyramids and, yes, the Taj Mahal, as being among the world's greatest constructed treasures.

Its cultural and iconic value, on the Opera House's 40th anniversary, was put at $4.6 billion,[126] while adding some $775 million to the Australian economy each year.

•

At least Utzon himself was able to witness much of the Opera House's growth to iconic status. He became the second architect to see his work World Heritage listed in his lifetime, after Oscar Niemeyer in 1987, the architect of the capital of Brazil, Brasilia.

After the turn of the century, Jørn Utzon seemed to rapidly get older and his health started to fail him, even as Lis Utzon also began to ail. In 2004, the couple moved back to Denmark for Lis to have cancer treatment, and though that was successful, not long afterwards a bad fall saw her needing hip surgery, which saw her in hospital for a further three months – leaving Jørn on his own in their Hellebaek home, away from her for an extended period really for the first time in nigh on 65 years. One day, when his daughter, Lin, called to check on him, the first thing he said in response to her asking how he was: 'There's an icicle outside my window. Like that icicle, I'm waiting for the sun to come home and melt me.'[127]

Oh, the poetry.

'That,' Lin says, 'summed up their relationship.'[128]

Of her mother, Lin says – 'She outlived him through sheer iron will. She knew she had to outlive him.'[129]

In the deep twilight of his life, Utzon gave an interview to *The Guardian*, where he was asked if there was no chance he might make a trip to Australia to see his masterpiece.

'No, I will not see it now,' he replied, 'which makes me sad. Every day I wake up and think of the Opera House. It gives me such pleasure that the building means so much to the people of Sydney and Australia – that makes me very happy.'[130]

Finally, in 2008, after 70 years with his Lis, Jørn Utzon died of a heart attack in his sleep at the age of 90.

The giant is gone.

That evening in Australia, on the orders of Premier Nathan Rees, Joe Cahill's successor five ALP Premiers down the track, the lights on the sails of the Opera House are dimmed, even as the flags on the Sydney Harbour Bridge flap listlessly at half-mast.

'There will be a formal memorial service for the architect,' the Premier announced, 'but as is tradition when the NSW Government deals with Utzon, it will be delayed, until next year.'[131]

Until it can be done absolutely *right*.

ENDNOTES

1 Weiley (dir.), *Autopsy on a Dream*, documentary, 1968.
2 *Sydney Opera House: Utzon Design Principles*, 2002, https://www.sydneyoperahouse.com/content/dam/pdfs/Utzon-Design-Principles.pdf, p. 18.
3 Messent, *Opera House Act One*, David Messent Photography, Sydney, 1997, p. 227.

Introduction

1 Utzon interview for TV documentary, 'The Building that Nearly Was', quoted in Messent, *Opera House Act One*, p. 103.
2 *Time* magazine, Vol. 186, No. 5, 2015, p. 11.

Prologue

1 Tench, *A Narrative of the Expedition to Botany Bay*, J. Debrett, London, 1789, p. 38.
2 Chambers, *A Treatise on Civil Architecture*, J. Haberkorn, London, p. iii.
3 Phillip, *The Voyage of Governor Phillip to Botany Bay*, John Stockdale, London, 1789, p. 47.
4 Phillip, *The Voyage of Governor Phillip to Botany Bay*, p. 47.
5 Bradley, *A Voyage to New South Wales: The Journal of Lieutenant William Bradley RN of HMS Sirius, 1786–1792*, Trustees of the Public Library of New South Wales, Sydney, 1969, p. 184.
6 Tench, *A Complete Account of the Settlement at Port Jackson Including An Accurate Description of the Situation of the Colony; of the Natives; and Of Its Natural Productions*, G. Nicol and J. Sewell, London, 1793, p. 34.
7 Tench, *A Complete Account of the Settlement at Port Jackson*, p. 83.
8 Heiss, 'Aboriginal Arts and Culture in Sydney', *Barani: Sydney's Aboriginal History*.
9 Hunter, *An Historical Journal of the Transactions at Port Jackson and Norfolk Island*, John Stockdale, London, 1793, p. 211.
10 Hunter, *An Historical Journal of the Transactions at Port Jackson and Norfolk Island*, p. 211 [reported speech].
11 Hunter, *An Historical Journal of the Transactions at Port Jackson and Norfolk Island*, p. 213.
12 Hunter, *An Historical Journal of the Transactions at Port Jackson and Norfolk Island*, p. 213.
13 Hunter, *An Historical Journal of the Transactions at Port Jackson and Norfolk Island*, p. 213.
14 Hunter, *An Historical Journal of the Transactions at Port Jackson and Norfolk Island*, p. 213 [tense changed].

15 Bradley, *A Voyage to New South Wales*, p. 231 [tense changed].

16 Hunter, *An Historical Journal of the Transactions at Port Jackson and Norfolk Island*, p. 213.

17 Hunter, *An Historical Journal of the Transactions at Port Jackson and Norfolk Island*, p. 213.

18 Hunter, *An Historical Journal of the Transactions at Port Jackson and Norfolk Island*, p. 213.

19 Fullagar, 'Bennelong in Britain', *Aboriginal History*, Vol. 33, 2009, p. 33.

20 Author's note: Although no contemporary source records this moment, the story of Bennelong wincing to hear classical music for the first time in London has remained an artefact of oral history ever since.

21 Messent, *Opera House Act One*, p. 49.

22 Messent, *Opera House Act One*, p. 43.

23 Messent, *Opera House Act One*, p. 51.

24 Messent, *Opera House Act One*, p. 49.

25 Messent, *Opera House Act One*, p. 51.

26 Messent, *Opera House Act One*, p. 57.

27 *The Sydney Morning Herald*, 22 October 1973, p. 10.

28 'Old Fort Macquarie', *Clarence and Richmond Examiner*, 10 August 1901, p. 4.

29 *Clarence and Richmond Examiner*, 10 August 1901, p. 4.

30 *The Sydney Morning Herald*, 22 September 1902, p. 5.

31 Towart, 'The Lily Whites', *Symbols of Solidarity*, Newsletter of the Trade Union Badge Collectors Society, Vol. 2, Issue 3, p. 15.

32 Towart, 'The Lily Whites', p. 15.

33 Towart, 'The Lily Whites', p. 15.

34 *Railway Voices*, a CD of Australian railway workers' stories with songs and poems, seen at: http://railwaystory.com/voices/voices9.htm

35 *The Sun*, 10 August 1917, p. 5.

36 *The Sydney Morning Herald*, 23 October 1959, p. 2.

37 Calter, 'Gateway to Mathematics: Equations of the St Louis Arch', *Nexus Network Journal: Architecture and Mathematics*, October 2006, Vol. 8, No. 2, p. 53.

38 Horne, 'Song for the Bridge', in *Art Deco from the National Collection: The World Turns Modern*, National Gallery of Australia, p. 6.

39 *The Sun*, 4 April 1932, p. 8.

40 *The Sun*, 4 April 1932, p. 8.

41 *The Sun*, 4 April 1932, p. 8.

42 *The Sun*, 4 April 1932, p. 8.

43 *The Sydney Morning Herald*, 19 March 1932, p. 1.

44 *The Sydney Morning Herald*, 19 March 1932, p. 1.

45 *The Sydney Morning Herald*, 24 January 1938, p. 3.

46 Michener, *Return to Paradise*, Random House, New York, 1951, p. 323.

47 Michener, *Return to Paradise*, p. 324.

Chapter 1

1 'Report of the Opera House Committee upon the Means of Financing the Cost of the Building the Proposed Opera house at Bennelong Point, Sydney', signed by Haviland and addressed to Cahill, in 'Working Papers – Sydney Opera House Executive Committee and Trust, 1954–1968', Series 19526, Item 4, State Records NSW, p. 3.

2 Ava Hubble, *The Strange Case of Eugene Goossens and Other Tales from the Opera House*, Collins Publishers Australia, Sydney, 1988, p. 54.

3 Mikami, *Utzon's Sphere: Sydney Opera House – How it was designed and built*, Shokokusha, Tokyo, 2001, p. 29.

4 Lin Utzon interview in documentary *Jørn Utzon: The Man and the Architect*, directed by Hansen and von Lowzow, 2019.

5 Francis, *The Gifted Knight: Sir Robert Garran, First Commonwealth Public Servant, Poet, Scholar and Lawyer*, ANU Press, Canberra, 1983, p. 2.

6 Inglis, *This is the ABC: The Australian Broadcasting Commission, 1932–1983*, Black Inc., 2006, p. 1.

7 *The Sydney Morning Herald*, 2 July 1932, p. 14.

8 Inglis, *This is the ABC*, p. 77.

9 Jørn Utzon in documentary *Jørn Utzon: The Man and the Architect*.

10 Lin Utzon interview in documentary *Jørn Utzon: The Man and the Architect*.

11 Chiu, 'China Receives Utzon', *Architectural Histories*, The Open Access Journal of the EAHN [reported speech].

12 Drew, *Utzon and the Sydney Opera House*, Inspire Press, Annandale, 2000, p. 23.

13 Drew, *The Masterpiece: Jørn Utzon, A Secret Life*, Hardie Grant Books, South Yarra, 2001, p. 18.

14 Drew, *The Masterpiece*, p. 18.

15 Yutang, *My Country and My People*, William Heinemann Ltd, London, 1936, pp. 272–73.

16 Charles Moses interview, Sydney Opera House Oral History Collection, AD 329.

17 Charles Moses interview, Sydney Opera House Oral History Collection.

18 *The ABC Weekly*, 19 January 1946, p. 11.

19 Messent, *Opera House Act One*, p. 66. Author's note: The idea had not taken off at the time, but Fuller had anticipated the coming trend – demand for live performances has only grown in the intervening years. In 1940, the National Theatre Movement of Australia had gone so far as to make a unanimous recommendation that a National Theatre be built on ... Bennelong Point, that conspicuous patch of land that's hosted corroborees since the Dreamtime (although not so much for the past 150 years).

20 *The ABC Weekly*, 19 January 1946, p. 11.

21 *The ABC Weekly*, 19 January 1946, p. 24.

22 Chandler, *Farewell, My Lovely*, Vintage, New York, 1992, p. 93.

23 *The Sydney Morning Herald*, 27 May 1946, p. 5.

24 *The Sydney Morning Herald*, 27 May 1946, p. 5.

25 *The Sydney Morning Herald*, 27 May 1946, p. 5.

26 *The Sydney Morning Herald*, 27 May 1946, p. 5 [reported speech].

27 *The Sydney Morning Herald*, 27 May 1946, p. 5.

28 *The Sunday Times*, 30 June 1946, p. 15.

29 *The Daily Telegraph*, 3 July 1947, p. 7.

30 *The Sydney Morning Herald*, 20 October 1948, p. 5.

31 Messent, *Opera House Act One*, p. 65.

32 Goossens, Belonging: *A Memoir*, ABC Books, Sydney, 2003, p. 24.

33 Goossens, *Belonging*, p. 24.

34 *The New York Times*, 11 October 2010.

35 Drew, *The Masterpiece*, p. 119.

36 Messent, *Opera House Act One*, p. 454 [reported speech].

37 Messent, *Opera House Act One*, p. 454 [reported speech].

38 *The Sydney Morning Herald*, 7 October 1948, p. 4.

39 *The Sydney Morning Herald*, 7 October 1948, p. 4.

40 Messent, *Opera House Act One*, p. 68.

41 Messent, *Opera House Act One*, p. 68.

42 *The Sydney Morning Herald*, 20 October 1948, p. 3.

43 *The Sydney Morning Herald*, 20 October 1948, p. 3.

44 Lin Utzon interview in documentary *Jørn Utzon: The Man and the Architect*.

45 Frampton, 'Jørn Utzon 2003 Laureate Biography', *The Architecture Pritzker Prize*, 2003.

46 Google Arts & Culture, *The Sydney Opera House: The Inspiration Behind the Scenes*.

47 Jan Utzon interview in documentary *Jørn Utzon: The Man and the Architect.*
48 Jan Utzon interview in documentary *Jørn Utzon: The Man and the Architect.*
49 Jan Utzon interview in documentary *Jørn Utzon: The Man and the Architect.*
50 Lin Utzon interview in documentary *Jørn Utzon: The Man and the Architect.*
51 Lin Utzon interview in documentary *Jørn Utzon: The Man and the Architect.*
52 Goossens, *Belonging*, p. 60.
53 Goossens, *Belonging*, p. 60.
54 *The Sun*, 10 June 1951, p. 38.
55 Major, *Joan Sutherland*, Queen Anne Press, London, 1987, p. 20.
56 Major, *Joan Sutherland*, p. 22.
57 Salter, 'The Conservatorium director and the witch', *The Sydney Morning Herald*, 3 July 2015.
58 Drury, *Pan's Daughter: The strange world of Rosaleen Norton*, William Collins, Sydney, 1988, p. 7.
59 Maloney and Grosz, *Australian Encounters*, Black Inc., Victoria, 2010, p. 116.

Chapter 2

1 *The Sydney Morning Herald*, 22 October 1954, p. 2.
2 Weiley (dir.), *Autopsy on a Dream.*
3 NSW Parliamentary Debates, *Hansard*, 19 August 1925, p. 243.
4 NSW Parliamentary Debates, *Hansard*, 19 August 1925, pp. 244–45.
5 NSW Parliamentary Debates, *Hansard*, 19 August 1925, p. 243.
6 Clune and Turner (eds), *The Premiers of New South Wales*, Vol. 2, 1901–2005, The Federation Press, Annandale, 2006, pp. 299–300.
7 Weiley (dir.), *Autopsy on a Dream.*
8 *Guyra Argus*, 28 August 1952, p. 8.
9 *The Armidale Express and New England General Advertiser*, 16 July 1952, p. 4.
10 *National Advocate*, 26 July 1952, p. 3.
11 *The Armidale Express and New England General Advertiser*, 30 July 1952, p. 3.
12 *The Armidale Express and New England General Advertiser*, 25 August 1952, p. 5.
13 Ziegler, *Sydney Builds an Opera House*, Oswald Ziegler Publications, Sydney, 1973, p. xx.
14 Ziegler, *Sydney Builds an Opera House*, p. 7.
15 Messent, *Opera House Act One*, p. 71.
16 Messent, *Opera House Act One*, p. 71.
17 Messent, *Opera House Act One*, p. 71.
18 Hubble, *The Strange Case of Eugene Goossens*, p. 57.
19 Messent, *Opera House Act One*, p. 72.
20 Charles Moses interview, Sydney Opera House Oral History Collection.
21 *The Daily Telegraph*, 28 November 1949, p. 10.
22 Charles Moses interview, Sydney Opera House Oral History Collection.
23 Hubble, *The Strange Case of Eugene Goossens*, p. 57.
24 Charles Moses interview, Sydney Opera House Oral History Collection [reported speech].
25 Charles Moses interview, Sydney Opera House Oral History Collection.
26 Charles Moses interview, Sydney Opera House Oral History Collection.
27 NSW Legislative Assembly, *Hansard, Estimates, 1954–55*, p. 1395.
28 'Report of the Proceedings of a Conference convened by the Premier and held in the Lecture Room, Public Library, Sydney, on 30th November 1954, concerning the question of the establishment of an Opera House in Sydney', in 'Working Papers – Sydney Opera House Executive Committee and Trust, 1954–1968', State Records NSW, Series 19526, Item 1, p. 6.
29 'Report of the Proceedings of a Conference', State Records NSW, p. 6.
30 'Report of the Proceedings of a Conference', State Records NSW, p. 7.
31 'Report of the Proceedings of a Conference', State Records NSW, p. 7.
32 'Report of the Proceedings of a Conference', State Records NSW, p. 7.

33 'Report of the Proceedings of a Conference', State Records NSW, pp. 7–8.

34 'Report of the Proceedings of a Conference', State Records NSW, p. 8.

35 'Report of the Proceedings of a Conference', State Records NSW, p. 9.

36 Messent, *Opera House Act One*, pp. 79–80.

37 Messent, *Opera House Act One*, p. 81.

38 Buttrose, *Words and Music*, Angus & Robertson, Sydney, 1984, p. 151.

39 Messent, *Opera House Act One*, p. 81.

40 *The Sydney Morning Herald*, 1 December 1954, p. 2.

41 Haviland, letter, 2 December 1954, Papers of Henry Ingham Ashworth, National Library of Australia, MS 4500, Correspondence, 1957–1964 (File 1) – Box 1, p. 1.

42 Charles Moses interview, Sydney Opera House Oral History Collection [reported speech].

43 Charles Moses interview, Sydney Opera House Oral History Collection.

44 Salter, *The Sydney Morning Herald*, 3 July 2015.

45 *The Sydney Morning Herald*, 23 October 1959, p. 8.

46 Charles Moses interview, Sydney Opera House Oral History Collection [reported speech].

47 Charles Moses interview, Sydney Opera House Oral History Collection.

48 Charles Moses interview, Sydney Opera House Oral History Collection.

49 Charles Moses interview, Sydney Opera House Oral History Collection.

50 Golding, *They Called Him Old Smoothie: John Joseph Cahill*, Australian Scholarly Publishing, 2009.

51 'Proposed new opera house for Sydney: Report of the Committee of the NSW Chapter of the Royal Australian Institute of Architects', in 'Working Papers – Sydney Opera House Executive Committee and Trust, 1954–1968', State Records NSW, Series 19526, Item 2, p. 3.

52 *The Sydney Morning Herald*, 18 May 1955, p. 2.

53 *The Sydney Morning Herald*, 9 June 1955, p. 2.

54 Salter, *The Sydney Morning Herald*, 3 July 2015.

55 Salter, *The Sydney Morning Herald*, 3 July 2015.

56 *The Sunday Telegraph*, 9 October 1955, p. 4.

57 'Notes of Important Matters Taken from the Minutes', Minutes of the Opera House Executive Committee, in 'Working Papers – Sydney Opera House Executive Committee and Trust, 1954–1968', 26 July 1955, State Records NSW, Series 19526, Item 2.

58 Messent, *Opera House Act One*, p. 87.

59 Messent, *Opera House Act One*, p. 87.

60 Messent, *Opera House Act One*, p. 87.

61 Messent, *Opera House Act One*, p. 85.

62 *The Sydney Morning Herald*, 4 June 1955, p. 2.

63 'Notes of Important Matters Taken from the Minutes', State Records NSW [reported speech].

64 'Notes of Important Matters Taken from the Minutes', State Records NSW [reported speech].

65 'Notes of Important Matters Taken from the Minutes', State Records NSW [reported speech].

66 'Notes of Important Matters Taken from the Minutes', State Records NSW [reported speech].

67 Messent, *Opera House Act One*, p. 462.

68 *The Daily Telegraph*, 4 October 1955, p. 8.

69 *The Daily Telegraph*, 4 October 1955, p. 9.

70 Department of Public Works, 'An International Competition for a National Opera House at Bennelong Point, Sydney, New South Wales, Australia: Conditions and Programme' ('Brown Book'), 1955, State Records NSW, NRS 12702.

71 Department of Public Works, 'Brown Book', p. 24.

72 Department of Public Works, 'Brown Book', p. 24.

73 Department of Public Works, 'Brown Book', p. 5.

74 *The Sydney Morning Herald*, 15 October 1973, p. 49.

75 *The Sydney Morning Herald*, 15 October 1973, p. 49.

76 Shakespeare, William, *Julius Caesar,* Act I, Scene II, Cambridge University Press, Cambridge, 1907, p. 10.

77 Giedion, 'Jörn Utzon and the Third Generation', *Zodiac*, No. 14, 1964.

78 Utzon, *Sydney Opera House: Utzon Design Principles*, p. 7.

Chapter 3

1 Charles Moses interview, Sydney Opera House Oral History Collection.

2 William Shakespeare, Hamlet, H. Holt, New York.

3 Ching, *Architecture: Form, Space and Order*, John Wiley & Sons, New Jersey, 2012, p. 407.

4 Richard Leplastrier interview in documentary, *Jørn Utzon: The Man and the Architect*.

5 Salter, *The Sydney Morning Herald*, 3 July 2015.

6 Salter, *The Sydney Morning Herald*, 3 July 2015.

7 Drury, *Pan's Daughter*, p. 87.

8 Drury, *Pan's Daughter*, p. 87.

9 Drury, *Pan's Daughter*, p. 88.

10 Charles Moses interview, Sydney Opera House Oral History Collection.

11 Charles Moses interview, Sydney Opera House Oral History Collection.

12 Craig, Department of Customs and Excise, Minute Paper, 14 March 1956, National Archives of Australia, NAA: A425, 1956/5842, Series number: A425.

13 Craig, Department of Customs and Excise.

14 Craig, Department of Customs and Excise.

15 Salter, *The Sydney Morning Herald*, 3 July 2015.

16 Salter, *The Sydney Morning Herald*, 3 July 2015.

17 Salter, *The Sydney Morning Herald*, 3 July 2015.

18 *The Sun*, 9 March 1956, p. 1 [reported speech].

19 Salter, *The Sydney Morning Herald*, 3 July 2015.

20 Salter, *The Sydney Morning Herald*, 3 July 2015.

21 'Report of the Police Department of New South Wales (Together with Appendices) For 1956', A. H. Pettifer, Government Printer, Sydney, 1957, pp. 5–6.

22 Salter, *The Sydney Morning Herald*, 3 July 2015.

23 *The Sun*, 9 March 1956, p. 1.

24 Hubble, *The Strange Case of Eugene Goossens*, p. 61.

25 *The Daily Telegraph*, 11 March 1956, p. 5.

26 *The Daily Telegraph*, 13 March 1956, p. 3.

27 *The Daily Telegraph*, 13 March 1956, p. 3.

28 *The Daily Telegraph*, 13 March 1956, p. 1.

29 *The Sydney Morning Herald*, 28 July 2011.

30 *The Sun*, 14 March 1956, p. 1.

31 National Library of Australia, Ashworth Papers, MS 4500, Box 9.

32 *The Daily Telegraph*, 23 March 1956, p. 3.

33 *The Daily Telegraph*, 23 March 1956, p. 3.

34 *The Daily Telegraph*, 23 March 1956, p. 3.

35 *The Daily Telegraph*, 23 March 1956, p. 3.

36 Salter, *The Sydney Morning Herald*, 3 July 2015.

37 Salter, *The Sydney Morning Herald*, 3 July 2015.

38 Messent, *Opera House Act One*, p. 104.

39 Drew, *The Masterpiece*, p. 107.

40 *The Sydney Morning Herald*, 13 May 1966, p. 3.

41 Utzon, *Sydney Opera House: Utzon Design Principles*, p. 9.

42 Dellora, *Utzon and the Sydney Opera House*, Penguin Group, Melbourne, 2013, p. 31 [reported speech].

43 *The Sydney Morning Herald*, 15 October 1973, p. 49.

44 Mikami, *Utzon's Sphere*, p. 29.

45 Utzon, 'The Use of Plateau and Element in Utzon's Works', 1962, from Guide to Utzon website.

46 Dellora, *Utzon and the Sydney Opera House*, p. 31.

47 Utzon, *Sydney Opera House: Utzon Design Principles*, p. 9.

48 *The Sun-Herald*, 13 March 1966, p. 1.

49 *The Sun-Herald*, 13 March 1966, p. 1.

50 *The Sun-Herald*, 13 March 1966, p. 45.

51 Goossens, *Belonging*, p. 139.

52 Goossens, *Belonging*, p. 139.

53 Goossens, *Belonging*, p. 140.

54 Goossens, *Belonging*, p. 140.

55 Goossens, *Belonging*, pp. 140–141.

56 Goossens, *Belonging*, p. 141.

57 *The Sydney Morning Herald*, 2 December 2008.

58 *The Sun-Herald*, 13 March 1966, p. 1.

59 *The Australian*, 27 December 1969, p. xx.

60 *The Sun-Herald*, 13 March 1966, p. 1.

61 *The Sydney Morning Herald*, 16 September 2014.

62 Department of Public Works, 'Brown Book', p. 7.

63 Department of Public Works, 'Brown Book', p. 5.

64 Department of Public Works, 'Brown Book', p. 6.

65 *The Sun-Herald*, 13 March 1966, p. 1.

66 Utzon, Sydney Opera House Competition Entry, 1956, Utzon Archives, Aalborg University & Utzon Center.

67 Messent, *Opera House Act One*, p. 95.

68 Jencks, *Modern Movements in Architecture*, Penguin, Harmondsworth, 1973, p. 197.

69 *The Australian*, 19 October 1973, p. 2.

70 *The Australian*, 19 October 1973, p. 2.

71 Fromont, *Jørn Utzon: The Sydney Opera House*, Electa Gingko, Corte Madera, 1998, p. 27.

72 Messent, *Opera House Act One*, p. 112.

73 Boyd, 'The Sydney Opera House', *Architecture Plus*, August 1973.

74 'Report of the Opera House Committee' in 'Working Papers – Sydney Opera House Executive Committee and Trust, 1954–1968', Series 19526, Item 4, State Records NSW, p. 2.

75 *The Sydney Morning Herald*, 19 January 1957, p. 2.

76 Charles Moses interview, Sydney Opera House Oral History Collection.

77 Parsons, 'Radical v. Conservative Architecture', *Meanjin Quarterly*, Vol. 26, No. 3, 1967, University of Melbourne, p. 342.

Chapter 4

1 van der Rohe, in Press Statement of the Museum of Modern Art, Retrospective Exhibition of the Architecture of Mies van der Rohe, 17 September 1947.

2 Weston, *Utzon: Inspiration, Vision, Architecture*, Edition Bløndal, Hellerup, 2002, p.

3 Hughes, 'Architecture: Australia's Own Taj Mahal', *Time* magazine, 8 October 1973, p. 48.

4 *The Sydney Morning Herald*, 30 January 1957, p. 2.

5 *The Sydney Morning Herald*, 30 January 1957, p. 2.

6 *The Sydney Morning Herald*, 30 January 1957, p. 2 [reported speech].

7 *The Sydney Morning Herald*, 30 January 1957, p. 2.

8 *The Sydney Morning Herald*, 30 January 1957, p. 2.

9 *The Sydney Morning Herald*, 30 January 1957, p. 2.

10 *The Sydney Morning Herald*, 30 January 1957, p. 2.

11 *The Sydney Morning Herald*, 30 January 1957, p. 2.

12 *The Sydney Morning Herald*, 30 January 1957, p. 2.

13 *The Sydney Morning Herald*, 30 January 1957, p. 2.

14 *The Sydney Morning Herald*, 30 January 1957, p. 2.

15 Author's note: Utzon's first name is pronounced 'Yern' in Danish but most Australians never learned to pronounce or spell it properly.

16 *The Sydney Morning Herald*, 9 January 1957, p. 1.

17 *The Daily Telegraph*, 30 January 1957, p. 10.

18 *The Sydney Morning Herald*, 30 January 1957, p. 3.

19 Charles Moses interview, Sydney Opera House Oral History Collection.

20 *The Sydney Morning Herald*, 30 January 1957, p. 3.

21 *The Sydney Morning Herald*, 30 January 1957, p. 3.

22 *The Sydney Morning Herald*, 30 January 1957, p. 3.

23 Drew, *Utzon and the Sydney Opera House*, p. 18.

24 'An International Competition for a National Opera House at Bennelong Point, Sydney, New South Wales, Australia: Assessors' Report', January 1957, in 'Working Papers – Sydney Opera House Executive Committee and Trust, 1954–1968', Series 19526, Item 4, State Records NSW, p. 1.

25 'An International Competition for a National Opera House', State Records NSW, p. 2.

26 Lin Utzon interview in documentary *Jørn Utzon: The Man and the Architect*.

27 Hubble, *The Strange Case of Eugene Goossens*, p. 98.

28 *The Sydney Morning Herald*, 30 January 1957, p. 1.

29 *The Daily Telegraph*, 30 January 1957, p. 1 [reported speech].

30 *The Daily Telegraph*, 30 January 1957, p. 1 [reported speech].

31 *The Daily Telegraph*, 30 January 1957, p. 1.

32 *The Sydney Morning Herald*, 30 January 1957, p. 1.

33 *The Sydney Morning Herald*, 30 January 1957, p. 1.

34 *The Sydney Morning Herald*, 30 January 1957, p. 3.

35 *The Sydney Morning Herald*, 30 January 1957, p. 3.

36 *The Sun*, 30 January 1957, p. 1.

37 *The Sydney Morning Herald*, 30 January 1957, p. 1.

38 Murray, *The Saga of Sydney Opera House: The Dramatic Story of the Design and Construction of the Icon of Modern Australia*, Routledge, Sydney, 2003, p. 7.

39 *The Daily Telegraph*, 4 February 1957, p. 1.

40 *The Sydney Morning Herald*, 30 January 1957, p. 3.

41 *The Sydney Morning Herald*, 30 January 1957, p. 1.

42 Watson (ed.), *Building a Masterpiece: The Sydney Opera House*, Powerhouse Publishing, Sydney, 2006, p. 67.

43 *The Sydney Morning Herald*, 30 January 1957, p. 3.

44 *The Sydney Morning Herald*, 15 October 1973, p. 49.

45 *The Sydney Morning Herald*, 30 January 1957, p. 2.

46 *The Sydney Morning Herald*, 31 January 1957, p. 2.

47 *The Sydney Morning Herald*, 31 January 1957, p. 2.

48 *The Sydney Morning Herald*, 31 January 1957, p. 2.

49 *The Sydney Morning Herald*, 31 January 1957, p. 2.

50 *The Sydney Morning Herald*, 31 January 1957, p. 2.

51 *The Sydney Morning Herald*, 31 January 1957, p. 2

52 Hubble, *The Strange Case of Eugene Goossens*, p. 9.

53 *The Daily Telegraph*, 8 February 1957, p. 2.

54 *The Sydney Morning Herald*, 2 February 1957, p. 2.

55 *The Sydney Morning Herald*, 2 February 1957, p. 2.

56 *The Daily Telegraph*, 2 February 1957, p. 2.

57 *The Daily Telegraph*, 1 February 1957, p. 2.

58 *The Australian*, 13 September 1965, p. 8.

59 *The Daily Telegraph*, 1 February 1957, p. 2.
60 *The Australian Women's Weekly*, 20 February 1957, p. 5.
61 *The Sydney Morning Herald*, 20 October 1991, p. 25.
62 *The Australian Women's Weekly*, 20 February 1957, p. 5.
63 *The Sun*, 26 February 1957, p. 7.
64 Kerr, *Sydney Opera House: a revised plan for the conservation of the Sydney Opera House and its site*, Sydney Opera House Trust, Sydney, 2003, p. 15.
65 Ashworth to Saarinen, letter, 28 February 1957, Ashworth Papers, NLA, MS 4500, Box 1, p. 1.
66 Saarinen to Ashworth, letter, 11 March 1957, Ashworth Papers, NLA, MS 4500, Box 1, p. 1.
67 Gilling, 'Utzon, the Institute and the Sydney Opera House: A Narrative of How the Resignation Affected the Profession and the Part Played by the Royal Australian Institute of Architects', 2002, SLNSW, MLMSS 7405, p. 6.
68 *The Sydney Morning Herald*, 2 February 1957, p. 9.
69 *The Sydney Morning Herald*, 2 February 1957, p. 9.
70 *The Daily Telegraph*, 7 February 1957, p. 9.
71 *The Sydney Morning Herald*, 4 February 1957, p. 2.
72 Jones, *Ove Arup: Masterbuilder of the Twentieth Century*, Yale University Press, New Haven, 2006, p. 1.
73 *The Times* (London), 30 January 1957, p. 5.
74 *The Times* (London), 30 January 1957, p. 5.
75 *The Times* (London), 30 January 1957, p. 5.
76 *The Times* (London), 30 January 1957, p. 5.
77 *The Times* (London), 30 January 1957, p. 5.
78 *The Sydney Morning Herald*, 1 February 1957, p. 2.
79 *The Daily Telegraph*, 2 February 1957, p. 2.
80 *Sydney Truth*, 3 February 1957, p. 1.
81 *The Sunday Telegraph*, 3 February 1957, p. 3.
82 Jones, *Ove Arup*, p. 175.
83 Messent, *Opera House Act One*, p. 103.
84 Messent, *Opera House Act One*, p. 103.
85 Martin to Ashworth, letter, Ashworth Papers, NLA, MS 4500, Box 1, Folder 2, p. 1.
86 Martin to Ashworth, letter, Ashworth Papers, NLA, MS 4500, Box 1, Folder 2, p. 1.
87 Jan Utzon interview in documentary *Jørn Utzon: The Man and the Architect*.
88 *The Sydney Morning Herald*, 2 February 1957, p. 2.
89 *The Sydney Morning Herald*, 2 February 1957, p. 2.
90 *The Sydney Morning Herald*, 2 February 1957, p. 2.
91 *The Sydney Morning Herald*, 2 February 1957, p. 2.
92 *The Daily Telegraph*, 31 January 1957, p. 2.
93 *The Daily Telegraph*, 1 February 1957, p. 2.
94 *The Sydney Morning Herald*, 1 February 1957, p. 2.
95 *The Sydney Morning Herald*, 4 February 1957, p. 2.

Chapter 5

1 Shakespeare, *The Plays of William Shakespeare*, Hurst, Robinson and Company, London, 1826, p. 347.
2 NSW Legislative Assembly, 28 August 1957, *Hansard*, p. 198.
3 *The Sunday Telegraph*, 10 February 1957, p. 3.
4 Letter from Utzon to Opera House Committee, 11 February 1957 in 'Working Papers – Sydney Opera House Executive Committee and Trust, 1954–1968', State Records NSW, Series 19526, Item 4, p. 1.
5 *The Sydney Morning Herald*, 15 February 1957, p. 2.

6 *The Sydney Morning Herald*, 15 February 1957, p. 2.

7 *The Sydney Morning Herald*, 19 February 1957, p. 2.

8 *The Sydney Morning Herald*, 23 February 1957, p. 2.

9 *The Sydney Morning Herald*, 23 February 1957, p. 2.

10 Hubble, *The Strange Case of Eugene Goossens*, p. 106.

11 NSW Legislative Assembly, 6 March 1957, Question without notice, *Hansard*, p. 3829.

12 Drew, *The Masterpiece*, p. 149.

13 *The Sydney Morning Herald*, 23 March 1957, p. 11.

14 Messent, *Opera House Act One*, p. 141.

15 *The Sydney Morning Herald*, 23 March 1957, p. 11.

16 *The Sydney Morning Herald*, 24 April 1957, p. 8.

17 *The Canberra Times*, 2 May 1956. p.5.

18 *The Sun-Herald*, 28 April 1957, p. 2.

19 *The Sydney Morning Herald*, 29 April 1957, p. 1.

20 *The Daily Mirror*, 27 April 1957, p. 1.

21 *The Sydney Morning Herald*, 21 March 1959, p. 2.

22 *The Sydney Morning Herald*, 29 April 1957, p. 2.

23 *The Daily Telegraph*, 29 April 1957, p. 3.

24 *The Sydney Morning Herald*, 29 April 1957, p. 1.

25 *The Daily Telegraph*, 29 April 1957, p. 3.

26 *The Daily Telegraph*, 2 May 1957, p. 3.

27 *The Sydney Morning Herald*, 2 May 1957, p. 3.

28 *The Sydney Morning Herald*, 6 May 1957, p. 5.

29 *The Sydney Morning Herald*, 2 May 1957, p. 3.

30 *The Sydney Morning Herald*, 2 May 1957, p. 3.

31 *The Sydney Morning Herald*, 3 May 1957, p. 3.

32 *The Sydney Morning Herald*, 6 May 1957, p. 5.

33 *The Sydney Morning Herald*, 2 May 1957, p. 2.

34 *The Sydney Morning Herald*, 17 June 1957, p. 1.

35 *The Sydney Morning Herald*, 17 June 1957, p. 1.

36 *The Sydney Morning Herald*, 17 June 1957, p. 1.

37 *The Sydney Morning Herald*, 17 June 1957, p. 1.

38 Messent, *Opera House Act One*, p. 125.

39 Jones, *Ove Arup*, p. 175.

40 Messent, *Opera House Act One*, p. 143.

41 Weiley (dir.), *Autopsy on a Dream*.

42 Messent, *Opera House Act One*, pp. 222–23 [reported speech].

43 Ove Arup interview, 28 September 1987, Sydney Opera House Oral History Collection.

44 Ove Arup interview, 28 September 1987, Sydney Opera House Oral History Collection.

45 Gilling, 'Utzon, the Institute and the Sydney Opera House', p. 83.

46 Ove Arup interview, 28 September 1987, Sydney Opera House Oral History Collection.

47 Baume, *The Sydney Opera House Affair*, Thomas Nelson, Sydney, 1967, p. 100.

48 Messent, *Opera House Act One*, p. 223 [reported speech].

49 Pitt, *The House*, Allen & Unwin, Sydney, 2018, p. 262 [reported speech].

50 Notes made by Haviland of a meeting with Premier Cahill, 2 July 1957, in 'Working Papers – Sydney Opera House Executive Committee and Trust, 1954–1968', State Records NSW, Series 19526, Item 4, p. 2.

51 Notes made by Haviland of a meeting with Premier Cahill, 2 July 1957, p. 2.

52 Notes made by Haviland of a meeting with Premier Cahill, 2 July 1957, p. 2.

53 'Notes of Important Matters Taken from the Minutes', Minutes of the Opera House Executive Committee, 2 July 1957, in 'Working Papers – Sydney Opera House Executive Committee and Trust, 1954–1968', State Records NSW, Series 19526, Item 4, p. 5.

54 Messent, *Opera House Act One*, pp. 79–80.

55 Drew, *The Masterpiece*, p. 259.

56 Martin to Ashworth, letter, 17 July 1957, in 'Working Papers – Sydney Opera House Executive Committee and Trust, 1954–1968', State Records NSW, Series 19526, Item 4, p. 1.

57 Martin to Ashworth, letter, 17 July 1957, p. 2.

58 Martin to Ashworth, letter, 17 July 1957, p. 2.

59 Messent, *Opera House Act One*, pp. 143–44.

60 Author's note: Yes, of course Sweden has a fair share of redheads. But in 1950s Australia, it was thought they were all blond.

61 *The Daily Telegraph*, 30 July 1957, p. 5.

62 *The Daily Telegraph*, 30 July 1957, p. 15.

63 *The Sydney Morning Herald*, 30 July 1957, p. 1.

64 *The Sydney Morning Herald*, 30 July 1957, p. 1.

65 *The Sydney Morning Herald*, 30 July 1957, p. 1.

66 *The Sydney Morning Herald*, 31 July 1957, p. 5.

67 *The Sydney Morning Herald*, 30 July 1957, p. 1.

68 *The Independent* (London), 24 October 1998.

69 *The Daily Telegraph*, 31 July 1957, p. 9.

70 *The Sydney Morning Herald*, 3 August 1957, p. 2.

71 *The Sydney Morning Herald*, 3 August 1957, p. 2.

72 *The Sydney Morning Herald*, 3 August 1957, p. 2.

73 *The Sydney Morning Herald*, 3 August 1957, p. 2.

74 *The Sydney Morning Herald*, 3 August 1957, p. 2.

75 *The Sydney Morning Herald*, 3 August 1957, p. 2.

76 Dellora, *Utzon and the Sydney Opera House*, pp. 15–16 [reported speech].

77 *The Daily Telegraph*, 31 July 1957, p. 9.

78 *The Sydney Morning Herald*, 19 August 1957, p. 6.

79 *The Sydney Morning Herald*, 19 August 1957, p. 6.

80 *The Daily Telegraph*, 5 August 1957, p. 3.

81 Wordsworth, *The Prelude or, Growth of a Poet's Mind; An Autobiographical Poem*, Edward Moxon, London, 1850, p. 299.

82 *The Sydney Morning Herald*, 31 October 1992, p. 166.

83 *The Sydney Morning Herald*, 24 August 1957, p. 10.

84 *The Sydney Morning Herald*, 31 October 1992, p. 166.

85 David Littlemore interview, February 1986, Sydney Opera House Oral History Collection, AD 329.

86 Stuart Littlemore interview with author, 10 December 2020.

87 *The Daily Telegraph*, 8 August 1957, p. 1.

88 *The Daily Telegraph*, 8 August 1957, p. 1.

89 *The Daily Telegraph*, 8 August 1957, p. 1.

90 *The Sydney Morning Herald*, 8 August 1957, p. 1.

91 *The Sydney Morning Herald*, 8 August 1957, p. 1.

92 *The Sydney Morning Herald*, 8 August 1957, p. 1.

93 *The Sydney Morning Herald*, 7 August 1957, p. 1.

94 *The Sydney Morning Herald*, 8 August 1957, p. 1.

95 Lin Utzon interview in documentary *Jørn Utzon: The Man and the Architect*.

96 Lis Utzon to Jørn Utzon, letter, in documentary *Jørn Utzon: The Man and the Architect*.

97 *The Sydney Morning Herald*, *Good Weekend Magazine*, 4 September 2014 [reported speech].

98 Opera House Executive Committee to Jørn Utzon, letter, August 1957, in 'Working Papers – Sydney Opera House Executive Committee and Trust, 1954–1968', State Records NSW, Series 19526, Item 4, p. 2.

99 *The Sydney Morning Herald*, *Good Weekend Magazine*, 4 September 2014.

100 *The Sydney Morning Herald, Good Weekend Magazine*, 4 September 2014 [reported speech].

101 Hubble, *The Strange Case of Eugene Goossens*, p. 110.

102 *The Sydney Morning Herald*, 22 August 1957, p. 4.

103 *The Sydney Morning Herald*, 22 August 1957, p. 4.

104 Drew, *The Masterpiece*, p. 159.

105 Drew, *The Masterpiece*, p. 159.

106 Mikami, *Utzon's Sphere*, p. 34.

Chapter 6

1 State Records NSW, 'Sydney Opera House– The Gold Book, Department of Public Works, NRS 12706/1, p. 3. https://www.records.nsw.gov.au/archives/magazine/galleries/sydney-opera-house-the-gold-book

2 *The Sydney Morning Herald*, 5 May 1959, p. 4.

3 Messent, *Opera House Act One*, p. 160.

4 *The Sydney Morning Herald*, 27 August 1957, p. 4.

5 Messent, *Opera House Act One*, p. 150.

6 NSW Legislative Assembly, 27 August 1957, *Hansard*, p. 149.

7 NSW Legislative Assembly, 26 September 1957, *Hansard*, p. 768.

8 NSW Legislative Assembly, 26 September 1957, *Hansard*, p. 769.

9 Messent, *Opera House Act One*, p. 152.

10 *The Daily Telegraph*, 13 September 1957, p. 2.

11 Messent, *Opera House Act One*.

12 Mikami, *Utzon's Sphere*, p. 35.

13 Drew, *The Masterpiece*, p. 159.

14 Messent, *Opera House Act One*, p. 153.

15 Messent, *Opera House Act One*, p. 153.

16 Drew, *The Masterpiece*, p. 190.

17 Messent, *Opera House Act One*, p. 143.

18 Arup and Jenkins, 'The Evolution and Design of the Concourse at the Sydney Opera House', *Proceedings of the Institution of Civil Engineers*, Vol. 41, Issue 3, 1 October 1968, p. 541 [reported speech].

19 Arup and Ronald, 'The Evolution and Design of the Concourse at the Sydney Opera House', p. 541 [reported speech].

20 Arup and Ronald, 'The Evolution and Design of the Concourse at the Sydney Opera House', p. 541 [reported speech].

21 Arup and Ronald, 'The Evolution and Design of the Concourse at the Sydney Opera House', p. 541 [reported speech].

22 Messent, *Opera House Act One*, p. 142.

23 Jones, *Ove Arup*, p. 184.

24 Jones, *Ove Arup*, p. 185.

25 Jan Utzon interview in documentary *Jørn Utzon: The Man and the Architect*.

26 Prip-Buus, 'Jørn Utzon', 3 March 2017, Drawing Matter website.

27 Mogens Prip-Buus interview in documentary, *Jørn Utzon: The Man and the Architect*.

28 Messent, *Opera House Act One*, p. 159.

29 'Sydney National Opera House – Red Book', 1958, State Records NSW, Department of Public Works, NRS 12707, Image 3.

30 *The Sydney Morning Herald*, 18 March 1963, p. 7 [reported speech].

31 *The Sydney Morning Herald*, 12 June 1958. p. 7.

32 Prip-Buus, 'Jørn Utzon', 3 March 2017.

33 Mikami, *Utzon's Sphere*, p. 34.

34 Mikami, *Utzon's Sphere*, p. 36.

35 Mogens Prip-Buus interview in documentary *Jørn Utzon: The Man and the Architect*.

36   Mikami, *Utzon's Sphere*, p. 36.
37   Mikami, *Utzon's Sphere*, p. 36.
38   Prip-Buus, 'Jørn Utzon', 3 March 2017.
39   Prip-Buus, 'Jørn Utzon', 3 March 2017.
40   Prip-Buus, 'Jørn Utzon', 3 March 2017.
41   Drew, *The Masterpiece*, p. 169.
42   Mikami, *Utzon's Sphere*, p. 41.
43   *Australian Financial Review*, 25 February 2016.
44   *The Sydney Morning Herald*, 6 February 1959, p. 4.
45   Mikami, *Utzon's Sphere*, p. 51.
46   Mikami, *Utzon's Sphere*, p. 52.
47   Mikami, *Utzon's Sphere*, p. 52.
48   *The Sydney Morning Herald*, 3 March 1959, p. 8.
49   Brooks, 'Unfinished Business', *The New Yorker Magazine*, 17 October 2005.
50   *The Sydney Morning Herald*, 3 March 1959, p. 8.
51   Zunz, 'Sydney Revisited', *The Arup Journal*, Vol. 23, No. 1, 1988, p. 5.
52   *The Sydney Morning Herald*, 3 March 1959, p. 1.
53   *The Australian*, 19 October 1973, p. 9.
54   'The Gold Book', State Records of New South Wales, p. 4.
55   Churchill, 'The End of the Beginning', a speech given at The Lord Mayor's Luncheon, Mansion House, 10 November 1942.

Chapter 7

1   *The Sydney Morning Herald*, 22 April 1959, p. 9.
2   *The Sydney Morning Herald*, 22 April 1959, p. 9.
3   *The Sydney Morning Herald*, 22 April 1959, p. 9.
4   *The Daily Telegraph*, 22 April 1959, p. 5.
5   *The Daily Telegraph*, 22 April 1959, p. 5.
6   Drew, *The Masterpiece*, p. 306.
7   *The Daily Telegraph*, 18 July 1959, p. 1.
8   *The Sydney Morning Herald*, 18 July 1959, p. 1.
9   *The Australian*, 19 October 1973, p. 2.
10   *The Sydney Morning Herald*, 31 October 1992, p. 166.
11   Paterson, *The Works of 'Banjo' Paterson*, Wordsworth Editions, London, 1995, p. 26.
12   Ian Mackenzie interview, Sydney Opera House Oral History Collection.
13   Mikami, *Utzon's Sphere*, p. 119.
14   Mikami, *Utzon's Sphere*, p. 119.
15   Pitt, *The House*, p. 160.
16   Willy Hall interview with author, 13 July 2021.
17   Pitt, *The House*, p. 161.
18   *The Sydney Morning Herald*, 22 October 1959, p. 1.
19   *The Sydney Morning Herald*, 22 October 1959, p. 1.
20   Pitt, *The House*, p. 162.
21   *The Daily Telegraph*, 23 October 1959, p. 1.
22   *The Daily Telegraph*, 23 October 1959, p. 1.
23   *The Sydney Morning Herald*, 23 October 1959, p. 8.
24   *The Sydney Morning Herald*, 23 October 1959, p. 8.
25   *The Sydney Morning Herald*, 23 October 1959, p. 8.
26   *The Daily Telegraph*, 24 October 1959, p. 3.
27   Hubble, *The Strange Case of Eugene Goossens*, p. 88.
28   Mikami, *Utzon's Sphere*, p. 57.
29   Mikami, *Utzon's Sphere*, p. 57.
30   *The Sydney Morning Herald*, 4 September 1959, p. 2.

31 *The Sydney Morning Herald*, 4 September 1959, p. 2.
32 Mikami, *Utzon's Sphere*, p. 121.
33 *The Sydney Morning* Herald, 23 March 1960, p. 4.
34 *The Sydney Morning Herald*, 23 March 1960, p. 4.
35 *The Sydney Morning Herald*, 3 March 1959, p. 8.
36 *The Sydney Morning Herald*, 23 March 1960, p. 4.
37 *The Sydney Morning Herald*, 23 March 1960, p. 4.
38 Thomson, Secretary and Executive Officer, Sydney Opera House Executive Committee Report, 'Sydney Opera House Executive Committee's reply to Criticism of the Opera House Project, 14 September 1962 –14 October 1962', NSW State Records, Series 12712, 4/8067, p. 9.
39 Ryan, Minister of Public Works to Cabinet, re: Contract for Stage Machinery, 10 January 1961, in 'Copies of Cabinet Minutes, Sydney Opera House 1961–1967', NSW State Records, Series 12692, 4/8037, p. 1.
40 Murray, *The Saga of Sydney Opera House*, p. 50.
41 Murray, *The Saga of Sydney Opera House*, p. 50.
42 *The Daily Telegraph*, 2 June 1960, p. 7.
43 *The Sydney Morning Herald*, 2 June 1960, p. 5.
44 *The Sydney Morning Herald*, 2 June 1960, p. 5.
45 *Australian Police Journal*, July 1962, Vol. 16, No. 3, p. 182 [reported speech].
46 *Australian Police Journal*, July 1962, Vol. 16, No. 3, p. 182.
47 *Australian Police Journal*, July 1962, Vol. 16, No. 3, p. 182.

Chapter 8

1   Zunz, 'Sydney Revisited', p. 5.
2   *The Sydney Morning Herald*, 24 March 1961, p. 10 [reported speech].
3   *The Sydney Morning Herald*, 24 March 1961, p. 10 [reported speech].
4   *The Sydney Morning Herald*, 20 October 1960, p. 12 [reported speech].
5   *The Sydney Morning Herald*, 17 August 1960, p. 4 [reported speech].
6   *The Sydney Morning Herald*, 20 October 1960, p. 12.
7   *The Sydney Morning Herald*, 17 August 1960, p. 4 [reported speech].
8   Author's note: Though the chloroform was never proven, that is the conclusion of the former Chief Prosecutor of the NSW Department of Public Prosecution, Mark Tedeschi, who has written the definitive book on it.
9   *The Sydney Morning Herald*, 8 July 1960, p. 1 [reported speech].
10 *The Daily Telegraph*, 8 July 1960, p. 2.
11 Tedeschi, *Kidnapped: The Crime that Shocked the Nation*, Simon and Schuster, NSW, 2015.
12 *The Daily Telegraph*, 8 July 1960, p. 2.
13 *The Sydney Morning Herald*, 22 March 1961, p. 6.
14 *The Sydney Morning Herald*, 22 March 1961, p. 6 [reported speech].
15 *The Daily Telegraph*, 8 July 1960, p. 1.
16 *The Sydney Morning Herald*, 25 September 1960, p. 3.
17 *The Daily Telegraph*, 9 July 1960, p. 2.
18 *The Daily Telegraph*, 9 July 1960, p. 1.
19 *The Daily Telegraph*, 9 July 1960, p. 1.
20 *The Daily Telegraph*, 9 July 1960, p. 1.
21 Hubble, *The Strange Case of Eugene Goossens*, p. 9.
22 *The Daily Telegraph*, 7 February 1957, p. 9.
23 *The Sydney Morning Herald*, 18 August 1960, p. 5.
24 *The Sydney Morning Herald*, 17 August 1960, p. 1.
25 *The Sydney Morning Herald*, 17 August 1960, p. 1.
26 Mikami, *Utzon's Sphere*, p. 122.
27 Mikami, *Utzon's Sphere*, p. 122.

28 Mikami, *Utzon's Sphere*, p. 122.
29 Mikami, *Utzon's Sphere*, pp. 122–23.
30 Mikami, *Utzon's Sphere*, p. 123.
31 Luck, Salter and Noad, *This Fabulous Century*, Lansdowne Press, Sydney, 1980, pp. 265–68.
32 *Australian Police Journal*, Vol. 16, No. 3, pp. 181–237.
33 Carter, 'The Sydney Opera House: What Went Wrong?', Royal Institute of British Architects, February 1967, p. 57.
34 Carter, 'The Sydney Opera House: What Went Wrong?', p. 57.
35 Carter, 'The Sydney Opera House: What Went Wrong?', p. 57 [tense changed].
36 Carter, 'The Sydney Opera House: What Went Wrong?', p. 57.
37 Tedeschi, *Kidnapped*, p. 119.
38 *The Sydney Morning Herald*, 1 April 1961, p. 5.
39 Messent, *Opera House Act One*, p. 103.
40 Jan Utzon interview in documentary *Jørn Utzon: The Man and the Architect*.
41 Messent, *Opera House Act One*, pp. 188–89.
42 *The Sydney Morning Herald*, 4 October 1960, p. 14.
43 Tedeschi. *Kidnapped*, p. 145.
44 *The Daily Telegraph*, 10 November 1960, p. 15.
45 'Ol' Man River', music: Jerome Kern; lyrics: Oscar Hammerstein II, 1927.
46 *The Daily Telegraph*, 10 November 1960, p. 15 [reported speech].
47 Keating, 'Building a Masterpiece: The Sydney Opera House', 10 August 2006.
48 Peters-Little, Curthoys and Docker (eds), *Passionate Histories: Myth, Memory and Indigenous Australia*, ANU Press, Canberra, p. 171.
49 *The Sydney Morning Herald*, 19 November 1960, p. 1.
50 Mark Tedeschi, personal papers.
51 *The Sydney Morning Herald*, 14 December 1960, p. 9.

Chapter 9

1   Drew, *The Masterpiece*, p. 10.
2   Baume, *The Sydney Opera House Affair*, pp. 121–22.
3   *The Australian*, 18 September 1965, p. 9.
4   Messent, *Opera House Act One*, p. 189.
5   Messent, *Opera House Act One*, p. 189.
6   Messent, *Opera House Act One*, p. 189 [reported speech].
7   Messent, *Opera House Act One*, p. 189.
8   Messent, *Opera House Act One*, p. 189.
9   Jenkins to Utzon, letter, 27 January 1961, Ashworth Papers, NLA, MS 4500, Box 1 Folder 2, p. 2.
10 Messent, *Opera House Act One*, p. 228.
11 *The New York Times*, 19 February 1961, p. 9.
12 Baume, *The Sydney Opera House Affair*, pp. 118–19.
13 *The Sydney Morning Herald*, 13 March 1966, p. 68.
14 *The Sydney Morning Herald*, 30 March 1961, p. 1.
15 *The Sydney Morning Herald*, 30 March 1961, p. 1.
16 Messent, *Opera House Act One*, p. 192.
17 Messent, *Opera House Act One*, p. 193.
18 Messent, *Opera House Act One*, p. 193.
19 Peter Jones, *Ove Arup: Masterbuilder of the Twentieth Century*, Yale University Press, New Haven, 2006, no page number.
20 Mogens Prip-Buus video interview, 'Jørn Utzon's Sydney Opera House', Drawing Matter.
21 Jones, *Ove Arup*, p. 185.
22 Messent, *Opera House Act One*, p. 142.

23 Mikami, *Utzon's Sphere*, p. 35.
24 Arup and Zunz, 'Sydney Opera House', *The Arup Journal*, October 1973, Issue 3, p. 10.
25 Messent, *Opera House Act One*, p. 242.
26 Arup and Zunz, 'Sydney Opera House', p. 10.
27 Prip-Buus, 'Jørn Utzon', 3 March 2017.
28 Mikami, *Utzon's Sphere*, p. 62.
29 Messent, *Opera House Act One*, p. 208.
30 Rice, 'A Celebration of the Life and Work of Ove Arup', *RSA Journal*, Vol. 137, No. 5395, June 1989, p. 426.
31 Messent, *Opera House Act One*, p. 244.
32 Messent, *Opera House Act One*, p. 244.
33 Messent, *Opera House Act One*, p. 244.
34 Shakespeare, *Hamlet*, H. Holt, New York, 1914, p. 15.
35 Brooks, 'Unfinished Business', *The New Yorker Magazine*.
36 Mikami, *Utzon's Sphere*, p. 65.
37 *Shakespeare, Hamlet*, p. 23.
38 Mikami, *Utzon's Sphere*, p. 65.
39 Mogens Prip-Buus interview, Drawing Matter.
40 Mikami, *Utzon's Sphere*, p. 65.
41 *The Australian*, 19 October 1973, p. 3.
42 *The Australian*, 19 October 1973, p. 3 [reported speech].
43 Messent, *Opera House Act One*, p. 243.
44 Mogens Prip-Buus interview, Drawing Matter.
45 Zunz, *An Engineer's Tale*, self-published, 2018, p. 101.
46 Utzon to Ashworth, letter, 29 September 1961, Ashworth Papers, NLA, MS 4500, Box 1, Folder 2, p. 2.
47 Mikami, *Utzon's Sphere*, p. 67.
48 Mikami, *Utzon's Sphere*, p. 67.
49 Arup to Ashworth, letter, 30 October 1961, Ashworth Papers, NLA, MS 4500, Box 1, Folder 2, p. 1.
50 Arup to Ashworth, letter, 30 October 1961, Ashworth Papers, NLA, MS 4500, Box 1, Folder 2, p. 1.
51 Arup to Ashworth, letter, 30 October 1961, Ashworth Papers, NLA, MS 4500, Box 1, Folder 2, pp. 2–3.
52 Arup to Ashworth, letter, 30 October 1961, Ashworth Papers, NLA, MS 4500, Box 1, Folder 2, pp. 3–4.
53 *The Sydney Morning Herald*, 1 July 1964, p. 2.

Chapter 10

1 *The Daily Telegraph*, 30 January 1957, p. 1.
2 *The Sydney Morning Herald*, 4 November 1962, p. 72.
3 Messent, *Opera House Act One*, p. 252.
4 Messent, *Opera House Act One*, p. 252.
5 Messent, *Opera House Act One*, p. 252.
6 Messent, *Opera House Act One*, p. 206.
7 Botros, 'Jack Zunz's Opera House', *Quadrant Online*, 6 July 2019.
8 *The Sun-Herald*, 13 March 1966, p. 67. Author's note: This is Utzon's explanation of the roof design as told to Professor Rasmussen in 1966, *I surmise he got used to giving a spiel when explaining the solution to people over the years.*
9 Messent, *Opera House Act One*, p. 22.
10 Messent, *Opera House Act One*, p. 257.
11 Messent, *Opera House Act One*, p. 104.
12 Messent, *Opera House Act One*, p. 104.

13 *The Sydney Morning Herald*, 1 May 1962, p. 7 [reported speech].
14 *The Sydney Morning Herald*, 1 May 1962, p. 7 [reported speech].
15 *The Daily Telegraph*, 7 May 1962, p. 15.
16 *The Sydney Morning Herald*, 1 May 1962, p. 7.
17 Drew, *The Masterpiece*, p. 203.
18 *The Sydney Morning Herald*, 29 May 1962, p. 4.
19 *The Sydney Morning Herald*, 1 June 1962, p. 1.
20 *The Sydney Morning Herald*, 1 June 1962, p. 1.
21 *The Sydney Morning Herald*, 6 June 1962, p. 1.
22 *The Sydney Morning Herald*, 1 June 1962, p. 1.
23 *The Sydney Morning Herald*, 5 June 1962, p. 2.
24 *The New York Times*, 11 October 2010.
25 *The Sydney Morning Herald, Good Weekend Magazine*, 3 July 1999.
26 Salter, 'Goossens, Sir Eugene Aynsley (1893–1962)', *Australian Dictionary of Biography*, National Centre of Biography, Australian National University, published first in hardcopy 1996, accessed online 13 November 2020.
27 Messent, *Opera House Act One*, p. 278.
28 *The Daily Telegraph*, 4 August 1962, p. 3.
29 *The Sydney Morning Herald*, 4 August 1962, p. 1.
30 *The Daily Telegraph*, 4 August 1962, p. 3.
31 *The Sydney Morning Herald*, 4 August 1962, p. 1.
32 *The Sydney Morning Herald*, 4 August 1962, p. 1.
33 Messent, *Opera House Act One*, p. 272.
34 Shakespeare, *Hamlet*, p. 67.
35 Jack Zunz interview, Sydney Opera House Oral History Collection.
36 Jack Zunz interview, Sydney Opera House Oral History Collection.
37 Jack Zunz interview, Sydney Opera House Oral History Collection.
38 *The Sydney Morning Herald*, 18 August 1962, p. 1.
39 *The Sydney Morning Herald*, 18 August 1962, p. 1.
40 *The Sydney Morning Herald*, 23 August 1962, p.6.
41 Zunz, *An Engineer's Tale*, p. 141.
42 Zunz, *An Engineer's Tale*, p. 141 [reported speech].
43 *The Sydney Morning Herald*, 23 August 1962, p. 7.
44 Zunz, *An Engineer's Tale*, p. 141.
45 *The Daily Telegraph*, 23 August 1962, p. 5.
46 Jack Zunz interview, Sydney Opera House Oral History Collection.
47 Jack Zunz interview, Sydney Opera House Oral History Collection.
48 Jack Zunz interview, Sydney Opera House Oral History Collection.
49 *The Sydney Morning Herald*, 25 August 1962, p. 1.
50 *The Sydney Morning Herald*, 25 August 1962, p. 1.
51 *The Sydney Morning Herald*, 25 August 1962, p. 1.
52 *The Sydney Morning Herald*, 25 August 1965, p. 1.
53 *The Sydney Morning Herald*, 25 August 1962, p. 2.
54 *The Sydney Morning Herald*, 25 August 1962, p. 2.
55 *The Sun-Herald*, 26 August 1962, p. 5.
56 *The Sun-Herald*, 26 August 1962, p. 5.
57 *The Sun-Herald*, 26 August 1962, p. 5.
58 *The Sun-Herald*, 26 August 1962, p. 5.
59 *The Daily Telegraph*, 25 August 1962, p. 3.
60 *The Sydney Morning Herald*, 5 September 1962, p. 1.
61 *The Sydney Morning Herald*, 5 September 1962, p. 1.
62 *The Sydney Morning Herald*, 5 September 1962, p. 1.
63 *The Sydney Morning Herald*, 5 September 1962, p. 6.

64 Heffron to Haviland, letter, 3 September 1962, Ashworth Papers, NLA, MS 4500, Box 1, Folder 2, p. 1.
65 *The Daily Telegraph*, 6 September 1962, p. 2.
66 *The Sydney Morning Herald*, 12 September 1962, p. 16.
67 Zunz, *An Engineer's Tale*, p. 144.
68 Messent, *Opera House Act One*, p. 207 [reported speech].
69 Messent, *Opera House Act One*, p. 207.
70 Messent, *Opera House Act One*, p. 402.
71 Messent, *Opera House Act One*, p. 402 [reported speech].
72 Nutt, 'Constructing a Legacy: Technological Innovation and Achievements', in Watson (ed.) *The Sydney Opera House: 40th Anniversary Edition*, Powerhouse Publishing, Sydney, 2013, p. 113.
73 *The Sunday Telegraph*, 21 October 1962, p. 4.
74 *The Sunday Telegraph*, 21 October 1962, p. 4.
75 Messent, *Opera House Act One*, p. 286.
76 Michael Lewis interview, 28 September 1987, Sydney Opera House Oral History Collection.
77 *The Sun-Herald*, 4 November 1962.
78 *The Sydney Morning Herald*, 4 November 1962, p. 72.
79 *The Sydney Morning Herald*, 4 November 1962, p. 72.
80 Mikami, *Utzon's Sphere*, p. 130.
81 Messent, *Opera House Act One*, p. 295.
82 Messent, *Opera House Act One*, p. 295.

Chapter 11

1 Baume, *The Sydney Opera House Affair*, p. 122.
2 Zunz, *An Engineer's Tale*, p. 149.
3 Messent, *Opera House Act One*, p. 297.
4 Jack Zunz interview, Sydney Opera House Oral History Collection.
5 Messent, *Opera House Act One*, p. 297.
6 Jones, *Ove Arup*, p. 208.
7 Michael Lewis interview, Sydney Opera House Oral History Collection.
8 Michael Lewis interview, Sydney Opera House Oral History Collection.
9 *The Sydney Morning Herald*, 4 March 1963. p. 1.
10 Drew, *The Masterpiece*, p. 245.
11 Drew, *The Masterpiece*, p. 245.
12 Drew, *The Masterpiece*, p. 245.
13 Drew, *The Masterpiece*, p. 245.
14 Drew, *The Masterpiece*, p. 245.
15 ABC, 'Chapter 13: 1963 – The Move to Sydney', *The Opera House Project*, 2012.
16 Drew, *The Masterpiece*, p. 246.
17 Dellora, *Utzon and the Sydney Opera House*, pp. 10–11.
18 *The Sydney Morning Herald*, 31 October 1992, p. 166.
19 *The Sydney Morning Herald*, 30 September 2020.
20 NSW Legislative Assembly, 6 March 1963, *Hansard*, p. 3102.
21 NSW Legislative Assembly, 6 March 1963, *Hansard*, p. 3108.
22 NSW Legislative Assembly, 6 March 1963, *Hansard*, p. 3108.
23 *The Sydney Morning Herald*, 7 March 1963, p. 4.
24 Charles Moses interview, Sydney Opera House Oral History Collection [reported speech].
25 Jack Zunz interview, Sydney Opera House Oral History Collection.
26 Jack Zunz interview, Sydney Opera House Oral History Collection.
27 *Sunday Mirror*, 17 March 1963, p. 1.
28 *Sunday Mirror*, 17 March 1963, p. 1.
29 *Sunday Mirror*, 17 March 1963, p. 1.

30 Messent, *Opera House Act One*, p. 325.
31 *The Sydney Morning Herald*, 24 March 1963, p. 1.
32 *The Sun-Herald*, 17 March 1963, p. 17 [tense changed].
33 Leplastrier, 'Jorn Utzon: the logbooks', *Architecture Australia*, 1 July 2010.
34 Oktay Nayman interview in documentary *Jørn Utzon: The Man and the Architect*.
35 Prip-Buus, *Letters from Sydney: The Sydney Opera House Saga Seen Through the Eyes of Utzon's Chief Assistant*, Edition Bløndal, Hellerup, 2000, p. 22.
36 Prip-Buus, *Letters from Sydney*, p. 28.
37 Prip-Buus, *Letters from Sydney*, p. 28.
38 Dellora, *Utzon and the Sydney Opera House*, pp. 11–12.
39 Botros, 'Jack Zunz's Opera House', *Quadrant Online*.
40 Baume, *The Sydney Opera House Affair*, p. 132.
41 Baume, *The Sydney Opera House Affair*, p. 132.
42 Baume, *The Sydney Opera House Affair*, p. 132.
43 Baume, *The Sydney Opera House Affair*, p. 133.
44 Baume, *The Sydney Opera House Affair*, p. 134.
45 Baume, *The Sydney Opera House Affair*, p. 135.
46 *The Sydney Morning Herald*, 4 December 1963, p. 4.
47 Messent, *Opera House Act One*, p. 326.
48 Messent, *Opera House Act One*, p. 327.
49 Messent, *Opera House Act One*, p. 307.
50 Michael Lewis interview, Sydney Opera House Oral History Collection.
51 Michael Lewis interview, Sydney Opera House Oral History Collection.
52 *The Daily Telegraph*, 30 May 1963, p. 5.
53 ABC, 'Chapter 14: Faltering Relationships', *The Opera House Project*, 2012.
54 Messent, *Opera House Act One*, p. 329.
55 Michael Lewis interview, Sydney Opera House Oral History Collection.
56 Michael Lewis interview, Sydney Opera House Oral History Collection.
57 Michael Lewis interview, Sydney Opera House Oral History Collection.
58 Michael Lewis interview, Sydney Opera House Oral History Collection.
59 Dellora, *Utzon and the Sydney Opera House*, pp. 12–13.
60 *The Sydney Morning Herald*, 31 October 1992, p. 166.
61 *The Sydney Morning Herald*, 31 October 1992, p. 166.
62 *The Sydney Morning Herald*, 31 October 1992, p. 166 [reported speech].
63 Jan Utzon interview in documentary, *Jørn Utzon: The Man and the Architect*.
64 Hubble, *The Strange Case of Eugene Goossens*, p. 88 [reported speech].
65 Baume, *The Sydney Opera House Affair*, p. 135.
66 Baume, *The Sydney Opera House Affair*, p. 137. Author's note: This is a summation of the four options proposed by Arup and Partners.
67 Baume, *The Sydney Opera House Affair*, p. 136.
68 Murray, *The Saga of Sydney Opera House*, p. 48.
69 *The Sydney Morning Herald*, 31 October 1992, p. 166.
70 *The Sydney Morning Herald*, 31 October 1992, p. 166.
71 *The Sun-Herald*, 28 July 1963, p. 31.
72 *The Sun-Herald*, 4 June 1963, p. 7.
73 Prip-Buus, *Letters from Sydney*, p. 37.
74 *The Sydney Morning Herald*, 19 June 1963, p. 3.
75 Messent, *Opera House Act One*, p. 314 [reported speech].
76 Messent, *Opera House Act One*, p. 314 [reported speech].
77 Messent, *Opera House Act One*, p. 315 [reported speech].
78 Brooks, 'Unfinished Business', *The New Yorker Magazine*, 17 October 2005.
79 Richard Leplastrier interview in documentary *Jørn Utzon: The Man and the Architect*.

80 Adams, *The Salmon of Doubt: Hitchhiking the Galaxy One Last Time*, Harmony Books, New York, 2002, p. 291.
81 Brooks, 'Unfinished Business', *The New Yorker*.
82 Messent, *Opera House Act One*, p. 188.
83 NSW Legislative Assembly, 22 August 1963, *Hansard*.
84 *The Sydney Morning Herald*, 15 October 1973, p. 38.
85 Messent, *Opera House Act One*, p. 307.
86 Murray, *The Saga of Sydney Opera House*, p. 47.
87 Murray, *The Saga of Sydney Opera House*, p. 47.
88 Murray, *The Saga of Sydney Opera House*, p. 47.
89 Jones, *Ove Arup*, p. 210.
90 Mikami, *Utzon's Sphere*, p. 130.
91 Gilling, 'Utzon, the Institute and the Sydney Opera House', p. 9.
92 Gilling, 'Utzon, the Institute and the Sydney Opera House', p. 9.
93 *The Sydney Morning Herald*, 24 January 1938, p. 3.
94 Prip-Buus, *Letters from Sydney*, p. 49.
95 Murray, *The Saga of Sydney Opera House*, p. 50.
96 Murray, *The Saga of Sydney Opera House*, p. 50.
97 Murray, *The Saga of Sydney Opera House*, pp. 50–51.

Chapter 12

1 *The Australian*, 18 September 1965, p. 9.
2 Yeomans, *The Other Taj Mahal: What Happened to the Sydney Opera House*, Longmans, London, 1968, p. 125.
3 *The Sydney Morning Herald*, 1 July 1964, p. 2.
4 Baume, *The Sydney Opera House Affair*, p. 122.
5 Drew, *The Masterpiece*, p. 233.
6 Drew, *The Masterpiece*, p. 313.
7 Murray, *The Saga of Sydney Opera House*, p. 54.
8 Prip-Buus, *Letters from Sydney*, p. 65.
9 Hubble, *The Strange Case of Eugene Goossens*, p. 110.
10 *The Sydney Morning Herald*, 29 April 1964, p. 4.
11 Murray, *The Saga of Sydney Opera House*, p. 53.
12 Murray, *The Saga of Sydney Opera House*, p. 53.
13 *The Sydney Morning Herald*, 14 June 1964, p. 32.
14 *The Sydney Morning Herald*, 22 August 1957, p. 4.
15 *The Sydney Morning Herald*, 18 June 1964, p. 1 [reported speech].
16 *The Sydney Morning Herald*, 18 June 1964, p. 1 [reported speech].
17 *The Sydney Morning Herald*, 18 June 1964, p. 1.
18 *The Sydney Morning Herald*, 18 June 1964, p. 1.
19 *The Sydney Morning Herald*, 18 June 1964, p. 4.
20 *The Sydney Morning Herald*, 18 June 1964, p. 4.
21 *The Sydney Morning Herald*, 19 June 1964, p. 5.
22 Weiley (dir.), *Autopsy on a Dream*.
23 *The Sydney Morning Herald*, 19 June 1964, p. 2.
24 *The Sydney Morning Herald*, 1 July 1964, p. 2.
25 *The Sydney Morning Herald*, 2 July 1964, p. 13.
26 Michael Lewis interview, Sydney Opera House Oral History Collection.
27 Michael Lewis interview, Sydney Opera House Oral History Collection.
28 Murray, *The Saga of Sydney Opera House*, p. 55.
29 Murray, *The Saga of Sydney Opera House*, p. 55.
30 Prip-Buus, *Letters from Sydney*, p. 62 [reported speech].
31 Prip-Buus, *Letters from Sydney*, p. 62 [reported speech].

32 Prip-Buus, *Letters from Sydney*, p. 62 [reported speech].
33 *The Sydney Morning Herald*, 26 July 1964, p. 15.
34 Michael Lewis interview, Sydney Opera House Oral History Collection.
35 Michael Lewis interview, Sydney Opera House Oral History Collection.
36 Michael Lewis interview, Sydney Opera House Oral History Collection.
37 Michael Lewis interview, Sydney Opera House Oral History Collection.
38 *The Sydney Morning Herald*, 24 July 1964, p. 1.
39 *The Sydney Morning Herald*, 24 July 1964, p. 1.
40 *The Sydney Morning Herald*, 24 July 1964, p. 1.
41 Prip-Buus, *Letters from Sydney*, p. 62.
42 *The Sydney Morning Herald*, 21 June 1964 p. 4.
43 Prip-Buus, *Letters from Sydney*, p. 62.
44 NSW Legislative Assembly, 8 April 1997, *Hansard*.
45 Prip-Buus, *Letters from Sydney*, p. 62.
46 Prip-Buus, *Letters from Sydney*, p. 62.
47 Murray, *The Saga of Sydney Opera House*, p. 56.
48 Murray, *The Saga of Sydney Opera House*, p. 56.
49 Baume, *The Sydney Opera House Affair*, pp. 46–47.
50 Drew, *The Masterpiece*, p. 260.
51 Brooks, 'Unfinished Business', *The New Yorker Magazine*.
52 Baume, *The Sydney Opera House Affair*, pp. 141–44.
53 Prip-Buus, *Letters from Sydney*, pp. 68–69.
54 *The Sun-Herald*, 1 November 1964, p. 27.
55 Prip-Buus, *Letters from Sydney*, p. 69.
56 NSW Legislative Assembly, 25 November 1964, *Hansard*, p. 2263.
57 NSW Legislative Assembly, 25 November 1964, *Hansard*, p. 2264.
58 NSW Legislative Assembly, 25 November 1964, *Hansard*, p. 2264.
59 NSW Legislative Assembly, 25 November 1964, *Hansard*, p. 2715.
60 *The Sydney Morning Herald*, 31 October 1992, p. 166.
61 *The Canberra Times*, 2 February 1986, p. 50.
62 Brooks, 'Unfinished Business', *The New Yorker Magazine*.
63 Brooks, 'Unfinished Business', *The New Yorker Magazine*.
64 Cochrane, 'Ralph Symonds Pty Ltd and the Sydney Opera House', Architectural Science Association, 1998.
65 Jones, *Ove Arup*, p. 216.
66 Gilling, 'Utzon, the Institute and the Sydney Opera House', p. 86.
67 Gilling, 'Utzon, the Institute and the Sydney Opera House', pp. 86–87.
68 Gilling, 'Utzon, the Institute and the Sydney Opera House', p. 87.
69 Baume, *The Sydney Opera House Affair*, p. 118.
70 Baume, *The Sydney Opera House Affair*, p. 118.
71 Baume, *The Sydney Opera House Affair*, p. 118.
72 Baume, *The Sydney Opera House Affair*, p. 119.
73 Baume, *The Sydney Opera House Affair*, pp. 120–21.
74 Baume, *The Sydney Opera House Affair*, p. 121.
75 Baume, *The Sydney Opera House Affair*, p. 121.
76 Baume, *The Sydney Opera House Affair*, pp. 121–22.
77 Baume, *The Sydney Opera House Affair*, p. 122.
78 Baume, *The Sydney Opera House Affair*, p. 122.
79 Utzon, Jørn, *Sydney Opera House: Utzon Design Principles*, 2002, p. 62.
80 Gilling, 'Utzon, the Institute and the Sydney Opera House', p. 9.
81 Murray, *The Saga of the Sydney Opera House*, p. 60.
82 *The Sydney Morning Herald*, 14 March 1965, p. 119.
83 Weiley (dir.), *Autopsy on a Dream*.

84 Utzon to Minister of Public Works, letter, 11 October 1965, in 'Copies of correspondence between Mr Utzon and the Minister, and notes of meetings, June 1965 – February 1966', AO NSW 4/7893, State Records NSW, pp. 2–3.
85 Weiley (dir.), *Autopsy on a Dream*.

Chapter 13

1 Baume, *The Sydney Opera House Affair*, p. 135.
2 Hughes, 'Twenty Years at the Sydney Opera House', p. 5, in Edward Farmer (NSW Government Architect from 1958), SLNSW, MLMSS 7703, Series 02: E. H. (Edward Herbert) Farmer files 15-36, ca. 1893, 1918–1993, Box 26, File 9.
3 Drew, *The Masterpiece*, p. 304.
4 *The Daily Telegraph*, 3 May 1965, p. 2.
5 *The Sydney Morning Herald*, 16 May 1965, p. 43.
6 David Littlemore interview, Sydney Opera House Oral History Collection.
7 Charles Moses interview, Sydney Opera House Oral History Collection.
8 Drew, *The Masterpiece*, p. 546.
9 Prip-Buus, *Letters from Sydney*, p. 82.
10 Drew, *The Masterpiece*, p. 299.
11 Charles Moses interview, Sydney Opera House Oral History Collection.
12 *The Sydney Morning Herald*, 5 June 1965, p. 1.
13 Jørn Utzon interview in the film, *The Edge of the Possible*, directed by Daryl Dellora, 1998.
14 Davis Hughes interview, Sydney Opera House Oral History Collection, May 1986.
15 Hughes, Minister of Public Works, Notes from interview with Utzon, 16 June 1965, in 'Copies of correspondence between Mr Utzon and the Minister, and notes of meetings, June 1965 – February 1966', State Records NSW, AO NSW 4/7893, p. 1.
16 Hughes to Utzon, letter, 7 July 1965, re: working arrangements, in 'Copies of correspondence between Mr Utzon and the Minister, and notes of meetings, June 1965 – February 1966', AO NSW 4/7893, State Records NSW, p. 1 [reported speech].
17 Charles Moses interview with Ava Hubble, 8 July 1986, Sydney Opera House Oral History Collection.
18 Hughes, Minister of Public Works, Notes from interview with Utzon, 16 June 1965, in 'Copies of correspondence between Mr Utzon and the Minister, and notes of meetings, June 1965 – February 1966', State Records NSW, AO NSW 4/7893, p. 1.
19 Hughes, Notes from interview with Utzon, 16 June 1965, p. 1.
20 *The Sydney Morning Herald*, 31 October 1992, p. 166.
21 Jørn Utzon interview in the film, *The Edge of the Possible*.
22 Hughes, Minister of Public Works, Notes from interview with Utzon, in 'Copies of correspondence between Mr Utzon and the Minister, and notes of meetings, June 1965 – February 1966', AO NSW 4/7893, State Records NSW, p. 1.
23 Prip-Buus, *Letters from Sydney*, p. 84.
24 Prip-Buus, *Letters from Sydney*, p. 84.
25 Prip-Buus, *Letters from Sydney*, p. 84.
26 Prip-Buus, *Letters from Sydney*, p. 84.
27 Utzon to Hughes, letter, 21 June 1965, re: tendering, in 'Copies of correspondence between Mr Utzon and the Minister, and notes of meetings, June 1965 – February 1966', AO NSW 4/7893, State Records NSW, p. 2.
28 Hughes to Utzon, letter, 7 July 1965, p. 1.
29 Hughes to Utzon, letter, 7 July 1965, in 'Copies of correspondence between Mr Utzon and the Minister, and notes of meetings, June 1965 – February 1966', State Records NSW, AO NSW 4/7893, pp. 1–2.
30 Hughes to Utzon, letter, 7 July 1965, p. 2.
31 Jones, *Ove Arup*, p. 220.
32 Hughes to Utzon, letter, 7 July 1965, p. 1.

33 Hughes to Utzon, letter, 7 July 1965, p. 2.

34 Utzon to Hughes, letter, 12 July 1965, in 'Copies of correspondence between Mr Utzon and the Minister, and notes of meetings, June 1965 – February 1966', AO NSW 4/7893, State Records NSW, p. 2.

35 Utzon to Hughes, letter, 12 July 1965, p. 4.

36 Utzon to Hughes, letter, 12 July 1965, p. 4.

37 Utzon to Hughes, letter, 12 July 1965, p. 6.

38 Prip-Buus, *Letters from Sydney*, p. 89.

39 Charles Moses, interview with Ava Hubble, 8 July 1986, Sydney Opera House Oral History Collection.

40 Davis Hughes interview, Sydney Opera House Oral History Collection, May 1986.

41 *The Sydney Morning Herald*, 31 October 1992, p. 166.

42 Baume, *The Sydney Opera House Affair*, p. 34 [reported speech].

43 Jones, *Ove Arup*, p. 221.

44 Spigelman, *Almost Full Circle – Harry Seidler*, Brandl & Schlesinger, Sydney, 2001, p. 239.

45 Hubble, *The Strange Case of Eugene Goossens*, p. 112.

46 *The Sydney Morning Herald*, 31 October 1992, p. 1.

47 *The Sydney Morning Herald*, *Good Weekend Magazine*, 4 September 2014.

48 *The Sydney Morning Herald*, 31 October 1992, p. 1.

49 Prip-Buus, *Letters from Sydney*, p. 110.

50 Prip-Buus, *Letters from Sydney*, p. 110.

51 ABC, 'Chapter 18: The Tenacity of Davis Hughes', *The Opera House Project*, 2012.

52 Wood to Hughes, confidential memo, 12 August 1965, Archives of NSW, 4/8070, p. 8.

53 ABC, 'The Tenacity of Davis Hughes', *The Opera House Project*, 2012.

54 Walker to Utzon, letter, 20 August 1965, re: copy of letter sent to Ove Arup & Partners, in 'Copies of correspondence between Mr Utzon and the Minister, and notes of meetings, June 1965 – February 1966', AO NSW 4/7893, State Records NSW, p. 1.

55 *The Sydney Morning Herald*, 2 January 1995, p. 12.

56 Brooks, 'Unfinished Business', *The New Yorker Magazine*.

57 Gilling, 'Utzon, the Institute and the Sydney Opera House', p. 15.

58 Murray, *The Saga of Sydney Opera House*, p. 62.

59 Gilling, 'Utzon, the Institute and the Sydney Opera House', p. 15.

60 Gilling, 'Utzon, the Institute and the Sydney Opera House', p. 16.

61 Gilling, 'Utzon, the Institute and the Sydney Opera House', p. 16.

62 Gilling, Report on luncheon conversation with Davis Hughes on 23 August 1965, in 'Miscellaneous correspondence relating correspondence of Mr. Utzon', NSW State Records, Series 12689, /16728, Item 164, p. 1X.

63 Gilling, 'Utzon, the Institute and the Sydney Opera House', p. 17 [reported speech].

64 Gilling, 'Utzon, the Institute and the Sydney Opera House', p. 17 [reported speech].

65 NSW Legislative Assembly, 24 August 1965, *Hansard*, p. 29.

66 *The Daily Telegraph*, 24 August 1965, p. 3.

67 Prip-Buus, *Letters from Sydney*, p. 119 [reported speech].

68 Gilling, 'Utzon, the Institute and the Sydney Opera House', p. 18 [reported speech].

69 Gilling, 'Utzon, the Institute and the Sydney Opera House', p. 18.

70 Gilling, 'Utzon, the Institute and the Sydney Opera House', p. 18.

71 Gilling, 'Utzon, the Institute and the Sydney Opera House', p. 18.

72 Prip-Buus, *Letters from Sydney*, p. 119 [reported speech].

73 Prip-Buus, *Letters from Sydney*, p. 119 [reported speech].

74 Prip-Buus, *Letters from Sydney*, p. 119.

75 Hughes to Utzon, letter, 25 August 1965, in 'Copies of correspondence between Mr Utzon and the Minister, and notes of meetings, June 1965 – February 1966', State Records NSW, AO NSW 4/7893, pp. 1–2.

76 Prip-Buus, *Letters from Sydney*, p 90.
77 Prip-Buus, *Letters from Sydney*, p. 119 [reported speech, tense changed].
78 Prip-Buus, *Letters from Sydney*, p. 120 [reported speech].
79 Utzon to Lewis, letter, 27 August 1965, re: design of auditoria, in 'Copies of correspondence between Mr Utzon and the Minister, and notes of meetings, June 1965 – February 1966', AO NSW 4/7893, State Records NSW.
80 Utzon to Hughes, letter re: working relationship, 27 August 1965, in 'Copies of correspondence between Mr Utzon and the Minister, and notes of meetings, June 1965 – February 1966', State Records NSW, AO NSW 4/7893, p. 1.
81 Utzon to Hughes, letter re: working relationship, 27 August 1965, p. 3.
82 Prip-Buus, *Letters from Sydney*, p. 120 [reported speech].
83 Gilling, 'Utzon, the Institute and the Sydney Opera House', p. 22.
84 Gilling, 'Utzon, the Institute and the Sydney Opera House', p. 23.
85 Gilling, 'Utzon, the Institute and the Sydney Opera House', p. 23.
86 *The Sydney Morning Herald*, 1 September 1965, p. 1.
87 *The Sydney Morning Herald*, 1 September 1965, p. 1.
88 *The Sydney Morning Herald*, 1 September 1965, p. 1.
89 *The Sydney Morning Herald*, 1 September 1965, p. 1.
90 Prip-Buus, *Letters from Sydney*, p. 120 [reported speech].
91 Prip-Buus, *Letters from Sydney*, p. 120.
92 Drew, *The Masterpiece*, p. 314
93 Elsa Atkins interview in documentary *Jørn Utzon: The Man and the Architect*.
94 Utzon to Hughes, letter re: Stage III, 13 September 1965, in 'Copies of correspondence between Mr Utzon and the Minister, and notes of meetings, June 1965 – February 1966, State Records NSW, AO NSW 4/7893, p. 1.
95 Hughes to Utzon, letter, 14 September 1965, in 'Copies of correspondence between Mr Utzon and the Minister, and notes of meetings, June 1965 – February 1966', State Records NSW, AO NSW 4/7893, p. 1.
96 Hughes to Utzon, letter, 14 September 1965, p. 1.
97 Hughes to Utzon, letter, 14 September 1965, p. 1.
98 *The Sydney Morning Herald*, 2 January 1995, p. 12.
99 Notes of meeting between Davis Hughes and Stanley Haviland, 22 September 1965, in 'Copies of correspondence between Mr Utzon and the Minister, and notes of meetings, June 1965 – February 1966', State Records NSW, AO NSW 4/7893, p. 1 [reported speech].
100 Notes of meeting between Hughes and Haviland, 22 September 1965, p. 1 [reported speech].
101 Notes of meeting between Hughes and Haviland, 22 September 1965, p. 1 [reported speech].
102 Notes of meeting between Hughes and Haviland, 22 September 1965, p. 1 [reported speech].
103 Sir Davis Hughes interview, Sydney Opera House Oral Project, May 1986.
104 Charles Moses, interview with Ava Hubble, 8 July 1986, Sydney Opera House Oral History Collection.

Chapter 14

1 Shakespeare, *The Tragedy of Hamlet Prince of Denmark*, Washington Square Press, New York, 1992, p. 209.
2 *The Australian*, 21 September 1965, p. 9.
3 Dellora, *Utzon and the Sydney Opera House*, pp. 14–15.
4 *The Sydney Morning Herald*, 31 October 1992, p. 1.
5 *The Australian*, 21 September 1966, p. 9.
6 *The Australian*, 21 September 1966, p. 9.
7 Mogens Prip-Buus interview in documentary *Jørn Utzon: The Man and the Architect*.
8 Gilling, 'Utzon, the Institute and the Sydney Opera House', p. 19.
9 Prip-Buus, *Letters from Sydney*, p. 121 [reported speech].

10 Hughes to Utzon, letter 1, 30 September 1965, in 'Copies of correspondence between Mr Utzon and the Minister, and notes of meetings, June 1965 – February 1966', State Records NSW, AO NSW 4/7893, p. 3.

11 Hughes to Utzon, letter 2, 30 September 1965, p. 2.

12 Prip-Buus, *Letters from Sydney*, p. 122.

13 Prip-Buus, *Letters from Sydney*, p. 122 [reported speech].

14 Weiley's personal blog. Author's note: John Weiley's narrative, published on his personal blog and accessed by me online in 2017, has since been taken down. Weiley kindly fact-checked and corroborated this material for me in 2021.

15 Ellis, 'The story of the missing Attenborough Opera House film', 29 July 2020.

16 Utzon to Hughes, letter 1, 11 October 1965, in 'Copies of correspondence between Mr Utzon and the Minister, and notes of meetings, June 1965 – February 1966', State Records NSW, AO NSW 4/7893, p. 1.

17 Utzon to Hughes, letter 1, 11 October 1965, p. 2.

18 Prip-Buus, *Letters from Sydney*, p. 123 [reported speech].

19 Utzon to Hughes, letter, 28 October 1965, in 'Copies of correspondence between Mr Utzon and the Minister, and notes of meetings, June 1965 – February 1966', State Records NSW, AO NSW 4/7893, p. 1.

20 Utzon to Hughes, letter, 28 October 1965, p. 1.

21 Gilling, 'Utzon, the Institute and the Sydney Opera House', p. 29 [reported speech].

22 Utzon to Hughes, letter 1, 1 November 1965, in 'Copies of correspondence between Mr Utzon and the Minister, and notes of meetings, June 1965 – February 1966', State Records NSW, AO NSW 4/7893, p. 1.

23 NSW Legislative Assembly, 3 November 1965, *Hansard*.

24 *The Daily Telegraph*, 4 November 1965, p. 7.

25 NSW Legislative Assembly, 3 November 1965, *Hansard*, pp. 1697–98.

26 *The Daily Telegraph*, 4 November 1965, p. 7.

27 Drew, *The Masterpiece*, p. 309.

28 *The Daily Telegraph*, 4 November 1965, p. 7.

29 *The Daily Telegraph*, 4 November 1965, p. 7.

30 Carter, 'The Sydney Opera House: What Went Wrong?', p. 63 [reported speech].

31 NSW Legislative Assembly, 3 November 1965, *Hansard*, p. 1696.

32 NSW Legislative Assembly, 3 November 1965, *Hansard*, p. 1728.

33 *The Sydney Morning Herald*, 4 November 1965, p. 2.

34 Revised notes of a meeting held in the office of the Minister for Public Works. Attendees: Hughes, Utzon, Haviland, Ashworth, J. [Colin] Humphrey (Director, Dept Public Works), and T. Walker (Secretary, Dept Public Works), B. Lloyd (Dept Public Works), in 'Copies of correspondence between Mr Utzon and the Minister, and notes of meetings, June 1965 – February 1966', State Records NSW, AO NSW 4/7893, p. 1 [reported speech].

35 Revised notes of a meeting held in the office of the Minister for Public Works, p. 2 [reported speech].

36 Revised notes of a meeting held in the office of the Minister for Public Works, p. 2.

37 Revised notes of a meeting held in the office of the Minister for Public Works, p. 2.

38 Revised notes of a meeting held in the office of the Minister for Public Works, p. 2.

39 Prip-Buus, *Letters from Sydney*, p. 126.

40 Prip-Buus, *Letters from Sydney*, p. 126 [reported speech].

41 Prip-Buus, *Letters from Sydney*, p. 126 [reported speech].

42 Prip-Buus, *Letters from Sydney*, p. 126 [reported speech].

43 Prip-Buus, *Letters from Sydney*, p. 126.

44 Prip-Buus, *Letters from Sydney*, p. 102.

45 Prip-Buus, *Letters from Sydney*, p. 127 [reported speech].

46 Prip-Buus, *Letters from Sydney*, p. 126 [reported speech].

47 Prip-Buus, *Letters from Sydney*, p. 128 [reported speech].

48 Prip-Buus, *Letters from Sydney*, p. 129.

49 *The Sydney Morning Herald*, 2 February 1957, p. 9.

50 *The Daily Telegraph*, 24 January 1966, p. 4.

51 Corbet Gore interview, 27 November 1986, Sydney Opera House Oral History Collection.

52 Michael Lewis interview, Sydney Opera House Oral History Collection.

53 Michael Lewis interview, Sydney Opera House Oral History Collection.

54 Michael Lewis interview, Sydney Opera House Oral History Collection.

55 Prip-Buus, *Letters from Sydney*, p. 108 [reported speech].

56 Prip-Buus, *Letters from Sydney*, p. 108 [reported speech].

57 ABC, 'Chapter 18: The Tenacity of Davis Hughes', *The Opera House Project*, 2012.

58 Prip-Buus, *Letters from Sydney*, p. 106.

59 Prip-Buus, *Letters from Sydney*, p. 106.

60 Drew, *The Masterpiece*, pp. 341–342.

61 Drew, *The Masterpiece*, pp. 340–341.

62 Drew, *The Masterpiece*, p. 344.

63 Prip-Buus, *Letters from Sydney*, p. 109.

64 Baume, *The Sydney Opera House Affair*, pp. 39–40.

65 Pitt, *The House*, p. 233 [reported speech].

66 Notes of a meeting held in the office of the Minister for Public Works, p. 3.

67 Prip-Buus, *Letters from Sydney*, p. 109 [reported speech].

68 Notes of a meeting held in the office of the Minister for Public Works, p. 3.

69 *The Sydney Morning Herald*, 31 October 1992, p. 166 [reported speech].

70 Drew, *The Masterpiece*, p. 344; Prip-Buus, *Letters from Sydney*, p. 109.

71 Messent, *Opera House Act One*, p. 438.

72 Jones, Peter, *Ove Arup: Masterbuilder of the Twentieth Century*, Yale University Press, New Haven, 2006, no page number.

73 Messent, *Opera House Act One*, p. 227.

74 Messent, *Opera House Act One*, p. 227.

75 Drew, *The Masterpiece*, p. 346.

76 Baume, *The Sydney Opera House Affair*, pp. 40–41.

77 Baume, *The Sydney Opera House Affair*, p. 41.

78 *The Australian*, 11 February 1967, p. 9.

Chapter 15

1 'Utzon Only', *Cross-Section*, March–April 1966, Issue No. 162, Extraordinary Issue, Journal of the University of Melbourne Department of Architecture, p. 5.

2 Dinesen, *Babette's Feast and Other Anecdotes of Destiny*, Vintage Books, 1988, p. 48.

3 *The Australian*, 13 February 1967, p. 9.

4 *The Canberra Times*, 2 March 1966. p. 3 [reported speech].

5 *The Canberra Times*, 2 March 1966. p. 3 [reported speech].

6 Yeomans, *The Other Taj Mahal*, p. 1.

7 Yeomans, *The Other Taj Mahal*, p. 146.

8 Pitt, *The House*, p. 239 [reported speech].

9 Pitt, *The House*, p. 239 [reported speech].

10 Pitt, *The House*, p. 239 [reported speech].

11 Yeomans, *The Other Taj Mahal*, p. 1.

12 *The Daily Telegraph*, 9 March 1966, p. 8.

13 Elsa Atkins interview in documentary *Jørn Utzon: The Man and the Architect*.

14 Richard Leplastrier interview in documentary *Jørn Utzon: The Man and the Architect*.

15 *The Sydney Morning Herald*, 15 October 1973, p. 49.

16 *The Sydney Morning Herald*, 15 October 1973, p. 49.

17 Confidential Cabinet Minute: Copy of letter received from Mr Jørn Utzon, 28 February 1966, to Davis Hughes, in 'Miscellaneous papers re: the Resignation of Mr. Utzon, 1964–1966', State Records NSW, AO NSW 4/7901, pp. 1–2.

18 Hubble, *The Strange Case of Eugene Goossens*, p. 89.

19 Hughes to Utzon, letter, 28 February 1966, in 'Miscellaneous papers re: the Resignation of Mr. Utzon, 1964–1966', State Records NSW, AO NSW 4/7901, p. 1.

20 Elsa Atkins interview in documentary *Jørn Utzon: The Man and the Architect.*

21 Mogens Prip-Buus interview in documentary *Jørn Utzon: The Man and the Architect.*

22 *The Sydney Morning Herald*, 1 March 1966, p. 1 [reported speech].

23 *The Sydney Morning Herald*, 1 March 1966, p. 1.

24 *The Sydney Morning Herald*, 1 March 1966, p. 1.

25 Lin Utzon interview in documentary *Jørn Utzon: The Man and the Architect.*

26 Gilling, 'Utzon, the Institute and the Sydney Opera House', p. 24 [reported speech].

27 *The Sydney Morning Herald*, 1 March 1966, p. 1.

28 *The Daily Telegraph*, 1 March 1966, p. 1.

29 *The Sydney Morning Herald*, 1 March 1966, p. 1.

30 *The Sydney Morning Herald*, 1 March 1966, p. 1.

31 *The Daily Telegraph*, 1 March 1966, p. 1.

32 *The Daily Telegraph*, 1 March 1966, p. 1.

33 *The Daily Telegraph*, 1 March 1966, p. 1.

34 *The Sydney Morning Herald*, 2 March 1966, p. 1.

35 NSW Legislative Assembly, 1 March 1966, *Hansard*, p. 3673.

36 *The Daily Telegraph*, 2 March 1966, p. 1.

37 *The Sydney Morning Herald*, 2 March 1966, p. 1.

38 NSW Legislative Assembly, 1 March 1966, *Hansard*, p. 3679.

39 *The Sydney Morning Herald*, 2 March 1966, p. 1.

40 NSW Legislative Assembly, 1 March 1966, *Hansard*, p. 3680.

41 *The Daily Telegraph*, 2 March 1966, p. 1.

42 *The Sydney Morning Herald*, 2 March 1966, p. 8.

43 NSW Legislative Assembly, 1 March 1966, *Hansard*, p. 3673.

44 Prip-Buus, *Letters from Sydney*, p. 111.

45 *The Daily Telegraph*, 2 March 1966, p. 14.

46 Gilling, 'Utzon, the Institute and the Sydney Opera House', p. 24 [reported speech].

47 Gilling, 'Utzon, the Institute and the Sydney Opera House', p. 24 [reported speech].

48 Gilling, 'Utzon, the Institute and the Sydney Opera House', p. 25.

49 Utzon, 'Items to be discussed with the Minister', 1 March 1966 by Mr Utzon, in 'Miscellaneous papers re: the Resignation of Mr. Utzon, 1964–1966', AO NSW 4/7901, State Records NSW, p. 1.

50 Utzon, 'Items to be discussed with the Minister', 1 March 1966, p. 1.

51 Gilling, 'Utzon, the Institute and the Sydney Opera House', p. 25.

52 Hughes, handwritten file note, 1 March 1966 (*author not stated and undated*), in 'Miscellaneous papers re: the Resignation of Mr. Utzon, 1964–1966', State Records NSW, AO NSW 4/7901, p. 4.

53 Gilling, 'Utzon, the Institute and the Sydney Opera House', p. 24.

54 Gilling, 'Utzon, the Institute and the Sydney Opera House', p. 25 [reported speech].

55 Gilling, 'Utzon, the Institute and the Sydney Opera House', p. 25 [reported speech].

56 Gilling, 'Utzon, the Institute and the Sydney Opera House', p. 25.

57 Gilling, 'Utzon, the Institute and the Sydney Opera House', p. 25 [reported speech].

58 Gilling, 'Utzon, the Institute and the Sydney Opera House', p. 29.

59 Gilling, 'Utzon, the Institute and the Sydney Opera House', p. 29.

60 *The Sydney Morning Herald*, 2 March 1966, p. 1.

61 *The Sydney Morning Herald*, 2 March 1966, p. 1.

62 *The Sydney Morning Herald*, 2 March 1966, p. 1.

63 *The Sydney Morning Herald*, 2 March 1966, p. 1.
64 'Phantom of the Opera House', *Australian Story*, 1 February 2016, directed by Ben Cheshire, ABC.
65 'Phantom of the Opera House', *Australian Story*, 1 February 2016.
66 *The Sydney Morning Herald*, 2 March 1966, p. 6.
67 *The Sydney Morning Herald*, 2 March 1966, p. 2.
68 *The Sydney Morning Herald*, 2 March 1966, p. 2.
69 *The Sydney Morning Herald*, 3 March 1966, p. 2.
70 Neville, Walsh and Sharp, OZ 26, OZ Publications Ink Ltd., Sydney, 1966, p. 20.
71 *The Sydney Morning Herald*, 26 March 2003.
72 'Utzon Only', *Cross-Section*, p. 7.
73 Gilling, 'Utzon, the Institute and the Sydney Opera House', p. 32.
74 Gilling, 'Utzon, the Institute and the Sydney Opera House', p. 29.
75 Gilling, 'Utzon, the Institute and the Sydney Opera House', p. 32 [reported speech].
76 Gilling, 'Utzon, the Institute and the Sydney Opera House', p. 32 [reported speech].
77 Prip-Buus, *Letters from Sydney*, p. 111.
78 *The Sydney Morning Herald*, 31 October 1992, p. 1.
79 Gilling, 'Utzon, the Institute and the Sydney Opera House', p. 33.
80 Gilling, 'Utzon, the Institute and the Sydney Opera House', p. 33.
81 Gilling, 'Utzon, the Institute and the Sydney Opera House', p. 36.
82 Gilling, 'Utzon, the Institute and the Sydney Opera House', p. 36.
83 *The Daily Telegraph*, 3 March 1966, p. 3.
84 *The Daily Telegraph*, 3 March 1966, p. 3.
85 Jones, *Ove Arup*, p. 226.
86 Jones, *Ove Arup*, p. 226.
87 'Utzon Only', *Cross-Section*, p. 2.
88 Weiley personal blog, accessed 2017.
89 'Utzon Only', *Cross-Section*, p. 2.
90 'Phantom of the Opera House', *Australian Story*, 1 February 2016.
91 *The Sydney Morning Herald*, 3 March 1966, p. 1.
92 *The Sydney Morning Herald*, 4 March 1966, p. 1.
93 *The Sydney Morning Herald*, 4 March 1966, p. 1.
94 *The Sydney Morning Herald*, 4 March 1966, p. 2.
95 *The Sydney Morning Herald*, 4 March 1966, p, 2.
96 *The Sydney Morning Herald*, 4 March 1966, p. 2.
97 *The Sydney Morning Herald*, 4 March 1966, p. 8.
98 *The Sydney Morning Herald*, 4 March 1966, p. 8.
99 *The Daily Telegraph*, 4 March 1966, p. 3.
100 Berger to Utzon, letter, 24 April 1966, Utzon Archives, p. 1.
101 Stephen, McNamara and Goad, *Douglas Snelling, Sydney Opera House letter, 1966, Modernism & Australia: Documents on Art, Design and Architecture 1917–1967*, The Miegunyah Press, Melbourne, 2006, pp. 964–65.
102 Stephen, McNamara and Goad, *Douglas Snelling*, pp. 964–65.
103 Stephen, McNamara and Goad, *Douglas Snelling*, pp. 964–65.
104 *The Sydney Morning Herald*, 5 March 1966, p. 1.
105 *The Sydney Morning Herald*, 5 March 1966, p. 1 [reported speech].
106 *The Sydney Morning Herald*, 5 March 1966, p. 1.
107 *The Daily Telegraph*, 5 March 1966, p. 1.
108 *The Canberra Times*, 5 March 1966, p. 5.
109 *The Sydney Morning Herald*, 5 March 1966, p. 1 [reported speech].
110 *The Canberra Times*, 5 March 1966, p. 5.
111 *The Sydney Morning Herald*, 5 March 1966, p. 1.
112 *The Sun-Herald*, 6 March 1966, p. 2.

113 Jack Zunz interview, Sydney Opera House Oral History Collection.
114 *The Sydney Morning Herald*, 2 March 1966, p. 1.
115 *The Sun-Herald*, 6 March 1966, p. 2.

Chapter 16

1 Weiley (dir.), *Autopsy on a Dream*.
2 Parsons, 'Radical v. Conservative Architecture: The Ruin of Utzon's Audacious Vision', *Meanjin Quarterly*, September 1967, 26 (3), pp. 339–46.
3 *The Sydney Morning Herald*, 8 March 1966, p. 1.
4 *The Sydney Morning Herald*, 8 March 1966, p. 1.
5 *The Daily Telegraph*, 8 March 1966, p. 1.
6 Weiley (dir.), *Autopsy on a Dream*.
7 *The Sydney Morning Herald*, 9 March 1966, p. 4.
8 *The Sydney Morning Herald*, 9 March 1966, p. 4.
9 *The Sydney Morning Herald*, 9 March 1966, p. 4.
10 *The Sydney Morning Herald*, 9 March 1966, p. 4.
11 Hansen and von Lowzow, *Jørn Utzon: The Man and the Architect*.
12 *The Sydney Morning Herald*, 9 March 1966, p. 4.
13 *The Age*, 9 March 1966, p. 4.
14 Hughes, 'Twenty Years at the Sydney Opera House', p. 4 [reported speech].
15 *The Sydney Morning Herald*, 9 March 1966, p. 4.
16 *The Daily Telegraph*, 9 March 1966, p. 8 [reported speech].
17 Gilling, 'Utzon, the Institute and the Sydney Opera House', p. 64.
18 Gilling, 'Utzon, the Institute and the Sydney Opera House', p. 44 [reported speech].
19 Gilling, 'Utzon, the Institute and the Sydney Opera House', p. 45 [reported speech].
20 Gilling, 'Utzon, the Institute and the Sydney Opera House', p. 45 [reported speech].
21 Gilling, 'Utzon, the Institute and the Sydney Opera House', p. 45.
22 Gilling, 'Utzon, the Institute and the Sydney Opera House', p. 45.
23 Gilling, 'Utzon, the Institute and the Sydney Opera House', p. 46.
24 *The Daily Telegraph*, 9 March 1966, p. 1.
25 *The Sydney Morning Herald*, 9 March 1966, p. 1.
26 *The Sydney Morning Herald*, 9 March 1966, p. 2.
27 Gilling, 'Utzon, the Institute and the Sydney Opera House', p. 47.
28 Gilling, 'Utzon, the Institute and the Sydney Opera House', p. 47.
29 Gilling, 'Utzon, the Institute and the Sydney Opera House', p. 48.
30 Botros, 'Jack Zunz's Opera House', *Quadrant Online*.
31 *The Daily Telegraph*, 10 March 1966, p. 2.
32 Gilling, 'Utzon, the Institute and the Sydney Opera House', p. 8.
33 Gilling, 'Utzon, the Institute and the Sydney Opera House', p. 49 [reported speech].
34 Gilling, 'Utzon, the Institute and the Sydney Opera House', p. 50.
35 'Utzon Only', *Cross-Section*, p. 5.
36 Gilling, 'Utzon, the Institute and the Sydney Opera House', p. 50 [reported speech].
37 Gilling, 'Utzon, the Institute and the Sydney Opera House', p. 51.
38 Gilling, 'Utzon, the Institute and the Sydney Opera House', p. 51.
39 Gilling, 'Utzon, the Institute and the Sydney Opera House', p. 51 [reported speech].
40 Gilling, 'Utzon, the Institute and the Sydney Opera House', p. 51 [reported speech].
41 Gilling, 'Utzon, the Institute and the Sydney Opera House', pp. 50–52. Author's note: While Gilling was not present at this meeting, he was later given a copy of the notes made at the meeting and quotes them verbatim in his narrative.
42 Gilling, 'Utzon, the Institute and the Sydney Opera House', p. 51.
43 Gilling, 'Utzon, the Institute and the Sydney Opera House', p. 51.
44 Gilling, 'Utzon, the Institute and the Sydney Opera House', p. 53.
45 Drew, *The Masterpiece*, pp. 363–64.

46 *The Daily Telegraph*, 11 March 1966, p. 3.

47 *The Sydney Morning Herald*, 11 March 1966, p. 2.

48 *The Sydney Morning Herald*, 11 March 1966, p. 2.

49 *The Sydney Morning Herald*, 12 March 1966, p. 2.

50 *The Sun-Herald*, 13 March 1966, p. 68.

51 *The Sydney Morning Herald*, 12 March 1966, p. 2.

52 *The Sydney Morning Herald*, 15 March 1966, p. 1.

53 *The Sydney Morning Herald*, 15 March 1966, p. 1.

54 *The Canberra Times*, 15 March 1966, p. 3.

55 ABC, 'Chapter 13: 1963 – The Move to Sydney', *The Opera House Project*, 2012.

56 Pitt, *The House*, p. 188.

57 *The Sydney Morning Herald*, 15 March 1966, p. 4.

58 *The Sydney Morning Herald*, 15 March 1966, p. 4.

59 *The Sydney Morning Herald*, 15 March 1966, p. 4.

60 *The Canberra Times*, 15 March 1966, p. 3 [reported speech].

61 *The Daily Telegraph*, 15 March 1966, p. 1.

62 Gilling, 'Utzon, the Institute and the Sydney Opera House', p. 53.

63 Gilling, 'Utzon, the Institute and the Sydney Opera House', p. 53.

64 'Utzon Only', *Cross-Section*, p. 3.

65 *The Daily Telegraph*, 16 March 1966, p. 8.

66 *The Daily Telegraph*, 16 March 1966, p. 8.

67 *The Daily Telegraph*, 16 March 1966, p. 8 [reported speech].

68 Watson, *The Poisoned Chalice: Peter Hall and the Sydney Opera House*, opusSOH Incorporated, Ballina NSW, 2017, p. 45.

69 Watson, 'The Poisoned Chalice', *Meanjin Quarterly*, Summer 2015.

70 *The Sydney Morning Herald*, 17 March 1966, p. 2.

71 *The Sydney Morning Herald*, 18 March 1966, p. 1.

72 *The Sydney Morning Herald*. 18 March 1966, p. 1.

73 David Littlemore interview, Sydney Opera House Oral History Collection.

74 *The Sydney Morning Herald*, 3 May 1986, p. 45.

75 *The Daily Telegraph*, 18 March 1966, p. 7.

76 *The Daily Telegraph*, 18 March 1966, p. 7.

77 *The Daily Telegraph*, 18 March 1966, p. 7.

78 *The Daily Telegraph*, 18 March 1966, p. 7.

79 Murray, *The Saga of Sydney Opera House*, p. 81.

80 Stuart Littlemore interview, 10 December 2020.

81 Stuart Littlemore interview, 8 December 2020.

82 *The Sydney Morning Herald*, 3 May 1986, p. 45.

83 David Littlemore interview, Sydney Opera House Oral History Collection.

84 Petition Relating to the Protest at the Treatment of Jørn Utzon, Museum of Applied Arts & Sciences, Sydney, Object No. 2007/39/4.

85 Lin Utzon interview in documentary *Jørn Utzon: The Man and the Architect*.

86 Lin Utzon interview in documentary *Jørn Utzon: The Man and the Architect*.

87 Jan Utzon interview in documentary *Jørn Utzon: The Man and the Architect*.

88 Richard Leplastrier interview in documentary *Jørn Utzon: The Man and the Architect*.

89 *A Woman's Day*, 21 March 1966.

90 *A Woman's Day*, 21 March 1966.

91 Lis Utzon to Jørn Utzon, letter, in documentary *Jørn Utzon: The Man and the Architect*.

92 Prip-Buus, *Letters from Sydney*, p. 113.

93 Gilling, 'Utzon, the Institute and the Sydney Opera House', p. 64.

94 *The Sydney Morning Herald*, 29 March 1966, p. 5 [reported speech].

95 *The Sydney Morning Herald*, 29 March 1966, p. 5.

96 Prip-Buus, *Letters from Sydney*, p. 114.

97 *The Sydney Morning Herald*, 31 October 1992, p. 1.

98 Peter Hall interview, 1973, Australian Film and Sound Archive [reported speech].

99 Jørn Utzon to Penelope Seidler, letter, 30 March 1966, Personal Papers of Penelope Seidler.

100 Hughes, 'Twenty Years at the Sydney Opera House', p. 22.

101 Watson, *The Poisoned Chalice*, p. 45.

102 'Phantom of the Opera House', *Australian Story*, 1 February 2016.

103 'Phantom of the Opera House', *Australian Story*, 1 February 2016.

104 Google Arts & Culture, *The Sydney Opera House: The Inspiration Behind the Scenes*, Peter Hall's Diary 1967, Hall Family Archives.

105 Watson, *The Poisoned Chalice*, p. 46.

106 'Phantom of the Opera House', *Australian Story*, 1 February 2016.

107 Google Arts & Culture, *The Sydney Opera House: The Inspiration Behind the Scenes*, Hall Family Archives [reported speech].

108 *The Sun-Herald*, 3 April 1966, p. 53.

109 *The Sydney Morning Herald*, 22 April 1966, p. 6.

110 *The Sydney Morning Herald*, 22 April 1966, p. 6.

111 *The Sydney Morning Herald*, 18 February 1967, p. 17.

112 *The Sydney Morning Herald*, 18 February 1967, p. 17.

113 *The Sydney Morning Herald*, 18 February 1967, p. 17.

114 *The Sydney Morning Herald*, 29 April 1966, p. 1.

115 *The Sydney Morning Herald*, 20 April 1966, p. 1.

116 *The Sydney Morning Herald*, 3 May 1986, p. 45.

117 Pitt, *The House*, pp. 262–63.

118 Pitt, *The House*, pp. 263–64.

119 *The Sydney Morning Herald*, 23 April 1966, p. 8.

120 Pickett, 'Opera House Models', 21 January 2013, Museum of Applied Arts & Sciences.

121 Drew, *The Masterpiece*, p. 371.

122 Richard Leplastrier interview in documentary *Jørn Utzon: The Man and the Architect*.

123 Richard Leplastrier interview in documentary *Jørn Utzon: The Man and the Architect*.

124 Richard Leplastrier interview in documentary *Jørn Utzon: The Man and the Architect*.

125 Botros, 'Jack Zunz's Opera House', *Quadrant Online* [reported speech].

126 Botros, 'Jack Zunz's Opera House', *Quadrant Online* [reported speech].

127 Botros, 'Jack Zunz's Opera House', *Quadrant Online* [reported speech].

128 Jack Zunz interview, Sydney Opera House Oral History Collection.

129 Botros, 'Jack Zunz's Opera House', *Quadrant Online*.

130 Mikami, *Utzon's Sphere*, p. 119.

131 Hubble, *The Strange Case of Eugene Goossens*, p. 72.

132 *The Sydney Morning Herald*, 12 August 2018.

133 Drew, *The Masterpiece*, p. 371.

134 *The Sydney Morning Herald*, 29 April 1966, p. 1.

135 Hubble, *The Strange Case of Eugene Goossens*, p. 20.

136 Zunz, *An Engineer's Tale*, p. 192.

137 Zunz, *An Engineer's Tale*, p. 192.

138 Baume, *The Sydney Opera House Affair*, p. 45.

139 Baume, *The Sydney Opera House Affair*, p. 45.

140 Jones, *Ove Arup*, p. 228.

141 Jones, *Ove Arup*, p. 228.

142 Baume, *The Sydney Opera House Affair*, p. 122.

143 Jack Zunz interview, Sydney Opera House Oral History Collection.

144 Weiley (dir.), *Autopsy on a Dream*.

145 Brooks, 'Unfinished Business', *The New Yorker Magazine*.

146 Pitt, *The House*, p. 267.

Chapter 17

1   *The Sydney Morning Herald*, 20 April 1966, p. 9.
2   *The Sydney Morning Herald*, 3 May 1986, p. 45.
3   Michael Lewis interview, Sydney Opera House Oral History Collection.
4   Ashbrook and Powers, *Puccini's 'Turandot': the end of the great tradition*, Princeton University Press, 1991, p. 131.
5   Mikami, *Utzon's Sphere*, p. 145.
6   Henry Hall interview with author, 12 July 2021.
7   *The Sydney Morning Herald*, 18 February 1967, p. 17.
8   *The Sydney Morning Herald*, 18 February 1967, p. 17.
9   *The Sydney Morning Herald*, 15 June 1968, p. 17.
10 *The Sydney Morning Herald*, 20 October 1983, p. 1.
11 *The Sydney Morning Herald*, 2 January 1995, p. 12.
12 *The Sydney Morning Herald*, 3 May 1986, p. 45.
13 Watson, 'The Poisoned Chalice', *Meanjin Quarterly*, Summer 2015.
14 Peter Hall interviewed by Hazel de Berg, 1973, in the Hazel de Berg collection.
15 Prip-Buus, *Letters from Sydney*, p. 115.
16 Gilling, 'Utzon, the Institute and the Sydney Opera House', p. 90.
17 Charles Moses interview, Sydney Opera House Oral History Collection.
18 Watson, *The Poisoned Chalice*, p. 53.
19 Peter Hall interviewed by Hazel de Berg, 1973.
20 Watson, 'The Poisoned Chalice', *Meanjin Quarterly*, Summer 2015.
21 *The Sydney Morning Herald*, 18 May 1966, p. 1.
22 Stuart Littlemore interview with author, 28 June 2021.
23 David Littlemore interview, Opera House Oral History Collection.
24 David Littlemore interview, Opera House Oral History Collection.
25 David Littlemore interview, Opera House Oral History Collection.
26 *The Sydney Morning Herald*, 3 May 1986, p. 45.
27 Peter Hall interviewed by Hazel de Berg, 1973.
28 *The Sydney Morning Herald*, 3 May 1986, p. 45.
29 *The Sydney Morning Herald*, 3 May 1986, p. 45.
30 *The Sydney Morning Herald*, 3 June 1966, p. 1.
31 *The Sydney Morning Herald*, 3 June 1966, p. 1.
32 *The Sydney Morning Herald*, 3 June 1966, p. 1.
33 Jones, *Ove Arup*, p. 60.
34 Baume, *The Sydney Opera House Affair*, pp. 26–27.
35 Baume, *The Sydney Opera House Affair*, p. 27.
36 Watson, *The Poisoned Chalice*, p. 53.
37 *The Australian*, 11 February 1967, p. 9.
38 Zunz, *An Engineer's Tale*, p. 194.
39 Zunz, *An Engineer's Tale*, p. 201.
40 Watson, *The Poisoned Chalice*, p. 73.
41 *The Sydney Morning Herald*, 3 May 1986, p. 43.
42 Drew, *The Masterpiece*, p. 313.
43 *The Sydney Morning Herald*, 27 February 1967, p. 2.
44 Jan Utzon interview in documentary *Jørn Utzon: The Man and the Architect*.
45 Jan Utzon interview in documentary *Jørn Utzon: The Man and the Architect*.
46 Jan Utzon interview in documentary *Jørn Utzon: The Man and the Architect*.
47 Oktay Nayman interview in documentary *Jørn Utzon: The Man and the Architect*.
48 *The Canberra Times*, 16 June 1966, p. 22.
49 *The Canberra Times*, 10 June 1966, p. 13.
50 *The Canberra Times*, 10 June 1966, p. 13.

51 David Littlemore interview, Opera House Oral History Collection.
52 *The Sydney Morning Herald*, 2 January 1995, p. 12.
53 *The Sydney Morning Herald*, 3 May 1986, p. 45.
54 Clune and Turner (eds), *The Premiers of New South Wales*, p. 357.
55 Clune and Turner (eds), *The Premiers of New South Wales*, p. 357.
56 *The Sydney Morning Herald*, 9 March 1966, p. 4.
57 Ellis, 'The Story of the Missing Attenborough Opera House Film', 29 July 2020.
58 Weiley personal blog, accessed 2017.
59 Weiley personal blog, accessed 2017.
60 Weiley personal blog, accessed 2017.
61 Vanhoenacker, 'What is a Tree Doing on Top of that Construction Site?', *Slate*, December 2013.
62 *The Sun-Herald*, 29 January 1967, p. 27.
63 *The Sun-Herald*, 29 January 1967, p. 27.
64 *The Sydney Morning Herald*, 18 February 1967, p. 17.
65 'Phantom of the Opera House', *Australian Story*, 1 February 2016.
66 Peter Hall interview, February 1986, Opera House Oral History Collection.
67 *The Sydney Morning Herald*, 23 March 1967, p. 5.
68 *The Australian*, 11 February 1967, p. 9.
69 Weiley (dir.), *Autopsy on a Dream*.
70 *The Australian*, 11 February 1967, p. 9.
71 *The Australian*, 14 February 1967, p. 9.
72 *The Sydney Morning Herald*, 1 March 1967, p. 12.
73 *The Sydney Morning Herald*, 1 March 1967, p. 12.
74 *The Sydney Morning Herald*, 1 March 1967, p. 12.
75 *The Sydney Morning Herald*, 1 March 1967, p. 12.
76 *The Sydney Morning Herald*, 1 March 1967, p. 12.
77 *The Sydney Morning Herald*, 27 October 1967, p. 2.
78 *The Sydney Morning Herald*, 1 March 1967, p. 12 [reported speech].
79 *The Sydney Morning Herald*, 1 March 1967, p. 12.
80 Watson, *The Poisoned Chalice*, p. 104.
81 *The Sydney Morning Herald*, 6 March 1967, p. 6.
82 Watson, *The Poisoned Chalice*, p. 109.
83 *The Sydney Morning Herald*, 15 October 1973, p. 49.
84 *The Sydney Morning Herald*, 9 March 1967, p. 6.
85 *Sydney Opera House: Utzon Design Principles*, 2002, p. 18.
86 *Time* (magazine), 8 October 1973, p. 48.
87 Messent, *Opera House Act One*, p. 438.
88 *The Sydney Morning Herald*, 1 February 1957, p. 2.
89 *The Sydney Morning Herald*, 4 February 1957, p. 2.
90 Charles Moses interview, Sydney Opera House Oral History Collection.
91 *The Sydney Morning Herald*, 3 May 1986, p. 45.
92 Murray, *The Saga of Sydney Opera House*, p. 94.
93 Mikami, *Utzon's Sphere*, p. 136.
94 Jack Zunz in video 'How Do You Solve a Problem Like the Sydney Opera House?', Perspectives, Arup.
95 Zunz, *An Engineer's Tale*, p. 195.
96 Watson, *The Poisoned Chalice*, p.103.
97 Watson, *The Poisoned Chalice*, p. 106.
98 Weiley (dir.), *Autopsy on a Dream*.
99 Watson, *The Poisoned Chalice*, p. 111.
100 Google Arts & Culture, *The Sydney Opera House: The Inspiration Behind the Scenes*, Peter Hall's Diary, Hall Family Archives [reported speech].

101 Google Arts & Culture, *The Sydney Opera House: The Inspiration Behind the Scenes*, Hall Family Archives.

102 Google Arts & Culture, *The Sydney Opera House: The Inspiration Behind the Scenes*, Peter Hall's Diary 1967, Hall Family Archives [reported speech].

103 Google Arts & Culture, *The Sydney Opera House: The Inspiration Behind the Scenes*, Peter Hall's Diary 1967, Hall Family Archives.

104 Google Arts & Culture, *The Sydney Opera House: The Inspiration Behind the Scenes*, Peter Hall's Diary 1967, Hall Family Archives [reported speech].

105 Google Arts & Culture, *The Sydney Opera House: The Inspiration Behind the Scenes*, Peter Hall's Diary 1967, Hall Family Archives [reported speech].

106 *The Australian*, 14 February 1967, p. 9.

107 Google Arts & Culture, *The Sydney Opera House: The Inspiration Behind the Scenes*, Peter Hall's Diary 1967, Hall Family Archives [reported speech].

108 Google Arts & Culture, *The Sydney Opera House: The Inspiration Behind the Scenes*, Hall Family Archives.

109 Google Arts & Culture, *The Sydney Opera House: The Inspiration Behind the Scenes*, Peter Hall's Diary 1967, Hall Family Archives [reported speech].

110 *The Sydney Morning Herald*, 27 October 1967, p. 1.

111 *The Sydney Morning Herald*, 27 October 1967, p. 1.

112 *The Sydney Morning Herald*, 27 October 1967, p. 2 [reported speech].

113 *The Sydney Morning Herald*, 27 October 1967, p. 2.

114 *The Sydney Morning Herald*, 15 October 1967, p. 49.

115 Zunz, *An Engineer's Tale*, p. 206.

116 Weiley (dir.), *Autopsy on a Dream*.

117 Weiley (dir.), *Autopsy on a Dream*.

118 Weiley (dir.), *Autopsy on a Dream*.

119 Weiley (dir.), *Autopsy on a Dream*.

120 Weiley (dir.), *Autopsy on a Dream*.

121 Dellora, *Utzon and the Sydney Opera House*, p. 47.

Chapter 18

1 Mikami, *Utzon's Sphere*, p. 145.

2 *The Sydney Morning Herald*, 21 February 1968, p. 5.

3 *The Sydney Morning Herald*, 17 February 1968, p. 1.

4 *The Sydney Morning Herald*, 17 February 1968, p. 1.

5 *The Sydney Morning Herald*, 17 February 1968, p. 2.

6 *The Sydney Morning Herald*, 20 February 1968, p. 5.

7 *The Sydney Morning Herald*, 20 February 1968, p. 5.

8 *The Sydney Morning Herald*, 20 February 1968, p. 5.

9 *The Sydney Morning Herald*, 20 February 1968, p. 5.

10 Weiley (dir.), *Autopsy on a Dream*.

11 Watson, *The Poisoned Chalice*, p. 117.

12 Antigone Hall interview with author, Sydney, 5 January 2021.

13 'Utzon Only', *Cross-Section*, p. 5.

14 Weiley (dir.), *Autopsy on a Dream*.

15 Weiley (dir.), *Autopsy on a Dream*.

16 Weiley (dir.), *Autopsy on a Dream*.

17 Weiley (dir.), *Autopsy on a Dream*.

18 Henry Hall interview with author, 12 July 2020.

19 Zunz, *An Engineer's Tale*, p. 206.

20 Zunz, *An Engineer's Tale*, p. 207.

21 Zunz, *An Engineer's Tale*, p. 207.

22 Weiley personal blog, accessed 2017.

23 *The Sydney Morning Herald*, 15 June 1968, p. 2.

24 *The Sydney Morning Herald*, 10 September 1968, p. 2.

25 *The Sydney Morning Herald*, 10 September 1968, p. 2.

26 *The Sydney Morning Herald*, 8 June 1969, p. 9.

27 *The Sydney Morning Herald*, 8 June 1969, p. 9.

28 'Phantom of the Opera House', *Australian Story*, 1 February 2016.

29 Penelope Hall interview with author, 7 July 2021.

30 Hubble, *The Strange Case of Eugene Goossens*, p. 116.

31 Mogens Prip-Buus interview in documentary *Jørn Utzon: The Man and the Architect*.

32 Frampton, 'Jørn Utzon 2003 Laureate Biography'.

33 Jack Mundey interview, Sydney Opera House Oral History Collection.

34 *The Australian*, 18 December 1972, p. 3.

35 Hughes, 'Twenty Years at the Sydney Opera House', p. 11.

36 Hughes, 'Twenty Years at the Sydney Opera House', p. 11.

37 *The Australian*, 18 December 1972, p. 3.

38 *The Australian*, 18 December 1972, p. 3.

39 Hughes, 'Twenty Years at the Sydney Opera House', p. 12.

40 *The Australian*, 18 December 1972, p. 3.

41 *The Sydney Morning Herald*, 18 December 1972, p. 1.

42 Hughes, 'Twenty Years at the Sydney Opera House', p. 10.

43 Hughes, 'Twenty Years at the Sydney Opera House', p. 10.

44 *The Sun-Herald*, 13 March 1966, p. 68.

45 Hughes, 'Twenty Years at the Sydney Opera House', p. 10.

46 Peter Hall interview in documentary *Jørn Utzon: The Man and the Architect*.

47 *The Australian*, 19 October 1973, p. 13.

48 Pitt, *The House*, p. 338.

49 Jørn Utzon interview in film *The Edge of the Possible*, 1998.

50 *The Sydney Morning Herald*, 6 March 1972, p. 3.

51 *The Sydney Morning Herald*, 6 March 1972, p. 3.

52 *The Sydney Morning Herald*, 6 March 1972, p. 3.

53 Hubble, *The Strange Case of Eugene Goossens*, p. 72.

54 Hubble, *The Strange Case of Eugene Goossens*, p. 72.

55 Hubble, *The Strange Case of Eugene Goossens*, p. 78.

56 *The Sydney Morning Herald*, 20 October 1973, p. 8.

57 Hubble, *The Strange Case of Eugene Goossens*, p. 71.

58 *The Sydney Morning Herald*, 21 August 1972, p. 8.

59 Hughes, 'Architecture: Australia's Own Taj Mahal', p. 48.

60 *The Sydney Morning Herald*, 19 October 1973, p. 2.

61 Excerpt from film, *Queen at the Opera House 1973*, National Film and Sound Archive of Australia, in Taylor, 'Sydney Opera House Opening'.

62 *The Canberra Times*, 22 October 1978, p. 3.

63 *The Canberra Times*, 22 October 1978, p. 3.

64 *The Sydney Morning Herald*, 20 April 1980, p. 33.

65 'Ben Blakeney', Obituary, Australian Federal Police, September 2018.

66 *The Sydney Morning Herald*, 22 October 1973, p. 10.

67 *The Sydney Morning Herald*, 22 October 1973, p. 10.

68 *The Sydney Morning Herald*, 22 October 1973, p. 10.

69 *The Sydney Morning Herald*, 22 October 1973, p. 10.

70 *The Sydney Morning Herald*, 22 October 1973, p. 10.

71 'Phantom of the Opera House', *Australian Story*, 1 February 2016.

72 *The Sydney Morning Herald*, 4 November 1962, p. 72.

73 Zunz, *An Engineer's Tale*, p. 228.

74 'Phantom of the Opera House', *Australian Story*, 1 February 2016.

75 *The Australian*, 19 October 1973, p. 9.

76 *The Australian*, 19 October 1973, p. 9.

77 *The Australian*, 19 October 1973, p. 14.

78 *The Australian*, 19 October 1973, p. 9.

79 *The Sunday Telegraph*, 21 October 1973, p. 3.

80 *The Sydney Morning Herald*, 21 October 1973, p. 3.

81 Hubble, *The Strange Case of Eugene Goossens*, p. 46.

Epilogue

1 Grant Norton, *Ten Materials that Shaped Our World*, Springer Nature, Switzerland, 2021, p. 119.

2 *The Sydney Morning Herald*, 20 October 1983, p. 1.

3 Hubble, *The Strange Case of Eugene Goossens*, p. 78.

4 Frampton, 'Jørn Utzon 2003 Laureate Biography', p. 3.

5 Frampton, 'Jørn Utzon 2003 Laureate Biography', p. 3.

6 Oktay Nayman interview in documentary *Jørn Utzon: The Man and the Architect*.

7 *The Sydney Morning Herald*, 31 October 1992, p. 166.

8 *The Sydney Morning Herald*, 31 October 1992, p. 166.

9 Lin Utzon interview in documentary *Jørn Utzon: The Man and the Architect*.

10 Jack Zunz interview, Sydney Opera House Oral History Collection.

11 Hubble, *The Strange Case of Eugene Goossens*, p. 81.

12 Hubble, *The Strange Case of Eugene Goossens*, p. 85.

13 Hubble, *The Strange Case of Eugene Goossens*, p. 96.

14 Hubble, *The Strange Case of Eugene Goossens*, p. 97.

15 Hubble, *The Strange Case of Eugene Goossens*, p. 10.

16 *The Sydney Morning Herald*, 4 January 1983, p. 1.

17 Hubble, *The Strange Case of Eugene Goossens*, p. 105.

18 Lin Utzon interview in documentary *Jørn Utzon: The Man and the Architect*.

19 Hubble, *The Strange Case of Eugene Goossens*, p. 105.

20 Hubble, *The Strange Case of Eugene Goossens*, p. 106.

21 Hubble, *The Strange Case of Eugene Goossens*, p. 106.

22 Hubble, *The Strange Case of Eugene Goossens*, p. 108.

23 Hubble, *The Strange Case of Eugene Goossens*, p. 108.

24 Hubble, *The Strange Case of Eugene Goossens*, p. 110.

25 Hubble, *The Strange Case of Eugene Goossens*, p. 112.

26 Hubble, *The Strange Case of Eugene Goossens*, p. 113.

27 Hubble, *The Strange Case of Eugene Goossens*, p. 113.

28 Hubble, *The Strange Case of Eugene Goossens*, p. 113.

29 *The Sydney Morning Herald*, 31 October 1992, p. 166.

30 *The Sydney Morning Herald*, 31 October 1992, p. 166.

31 Lin Utzon interview in documentary *Jørn Utzon: The Man and the Architect*.

32 *The Sydney Morning Herald*, 31 October 1992, p. 166.

33 *The Sydney Morning Herald*, 31 October 1992, p. 166.

34 *The Sydney Morning Herald*, 31 October 1992, p. 166.

35 *The Sydney Morning Herald*, 31 October 1992, p. 166.

36 *The Sydney Morning Herald*, 31 October 1992, p. 166.

37 Lin Utzon interview in documentary *Jørn Utzon: The Man and the Architect*.

38 Brooks, 'Unfinished Business', *The New Yorker Magazine*.

39 Brooks, 'Unfinished Business', *The New Yorker Magazine*.

40 Utzon, *Sydney Opera House: Utzon Design Principles*, p. 28.

41 Utzon, *Sydney Opera House: Utzon Design Principles*, p. 40.

42 Utzon, *Sydney Opera House: Utzon Design Principles*, p. 57.

43 *The Sydney Morning Herald*, 3 August 1957, p. 2.

44 Lin Utzon interview in documentary, *Jørn Utzon: The Man and the Architect*.
45 *The Guardian*, 10 October 2005.
46 Brooks, 'Unfinished Business', *The New Yorker Magazine*.
47 Watson (ed.), *Building a Masterpiece*, Foreword, (no page numbers).
48 'Bjarke Ingels on Jørn Utzon', video, produced by Kaspar Astrup Schröder, Louisiana Channel, Louisiana Museum of Modern Art, 2018.
49 'Bjarke Ingels on Jørn Utzon', video, 2018.
50 Ove Arup interview, Sydney Opera House Oral History Collection.
51 'Sydney Opera House Special Issue', *The Arup Journal*, Vol. 8, No. 3, October 1973, p. 2.
52 *The Sydney Morning Herald*, 19 December 2018.
53 Sir Jack Zunz obituary, *The Guardian*, 3 January 2019.
54 Botros, 'Jack Zunz's Opera House', *Quadrant Online*.
55 Botros, 'Jack Zunz's Opera House', *Quadrant Online*.
56 Hughes, 'Twenty Years at the Sydney Opera House', p. 7.
57 Hughes, 'Twenty Years at the Sydney Opera House', p. 19.
58 Hughes, 'Twenty Years at the Sydney Opera House', p. 7.
59 Hughes, 'Twenty Years at the Sydney Opera House', p. 2.
60 'Jørn Utzon dies at 90; Danish architect of Sydney Opera House', *Los Angeles Times*, 30 November 2008.
61 Hughes, 'Twenty Years at the Sydney Opera House', p. 3.
62 Hughes, 'Twenty Years at the Sydney Opera House', p. 7.
63 NSW Legislative Assembly, 30 April 2003, *Hansard*, p. 123.
64 Jørn Utzon interview in the film, *The Edge of the Possible*.
65 *The Sydney Morning Herald*, 14 October 2006.
66 *The Sydney Morning Herald*, 14 October 2006.
67 *The Sydney Morning Herald*, 14 October 2006.
68 *The Sydney Morning Herald*, 14 October 2006.
69 'Phantom of the Opera House', *Australian Story*, 1 February 2016.
70 'Phantom of the Opera House', *Australian Story*, 1 February 2016.
71 *The Sydney Morning Herald*, 3 May 1986, p. 45.
72 Antigone Hall interview with author, 5 January 2021.
73 Lumby, 'Hall, Peter Brian (1931–1995)', *Australian Dictionary of Biography*, National Centre of Biography, Australian National University, published online 2019.
74 'Phantom of the Opera House', *Australian Story*, 1 February 2016.
75 Henry Hall interview with author, 12 July 2021.
76 Penelope Hall interview with author, 9 August 2021.
77 'Phantom of the Opera House', *Australian Story*, 1 February 2016.
78 'Phantom of the Opera House', *Australian Story*, 1 February 2016.
79 'Unseen Utzon' video, research and animation by Philip Nobis, 1994.
80 *The Sydney Morning Herald*, 2 January 1995, p. 12.
81 *The Sydney Morning Herald*, 2 January 1995, p. 12.
82 *The Canberra Times*, 1 December 1994, p. 10.
83 *The Sydney Morning Herald*, 2 January 1995, p. 12.
84 'Phantom of the Opera House', *Australian Story*, 1 February 2016.
85 Watson, 'The Poisoned Chalice', *Meanjin Quarterly*, Summer 2015.
86 'Phantom of the Opera House', *Australian Story*, 1 February 2016.
87 Antigone Hall interview with author, 9 August 2021.
88 Watson, 'The Poisoned Chalice', *Meanjin Quarterly*, Summer 2015.
89 Lumby, 'Hall, Peter Brian (1931–1995)'.
90 Charles Moses interview, Sydney Opera House Oral History Collection.
91 'An architect of foresight', *The Sydney Morning Herald*, 29 November 1991, p. 9.
92 Prip-Buus, *Tiden med Utzon (My Time with Utzon)*, Kunstakademiets Arkitektskoles Forlag, Aarhus, 2011, [n/a].

93 *The Sydney Morning Herald*, 18 November 2020.

94 *The Sydney Morning Herald*, 18 November 2020.

95 *The Sydney Morning Herald*, 20 September 2013.

96 *The Sydney Morning Herald*, 20 September 2013.

97 Nutt, 'Constructing a Legacy: Technological Innovation and Achievements', in Watson (ed.) *Building a Masterpiece*, p. 121.

98 'Officers of the Order of Australia', *The Age*, 26 January 1998, p. 13.

99 The Institution of Engineers Australia, Newsletter of the National Committee on Engineering Heritage, No. 8, November 1998.

100 *The Sydney Morning Herald*, 16 September 1989, p. 11.

101 Ted Farmer Obituary, *Architecture Australia*, September 2001.

102 Drury, *Rosaleen Norton's Contribution to The Western Esoteric Tradition*, 2008.

103 Drury, *Pan's Daughter*, p. xx.

104 'Bazil Harold Parker Thorne', Find a Grave Memorial website.

105 Ellis, 'The Story of the Missing Attenborough Opera House Film', July 2020.

106 Hubble, *The Sydney Opera House: More than Meets the Eye*, Weldon, 1989, p. 17.

107 Charles Moses interview, Sydney Opera House Oral History Collection.

108 'Report of the Proceedings of a Conference convened by the Premier and held in the Lecture Room, Public Library, Sydney, on 30th November 1954, concerning the question of the establishment of an Opera House in Sydney', in 'Working Papers – Sydney Opera House Executive Committee and Trust, 1954–1968', State Records NSW, Series 19526, Item 1, pp. 6–7.

109 *The Courier Mail*, 23 October 2013.

110 Brooks, 'Unfinished Business', *The New Yorker Magazine*.

111 Hughes, 'Architecture: Australia's Own Taj Mahal', p. 48.

112 Martin to Ashworth, letter, 17 July 1957, in 'Working Papers – Sydney Opera House Executive Committee and Trust, 1954–1968', State Records NSW, Series 19526, Item 4, p. 1.

113 King, 'This is not an Opera House', *The Monthly*, October 2017.

114 Kamenev, 'Sydney's Opera House: Easy on the Eyes, Not the Ears', *Time* magazine, 19 October 2011.

115 Watson, *The Poisoned Chalice*, p. 23.

116 Drew, 'Romanticism Revisited: Jørn Utzon's Opera House Revisited', *Architectural Theory Review*, 2007, Vol. 12, Issue 2, p. 121.

117 Watson, *The Poisoned Chalice*, p. 23.

118 *The Sydney Morning Herald*, 29 September 1973, p. 1.

119 *The Age*, 15 April 2002.

120 *The Sydney Morning Herald*, 26 April 1980, p. 17.

121 *The Sydney Morning Herald*, 31 October 1992, p. 166.

122 Gillard-Estrada, '"Consummate Too Too": On the Logic of Iconotexts Satirising the "Aesthetic Movement"', *Sillages critiques*, Vol. 21, 2016.

123 'The Utzon and Le Corbusier Tapestry', https://www.sydneyoperahouse.com/give/stories/le-corbusier.html

124   ABC News, 6 October 2018.

125 Glancey, 'Sydney Opera House: An Architectural Marvel', BBC Culture, 2014.

126 'How do you value an icon? The Sydney Opera House: economic, cultural and digital value', Report, Deloitte, 2013.

127 Lin Utzon interview in documentary *Jørn Utzon: The Man and the Architect*.

128 Lin Utzon interview in documentary *Jørn Utzon: The Man and the Architect*.

129 Lin Utzon interview in documentary *Jørn Utzon: The Man and the Architect*.

130 *The Guardian*, 10 October 2005.

131 *The Australian*, 30 November 2008.

BIBLIOGRAPHY

Books

Adams, Douglas, *The Salmon of Doubt: Hitchhiking the Galaxy One Last Time*, Harmony Books, New York, 2002

Ashbrook, William and Powers, Harold, *Puccini's 'Turandot': the end of the great tradition*, Princeton University Press, 1991

Baume, Michael, *The Sydney Opera House Affair*, Thomas Nelson, Sydney, 1967

Buttrose, Charles, *Words and Music*, Angus & Robertson, Sydney, 1984

Chambers, William, *A Treatise on Civil Architecture*, J. Haberkorn, London, 1759

Chandler, Raymond, *Farewell, My Lovely*, Vintage, New York, 1992

Ching, Francis, *Architecture: Form, Space and Order*, John Wiley & Sons, New Jersey, 2012

Clune, David and Turner, Ken (eds), *The Premiers of New South Wales*, Vol. 2, 1901–2005, The Federation Press, Annandale, 2006

Dellora, Daryl, *Utzon and the Sydney Opera House*, Penguin Group, Melbourne, 2013

Dinesen, Isak, *Babette's Feast and Other Anecdotes of Destiny*, Vintage Books, 1988

Drew, Philip, *Utzon and the Sydney Opera House*, Inspire Press, Annandale, 2000

Drew, Philip, *The Masterpiece: Jørn Utzon, A Secret Life*, Hardie Grant Books, South Yarra, 2001

Drury, Nevill, *Pan's Daughter: The strange world of Rosaleen Norton*, William Collins, Sydney, 1988

Duek-Cohen, Elias, *Utzon and the Sydney Opera House: Statement in the Public Interest*, Morgan Publications, Sydney, 1967

Francis, Noel, *The Gifted Knight: Sir Robert Garran, First Commonwealth Public Servant, Poet, Scholar and Lawyer*, ANU Press, Canberra, 1983

Fromont, Francoise, *Jørn Utzon: The Sydney Opera House*, Electa Gingko, Corte Madera, 1998

Golding, Peter, *They Called Him Old Smoothie: John Joseph Cahill*, Australian Scholarly Publishing, 2009

Goossens, Renée, *Belonging: A Memoir*, ABC Books, Sydney, 2003

Grant Norton, M., *Ten Materials that Shaped Our World*, Springer Nature, Switzerland, 2021

Hubble, Ava, *The Strange Case of Eugene Goossens and Other Tales from the Opera House*, Collins Publishers Australia, Sydney, 1988

Hubble, Ava, *The Sydney Opera House: More than Meets the Eye*, Weldon, Sydney, 1989

Hunter, John, *An Historical Journal of the Transactions at Port Jackson and Norfolk Island*, John Stockdale, London, 1793

Inglis, Ken, *This is the ABC: The Australian Broadcasting Commission, 1932–1983*, Black Inc., 2006

Jencks, Charles, *Modern Movements in Architecture*, Penguin, Harmondsworth, 1973

Jones, Peter, *Ove Arup: Masterbuilder of the Twentieth Century*, Yale University Press, USA, 2006

Kerr, James Semple, *Sydney Opera House: a revised plan for the conservation of the Sydney Opera House and its site*, Sydney Opera House Trust, Sydney, 2003

Luck, Peter; Salter, David and Noad, Carolyn, *This Fabulous Century*, Lansdowne Press, Sydney, 1980

Major, Norma, *Joan Sutherland*, Queen Anne Press, London, 1987

Maloney, Shane and Grosz, Chris, *Australian Encounters*, Black Inc., Victoria, 2010.

Messent, David, *Opera House Act One*, David Messent Photography, Sydney, 1997

Michener, James A., *Return to Paradise*, Random House, New York, 1951

Mikami, Yuzo, *Utzon's Sphere: Sydney Opera House – How it was designed and built*, Shokokuska, Tokyo, 2001

Murray, Peter, *The Saga of Sydney Opera House: The Dramatic Story of the Design and Construction of the Icon of Modern Australia*, Routledge, Sydney, 2003

Paterson, Andrew Barton, *The Works of 'Banjo' Paterson*, Wordsworth Editions, London, 1995

Peters-Little, Frances; Curthoys, Ann; and Docker, John (eds), *Passionate Histories: Myth, Memory and Indigenous Australia*, ANU Press, Canberra, 2010

Phillip, Arthur, *The Voyage of Governor Phillip to Botany Bay*, John Stockdale, London, 1789

Pitt, Helen, *The House*, Allen & Unwin, Sydney, 2018

Prip-Buus, Mogens, *Letters from Sydney: The Sydney Opera House Saga Seen Through the Eyes of Utzon's Chief Assistant*, Blondal, Marieveji, 2000

Prip-Buus, Mogens, *Tiden med Utzon (My Time with Utzon)*, Kunstakademiets Arkitektskoles Forlag, Aarhus, 2011

Shakespeare, William, *Hamlet*, H. Holt, New York, 1914

Shakespeare, William, *Julius Caesar*, Act I, Scene II, Cambridge University Press, Cambridge, 1907

Shakespeare, *The Plays of William Shakespeare*, Hurst, Robinson and Company, London, 1826

Shakespeare, *The Tragedy of Hamlet Prince of Denmark*, Washington Square Press, New York, 1992

Spigelman, Alice, *Almost Full Circle – Harry Seidler*, Brandl & Schlesinger, Sydney, 2001

Stephen, Ann; McNamara, Andrew and Goad, Philip, *Douglas Snelling, Sydney Opera House letter, 1966, Modernism & Australia: Documents on Art, Design and Architecture 1917–1967*, The Miegunyah Press, Melbourne, 2006

Tedeschi, Mark, *Kidnapped: The Crime that Shocked the Nation*, Simon and Schuster, NSW, 2015, [ebook]

Tench, Watkin, *A Complete Account of the Settlement at Port Jackson Including An Accurate Description of the Situation of the Colony; of the Natives; and Of Its Natural Productions*, G. Nicol and J. Sewell, London, 1793

Tench, Watkin, *A Narrative of the Expedition to Botany Bay*, J. Debrett, London, 1789

Watson, Anne (ed.), *Building a Masterpiece: The Sydney Opera House*, Powerhouse Publishing, Sydney, 2006

Watson, Anne, *The Poisoned Chalice: Peter Hall and the Sydney Opera House*, opus SOH Incorporated, Ballina NSW, 2017

Watson, Anne (ed.), *The Sydney Opera House: 40th Anniversary Edition*, Powerhouse Publishing, Sydney, 2013

Weston, Richard, *Utzon: Inspiration, Vision, Architecture*, Edition Blondal, Hellerup, 2002

Wordsworth, William, *The Prelude or, Growth of a Poet's Mind; An Autobiographical Poem*, Edward Moxon, London, 1850

Yeomans, John, *The Other Taj Mahal: What Happened to the Sydney Opera House*, Longmans, London, 1968

Yutang, Lin, *My Country and My People*, William Heinemann Ltd, London, 1936

Ziegler, Oswald, *Sydney Builds an Opera House*, Oswald Ziegler Publications, Sydney, 1973

Zunz, Jack, *An Engineer's Tale*, self-published, 2018

Journal and Magazine Articles

Arup, Ove and Jenkins, Ronald, 'The Evolution and Design of the Concourse at the Sydney Opera House', *Proceedings of the Institution of Civil Engineers*, Vol. 41, Issue 3, 1 October 1968

Arup, Ove and Zunz, Jack, 'Sydney Opera House', *The Arup Journal*, Issue 3, October 1973

Australian Police Journal, Vol. 16, No. 3, July 1962

Botros, Andrew, 'Jack Zunz's Opera House', *Quadrant Online*, 6 July 2019, https://quadrant.org.au/magazine/2019/06/jack-zunzs-opera-house/

Bradley, *A Voyage to New South Wales: The Journal of Lieutenant William Bradley RN of HMS Sirius, 1786–1792*, Trustees of the *Public* Library of New South Wales, Sydney, 1969

Boyd, Robin, 'The Sydney Opera House', *Architecture Plus* magazine, Informat Publishing Corporation, August 1973

Brooks, Geraldine, 'Unfinished Business', *The New Yorker Magazine*, 17 October 2005

Calter, Paul, 'Gateway to Mathematics: Equations of the St Louis Arch', *Nexus Network Journal: Architecture and Mathematics*, Vol. 8, No. 2, October 2006

Carter, John, 'The Sydney Opera House: What Went Wrong?', Royal Institute of British Architects, February 1967

Chiu, Chen-Yu, 'China Receives Utzon', *Architectural Histories*, The Open Access Journal of the EAHN, https://journal.eahn.org/articles/10.5334/ah.182/#n8

Drew, Philip, 'Romanticism Revisited: Jørn Utzon's Opera House Revisited,' *Architectural Theory Review*, 2007, Vol. 12, Issue 2

Fullagar, Kate, 'Bennelong in Britain', *Aboriginal History*, Vol. 33, 2009

Giedion, Siegfried, 'Jörn Utzon and the Third Generation', *Zodiac*, No. 14, 1964

Gillard-Estrada, '"Consummate Too Too": On the Logic of Iconotexts Satirizing the "Aesthetic Movement"', *Sillages critiques*, 21, 2016, http://journals.openedition.org/sillagescritiques/5041

Glancey, Jonathan, 'Sydney Opera House: An Architectural Marvel', BBC Culture, 2014

Hughes, Robert, 'Architecture: Australia's Own Taj Mahal', *Time* magazine, 8 October 1973

Institution of Engineers Australia, Newsletter of the National Committee on Engineering Heritage, No. 8, November 1998 https://www.engineersaustralia.org.au/sites/default/files/resource-files/2017-01/eha%20newsletter%208.pdf

Kamenev, Marina, 'Sydney's Opera House: Easy on the Eyes, Not the Ears', *Time*, 19 October 2011, http://content.time.com/time/world/article/0,8599,2097247,00.html

King, Darryn, 'This is not an Opera House,' *The Monthly*, October 2017, https://www.themonthly.com.au/issue/2017/october/1506780000/darryn-king/not-opera-house#mtr

Leplastrier, Richard, 'Jørn Utzon: the logbooks', *Architecture Australia*, 1 July 2010, https://architectureau.com/articles/books-73/

Neville, Richard; Walsh, Richard and Sharp, Martin, OZ 26, OZ Publications Ink Ltd., Sydney, 1966

Parsons, Philip, 'Radical v. Conservative Architecture', *Meanjin*, Vol. 26, No. 3, 1967, University of Melbourne

Parsons, Philip, 'Radical v. Conservative Architecture: The Ruin of Utzon's Audacious Vision', *Meanjin Quarterly*, September 1967, 26 (3)

Rice, Peter, 'A Celebration of the Life and Work of Ove Arup', *RSA Journal*, Vol. 137, No. 5395, June 1989

Salter, David, 'The Conservatorium director and the witch', *The Sydney Morning Herald*, 3 July 2015, https://www.smh.com.au/lifestyle/the-conservatorium-director-and-the-witch-20150702-gi3h8y.html

Sydney Opera House Special Issue, *The Arup Journal*, Vol. 8, No. 3, October 1973

Towart, Neil, 'The Lily Whites', *Symbols of Solidarity*, Newsletter of the Trade Union Badge Collectors Society, Vol. 2, Issue 3

'Utzon Only', *Cross-Section*, March–April 1966, Issue No. 162, Extraordinary Issue, Journal of the University of Melbourne Department of Architecture

Watson, Anne, 'The Poisoned Chalice', *Meanjin Quarterly*, Summer 2015

Vanhoenacker, Mark, 'What is a Tree Doing on Top of that Construction Site?', *Slate*, December 2013, https://slate.com/human-interest/2013/12/why-do-construction-workers-top-building-sites-with-undecorated-christmas-trees.html

Zunz, 'Sydney Revisited', *The Arup Journal*, Vol. 23, No. 1, 1988

Newspapers and Magazines

A Woman's Day
Clarence and Richmond Examiner
Good Weekend Magazine
Guyra Argus
National Advocate
Sydney Truth
The ABC Weekly
The Age
The Armidale Express and New England General Advertiser
The Australian
The Australian Financial Review
The Australian Women's Weekly
The Canberra Times
The Courier Mail
The Daily Mirror
The Daily Telegraph
The Guardian
The Independent (London)
The New York Times
The Sun
The Sunday Telegraph
The Sunday Times
The Sun-Herald
The Sydney Morning Herald
Time magazine
The Times (London)

Archives/State Collections

Australian Film and Sound Archive, Audio interview with Peter Hall, 1973

National Archives of Australia, NAA, N. P. Craig, Department of Customs and Excise, Minute Paper, 14 March 1956, A425, 1956/5842

National Library of Australia, Papers of Henry Ingham Ashworth

National Library of Australia, Hazel de Berg collection, Peter Hall interviewed by Hazel de Berg [1973] https://nla.gov.au/nla.obj-245878880/listen

NSW Legislative Assembly, *Hansard*

NSW Parliamentary Debates, *Hansard*

'Report of the Police Department of New South Wales (Together with Appendices) For 1956', A. H. Pettifer, Government Printer, Sydney, 1957

Seidler, Penelope, personal papers

State Library of NSW, Davis Hughes, 'Twenty Years at the Sydney Opera House', in Edward Farmer (NSW Government Architect from 1958), SLNSW, MLMSS 7703, Series 02: E. H. (Edward Herbert) Farmer files 15-36, ca. 1893, 1918–1993, Box 26, File 9

State Records NSW, 'Copies of correspondence between Mr Utzon and the Minister, and notes of meetings, June 1965 – February 1966', AO NSW 4/7893

State Records NSW, Department of Public Works, 'An International Competition for a National Opera House at Bennelong Point, Sydney, New South Wales, Australia: Conditions and Programme' ('Brown Book'), 1955, NRS 12702

State Library of NSW, Gilling, Ronald, 'Utzon, the Institute and the Sydney Opera House: A Narrative of How the Resignation Affected the Profession and the Part Played by the Royal Australian Institute of Architects', 2002, MLMSS 7405

State Records NSW, 'Miscellaneous correspondence relating correspondence of Mr. Utzon,' Series 12689, /16728

State Records NSW, Norman Ryan, Minister of Public Works to Cabinet, re: Contract for Stage Machinery, 10 January 1961, in Copies of Cabinet Minutes, Sydney Opera House 1961–1967, Series 12692, 4/8037

State Records NSW, 'Sydney National Opera House – Red Book', 1958, Department of Public Works, NRS 12707, https://gallery.records.nsw.gov.au/index.php/galleries/sydney-opera-house/sydney-opera-house-the-red-book/.

State Records NSW, 'Sydney Opera House Executive Committee's reply to Criticism of the Opera House Project, 14 September 1962 – 14 October 1962', Series 12712, 4/8067

State Records NSW, 'Sydney Opera House – The Gold Book', Department of Public Works, NRS 12706/1, https://www.records.nsw.gov.au/archives/magazine/galleries/sydney-opera-house-the-gold-book

State Records NSW, 'Working Papers – Sydney Opera House Executive Committee and Trust, 1954–1968', Series 19526

Sydney Opera House Oral History Collection

Tedeschi, Mark, personal papers

Utzon Archives, Aalborg University & Utzon Center, Sydney Opera House Competition Entry, 1956, https://www.utzon-archives.aau.dk/documents/Folios/competition-drawings-by-jorn-utzon/SZ112_02.jpg.html

Online Sources

ABC, *The Opera House Project*, http://theoperahouseproject.com

Australian Federal Police, 'Ben Blakeney', Obituary, September 2018, https://www.afp.gov.au/node/2066

Churchill, 'The End of the Beginning', a speech given at The Lord Mayor's Luncheon, Mansion House, 10 November 1942, http://www.churchill-society-london.org.uk/EndoBegn.html

Cochrane, John, 'Ralph Symonds Pty Ltd and the Sydney Opera House', Architectural Science Association, 1998, http://anzasca.net/wp-content/uploads/2014/08/ANZASCA-1998-Cochrane-SydneyOperaHouse.pdf

Deloitte report, 'How do you value an icon? The Sydney Opera House: economic, cultural and digital value,' Deloitte, 2013, https://www2.deloitte.com/content/dam/Deloitte/au/Documents/Economics/deloitte-au-economics-how-do-you-value-icon-2013.pdf

Drury, Nevill, *Rosaleen Norton's Contribution to The Western Esoteric Tradition*, 2008 https://ogma.newcastle.edu.au/vital/access/services/Download/uon:2752/ATTACHMENT02

Ellis, Dominic, 'The story of the missing Attenborough Opera House film,' 29 July 2020, https://www.sydneyoperahouse.com/digital/articles/community/missing-attenborough-opera-house-film-autopsy-on-a-dream.html

https://www.findagrave.com/memorial/191863169/bazil-harold_parker-thorne

Frampton, Kenneth, 'Jørn Utzon 2003 Laureate Biography', *The Architecture Pritzker Prize*, 2003, https://www.pritzkerprize.com/sites/default/files/inline-files/2003_bio.pdf

Google Arts & Culture, *The Sydney Opera House: The Inspiration Behind the Scenes* https://artsandculture.google.com/story/the-sydney-opera-house-the-inspiration-behind-the-scenes/sgXh63bUjd6gRw?hl=en

Heiss, Anita, 'Aboriginal Arts and Culture in Sydney,' *Barani: Sydney's Aboriginal History*, https://www.sydneybarani.com.au/sites/aboriginal-arts-and-culture-in-sydney/

Horne, H. E., 'Song for the Bridge', in 'Art Deco from the National Collection: *The World Turns Modern*', National Gallery of Australia, https://nga.gov.au/education/resources/artdeco/artdeco_edresource.pdf

Keating, Paul, 'Building a Masterpiece: The Sydney Opera House', 10 August 2006 http://www.keating.org.au/shop/item/building-a-masterpiece-the-sydney-opera-house---10-august-2006

Lumby, Roy, 'Hall, Peter Brian (1931–1995)', *Australian Dictionary of Biography*, National Centre of Biography, Australian National University, http://adb.anu.edu.au/biography/hall-peter-brian-23687/text32631, published online 2019

Petition Relating to the Protest at the Treatment of Jørn Utzon, Museum of Applied Arts & Sciences, Object No. 2007/39/4, https://collection.maas.museum/object/364757

Pickett, 'Opera House Models', 21 January 2013, Museum of Applied Arts & Sciences, https://maas.museum/inside-the-collection/2013/01/21/opera-house-models/

Prip-Buus, Mogens, 'Jørn Utzon', 3 March 2017, Drawing Matter, https://drawingmatter.org/mogens-prip-buus-utzon/

Railway Voices, a CD of Australian railway workers' stories with songs and poems, http://railwaystory.com/voices/voices9.htm

Salter, David, 'Goossens, Sir Eugene Aynsley (1893–1962)', *Australian Dictionary of Biography*, National Centre of Biography, Australian National University, http://adb.anu.edu.au/biography/goossens-sir-eugene-aynsley-10329/text18283, published first in hardcopy 1996, accessed online 13 November 2020.

Utzon, Jørn, *Sydney Opera House: Utzon Design Principles*, 2002, https://www.sydneyoperahouse.com/content/dam/pdfs/Utzon-Design-Principles.pdf

Utzon, 'The Use of Plateau and Element in Utzon's Works', Guide to Utzon website, 1962, http://www.utzonphotos.com/philosophy/the-use-of-plateau-and-element-in-utzons-works/

van der Rohe, Mies, Press Statement of the Museum of Modern Art, Retrospective Exhibition of the Architecture of Mies van der Rohe, 17 September 1947, https://assets.moma.org/documents/moma_press-release_325576.pdf

Songs

'Ol' Man River', music: Jerome Kern; lyrics: Oscar Hammerstein II, Universal Music Publishing Group, 1927

TV, Film and Video

Arup Perspectives, 'How Do You Solve a Problem Like the Sydney Opera House?', https://www.arup.com/perspectives/sir-jack-zunz

Cheshire, Ben (dir.), 'Phantom of the Opera House', *Australian Story*, 1 February 2016, ABC

Dellora, Daryl (dir.), *The Edge of the Possible*, 1998

Hansen, Lene Borch and von Lowzow, Anna (dir.), *Jørn Utzon: The Man and the Architect*, 201

National Film and Sound Archive of Australia, excerpt from film, *Queen at the Opera House 1973*, in Taylor, 'Sydney Opera House Opening', https://www.nfsa.gov.au/latest/sydney-opera-house-opening-news-photographs-home-movie

Nobis, Philip (research and animation) 'Unseen Utzon' video, 1994, https://www.youtube.com/watch?v=aU6oQpHfDz8

Prip-Buus, Mogens, video interview, Drawing Matter, https://vimeo.com/265976565

Schröder, Kaspar Astrup (producer), 'Bjarke Ingels on Jørn Utzon', video, Louisiana Channel, Louisiana Museum of Modern Art, 2018, https://channel.louisiana.dk/video/bjarke-ingels-on-j%c3%b8rn-utzon

Weiley, John, *Autopsy on a Dream*, documentary, 1968

INDEX

549